Dreams
and
Inward
Journeys

A Rhetoric and Reader for Writers

Sixth Edition

Marjorie Ford
Stanford University

Jon Ford
De Anza College

PEARSON
Longman

New York Boston San Francisco
London Toronto Sydney Tokyo Singapore Madrid
Mexico City Munich Paris Cape Town Hong Kong Montreal

Senior Acquisitions Editor: Lynn M. Huddon
Senior Marketing Manager: Sandra McGuire
Production Manager: Denise Phillip
Project Coordination, Text Design,
    and Electronic Page Makeup: WestWords, Inc.
Cover Designer/Manager: Wendy Ann Fredericks
Cover Art: From a Thousand and One Nights 1, 1984
    (oil on canvas). Al-Attar, Suad (Contemporary Artist),
    Private collection Iraqi. Bridgeman Art Library, New York, NY
Photo Researcher: Chrissy McIntyre
Manufacturing Buyer: Lucy Hebard
Printer and Binder: R. R. Donnelley & Sons, Inc.
Cover Printer: Phoenix Color Corporation

For permission to use copyrighted material, grateful acknowledgment is made to the
copyright holders on pp. 572–574, which are hereby made part of this copyright page.

Library of Congress Cataloging-in-Publication Data

Ford, Marjorie (Marjorie A.)
  Dreams and inward journeys : a rhetoric and reader for writers / Marjorie Ford,
Jon Ford.—6th ed.
    p. cm.
  Includes bibliographical references and index.
  ISBN 0-321-36602-6 (pbk.)
  1. College readers. 2. Report writing—Problems, exercises, etc. 3. English language—
Rhetoric—Problems, exercises, etc. I. Ford, Jon. II. Title.
PE1417.F63 2006
808'.0427—dc22

                                                                    2005034826

Please visit us at www.ablongman.com

ISBN 0-321-36602-6

1 2 3 4 5 6 7 8 9 10—DOC—09 08 07 06

Contents

1 DISCOVERING OURSELVES IN WRITING AND READING   1

Readings

Student Writing

2 PLACES IN NATURE   65

Revising Initial Descriptions
Establishing Vantage Point and Tone
Thinking About Your Purpose and Audience

Readings

"Lately I had looked for you everywhere
But only night's smooth stare gazed back."

"I knew and abided by the rules of the game I was playing—the weather
and animal rules, the time rules, the danger rules, the social rules with my
shipmates. I was alert but also ecstatic."

"We are sitting on an island in the American River, right in the middle of
. . . a metropolitan area of well over a million people, but my husband and
I like to preserve our mutual delusion."

"The spatterings glisten like enormous, otherworldly fireworks as they sail
through the shadowed air."

"At one point I was balanced on the unsteady ladder in the predawn
gloaming, stepping tenuously from one bent rung to the next, when the ice
supporting the ladder on either end began to quiver as if an earthquake
had struck."

"The power of nature is the power of a life in association. Nothing stands
alone. . . . Each organism is rooted in its own biological niche, drawing its
power from its relationship to other organisms."

"If our culture is out of balance with nature, everything about our lives is
affected: family, workplace, school, community—all take on a crazy shape."

Student Writing

3 JOURNEYS IN MEMORY   119

Readings

"All praises All praises
I am the one who would save."

Linda Seger, "Universal Stories" (essay)   191

"A myth is a story 'more than true'. . . . It's a story that connects and
speaks to us all."

Gabriel García Márquez, "The Handsomest Drowned Man in the World: A Tale for Children" (fiction)   198

"The Captain . . . would say in fourteen languages, look there, where the
wind is so peaceful now that it's gone to sleep beneath the beds, over there,
where the sun's so bright that the sunflowers don't know which way to turn,
yes, over there, that's Esteban's village."

Marcelo Gleiser, "The Myths of Science—Creation" (essay)   203

"All cultures have attempted to provide an answer to the mystery of
creation, and our modern scientific model is no exception. Perhaps more
surprisingly, there is an intriguing correspondence between answers suggested
by mythic narratives and those suggested by scientific research."

Portfolio of Creation Myths   208

These myths from cultures around the world celebrate the mystery of creation
and embody core values and beliefs in imaginative stories of the origins of
the world, its creatures, and human beings.

Genesis 2:4–23 (Old Testament of the Hebrew Bible)   208

"How the Sun Was Made: Dawn, Noontide and Night" (Australian Aboriginal)   209

"The Pelasgian Creation Myth" (Ancient Greek)   210

"The Chameleon Finds" (Yao-Bantu, African)   211

"Spider Woman Creates the Humans" (Hopi, Native American)   212

"The Beginning of the World" (Japanese)   213

Bruno Bettelheim, "Fairy Tales and the Existential Predicament" (essay)   215

"[T]he form and structure of fairy tales suggest images to children by which
they can structure their daydreams and with them give better direction to
their life."

Student Writing

Readings

Student Writing

"Any repair of our fractured world must start with individuals who have the insight and courage to own their own shadow."

"Many a man would have even blazoned such irregularities as I was guilty of; but from the high views that I had set before me, I regarded and hid them with an almost morbid sense of shame."

"An internal debate ensues between two of my selves: the teen girl who loves to torture herself with unfavorable comparisons to others, and the concerned guru."

"Treating our adversaries as potential allies need not entail unthinking acceptance of their actions. Our challenge is to call forth the humanity with each adversary, while preparing for the full range of possible responses."

"I told them. . . . to go beyond retributive justice to restorative justice, to move on to forgiveness, because without it there was no future."

Student Writing

"Identity is more than skin deep."

"Despite my pride in my identity, being Asian American has forced me to deal with situations that have made me feel excluded from both Asian and American cultures."

8   POP DREAMS   459

Readings

Student Writing

9   VOYAGES IN SPIRITUALITY   524

Readings

Student Writing

Contents by Strategies and Modes

Process Analysis

Example and Illustration

Comparison and Contrast

Classification

Definition

Causal Analysis

Argument

Interpretation and Evaluation

Research Writing

Literary Fiction

Poetry

To the Instructor

Dreams and Inward Journeys began as an experiment; we wanted to create a textbook for students that would encourage them to explore their inner worlds of dreams, fantasies, and the unconscious mind as well as the way society influenced those worlds through cultural artifacts such as poems, stories, and essays, as well as through popular culture such as mythology, films, and television. We wanted students to learn to become more engaged in the acts of reading and writing while feeling themselves empowered as agents of social change, which grows out of greater self-knowledge and understanding of the dynamic relationship between inner and outer worlds. Our commitment to this work has been rewarded through the success of *Dreams and Inward Journeys,* which is now entering its sixth edition, and by the enthusiastic response we have received from the many instructors and students who have used the book in their classes and in our own.

Gathering the new materials and writing this edition of *Dreams and Inward Journeys,* we have felt very fortunate to have the opportunity to continue following our dreams. In this new edition we have built on the pedagogical foundation put in place by the earlier editions. We continue to support a creative approach to teaching writing and reading that acknowledges the role and importance of the unconscious mind, of dreams, of the imagination, of the heart connected to the reasoning mind. We have seen our students' writing develop as they have experimented with different writing projects and genres, from reflective essays that are primarily based on personal experiences to essays based on the traditional modes such as comparison, causal analysis, and definition, to ambitious argument and research papers that involve synthesis of diverse perspectives on social issues.

As in previous editions of *Dreams,* we have enjoyed applying these assumptions in shaping the text around the theme of dreams, a topic that is intriguing, revealing, and challenging. *Dreams and Inward Journeys* presents a rich mixture of essays, stories, poems, and student writings thematically focused on dream-related topics such as writing, reading, nature, memory, myths, obsessions, the double, sexuality, gender roles, technology, popular culture, and spirituality. Each chapter features rhetorical advice and strategies for writing and critical thinking. All of the included selections have personal and social meanings that encourage students to think about and develop new ways of seeing and understanding themselves in relation to fundamental social issues as well as universal human concerns.

Special features of the sixth edition include the following:

- Thirty-six new readings that continue to develop and update the text's thematic concept with more particular attention to social and political issues.
- A rhetorical advice section that opens each chapter and provides students with one particular writing and thinking strategy.
- Three chapters that take a very different direction and that contain many new readings: Chapter 2, "Places in Nature"; Chapter 8, "Pop Dreams"; and Chapter 9, "Voyages in Spirituality."
- Classical artwork and photography that support the theme of each chapter, with related prompts that generate prewriting activities and informal and formal writing projects.
- One or two student essays in each chapter that present students' perspectives on the topics raised in the chapter and provide models of the rhetorical strategy outlined at the beginning of each chapter. Four of the student essays in the book are documented argumentative research papers.
- Information on keeping a dream journal as well as journal writing prompts before each reading to encourage informal, expressive, and spontaneous thinking and writing.
- One poem per chapter that explores the chapter's theme in a concrete, expressive, and literary form.
- New "Connection" questions as well as "Questions for Discussion" and "Ideas for Writing."
- "Topics for Research and Writing" questions at the end of each chapter. These questions give students suggestions for research and longer writing assignments, as well as film and URL suggestions for further viewing/reading/research.
- Two Web sites related to each selection to encourage students to do further research on the topics raised in the reading.

Supplements

An Instructor's Manual is available to teachers who adopt the sixth edition of *Dreams and Inward Journeys*. The Instructor's Manual presents instructors with three possible course constructions as well as teaching suggestions and possible responses to the study questions for each reading.

mycomplab 2.0

MyCompLab 2.0 (www.mycomplab.com) offers engaging new resources in grammar, writing, and research for composition students and instructors. This market-leading composition Web resource includes grammar diagnostics; over 3500 grammar questions; video-, image-, and Web-based writing activities organized by different writing purposes; Exchange, an online peer review and instructor grading program; a Model Documents gallery; the highly acclaimed Avoiding Plagiarism tutorial; ResaeachNavigator™ with AutoCite bibliography maker program and searchable databases of credible academic sources; and access to Longman's English Tutor Center. New Gradetracker system, in the

Web site version of MyCompLab, tracks student results for all exercises and activities on the site.

Acknowledgments

First, we thank our reviewers around the country whose advice guided us in this revision: Dawn Comer, Albion College; Michael Hyde, Fashion Institute of Technology; Gina Ladinsky, Santa Monica College; Ronald Layne, Sandhills Community College; Karen Petit, Bristol Community College; Suzanne Shepard, Broome Community College; and Ruthe Thompson, Southwest Minnesota State University.

We also give thanks to our editor, Lynn Huddon, who has helped us to interpret and apply the advice of the critics and to continue to help us develop the creative vision of the book. We thank Jami Darby of WestWords for her consistently supportive supervision of the manuscript's proofreading and production, and we thank Randie Wann for her help with writing new text for the Instructor's Manual. We thank our students at Stanford University and DeAnza College who have provided many valuable insights into ways that we could develop the manuscript's themes and keep the text lively. We are especially grateful to the students at DeAnza College, Norman Chung and Karen Methot-Chun, who wrote new essays for this edition, spending much time outside of their required writing assignments to produce works that we think will inspire your student writers.

We thank our friends who have provided encouragement and love. Finally, we thank our loving children, Michael and Maya, whose lives bring us joy on a daily basis and make our own lives complete, and our grandchild, Elijah Ford, a dream of a baby.

Marjorie Ford
Jon Ford

To the Student

Nothing said to us, nothing we can learn from others, reaches us so deep as that which we find in ourselves.

THEODORE REIK

Each person has a unique understanding of the role and importance of dreams. We may value and analyze the dreams we have while asleep, our daytime fantasies, our hopes and aspirations, our belief in the power of our own imagination and creativity. The lyrics of popular songs, the plots of movies and novels, advertisements, and travel literature—all speak of the power of dreams and promise fulfillment of fantasies, romance, success, or peace of mind. As you think more about the presence and importance of dreams in your personal life and culture, you will begin to discover even more subtle meanings. Just as everyone dreams while sleeping, each person has a personal dream or vision that guides his or her waking life. Perhaps it is a dream that one is just starting to explore, a dream that one has been working to accomplish, or a dream that has just "come true."

We have designed this text using the concept of the dream as a common meeting ground, one that we hope will encourage you to better understand yourself, your family, friends, college, and professional acquaintances—and the world in which you live. Dreams and the insights they bring from the inner self, with the universality of their patterns, imagery, and meaning, also present a central metaphor that can be likened to the writing process, which is often an inward journey that involves the imagination, creativity, and vision.

Dreams and Inward Journeys: A Reader for Writers, sixth edition, is composed of nine chapters. Each chapter presents an aspect of the book's theme as well as a writing strategy that we think will help you to understand yourself and your world while improving your writing fluency and skills. The earlier chapters ask you to reflect on your personal experiences as a reader and as a writer. As you progress through the book, you will be asked to relate your personal and imaginative experiences to the social and cultural realities that also help to shape your identity and values.

In Chapter 1, "Discovering Ourselves in Writing and Reading," you will explore the ways in which reading is an active process that encourages the reader to understand and clarify her or his inner resources and values in relation to the values and experiences that have been recorded in a text. The reading strategies introduced discuss techniques for activating and enriching your reading and language experience. We also emphasize how reading is closely related to writing, which is presented as a process that is often chaotic in its initial stages, but powerful and rewarding. Writing and revising help a writer to understand himself or herself better and to clarify thoughts and feelings, while at the same time communicating what is most important to you to a real audience of readers. The writing techniques explained will help you to overcome writing-related anxieties and fears and to get you started on your writing. The dream journal project introduced in this chapter will provide you with the opportunity to discover the similarities between the writing process and dreaming—to discover the concerns of your unconscious mind.

In Chapter 2, "Places in Nature," the essays invite you to reflect on the way nature can inspire and help you reflect on places in nature you have visited, in order to better grasp the essential connections between human beings and the world around us. The selections in this chapter present a variety of experiences in nature that brought the writer to a revelation about the beauty of the natural world: the challenges of viewing magnificent natural refuges and formations, and the wisdom that natural creatures show us when we watch, listen to, and recognize how they organize and value their own worlds. The strategies that we focus on—observing and capturing details, using words and images (both literally as well as metaphorically), and the essential power of revision through thinking about communicating with your audience—will help you to create striking descriptive accounts of what you see and how you have been affected by particular places in the natural world.

The readings in Chapter 3, "Journeys in Memory," explore how early experiences and memories, especially those inner experiences that are rooted in dreams, fantasies, or even obsessions, influence one's sense of self. The readings included in this section also suggest that stories created and remembered from childhood help to shape personal myths. At the same time, we include readings that examine what constitutes a person's store of memories, including both firsthand experience as well as imagined scenes, stories we are told, and media intake. In this chapter, we discuss creative strategies for writing effective narratives. These strategies will help you when you write about your dreams and memories.

Chapter 4, "Dreams, Myths, and Fairy Tales," will help you develop perspective on your inward journey so that you can place it in a broader social and cultural context. Seeing how your self-concept and values have been influenced by ancient and popular myths and fairy tales may encourage you to seek out new meanings in your life experiences. Because you will be asked to compare different versions of myths and tales, in this chapter we discuss strategies used in comparison writing as well as approaches to making clear evaluative statements.

The readings included in Chapter 5, "Obsessions and Transformation," explore situations and syndromes in which people are overwhelmed by negative and obsessive thoughts and behaviors. Readings also show how destructive obsessions can be transformed positively into greater self-understanding, through healing dreams and mental and physical guidance. The thinking and writing strategies discussed in this chapter will help you to define and draw distinctions among complex concepts such as dreams, myths, obsessions, and fantasies. We also explore some common misuses of words and some barriers to clear communication, as well as the difference between the private and public meanings and associations of words.

Chapter 6, "Journeys in Sexuality and Gender," explores issues of gender and sexuality as they influence an individual's self-concept and role in society. The readings also examine ways that sexuality is reflected in dreams and emotional life, as well as the way that sexual feelings are channeled through myths and rituals. The chapter also focuses on issues of conflict between different genders, particularly in terms of family roles and responsibilities. The writing and thinking strategy presented in this chapter, causal analysis, will help you to analyze and interpret the readings and will provide you with a structure for composing the essays you will be asked to write in response to the readings.

Chapter 7, "The Double/The Other," begins with a discussion of the double-sided nature of the human personality and presents readings, including a variety of classic stories, many of which are based on dreams or fantasies. These essays and stories reflect different forms of the dualistic struggle within the human mind: the good self as opposed to the evil self, the rational self as opposed to the irrational self. The writing strategies in this chapter focus on how to create a balanced argument through exploring opposing viewpoints, empathizing with your audience, making decisions, and taking a final position of your own.

To what extent have your self-image and mental well-being been influenced by the pop dreams and celebrity figures of our mass culture? What happens to those people who don't choose to fit into, or who feel excluded from, the predominant dream of their society? These are some of the questions that are considered in the readings included in Chapter 8, "Pop Dreams." The research writing strategies covered will help you to analyze social issues and to think critically about outside sources of opinion while maintaining your own personal perspective and sense of voice in research writing.

Our final chapter is called "Voyages in Spirituality." Here you will find that spiritual dreams and visions often come to us when least expected, and you will read essays by practitioners of living or action spirituality, who seek to use their spiritual convictions to help other people in need of hope for a positive direction in life. Synthesis and problem solving, the writing strategies presented in this chapter, will help to reinforce your understanding of the chapter's readings and guide you in developing complex, creative essays.

Our experiences as writing teachers continue to confirm the importance of providing students with many opportunities to share their writing with their peers. We have included student essays for you to discuss in class. We hope, too, that you will share your own writing. We believe that you can gain confidence and motivation when you work on your writing with your peers and your instructor.

Although writing is a demanding and challenging activity, it can be a valuable and meaningful experience when you feel you are writing about something vital that engages your mind and your emotions. We have worked to provide opportunities for this type of engagement through the materials and activities included in this text. We hope that *Dreams and Inward Journeys* will guide and help you to uncover and understand more fully your personal and public dreams.

Marjorie Ford
Jon Ford

Discovering Ourselves in Reading and Writing 1

Penny Kaela Bauer
"Gifts from Wise Women and Men: 'Bill'"

Raised in California and currently residing in Washington, Penny Bauer worked for 25 years as a marriage counselor before becoming a professional photographer. Bauer describes her series of photographs of the hands of older men and women as a "vision [of] a circle of elders from different cultures whose hands offer gifts of support as we pursue our dreams."

JOURNAL

Write about your thoughts as you engage in the act of reading or writing. Do you easily become distracted, or do you often find yourself in a deep state of concentration in which you are able to screen out external sounds and ideas unrelated to your work?

Writing itself is one of the great, free human activities. . . . For the person who follows what occurs to him with trust and forgiveness, the world remains always ready and deep, an inexhaustible environment, with the combined vividness of an actuality and flexibility of a dream.
WILLIAM STAFFORD
The Way of Writing

A dream which is not understood is like a letter which is not opened.
The Talmud

Looking back, it's clear to me that I was reading as a creator, bringing myself . . . to a collaboration with the writer in the invention of an alternate world.
PETE HAMILL
D'Artagnan on Ninth Street:
A Brooklyn Boy at the Library

A PROCESS VIEW OF WRITING AND READING

When people write and read, they are concerned with self-discovery just as they are when they explore their dreams. Both writing and reading are complex processes that a reader controls consciously and also experiences unconsciously. These processes, for most of us, begin almost at the same time, although we may have experienced having our parents or preschool teachers read to us before we actually began to study our ABCs and learn to write and to read. In the act of writing, an internal conversation takes place between what we read and our own inner experiences and ideas that helps us to come up with the words we put down on the page. Similarly, in the act of reading, as in a conversation, a dialogue takes place between the voice of the inner self and the voice of the text being read. A good conversation with a text can lead to the development and clarification of the writer's and the reader's values and ideas. Both reading and writing require some formal understanding of literary conventions and language codes. To write well, we must have done some reading: the more the better. Likewise, writing down our responses to what we read helps to clarify our interpretations and evaluations of complex texts.

Because the processes are so interrelated, we could begin our discussion with either writing or reading. Since the course you are probably taking now is a "writing class," we will start with writing and move outward to the more public, responsive dimension of reading and writing about what we read.

The Writing Process and Self-Discovery

William Stafford has said that "writing itself is one of the great, free human activities. There is scope for individuality, and elation, and discovery, in writing." At the same time, a good writer is also a patient craftsperson. Writing makes demands on both the creative and the rational sides of the mind. From the creative and intuitive mind, it summons forth details, images, memories, dreams, and feelings; from the rational and logical mind, it demands planning, development, evidence, rereading, rethinking, and revision.

Perhaps it is this basic duality associated with the act of writing that can sometimes make it feel like a complex and overwhelming task. Practicing and studying particular writing strategies such as those presented in each chapter of *Dreams and Inward Journeys*, along with drafting, revising, and sharing your writing with your peers and instructor, will help you to develop your self-confidence. As a writer you need to be aware of the feelings and fears of your unconscious self as well as the expectations of your rational mind. Balancing these two sides of your mind—knowing when, for example, to give your creative mind license to explore while controlling and quieting your critical mind—is an important part of the challenge of developing self-confidence and learning to write well.

Stages of the Writing Process

Most professional and student writers benefit from conceptualizing writing as a process with a number of stages. Although these stages do not need to be rigidly separated, an awareness of the different quality of thoughts and feelings that usually occur in each of the stages of writing is useful. Having a perspective on your writing process will encourage you to be patient and help you create a finished piece of writing that speaks clearly about your own concerns, values, and opinions. The stages of the writing process include the prewriting, drafting, and revision phases. As you become a more experienced and skillful writer, you may find that you want to adapt this process to the goals of your writing assignment. Perhaps you will find that you need to spend more time in preliminary reading to collect background information for a research essay, or that you don't have as much time to spend on prewriting if you are working on an essay that must be completed in a shorter time frame or during an in-class exam.

As preparation for writing the initial draft of an essay, prewriting allows you to pursue a variety of playful, creative activities that will help you to generate ideas and understand what you want to say about your subject. Drafting is your rapid first "take" on your topic and should be done after you have concentrated on your paper's subject and thought about the thesis or core concept around which you want to center the ideas and examples of your essay. You may find, however, that as you write your first draft, your thesis and focus shift or even change dramatically. Don't be concerned if this happens. Many professional writers have learned that although they begin the drafting phase feeling that they have a focus and thesis, the actual process of writing the draft changes their initial plan. Rewriting is a natural part of the writing process. As you return to your draft and continue to work to shape your thoughts into clear sentences, they will better capture your inner feelings and ideas.

While you will need to rewrite to clarify your thinking and ideas, the process of revision can also be approached in stages. They include revising for your paper's overall shape and meaning, which may involve outlining the rough draft; rearranging whole paragraphs or ideas and examples; developing and cutting redundancy within paragraphs; refining and clarifying sentences and individual words; and, finally, proofreading for grammar, spelling, and punctuation. The revision and editing stages of writing have become more exciting and less tedious since the invention of the computer and word processing software. Now your computer can help you because it includes commands for cutting and pasting text, outliners, spelling and grammar checkers, word and paragraph counters, and global search and replace functions that make it easier to correct any aspect of the entire essay. But revision is still a time-consuming and important element of the writing process, for it is through revision and editing that your essay moves from an approximate statement of a thought or insight into a well-crafted and moving verbal expression of your thoughts and purpose.

Strategies for Prewriting

Because writing begins with prewriting, we have chosen to focus on this stage here, at the beginning of your journey as a writer. The prewriting stage is enjoyable for those who enjoy creative expression, and helpful for people who don't have much confidence in themselves as writers, who feel it is hard to get warmed up to the task. If you are apprehensive about writing and don't see yourself as a creative thinker, prewriting activities may help you to discover new or forgotten images, memories, and ideas, as well as to make connections you may never have anticipated. You may find yourself liberating a creative spirit hidden in the recesses of your mind. You are the only person who needs to read and evaluate your prewriting; at this stage, you determine what seems interesting and relevant.

Prewriting also makes the writing of later drafts easier because it helps you to clarify and organize your thoughts before they are put into a formal format. Drawing, freewriting, invisible writing, brainstorming, clustering, and journal keeping are all effective prewriting techniques that will help you to discover what you really want and need to say. Like the later stages of writing, all of these techniques can be practiced with a pencil, a pen, or sophisticated computer software. Although some students continue to feel more comfortable and natural when prewriting with pencil or pen, those who are familiar with the computer and have good keyboarding skills often find it helpful to do many of their prewritings on the computer so that they can save and possibly transform their initial ideas into details, images, and sentences for their drafts.

Drawing   Drawing a picture in response to a topic can help you understand what you think and feel. In the drawings in response to a topic included in this text, students used a computer program to capture their writing processes and responses to readings, but you may feel more comfortable using colored pencils, watercolors, charcoal, or ink. A number of professional writers have spoken of the value of drawing as a way to develop ideas or understand a new text. In *The Nature and Aim of Fiction*, Flannery O'Connor maintains, "Any discipline can help your writing . . . particularly drawing. Anything that helps you to see, anything that makes you look." While drawing an image from a complex text you are reading, you will be able to focus your thoughts on the details that may have already unconsciously captured your imagination. This process of drawing about a piece of writing will increase your engagement with it and help you clarify your response as you make that response more tangible.

Freewriting   A freewrite can start anywhere and usually lasts from 5 to 15 minutes. During these brief writing sessions, it is important to continue to write and not to censor any idea or feeling that comes to your mind. If you seem to run out of thoughts, just write, "I have no more to say," or anything you wish until a new thought emerges. After ten minutes of freewriting, read what you have written and try to sum up the central idea or feeling of the piece. You can then proceed to another freewrite, using the summary statement as a new starting point. Writers often do several freewrites before they decide how to focus their thoughts.

Invisible Writing   With invisible writing, the writer creates "invisible" words, or words that can't be seen while the writer is working. Some writers never even look at the words generated in an invisible writing exercise but instead use the exercise as a rehearsal, a building of mental pathways that will make the actual writing of their paper less halting and painful. Many writers find new insights in their thoughts that were produced invisibly. Invisible writing can be done by writing on the back of a piece of carbon paper onto a piece of notebook paper or by keyboarding with a dimmed computer screen. While you are freewriting and doing invisible writing, do not consciously pay attention to central ideas, relationships between ideas, organizational patterns, or grammatical or spelling errors. Concentrate instead on getting your ideas and feelings out in words.

Brainstorming   Brainstorming, which can be done effectively in groups or individually, involves writing a list of words, phrases, ideas, descriptions, thoughts, and questions that come to your mind in response to a topic or issue. As in freewriting, it is essential not to stop to censor, judge, or correct

A raindrop begins as a suspension of water. The instant it explodes upon a surface, it spreads and touches everything around it. Just as its potential for expansion increases the farther it falls, my writing process takes shape the deeper it progresses. At first, I begin with nothing, like the blank regions in this background. Then, an idea buds, and I find that the crescendo of my thoughts is like the descent of this raindrop, until it finally bursts and my idea flowers into a new creation. Just as the water is transformed into a broad palette of colors, my writing welcomes potential and growth in various forms.

ideas or feelings. The process of listing will, itself, bring up new ideas and associations. Ideas will build on one another, leading to thoughts that are original and fresh, while creating a list will help you to see relationships between ideas that may have previously seemed disconnected. When your list is complete, normally in 15 to 20 minutes, go back to find patterns of thought or main ideas that you have uncovered. Bracketing or circling related ideas and details may help you form an organizational plan. Through brainstorming, you can formulate a rough outline for your essay that will guide you in the drafting phase of writing.

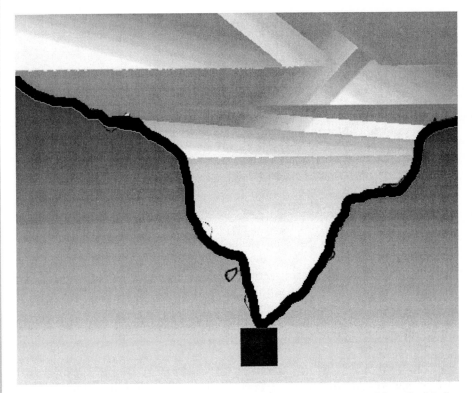

You should "read" my picture from top to bottom. My writing process, as with anybody's, begins with human creativity, an entity as vast and varied as the endless blue skies. When I am called upon to write, I channel my creativity amidst a sea of red, seething frustration. I constantly try to convey my thoughts exactly to my reader, a tedious process. As the channel narrows, the frustration decreases in intensity and I get closer to my final product. At last, when the channel reaches its apex, my pains are rewarded. The result is green, new and fresh, and square, rigid to my expectations.

Clustering Clustering, or mapping, closely reflects the way the mind functions in making nonlinear connections between ideas. Combined with brainstorming or freewriting, clustering can also help you to perceive relationships between ideas. Start your cluster by placing the topic to be explored in the center of the page. Draw a circle around it, and then draw lines out from your central circle in different directions to connect it with other circles containing additional ideas, phrases, or clues to experiences. The words in these circles will naturally develop their own offshoots as new associations emerge. The pattern being created by the clustering process continually changes in complex ways because any new idea will relate to all of the ideas already recorded. As in freewriting, clustering should be done without stopping. Once the cluster feels completed to you, write for a few minutes about what you have discovered. Completing a cluster and a related freewrite can help you understand how you want to focus your topic and organize the major relationships between ideas, examples, and details.

Journal Keeping   Daily writing in a notebook or journal will help you develop a record of your thoughts and feelings. Keeping a journal is similar to the type of prewriting assignments we have just discussed in that it allows you freedom to explore parts of your inner world, knowing that your writing will not be evaluated. Keeping a journal of your responses to the journal topics and study questions in a text, using either a small notebook or a computer, is one of the most effective ways to develop your confidence and skills as a writer. Both of the student essays included in this chapter were developed from journal entries that focused on strong inner experiences and images that initially seemed very private but were clarified and made public through drafting, revising, peer sharing, and more revision.

The Dream Journal   Because this text has been developed around the theme of dreams, and because the process of understanding your dreams may lead you to new insights and images that you may find useful in more formal writing, we recommend that you extend your journal keeping into the night world by writing down your dreams—a process used by many professional writers. Through keeping a dream journal, you can improve your ability to recall dreams, and you can capture unconscious images that intrigue or possibly disturb you. Perhaps, too, you will notice more similarities between your dream images and some of the dreamlike stories in this text. Your appreciation of metaphors and symbols will increase.

By keeping your dream journal, you will also realize how understanding your writing process is similar to understanding your dreams. The first written draft of your dream is like a prewrite of an essay: a set of strong, if chaotic, images that you can work with thoughtfully and creatively. As you bring form and meaning to a dream through analysis and interpretation, you bring form and meaning to an essay through drafting and revising those first generative ideas that begin the process of writing an essay, story, or poem.

Keep your dream journal at your bedside along with a pen or dark pencil. The best time to write in your dream journal is in the early morning or immediately on awaking from a vivid dream. Some students have even used a tape recorder to capture their "dream voice," its sounds and rhythms. Try to write in your dream journal three or four times a week, even if you have only a dim or fleeting image or impression to record. Write down all the details you can remember, indicating a shift, jump in time, or unclear portion of the dream with ellipses or a question mark. Try not to censor or "clean up" the dream imagery, even if the thinking seems illogical, chaotic, or even embarrassing to you. Avoid interpreting your dream as you are recording it, although you might list in the margins any associations that immediately come to mind in relation to the images as you record them. Later, as you reread your dream journal entries over a period of several days, you may see patterns and more complex associations emerging, and you may want to write about them.

Your Computer: Developing an Important Writing Partnership

Most students come to their college writing classes with basic computer skills. Your computer can help to facilitate and streamline your writing process. Computers are not just keyboarding tools or drivers for printing out text. In the later stages of revising and editing, computers are invaluable, making it possible for you to reorganize your paper easily by moving around large sections of your essay, adding concise examples and details, and fine-tuning grammar, syntax, and word choice. The spell-checker on your computer will help you prepare your draft for final presentation, while an online dictionary and thesaurus make it possible to find just the right word for precise and powerful expression. Some students find that the flexibility that computers provide to generate new ideas; experiment; change sentences, paragraphs, details, and examples; and refine major ideas helps them to overcome writing blocks.

In fact, all of the strategies for prewriting mentioned here, particularly the technique of invisible writing, can be completed and saved on a computer. Other exploratory techniques work only on a computer, such as engaging in an online conversation on a subject for writing using a chat program or e-mail, and then saving the conversation for later use. You might decide to copy sections from any of your prewritings into the first or a later draft of your essay; this is much easier to do if you write them on a computer rather than on a piece of paper.

Prewriting strategies are more frequently used in the generative stage of the writing process, but we encourage you to use these techniques whenever you feel yourself getting blocked in your work. During the drafting stage of writing, or even after an instructor has returned your paper to you with corrections on it and you are working on a major revision, the exercises discussed above can continue to help you keep in touch with what you really want to say—with your own inner voice.

Discovering Ourselves in Reading: The Reading Process

Once absorbed in the complex mental process of reading, readers desire to identify with the characters, the ideas, the emotions, and the cultural and social assumptions of the text. Readers then are able to experience new and different realities vicariously; these encounters can contribute to the reader's personal growth as they present new intellectual and emotional experiences that help readers to build their inner resources. As a person becomes a better reader and develops a richer life through reading, his or her writing may also become more fluent and varied as the reader becomes more conscious of public values, opinions, and cultures that are different from his or her personal experiences.

Writing is one of the most valuable ways to respond to what you read. Writing about what you're reading will help you articulate and clarify your responses and will improve your writing as you develop your writer's voice through connecting to the words and thoughts of others. As with any form of writing, responses to reading can move through a series of phases or stages, each one building upon the next, moving gradually from prereading strategies to interpretation and evaluation.

Prereading/Early Reading

In the prereading phase, you examine what you plan to read, browsing through titles and subheadings, and noting epigraphs, topic sentences, headnotes, and footnotes, just as you probably did when you first picked up this textbook. Prereading can be a very helpful process if you combine it with writing down basic questions that you have during this initial browsing stage. Does this work seem like fact or fiction? Was it written recently or in the distant past? Is its style experimental or traditional? Is the writer American, or is he or she from a different culture and country? Is the writer male or female? Is the subject a familiar one? Do you need more background knowledge to understand the subject? Asking and answering such questions can help you become involved with the text and can help put you into a receptive frame of mind.

After previewing the work, proceed to the second part of the first stage in reading, the "early reading" phase. In this phase, as in writing a first draft, you simply plunge in, reading the work quickly to get an overall sense of its meaning, perhaps noting a few key passages or putting a question mark by an idea or detail that seems unfamiliar or confusing. At this stage of reading, avoid negative preconceptions about the content of the reading; don't tell yourself, "This is about a subject in which I have absolutely no interest." Try instead to be open to the reading. Avoid evaluating the text before you give yourself a chance to become engaged with it.

Personal and Interpretive Response

In this second stage, the interpretive response phase, put the reading aside for a moment and write down a few immediate, personal reactions: Is this piece what I expected it to be? Did it make me angry? Sad? Elated? How did the piece challenge me? What didn't I understand after the first reading? Reread your notes and questions before attempting another reading. The second time, read more slowly and reflectively. Try to answer some of your initial questions as well as to move toward an overview and interpretation of the piece as a whole—its meaning, or your view of its meaning at this stage in your reading.

Look for those patterns that support an interpretation or view of the work: metaphors, plot and subplot, character relationships and conflicts, point of view, evolving personae, and narrative voice. Mark your book, placing circles around and drawing lines to connect ideas and images that you believe form a pattern of meaning. Ask yourself how much of the work is meant to be responded to literally, and how much is meant to be considered as ironic or symbolic. Record responses to this stage of the reading process in writing, including some particular quotations and references to the text. Also compare your reactions at this stage of reading with your written responses to the first reading of the text. You will probably find that your ideas have deepened considerably and that you have a more complete and interpretive view of the work than you did initially.

Critical and Evaluative Response

For the third stage in your reading/writing process, the "critical" phase, reread the story again more rapidly, after reviewing your second written response and your textual references. Now write a final response, clarifying how this reading confirms, expands on, or causes you to question or revise your earlier readings. Using particular elements in the text that you noticed in your earlier readings as evidence, try to draw some larger evaluative conclusions about the work and your response to it: Is your overall response to the values, ideas, and emotions in the work positive or negative? How do you feel about the unity of the piece, its quality as writing? How do the values of this selection reflect or illuminate issues of concern to you and to your community? Was there something new and special about the experience of reading this work? Did it remind you of or seem to build upon other, similar works with which you are familiar? After finishing the text, did you want to read more by this writer or learn more about the theme of the work by reading related works by other writers? Would you recommend the work to other readers?

"Reading" Nonprint, Multimedia, and Online Texts

Although some theorists believe that the traditional act of reading is passé in this electronic age, the perceptual and critical thinking process for decoding, analyzing, interpreting, and evaluating materials that involve images along with printed words or even with no words at all is not as different from book reading as it might seem. Whether you are reading a book, watching a film, viewing a television show, or scrolling through Web pages, you need to pay close attention to all available clues for meaning. You will need to look for patterns of imagery, symbols, significant character interaction, plotlines, and crucial meaning statements, whether in the form of speeches by characters, key bits of dialogue, or voice-overs (in the case of a film).

Whether reading a book, viewing a film, or examining a Web page, you also need to know something about the author (director/screenwriter, in the case of a film; or, in the case of many Web pages, the organization that has produced the page and its objectives). You need to know how this work builds on other works by the same writer or organization, as well as what cultural assumptions and traditions (of writing, filmmaking, or multimedia) the work issues from.

Finally, whether you are reading a book, watching a film or TV show, or even cruising the Internet, you need the opportunity for a second reading/viewing, to get closer to the work through repeated exposure to grasp its full significance and to make interpretations and connections with other similar works. While this is easier to do with a book, you can always watch a film a second time and take notes, videotape a TV show, or, in the case of Web pages, bookmark the page or save the text for instant replay later on. Note that in nonprint media or multimedia, you have to learn to read visual images for meaningful forms, symbols, intellectual suggestions, and emotional impact, just as you examine the words in a written text closely for their connotations or shadings of meaning. In multimedia, you need to be alert to a complex interplay between words, images, and even sounds.

What makes a person a good reader, interpreter, and judge of electronic media is precisely the kind of good study habits that an experienced reader brings to a book. You need to resist the passive mood many people sink into in front of TV sets or the "surf" mentality that involves clicking rapidly and restlessly from one link to another on the Internet. When studying media, writing can be an especially helpful way to develop critical responses. Try keeping a journal of media you watch and listen to, responding actively by using the kind of entries suggested above in the section on keeping a reader's journal: preliminary responses and entries, interpretive entries, and evaluative entries for a repeated viewing of material that looks interesting. In this way, you can become a strong reader, sensitive to the world of books as well as an able critic of the electronic media that surround us daily, which at times overwhelm our abilities to respond or to take a position.

In reading and writing about the essays, stories, and poems selected for this textbook as well as the different media that you encounter, try to practice the slow, three-stage reading and written response process outlined above, taking time to write down questions and responses in your notebook and in the margins of the text. Give yourself enough time to absorb and think about what you have read and viewed. Your patience will yield you both heightened understanding as well as deeper pleasure in all your learning experiences.

T H E M A T I C I N T R O D U C T I O N :
D I S C O V E R I N G O U R S E L V E S
I N W R I T I N G A N D R E A D I N G

W riting and reading can be described as inward journeys. Discovering what resides within your mind and your spirit begins anew each time you start a writing or reading project. Many people find it difficult to begin, wondering how they will be able to untangle all of their thoughts and feelings, and how they will finally decide on the most accurate words and sentence patterns to make their statement clear and compelling. You may feel overwhelmed by the possibilities of all that is waiting to be discovered within you, and, at the same time, you may feel a sense of wonder and excitement, anticipating pleasures and rewards of uncovering and expressing new parts of your mind, imagination, and spirit.

The complex feelings often experienced at the beginning of the writing/reading process have been eloquently described by many authors whose language, images, and ideas can serve as your guides. They experience writing and reading as processes of self-discovery and self-understanding that are rooted in their unconscious and conscious mind, in their dreams and memories of childhood, and in their everyday lives and goals. At the same time, reading and writing are about communication with the public world as well as the inner world.

This chapter's readings begin with a poem by Denise Levertov, "The Secret," in which she examines the mysterious relationship that authors have with readers who discover wisdom through the imaginative texts they read, wisdom that the author herself may be unaware of. In the selection that follows, "The Symbolic Language of Dreams," popular novelist Stephen King discusses the ways in which his dreams have helped him to solve problems that he has had in writing.

In our next essay, "A Matter of Trust," Ursula Le Guin focuses on issues of audience consideration in the revision stage of writing. In contrast, Virginia Woolf, in her classic essay "Professions for Women," contextualizes the writing process by exploring ways that social, economic, and gender status have an impact on a person's ability to express herself openly and to write freely. In her essay "Mother Tongue," best-selling novelist Amy Tan focuses on the importance of language and family culture in writing, revealing how she developed her writing talents by incorporating all that she and her mother, a nonnative speaker, knew about language and about life.

Reading can be a very active, intriguing, and creative process. Several of the authors in this chapter reflect on the ways that reading plays a part in the development of the reader's inner life and imagination. Frederick Douglass, in "Learning to Read and Write," shares his passion for reading from the perspective of a former slave; he speaks of his awakening to freedom through the knowledge he uncovers in the signs, books, and periodicals of his time. In contrast, in "Don't Look Back," software entrepreneur and digital composer Steven Holtzman argues that we can't turn our backs on the new ways that reading is presented to us through technology. Finally, in his essay, "Hell's Bibliophiles," college English professor John Ramsay presents an approach that could make reading more exciting for "aliterate" Americans who choose to read as little as possible despite modern technology's ability to provide quick access to an abundance of information.

The two student essays that conclude this chapter give further insights into how writing and reading shape an individual's inner growth and identity. Joyce Chang, in her essay "Drive Becarefully," a response to Amy Tan's "Mother Tongue," discusses Chang's inner struggle to accept her mother's language as fundamental to both of their identities. In the final student essay, Molly Thomas responds to Steven Holtzman's "Don't Look Back" by pointing out some of the contradictions she sees in his position on the electronic media and its impact on our culture.

As you embark on your journey through the readings in this chapter, we hope that you will reflect on the universal yet changing nature of writing and reading. We know that these interrelated processes have the power to engage your mind in lively, imaginative, and provocative adventures.

Denise Levertov

The Secret

Born in England, Denise Levertov (1923–1998) moved to the United States in 1948 after serving as a nurse in World War II. She was active in anti–Vietnam War protests in the 1960s and taught in the English Department at Stanford University from 1982 to 1993. Levertov published many volumes of poetry that explore social, mystical, and natural themes, as well as several prose books and translations of poetry. Her collections include Freeing the Dust *(1975),* Candles in Babylon *(1982),* Sands of the Well *(1996), and* This Great Unknowing: Last Poems *(1999). The following poem, "The Secret," from* O Taste and See *(1962), explores the relationship between a writer, a text, and ordinary readers.*

JOURNAL

Write about a reading experience that helped you to discover a secret about yourself, the world, or life itself.

Two girls discover
the secret of life
in a sudden line of
poetry.

5 I who don't know the
secret wrote
the line. They
told me

(through a third person)
10 they had found it
but not what it was
not even

what line it was. No doubt
by now, more than a week
15 later, they have forgotten
the secret,

the line, the name of
the poem. I love them
for finding what
20 I can't find,

and for loving me
for the line I wrote,
and for forgetting it
so that

25 a thousand times, till death
finds them, they may
discover it again, in other
lines

in other
30 happenings. And for
wanting to know it,
for

assuming there is
such a secret, yes,
35 for that
most of all.

QUESTIONS FOR DISCUSSION

1. How is it that the young girls can "discover" the secret of life in a line of poetry? What does this suggest about both the concentrated nature of poetry and how we come to "understand" it?
2. Why can't the writer in the poem "know" the secret that young girls have found? What does this suggest about the unique experiences of writer and readers for a written work?
3. What does the writer suggest about the relationship between imaginative texts and life experience when she predicts that the young readers will forget the "secret," only to find it later "in other / lines / in other / happenings"? Does this remind you of your own reading experiences? How? Why?
4. Why does the writer in the poem "love" her readers? Why do they "love" her? What is meant by love in this context, and how is love a significant aspect of the felt relationship between a writer and her reading audience?
5. Why does the writer love the young readers especially for "wanting to know" the secret of life and for assuming there is such a secret? What do these key concepts imply about the importance of values and faith to the reading experience? Would a reader who believes there is no secret to life and/or doesn't care about such secrets be likely to enjoy or fully understand imaginative texts?
6. Levertov uses very short, irregular lines and brief stanzas to organize and shape this poem. How do her line lengths and the breaks between lines and stanzas help to emphasize her thought process and the subject matter of the poem?

CONNECTION

Compare Levertov's views on the potential importance of literature to a reader with the ideas on reading in "Hell's Bibliophiles" (see page 50).

IDEAS FOR WRITING

1. Develop your journal entry above into an essay about a "secret" you learned through reading. Return to the original text if possible and reread it. How does the secret it captures appear different now than it did when you first read the poem?
2. Write a persuasive essay in which you write to an audience of skeptical young people who don't believe they can find the "secret to life" in poems and books. What other important rewards can reading provide them?

RELATED WEB SITES

Modern American Poetry Site: Denise Levertov
`www.english.uiuc.edu/maps/poets/g_l/levertov/levertov.htm`
This site, devoted to Denise Levertov, contains some of her poems and analysis of poems, speeches and essays by Levertov, interviews with her, as well as external links to more information.

Favorite Poem Project
www.favoritepoem.org/theproject/index.html
This online project, initiated by Poet Laureate Robert Pinsky, features videos of
ordinary people reading and sometimes commenting on poems that have had
a profound effect on their lives. Text versions of the poems are also included.

Stephen King

The Symbolic Language of Dreams

*Stephen King (b. 1947) is originally from Portland, Maine, where he continues to
reside. After graduating from the University of Maine in 1970 with a B.A. in English, King taught high school and worked at odd jobs before finding time to write
his first novel,* Carrie *(1974), an immediate best-seller that was made into a classic horror film. King has continued to be one of the most popular contemporary
writers of horror novels. Some of his best-known works include* The Shining
(1977; film version 1980), Firestarter *(1980; film version 1984),* Misery
(1987; film version 1990), The Dark Half *(1989),* Desperation *(1996),* The
Girl Who Loved Tom Gordon *(1999),* Hearts in Atlantis *(1999; film version
2001), and* The Dream Catcher *(2001). In the following essay, King describes
some of the ways dreams have helped him with his writing.*

JOURNAL

Write about how one of your dreams or intuitions helped you to solve a writing
problem or to understand an issue in your life.

One of the things that I've been able to use dreams for in my stories is to
show things in a symbolic way that I wouldn't want to come right out and
say directly. I've always used dreams the way you'd use mirrors to look at something you couldn't see head-on—the way that you use a mirror to look at your
hair in the back. To me that's what dreams are supposed to do. I think that
dreams are a way that people's minds illustrate the nature of their problems.
Or maybe even illustrate the answers to their problems in symbolic language.

When we look back on our dreams, a lot of times they decompose as soon as
the light hits them. So, you can have a dream, and you can remember very
vividly what it's about, but ten or fifteen minutes later, unless it's an extraordinarily vivid dream or an extraordinarily good dream, it's gone. It's like the
mind is this hard rubber and you really have to hit it hard to leave an impression that won't eventually just erase.

One of the things that we're familiar with in dreams is the sense that familiar or prosaic objects are being put in very bizarre circumstances or situations.

And since that's what I write about, the use of dreams is an obvious way to create that feeling of weirdness in the real world. I guess probably the most striking example of using a dream in my fiction was connected to the writing of *Salem's Lot.*

Now, I can think of only maybe five or six really horrible nightmares in the course of my life—which isn't bad when you think that that life stretches over 44 years—but I can remember having an extremely bad dream when I was probably nine or ten years old.

5   It was a dream where I came up a hill and there was a gallows on top of this hill with birds all flying around it. There was a hangman there. He had died, not by having his neck broken, but by strangulation. I could tell because his face was all puffy and purple. And as I came close to him he opened his eyes, reached his hands out and grabbed me.

I woke up in my bed, sitting bolt upright, screaming. I was hot and cold at the same time and covered with goosebumps. And not only was I unable to go back to sleep for hours after that, but I was really afraid to turn out the lights for weeks. I can still see it as clearly now as when it happened.

Years later I began to work on *Salem's Lot.* Now, I knew that the story was going to be about a vampire that came from abroad to the United States and I wanted to put him in a spooky old house. I got about that far in my thinking and, by whatever way it is that your mind connects things, as I was looking around for a spooky house, a guy who works in the creative department of my brain said, Well what about that nightmare you had when you were eight or nine years old? Will that work? And I remembered the nightmare and I thought, Yes, it's perfect.

I turned the dead man into a guy named Hubie Marston who owned a bad house and pretty much repeated the story of the dream in terms of the way he died. In the story, Hubie Marston hangs himself. He's some sort of black artist of the Aleister Crowley kind—some sort of a dark magician—and I kind of combined him with a stock character in American tabloidism—the wealthy guy who lives and dies in squalor.

For me, once the actual act of creation starts, writing is like this high-speed version of the flip books you have when you're a kid, where you mix and match. The cover of the book will say, "You Can Make Thousands of Faces!" You can put maybe six or seven different eyes with different noses. Except that there aren't just thousands of faces, there are literally billions of different events, personalities, and things that you can flip together. And it happens at a very rapid rate. Dreams are just one of those flip strips that you can flip in there. But they also work in terms of advancing the story.

10   Sometimes when I write I can use dreams to have a sort of precognitive effect on the story. Precognitive dreams are a staple of our supernatural folklore. You know, the person who dreamed that flight 17 was going to crash and changed his reservation and sure enough, flight 17 crashed. But it's like those urban fairy tales: you always hear somebody say, "I have a friend that this happened to." I've never actually heard anyone say, "This happened to *me*."

The closest that I can come to a precognitive experience is that I can be in a situation where a really strong feeling of déjà vu washes over me. I'm sure that I've been there before. A lot of times I make the association that, at some point, I had a dream about this place and this series of actions, and forgot it with my conscious mind when I awoke.

Every now and then dreams can come in handy. When I was working on *It*—which was this really long book—a dream made a difference.

I had a lot of time and a lot of my sense of craft invested in the idea of being able to finish this huge, long book. Now, when I'm working on something, I see books, completed books. And in some fashion that thing is already there. I'm not really making it so much as I am digging it up, the way that you would an artifact, out of the sand. The trick is to get as much of that object as you possibly can, to get the whole thing out, so it's usable, without breaking it. You always break it somewhat—I mean you never get a complete thing—but if you're really careful and if you're really lucky, you can get most of it.

When I'm working I never know what the end is going to be or how things are going to come out. I've got an idea what direction I want the story to go in, or hope it will go in, but mostly I feel like the tail on a kite. I don't feel like the kite itself, or like the wind that blows on the kite—I'm just the tail of it. And if I know when I sit down what's happening or what's going to happen, that day and the next day and the day after, I'm happy. But with *It* I got to a point where I couldn't see ahead any more. And every day I got closer to the place where this young girl, who was one of my people—I don't think of them as good people or bad people, just my people—was going to be and they were going to find her.

I didn't know what was going to happen to her. And that made me extremely nervous. Because that's the way books don't get done. All at once you just get to a point where there is no more. It's like pulling a little string out of a hole and all at once it's broken and you don't get whatever prize there was on the end of it.

So I had seven, eight hundred pages and I just couldn't stand it. I remember going to bed one night saying, I've got to have an idea. I've got to have an idea! I fell asleep and dreamed that I was in a junk yard, which was where this part of the story was set.

Apparently, I was the girl. There was no girl in the dream. There was just me. And there were all these discarded refrigerators in this dump. I opened one of them and there were these things inside, hanging from the various rusty shelves. They looked like macaroni shells and they were all just sort of trembling in a breeze. Then one of them opened up these wings, flew out and landed on the back of my hand. There was a sensation of warmth, almost like when you get a subcutaneous shot of Novocain or something, and this thing started to turn from white to red. I realized it had anesthetized my hand and it was sucking my blood out. Then they all started to fly out of this refrigerator and to land on me. They were these leeches that looked like macaroni shells. And they were swelling up.

I woke up and I was very frightened. But I was also very happy. Because then I knew what was going to happen. I just took the dream as it was and put it in the book. Dropped it in. I didn't change anything.

In the story "The Body," there's an incident where several boys find themselves covered with leeches. That was something that actually happened to me. There's a lot of stuff in "The Body" that's just simply history that's been tarted up a little bit. These friends and I all went into this pond about a mile and half from the house where I grew up and when we came out we were just covered with those babies. It was awful. I don't remember that I had nightmares about the incident then but of course I had this leech dream years later.

I really think what happened with this dream was that I went to sleep and the subconscious went right on working and finally sent up this dream the way that you would send somebody an interoffice message in a pneumatic tube.

In the Freudian sense, I don't think there is any subconscious, any unconscious where things are going on. I think that consciousness is like an ocean. Whether you're an inch below the surface or whether you're down a mile and half deep, it's all water. All H_2O.

I think that our minds are the same nutrient bath all the way down to the bottom and different things live at different levels. Some of them are a little bit harder to see because we don't get down that deep. But whatever's going on in our daily lives, our daily thoughts, the things that the surface of our minds are concerned with eddy down—trickle down—and then they have some sort of an influence down there. And the messages that we get a lot of times are nothing more than symbolic reworkings of the things that we're concerned with. I don't think they're very prophetic or anything like that. I think a lot of times dreams are nothing more than a kind of mental or spiritual flatulence. They're a way of relieving pressure.

One way of looking at this water metaphor might be to talk about jumbo shrimp, everybody's favorite oxymoron. They're the big shrimp that nobody ate in restaurants until 1955 or 1960 because, until then, nobody thought of going shrimping after dark. They were there all the time, living their prosaic shrimp lives, but nobody caught them. So when they finally caught them it was, "Hello! Look at this. This is something entirely new." And if the shrimp could talk they'd say, "Shit, we're not new. We've been around for a couple of thousand years. You were just too dumb to look for us."

A slightly different way of looking at this is that there are certain fish that we get used to looking at. There are carp, goldfish, catfish, shad, cod—they're fish that are more or less surface fish. They go down to a depth of maybe fifty, sixty, or a hundred feet. People catch them, and we get used to seeing them. Not only do we see them in aquariums or as pictures in books, we see them on our plates. We cook them. We see them in the supermarket in the fish case. Whereas if you go down in a bathysphere, if you go down real deep, you see all these bright fluorescent, weird, strange things with membranous umbrellas and weird skirts that flare out from their bodies. Those are creatures that we don't see very often because they explode if we bring them up close to the surface. They are to surface fish what dreams are to our surface thoughts. Deep fish are like dreams of surface fish. They change shape, they change form.

25   There are dreams and there are deep dreams. There are dreams where you're able to tap sources that are a lot deeper. I'm sure that if you wanted to extend this metaphor you could say that within the human psyche, within human thought, there really are Mindanao trenches, places that are very very deep, where there are probably some extremely strange things floating around. And what the conscious mind brings up may be the equivalent of an exploded fish. It may just be a mess. It may be something that's gorgeous in its own habitat but when it gets up to the sun it just dries out. And then it's very gray and dull.

    I remember about six months ago having this really vivid dream.

    I was in some sort of an apartment building, a cheesy little apartment building. The front door was open and I could see all these black people going back and forth. They were talking and having a wonderful time. Somebody was playing music somewhere. And then the door shut.

    In the dream I went back and got into bed. I think I must have shut the door myself. My brother was in bed with me, behind me, and he started to strangle me. My brother had gone crazy. It was awful!

    I remember saying, with the last of my breath, "I think there's somebody out there." And he got up from the bed and went out. As soon as he was out I went up and closed the door and locked it. And then I went back to bed. That is, I started to lie down in this dream.

30   Then I began to worry that I hadn't really locked the door. This is the sort of thing that I'm always afraid of in real life. Did I turn off the burners on the stove? Did I leave a light on when I left the house? So, I got up to check the door and sure enough it was unlocked. I realized that he was still in there with me. Somewhere.

    I screamed in the dream, "He's still in the house." I screamed so loud I woke myself up. Except I wasn't screaming when I woke up. I was just sort of muttering it over and over again: He's in the house, he's in the house. I was terrified.

    Now, I keep a glass of ice water beside the bed where I sleep and the ice cubes hadn't melted yet, so it had happened almost immediately after I fell asleep. That's usually when I have the dreams that I remember most vividly.

    Part of my function as a writer is to dream awake. And that usually happens. If I sit down to write in the morning, in the beginning of that writing session and the ending of that session, I'm aware that I'm writing. I'm aware of my surroundings. It's like shallow sleep on both ends, when you go to bed and when you wake up. But in the middle, the world is gone and I'm able to see better.

    Creative imaging and dreaming are just so similar that they've got to be related.

35   In a story like "The Body" or *It*, which is set around the late fifties or the early sixties, I'm literally able to regress so that I can remember things that I'd forgotten. Time goes by and events pile up on the surface of your mind like snow, and it covers all these other previous layers. But if you're able to put yourself into that sort of semidreaming state—whether you're dreaming or whether

you're writing creatively the brainwaves are apparently interchangeable—you're able to get a lot of that stuff back. That might be deep dreaming.

I'm aware, particularly in recent years, how precious that state is, I mean the ability to go in there when one is awake. I'm also aware, as an adult, of the vividness of my sleeping dreams when I have them. But I don't have any way of stacking up the number of dreams that I have as opposed to anybody else. My sense is I probably dream a little bit less at night because I'm taking off some of the pressure in the daytime. But I don't have an inherent proof of that.

I can remember finding that state for the first time and being delighted. It's a little bit like finding a secret door in a room but not knowing exactly how you got in. I can't remember exactly how I first found that state except that I would sit down to write every day, and I would pretty much do that whether the work went well or the work went badly. And after doing that for a while it was a little bit like having a posthypnotic suggestion.

I know that there are certain things that I do if I sit down to write: I have a glass of water or I have a cup of tea. There's a certain time I sit down around eight o'clock—or 8:15 or 8:30—somewhere within that half-hour every morning. I have my vitamin pill; I have my music; I have my same seat; and the papers are all arranged in the same places. It's a series of things. The cumulative purpose of doing those things the same way every day seems to be a way of saying to the mind: you're going to be dreaming soon.

It's not really any different than a bedtime routine. Do you go to bed a different way every night? Is there a certain side that you sleep on? I mean I brush my teeth. I wash my hands. Why would anybody wash their hands before they go to bed? I don't know. And the pillows: the pillows are supposed to be pointed a certain way. The open side of the pillowcase is supposed to be pointed *in* toward the other side of the bed. I don't know why.

40   And the sleeping position is the same: turn to the right, turn to the left. I think it's a way of your mind saying to your body, or your body saying to your mind—maybe they're communicating with each other saying—we're gonna go to sleep now. And probably dreaming follows the same pattern if you don't interrupt it with things like drug use, alcohol, or whatever.

The dreams that I remember most clearly are almost always early dreams. And they're not always bad dreams. I don't want to give you that impression. I can remember one very clearly. It was a flying dream. I was over the turnpike and I was flying along wearing a pair of pajama bottoms. I didn't have any shirt on. I'm just buzzing along under overpasses—*kazipp*—and I'm reminding myself in the dream to stay high enough so that I don't get disemboweled by car antennas sticking up from the cars. That's a fairly mechanistic detail but when I woke up from this dream my feeling was not fear or loathing but just real exhilaration, pleasure and happiness.

It wasn't an out of control flying dream. I can remember as a kid, having a lot of falling dreams but this is the only flying dream that I can remember in detail.

I don't have a lot of repetitive dreams but I do have an anxiety dream: I'm working very hard in a little hot room—it seems to be the room where I lived as

a teenager—and I'm aware that there's a madwoman in the attic. There's a little tiny door under the eave that goes to the attic, and I have to finish my work.
I have to get that work done or she'll come out and get me. At some point in
the dream that door always bursts open and this hideous woman—with all this
white hair stuck up around her head like a gone-to-seed dandelion—jumps out
with a scalpel.

And I wake up.

45   I still have that dream when I'm backed up on my work and trying to fill all
these ridiculous commitments I've made for myself.

QUESTIONS FOR DISCUSSION

1. King says, "I think that dreams are a way that people's minds illustrate the
   nature of their problems. Or maybe even illustrate the answers to their
   problems in symbolic language." How does he develop this insight about
   dreams through the personal examples provided in the essay?
2. Discuss several different ways in which King uses his dreams in his writing.
   Which approach seems to have been most productive for him?
3. King is known as a vivid and detailed writer, particularly in the construction of the fantasy scenes in his novels. Give examples of King's use of specific detail and effective choice of language in describing the dreams he
   refers to in this essay.
4. What conclusions about the way in which the mind functions does King
   develop through his metaphors of the mind as an ocean, as a nutrient bath,
   and as water? What different roles do the analogies he makes with jumbo
   shrimp and different kinds of fish play in his explanations?
5. What relationship does King find between his process of writing and his
   process of dreaming? Why does King believe that "creative imaging and
   dreaming are just so similar that they've got to be related"? Explain why
   you agree or disagree with him.
6. Although King is primarily a novelist, how do you think you will be able to
   use his insights about the role of dreams in your own writing?

CONNECTION

Compare and contrast King's and Woolf's use of their dreams and fantasies in
their writing (see page 28).

IDEAS FOR WRITING

1. Write down a dream or nightmare that is vivid in your mind but that has
   never been recorded in words; then write an analysis of the dream. Discuss what you have learned about yourself from recording the dream.
2. King gives us a good sense of the types of dreams that he has, the impact
   that his dreams have had on him, and the detailed fabric of his dreams.
   Write an essay in which you compare and contrast your dreams to King's

dreams. What does this comparison and contrast suggest to you about how dreams might have a significant impact on waking life?

RELATED WEB SITES

Stephen King
www.stephenking.com
This official site for author Stephen King provides the latest news about the author as well as relevant links. The site also includes information on Steven King's past and his upcoming projects.

Online Symbolism Dictionary
**www.umich.edu/~umfandsf/symbolismproject/symbolism.html/
index.html**
This online dictionary of symbols in dreams, literature, and the visual arts will serve as a helpful guide to readers, writers, or curious dreamers. Browse or search by key word.

Ursula Le Guin

A Matter of Trust

Ursula Le Guin (b. 1929) studied literature at Radcliffe, where she earned a B.A. degree, and went on to earn her M.A. from Columbia University in 1952. After being awarded a Fulbright fellowship, she studied in France; she now lives in Portland, Oregon. Le Guin is the author of more than 100 short stories, 2 collections of essays, several volumes of poetry, and 19 novels including the Earthsea *trilogy, which won the National Book Award in 1973. Some of her best-known books include* The Left Hand of Darkness *(1969) and* The Dispossessed *(1974). She also writes essays on language, the imagination, and the craft of writing, most recently* Dancing at the Edge of the World: Thoughts on Words, Women, Places *(1996), and* The Waves of the Mind: Talks and Essays on the Writer, Reader and the Imagination *(2004), where the selection that follows can be found. In "A Matter of Trust," Le Guin gives advice to beginning authors on the kind of relationship that develops between a writer and his or her readers after the first draft of a work is completed.*

JOURNAL

Write about the experience of revising a draft for a story or essay. What strategies have you used to make your work clearer and more engaging during the revision stage of writing?

A story is a collaboration between teller and audience, writer and reader. Fiction is not only illusion, but collusion.

Without a reader there's no story. No matter how well written, if it isn't read it doesn't exist as a story. The reader makes it happen just as much as the writer does. Writers are likely to ignore this fact, perhaps because they resent it.

The relationship of writer and reader is popularly seen as a matter of control and consent. The writer is The Master, who compels, controls, and manipulates the reader's interest and emotion. A lot of writers love this idea.

And lazy readers want masterful writers. They want the writer to do all the work while they just watch it happen, like on TV.

5   Most best-sellers are written for readers who are willing to be passive consumers. The blurbs on their covers often highlight the coercive, aggressive power of the text—compulsive page-turner, gut-wrenching, jolting, mind-searing, heart-stopping—what is this, electroshock torture?

From commercial writing of this type, and from journalism, come the how-to-write clichés, "Grab your readers with the first paragraph," "Hit them with shocker scenes," "Never give them time to breathe," and so on.

Now, a good many writers, particularly those entangled in academic programs in fiction, get their intellect and ego so involved in what they're saying and how they're saying it that they forget that they're saying it to anyone. If there's any use in the grab-'em-and-wrench-their-guts-out school of advice, it's that it at least reminds the writer that there is a reader out there to be grabbed and gutted.

But just because you realise your work may be seen by somebody other than the professor of creative writing, you don't have to go into attack mode and release the Rottweilers. There's another option. You can consider the reader, not as a helpless victim or a passive consumer, but as an active, intelligent, worthy collaborator. A colluder, a co-illusionist.

Writers who choose to try to establish mutual trust believe it is possible to attract readers' attention without verbal assault and battery. Rather than grab, frighten, coerce, or manipulate a consumer, collaborative writers try to interest a reader. To induce or seduce people into moving with the story, participating in it, joining their imagination with it.

10   Not a rape: a dance.

Consider the story as a dance, the reader and writer as partners. The writer leads, yes; but leading isn't pushing; it's setting up a field of mutuality where two people can move in cooperation with grace. It takes two to tango.

Readers who have only been grabbed, bashed, gut-wrenched, and electroshocked may need a little practice in being interested. They may need to learn how to tango. Once they've tried it, they'll never go back among the pit bulls.

Finally, there is the difficult question of "audience": In the mind of the writer planning or composing or revising the work, what is the presence of the potential reader or readers? Should the audience for the work dominate the writer's mind and guide the writing? Or should the writer while writing be utterly free of such considerations?

I wish there were a simple sound bite answer, but actually this is a terribly complicated question, particularly on the moral level.

15   Being a writer, conceiving a fiction, implies a reader. Writing is communication, though that's not all it is. One communicates *to* somebody. And what people want to read influences what people want to write. Stories are drawn out of writers by the spiritual and intellectual and moral needs of the writer's people. But all that operates on a quite unconscious level.

Once again it's useful to see the writer's work as being done in three stages. In the approach stage, it may be essential to think about your potential audience: who is this story for? For instance, is it for kids? Little kids? Young adults? Any special, limited audience calls for specific kinds of subject matter and vocabulary. All genre writing, from the average formula romance to the average *New Yorker* story, is written with an audience in mind—an audience so specific it can be called a market.

Only the very riskiest kind of fiction is entirely inconsiderate of the reader/market, saying, as it were, I will be told, and somebody, somewhere, will read me! Probably 99 percent of such stories end up, in fact, unread. And probably 98 percent of them are unreadable. The other 1 or 2 percent come to be known as masterpieces, usually very slowly, after the brave author has long been silent.

Consciousness of audience is limiting, both positively and negatively. Consciousness of audience offers choices, many of which have ethical implications— puritanism or porn? shock the readers or reassure them? do something I haven't tried or do my last book over?—and so on.

The limitations imposed by aiming at a specific readership may lead to very high art; all craft is a matter of rules and limitations, after all. But if consciousness of audience *as market* is the primary factor controlling your writing, you are a hack. There are arty hacks and artless hacks. Personally I prefer the latter.

20   All this has been about the approach stage, the what-am-I-going-to-write stage. Now that I know, dimly or exactly, who I'm writing for—anything from my granddaughter to all posterity—I start writing. And now, at the writing stage, consciousness of audience can be absolutely fatal. It is what makes writers distrust their story, stick, block, start over and over, never finish. Writers need a room of their own, not a room full of imaginary critics all watching over their shoulders saying "Is 'The' a good way to start that sentence?" An overactive internal aesthetic censor, or the external equivalent—what my agent or my editor is going to say—is like an avalanche of boulders across the story's way. During composition I have to concentrate entirely on the work itself, trusting and aiding it to find its way, with little or no thought of what or who it's for.

But when I get to the third stage, revision and rewriting, it reverses again: awareness that somebody's going to read this story, and of who might read this story, becomes essential.

What's the goal of revision? Clarity—impact—pace—power—beauty . . . things that imply a mind and heart *receiving* the story. Revision clears unnecessary obstacles away so the reader can receive the story. That is why the comma is important. And why the right word, not the approximately right word, is important. And why consistency is important. And why moral implications are important. And all the rest of the stuff that makes a story readable, makes it live. In revising, you must trust yourself, your judgment, to work with the receptive intelligence of your potential readers.

You also may have to trust specific actual readers—spouse, friends, workshop peers, teachers, editors, agents. You may be pulled between your judgment and theirs, and it can be tricky to arrive at the necessary arrogance, or the necessary humility, or the right compromise. I have writer friends who simply cannot hear any critical suggestions; they drown them out by going into defensive explanation mode: *Oh, yes, but see, what I was doing*—are they geniuses or just buttheaded? Time will tell. I have writer friends who accept every critical suggestion uncritically, and end up with as many different versions as they have critics. If they meet up with bullying, manipulative agents and editors, they're helpless.

What can I recommend? Trust your story; trust yourself; trust your readers—but wisely. Trust watchfully, not blindly. Trust flexibly, not rigidly. The whole thing, writing a story, is a high-wire act—there you are out in midair walking on a spiderweb line of words, and down in the darkness people are watching. What can you trust but your sense of balance?

Questions for Discussion

1. What is the significance of "collaboration" in this essay? Who and what must the writer collaborate with, according to Le Guin? Why do writers somtimes "ignore" or "resent" this need for collaboration?

2. What relationship to the reader is present in the strategies of writers of "bestsellers"? Why is this relationship inadequate in more sophisticated writing?

3. Why does Le Guin believe that a fictional work can be narrowed and weakened by a conscious attempt by a writer to master and manipulate readers' feelings? Do you think her advice for fiction writers relevant to writers of nonfiction essays? Why or why not? Explain.

4. What does Le Guin believe should be the ideal relationship between writer and reader? What image of the reader should the writer maintain, and why? What does Le Guin mean by her metaphor "Not a rape: a dance?"

5. What does Le Guin believe is the major goal of revision, and why does she believe that thinking about audience is most important in the revision stage of writing? Do you think what she says here about audience is also applicable to nonfiction writing such as essays?

6. Aside from the intended general audience of the piece, what kinds of individuals and groups should a writer trust during the revision stage? Why is it so important for the writer to listen to these people? What happens when a writer listens *too* much to advice on revision? Why is writing "a high-wire act"?

CONNECTION

Compare Ursula Le Guin's ideas on the role of audience in the reading/writing process with those of Denise Levertov (see page 14).

IDEAS FOR WRITING

1. Write an essay about your own writing process, using examples from one or more of your recent essays or stories. Do you use any strategies similar to those in "A Matter of Trust" to guide you through the stages of writing your own works? Which of Le Guin's strategies would you like to try out in future writing projects?

2. Write an essay in which you examine the idea of audience in writing. How important do you think it is to keep your audience in mind while writing? Do some outside reading about the role of audience: what areas of disagreement are there on the subject? Do you agree with Le Guin that the issue of audience is "a terribly complicated question," or is this only true for fiction writers?

RELATED WEB SITES

Official Web Site of Ursula K. Le Guin

`www.ursulakleguin.com/UKL_info.html`

This official Web site contains interviews, a biography, a bibliography, articles on writing, pictures, maps, poems, and other information related to Ursula Le Guin and her work.

The Writer's Audience

`www.boisestate.edu/wcenter/ww76.htm`

`www.boisestate.edu/wcenter/ww77.htm`

These two online articles published by the Boise State University Writing Center examine the history of audience theory in the writing/reading process and make some practical suggestions for effective audience communication.

Virginia Woolf

Professions for Women

Virginia Woolf (1882–1941) grew up in London as the daughter of the eminent Victorian literary critic and agnostic Leslie Stephen. Since women were not sent to school at that time, she educated herself in her father's extensive library. As a young woman, Woolf was a member of the intellectual circle known as the Bloomsbury group. Woolf is best known for her experimental, stream-of-consciousness novels Mrs. Dalloway *(1925),* To the Lighthouse *(1927), and* The Waves *(1931).*

Her extended essay, A Room of One's Own *(1929), is considered one of the most important feminist texts of the twentieth century. The essay that follows, "Professions for Women," reflects Woolf's deep concern about the status of women writers in any society dominated by males. The essay was first delivered in 1925 to a professional women's club and is included in* Death of a Moth and Other Essays *(1942).*

JOURNAL

Discuss what it would be like to have your own special writing room. What would the room be like? Where would it be? How might you furnish it?

When your secretary invited me to come here, she told me that your Society is concerned with the employment of women and she suggested that I might tell you something about my own professional experiences. It is true I am a woman: it is true I am employed; but what professional experiences have I had? It is difficult to say. My profession is literature; and in that profession there are fewer experiences for women than in any other, with the exception of the stage—fewer, I mean, that are peculiar to women. For the road was cut many years ago—by Fanny Burney, by Aphra Behn, by Harriet Martineau, by Jane Austen, by George Eliot—many famous women, and many more unknown and forgotten, have been before me, making the path smooth, and regulating my steps. Thus, when I came to write, there were very few material obstacles in my way. Writing was a reputable and harmless occupation. The family peace was not broken by the scratching of a pen. No demand was made upon the family purse. For ten and sixpence one can buy paper enough to write all the plays of Shakespeare—if one has a mind that way. Pianos and models, Paris, Vienna and Berlin, masters and mistresses, are not needed by a writer. The cheapness of writing is, of course, the reason why women have succeeded as writers before they have succeeded in the other professions.

But to tell you my story—it is a simple one. You have only got to figure to yourselves a girl in a bedroom with a pen in her hand. She had only to move that pen from left to right—from ten o'clock to one. Then it occurred to her to do what is simple and cheap enough for all—to slip a few of those pages into an envelope, fix a penny stamp in the corner, and drop the envelope into the red box at the corner. It was thus that I became a journalist; and my effort was rewarded on the first day of the following month—a very glorious day it was for me—by a letter from an editor containing a cheque for one pound ten shillings and sixpence. But to show you how little I deserve to be called a professional woman, how little I know of the struggles and difficulties of such lives, I have to admit that instead of spending that sum upon bread and butter, rent, shoes and stockings, or butcher's bills, I went out and bought a cat—a beautiful cat, a Persian cat, which very soon involved me in bitter disputes with my neighbours.

What could be easier than to write articles and to buy Persian cats with the profits? But wait a moment. Articles have to be about something. Mine, I seem to remember, was about a novel by a famous man. And while I was writing this review, I discovered that if I were going to review books I should need to do battle with a certain phantom. And the phantom was a woman, and when I came to know her better I called her after the heroine of a famous poem, The Angel in the House. It was she who used to come between me and my paper when I was writing reviews. It was she who bothered me and wasted my time and so tormented me that at last I killed her. You who come of a younger and happier generation may not have heard of her—you may not know what I mean by the Angel in the House. I will describe her as shortly as I can. She was intensely sympathetic. She was immensely charming. She was utterly unselfish. She excelled in the difficult arts of family life. She sacrificed herself daily. If there was a chicken, she took the leg; if there was a draught she sat in it—in short she was so constituted that she never had a mind or a wish of her own, but preferred to sympathize always with the minds and wishes of others. Above all—I need not say it—she was pure. Her purity was supposed to be her chief beauty—her blushes, her great grace. In those days—the last of Queen Victoria—every house had its Angel. And when I came to write I encountered her with the very first words. The shadow of her wings fell on my page; I heard the rustling of her skirts in the room. Directly, that is to say, I took my pen in hand to review that novel by a famous man, she slipped behind me and whispered: "My dear, you are a young woman. You are writing about a book that has been written by a man. Be sympathetic; be tender; flatter; deceive; use all the arts and wiles of our sex. Never let anybody guess that you have a mind of your own. Above all, be pure." And she made as if to guide my pen. I now record the one act for which I take some credit to myself, though the credit rightly belongs to some excellent ancestors of mine who left me a certain sum of money—shall we say five hundred pounds a year?—so that it was not necessary for me to depend solely on charm for my living. I turned upon her and caught her by the throat. I did my best to kill her. My excuse, if I were to be had up in a court of law, would be that I acted in self-defence. Had I not killed her she would have killed me. She would have plucked the heart out of my writing. For, as I found, directly I put pen to paper, you cannot review even a novel without having a mind of your own, without expressing what you think to be the truth about human relations, morality, sex. And all these questions, according to the Angel in the House, cannot be dealt with freely and openly by women; they must charm, they must conciliate, they must—to put it bluntly—tell lies if they are to succeed. Thus, whenever I felt the shadow of her wing or the radiance of her halo upon my page, I took up the inkpot and flung it at her. She died hard. Her fictitious nature was of great assistance to her. It is far harder to kill a phantom than a reality. She was always creeping back when I thought I had despatched her. Though I flatter myself that I killed her in the end, the struggle was severe; it took much time that had better have been spent upon learning Greek grammar; or in roaming the world in search of adventures. But it was a real experience; it was an experience that was bound to befall all women writers at that time. Killing the Angel in the House was part of the occupation of a woman writer.

But to continue my story. The Angel was dead; what then remained? You may say that what remained was a simple and common object—a young woman in a bedroom with an inkpot. In other words, now that she had rid herself of falsehood, that young woman had only to be herself. Ah, but what is "herself"? I mean, what is a woman? I assure you, I do not know. I do not believe that you know. I do not believe that anybody can know until she has expressed herself in all the arts and professions open to human skill. That indeed is one of the reasons why I have come here—out of respect for you, who are in process of showing us by your experiments what a woman is, who are in process of providing us, by your failures and successes, with that extremely important piece of information.

5   But to continue the story of my professional experiences. I made one pound ten and six by my first review; and I bought a Persian cat with the proceeds. Then I grew ambitious. A Persian cat is all very well, I said; but a Persian cat is not enough. I must have a motor car. And it was thus that I became a novelist— for it is a very strange thing that people will give you a motor car if you will tell them a story. It is a still stranger thing that there is nothing so delightful in the world as telling stories. It is far pleasanter than writing reviews of famous novels. And yet, if I am to obey your secretary and tell you my professional experiences as a novelist, I must tell you about a very strange experience that befell me as a novelist. And to understand it you must try first to imagine a novelist's state of mind. I hope I am not giving away professional secrets if I say that a novelist's chief desire is to be as unconscious as possible. He has to induce in himself a state of perpetual lethargy. He wants life to proceed with the utmost quiet and regularity. He wants to see the same faces, to read the same books, to do the same things day after day, month after month, while he is writing, so that nothing may break the illusion in which he is living—so that nothing may disturb or disquiet the mysterious nosings about, feelings round, darts, dashes and sudden discoveries of that very shy and illusive spirit, the imagination. I suspect that this state is the same both for men and women. Be that as it may, I want you to imagine me writing a novel in a state of trance. I want you to figure to yourselves a girl sitting with a pen in her hand, which for minutes, and indeed for hours, she never dips into the inkpot. The image that comes to my mind when I think of this girl is the image of a fisherman lying sunk in dreams on the verge of a deep lake with a rod held out over the water. She was letting her imagination sweep unchecked round every rock and cranny of the world that lies submerged in the depths of our unconscious being. Now came the experience, the experience that I believe to be far commoner with women writers than with men. The line raced through the girl's fingers. Her imagination had rushed away. It had sought the pools, the depths, the dark places where the largest fish slumber. And then there was a smash. There was an explosion. There was foam and confusion. The imagination had dashed itself against something hard. The girl was roused from her dream. She was indeed in a state of the most acute and difficult distress. To speak without figure she had thought of something, something about the body, about the passions which it

was unfitting for her as a woman to say. Men, her reason told her, would be shocked. The consciousness of what men will say of a woman who speaks the truth about her passions had roused her from her artist's state of unconsciousness. She could write no more. The trance was over. Her imagination could work no longer. This I believe to be a very common experience with women writers—they are impeded by the extreme conventionality of the other sex. For though men sensibly allow themselves great freedom in these respects, I doubt that they realize or can control the extreme severity with which they condemn such freedom in women.

These then were two very genuine experiences of my own. These were two of the adventures of my professional life. The first—killing the Angel in the House—I think I solved. She died. But the second, telling the truth about my own experiences as a body, I do not think I solved. I doubt that any woman has solved it yet. The obstacles against her are still immensely powerful—and yet they are very difficult to define. Outwardly, what is simpler than to write books? Outwardly, what obstacles are there for a woman rather than for a man? Inwardly, I think, the case is very different; she has still many ghosts to fight, many prejudices to overcome. Indeed it will be a long time still, I think, before a woman can sit down to write a book without finding a phantom to be slain, a rock to be dashed against. And if this is so in literature, the freest of all professions for women, how is it in the new professions which you are now for the first time entering?

Those are the questions that I should like, had I time, to ask you. And indeed, if I have laid stress upon these professional experiences of mine, it is because I believe that they are, though in different forms, yours also. Even when the path is nominally open—when there is nothing to prevent a woman from being a doctor, a lawyer, a civil servant—there are many phantoms and obstacles, as I believe, looming in her way. To discuss and define them is I think of great value and importance; for thus only can the labour be shared, the difficulties be solved. But besides this, it is necessary also to discuss the ends and the aims for which we are fighting, for which we are doing battle with these formidable obstacles. Those aims cannot be taken for granted; they must be perpetually questioned and examined. The whole position, as I see it—here in this hall surrounded by women practising for the first time in history I know not how many different professions—is one of extraordinary interest and importance. You have won rooms of your own in the house hitherto exclusively owned by men. You are able, though not without great labour and effort, to pay the rent. You are earning your five hundred pounds a year. But this freedom is only a beginning; the room is your own, but it is still bare. It has to be furnished; it has to be decorated; it has to be shared. How are you going to furnish it, how are you going to decorate it? With whom are you going to share it, and upon what terms? These, I think are questions of the utmost importance and interest. For the first time in history you are able to ask them; for the first time you are able to decide for yourselves what the answers should be. Willingly would I stay and discuss those questions and answers—but not tonight. My time is up; and I must cease.

QUESTIONS FOR DISCUSSION

1. Explain why Woolf's opening paragraph is ironic. Is her use of irony effective? Explain.
2. Describe the angellike phantom that torments Woolf when she tries to write reviews of men's work. What does the angel represent for Woolf? Do you ever think that you, too, have an angellike figure that sometimes controls your thoughts and actions?
3. Why is it so difficult for Woolf to kill the phantom angel? Why was killing the phantom angel an important concern of any woman writer of Woolf's age? Do you think that women writers today still struggle against a phantom angel?
4. How does Woolf get into her writer's frame of mind? Why does Woolf rely on her unconscious mind when she writes? What rouses the woman from her artist's state of unconsciousness? Do women today still face this type of obstacle?
5. Why does Woolf rely on metaphors and images (such as the phantom angel and the young girl who wants to write becoming "the image of a fisherman lying sunk in dreams on the verge of a deep lake with a rod held out over the water") to illustrate her ideas about writing? Are her metaphors and images persuasive and effective? Explain.
6. Why does Woolf think that the inward obstacles women writers face are the hardest to overcome? In your own life as a writer, what are the most difficult challenges that you must overcome?

CONNECTION

Compare Woolf's advice to writers to Ursula Le Guin's comments about the writer and her audience in "A Matter of Trust." Whose advice is more useful? Which is most inspirational, and why?

IDEAS FOR WRITING

1. Write an essay that discusses the relevance of Woolf's ideas for men who are struggling to become writers.
2. Create your own phantom angel, the visual and mental image that tries to keep you from expressing yourself in your writing. Begin by drawing (with pens and paper or on a computer program) this inner critic. Then write a dialogue between your inner critic and your creative self. In conclusion, write a paragraph that discusses what you learned from this activity.

RELATED WEB SITES

Virginia Woolf

`http://hubcap.clemson.edu/aah/ws/vw6links.html`

Learn about Virginia Woolf at this Web site of links to useful research materials about the author. It includes not only large collections of links but also courses and course materials, chronologies, online texts, bibliographies, and books on Woolf.

Feminist Theory—An Overview
`www.victorianweb.org/victorian/gender/femtheory.html`
Visit "The Victorian Web" and read a brief overview of feminist theory. Link
to information about gender studies as well as other various topics surrounding "The Victorians."

Amy Tan

Mother Tongue

*Born in Oakland, California, in 1952 to immigrant parents, Amy Tan received
an M.A. (1974) from San Jose State University, where she studied linguistics. Her
first best-selling novel,* The Joy Luck Club *(1989), was inspired by the stories
told by Chinese American women of her mother's generation. Tan has written three
other novels—*The Kitchen God's Wife *(1991),* The One Hundred Secret
Senses *(1995), and* The Bonesetter's Daughter *(2001)—as well as a number
of essays in which she explores cultural and linguistic issues. As you read the following essay, notice how Tan uses her experiences growing up bilingual in a Chinese American family to challenge the traditional expectations of academic writing
achievement tests.*

JOURNAL

In her essay, Amy Tan states that she is "fascinated by language in daily life." Discuss several striking examples of creative uses of language that you have noticed
recently in your everyday life or in conversations with friends.

I am not a scholar of English or literature. I cannot give you much more
than personal opinions on the English language and its variations in this
country or others.

I am a writer. And by that definition, I am someone who has always loved
language. I am fascinated by language in daily life. I spend a great deal of my
time thinking about the power of language—the way it can evoke an emotion,
a visual image, a complex idea, or a simple truth. Language is the tool of any
trade. And I use them all—all the Englishes I grew up with.

Recently, I was made keenly aware of the different Englishes I do use. I was
giving a talk to a large group of people, the same talk I had already given to
half a dozen other groups. The nature of the talk was about my writing, my life,
and my book, *The Joy Luck Club.* The talk was going along well enough, until I
remembered one major difference that made the whole talk sound wrong. My
mother was in the room. And it was perhaps the first time she had heard me

give a lengthy speech, using the kind of English I have never used with her. I was saying things like, "The intersection of memory upon imagination" and "There is an aspect of my fiction that relates to thus-and-thus"—a speech filled with carefully wrought grammatical phrases, burdened, it suddenly seemed to me, with nominalized forms, past perfect tenses, conditional phrases, all the forms of standard English that I had learned in school and through books, the forms of English I did not use at home with my mother.

Just last week, I was walking down the street with my mother, and I again found myself conscious of the English I was using, the English I use with her. We were talking about the price of new and used furniture, and I heard myself saying this: "Not waste money that way." My husband was with us as well, and he didn't notice any switch in my English. And then I realized why. It's because over the twenty years we've been together, I've often used that same kind of English with him, and sometimes he even uses it with me. It has become our language of intimacy, a different sort of English that relates to family talk, the language I grew up with.

5   So you'll have some idea of what this family talk I heard sounds like I'll quote what my mother said during a recent conversation which I videotaped and then transcribed. During this conversation, my mother was talking about a political gangster in Shanghai who had the same last name as her family's, Du, and how the gangster in his early years wanted to be adopted by her family, which was rich by comparison. Later, the gangster became more powerful, far richer than my mother's family, and one day showed up at my mother's wedding to pay his respects. Here's what she said in part:

"Du Yusong having business like fruit stand. Like off the street kind. He is Du like Du Zong—but not Tsung-ming Island people. The local people call putong, the near east side, he belong to that side local people. That man want to ask Du Zong father take him in like become own family. Du Zong father wasn't look down on him, but didn't take seriously, until that man big like become a mafia. Now important person, very hard to inviting him. Chinese way, came only to show respect, don't stay for dinner. Respect for making big celebration, he shows up. Man gives lots of respect. Chinese custom. Chinese social life that way. If too important won't have to stay too long. He come to my wedding. I didn't see, I heard it. I gone to boy's side, they have YMCA dinner. Chinese age I was nineteen."

You should know that my mother's expressive command of English belies how much she actually understands. She reads the *Forbes* report, listens to *Wall Street Week,* converses daily with her stockbroker, reads all of Shirley MacLaine's books with ease—all kinds of things I can't begin to understand. Yet some of my friends tell me they understand 50 percent of what my mother says. Some say they understand 80 to 90 percent. Some say they understand none of it, as if she were speaking pure Chinese. But to me, my mother's English is perfectly clear, perfectly natural. It's my mother tongue. Her language, as I hear it, is vivid, direct, full of observation and imagery. That was the language that helped shape the way I saw things, expressed things, made sense of the world.

Lately, I've been giving more thought to the kind of English my mother speaks. Like others, I have described it to people as "broken" or "fractured" English. But I wince when I say that. It has always bothered me that I can think of no way to describe it other than "broken," as if it were damaged and needed to be fixed, as if it lacked a certain wholeness and soundness. I've heard other terms used, "limited English," for example. But they seem just as bad, as if everything is limited, including people's perceptions of the limited English speaker.

I know this for a fact, because when I was growing up, my mother's "limited" English limited *my* perception of her. I was ashamed of her English. I believed that her English reflected the quality of what she had to say. That is, because she expressed them imperfectly her thoughts were imperfect. And I had plenty of empirical evidence to support me: the fact that people in department stores, at banks, and at restaurants did not take her seriously, did not give her good service, pretended not to understand her, or even acted as if they did not hear her.

10   My mother had long realized the limitations of her English as well. When I was fifteen, she used to have me call people on the phone to pretend I was she. In this guise, I was forced to ask for information or even to complain and yell at people who had been rude to her. One time it was a call to her stockbroker in New York. She had cashed out her small portfolio and it just so happened we were going to go to New York the next week, our very first trip outside California. I had to get on the phone and say in an adolescent voice that was not very convincing, "This is Mrs. Tan."

And my mother was standing in the back whispering loudly, "Why he don't send me check, already two weeks late. So mad he lie to me, losing me money."

And then I said in perfect English, "Yes, I'm getting rather concerned. You had agreed to send the check two weeks ago, but it hasn't arrived."

Then she began to talk more loudly. "What he want, I come to New York tell him front of his boss, you cheating me?" And I was trying to calm her down, make her be quiet, while telling the stockbroker, "I can't tolerate any more excuses. If I don't receive the check immediately, I am going to have to speak to your manager when I'm in New York next week." And sure enough, the following week there we were in front of this astonished stockbroker, and I was sitting there red-faced and quiet, and my mother, the real Mrs. Tan, was shouting at his boss in her impeccable broken English.

We used a similar routine just five days ago, for a situation that was far less humorous. My mother had gone to the hospital for an appointment, to find out about a benign brain tumor a CAT scan had revealed a month ago. She said she had spoken very good English, her best English, no mistakes. Still, she said, the hospital did not apologize when they said they had lost the CAT scan and she had come for nothing. She said they did not seem to have any sympathy when she told them she was anxious to know the exact diagnosis, since her husband and son had both died of brain tumors. She said they would not give her any more information until the next time and she would have to make another appointment for that. So she said she would not leave until the doctor called daughter. She wouldn't budge. And when the doctor finally called her daughter, me, who spoke in perfect English—lo and behold—we had assurances the CAT scan would be found, promises that a conference call on Monday would be held, and apologies for any suffering my mother had gone through for a most regrettable mistake.

15   I think my mother's English almost had an effect on limiting my possibilities in life as well. Sociologists and linguists probably will tell you that a person's developing language skills are more influenced by peers. But I do think that the language spoken in the family, especially in immigrant families which are more insular, plays a large role in shaping the language of the child. And I believe that it affected my results on achievement tests, IQ Tests, and the SAT. While my English skills were never judged as poor, compared to math, English could not be considered my strong suit. In grade school I did moderately well, getting perhaps B's, sometimes B-pluses, in English and scoring perhaps in the sixtieth or seventieth percentile on achievement tests. But those scores were not good enough to override the opinion that my true abilities lay in math and science, because in those areas I achieved A's and scored in the ninetieth percentile or higher.

This was understandable. Math is precise; there is only one correct answer. Whereas, for me at least, the answers on English tests were always a judgement call, a matter of opinion and personal experience. Those tests were constructed around items like fill-in-the-blank sentence completion, such as "Even though Tom was ___, Mary thought he was ___." And the correct answer always seemed to be the most bland combinations of thoughts, for example, "Even though Tom was shy, Mary thought he was charming," with the grammatical structure "even though" limiting the correct answer to some sort of semantic opposites, so you wouldn't get answers like, "Even though Tom was foolish, Mary thought he was ridiculous." Well, according to my mother, there were very few limitations as to what Tom could have been and what Mary might have thought of him. So I never did well on tests like that.

The same was true with word analogies, pairs of words in which you were supposed to find some sort of logical, semantic relationship—for example, "*Sunset* is to *nightfall* as ___ is to ___." And here you would be presented with a list of four possible pairs, one of which showed the same kind of relationship: *red* is to *stoplight, bus* is to *arrival, chills* is to *fever, yawn* is to *boring.* Well, I could never think that way. I knew what the tests were asking, but I could not block out of my mind the images already created by the first pair "*sunset* is to *nightfall*"—and I would see a burst of colors against a darkening sky, the moon rising, the lowering of a curtain of stars. And all the other pairs of words—red, bus, stoplight, boring—just threw up a mass of confusing images, making it impossible for me to sort out something as logical as saying: "A sunset precedes nightfall" is the same as "a chill precedes a fever." The only way I would have gotten that answer right would have been to imagine an associative situation, for example, my being disobedient and staying out past sunset, catching a chill at night, which turns into feverish pneumonia as punishment, which indeed did happen to me.

I have been thinking about all this lately, about my mother's English, about achievement tests. Because lately I've been asked, as a writer, why there are not more Asian-Americans represented in American literature. Why are there few Asian-Americans enrolled in creative writing programs? Why do so many Chinese students go into engineering? Well, these are broad sociological questions I can't begin to answer. But I have noticed in surveys—in fact, just last week—that Asian students, as a whole, always do significantly better on math achievement tests than in English. And this makes me think that there are other Asian-American students whose English spoken in the home might also be described as "broken" or "limited." And perhaps they also have teachers who are steering them away from writing and into math and science, which is what happened to me.

Fortunately, I happen to be rebellious in nature and enjoy the challenge of disproving assumptions made about me. I became an English major my first year in college, after being enrolled as pre-med. I started writing nonfiction as a freelancer the week after I was told by my former boss that writing was my worst skill and I should hone my talents toward account management.

20   But it wasn't until 1985 that I finally began to write fiction. And at first I wrote using what I thought to be wittily crafted sentences, sentences that would finally prove I had mastery over the English language. Here's an example from the first draft of a story that later made its way into *The Joy Luck Club,* but without this line: "That was my mental quandary in its nascent state." A terrible line, which I can barely pronounce.

Fortunately, for reasons I won't get into today, I later decided I should envision a reader for the stories I would write. And the reader I decided upon was my mother, because these were stories about mothers. So with this reader in mind—and in fact she did read my early drafts—I began to write stories using all the Englishes I grew up with: the English I spoke to my mother, which for lack of a better term might be described as "simple"; the English she used with me, which for lack of a better term might be described as "broken"; my translation of her Chinese, which could certainly be described as "watered down"; and what I imagined to be her translation of her Chinese if she could speak in perfect English, her internal language, and for that I sought to preserve the essence, but neither an English nor a Chinese structure. I wanted to capture what language ability tests can never reveal: her intent, her passion, her imagery, the rhythms of her speech and the nature of her thoughts.

Apart from what any critic had to say about my writing, I knew I had succeeded where it counted when my mother finished reading my book and gave me her verdict: "So easy to read."

QUESTIONS FOR DISCUSSION

1. Tan discusses her awareness of using language differently when speaking with different audiences and on different occasions. Keep a log for several

days that records the situations when you change the way you use English for a specific group of friends, teachers, relatives, or a work situation. Share your observations and conclusions with your classmates.

2. Why is Tan critical of the descriptive term "limited English"? How did this term influence her perception of her own mother?

3. Why is the article entitled "Mother Tongue"? What do Tan's examples about how she would often speak for her mother suggest?

4. Why is Tan critical of the achievement tests she was given as an adolescent? Do you agree or disagree with her point of view and conclusions? Explain your point of view.

5. Why does Tan believe that high school teachers encourage Asian students to study math and science rather than writing? How does she explain her success as a writer in spite of the evaluations provided by her teachers and former employer?

6. According to Tan, what is the real test of a writer? What advice does Tan offer to the person who aspires to be a successful writer?

CONNECTION

Compare Tan's views on the role of different "Englishes" in her writer's life and in her relationship with her mother with the views of Joyce Chang in her essay "Drive Becarefully" (see page 57).

IDEAS FOR WRITING

1. "I am a writer. And by that definition, I am someone who has always loved language. I am fascinated by language in daily life." Develop Tan's ideas on language into an essay, using personal experiences and examples from your reading that illustrate language's complexity and power.

2. Write an essay in which you discuss how your rebellion against a cultural or social myth helped you to develop a skill or talent that is both useful and rewarding.

RELATED WEB SITES

Amy Tan
www.luminarium.org/contemporary/amytan/
This extensive online resource on author Amy Tan includes interviews, book reviews, essays, links, and biographical information.

Asian American Studies Resources
http://sun3.lib.uci.edu/~dtsang/aas2.htm
This site contains hundreds of links to topics in Asian American studies, such as bibliographies, magazines, journals, audiovisual resources, research institutes, programs, and libraries.

Frederick Douglass

Learning to Read and Write

An important figure in the history of African American thought and writing, Frederick Douglass (1818–1895) was born in Maryland into slavery. After escaping to the North, he wrote of his journey to freedom in The Narrative Life of Frederick Douglass *(1845). He also became the publisher of two radical newspapers,* North Star *and the* Frederick Douglass Paper, *which had a very significant impact on the antislavery movement. Douglass helped hundreds of slaves make their way to freedom on the Underground Railroad. During the Civil War Douglass served as an advisor to President Abraham Lincoln, and after 1872, he served as an international diplomat. In the short excerpt from his autobiography included below, Douglass describes how learning to read developed his intellect, pride, and resourcefulness.*

JOURNAL

How did you learn to read? What do you appreciate most about reading?

I lived in Master Hugh's family about seven years. During this time, I succeeded in learning to read and write. In accomplishing this, I was compelled to resort to various stratagems. I had no regular teacher. My mistress, who kindly commenced to instruct me, had, in compliance with the advice and direction of her husband, not only ceased to instruct, but had set her face against my being instructed by any one else. It is due, however, to my mistress to say of her, that she did not adopt this course of treatment immediately. She at first lacked the depravity indispensable to shutting me up in mental darkness. It was at least necessary for her to have some training in the exercise of irresponsible power, to make her equal to the task of treating me as though I were a brute.

My mistress was, as I have said, a kind and tender-hearted woman; and in the simplicity of her soul she commenced, when I first went to live with her, to treat me as she supposed one human being ought to treat another. In entering upon the duties of a slaveholder, she did not seem to perceive that I sustained to her the relation of a mere chattel, and that for her to treat me as a human being was not only wrong, but dangerously so. Slavery proved as injurious to her as it did to me. When I went there, she was a pious, warm, and tender-hearted woman. There was no sorrow or suffering for which she had not a tear. She had bread for the hungry, clothes for the naked, and comfort for every mourner that came within her reach. Slavery soon proved its ability to divest her of these heavenly qualities. Under its influence, the tender heart became stone, and the lamb-like disposition gave way to one of tiger-like fierceness. The first step in her downward course was in her ceasing to instruct me. She now commenced to practise her husband's precepts. She finally became even more violent in her opposition than her husband himself. She was not satisfied with simply doing as well as he had commanded; she seemed anxious to do better. Nothing seemed to make her more angry than to see me with a newspaper. She seemed to think that here lay the danger. I have had her rush at me with a face made all up of fury, and snatch from me a newspaper, in a manner that fully revealed her apprehension. She was an apt woman; and a little experience soon demonstrated, to her satisfaction, that education and slavery were incompatible with each other.

From this time I was most narrowly watched. If I was in a separate room any considerable length of time, I was sure to be suspected of having a book, and was at once called to give an account of myself. All this, however, was too late. The first step had been taken. Mistress, in teaching me the alphabet, had given me the *inch,* and no precaution could prevent me from taking the *ell.*

The plan which I adopted, and the one by which I was most successful, was that of making friends of all the little white boys whom I met in the street. As many of these as I could, I converted into teachers. With their kindly aid, obtained at different times and in different places, I finally succeeded in learning to read. When I was sent on errands, I always took my book with me, and by doing one part of my errand quickly, I found time to get a lesson before my return. I used also to carry bread with me, enough of which was always in the house, and to which I was always welcome; for I was much better off in this regard than many of the poor white children in our neighborhood. This bread I used to bestow upon the hungry little urchins, who, in return, would give me that more valuable bread of knowledge. I am strongly tempted to give the names of two or three of those little boys, as a testimonial of the gratitude and affection I bear them; but prudence forbids;—not that it would injure me, but it might embarrass them; for it is almost an unpardonable offence to teach slaves to read in this Christian country. It is enough to say of the dear little fellows, that they lived on Philpot Street, very near Durgin and Bailey's shipyard. I used to talk this matter of slavery over with them. I would sometimes say to them, I wished I could be as free as they would be when they got to be men. "You will be free as soon as you are twenty-one, *but I am a slave for life!* Have not I as good a right to be free as you have?" These words used to trouble them; they would express for me the liveliest sympathy, and console me with the hope that something would occur by which I might be free.

5   I was now about twelve years old, and the thought of being *a slave for life* began to bear heavily upon my heart. Just about this time, I got hold of a book entitled "The Columbian Orator." Every opportunity I got, I used to read this book. Among much of other interesting matter, I found in it a dialogue between a master and his slave. The slave was represented as having run away from his master three times. The dialogue represented the conversation which took place between them, when the slave was retaken the third time. In this dialogue, the whole argument in behalf of slavery was brought forward by the master, all of which was disposed of by the slave. The slave was made to say

some very smart as well as impressive things in reply to his master—things which had the desired though unexpected effect; for the conversation resulted in the voluntary emancipation of the slave on the part of the master.

In the same book, I met with one of Sheridan's mighty speeches on and in behalf of Catholic emancipation. These were choice documents to me. I read them over and over again with unabated interest. They gave tongue to interesting thoughts of my own soul, which had frequently flashed through my mind, and died away for want of utterance. The moral which I gained from the dialogue was the power of truth over the conscience of even a slaveholder. What I got from Sheridan was a bold denunciation of slavery, and a powerful vindication of human rights. The reading of these documents enabled me to utter my thoughts, and to meet the arguments brought forward to sustain slavery; but while they relieved me of one difficulty, they brought on another even more painful than the one of which I was relieved. The more I read, the more I was led to abhor and detest my enslavers. I could regard them in no other light than a band of successful robbers, who had left their homes, and gone to Africa, and stolen us from our homes, and in a strange land reduced us to slavery. I loathed them as being the meanest as well as the most wicked of men. As I read and contemplated the subject, behold! that very discontentment which Master Hugh had predicted would follow my learning to read had already come, to torment and sting my soul to unutterable anguish. As I writhed under it, I would at times feel that learning to read had been a curse rather than a blessing. It had given me a view of my wretched condition, without the remedy. It opened my eyes to the horrible pit, but to no ladder upon which to get out. In moments of agony, I envied my fellow-slaves for their stupidity. I have often wished myself a beast. I preferred the condition of the meanest reptile to my own. Any thing, no matter what, to get rid of thinking! It was this everlasting thinking of my condition that tormented me. There was no getting rid of it. It was pressed upon me by every object within sight or hearing, animate or inanimate. The silver trump of freedom had roused my soul to eternal wakefulness. Freedom now appeared, to disappear no more forever. It was heard in every sound, and seen in every thing. It was ever present to torment me with a sense of my wretched condition. I saw nothing without seeing it, I heard nothing without hearing it, and felt nothing without feeling it. It looked from every star, it smiled in every calm, breathed in every wind, and moved in every storm.

I often found myself regretting my own existence, and wishing myself dead; and but for the hope of being free, I have no doubt but that I should have killed myself, or done something for which I should have been killed. While in this state of mind, I was eager to hear anyone speak of slavery. I was a ready listener. Every little while, I could hear something about the abolitionists. It was some time before I found what the word meant. It was always used in such connections as to make it an interesting word to me. If a slave ran away and succeeded in getting clear, or if a slave killed his master, set fire to a barn, or did any thing very wrong in the mind of a slaveholder, it was spoken of as the fruit of *abolition*. Hearing the word in this connection very often, I set about learning what it meant. The dictionary afforded me little or no help. I found it was "the act of abolishing," but then I did not know what was to be abolished. Here I was perplexed. I did not dare to ask any one about its meaning, for I was satisfied that it was something they wanted me to know very little about. After a patient waiting, I got one of our city papers, containing an account of the number of petitions from the north, praying for the abolition of slavery in the District of Columbia, and of the slave trade between the States. From this time I understood the words *abolition* and *abolitionist,* and always drew near when that word was spoken, expecting to hear something of importance to myself and fellow-slaves. The light broke in upon me by degrees. I went one day down on the wharf of Mr. Waters; and seeing two Irishmen unloading a scow of stone, I went, unasked, and helped them. When we had finished, one of them came to me and asked me if I were a slave. I told him I was. He asked, "Are ye a slave for life?" I told him that I was. The good Irishman seemed to be deeply affected by the statement. He said to the other that it was a pity so fine a little fellow as myself should be a slave for life. He said it was a shame to hold me. They both advised me to run away to the north; that I should find friends there, and that I should be free. I pretended not to be interested in what they said, and treated them as if I did not understand them; for I feared they might be treacherous. White men have been known to encourage slaves to escape, and then, to get the reward, catch them and return them to their masters. I was afraid that these seemingly good men might use me so; but I nevertheless remembered their advice, and from that time I resolved to run away.

QUESTIONS FOR DISCUSSION

1. Why does the relationship between Frederick Douglass and his mistress change? What is the nature of their power struggle?
2. How did Douglass learn to read?
3. Discuss two of the incidents from the selection that show that Douglass has resourcefulness and an understanding of human nature, as well as an ability to listen, think critically, and learn from his experience.
4. Why does Douglass grow more and more tormented by what he is reading and thinking? How does he combat his deep feelings of frustration and despair on his journey to becoming an educated and free man?
5. Why and how does Douglass finally join the abolitionists' cause?
6. What connections between education and freedom does Douglass make in this excerpt from his autobiography? What relationships have you seen between education and freedom in your own life?

CONNECTION

Compare John G. Ramsay's and Douglass's views on the importance of reading. Why do you think reading was more important to Douglass than it is for many young people today (see page 50)?

IDEAS FOR WRITING

1. Becoming educated through reading allowed Douglass to gain his freedom and help many other slaves to gain their freedom. Write an essay that explores different ways in which your education through reading has helped you to gain more freedom and independence.
2. Using the resources at your college library and on the Internet, find out more about how slaves learned to read and write, and how their education helped them to gain their freedom.

RELATED WEB SITES

Frederick Douglass
`www.history.rochester.edu/class/douglass/home.html`
This biography of Frederick Douglass by Sandra Thomas will give you more insight into the struggles and challenges that Douglass overcame in his fight to gain his own freedom and the freedom of his people.

Frederick Douglass National Historic Site
`www.nps.gov/frdo/freddoug.html`
The Frederick Douglass National Historic Site is dedicated to preserving the legacy of the most famous African Americans of the nineteenth century. The museum is located at the final home that Douglass purchased in 1877, which he named Cedar Hill.

Frederick Douglass Papers
`www.iupui.edu/~douglass/`
Housed at Indiana University–Purdue University at Indianapolis, the Frederick Douglass Papers project collects and publishes his speeches and writings.

Steven Holtzman

Don't Look Back

Steven Holtzman (b. 1947) is interested in computers, philosophy, and creativity. He holds both an undergraduate degree in Western and Eastern philosophy and a Ph.D. in computer science from the University of Edinburgh. He is also founder and vice president of Optimal Networks in Palo Alto, California. Using computer techniques, he has composed a number of musical works that have been performed in Europe and the United States, some of which can be found on a CD he has produced, Digital Mantras *(Shriek! Records, 1994). He also has written two books that examine the new types of creative expression possible in the age of computers and cyberspace:* Digital Mantras: The Language of Abstract and Virtual Worlds *(1994), and* Digital Mosaics: The Aesthetics of Cyberspace *(1997).*

Holtzman's books are aesthetically appealing as well as intellectually provocative. In the following excerpt from Digital Mosaics, *he argues that we can't turn our backs on today's digital technology as it is already an inextricable part of our lives.*

JOURNAL

Write about your experience with reading books and other texts online. Have you found this kind of reading rewarding?

For centuries, the book has been the primary vehicle for recording, storing, and transferring knowledge. But it's hard to imagine that paper will be the preferred format in a hundred years. Digital media will marginalize this earlier form of communication, relegating it to a niche just as music CDs have replaced LPs. The book will be forced to redefine itself, just as TV forced radio to redefine itself, and radio and TV together transformed the newspaper's role. The process is survival of the fittest—competition in the market to be a useful medium. Whatever the book's future is, clearly its role will never be the same. The book has lost its preeminence.

The print medium of newspaper is also fading. Almost every major newspaper in the United States is experiencing significant declines in circulation. (The exception is *USA Today*—characterized by itself as "TV on paper.") More than 70 percent of Americans under the age of thirty don't read newspapers. And this trend isn't about to change.

The powers of the media business today understand this. As part of the frenzied convergence of media, communications, and the digital world, we're witnessing a dizzying tangle of corporate alliances and mega-mergers. Companies are jockeying for position for this epochal change. The list includes many multibillion-dollar companies—AT&T, Bertelsmann, Disney, Microsoft, Time Warner, Viacom—and many, many more small startup technology companies. They all want to position themselves as preeminent new media companies.

Clinging to the Past

Members of the literary establishment can also see this imminent change. Yet, for the most part, they take a dim view of these new digital worlds. Beyond the loss of their cherished culture, what disturbs many critics is that they find new digital media like CD-ROMs and the World Wide Web completely unsatisfying.

5   The literacy critic Sven Birkerts eloquently laments that the generation growing up in the digital age is incapable of enjoying literature. Teaching at college has brought Birkerts to despair because his students aren't able to appreciate the literary culture he so values. After only a proudly self-confessed "glimpse of the future" of CD-ROMs, he declares he is "clinging all the more tightly to my books."

The disillusionment with the digital experience is summed up by the *New York Times Book Review* critic Sarah Lyall. She complains that multimedia CD-ROMs still don't come close to matching the experience of reading a paper-and-print book while curled up in a chair, in bed, on the train, under a tree, in an airplane. . . . After all, the modern book is the result of centuries of trial and error during which people wrote on bark, on parchment, on vellum, on clay, on scrolls, on stone, chiseling characters into surfaces or copying them out by hand.

Okay, I thought as I read Birkerts and Lyall, these are members of a dying cultural heritage who—like seemingly every generation—are uncomfortable with new. Unable to shift their perspective, they'll be casualties of change. After all, Birkerts boasts that he doesn't own a computer and still uses only a typewriter.

Birkerts clings not to his books, but to the past. I was reminded of a comment by the cultural critic William Irwin Thompson, who is also wary of the consequences of digital technology:

It is not the literary intelligentsia of *The New York Review of Books* [or *The New York Times,* as the case may be] that is bringing forth this new culture, for it is as repugnant to them as the Reformation was to the Catholic Church. . . . This new cyberpunk, technological culture is brought forth by Top and Pop, electronic science and pop music, and both the hackers and the rockers are anti-intellectual and unsympathetic to the previous Mental level expressed by the genius of European civilization.

This helped me dismiss the backlash from those looking in the rearview mirror. But then I came across a book by Clifford Stoll.

Muddier Mud

10 Stoll, who was introduced to computers twenty years ago, is a longtime member of the digerati. In his book *Silicon Snake Oil,* he claims to expose the true emptiness of the digital experience.

In opening, Stoll explains that "every time someone mentions MUDs [multi-user dungeons, a type of interactive adventure game] and virtual reality, I think of a genuine reality with muddier mud than anything a computer can deliver." Stoll then nostalgically recounts the story of the first time he went crawling through caves in his college days. "We start in, trailing a string through the muddy tunnel—everything's covered with gunk, as are the six of us crawling behind [the guide]. Not your ordinary slimy, brown, backyard mud, either. This is the goop of inner-earth that works its way into your hair, socks, and underwear."

Stoll's general theme: "You're viewing a world that doesn't exist. During that week you spend online, you could have planted a tomato garden. . . . While the Internet beckons brightly, seductively flashing an icon of knowledge-as-power, this nonplace lures us to surrender our time on earth."

I suppose this excludes any experience that might distract us from the real—a novel, a Beethoven symphony, a movie. (A tomato garden?)

And then we get the same theme that Birtkerts and Lyall hit on.

I've rarely met anyone who prefers to read digital books. I don't want my morning newspaper delivered over computer, or a CD-ROM stuffed with National Geographic photographs. Call me a troglodyte; I'd rather peruse those photos alongside my sweetheart, catch the newspaper on the way to work, and page through a real book. . . . Now, I'm hardly a judge of aesthetics, but of the scores of electronic multimedia productions I've seen, I don't remember any as being beautiful.

A CD-ROM Is Not a Book

15   These laments totally miss the point. No, a CD-ROM isn't a book. Nor is a virtual world—whether a MUD or a simulation of rolling in the mud—the same as the real experience. This is *exactly* the point! A CD-ROM isn't a book; it's something completely new and different. A MUD on the Internet isn't like mud in a cave. A virtual world isn't the real world; it offers possibilities unlike anything we've known before.

Birkerts, Lyall, and Stoll dismiss the digital experience to justify staying in the familiar and comfortable worlds of their past. Yet what's exciting to me about these digital worlds is precisely that they're new, they're unfamiliar, and they're our future.

It's not that I disagree with the literati's assertions. We will lose part of our literary culture and tradition. Kids today are so attuned to the rapid rhythms of MTV that they're unresponsive to the patient patterns of literary prose. They are indeed so seduced by the flickeringly powerful identifications of the screen as to be deaf to the inner voices of print. Literary culture—like classical music and opera—will become marginalized as mainstream culture pursues a digital path.

There never will be a substitute for a book. And today's multimedia CD-ROM—even surfing the World Wide Web—is still for the most part a static and unsatisfying experience. But it's rather early to conclude anything about their ultimate potential.

Patience Is a Virtue

It puzzles me that there are people who expect that, in almost no time at all, we'd find great works by those who have mastered the subtleties of such completely new digital worlds. We are seeing the first experiments with a new medium. It took a long time to master the medium of film. Or the book, for that matter. It will also take time to master new digital worlds.

20   It's challenging to create a multimedia digital world today. The enabling technologies that will make radically new digital worlds possible—Java, VRML, and a string of acronymic technologies—are still emerging. Artists, writers, and musicians must also be software programmers. Today, a rare combination of passion, artistry, and technical knowledge is required. Yet, over time, these skills will become common. Even more important than the technical mastery of new digital media, a new conceptual framework and aesthetic must also be established for digital worlds.

When this conceptual and technical mastery is achieved, we'll discover the true possibilities of digital expression. In a few decades—or possibly in just five years—we'll look on today's explorations as primitive. Until then, we will continue to explore these new digital worlds and seek to learn their true potential.

Embracing the Digital

There will be nothing to replace the reading of a book or newspaper in bed. Curling up by a fireside to read a poem with an electronic tablet won't have the same intimacy as doing so with a book. But curling up by a fireside with an electronic tablet is itself simply an example of substituting electronic technology for an existing medium—extrapolating from today's flat-paneled handheld computers to an "electronic book." We need to develop a new aesthetic—a digital aesthetic. And the emerging backlash from the literati makes clear to me how urgently we need it.

When we've mastered digital media, we won't be talking about anything that has much to do with the antiquated form of the book. I imagine myself curled up in bed with laser images projected on my retinas, allowing me to view and travel through an imaginary three-dimensional virtual world. A story about the distant past flashes a quaint image of a young woman sitting and reading a book, which seems just as remote as the idea of a cluster of Navajo Indians sitting around a campfire and listening to a master of the long-lost tradition of storytelling. In a hundred years, we'll think of the book as we do the storyteller today.

Will we lose a part of our cultural heritage as we assimilate new media? No doubt. Is this disturbing? Absolutely. Today's traditional media will be further marginalized. Is there much value in decrying an inevitable future? Probably not. The music of *today* is written on electric instruments. Hollywood creates our theater. And soon digital media will be *our* media. Digital technology and new digital media—for better or worse—are here to stay.

25   That's not to say that all things digital are good. Perhaps, like the Luddites in Britain during the first half of the nineteenth century, the literati raise a flag of warning, raise awareness, and create debate, debunking some of the myths of a utopian digital future. But in the end, for better or for worse, the efforts of the Luddites were futile when it came to stopping the industrial revolution.

Likewise, today you can't turn off the Internet. Digital technology isn't going away. There are already thousands of multimedia CD-ROMs and hundreds of thousands of sites on the World Wide Web; soon there will be thousands of channels of on-demand digital worlds.

Digital technology is part of our lives, a part of our lives that we know will only continue to grow. We can't afford to dismiss it. Rather we must embrace it—not indiscriminately, but thoughtfully. We must seize the opportunities generated by the birth of a new medium to do things we've never been able to do before. Don't look back.

QUESTIONS FOR DISCUSSION

1. Why does Holtzman believe that the power and popularity of books and newspapers are fading? Do you agree?
2. According to William Thompson, why do the members of the "literary intelligentsia" find the "new culture" of CD-ROMs and the Internet to be repugnant? What other reasons for the rejection might there be?
3. What is computer scientist Cliff Stoll's primary reason for rejecting the Internet as a learning experience? How does Holtzman attempt to refute Stoll? Is he successful? With whose point of view do you agree?
4. What features of the book do the traditional critics such as Birkerts consider to be irreplaceable? Do these critics have valid arguments? Explain.
5. What do you think Holtzman means by his concluding statement that we must embrace digital media "not indiscriminately, but thoughtfully"? Do you think his essay is a good example of the thoughtful approach he recommends? Explain your point of view.

CONNECTION

Compare Holtzman's view of reading and its significance with those of John G. Ramsay. How would Holtzman respond to Ramsay's suggestions for encouraging young people to read more deeply and enthusiastically (see page 50)?

IDEAS FOR WRITING

1. Write an essay in which you compare your own experience with the World Wide Web or a learning program on a multimedia CD-ROM disk to reading a regular book or textbook on the same subject. Which experience did you find more useful and worthwhile? Use examples to support your ideas.
2. Write an essay that predicts the changing roles that books and printed media will play in contrast to the roles of the Internet and other digital media in the next five years. Consider specific environments such as the home, schools, the workplace, and governmental agencies.

RELATED WEB SITES

Steven Holtzman
www.beatrice.com/interviews/holtzman/
Learn more about the author, Steven Holtzman, and his ideas on the revolution of art and writing in the "new digital media age."

The Scene! Digital Expression
www.inthescene.com/digitexp/
This Web site shares new writing, art, and music "in the digital realm." Here one can view the latest in digital expressions from artists, musicians, and writers.

John G. Ramsay

Hell's Bibliophiles: The Fifth Way of Looking at an Aliterate

John G. Ramsay completed his Ph.D. at the State University of New York at Buffalo in 1984. He is currently the chair of the Educational Studies Department at Carleton College, where he also teaches courses in educational research and on topics such as the history of African American education in the United States. Ramsey lives in Northfield, Minnesota, and serves as treasurer of the local school board. For the academic year 2003–2004, he was honored to become a participant in the American Council on Education (ACE), which prepares fellows to assist administrators on key issues at their college. Ramsay has published articles in many academic journals and is coeditor of the Biographical Dictionary of Modern American Educators *(1997). The essay included below examines the phenomenon of aliteracy and refutes some of the stereotypes of the "aliterate" individual.*

JOURNAL

Do you consider yourself an "aliterate," that is, a person who knows how to read but seldom reads a book unless forced to? Do you have friends who are aliterates? Why don't you or other people you know like to read?

The word "aliterate" has an edge that puts me on edge. I don't find it as frightful as "amoral," but the two words affect my fear gland in much the same way. They both invite me to worry about a void. An amoralist is someone who lacks sensibility, who doesn't care about (or even recognize) distinctions between right and wrong. An aliterate is usually cast as someone who doesn't care about what others write, and is therefore suspected of being lazy. Definitions of amoralism are careful not to speculate about the origins of this void, but they highlight deviation from a commonly accepted norm of caring about ethical distinctions. The aliterate, I'd suggest, faces the same tacit accusation of deviation from a culture that considers a literate life as normal, desirable, and good.

A first way of looking at an aliterate is through the eyes of cartoonists. Aliterates are always good for a laugh in sophisticated literacy circles, such as in the pages of the *New Yorker* magazine. For example, you might recall William Hamilton's 1994 cartoon depicting a grandmotherish figure in a bookstore saying to the clerk: "It's for a young woman in the generation that knows how to read but doesn't feel like it."

Then there's Arnie Levin's take on the daily dilemma of reading for busy adults. A guy is standing outside a bookstore with his guardian angel whispering in his ear, "Read the book!" And at the same time a horned figure with a pitch fork is whispering in his other ear, "See the movie!"

Other cartoonists invite us to chuckle about the cultural gulf between readers and non-readers. Warren Miller has a middle-aged couple walking through a vacant apartment with wall after wall of empty bookshelves. The woman is asking the real estate broker: "Holy cow! What kind of crazy people used to live here anyway?"

5   A famous quote by Mark Twain captures the bewildered frustration of the literate as he gazes at the aliterate: "The man who does not read good books has no advantage over the man who can't read them." His point is that aliteracy is a chosen form of illiteracy, and therefore borders on being a self-inflicted handicap—a radical rejection of literate and literary culture and the recorded wisdom of the ages.

The very word aliteracy is a charge of indifference, self-absorption, or insularity. It is fashionable now to suggest that words "have an agenda," and I think aliteracy certainly does. It is clear that aliteracy, the word, has a credenda—set of doctrines to be believed in as articles of faith. There are two elements in this belief: 1) that a wonderful gift—the ability to read—is being wasted, and 2) that such a waste is both baffling and—as with any wasted skill or talent—morally charged.

These are the particular assumptions about aliteracy that I want to question here. Does an aliterate really think of reading as a wonderful gift? Do aliterates feel a sense of bafflement too? Are they wounded by the indignation of the highly literate? What can we learn if we think about aliteracy as a complicated cultural question, rather than simply a knee-jerk accusation of deficiency? And how can we harness what we learn to help us approach the many students we encounter who appear indifferent to reading?

A second way of looking at an aliterate is through the eyes of the International Reading Association (IRA). This literacy organization, interestingly, views aliteracy with a rather cartoonish quality. The IRA's Literacy Dictionary defines aliteracy as the "lack of the reading habit in capable readers." This definition encourages us to think about literacy as essentially a work-ethic problem among skilled readers. The IRA locates the problem within individuals, who, as the definition suggests, have no one to blame but their weak-willed selves. The circularity of the aliterate's logic seems lost on the IRA: If these non-readers would only get into the habit of reading, then they'd have the habit of reading, and wouldn't squander their capacity.

Reading professional Larry Mikulecky coined the term aliteracy in 1979. The original formulation included an intensifying phrase: "Lack of the reading habit; especially, such a lack in capable readers who choose not to read." Mikulecky underscored the theme of wasted capability by insisting that it is a willful wasting, rather than mere casual apathy. He then went on to put a new spin on Twain's point. He wrote: "Aliteracy may guarantee continued, lifelong, functional illiteracy."

10   So definitions matter—they carry both credendas and agendas. Try this thought experiment. Suppose the IRA's definition of aliteracy were the following: "An aversion to reading among weak readers." How would that definition change the questions we ask about our students who have a fragile attachment

to texts? I would begin by asking: 1) How did these kids learn to dislike reading in the first place? 2) Which of their reading skills seem to be overmatched by the texts we ask them to read? These are questions that can move us along in a way that the IRA's implication of sloth cannot. If we're going to make progress on understanding the mystery beneath the superficial indifference we see in our classrooms, we're going to have to defuse this 23-year-old credenda about aliteracy. We are going to have to put a different set of faces on aliterates. And we are going to have to challenge our culture's mental models of what aliteracy is and how it works.

A third way of looking at an aliterate is to look in the mirror and try to understand it from the inside out. This is not an easy thing to do. Once we are literate it is difficult to sympathetically recall what it was like to be indifferent to the power and beauty of words on a page. Our ears know that there is a difference between the mocking snickers that cartoons provoke and the nervous laughter that mirrors elicit.

If we are going to help our students, we must think of these differences between us, the literate, and them, the aliterate, as bridgeable differences of degree, rather than as insurmountable differences of kind. To do so, it may be useful to resurrect a remote state of mind—an aliterate chapter in our own lives. I say "chapter" because we need to remember that to grow up in any literate culture is to be coerced into caring about reading. In the long career of any reader, there are many moments when we feud with the text, and it is important to understand these feuds rather than to dismiss the feuders as possessing low and irredeemable intellectual status. Getting a glimpse of the aliterate within can be an important first step toward working well with fragile readers in our classrooms. Try another thought experiment: What aliterate chapter do you recall in your own life? What was it about? How did you move out of it?

I began high school as an avid reader, but I read with the same ear I used to listen to sporting events on the radio. I read to hear the voice, the official play-by-play of a contest on a field I could only imagine. For me, reading was listening to a game broadcast on a faintly received station. Consequently, I would fiddle with the tuner, then the volume, and eventually the voice of the writer came in louder and clearer. I assumed that my job as a reader was to absorb the action, and to learn who won and lost. The goal of reading, so I believed, was to identify the heroes, the goats, and the final score.

I was pretty good at this "sponging the events" kind of reading, and it gave me a chance to hone the skill of reading for multiple-choice tests: a) plot; b) character; c) setting; d) details. I sailed through the summer reading exams administered during the first week of school each year. I gloated while my buddies struggled to recall what actually happened in *Teahouse of the August Moon*.

15   Recall, I could do, but if the task required a kind of reading more subtle than a sturdy memory could furnish, I was sunk. As a high school senior I tried to write an extra-credit essay about several of J.D. Salinger's characters to no avail. I turned in nine pages of inconclusive ramblings about Franny, Zooey, and Seymour Glass. Then I prayed my teacher would reward the sincerity of my sweat. He didn't.

And so in December 1969, I stood shivering in a snow-storm, a frosh in a reading rut, hitchhiking home for the holidays to await my first grade report from college. I had been unable to pierce any meaning from three of my textbooks—psychology, biology, and statistics. I didn't have a study skills problem. I had tutors in bio and stat. I had dim, surface-level understandings. But I could not read for comprehension. I hated reading the stuff, often falling asleep in the library without a memorized definition to my name.

What happened next saved me. I was offered a ride east on Interstate 80 by two women from my college who were deep in conversation about how thoughtful people read books. They were talking animatedly about one of their friends, an intellectual maverick who had written all of her end-of-semester papers about different aspects of a single book—Ken Kesey's *One Flew Over the Cuckoo's Nest*. My first reaction was a mixture of outrage and awe. Could you really get away with that sort of thing in college? The dean of students was on my case for tossing a few water balloons, while something like this was going on?

I had never met anyone with this level of literary audacity. But in my dense and plodding way, I began to imagine how she might read. I'm convinced it was the Salinger fiasco, coupled with the frustrations of my first semester, that made me an especially attentive eavesdropper that night. I sat staring out the back seat window, listening in amazement, hungering for a way out of a literacy limbo that I couldn't even name. I listened as they celebrated the craft and sheer nerve of their friend: "And then in her political science paper, she wrote about how McMurphy undermines the authority structure of the hospital." I remember thinking: "So this is it. This is how you do college. This is how you read."

I'd like to report that my academic performance improved dramatically during the spring semester. It didn't. What did happen, though, was that the eavesdropping episode pushed me beyond the broadcast model of reading that had served me for good and ill for so long. In its place was the vague outline of constructing a tool box—reading as the gathering of useful objects to think, talk, and write with. This was what the maverick seemed to be doing with *Cuckoo's Nest*—stripping it for ideas and values. Then she used what she found to illustrate, elaborate, or cast doubt upon some other set of ideas and values in an entirely different course. It sounded daring and scary. I couldn't wait to try it.

20   I was also struck by the passion that the maverick felt for Kesey's mind, the world that he had invented. That spring I began to dwell on the strange and private business that transpired between readers and writers—the silent courtship of reading. I started to notice who was reading whom, and to wonder about what was going on between these couples as they strolled hand-on-binding across campus. And I began to wonder if I, too, could profitably read those books.

Last year I taught a senior seminar on the personal essay. In it, I asked my students to write about their careers as readers and non-readers. I had never given this assignment before, and did not know if we had enough mutual trust for serious reflection and candor. Would my students be willing to trade on private memories to enter a conversation about what reading had meant to them? This is what I learned.

They remembered fondly the rites of passage that comprise our reading lives—finishing an entire chapter in a day, and binge-reading a single author, like Gary Paulson or Roald Dahl. They also remembered being infected, and having their imaginations fully inhabited, by particular books like *Anne of Green Gables*. One young woman wrote, "At one point, Anne explained the significance of her name being spelled with an 'e' at the end; with an 'e' the name 'Anne' had elegance; without it, 'Ann' was plain. My own middle name Ann had no 'e' and became burdensome, and I begged my parents to allow me to have it changed."

I was pleased to find a common theme that I call the thirst for significant reading. The idea is this: If you're going to ask me to invest the time in reading in the first place, give me something weighty, important, or even troubling. One young woman wrote of discovering James Baldwin at Carleton, and linked it to the memory of her parents smuggling Marxist books into Taiwan when she was a child. She wrote: "Over the past four years I have gotten to know Baldwin as an artist-sociologist who I find more eloquent and also more profound than anyone else I have ever read. He renewed my faith in the novel and underlined my demand for piercing analysis. When I think about my parents disguising books in clothes to go to Taiwan, and myself hiding books in the frame of my backpack in Ireland, that is the weight I want to everything I read." I was glad I had not read this daunting challenge when I was designing the syllabus.

There were strong counter-themes in these essays as well. One was about reading slowness, time pressures, and similar frustrations. One student began her essay with: "I have a visual kinetic failure: an inability to translate written words directly from sight to comprehension. For me, the extra step involves saying the words either out loud or silently to myself. This makes me a dismally slow reader, and skimming or speed-reading is virtually impossible. Perseverance saw me through, but I began to associate stress and rush with reading. The thought of books left a bad taste in my mouth."

25   Another student was even more viscerally expressive about being a slow reader: "In high school I learned to hate books. I resented them. These objects that used to hold so much excitement now promised it but did not deliver. They discriminated against me because I was not speedy enough to read them cover to cover while still understanding their meaning."

These students drew a sharp nostalgic distinction between the leisurely joy of reading during their childhoods and the high-stress, low-learning "assigned reading" of high school and college. One young woman wrote: "I miss my life when books were wonderful and I resent having been made to feel like they are a chore." One young man wrote: "I'm always cautious about assigned readings. To a large extent teachers have a good idea of what types of literature are appropriate for students. However, in my early years, that was not the case and many works were lost upon my unfocused and impatient pint-sized brain. I read because it was assigned for class."

The last quote captures the uncertainty that many students feel about their futures with books. My students knew that their frustrations with my assigned readings would be behind them in a couple of weeks. But they didn't know quite what the future would hold. One woman wrote: "I have wanted to be a writer all my life but being so discouraged about reading and my struggle with writing essays in high school sufficiently deterred me. I am not a writer. I am not a reader. But I will read and write all my life, in spite of the clock (which is ticking), and because of my adopted belief in the hallowed, elusive benefits of books."

I came away from these essays heartened by the passion my students feel for their reading lives. But I was saddened by the disconnect between those lives and the assigned readings of high school and college. I recommend asking this reading-career question widely and then trying to decipher the answers by course and department. We have a lot to learn from both the joys and exasperations of our students, but next time I will ask this question up front as a short diagnostic, rather than at the end as a graded assignment.

Notice how the definition of aliteracy would change if it were written to describe the experiences of some of my students. Instead of the "lack of the reading habit," it would be more accurate to talk of the "loss of the reading habit." Instead of "incapable readers," it would make more sense to say "in slow and frustrated readers." Instead of "who choose not to read," it would be more truthful to write "who choose to read despite feeling enormous stress, confusion, and pressure." This is the fourth way of looking at an aliterate—from the struggling reader's point of view.

30   When the African-American essayist Gayle Pemberton was in her first year of college, she heard a talk given by Ralph Ellison. Ellison had fallen out of favor with some black militant students and during his presentation they jeered him. Pemberton felt ashamed that she could not come to Ellison's defense. She writes: "I was several years too young and underread to take on the battle."

Underread—what a fabulous word! *Webster's Third International* defines it as, "To read with less than full or due understanding, appreciation, or alertness." To take this definition seriously is to understand what the ultra-literate share with the allegedly aliterate. We are all underread. We are eternally underread. It's nothing to be ashamed of. Underread suggests bridgeable differences of degree.

Here's my concluding suggestion: Build a course about the long and complicated journey of the reading life, and they will come. My own version of this course will be titled Hell's Bibliophiles. I've borrowed the title, you won't be surprised, from a Michael Maslin cartoon. It depicts a group of rough-and-tumble guys browsing in a bookstore, gently caressing the classics and the new releases. They are all wearing motorcycle jackets that have "Hell's Bibliophiles" written on the back.

The joke is a play on the cliché, "Don't judge a book by its cover." But beneath the joke, Maslin implies an interesting question: How do we do this? How do we recruit gangs of readers? How do we reach students with an attitude, students aligned against literate culture, and convince them to make their peace with it and us? I'd teach this course as a freshman seminar, and the course description would read something like this:

"Hell's Bibliophiles. This course is intended for students with a bad attitude about reading. It will be conducted seminar-style and will require you to disclose how it was that you learned to dislike reading. This is not a remedial reading course, though it might remedy whatever loss you may feel for having fallen out of love with reading. You'll be required to read personal essays, short fiction, and poems about growing up in a culture that coerces you to place a high value on literacy, and a low value on literariness. You'll have to write short personal essays in response to the readings and discussions. You will be expected to contribute to the building of a community of readers, or be willing to argue why such an activity would be a waste of time."

35   In teaching this course, my fantasy is to portray Attila the Hun in a Frank Cotham cartoon. The cartoon depicts Attila returning from a raid with loot, turning on his horse and calling out to his followers: "Did anyone plunder something good to read?"

QUESTIONS FOR DISCUSSION

1. What is the popular stereotype of or "accusation" against the aliterate, and why does this viewpoint disturb Ramsay? Do you agree or disagree with him? Why?
2. Where and how does Ramsay use references to cartoons in his essay? Do you think that illustrating the essay with reproductions of cartoons as opposed to just quoting from them would make the essay more effective? Why or why not? Explain.
3. Ramsay structures his essay around five different ways of "looking at an aliterate." Is this an effective approach to arranging ideas? What are the five ways, and why are they introduced in the sequence found in the essay?
4. How does Ramsay use quotations from definitions of aliteracy by the IRA and Larry Mikulecky to illustrate the contradictions and negativity in contemporary views of the aliterate?
5. How effective and relevant is Ramsay's narrative of his own early experience as an aliterate? What did you learn from his story? What did you learn from the comments of his students about their own feelings about reading?
6. Describe Ramsay's idea for a course called Hell's Bibliophiles. Why is this "not a remedial reading course"? Does it seem like a useful project? Why or why not?

CONNECTION

Compare Ramsey's ideas for causes of the current lack of interest among youth in reading and books with those of Steven Holtzman in "Don't Look Back" (see page 44).

IDEAS FOR WRITING

1. Write an essay about your own "reading story": What events and activities in your life led you to want to read or to dislike reading? Do you consider yourself to be or to have been at some point in the past an "aliterate"? Why or why not?
2. Ramsay ends his essay with his idea for a course designed to encourage aliterate students to want to read. Do some research in this area and write an essay that describes and explains several strategies that a teacher might

use to get students excited about reading, particularly those who are used to doing their reading by skimming text on the Internet.

RELATED WEB SITES

Help Me Read
www.helpmeread.org/tutors/aliteracy.html
The Help Me Read Web site has links to articles, books, tutoring tips, and advice for parents on combating aliteracy.

When Students Do Not Feel Motivated
http://curry.edschool.virginia.edu/go/clic/nrrc/ rspon_r8.html
An article by Penny Oldfather of the University of Georgia explains how a positive classroom culture and teachers who try to attain an empathetic understanding of their unmotivated students' perceptions can help them accept and become engaged with literacy learning.

Joyce Chang

Drive Becarefully

Student writer Joyce Chang (b. 1975) was raised in northern California. Living in a predominantly white neighborhood and growing up in a traditional, close-knit Asian family, Chang struggled to integrate her Chinese heritage with mainstream American culture. In the essay that follows, written originally for an introductory writing class, she explores the problem of coming to terms with her mother's non-standard English in light of reading Amy Tan's essay, "Mother Tongue."

"My mother's 'limited' English limited my perception of her. I was ashamed of her English." Amy Tan's self-evaluation in her essay, "Mother Tongue," clung to my conscience as I continued reading. I could have said those words myself. I have definitely thought those words a million times. Like Tan, I too used to be ashamed of my mother's English. I used to shudder whenever I heard an incorrect verb tense, misplaced adverb, or incorrect pronoun come from her lips. Like many people, I couldn't look beyond my mother's incorrect grammar to see the intent and beauty behind her words.

My mother immigrated to the United States in the 1970s, speaking only a few words of English. As time went on, she gradually learned more and more words, although her sentence structure remained very basic. As a young working woman and mother of two, my mother didn't have much of a chance to improve her grammar. Taking ESL courses was not one of her immediate concerns—trying to beat rush hour Chicago traffic to get home in time to make dinner was what she worried about. So my mother went on using phrases like "He go to the store."

Since I had the advantage of being born and raised in the United States, my English abilities quickly surpassed those of my mother by the time I was in grade school. I knew all about auxiliary verbs, the subjunctive, and plurals—my mother didn't. I could form sentences like "He treated her as if she were still a child." For my mother to convey that same idea, she could only say, "He treat her like child."

My mother's comprehension of the English language was comparable to her speaking abilities. When I was with her, I learned early on not to try any of the complicated, flowery, descriptive sentences that I had been praised for in school. Anything beyond a simple subject-verb-object construction was poorly received. When I was very young, I did not think much about having to use a different English with my mother. The two Englishes in my life were just different—one was not better than the other. However, that feeling quickly changed in third grade.

5   My young mind could not always switch between the two Englishes with ease. I usually knew which English belonged in which world, but sometimes my Englishes crossed over. I remember one day in third grade when I was supposed to bring something for a "cultural show-and-tell." It must have been sometime in winter—around Chinese New Year. My mother had given me a "red bag" for show-and-tell. A "red bag" is an envelope that contains money. Chinese people give and receive these envelopes of money as gifts for the new year. As my mother described it to me, "The bag for good fortune . . . you rich for New Year." When I tried to explain the meaning of the red envelope to my class, I used my mother's words, "The bag for good fortune. . . . " I do not think my classmates noticed my grammatical shortcomings, or maybe they did notice but chose not to comment. In any case, my teacher had an alarmed look on her face and sharply demanded, "What did you say?" She seemed to be in complete bewilderment at how one of her students who spoke "good English" could suddenly speak "bad English." Thinking that she just didn't hear me the first time, I innocently repeated the exact same phrase I had said before.

"Where did you learn *that* English?" she questioned. "It's wrong! Please speak correctly!" she commanded.

After her admonishment, it took me a while to continue speaking. When I finally opened my mouth to utter my first word, all I could think of was, "I hope this is correct." I was relieved when I finished with no further interruptions.

Hearing my teacher say that my mother's English was wrong had a lasting impression on me. When I went home that day, all I could think about when my mother spoke was the "wrongness" of her English, and the "wrongness" of her as a person. I took her awkward phrases, sentence fragments, and other incorrect phrases as a sign that she somehow was "incorrect." I became irritated with her when she made grammatical mistakes at home. I became ashamed of her when she made those same mistakes outside of the house.

By the time I entered high school I was tired of being ashamed of my mother's English. I thought I would do her a favor and take on a mission to improve her English. The mission turned out to be a lot more difficult than I thought it would be. No matter how many times I would tell her something that she said was wrong, she would still say the same phrase over and over again. For example, whenever I left the house, my mother would say, "Drive becarefully." After the first time she said that, I told her it was wrong. I would then add, "The correct way to say that is 'drive carefully' or 'be careful driving.'" She would then nod and say good-bye. However, the next day as I headed out the door, mother would come up to me and say "drive becarefully" again. I would get incredibly frustrated because she never seemed to learn. I was glad, however, that at least I was the only one to hear such an "incorrect" statement.

10   One day, however, a friend of mine was with me as we headed out the door. As usual my mother screamed out "drive becarefully" as we walked toward the car. I immediately rolled my eyes and muttered, "It's 'drive carefully.' Get it right."

Later, as I drove my friend back home, she asked me a question that I will never forget. "Is it your mom who wants to improve her English or is it you who wants to 'improve' her?" I was stunned at first by my friend's question. I had no response. After a lot of thinking, I realized my friend was right. My mom was satisfied with her English. She could convey her thoughts and didn't care that she did it in a way that was different from the standard. She had no problem with her use of language—I did.

After that conversation, I began to accept the idea that there are many different Englishes and that one is not necessarily better than the other. As long as a person is understood, it is not necessary to speak textbook perfect English. Presently, I am very concerned with how people treat others who speak "limited" English. I understand how easy it is to misperceive and mistreat people. In her essay "Mother Tongue," Tan also writes about how people are perceived differently just because of their "limited" English. She describes the problems her mother encounters day to day, "people in department stores, at banks, and at restaurants did not take her seriously, did not give her good service, pretended not to understand her, or even acted as if they did not hear her." Although I am very angry when I read about how a person with "limited" English is mistreated, I still understand how it is all too easy for a person not to take someone seriously when he/she does not speak the same English as that person. It is also easy to assume a person who speaks "broken" English wants someone to help him "fix" it.

Now, when I find myself talking with people who speak "another" English, I try to look for the meaning, the intent of what they say, and ignore the perhaps awkward structure of their statements. Also when I encounter someone who speaks an English different from my own, I try not to assume that he or she wants to "improve" it.

As Tan concludes her essay, the importance of what is spoken lies in a person's ". . . intent . . . passion . . . imagery . . . and the nature of . . . thoughts." These are the things I now look for when someone speaks to me. Incorrect verb tenses, misplaced adverbs, and incorrect pronouns are less significant issues. As I begin to realize this more, I feel more comfortable with not only my mom's different English but my own. My mom's English is the one I grew up with at home. It is one of the Englishes I speak.

15   The other day I went home to help my mom run errands.
"Go to store," she said.
"Buy what?"
"Juice and eggs. Drive becarefully!" my mom warned.
I couldn't help but to smile. I like hearing that now.

QUESTIONS FOR DISCUSSION

1. How has Chang applied insights and experiences of Amy Tan in "Mother Tongue" to her own relationship with her mother?
2. Could you identify with any aspects of Chang's feelings and attitudes about her mother's English or with her struggle to accept her mother for who she is rather than to "fix her"?
3. Do you agree or disagree with Chang's teacher's attitude and her definition of correct English? Explain your point of view.
4. Do you agree or disagree with Chang's conclusion, "As long as a person is understood, it is not necessary to speak textbook perfect English"?

Molly Thomas

Response to "Don't Look Back"

Student writer Molly Thomas wrote the following essay after reading "Don't Look Back," a reading selection included in this chapter. In the essay that follows, notice how she writes using a number of the response strategies suggested at the beginning of the chapter: giving some background on the piece and its central debate, then moving to analyze some of its strategies of refutation and audience, and finally taking her own evaluative position on the piece itself and the larger debate over technology and the book.

Today the debate over the long-lasting effects of digital technology on literacy and the culture of the book provoke many heated and widespread disputes that often pit different generations against one another. In "Don't Look Back," a chapter from his book *Digital Mosaics*, Steven Holtzman heralds the onset of the digital age and the opportunities it will provide, dismissing the extreme negative critics of digital learning and culture even as he expresses regret about its potential effects on the high culture of books and print literacy. Holtzman's arguments are subtly contradictory enough to undermine some of his initial claims supporting technology.

In both the pro and antitechnology sides of the argument, there is an impending feeling that the spread of digital technology is inevitable. For Holtzman, this fact rests on the nature of the technology itself. He writes, "For centuries, the book has been the primary vehicle for recording, storing, and transferring knowledge. But it's hard to imagine that paper will be the preferred format in

100 years." In Holtzman's model, technology takes the more active role, driven by sheer Darwinian evolution and a search for convenience. As is the case with most technological developments, digital technology itself develops at a rate far faster than the consideration of its moral and cultural implications. For Holtzman, the argument seems to be simply over the technology itself, the actual practical differences between writing information on a piece of paper versus a computer. Later on in his argument, Holtzman goes on to compare the opponents of digital technology to the machine-smashing Luddites who rebelled against the rise of industrialization in nineteenth century Britain. The connotation today of a "Luddite" is of someone who appears antiquated in his or her approach to the world and as a result out of tune with reality. According to this view, people may have a say in how technology is created, but once it is in circulation it becomes self-propagating and as a result any opposition to its spread is futile.

In disqualifying opposition to his pro-digital argument, Holtzman quotes critic William Irwin Thompson who observes, "This new cyberpunk, technological culture is brought forth by . . . electronic science and pop music, and both the hackers and the rockers are anti-intellectual and unsympathetic to the previous Mental level expressed by the genius of European civilization." For Thompson, these digital advancements are less about the technology itself and instead are more defined by the community that fosters technological growth. This opinion is clearly very one-sided, and easy to refute as it only attributes digital creativity to those who have been traditionally classified as outlying, destructive and "anti-intellectual" deviants of modern culture such as hackers and rockers. From this perspective, the debate over digital technology versus books is less about the technology itself; it rather centers on how technology is fostered by a disinterest or aversion to learning and the intellectual.

Holtzman goes on to cite another dissenting opinion of technology from author Clifford Stoll who argues, "During that week you spend online, you could have planted a tomato garden. . . . While the Internet beckons brightly, seductively flashing an icon of knowledge-as-power, this nonplace lures us to surrender our time on earth." Holtzman is right to point out ironically that books and symphonies similarly deter us from direct, physical ways of acquiring knowledge through observation and action, although he could have developed his critique further. Stoll's imagery of the Internet seducing its youthful viewers is really a stereotype or cartoon image of evil technological tools that inevitably alienate youngsters from the world of experiential learning. Stoll is creating an either-or dilemma in response to technology: Why should manual labor provide more essential understanding than the Internet, rather than an equal and complementary insight into the world around us and the distant worlds of foreign cultures, geographies, and planetary systems?

5   Despite his deft refutation of Stoll, Holtzman's argument loses some of its power through the use of rhetorical strategies that suggest his audience is predominantly one that shares his point of view. For example, after excerpting Thompson's quote on "cyberpunks" Holtzman states his response very briefly: "This helped me dismiss the backlash from those looking in the rearview mirror." Throughout the first half of his piece, Holtzman creates a distance between

himself and those who espouse an anti-digital perspective by creating a casual dialogue-like tone between himself and the reader as he walks through the process of reaffirming his own beliefs. Again we see from the use of dismissive words like "rearview mirror" and "backlash" that those who are responding as antiquated "Luddites" are only protesting a technology that has and will inevitably spread.

However, Holtzman seems to draw back from fully supporting technology-based culture and learning by espousing some of the rhetoric associated with the opposing side of the debate. He writes, "There never will be a substitute for a book. And today's multimedia CD-ROM—even surfing the World Wide Web—is still for the most part a static and unsatisfying experience." It's true that no technology will be able to replicate a book exactly, but it's certainly an exaggeration to suggest that multimedia provides an "unsatisfying experience." Like the authors he criticizes, Holtzman seems to make a hierarchical distinction between reading and using the Internet. It might have helped for him to qualify this statement by specifying in what ways books *and* the Internet can be both rewarding and not. Holtzman goes on to inquire, "Will we lose part of our cultural heritage as we assimilate new media? No doubt. Is this disturbing? Absolutely." Here again, he fails to explain exactly what will be lost and what new culture might replace it. Although Holtzman begins his piece by suggesting that his argument is fundamentally one over the fated evolution of technology, he ends by conceding that books still give us insight into a world that will never be matched by technology.

Why is it, then, that books are unquestioningly associated with learning and intellectual growth while technology becomes defined as just the opposite? The answer lies in the fact that learning itself is frequently viewed as a tool of privilege; those who feel that the digital world is alien to them in turn cling to traditional means of learning that they do understand, means which are slowly becoming alien to today's youngest generations. As Holtzman concedes, "Kids today are so attuned to the rapid rhythms of MTV that they're unresponsive to the patient patterns of literary prose. . . . Literary culture—like classical music and opera—will become marginalized as mainstream culture pursues a digital path." Unlike the technological arguments that we saw earlier, the distinction he now makes seems more class-based. It would be sad indeed if books did meet the same fate that classical music and opera have met in modern culture, if they become part of a culturally elitist group that excludes its membership from mass culture. Holtzman cites one writer who prides himself in using only a typewriter and not even owning a computer. Many, like this writer, hide behind the façade of intellectualism to avoid integrating themselves into the digital world. In a sense, Holtzman seems to accept this position by similarly classifying books into a unique, unchanging and irreplaceable aspect of culture instead of seeing them as an evolving means of cultural communication. It's only when the cultures of readers and technology users become polarized that we really have to worry about one group having a superficial relationship with their surrounding world.

While opponents of the digital revolution claim that technology is "dumbing us down" and drawing us away from real learning, the reality is quite different. To the average person with access to an inexpensive home computer and a modem, the Internet alone has opened up doors to more sources of knowledge than anyone in history has ever had access to. For thousands of years, this type of access to vast knowledge contained previously only in world-class libraries has been limited by access to high-level literacy and quality education to a lucky few. Today the Internet has become the digital printing press of our generation. It's unfortunate, then, that there are those who still wish to deter the development of digital technology, and in turn maintain access to knowledge and learning as a privilege, not a right. Now that this privilege has become a widespread commodity, we shouldn't discourage its growth; rather we should help it to evolve into a universal tool for cultural expression.

QUESTIONS FOR DISCUSSION

1. In the first paragraph, how clearly does Thomas state both the subject of Holtzman's essay and his perspective on the debate between pro- and antitechnology forces? Is her position on the essay clear?

2. In the second paragraph, how does Thomas use references to "Luddites" and Darwinian evolution theories to contrast the conflicting positions on technology of Holtzman and his opponents? Is her explanation of these terms clear?

3. Thomas uses both paraphrase and direct quoting from Holtzman's essay, as well as quoting and paraphrasing some of his critics. How effectively are these quotations and paraphrases used? Are there places where you would have liked to see quoting rather than paraphrasing, or more introduction or explanation of a quotation?

4. In the two paragraphs before the conclusion, Thomas criticizes Holtzman for conceding too much to the antitechnology argument, which comes from a "high culture," traditional perspective. Does her criticism seem justified? Why or why not?

TOPICS FOR RESEARCH AND WRITING

1. Drawing on evidence from the selections in this chapter such as the essays by King, Woolf, and Le Guin, as well as outside research and your own experiences, write an essay that examines the role of dreams and the unconscious mind in the reading and writing processes.

2. Although several authors in this chapter discuss ways in which they have been influenced to become readers and writers, in contrast, John Ramsay discusses reasons why people in today's society feel a lack of motivation to practice higher literacy skills and seldom read books at all. Taking into consideration the experiences of these writers as well as those of others you have read about or interviewed, write an essay in which you examine some of the influences that either encourage or discourage a person's interest in becoming a reader and/or a writer.

3. Tan, Woolf, and King value reading and writing as processes of self-discovery and healing. Write an essay in which you explore this perspective on reading and writing, taking into account these writers' ideas, those of other writers you read about, as well as your own experiences.

4. Woolf and Levertov examine the social, ethical, and spiritual values involved in the art of writing. Taking into account their ideas and those of other authors, discuss some of the ways that reading and writing have a positive influence on beliefs, values, and social behavior.

5. Writers in the chapter such as Le Guin, King, and Woolf present insights into the nature of creativity and the creative process. After doing some further research into this issue, write an essay in which you present and evaluate several current theories about creative thinking and the creative process in writing.

6. Holtzman suggests that the wide availability of computers, e-mail, and Internet chat groups is changing the way writers work and relate to their audience. After doing some research into new Web-based literary ideas, writers' groups, and online publications, write an essay about new directions for writing and interactions of writers and audiences that are arising as a direct result of the cyber-space revolution.

7. See one of the following films that approach the life of the writer and/or the reader: *The Postman, Naked Lunch, Misery, The Color Purple, Shakespeare in Love, Finding Forrester, Wonder Boys, Dead Poet's Society, The Swimming Pool, Sylvia, Adaptation,* and *Neverland.* Making reference to such elements of the film as plot, dialogue, voice-over, characters, images, and visual symbolism, write an essay that discusses the ways in which the film explores the inner world of the writer and/or the reader.

Places in Nature 2

Vittorio Stella (1859–1943), "On the Glacier Blanc" (1880s)

From Biella, Italy, Vittorio Stella was a specialist in mountain photography who traveled throughout the world. His work was reproduced by many geographical societies and influenced American nature photographers such as Ansel Adams. In "On the Glacier Blanc," Stella shows a group of mountain adventurers halted by a chasm in the French alps.

JOURNAL

Write a description of a scene from nature as you imagine it; then reflect on what readings or images you have had contact with that may have led you to depict it in this manner.

It is the marriage of the soul with Nature that makes the intellect fruitful, and gives birth to the imagination.

HENRY DAVID THOREAU

Did they dream? What are penguin dreams? Food and famine, ice floes, lunging leopard seals?

DIANE ACKERMAN

The open space of democracy provides justice for all living things—plant, animals, rocks, rivers, as well as human beings.

TERRY TEMPEST WILLIAMS

OBSERVING NATURE AND WRITING DESCRIPTIONS

When we describe, we try to create powerful impressions of our experiences so that others can share our visions, feeling what we have felt, seeing through our eyes, and sharing other senses as well—hearing, taste, smell, and touch. Descriptions need to be written with great care to detail, in specific language, and with much thought as to the choice of material in order to communicate your meaning to your audience.

Observing

The more awake and alert your senses are to the world around you, the more fully you experience your world, and the more likely it is that you will be able to collect the relevant, unique, and interesting details needed to create an evocative and expressive description. To train your senses to be receptive to your surroundings and to help you write a vivid description, spend some time in quiet observation of a particular object or place you want to describe. Try observing your subject from various perspectives, walking around it, looking at it in different lights, and experiencing it through your different senses. Can you listen to it? Touch it? Smell it? While you observe, try asking yourself these questions: Why am I doing this observation? How do I feel about my subject? How do my feelings influence the way I perceive the subject? Spend ten minutes or so in quiet observation before you begin to write; then jot down as many details as you can about your subject. Read your list over to see if you can add more sensory details. Share your list of details with a classmate who may be able to help you to think about details you had forgotten.

Words and Images

Writer Annie Dillard has noted, "Seeing is . . . verbalization." When describing a person, place, thing, or even something so seemingly imprecise as an emotion, it is important to verbalize your response using specific, carefully chosen words. When you use words effectively, you can create a series of images, or sensory clusters of detail, which, taken together, convey to your readers an intimate or intense description of your experiences. Notice how in the following example from her travel memoir *Russian Journal*, Andrea Lee used a series of images that evoke specific colors ("gold," "yellow"), a sense of touch ("stuck," "cold"), a concrete impression of textures and forms ("decayed" "grotesque," "peeling front"), and a specific place or area ("a mansion in the Arbat"): "In Moscow I found more demanding pleasures of nature and architecture: rain on the gold domes inside the Kremlin walls, yellow leaves stuck to a wet pavement; a decayed stone grotesque on the peeling front of a mansion in the Arbat; a face in a subway crowd."

An image may be clarified by a comparison (a simile or a metaphor) that helps to explain more fully the quality of an experience by linking it imaginatively or literally to other, related experiences or things. This is a technique Farley Mowat uses in his essay "Learning to See" to capture his confusion as he notices something mysterious and white that looks like a feather boa at first, yet turns out to be the tails of two huge, playful wolves: "Without warning, both boas turned toward me; began rising higher and higher, and finally revealed themselves as the tails of two wolves beginning to top the esker." A reader of such a comparison is imaginatively drawn into the image and the author's attempt to create meaning for it. Use specific images and comparisons in your writing in order to invite your readers to become imaginatively engaged in your thoughts and descriptions.

Revising Initial Descriptions

Look back through your journal to find several descriptive passages of physical objects, places, people, or moods. Try to replace observations or descriptions, in particular any words that now seem too general, generic, or imprecise, with specific, concrete, close-up words or with imaginative images and comparisons that will involve your readers' minds and emotions. In the following two paragraphs written by a student, notice the differences between the initial version, in which the student describes a cattle feedlot in generalized terms, and the second paragraph, which presents a more vivid and emotionally involving description of the same scene.

Original Version   Once I visited a feedlot. In and around the wood and metal barn at the center of the lot were stalls where a number of, dull-colored, dirty, smelly cattle were penned, eating from long metal troughs.

Approximately 50 animals per pen were huddled in four structures sur-rounding the barn.

Revised Version   Last winter I had the depressing experience of visiting a feedlot. A ramshackle, unpainted oak barn leaned against the yellowish metal of a prefabricated structure, the juxtaposed structures clashing like images from a nightmare. The cattle huddled in dejected, segregated groups of approximately 50 animals per pen in four battered wooden structures surrounding the barn. The dull-colored, dusty cattle blended into the un-painted desolation of the winter day, standing in munching fortitude before a long metal trough extending the entire length of their outdoor prison. Their jaws worked with ceaseless rhythm: a lifestyle of breathing, chewing; breathing, chewing.

Establishing Vantage Point and Tone

A descriptive writer, like a painter or a photographer, is interested in estab-lishing a coherent, unified impression. To create this impression, it is neces-sary to focus the description from a particular vantage point, to let the reader see the scene from one special window. The student writer above began her description of the feedlot from a distance, gradually moved closer to the cattle, and concluded with a close look at their endlessly chewing jaws.

Notice how Annie Dillard in her essay "A Field of Silence" (from Chapter 9 of this book) begins her account of a visionary experience that takes place on a farm she enjoys visiting. First, she establishes a clear geo-graphical, spatially precise backdrop for her subsequent description: "I loved the place, and still do. It was an ordinary farm, a calf raising, hay making farm, and very beautiful. Its flat, messy pastures ran along one side of the central position of a quarter-mile road in the central part of an island, an island in Puget Sound, so that from the high end of the road you could look west toward the Pacific." While Dillard establishes a clear vantage point in the passage above, she also draws us into her description of a free, open environment through the positive emotions that she associates with her subject: "I loved the place, and still do." As you write descriptions, re-member to pay close attention to the emotional associations evoked by the physical qualities of the subject you are describing, as the student writing about a feedlot does through her use of emotional words such as "depress-ing," "huddled," and "desolate," or as Dillard does in her use of paradoxical words such as "ordinary" and "beautiful" to describe the complex impres-sion made upon her by the farm.

Thinking About Your Purpose and Audience

Although descriptions are often written for the pleasure of capturing an experience with accuracy, description serves other purposes in writing, depending in part upon the occasion for and intended audience of the piece. The selection from the student essay on a feedlot, for example, was intended to make a comment on the nature of apathy, and was directed to an audience of students and city dwellers who might never have seen a feedlot. By including details appropriate to the dull existence of the cattle on the lot, the student both shocks and prepares her audience for a commentary on human apathy and indifference. Annie Dillard has a very different purpose for her description in her essay "A Field of Silence": to make the remote farm reflect "ordinary" beauty, which heightens the contrast that she will introduce later in the essay between familiar peace and contentment, and the otherworldly intensity of a vision she had one morning while exploring the farm. Dillard assumes that her readers share her interest in nature and visionary experience, whereas the student writer assumes that her classmates would naturally share her feelings of outrage and anger over the unfortunate condition of cattle in the feedlot. Try taking a look at some of the descriptive writing in this chapter and ask yourself what assumptions the authors are making about the tastes, needs, and interests of their readers, particularly as regards the level of involvement with nature that the readers have. How do the writers try to satisfy these needs by the details and images they have chosen to include in their essays?

Now that you have had some practice in observing a familiar place or object and in selecting a purpose and tone, audience, and vantage point, you are ready to write a precise, imaginative, and expressive description of a place that holds strong meaning for you. Finding the words to describe what you see and selecting the pertinent details, images, and comparisons to clarify and support your ideas and opinions are skills that you will need to master as you continue to improve your ability to describe. As you become more adept at using these strategies, you will discover above all that powerful writing is also writing that reveals, that lights up the darkness around you.

THEMATIC INTRODUCTION: PLACES IN NATURE

Nature has always had the power to nourish, heal, and inspire. Many naturalists believe that nature is our greatest teacher, embodying the truth through the dangers, challenges, and beauty it presents to us: a remarkable sunset, an isolated beach at dawn, ancient rock formations in the desert, as well as a devastating earthquake, flood, or forest fire. Nature is extraordinary with the power to nourish and to destroy. Despite our efforts to control nature for our own benefit, it continues to act upon us, to have the last word, for we are inextricably a part of it. Yet how often do we think seriously about the natural world, pause to observe its beauty and its laws, or play in it as active participants? Most of us live in communities that are largely defined by laws and technology. Intent on getting through our daily routines and on maintaining a comfortable lifestyle, we easily forget about how much the natural world has to provide: adventure, beauty, perspective, and peace. Nature is in great part what we are, where we came from, and where we are going as we move through the places in our lives.

The selections in this chapter present a variety of experiences and places in nature that will give the reader insights about the beauty and interdependence of the natural world. The writers we have included have experienced nature firsthand; many of them are trained scientists, explorers, and naturalists. They rely on close observations, vivid descriptions, and intense inner awareness to create the moments of revelation that make up the texts that follow.

The chapter opens with Naomi Shihab Nye's poem "Fireflies," which offers a vivid portrait of creatures in nature that seem to be disappearing as they are increasingly pushed back from the urban areas in which most people dwell. In the next selection, "Deep Play," poet and naturalist Diane Ackerman shares her experience of observing a group of penguins in Antarctica, and introduces us to her philosophy of "deep play," a very engaged, imaginative way to find one's place in the natural world. In a more familiar natural setting within a large city, Mary Mackey's essay "The Distant Cataract" describes the birds, animals, and people that are able to enjoy quiet moments in nature without traveling far from home.

In our next essays, adventurers and travel writers Donovan Webster and Jon Krakauer describe their challenging adventures exploring two of nature's most breathtaking and dangerous terrains. "Inside the Volcano" is Webster's account of his climb down into a high volcano in the South Pacific, while in "The Khumbu Icefall," Jon Krakauer describes the challenges and practical strategies of climbing the most demanding and terrifying glacial icefall on the route to Mount Everest.

The two essays that follow, Terry Tempest Williams's "Ground Truthing" and Theodore Roszak's "The Nature of Sanity: Mental Health and the

Outdoors," take a more activist and philosophical approach to finding a place for oneself in nature. Williams provides a vivid description both of the Alaska National Wildlife Refuge and the struggle to keep it off-limits to exploitation by the building of oil fields and pipelines, while ecopsychologist Roszak argues for the psychologically healing results of sustained contact with the natural world.

The two student essays that conclude this chapter take very different approaches to writing about nature. In "Strawberry Creek," student writer David Kerr describes a childhood excursion into an underground natural world long hidden from surface explorers in the city above, while in "Visualizing Our Environment," Sheila Walsh examines how modern artists are drawing attention to environmental issues through their visual displays.

Powerful writing is nurtured through connections: between the inner world of dreams and the imagination, between the worlds of experience and knowledge, and between one's own feeling for and mastery of the conventions of language and written expression. As you gain more experience expressing and crafting your ideas about yourself, the natural world around you, and your hopes for the future, we hope that writing will become a vital and versatile means for expressing your thoughts, feelings, hopes, and visions.

Naomi Shihab Nye

Fireflies

Naomi Shihab Nye was born in St. Louis, Missouri, in 1952, to a Palestinian father and an American mother. Her family moved to Jerusalem when she was 14 and several years later to San Antonio, Texas, where she finished her B.A. at Trinity University in 1974 and began her career as a freelance writer and poet. Twice she has visited the Middle East and Asia for the United States Information Agency to encourage international goodwill through the arts. Currently Nye lives in San Antonio with her husband and son. Her poems and short stories have appeared in various journals and reviews throughout North America, Europe, and the Middle and Far East. Her recent books of poems include Red Suitcase *(1994),* Fuel *(1998), and* 19 Varieties of Gazelle: Poems of the Middle East *(2002). Nye has a strong sense of place and the need for natural preservation, which are evident in her poem "Fireflies," set in the hill country around San Antonio.*

JOURNAL

Describe a natural creature you have seen or read about that now is rare or extinct. What do you feel about its loss?

Lately I had looked for you everywhere
but only night's smooth stare gazed back.

Some said DDT had cupped your glow
in its sharp mouth and swallowed.
5   The loneliness of growing up
held small soft pockets you could have filled.

This summer I took my son
to the Texas hills where you startled us at dark,
ancestral droves swirling about our heads.
10   He thought you held kerosene lamps
the size of splinters. He wanted to borrow one,
just for a second, he said.
My head swooned in the blink of your lives.

Near a cedar-shaded stream where by day
15   fish rise for crumbled lumps of bread,
you were saving us from futures bereft
of minor lovely things.
You're singing, my boy said that night.
Why are you singing? He opened his hands.
20   I sang to the quiet rise of joy,
to little light.

QUESTIONS FOR DISCUSSION

1. In the poem's initial address to the missing fireflies, what is implied about the significance of their disappearance by the metaphors "only night's smooth stare gazed back" and the "small soft pockets you could have filled"?

2. What metaphor does the speaker create for DDT in lines 3 and 4? What is the effect of this metaphor as a comment on insecticides and their impact on nature?

3. What is the effect of the speaker's reference to "ancestral droves" of fireflies "swirling about our heads" in the Texas hills? What does this line suggest about the irony of the "extinction" of the fireflies?

4. What does the son's thought of the fireflies as holding "kerosene lamps/the size of splinters" reveal about the impact of natural creatures on the imagination?

5. Why does the speaker believe that the fireflies she sees are "saving us"? From what are they saving us?

6. Why does the speaker sing at the end of the poem? How does the content of her song relate to the poem as a whole and to her son's final question?

CONNECTION
Compare the implied views on the psychological importance of closeness to nature in Nye's poem with those of Theodore Roszak in "The Nature of Sanity: Mental Health and the Outdoors" (see page 103).

IDEAS FOR WRITING

1. Write a descriptive essay about a close encounter with a natural creature that took you by surprise. Describe your feelings about the encounter—how did it change you?
2. Do some research into the disappearance or increasing rareness of a particular creature you have seen or read about. Try to draw some conclusions about what has led to the approaching extinction, and, if possible, suggest something that could be done to preserve it.

RELATED WEB SITES

A Conversation with Naomi Shihab Nye
`www.soemadison.wisc.edu/ccbc/authors/experts/nye.asp`
In this interview, Nye discusses her early interest in nature and the perceptual basis of her writer's imagination.

Fireflies in Houston
`www.burger.com/firefly.htm`
Attorney Donald Burger started this site to help in his activist efforts to bring back fireflies to Houston, Texas. His site has a great deal of information about fireflies and links to many other sites that contain facts about fireflies, their scientific value, and the effort to preserve them.

Diane Ackerman

Deep Play

Diane Ackerman was born in 1948 and attended Pennsylvania State University (B.A., 1970) and Cornell University (M.F.A., 1973). She has taught at many universities and colleges, including the College of William and Mary, Columbia University, and Cornell University. Ackerman received the Academy of American Poet's Lavan Award and grants from the National Endowment for the Arts and the Rockefeller Foundation. Her essays about nature have appeared in the National Geographic, *the* New Yorker, *the* New York Times, *and other journals. Her book* A Natural History of the Senses *(1991) was a national best-seller and became the basis for a PBS television series called* Mystery of the Senses, *which*

Diane Ackerman narrated. Her most recent works include the poetry volume
Origami Bridges: Poems of Psychoanalysis and Fire *(2002), and the prose
works* A Natural History of Love *(1995),* A Slender Thread *(1998), and*
Alchemy of the Mind *(2004). In the selection that follows from* Deep Play
*(2000), Ackerman presents an imaginative description of Antarctic penguins that
exemplifies her concept of "deep play" in relation to the natural world.*

JOURNAL

Using as many figurative comparisons as you can, describe a type of play that
you have engaged in outdoors in the natural world. What did you gain or learn
from this type of play?

All alone at the rim of the known world, they stood like brightly uniformed
sentinels and stared out to sea. What did they watch for across the
windswept white deserts and galloping tar-blue waves? What signposts did they
remember that would guide them home after a long oceanic wandering? A certain shade of bay water, a dialect of current, a familiar arpeggio of ice-glazed
rock? Returning to a thousandfold teeming mass of penguins, did they recognize the relief map of a spouse's face? Did they dream? What are penguin
dreams? Food and famine, ice floes, lunging leopard seals?

Standing in the blustery Antarctic wind, while a vast city-state of penguins
milled noisily around me, I was surprised by everything—the number of penguins, whose raucous calls blurred into a symphonic screech; the brutality of
the cold biting through my jacket; the way my mind obsessed about how penguins view life; the unexpected voluptuousness of the vista. I had always imagined them living among ice palaces in windswept rookeries of monotone white,
but I discovered that their world danced with minute prisms. More colorful
than a rain forest, snow's never-ending white contains all colors, could we but
see them. And in such extreme cold one can, which I learned with the force of
a revelation. Because the surgical winds were blowing sharp as a scalpel, clouds
couldn't form in the frigid air. But suddenly, out of the brilliant blue emptiness, snow began falling in a confetti-sparkle of diamond dust. I was standing
inside a kaleidoscope. What did those emperor penguins make of it? I wondered. Or of me, for that matter. After all, their world was half the man-devils'
and half their own. Clothed in brilliant red parkas, spawned from the sides of a
colossal metal fish that floated upon the water, my shipmates and I had arrived
to stalk without killing, while gabbling among ourselves, sometimes clicking
and clacking—tall gangly creatures who stomped slowly through snow and
never slid downhill on our bellies, or used beaks as ice picks when climbing a
steep slope, or swam fast after catapulting into the sea. We were baritone beings who dragged, drove, wore, and carried an endless array of things. I felt
ashamed of my belongings—some objects for survival, but others merely for a
sense of connectedness to the known world, a symbolic trail to my past. As my

sense of identity began to seep out of me and extend itself to the penguins, I realized that they were the ultimate ascetics, creatures that possessed nothing, nested with nothing, traded nothing, carried nothing but their young.

Far from home, extravagantly unencumbered, they reminded me of the colorful thrall I'd left behind—cities and temptations, a carnival of possessions, blooming landscapes, family cares and errands, the elaborate rules of social dressage. Perhaps that's why I found myself free-associating in homely comparisons. They looked formal as waiters, or ceremonial as a village of totem poles, or they did a Chaplinesque walk, or glowed like Hopi kachinas carved to symbolize the soul of the wilderness. I did not find them human, I knew they did not choose to be stately, deliberate, and imposing. They stood doll-like, their legs set close to their tails; they were upright by design, growing large and burly enough to dive deep through frigid waters to feast on squid. Letting my mind spin on into caricature, I fancied them monarchs of all they surveyed, riding ice-floe coaches, and wearing a royal purple that came, not from sea snails, but from the atmosphere itself, when the cloak of night descended over them.

Untethered, my mind roamed the ice floes for hours, devouring each moment, far from any trace of past or future, unacquainted with my body, light as diamond dust. My gaze slid easily from the ice beneath the penguins' feet up their torpedo-shaped bodies, where pale lemon shirtfronts grade to sunrise gold at the neck, around their orange-gold crowns and lilac bills, then at last up to the star-encrusted heavens. Their ways may be mucky and bird-physical, but a saintly aura clung to them. Perhaps it was their vigil in that harsh desert. Living beacons, they brought life to a desolate part of the planet, and reminded me how rugged, how durable life is. Life that can evolve around volcanic lips in the deepest sea trenches. Life that can thrive on mountaintops high as the jet stream. Life that endures with grace even at the ends of the earth. For emperors never touch land. They live out their lives standing sentry on shelf ice. For hours I stood watching them as hypnotically as they watched the sea, wholly absorbed by their starch and vitality. Haloed in blue, they carried the sky on their shoulders. They alone seemed to connect the earth and night.

5   For the most part, the details of that new world recorded themselves on my senses. When thought happened, it bedeviled me. Why did penguins so fascinate me that I had studied them exhaustively in books, raised baby penguins in a seaquarium, traveled the length of a continent, survived physical hardships, and sailed over staggering oceans just to witness them and their dazzlingly remote landscape? I was intrigued by their protective zeal. They are such devoted parents that they will even pick up frozen or ruined eggs and try to incubate them—or try to incubate stones, or an old dead chick. Committed, self-sacrificing, they brave raging blizzards and ocean hazards in stultifying cold to fledge one fluffy, owl-faced chick. I was beguiled by the thought of hot-blooded beings ruling a world of ice, which they had adapted to in ingenious ways. Without their inner campfires, emperors would freeze to rubble. Yet cold didn't seem to bother them as much as heat. Toasty underneath thick layers of blubber, watertight and airtight, they lived inside feather comforters they could never toss aside.

At the coldest spot on earth, scoured by 200 mph winds and temperatures falling toward –100°F, how odd to see penguins battle heatstroke by blushing, panting, ruffling their feathers, lying on their bellies, exposing their underarms. I was captivated by the rare, altogether-in-the-raw, availability of emperors. No animal is more vulnerable, more open to life's vicissitudes and the roughest weathers. Wholly visible on the shelf ice, they did not fly away like the forest or jungle birds I had known, which quickly became silhouettes in the tree canopy, destined to be studied one glimpse at a time. I was dumbfounded by how beautifully the emperors flew in water—fluent, streamlined, magnificently aquatic—gliding through realms I could only guess at. Above all, they enchanted me because they were still feathered mysteries.

If someone had broken the spell of that magical day, I could easily have given my name and other particulars, but I would only gradually have emerged into my familiar world. It would have felt like surfacing from a deep-sea dive, or landing on earth after a week in orbit. I could have moved quickly and decisively if I needed to—if anything, I felt stronger than usual, more adroit, better informed. I knew and abided by the rules of the game I was playing—the weather and animal rules, the time rules, the danger rules, the social rules with my shipmates. I was alert but also ecstatic. My mood was a combination of clarity, wild enthusiasm, saturation in the moment, and wonder. In that waking trance, I was enjoying a thrilling form of play, one I've come to relish throughout my life, and have often chronicled in my books. Over the years, I've become increasingly aware of what play, and especially deep play, has meant to me, to all of us. We long for its heights, which some people often visit and others must learn to find, but everyone experiences as replenishing. Opportunities for deep play abound. In its thrall we become ideal versions of ourselves.

QUESTIONS FOR DISCUSSION

1. What kind of initial speculations does Ackerman make about the penguins she encounters in Antarctica? Do you consider her questions about the penguins serious, playful, imaginative—or some combination of the three? Explain your response.

2. What metaphors and similes does Ackerman use to describe the penguins? How do these metaphors add to your understanding and appreciation of the penguins as a species?

3. How does Ackerman use descriptive and figurative language to contrast and compare the world of the penguins to that of the human explorers who share it with them? What do we learn about the "man-devils" and about ourselves in relation to nature through her descriptions?

4. Why do the penguins make Ackerman feel ashamed of her usual lifestyle? What lesson about life do they teach her as her "mind roam[s] the ice floes"?

5. Why does the fact that the penguins are "feathered mysteries" so enchant Ackerman? Indicate some of the aspects of the penguins that are particularly mysterious and intriguing to her.

6. In her final paragraph, Ackerman introduces and hints at the significance of deep play. What does she seem to feel is particularly beneficial about deep play, and how does the selection as a whole exemplify the concept?

CONNECTION

Compare Ackerman's sense of play and whimsy in her description of the penguins with Mary Mackey's description of human and animal life on the Sacramento River. How does each writer capture a unique sense of place in her descriptions? (See page 73.)

IDEAS FOR WRITING

1. Write an essay in which you develop your initial journal entry into a descriptive essay that is designed to illustrate the concept of "deep play" in the natural world and its benefits for human beings.
2. Write an essay about a "natural mystery" that has always intrigued you. Define the mystery and give several kinds of possible explanations for it, using both your own experience and research to come to a fuller understanding of the issue.

RELEVANT WEB SITES

At Play with Diane Ackerman
www.januarymagazine.com/profiles/ackerman.html
In this interview with *January Magazine,* Diane Ackerman discusses her work habits, her interests, her family life, her poetry, and her book *Deep Play.*

Antarctic Connection Site
www.antarcticconnection.com/antarctic/wildlife/index.shtml
This Antarctica site gives information on travel, climate, geography, history and research projects, as well the variety of wildlife there, including many types of birds (including penguins), seals, and whales.

Mary Mackey

The Distant Cataract About Which We Do Not Speak

Mary Mackey was born in 1945 and raised in Indianapolis, Indiana. She graduated magna cum laude *from Harvard University (1966) and received her Ph.D. in comparative literature from the University of Michigan (1970). Her interest in travel, nature, and ecology led her to live in Costa Rica and the Dominican Republic during the 1970s. She has lectured at many institutions, including*

Harvard and the Smithsonian; currently she is a professor of English at California State University, Sacramento. Mackey has published screenplays, four books of poetry, and nine novels that have sold over a million copies. She is most widely known for the novels in the Earthsong Trilogy *(1993–1998). Much of her writing is rooted in her love and respect for the earth. In the selection that follows, Mackey describes her observations of birds and people along the Sacramento River in an urban area.*

Write descriptively about an experience you have had watching birds or other natural creatures and observing their behavior.

The air is full of drifting cottonwood seeds; the water is turning from translucent green to puddled copper; it is 105 degrees Fahrenheit; and once again I am about to sneak up on the ducks disguised as one of their own. Donning a blue baseball cap and a pair of sunglasses, I slip into the river, sink until my nose is just above the surface, and begin to do a slow, underwater breast-stroke toward a flock of mallards.

The water comes from Sierra snowmelt that has been held behind Folsom dam like a cache of liquid ice. Even in mid-July, it is still so cold, it takes my breath away, but over the years I have learned that, if I grit my teeth and keep swimming, my body will gradually acclimatize.

The mallards do not notice my approach. They never do. Perhaps ducks are nearsighted, perhaps they have a limited ability to sort out foreground and background, perhaps they are too busy dunking under to grab a beak-full of duckweed, or perhaps they just don't give a damn. I have never been sure why they always fail to notice the weird thing moving toward them, particularly on days like today when I approach against the current. Logically, I cannot possibly be a log or even a lost beach ball.

I swim nearer. No one looks up. The mallards continue to quack and duck their heads under the water. Over to the left, a male is engaged in a display of splashing and wing beating aimed at impressing a female who appears to be more interested in grooming her tail feathers. I take a few more strokes and float silently into the middle of the flock. The water is so clear I can see tadpoles scattering beneath me in all directions. The shadow of a large fish, a carp perhaps, slides under my feet. I am now close enough that I could reach out and grab the legs of the nearest drake, but I am a duck-observer, not a duck-eater.

5   For a moment, I relish my presence among them. Again, I wonder why they are not seeing me. Does the bill on my baseball cap make me look like a large mallard? Does their universe include the possibility of a bright blue duck with no eyes or tail feathers?

Suddenly, a female with six tiny ducklings trailing behind her paddles toward me, freezes and does a double take. *That THING is definitely not a duck!*

She gives a terrified squawk and my cover is blown. Instantly, all hell breaks loose. Quacking in panic, the ducks scatter like swimmers who have just realized that the log floating toward them is actually a crocodile. Most of the flock takes to the air; the mothers lead their ducklings into the reeds and disappear.

Finding myself alone again with only a few floating feathers to keep me company, I turn and begin to swim back toward the island, still keeping a low profile. Sometimes on the return trip, I see other animals. I cannot get anywhere near the four-foot tall blue herons who are too smart and much too wary to be taken in; but once a green heron actually perched on my cap for a moment, perhaps mistaking me for a small, blue island. On another occasion, near dusk, I looked up and there on the bank, staring at me with unguarded curiosity, was a large buck with a fine rack of antlers. Once, only once, I saw a coyote playing catch with a stick.

Only a week ago as I swam in a warmer backwater, something sneaked up on me. It was not, thank goodness, a rattlesnake. I have only seen one of those in the seventeen-some years I have been coming here and one was enough to last a lifetime; but it gave me quite a start nevertheless. I was swimming under the cottonwoods toward a patch of ripe blackberries that can only be pillaged by water, when I heard a huge smack behind me. I did exactly what the ducks do under such circumstances: I squawked and began to paddle toward safety only to discover that I was sharing the lagoon with a large beaver.

I have no idea why she was out in mid-afternoon. As a rule, beavers are crepuscular creatures. When we paddle our canoe back to the boat launch after sunset, we often encounter as many as twenty of them: large, plump, shadowy balls that slap their tails on the water like a rhythm band as we float by. But this one was up early, and she did not enjoy sharing the lagoon. For a few minutes she swam circles around me, slapping and diving. Then, to my great relief, she slid under water and disappeared. I have never heard of anyone being attacked by a beaver, but I got a good look at her, and just for the record, beaver teeth, when seen up close, are formidable.

10　　But today, I make it back to the island without encountering anything more than a small muskrat and a swarm of Bluetail flies. Stumbling out of the water across a spread of small, unreasonably sharp stones, I towel off, sit down in a lawn chair, pick up the thermos, and pour myself a cup of iced tea. In a few minutes my husband, who originally introduced me to this place, swims up and joins me. We sit, chatting, drinking tea, eating cold melons, and waiting for the sun to set; and in the distance, as always, we hear the sound of The Distant Cataract About Which We Do Not Speak.

Of course, it is not really the sound of a cataract. It is the roar of rush-hour traffic, half of it crossing the Howe Avenue Bridge, half of it crossing the bridge at Watt. We are sitting on an island in the American River, right in the middle of Sacramento, the state capital, a metropolitan area of well over a million people, but my husband and I like to preserve our mutual delusion. We have agreed to imagine we are not a five-minute drive from our home and a twenty-minute walk from the university where we both teach, but instead in some remote part of California where just out of sight a magnificent waterfall foams down into a green pool.

The American River Parkway makes this fantasy amazingly easy. For over thirty miles, it runs through the heart of the city from Folsom Lake to the point where the American River joins the Sacramento. This is a town where if you float in a canoe or sit on an island below the levees you cannot see houses (except in a few places where, alas, the zoning restrictions are being violated). This is a town where some state employees kayak to work; where, no matter how hot it gets, you can get goose bumps and blue lips just by going for a swim.

Over the years, we have seen Hmong families in brightly embroidered, traditional dress picnicking on the banks. We have come upon a circle of Samoans, up to their chests in water, drinking cold beers and singing "Under The Boardwalk" in perfect harmony. When we launch our canoe, we often find ourselves having conversations in Spanish with recent immigrants from Mexico or Central America. About seventy-five thousand Russians live in Sacramento County, many of them Baptists. We have watched them build huts of reeds and flowers and carry flowered crosses out into the water as part of their baptismal rituals. African-American congregations baptize here too, dressed in white robes. Like the Russians, they sing hymns and pray. I am always moved when I hear them. This, I think, is the spiritual heart of the river.

Once, during a January when it looked as if the levees might break, my husband and I came upon a pile of candy wrapped in gold foil, pineapples and oranges sliced in half, several beheaded guinea fowl, a pack of matches and a handful of popcorn—traditional offerings made to the goddess Oxum by devotees of the African-Brazilian religion Candomblé. On another occasion, we went down to the river to launch our canoe and found the parking lot occupied by a Russian Orthodox priest and his congregation. The priest appeared to be blessing the river with incense. A procession made its way to the edge of the river bearing banners painted with holy icons. I believe their prayers were in Old Slavonic.

15   But nothing can compare to a night in early August when my husband and I came to the river and found it full of small, floating lanterns. A Japanese priest stood at the boat launch chanting as the lanterns drifted toward him and his congregation. We found out later that this is a traditional ceremony for souls lost at sea, but that now it is done to commemorate those who died at Hiroshima and Nagasaki in August of 1945. Above the lanterns, a full moon rose into the sky, bright and large as a second sun. The flames swirled in the current, the night primroses blossomed, the beavers were silent, and for a few moments the American was a river of light.

QUESTIONS FOR DISCUSSION

1. What makes Mackey's description of her experience of swimming among the ducks particularly vivid and memorable? Point out effective descriptions of the physical setting and the ducks' behavior.

2. How does Mackey attempt to understand what the ducks perceive as she swims among them? What are her speculations about why they seem not to notice her? Do you think her speculations have validity, or do they seem to be a type of mental play?

3. What does Mackey recall about previous encounters with animals on her swims in the lagoon? At what point does she behave like the ducks do when they are frightened by her presence? What is the significance of this role reversal?

4. What is the "cataract" mentioned in the title, and why does Mackey wait so long to reveal its significance? Why does the title reveal about her attitude toward urban life?

5. What does Mackey believe to be the "spiritual heart of the river"? Why does she believe this? Give examples of Mackey's experiences of spiritual rituals and events she witnesses along the river.

6. This essay takes place along the American River. How does the essay as a whole make an implied comment about the American dream of nature, spirituality, and renewal for both immigrants and native-born citizens? Note particularly the language of the essay's final sentence, which concludes with the words "for a few moments the American was a river of light."

CONNECTION

Compare and contrast the use and description of water in the creation of a sense of place in nature in Mary Mackey's essay and that of Terry Tempest Williams in this chapter (see page 94).

IDEAS FOR WRITING

1. Write a descriptive essay about an experience you have had on a river, in a park, or in some other natural spot shared by people and animals. What kind of conflicts or harmony did you notice between the species? What did you learn from this experience?

2. Mackey's essay has implications for urban design, providing an example of a vibrant and successful integration of nature into urban life. Write an essay in which you describe and comment on another city that has accomplished something like what Sacramento has done with the American River through preservation and recreation access to a body of water or a park area.

RELATED WEB SITES

The Official Mary Mackey Home Page
`www.csus.edu/indiv/m/mackeym/`
Visit Mary Mackey's home page and find prose and poetry by her, a biography, and links to other related sites.

The American River Parkway Foundation
`www.arpf.org/`
This site contains information about the foundation that makes possible the
American River urban park area described in Mary Mackey's essay. The site
contains maps, photos, links, newsletter archives, and donation opportunities.

Donovan Webster

Inside the Volcano

After studying at Kenyon College and Middlebury College, Donovan Webster de-
voted himself to a career in writing and travel. He has been a senior editor for
Outside *magazine, and has written for such national publications as the*
National Geographic, *the* New Yorker, *the* New York Times Magazine, *and*
the Smithsonian. *His book on landmines and other leftover toxics from wars,*
Aftermath: Cleaning Up a Century of World War *(1996), won the Lionel*
Gelber Prize *in 1997 and was made into a documentary film in 2001. He has also*
written a history of relations between China, Burma, and India during World
War II, The Burma Road *(2003). The essay that follows describes Webster's ex-*
perience of being lowered into an active volcanic cone on an island in the South
Pacific.

> **JOURNAL**
>
> Write a description of an unusual natural spot you have visited, trying to choose
> descriptive details that create a unified impression of the place as well as your re-
> sponse to it.

The volcano's summit is a dead zone, a cindered plain swirling with poiso-
nous chlorine and sulfur gases, its air further thickened by nonstop siftings
of new volcanic ash. No life can survive this environment for long. On the ash
plain's edge, always threatening to make the island an aboveground hell, sit
two active vents, Marum and Benbow, constantly shaking the earth and spewing globs of molten rock into the air. Yet across the black soil of the plain come
all nine of us, a team of explorers, photographers, a film crew, a volcanologist,
and me. We have hacked through dense jungles on this island called Ambrym,
one of some eighty islands making up the South Pacific nation of Vanuatu, and
entered this inhospitable landscape to camp and explore for two weeks. We've
tightroped up miles of eroded, inches-wide ridgeline—with deep canyons
plummeting hundreds of feet on either side—to totter at the lip of the volcanic
pit of Benbow. The pit's malevolent red eye—obscured by gases and a balcony
ledge of new volcanic rock—sits just a few hundred feet below.

"Okay, your turn," Chris Heinlein shouts above the volcano's roar.

A sinewy and friendly German engineer, Heinlein hands me the expedition's climbing rope, which leads down, inside the volcano. Clipping the rope into a rappelling device on my belt—which helps control my descent—I step into the air above the pit.

A dozen feet of rope slips between my gloved fingers. I lower myself into the volcano. Acidic gas bites my nose and eyes. The sulfur dioxide is mixing with the day's spitting drizzle, creating a sulfuric-acid rain so strong it will eat the metal frames of my eyeglasses within days, turning them to crumbly rust. The breathing of Benbow's pit is deafening, like up-close jet engines mixed with a cosmic belch. Each new breath from the volcano heaves the air so violently my ears pop in the changing pressure—then the temperature momentarily soars. Somewhere not too far below, red-hot, pumpkin-size globs of ejected lava are flying through the air.

5   I let more rope slip. With each slide deeper inside, I can only wonder: Why would anyone *do* this? And what drives the guy on the rope below me—the German photographer and longtime volcano obsessive Carsten Peter—to do it again and again?

We have come to see Ambrym's volcano close up and to witness the lava lakes in these paired pits, which fulminate constantly but rarely erupt. Yet suspended hundreds of feet above lava up to 2,200 degrees Fahrenheit that reaches toward the center of the Earth, I'm also discovering there's more. It is stupefyingly beautiful. The enormous noise. The deep, orangy red light from spattering lava. And those dark and brittle strands called Pele's hair: Filaments of lava that follow large blobs out of the pit, they cool quickly in the updraft and create six-inch-long, glassy threads that drift on the wind. It is like nowhere else on Earth.

Our first night on Ambrym we make camp in a beachside town called Port-Vato at the base of the 4,167-foot-high volcano. Shortly after sunrise the next morning, at the start of a demanding hike up the side of the volcano—walking a dry riverbed through thick jungle—I try to extract Peter's reasons for coming. As we crunch along the floor of black volcanic cinders, scrambling over shiny cliffs of cold lava that become waterfalls in the rainy season, Peter, forty-one, is grinning with excitement. Overhead dark silhouettes of large bats called flying foxes crease the morning sky like pterodactyls.

"I was fifteen years old and on vacation in Italy with my parents. They took me to see Mount Etna," he says. "As soon as I saw it, I was drawn to the crater's edge. I was *fascinated*. My parents went back to the tour bus. They honked the horn for me to come—but I couldn't leave. I edged closer, seeing the smoke inside, imagining the boiling magma below. At that moment I became infected."

Since then Peter has traveled the world examining volcanoes. His trips have taken him to Iceland, Ethiopia, Indonesia, Hawaii, and beyond. "And of course," he says, "I have been back to Etna, my home volcano, many times."

10   Using single-rope descending and climbing techniques developed by cave explorers and adapted for volcanoes, Peter has been dropping into volcanoes

now for nearly a decade. "The size and power of a volcano is like nothing else on Earth," he says. "You think you understand the Earth and its geology, but once you look down into a volcanic crater and see what's there, well, you realize you will never completely understand. It is that powerful. That big." He grins. "You'll find out what I mean, I think."

After a five-hour walk uphill I get my first glimpse of that power as the expedition emerges from the steep, heavily vegetated sides of the volcano's cone and onto the caldera. In the course of a few hundred yards the trail flattens out, and the palm trees and eight-foot-tall cane grasses that lushly lined the trail behind us become gnarled and dead, their life force snuffed by a world of swirling gas clouds and acid rain.

This is Ambrym's ash plain. Seven miles across, it's a severely eroded ash-and-lava cap hundreds of feet thick. Across the plain Benbow and Marum jut almost a thousand feet into the sky.

To protect ourselves from the harsh environment, our team quickly establishes a base camp near the caldera's edge. Shielded behind a low bluff separating the caldera from the jungle, the camp stretches through a grove of palms and tree-size ferns, the black soil dotted with purple orchids bobbing on long green stalks. For the remainder of this first afternoon we set up tents and create acid-rain-tight storage areas. The camp is a paradise perched on the edge of disaster. As night falls, we eat chicken soup fortified with cellophane noodles and plan tomorrow's exploration, the volcano rumbling regularly in the background as we talk.

After dinner we follow Carsten Peter to the edge of the ash plain and watch the vents light the gas clouds, wreathing each peak in ghostly red glows. "Look there," Peter says, pointing to a third red cauldron halfway up Marum's side. "That must be Niri Taten. Tomorrow we'll start there."

15   All night long the rumbling keeps awakening us. Just a few miles away lava boils and the Earth roars while each of us—lying quietly in a flimsy tent—anxiously dreams of those swirling red clouds. Tomorrow night at this time, I resolve as I drift off to sleep once again, one thing is certain: It will have been a day like none I've ever had.

In the morning, shortly after a sunrise breakfast, we strike out toward Niri Taten, several miles uphill. As we follow dry and eroded riverbeds toward the volcanic cones, a gentle rain falls.

"What does Niri Taten mean?" I ask our local guide, Jimmy.

"Niri Taten is a small pig," he replies. "A small mad pig. A crazy pig. A small pig that causes trouble to men."

Haraldur Sigurdsson, one of the world's premier volcanologists, walks alongside me in the dry riverbed, examining sheer cliff faces. He points out strata of tephra, a mixture of volcanic material. By examining these layers, volcanologists can tell a volcano's level of activity. Larger and coarser tephra far from a volcanic pit means a more powerful volcano, since heavier matter is thrown farther as more explosive energy is supplied.

20　　It's true. The closer we hike to the craters, the more the character of the riverbed beneath our feet changes from silty black grit to charcoal-size stones— not unlike old-time furnace clinkers. "Each volcano has its own chemical fingerprint," Sigurdsson says. "Each volcano's mineral and elemental content is different because of the nature of the volcano itself: its rock and the shape of its vent. It helps volcanologists a lot in their study."

"Like the Tambora eruption of 1815 in Indonesia," Sigurdsson says. "We've found Tambora ash by its particular chemical signature almost everywhere on Earth. One of that magnitude happens about every thousand years." The Tambora explosion is said to have given off so much ash and sulfur dioxide— both of which blocked and reflected sunlight—that 1816 was a "year without a summer" across much of the world. There was crop-killing frost throughout the summer in New England. In northern Europe harvests were a disaster.

Suddenly, from two miles upwind behind us, Benbow gives a huge belch. We turn to look back. "Uh-oh" Sigurdsson says. "Ashfall on the way." Instead of the usual bluish white clouds of steam and gas, the plume issuing from the cone is heavy and black, trailing earthward in a dark curtain. Slowly it drifts our way on the wind. Five minutes later the ashfall finds us, covering our rucksacks, clothing, faces, boots, and ponchos with a sandy grit the color of wet cocoa mix.

Under the ashfall we climb Marum, pressing forward through the dead volcanic soil for another hour. Each step takes us closer to Niri Taten, a crater that tunnels straight down into the basaltic rock like a massive, steaming worm burrow 200 yards across. As we approach, a rising wind and thick clouds of chlorine gas force us to pause and pull on safety helmets and industrial-style gas masks that cover our noses and mouths. Without them, between the flying bits of stone and grit carried on the fifty-mile-an-hour winds and the thick clouds of gas roaring upward from the vent, time spent near the pit's lip would be painfully dangerous if not impossible.

Even with these protections the howling wind and gas often force us to shut our eyes and suspend breathing until the heaviest gas clouds pass. We lean against the high winds, brace at the crater's edge, and look inside.

25　　Five hundred feet below, the vent's opening is obscured by rocky ledges. But if we can't see the lava itself, there is a consolation. Every inch of rocky surface inside the vent's cone is painted with color. Sunshine yellow sulfur coats some of the crater's sheer rock faces. Iron washes other sections of rock with flaming orange. Pastel green deposits of manganese glaze rock nearest the vent, like a carpet of immortal moss. Other patches of stone have been bleached white by chlorine and fluorine gases pouring from the vent.

Besides the wind and dangerous concentration of gases, the edges of Niri Taten are too crumbly to allow safe descent. Anyone climbing down a rope inside the crater could be dislodging loose boulders, some the size of cars, that could crash on anyone below. Carsten Peter pulls out his camera and long lens—whose coating immediately becomes corroded in the noxious air. The howling gusts twice knock expedition members to the ground.

After an hour it's decided that we should examine the Marum crater itself. "We can get two volcanoes in one day!" Carsten Peter says with glee. Our helmeted heads tucked down, we continue breathing scuba-diver slow into our masks for maximum benefit, and we push on.

The walk to Marum's opening isn't far, but what it lacks in distance it makes up for in danger. No matter which route you choose, you have to traverse the mountain's steep slopes, many of which are gouged with deep, unclimbable erosion gullies. We decide to cross where the gullies are smallest: along Niri Taten's knife-edged lip, within a foot of a sheer drop into the crater.

We step gingerly where the slope looks most reliable, but our footing remains dangerously slick. The slope's top layer is crumbly tephra, sometimes as big as charcoal briquettes. Making things more difficult, we've moved downwind of Niri Taten. All around us clouds of sulfur dioxide, chlorine, and fluorine gases swirl so thick they sometimes obscure our vision and force us to stop and bury our gas-masked faces inside our arms for extra protection.

30   It's a slog. Minutes stretch into an hour. Every step could be our last. Finally we reach the summit of the crater's edge and begin down its other side. Protected by the lip behind us, the environment changes. Sunshine blankets the tilting black ash, and the cold gales calm into balmy breezes.

Two expedition members, Franck Tessier and Irène Margaritis, hustle downslope with me toward Marum. As we approach its lip, the thirty-nine-year-old Tessier—a genial and easygoing French biologist with impressive rope and rock-climbing skills honed by years of adventures like this one—rips off his gas mask and begins to hoot with pleasure.

I know why. Ahead of us Marum's volcanic pit stretches as open and clear as a visionary's painting. In the pit, three step-down ledges—each deeper and wider than the one uphill of it—are marbled with layers of black ash and pale, bleached basaltic andesite. The layers of lava inside the vent form as a crust over a cooling lava lake that gets blown out like a massive champagne cork when volcanic activity resumes. Small wall vents called fumaroles—created where heated groundwater and escaping volcanic gas reach the surface—let off steady plumes of steam. Inside Marum's crater it looks as if the world is being born.

And there, in the bottom of the third and largest pit—some 1,200 feet below—sits the lava lake. Its fury pushes lava through three skylight holes in a roof that partly covers the lake like a canopy. Bright orange and red spatters fly unpredictably from the circular opening of the largest skylight, a hole perhaps fifty yards across.

Lava is three times as dense as water. Despite its up to 2,200 degrees-Fahrenheit heat, lava moves, burbles, and flies through the air with the consistency of syrup. Every few minutes huge molten blobs seem to soar in slow motion. A second or two later a noise from beneath the earth—a rumbling *booooom*—fills the pit and rolls across the sculpted ash plain beyond. It's mesmerizing: lava sloshing back and forth, bubbles emerging and popping like a thick stew. As we survey Marum's lip and crater, I can't take my eyes off the lava. Suddenly I understand Peter's obsession. As evening cloaks the pit's deepest recesses in shade, the lava lake and explosive bubbles glow more seductively. The spatterings glisten like enormous, otherworldly fireworks as they sail through the shadowed air.

35   Dangling inside Benbow's crater the following afternoon, I have time to reflect. This morning we followed the narrow ridge to Benbow's pit—which was firm enough to climb down. We fixed our rope, ate lunch in a spitting acid rain, and began our descent into the volcano.

Now, on the rope below me, Carsten Peter works his way deeper inside the crater. I let more rope slide through my hands, easing myself deeper as well.

With each drop the air shakes more violently; the clouds of poison gas grow thicker. Waves of pressurized air rumble past me.

Grasping the rope tightly, I halt my descent at the edge of an overhung cliff and stare deeper inside. The lava lake waits below, ejecting orange bombs and smaller drops. Then, in a heartbeat, a wall of thick clouds blows between me and the pit, enveloping everything around me in a world of gray. In the shuddering air and disorienting noise, gravity, direction, and time seem to fade away. There is only the volcano, its existence a direct result of two tectonic plates colliding below me. Benbow roars again. The earth shakes.

In this moment I know I've gotten close enough to the fire at the center of the Earth. At that same second the clouds part and Benbow reappears. Fumaroles smoke, and steam swirls from the pit's walls. The Technicolor wash swarms around me like a kaleidoscope. Below, Carsten Peter hits the end of the rope just above Benbow's explosive vent. He pulls a camera from his bag and lifts it to his eye.

40   Torrential rains will frustrate another attempt to explore Benbow. Then dissension breaks out among some of the expedition's porters who helped carry gear up the volcano's steep cone, and it becomes clear that the team will have to leave Ambrym as soon as possible. In a last-ditch, eighteen-hour marathon, team members drop 1,200 feet into Marum and photograph its lava lake nonstop. They emerge from the crater and find a fractious camp. Jimmy cannot persuade the disgruntled porters to bend, and the tension escalates. With a satchel full of photographs, Carsten Peter finally agrees to abandon the volcano—even as he vows to return.

QUESTIONS FOR DISCUSSION

1. Explain how Webster's opening paragraph uses descriptive detail to provide the background, setting, and purpose of his essay.
2. The paragraphs that follow the introduction bring the reader into the volcano along with the other climbers. Point out how Webster uses details that appeal to all of the senses in order to evoke the atmosphere of the volcano and its physical impact.

3. Comment on the way Webster uses details and dialogue to characterize the other explorers on his expedition, particularly Carsten Peter, the "long-time volcano obsessive." How do these characters engage readers' interest while helping them to better understand the nature of volcanoes?
4. How does Webster use contrast and color description to bring out the beauty of particular aspects of the volcano's interior? Give examples.
5. How does the description of the lava in the Marum volcanic pit prepare the reader for Webster's realization, "Suddenly I understand Peter's obsession"?
6. Examine the final paragraphs of the essay. How is Webster's response to the volcano similar to Peter's, yet ultimately different? Point out details and word choice that underscore the two men's different levels of engagement.

CONNECTION

Compare Webster's description of a hazardous "extreme" natural place with that of Jon Krakauer in "The Khumbu Icefall." How do the authors use description differently to appeal to their respective audiences (see page 89)?

IDEAS FOR WRITING

1. Develop your journal writing into an essay in which you create a dramatic descriptive account of a visit to an unusual natural place. Reflect at the end on what seeing this place and engaging in it with all of your senses has meant to you.
2. After looking at some back issues of *National Geographic,* write an essay in which you analyze "Inside the Volcano," pointing out specific aspects of its descriptive style, characterization, and information that would appeal strongly to the publication's readers.

RELATED WEB SITES

"War Without End?" By Donovan Webster
www.archipelago.org/vol7-2/webster.htm
In the winter of 2005, the online magazine *Archipelago* published this article by Donovan Webster about the terrorist conflict on a tiny, pristine island in the Philippines. It is interesting to see how Webster's writing differs when he works for a more politically conscious, less commercial publication than *National Geographic.*

Michigan Technological University Volcanoes Page
www.geo.mtu.edu/volcanoes/
Visit the "MTU Volcanoes" Web site to find out "anything you ever wanted to know about volcanoes" and about specific volcanoes all around the world.

Jon Krakauer

The Khumbu Icefall

Jon Krakauer was born in 1954 and raised in Corvallis, Oregon. He traces his obsession with mountain climbing to his first climbing experiences when he was only 8 years old. After graduating from college in 1975, in 1981 he began his career as a journalist writing about the outdoors. A collection of his essays was published in Eiger Dreams *(1992). Other books by Krakauer include* Into the Wild *(1996);* The Land of White Death: An Epic Story of Survival in the Siberian Arctic *(2000); and* Under the Banner of Heaven: A Story of Violent Faith *(2004). In the following excerpt from his best-selling account of a failed climbing expedition to Mount Everest,* Into Thin Air *(1997), Krakauer uses closely observed description to capture one of the most dramatic episodes in the days leading up to the deadly summit attempt.*

JOURNAL

Try to get inside the mind of a mountain climber and imagine his or her thoughts and feelings before embarking on a challenging climb. Imagine what has led this person to risk his or her life just to "get to the top."

O ur route to the summit would follow the Khumbu Glacier up the lower half of the mountain. From the *bergschrund** at 23,000 feet that marked its upper end, this great river of ice flowed two and a half miles down a relatively gentle valley called the Western Cwm. As the glacier inched over humps and dips in the Cwm's underlying strata, it fractured into countless vertical fissures— crevasses. Some of these crevasses were narrow enough to step across; others were eighty feet wide, several hundred feet deep, and ran half a mile from end to end. The big ones were apt to be vexing obstacles to our ascent, and when hidden beneath a crust of snow they would pose a serious hazard, but the challenges presented by the crevasses in the Cwm had proven over the years to be predictable and manageable.

The Icefall was a different story. No part of the South Col route was feared more by climbers. At around 20,000 feet, where the glacier emerged from the lower end of the Cwm, it pitched abruptly over a precipitous drop. This was the infamous Khumbu Icefall, the most technically demanding section on the entire route.

The movement of the glacier in the Icefall has been measured at between three and four feet a day. As it skids down the steep, irregular terrain in fits and starts, the mass of ice splinters into a jumble of huge, tottering blocks called

---

*A *bergschrund* is a deep slit that delineates a glacier's upper terminus; it forms as the body of ice slides away from the steeper wall immediately above, leaving a gap between glacier and rock.

seracs, some as large as office buildings. Because the climbing route wove under, around, and between hundreds of these unstable towers, each trip
through the Icefall was a little like playing a round of Russian roulette: sooner
or later any given serac was going to fall over without warning, and you could
only hope you weren't beneath it when it toppled. Since 1963, when . . . Jake
Breitenbach was crushed by an avalanching serac to become the Icefall's first
victim, eighteen other climbers had died here.

The previous winter, as he had done in winters past, Hall had consulted with
the leaders of all the expeditions planning to climb Everest in the spring, and
together they'd agreed on one team among them who would be responsible
for establishing and maintaining a route through the Icefall. For its trouble,
the designated team was to be paid $2,200 from each of the other expeditions
on the mountain. In recent years this cooperative approach had been met with
wide, if not universal, acceptance, but it wasn't always so.

5   The first time one expedition thought to charge another to travel through
the ice was in 1988, when a lavishly funded American team announced that
any expedition that intended to follow the route they'd engineered up the
Icefall would have to fork over $2,000. Some of the other teams on the moun-
tain that year, failing to understand that Everest was no longer merely a mountain but a commodity as well, were incensed. And the greatest hue and cry
came from Rob Hall, who was leading a small, impecunious New Zealand
team.

Hall carped that the Americans were "violating the spirit of the hills" and
practicing a shameful form of alpine extortion, but Jim Frush, the unsentimen-
tal attorney who was the leader of the American group, remained unmoved.
Hall eventually agreed through clenched teeth to send Frush a check and was
granted passage through the Icefall. (Frush later reported that Hall never
made good on his IOU.)

Within two years, however, Hall did an about-face and came to see the logic
of treating the Icefall as a toll road. Indeed, from 1993 through '95 he volunteered to put in the route and collect the toll himself. In the spring of 1996 he
elected not to assume responsibility for the Icefall, but he was happy to pay the
leader of a rival commercial* expedition—a Scottish Everest veteran named
Mal Duff—to take over the job. Long before we'd even arrived at Base Camp, a
team of Sherpas employed by Duff had blazed a zigzag path through the seracs,
stringing out more than a mile of rope and installing some sixty aluminum ladders over the broken surface of the glacier. The ladders belonged to an enter-
prising Sherpa from the village of Gorak Shep who turned a nice profit by
renting them out each season.

---

*Although I use "commercial" to denote any expedition organized as a money-making venture, not all
commercial expeditions are guided. For instance, Mal Duff—who charged his clients considerably less
than the $65,000 fee requested by Hall and Fischer—provided leadership and the essential infrastructure
necessary to climb Everest (food, tents, bottled oxygen, fixed ropes, Sherpa support staff, and so on) but
did not purport to act as a guide; the climbers on his team were assumed to be sufficiently skilled to get
themselves safely up Everest and back down again.

So it came to pass that at 4:45 a.m. on Saturday, April 13, I found myself at the foot of the fabled Icefall, strapping on my crampons in the frigid predawn gloom.

Crusty old alpinists who've survived a lifetime of close scrapes like to counsel young protégés that staying alive hinges on listening carefully to one's "inner voice." Tales abound of one or another climber who decided to remain in his or her sleeping bag after detecting some inauspicious vibe in the ether and thereby survived a catastrophe that wiped out others who failed to heed the portents.

10   I didn't doubt the potential value of paying attention to subconscious cues. As I waited for Rob to lead the way, the ice underfoot emitted a series of loud cracking noises, like small trees being snapped in two, and I felt myself wince with each pop and rumble from the glacier's shifting depths. Problem was, my inner voice resembled Chicken Little: it was screaming that I was about to die, but it did that almost every time I laced up my climbing boots. I therefore did my damnedest to ignore my histrionic imagination and grimly followed Rob into the eerie blue labyrinth.

Although I'd never been in an icefall as frightening as the Khumbu, I'd climbed many other icefalls. They typically have vertical or even overhanging passages that demand considerable expertise with ice ax and crampons. There was certainly no lack of steep ice in the Khumbu Icefall, but all of it had been rigged with ladders or ropes or both, rendering the conventional tools and techniques of ice climbing largely superfluous.

I soon learned that on Everest not even the rope—the quintessential climber's accoutrement—was to be utilized in the time-honored manner. Ordinarily, one climber is tied to one or two partners with a 150-foot length of rope, making each person directly responsible for the life of the others; roping up in this fashion is a serious and very intimate act. In the Icefall, though, expediency dictated that each of us climb independently, without being physically connected to one another in any way.

Mal Duff's Sherpas had anchored a static line of rope that extended from the bottom of the Icefall to its top. Attached to my waist was a three-foot-long safety tether with a carabiner, or snap-link, at the distal end. Security was achieved not by roping myself to a teammate but rather by clipping my safety tether to the fixed line and sliding it up the rope as I ascended. Climbing in this fashion, we would be able to move as quickly as possible through the most dangerous parts of the Icefall, and we wouldn't have to entrust our lives to teammates whose skill and experience were unknown. As it turned out, not once during the entire expedition would I ever have reason to rope myself to another climber.

If the Icefall required few orthodox climbing techniques, it demanded a whole new repertoire of skills in their stead—for instance, the ability to tiptoe in mountaineering boots and crampons across three wobbly ladders lashed end to end, bridging a sphincter-clenching chasm. There were many such crossings, and I never got used to them.

15   At one point I was balanced on an unsteady ladder in the predawn gloaming, stepping tenuously from one bent rung to the next, when the ice supporting the ladder on either end began to quiver as if an earthquake had struck. A moment later came an explosive roar as a large serac somewhere close above came crashing down. I froze, my heart in my throat, but the avalanching ice passed fifty yards to the left, out of sight, without doing any damage. After waiting a few minutes to regain my composure I resumed my herky-jerky passage to the far side of the ladder.

The glacier's continual and often violent state of flux added an element of uncertainty to every ladder crossing. As the glacier moved, crevasses would sometimes compress, buckling ladders like toothpicks; other times a crevasse might expand, leaving a ladder dangling in the air, only tenuously supported, with neither end mounted on solid ice. Anchors* securing the ladders and lines routinely melted out when the afternoon sun warmed the surrounding ice and snow. Despite daily maintenance, there was a very real danger that any given rope might pull loose under body weight.

But if the Icefall was strenuous and terrifying, it had a surprising allure as well. As dawn washed the darkness from the sky, the shattered glacier was revealed to be a three-dimensional landscape of phantasmal beauty. The temperature was six degrees Fahrenheit. My crampons crunched reassuringly into the glacier's rind. Following the fixed line, I meandered through a vertical maze of crystalline blue stalagmites. Sheer rock buttresses seamed with ice pressed in from both edges of the glacier, rising like the shoulders of a malevolent god. Absorbed by my surroundings and the gravity of the labor, I lost myself in the unfettered pleasures of ascent, and for an hour or two actually forgot to be afraid.

Three-quarters of the way to Camp One, Hall remarked at a rest stop that the Icefall was in better shape than he'd ever seen it: "The route's a bloody freeway this season." But only slightly higher, at 19,000 feet, the ropes brought us to the base of a gargantuan, perilously balanced serac. As massive as a twelve-story building, it loomed over our heads, leaning 30 degrees past vertical. The route followed a natural catwalk that angled sharply up the overhanging face: we would have to climb up and over the entire off-kilter tower to escape its threatening tonnage.

Safety, I understood, hinged on speed. I huffed toward the relative security of the serac's crest with all the haste I could muster, but since I wasn't acclimatized my fastest pace was no better than a crawl. Every four or five steps I'd have to stop, lean against the rope, and suck desperately at the thin, bitter air, searing my lungs in the process.

20   I reached the top of the serac without it collapsing and flopped breathless onto its flat summit, my heart pounding like a jackhammer. A little later,

---

*Three-foot-long aluminum stakes called pickets were used to anchor ropes and ladders to snow slopes. When the terrain was hard glacial ice, "ice screws" were employed: hollow, threaded tubes about ten inches long that were twisted into the frozen glacier.

around 8:30 a.m., I arrived at the top of the Icefall itself, just beyond the last of the seracs. The safety of Camp One didn't supply much peace of mind, however: I couldn't stop thinking about the ominously tilted slab a short distance below, and the fact that I would have to pass beneath its faltering bulk at least seven more times if I was going to make it to the summit of Everest. Climbers who snidely denigrate this as the Yak Route, I decided, had obviously never been through the Khumbu Icefall.

QUESTIONS FOR DISCUSSION

1. According to Krakauer, what factors make climbing the Khumbu Icefall the most demanding challenge on the route to the summit of Mount Everest?
2. Why has the icefall been made into a toll road? Does this seem like an overcommercialization of a natural place? Is it necessary?
3. Why does Krakauer reflect on the alpine climbers who listen to their inner voices, or subconscious, before embarking on a dangerous journey? How does Krakauer handle his fear?
4. Give examples of Krakauer's use of descriptive detail in passages where he tries to give clear impressions of the terrain of the glacier and the placements of the ladders. Do you get a good sense of what it was like to climb the ladders? Could he have included other details?
5. Give examples of ways that Krakauer uses description to clarify the different techniques of ice climbing used on the Khumbu Icefall as well as the glacier's "continual and often violent state of flux."
6. In this climb two highly respected climbers, Rob Hall and Scott Fisher, died when they were caught in a storm at the summit. Give examples of physical and emotional observations made by Krakauer here that could be said to foreshadow the disaster that lies ahead.

CONNECTION

Compare Krakauer's use of descriptive detail with that of Diane Ackerman (see page 73). What different purpose does the description serve in these two very different accounts of extreme climates?

IDEAS FOR WRITING

1. Write a paper about a natural challenge that you have experienced or that you intend to experience. What will or did you do? How did you or are you preparing yourself? Why did you or why are you going on this journey? If you have completed this journey, what did you learn? What insights did you gain?
2. Describe an ordinary process that you participate in that could be said to be dangerous at times, such as driving in heavy traffic in the rain or snow through a mountain pass. Describe the process involved in this activity in

clear details, indicating some of the close calls you have had performing the activity. Provide insights into your feelings of fear and exhilaration.

Jon Krakauer
`http://archive.salon.com/directory/topics/jon_krakauer/`
Here at the archive for *Salon* online magazine can be found a number of articles on the controversy over Krakauer's reporting in his book *Into Thin Air* and the possible impact of his presence as a professional journalist on the disastrous expedition the book describes.

Mount Everest
`www.mnteverest.net`
Information about Mount Everest can be found at this extensive Web site devoted to the world's highest peak. The site includes several interesting links for climbers and trekkers.

Terry Tempest Williams

Ground Truthing

Terry Tempest Williams (b. 1955) was raised in Nevada and attended Teton Science School, where she earned a B.A. in English and an M.A. in environmental education. She now works as a naturalist for the Utah Museum of Natural History and lives with her husband in the mountains outside of Salt Lake City, Utah. She is a highly respected nature writer and environmental activist who is involved with protests over nuclear testing and its impact on public health and cancer rates in the desert states. Her works include Coyote's Canyon *(1989);* Desert Quartet *(1995);* Red: Patience and Passion in the Desert *(2001); and* The Open Space for Democracy *(2004). The selection that follows concerns the struggle to preserve the Alaska National Wildlife Refuge from oil drilling; notice Williams's persuasive use of descriptive writing about the beauty of this pristine wilderness area.*

JOURNAL

Write about your views on prohibition of oil drilling and other energy prospecting in wilderness or national park areas.

Ground Truthing: The use of a ground survey to confirm findings of aerial imagery or to calibrate quantitative aerial observations; maps; walking the ground to see for oneself if what one has been told is true; near surface discoveries.

The arctic is balancing on an immense mirror. The water table is visible. Pools of light gather: lakes, ponds, wetlands. The tundra is shimmering. One squints perpetually.

Drinking from the river—I am drinking from the river—this tincture of glaciers, this press of ice warmed by the sun. My arid heart has been waiting for decades, maybe three, for the return of this childhood pleasure of drinking directly from the source.

When my father asks me what it was like to visit the Arctic National Wildlife Refuge, I will simply say, "We drank from the river."

5   Experience opens us, creates a chasm in our heart, an expansion in our lungs, allowing us to pull in fresh air to all that was stagnant. We breathe deeply and remember fear for what it is—a resistance to the unknown.

It is a day of walking. Most decide to climb an unnamed peak. Cindy Shogan and I choose a more modest hike where we can find a vantage point to watch animals. To our great surprise, our attention focuses not on big mammals, but poppies.

We are on our bellies for a ground squirrel's look. Tissue-like petals form a yellow cup that literally holds light which translates to heat as the flowers turn their heads to continuously follow the sun. The blossom is supported on a threadlike stem. The poppies we meet have survived the pounding rains and brutal winds of the past three days. Not a petal is torn or tattered. They simply raise their heads toward the sun and lure in flies with the seduction of warmth.

Cindy, the executive director of the Alaska Wilderness League, is one of the smartest strategists of her generation. She talks about the political challenges presented by the Bush administration and their relentless drive to drill for oil in the Arctic National Wildlife Refuge.

I ask her what she fears most. Ever the optimist, Cindy says, "We're not going to lose the Arctic, it's just the opposition's endless bombardment and trickery." Alaska's senior senator, Ted Stevens, head of the powerful Appropriations Committee, is now planning to attach his drilling proposal to any piece of legislation that can be bought, from energy to transportation.

10   This is Cindy's first trip to the refuge. We are here to see the lands left in limbo, coldly referred to in Washington as "the 1002" (ten-o-two), a number referring to a particular amendment which says that these 1.2 million acres within the Arctic National Wildlife Refuge could be opened for oil and gas development. These disputed lands are part of the Coastal Plain, where the great caribou migrations occur—the long sweep of land that stretches from the foothills of the Brooks Range to the Beaufort Sea.

Cindy and I discuss the story of Subhankar Banerjee, a talented young photographer from India who quit his job, cashed in his savings in 2000, and has

been taking pictures of the Arctic ever since. He recently published a book titled *Arctic National Wildlife Refuge: Seasons of Life and Land.*

In March 2003, during the budget debate, U.S. Senator Barbara Boxer introduced an amendment to prevent consideration of drilling in the refuge
from being added to the bill. She held Banerjee's book up on the Senate floor
as an example of the elegance of this place and why it deserves protection. She
then invited members to visit Mr. Banerjee's upcoming show at the Smithsonian Institution. Ted Stevens took note and said, "People who vote against this
today are voting against me, and I will not forget it." Boxer's amendment
passed anyway.

A few weeks later, the show Subhankar Banerjee had been promised by the
Smithsonian, which was to hang in a central location near the rotunda, had
suddenly been relegated to the basement. Evocative captions offering a rationale for conservation with quotations by Peter Matthiessen, David Allen Sibley,
Jimmy Carter, and others had been removed and replaced with perfunctory labels such as "Buff-breasted Sandpiper: Coastal plain of the Jago River." A cry of
foul play went out in Washington and in May 2003, Senator Richard Durbin
used a hearing on the Smithsonian's budget to question whether outside influence had been used to move Subhankar's exhibition.

It was Cindy and the Alaska Wilderness League that placed a copy of
Subhankar Banerjee's book in Senator Boxer's hands. It was also Cindy who
nudged Senator Durbin for an investigation. She did not tell me these facts. I
had to find these details in the press.

15   Subhankar Banerjee has become, unwittingly, a celebrity photographer who
bears the distinction of being censored by the United States government. For
what? The threat of beauty.

In the open space of democracy, beauty is not optional, but essential to our
survival as a species.

In a few days, we will reach the confluence of the Marsh Fork and the Canning River. The Canning is the fluid western boundary of the Arctic National
Wildlife Refuge that determines where one can now drill and where one cannot. It will carry us into the heart of this national debate. Right now, the rallying cry and corruption of politics seem a world apart from the world we are in,
because in the rock-hard, ice-sculpted reality of the Arctic—they are.

Arctic still life: a caribou antler, laced with lichen, orange and yellow, is
wrapped around a dwarf willow which now provides shade and shelter for what
was once held high in motion.

Cindy finds a piece of quiviut, musk ox hair, and hands it to me.

20   What will we make of the life before us? How do we translate the gifts of solitary beauty into the action required for true participatory citizenship?

Brooks Yeager, Cindy's husband, has just come down the mountain. He
was assistant secretary for policy in the Department of the Interior during the
Clinton administration, when he labored long and hard on behalf of the Arc-

tic. He has tender eyes and this trip for him, as it is for all of us, is a "ground truthing" to see if what he has fought for and imagined is true. He knows first-hand how politics translates into policy and how much is bargained away in bills before Congress.

More rain. More stories. They pop open like umbrellas. Jim Campbell, our guide, tall and lean, with gray, cropped hair and large, skilled hands, crouches down over the stove to make coffee. He knows wilderness intimately, the wilderness of war and the wilderness of peace. For more than twenty years, he has traversed the Brooks Range by foot, run its rivers, and camped night after night in the buoyancy of the tundra.

He tells of coming home from Vietnam in 1968, walking into his father's tavern in Pennsylvania, still in uniform, completely disoriented. A few weeks later, he found himself holding the security line in Chicago at the Democratic Convention and fighting the antiwar protesters. "Nothing made sense," he says. "Nothing." And then, just a year or so ago, he attended a ceremony for Vietnam veterans in Fairbanks, Alaska. "Welcome home," a woman said to him. Jim paused, holding back emotion. "It was the first time I had heard those words."

Light shifts. An opening is created. We step outside the cook tent and place four topographical maps that encompass the 19.5 million acres of the Arctic National Wildlife Refuge on the ground to see where we are and where we are going. We will cover another ten to fifteen miles on the river today. In a week, we will be camping on the Coastal Plain.

25   Scale cannot be registered here in human terms. It is geologic, tectonic, and planetary. Stegosaurus-like ridgelines form the boundaries of our passage. Ribbon-like waterfalls cascade for miles down cliffs. What I thought was a swallow became an eagle. Weather changes minute by minute. Gray tumultuous clouds weave themselves into patterns of herringbone, yet a strange softness abides, even in the razor-cut terror of this rugged terrain.

Coming into the confluence where the Marsh Fork meets the Canning River feels celebratory. It is a great flooding, far and wide. Blinding light ricochets off platinum strands of water. Braided rivers, braided energies. Wild waters intertwine. We pull the boat over a few rock gardens until we find the deeper channels. The roots of silver-leafed willows, exposed in the cut bank, tremble like the nervous system of the Arctic.

I cannot sleep and slip from the comfort of our tent to face the low, diffused glow of midnight. All colors bow to the gentle arc of light the sun creates as it strolls across the horizon. Green steppes become emerald. The river, lapis. A patch of cotton grass ignites. My eyes catch the illumined wings of a tern, an Arctic tern, fluttering, foraging above the river—the embodiment of grace, suspended. The tern animates the vast indifference with its own vibrant intelligence. Black cap; blood-red beak pointed down; white body with black-tipped wings. With my eyes laid bare, I witness a bright thought in big country. While everyone is sleeping, the presence of this tern hovering above the river, alive, alert, engaged, becomes a vision of what is possible.

On this night, I met the Arctic Angel and vowed the 22,000 miles of her migratory path between the Arctic and Antarctica would not be in vain. I will remember her. No creature on Earth has spent more time in daylight than this species. No creature on Earth has shunned darkness in the same way as the Arctic tern. No creature carries the strength and delicacy of determination on its back like this slight bird. If air is the medium of the Spirit, then the Arctic tern is its messenger.

What I know is this: when one hungers for light it is only because one's knowledge of the dark is so deep.

30   A grizzly has just circled the rock. Tom Campion spotted him first from the river. We stop, tie down our boats, and hike to a knoll where we can watch from a safe distance, separated by a ravine. The grizzly is pawing the ground for roots. The bear is oblivious to us. We are not oblivious of the bear. We sit down and eat lunch, mindful of where and how the grizzly is moving. An upland sandpiper cries, circles us, and raises her wings as she lands. Light breaks through clouds and catches the bear's honey-colored coat, with a brown line traveling down his hump and back. His massive body, moving in all its undulating power, makes my blood quiver. I note his small eyes, his large head, and the length of his claws, perfect for digging. Another hour flies. We eat and watch as he eats and saunters. The wind shifts, the bear looks up, stands, and sniffs the air. We freeze. He turns and runs downhill.

It is called "Bear Shaman"—an Iñupiat sculpture carved out of soapstone. At one end is Man, crouched close to the earth. At the other end is Bear, in search of prey. Both Man and Bear live inside the same body. Their shared heart determines who will be seen and who will disappear. Shape-shifting is its own form of survival.

For several days, we have been floating the Canning River. In the end, we will have covered almost 125 miles. We are now camped on the famed 1002 lands. On one side of the river is the Arctic National Wildlife Refuge. On the other side are the Alaska State lands where oil and gas exploration is underway. Keep walking west and you'll bump into Prudhoe Bay.

I thought I saw a musk ox across the river. It was an empty oil drum.

The Arctic is made up of dreams. And not everyone's is the same. My dream of the Arctic National Wildlife Refuge was planted in my heart by Mardy Murie. The year was 1974. The place was Moose, Wyoming, at the Murie Ranch where the famed naturalists, Olaus and Adolph, with their wives, Mardy and Louise, made their home at the base of the Tetons.

35   I was a student at the Teton Science School. I was eighteen years old. Mardy introduced us to Alaska through her stories of growing up in Fairbanks, of Olaus's field work studying caribou for the U.S. Fish and Wildlife Service in

1920. She showed us her slides of their summer on the Sheenjek River in 1956 with Olaus, Brina Kessel, Bob Krear, and George Schaller. She shared with us their dream of Arctic protection, and the dedication of their group of friends, including Bob Marshall, Ed Zahnhiser, George Collins, Lowell Sumner, Starker Leopold, writers Sigurd Olson and Lois Crisler, and Supreme Court Justice William O. Douglas, along with local conservationists Celia Hunter and Ginny Wood, who helped build a state and national constituency for the creation of the Arctic National Wildlife Range, placing pressure on Congress until it was created in 1960.

Revolutionary patience. This community of Americans never let go of their wild, unruly faith that love can lead to social change. The Muries believed that the protection of wildlands was the protection of natural processes, the unseen presence in wilderness. The Wilderness Act, another one of their dreams, was signed in 1964.

It was Mardy who inspired me to join her and a thousand others on June 5, 1977, to attend the Alaska Lands Hearings in Denver, Colorado. I hitched a ride with friends; we slept on the floor of a church. The next morning, road weary, we cleaned ourselves up and found seats inside the capitol building. This was one of the many regional hearings conducted by the House Interior Subcommittee on General Oversight and Alaskan Lands.

Those who wanted to offer testimony signed up. Mardy was among the first to be called forward. I remember her white braided hair, her poise, her strength. Her love of Alaska transcended her words. When she stood before the presiding congressman, Representative John Seiberling, her whole history and community stood with her.

"I am testifying as an emotional woman," I can still remember her saying, "and I would like to ask you, gentlemen, what's wrong with emotion?"

40   Perhaps she was remembering the emotion in Olaus's voice when he testified before the Senate two decades earlier and said:

> We long for something more, something that has a mental, a spiritual impact on us. This idealism, more than anything else, will set us apart as a nation striving for something worthwhile in the universe. It is inevitable, if we are to progress as people in the highest sense, that we shall become ever more concerned with the saving of the intangible resources, as embodied in this move to establish the Arctic Wildlife Range.

I have held this dream of visiting the Arctic for thirty years. That the refuge has become a symbol for how we define our national priorities is a testament to its innate power. That it continues to survive, resist, and absorb our own greed and economic tensions, year after year, is evidence of the force of love that has protected these wildlands for generations.

As the Brooks Range recedes behind us, I am mindful that Mardy is approaching 101 years of age. She has never shed her optimism for wild Alaska. I am half her age and my niece, Abby, is half of mine. We share her passion for this order of quiet freedom.

America's wildlands are vulnerable and they will always be assailable as long as what we value in this nation is measured in monetary terms, not spiritual ones.

What are we willing to give our lives to if not the perpetuation of the sacred? Can we continue to stand together in our collective wisdom and say, these particular lands are inviolable, deserving protection by law and the inalienable right of safe passage for all beings that dwell here? Wilderness designation is the promise of this hope held in trust.

The open space of democracy provides justice for all living things—plants, animals, rocks, and rivers, as well as human beings.

We are camped on Shublik Island, another part of the 1002 lands, what Cindy and Brooks call "the soul of the Arctic." Cindy has the maps out, looking at Red Hill and the miles we paddled yesterday on the river, close to twenty-five. It was a long, arduous day and our muscles ache.

45   A fragrance drifts across the Canning. Without thought, each of us begins breathing deeply. Sighs emerge on the exhale. We are being drugged by perfume. An innocence is wafting on the wind. I am weeping and I don't know why. Brooke stands up in our boat and points. The plains are magenta all the way to the horizon, a blanket of petals, pink and violet variations of wild sweet pea.

When I ask Carol Kasza to describe the Arctic National Wildlife Refuge in one word, she doesn't hesitate. "Wholeness," she says. I am in the back of the boat with her as she steers us ahead to our last camp.

"It's not just the refuge or ANWR, the 1002, the National Petroleum Reserve Area, or any of the other throwaway names that are being bantered about in Washington," she explains, "but the entire region of what lives and breathes in the shadow of the Brooks Range with all its peaks and valleys, braided rivers, and coastlines. It's this layered sense of wilderness, the uninterrupted vistas without man's hand on it.

"If we choose to continue to only focus on particular areas, then this whole region becomes part of an intellectual and political project of fragmentation. Do we have to keep cutting it up into smaller and smaller bits and pieces until we finally call it a compromise? The Arctic National Wildlife Refuge is already a compromise—it was in 1960 and again in 1980."

Carol, a woman in her fifties, is as fierce and wise and beautiful as the lines that give her face expression. She is a woman who has made her work her passion and has brought her whole family into her explorer's heart.

50   "I want to hear a different discussion," she says. "I want people to ask, 'How does it feel to be in this country? What do you remember here that you have otherwise forgotten? Why do we want to destroy or diminish anything that inspires us to live more honestly?'"

The sanctity of solitude: I sit above a lake after a long walk up the steppe and then north across the tundra. Two swans are mirrored in the water.

A long-tailed jaeger sits next to me. I try not to move. With my legs crossed and my eyes barely open, I enter the space of meditation. A wolf howls. My body leaps. The jaeger flies. Fear floods my heart. Presence creates presence. I am now alert. To feel yourself prey is to be shocked back into the reality of the Arctic's here and now.

55   This is what I have learned in these short weeks in the refuge:

You cannot afford to make careless mistakes, like meditating in the presence of wolves, or topping your boots in the river, or losing a glove, or not securing your tent down properly. Death is a daily occurrence in the wild, not noticed, not respected, not mourned. In the Arctic, I've learned ego is as useless as money.

Choose one's traveling companions well. Physical
strength and prudence are necessary. Imagination
and ingenuity are our finest traits.
Expect anything.
You can change your mind like the weather.
Patience is more powerful than anger. Humor is
more attractive than fear.
Pay attention. Listen. We are most alive when
discovering.
Humility is the capacity to see.
Suffering comes, we do not have to create it.
We are meant to live simply.
We are meant to be joyful.
Life continues with and without us.
Beauty is another word for God.

Here is my question: what might a different kind of power look like, feel like? And can power be distributed equitably among ourselves, even beyond our own species?

The power of nature is the power of a life in association. Nothing stands alone. On my haunches, I see a sunburst lichen attached to limestone; algae and fungi are working together to break down rock into soil. I cannot help but recognize a radical form of democracy at play. Each organism is rooted in its own biological niche, drawing its power from its relationship to other organisms. An equality of being contributes to an ecological state of health and succession.

"We can only attain harmony and stability by consulting ensemble," writes Walt Whitman. This is my definition of community, and community interaction is the white-hot center of a democracy that burns bright.

60   Within the refuge, if I rotate slowly in place, what I see is a circumference of continuity. What I feel is a spiritual cohesion born out of wholeness. It is organic, cellular. I am at home in the peace of an intact world. The open space of democracy is not interested in hierarchies but in networks and systems where

power is circular, not linear; a power reserved not for an entitled few, but shared and maintained by many. Public lands are our public commons and they belong to everyone. We enter these sacred lands soulfully and remember what it is we have forgotten—the gift of time and space. The Arctic National Wildlife Refuge is the literal open space of democracy. The privilege of being here is met with the responsibility I feel to experience and express its compounding grace.

Raw, wild beauty is a deeply held American value. It is its own declaration of independence. Equality is experienced through humility. Liberty is expressed through the simple act of wandering.

3:00 a.m. Divine light. I am called out of the tent by the sun. I walk north, blinded by its radiance. On top of the ridge, I see two figures—human—Jim and Kyle. I wave. They wave back. Kyle raises his arms above his head with bent elbows. I understand. Caribou. I walk briskly up toward the men.

"Thousands upon thousands of caribou," Jim says. I turn. My binoculars scan the landscape for several minutes. Heads, antlers, backs, tails, legs, hooves, one caribou merges into another. Calves are jumping next to their mothers. It is an endless stream of animals walking across the tundra. Without field glasses, they register as a heat wave. I cannot take my eyes off them.

Jim and Kyle walk down to the flats and wake everyone. One by one, they rise from their tents. They rise to a rainbow, and another. A double rainbow is arching over the plains in Arctic light and we watch, as human beings have always watched, the great herds in motion.

QUESTIONS FOR DISCUSSION

1. How does the second part of the initial definition of "ground truthing" suggest a dimension of political truth/falsehood to the process of "seeing for yourself"? How has the Alaskan wilderness, the subject of this essay, become a politicized space about which untruths have been told?
2. What is revealed about the water in the Alaskan refuge area at the beginning of the essay? How does the water and its "mirror" quality become symbolic of the entire refuge area and its value to humanity?
3. Discuss the importance of Subhankar Banerjee's photographs in the effort to preserve the Alaskan wilderness. Do you agree with Williams's comment that beauty is "essential to our survival as a species"?
4. How do Williams's descriptions of the flora, fauna, and landscape of the Alaskan wilderness area help make her point that it is worth preserving in its current pristine state? Give examples of effective descriptive passages.
5. Indicate how Williams's examples of stories and dreams connected to the Alaskan wilderness help to make her points about the uniqueness and spiritual power of the place.
6. What lessons did Williams learn in her time at the Refuge? Why is this place and the experience of it so important for democracy and the sense of community for Americans?

CONNECTION

Compare Williams's description about the benefits of wilderness to our psychological and spiritual awareness with the ideas in Theodore Roszak's essay in this chapter (see below).

IDEAS FOR WRITING

1. Do some research into Subhankar Banerjee's exhibition of nature photographs at the Smithsonian as well as other artistic representations of nature, then write an essay in which you evaluate how successful these artworks have been at building enthusiasm for environmental preservation and the establishment of national parks.
2. In mid-2005, the Alaskan National Wildlife Refuge was opened to drilling on a limited basis. Do some research into this issue: Do you believe that the drilling as currently planned will do serious damage to the Refuge and to the values it represents? Why or why not?

RELEVANT WEB SITES

Interview with Terry Tempest Williams: The Politics of Place
`www.scottlondon.com/insight/scripts/ttw.html`
In this interview with Scott London, Terry Tempest Williams discusses her recent writing and her activism in regard to the preservation of natural places.

Arctic National Wildlife Refuge
`http://arctic.fws.gov/tkg2003.htm`
This government site examines the history, native cultures, wildlife, and visitor opportunities for this pristine region.

Alaska Wilderness League Site
`www.alaskawild.org`
This activist site seeks to mobilize support against drilling and development of the Alaskan wilderness and the Arctic National Wildlife Refuge.

Theodore Roszak

The Nature of Sanity: Mental Health and the Outdoors

Theodore Roszak was born in 1933 in Chicago, Illinois. He earned his B.A. at the University of California, Los Angeles, in 1955 and his Ph.D. at Princeton University. He served for two years as the editor of the Peace News *in London, taught at Stanford University as an instructor in history from 1959 to 1963, and currently is a professor of history at California State University, Hayward, where he also serves as director of the Ecopsychology Institute. Roszak's books include* The Making of the Counter Culture *(1969),* The Voice of the Earth: An Exploration of Ecopsychology *(1992),* The Cult of Information *(1994), and* The Longevity Revolution *(2001). The following essay explores Roszak's ideas on the relationship between nature and mental health that have formed the basis of the ecopsychology movement for which he is a leading advocate.*

JOURNAL

Write about your feelings before, during, and after a stay in the outdoors or in a rural area. How did your emotional/mental state change, and what particular aspects of outdoor life had a special influence on you?

Funny how psychiatrists are absolutely inspired when it comes to mapping sexual dysfunction, but fail to chart the strong emotional bond we have with the natural habitat. It's time for an environmentally based definition of mental health. So the next time you're feeling down, take yourself off to the woods for a few days.

I recently attended a meeting of the International Rivers Network, a San Francisco-area environmental group. The featured speaker was Dan Beard, head of the U.S. Bureau of Reclamation. After detailing the ways in which big dams have devastated natural watersheds and riverine cultures, he ended with an appeal: "Somehow we have got to convince people that projects like this are crazy." There was applause all around.

"Crazy" . . . in the presence of environmental horrors, the word leaps to mind. Depleting the ozone is "crazy," killing off the rhinos is "crazy," destroying rain forests is "crazy." Our gut feeling is immediate, the judgment made with vehemence. "Crazy" is a word freighted with strong emotion.

Inflicting irreversible damage on the biosphere might seem to be the most obvious kind of craziness. But when we turn to the psychiatric literature of the modern Western world, we find no such category as ecological madness.

5   The American Psychiatric Association lists more than 300 mental diseases in its *Diagnostic and Statistical Manual.* Among the largest of DSM categories is sex. In mapping sexual dysfunction, therapists have been absolutely inspired. We have sexual aversion disorder, female sexual arousal disorder, hypoactive sexual desire disorder (male and female), gender identity disorder, transient stress-related cross-dressing behavior, androgen insensitivity syndrome, fetishism, transvestic fetishism, transvestic fetishism with gender dysphoria, voyeurism, frotteurism, pedophilia (six varieties), and paraphiliac telephone scatologia.

Granted, the DSM bears about the same relationship to psychology as a building code bears to architecture. It is nonetheless revealing that the volume contains only one listing remotely connected to nature: seasonal affective disorder, a depressive mood swing occasioned by seasonal changes. Even here, nature comes in second: If the mood swing reflects seasonal unemployment, economics takes precedence as a cause.

Psychotherapists have exhaustively analyzed every form of dysfunctional family and social relations, but "dysfunctional environmental relations" does not exist even as a concept. Since its beginning, mainstream Western psychology has limited the definition of mental health to the interpersonal context of an urban industrial society: marriage, family, work, school, community. All that lies beyond the citified psyche has seemed of no human relevance—or perhaps too frightening to think about. "Nature," Freud dismally concluded, "is eternally remote. She destroys us—coldly, cruelly, relentlessly." Whatever else has been revised and rejected in Freud's theories, this tragic sense of estrangement from nature continues to haunt psychology, making the natural world seem remote and hostile.

Now all is changing. In the past 10 years, a growing number of psychologists have begun to place their theory and practice in an ecological context. Already ecopsychology has yielded insights of great value.

For one thing, it has called into question the standard strategy of scaring, shaming, and blaming that environmentalists have used in addressing the public since Rachel Carson wrote *Silent Spring*. There is evidence this approach does more harm than good—especially if, as ecopsychologists suggest, some environmentally destructive behavior bears the earmarks of addiction.

10   Take consumption habits. In ecopsychology workshops, people frequently admit their need to shop is "crazy." Why do they buy what they do not need? A common answer is, "I shop when I'm depressed. I go to the mall to be among happy people." Buying things is strictly secondary—and in fact does little to relieve the depression.

Some ecopsychologists believe that, as with compulsive gamblers, the depression that drives people to consume stems not from greed but from a sense of emptiness. This void usually traces back to childhood experiences of inadequacy and rejection; it may have much to do with the typically middle-class need for competitive success. The insecurity born of that drive may grow into a hunger for acquisition that cannot be satisfied even when people have consumed so much that they themselves recognize they are behaving irrationally.

If the addiction diagnosis of overconsumption is accurate, then guilt-tripping the public is worse than futile. Faced with scolding, addicts often resort to denial—or hostility. That makes them prey for antienvironmentalist groups like the Wise Use Movement, which then persuade an aggravated public to stop paying attention to "grieving greenies" and "ecofascists" who demand too much change too quickly.

As every therapist knows, addictive behavior cannot be cured by shame, because addicts are already deeply ashamed. Something affirmative and environmentally benign must be found to fill the inner void. Some ecopsychologists believe the joy and solace of the natural world can itself provide that emotional sustenance. Some, therefore, use wilderness, restoration projects, or gardens as a new "outdoor office."

"Nature heals" is one of the oldest therapeutic dicta. Ecopsychologists are finding new ways to apply that ancient insight. Over a century ago, Emerson lamented that "few adult persons can see nature." If they could, they would know that "in the woods, we return to reason and faith. There I feel that nothing can befall me in life, no disgrace or calamity . . . which nature cannot repair."

15   Why have therapists made so little of this obvious resource? When highly stressed people are asked to visualize a soothing scene, nobody imagines a freeway or a shopping mall. Rather, images of wilderness, forest, seascape, and starry skies invariably emerge. In taking such experiences seriously, ecopsychologists are broadening the context of mental health to include the natural environment. They are hastening the day when calling our bad environmental habits "crazy" will be more than a rhetorical outburst. The word will have behind it the full weight of considered professional consensus.

This, in turn, could be of enormous value in opening people to our spiritual, as well as physical, dependence upon nature. The time may not be far off when environmental policy-makers will have something more emotionally engaging to work with than the Endangered Species Act. They will be able to defend the beauties and biodiversity of nature by invoking an environmentally based definition of mental health. We might then see an assault upon endangered species or old-growth forest as an assault upon the sanity of a community, upon children, or upon our species as a whole.

In devastating the natural environment, we may be undermining a basic requirement of sanity: our sense of moral reciprocity with the nonhuman environment. Yet ecopsychology also offers hope. As ecocidal as our behavior may have become, our bond with the planet endures; something within us voices a warning.

Ecopsychologists have begun to detect in people evidence of an unspoken grieving for the great environmental losses the world is suffering. Sometimes, indeed, clients themselves demand to have that sense of loss taken seriously in their therapy. In a letter to *Ecopsychology Newsletter,* one reader reports how she confessed her anxiety for our environmental condition to her psychiatrist. "I felt depressed that things had gotten so bad I could no longer drink tap water safely." Her therapist, all too typically, dismissed her feelings as an "obsession with the environment." That judgment eventually drove the client to seek help elsewhere and finally toward a commitment to the environmental movement.

Denying the relevance of nature to our deepest emotional needs is still the rule in mainstream therapy, as in the culture generally. It is apt to remain so until psychologists expand our paradigm of the self to include the natural habitat—as was always the case in indigenous cultures, whose methods of healing troubled souls included the trees and rivers, the sun and stars.

20   At a conference titled "Psychology As If the Whole Earth Mattered" at Harvard's Center for Psychology and Social Change, psychologists concluded that "if the self is expanded to include the natural world, behavior leading to destruction of this world will be experienced as self-destruction."

Such an intimate connection with the earth means taking our evolutionary heritage seriously and putting it in an ecological framework. Ecopsychology reinforces insights from naturalists like E. O. Wilson, who suggests that we possess "an innately emotional affiliation with all living organisms"—biophilia—that inclines us toward fostering biodiversity.

If our culture is out of balance with nature, everything about our lives is affected: family, workplace, school, community—all take on a crazy shape. For this reason, ecopsychology does not seek to create new categories of pathology, but to show how our ecological disconnection plays into all existing ones. For example, the DSM defines "separation anxiety disorder" as "excessive anxiety concerning separation from home and from those to whom the individual is attached." But no separation is more pervasive in this Age of Anxiety than our disconnection from the natural world.

Freud coined the term reality principle to designate that objective order of things to which the healthy psyche must adapt if it is to qualify as "sane." Writing in a pre-ecological era, he failed to include the biosphere. Ecopsychology is seeking to rectify that failure by expanding the definition of sanity to embrace the love for the living planet that is reborn in every child.

QUESTIONS FOR DISCUSSION

1. What is the DSM, and why does Roszak believe that it contains so few references to the impact of nature on mental health? Do you agree with his explanation of this absence? Can you think of other reasons for it?

2. Why are psychologists just now starting to question the use by environmentalists of tactics of "scaring, shaming, and blaming"? Do you agree that this approach could have a negative emotional impact?

3. What is Roszak's view of the ecologically destructive practice of overconsumption? Do you agree with his views on the cause of overconsumption in the form of compulsive shopping?

4. In Roszak's view and those of other ecopsychologists, how can nature help fill the "inner void"? Do you agree that "nature heals"? Explain.

5. What do you think Emerson meant when he said over a hundred years ago that "few adult persons can see nature"? Does this statement suggest a literal or figurative type of seeing? Do you think the situation is worse today, in an age of vibrant nature photography and film? Why or why not?

6. How does naturalist E. O. Wilson's theory of human beings' "innately emotional affiliation with all living organisms" suggest a flaw in the DSM concept of "separation anxiety disorder"? Do you agree with Wilson's belief?

CONNECTION

Compare Roszak's ideas on the healing and mental health influences of contact with nature with the ideas and experiences portrayed in Diane Ackerman's "Deep Play" (see page 73).

IDEAS FOR WRITING

1. Develop your journal entry into a personal essay about how being in nature has helped you "heal" or to feel more emotionally complete and con-
tented. Use descriptions and examples from experience.
2. Write an essay in response to Roszak's ideas and those of Emerson and
Wilson about the ability of nature to help us find mental stability and
fulfillment. Which of their ideas made the strongest impression on you,
and why?

RELATED WEB SITES

International Community for Ecopsychology
`www.ecopsychology.org/index.html#ice`
The Web site for this organization features a large annotated bibliography of
background information, books, articles, and active figures in the field of
ecopsychology.

Interview with Theodore Roszak
`www.williamjames.com/transcripts/roszak.htm`
In this three-part interview with Dr. Jeffery Mishlove in the series Thinking
Allowed: Conversations on the Leading Edge of Knowledge and Discovery,
Theodore Roszak shares his views on ecological and spiritual crisis, tradi-
tional psychology, and the ecopsychology movement.

David Kerr

Strawberry Creek: A Search for Origins

*David Kerr, a longtime resident of Berkeley, California, wrote the following paper
for his critical thinking class and published it in a class anthology on nature. In
his paper, he uses his own boyhood explorations in an attempt to understand and
to define the history and secret pattern of a buried urban creek.*

On warm summer days as if there were some great parental conspiracy, my
friends and I would be sent out of our respective homes to "get some
sun" and "go for a hike and explore nature." The irony of these requests
would be that we would very often explore nature without ever getting any sun
at all.

Once we decided to trace Strawberry Creek from the flatlands where I lived
to its hidden beginnings. This had to be done underground. Our starting point
was alongside a road in lower Berkeley (we often called lower Berkeley the flatlands or flats). Here the creek exited a tunnel on its way to the Bay. At an early
period in the city's history, those in charge of such things decided to bury all of

the creeks in the flatlands in order to build homes there as well as all over downtown. Even though the creeks had been covered over, they still flowed through these now ancient tunnels, perfect kid-size tunnels with small tunnel mouths.

Armed with flashlights, candles, lighters and matches, we entered the tunnel for Strawberry Creek at a small, partially concealed outlet on the side of the road among the bushes. Our plan was to wind our way through the city underground. A big part of the adventure for us was finding out if this was truly the same Strawberry Creek that coursed through the university and Strawberry Canyon. There was no other way of knowing without tracing the creek backwards.

Entering the tunnel we tried to balance ourselves on any flat rocks we could find, some of which were covered with a fine green moss from the occasional flow of water that passed over them. We tried our best to stay dry, something that was to be a losing battle. Inside, we discovered that there was a small dry ledge upon which we could walk. Our strange mixture of lights created long and short dancing shadows on the walls and on the rushing water. The rocks in the creek seemed almost alive as our flashlight beams crossed over them. The whole scene was straight out of some old horror movie, making us all a little nervous.

5   In the tunnel, we discovered after a short while that there were a number of side tunnels. In the hope of finding out what these side tunnels were for, we entered one. There was no flowing water as in the main tunnel; this tunnel was dry. The ground was very smooth and silky with soft ripples like an ancient ocean bed hidden for years. As our steps left the impressions of our tennis shoes, it was like being the first man on the moon. Someone in the group, not being able to resist, argued, "I'm just sure that this has nothing to do with the creek. We're following an old sewer line. Let's turn back before someone decides to flush." I replied, "I don't think so; I'm sure it would smell if that were true."

As we continued on, we could see the roots of trees dangling down above our heads. Leonard observed, "Don't you feel like you're in a cartoon or something?" He grabbed a large root and started to swing around from it. I asked, "What the hell do you think you're doing, Leonard?" He came back with authority, "Trying to pull the tree into the tunnel of course." Well, there was no arguing with that, so we let him swing. This little side tunnel somehow ended up back at the main tunnel; at least we hoped this was the main tunnel. Here it was not so easy to walk as in the side tunnels, because there was flowing water and no dry, silted mud to walk on.

More often than not, as we traversed the tunnel, we had to walk in the creek water because the dry edges had become too small to walk on. As we walked with the creek water rushing over our feet and soaking our shoes, we started making jokes about coming across giant rats or some great albino alligator who would gobble us up. We had heard stories of children bringing back alligators from Florida that end up in the sewers of New York. These alligators supposedly attack sewer workers there; so why not here? Never mind that we are on the other side of the country. Then of course there were the giant mutant rats lurking around the next bend. It had to be true. My friend Leonard also pointed out that in this great exploration of nature, "Strawberry Creek does run through the university." He commented with his best all-knowing voice, "Some careless student has dumped something radioactive into the creek." This without question had given birth to giant mutant rats which were certainly going to eat us for a tasty little snack. We never did get eaten; we did, on the other hand, come to the end of the tunnel at the entrance of the university. At least one mystery was solved: It is the same creek.

Strawberry Creek enters the tunnel at the university around Center and Oxford streets where we had just exited. The creek at this point is surrounded by a small grove of redwoods through which the sun was still shining as we emerged. It was a bit of a shock to see the sun again after having spent the last few hours underground. We were tired and a bit wet; nonetheless, we were only half done in our search for the creek's origins.

As we followed the creek through the university, we wound around buildings and under bridges rather than underground. The creek led us through different groves of trees, some bay laurel, some redwood and some live oak. At a point near the Life Sciences building, there is a calm area that has created a pond. There is an abundance of water life here; it provided a momentary stop in our search. We cupped our hands and tried to scoop up water striders. They raced away the second our hands touched the water, yet always returned (as if to torture us) to where we had placed our hands in the water. Somehow we were never able to capture any at all. After giving up our efforts with the water striders, we followed the creek to the other side of the campus. Here, much to our dismay, we could no longer follow the creek; the tunnel under the stadium was too small for us. Crossing over to the other side of the stadium we tried to pick up Strawberry Creek where it starts before it enters the tunnel. I don't remember whether we ever found that end of the tunnel, but we eventually picked up our journey for the origins of the creek in Strawberry Canyon.

10   As we hiked up the canyon alongside the creek, the creek started to split into different tributaries. We followed one of them, which led us to a fenced area, the botanical gardens for the university. Unable to continue here, we followed a fire trail that this part of the creek had led us to. As we hiked up the trail, we could see another part of the creek continuing up the canyon. This again led us to another part of the botanical gardens fence through which we could pass.

At this point, we gave up our search for the mythical origins of Strawberry Creek, yet we continued on to a part of the canyon called Woodbridge Memorial Grove. When we arrived at this small grove of redwoods with its tilted bay tree from which we, as others have, once hung a rope to swing from, we found our rope had once again been cut away from the tree. The day was gone, so we headed home where dinner awaited.

QUESTIONS FOR DISCUSSION

1. How does David Kerr's essay add to our sense of definition and understanding of Strawberry Creek through the process of exploration? Give

examples from the essay of what it taught you about the history, origins, and form of the creek.

2. Kerr writes his essay from the point of view of several children on a nature expedition. How does he capture the voice and typical sense of expression and concerns of children in nature?

3. Kerr uses dialogue in his essay not only to capture the way children speak, but also to communicate some observations about the creek. Give examples of effective uses of dialogue in the essay.

4. Give examples of closely observed, clear description from the essay that adds to your understanding of the creek and its surrounding environment.

5. It could be argued that Kerr's essay has no conclusion; the friends simply give up and go home for supper. Do you consider this an effective ending, or would you rather have seen a more formal conclusion that emphasized Kerr's understanding of the creek? Would you have advice for Kerr on this point?

Sheila Walsh

Visualizing Our Environment: Communication of Environmental Issues Through Visual Arts

Sheila Walsh was a first-year student majoring in biology and minoring in studio art when she wrote the following research proposal for her introductory composition course. As an undergraduate doing research at the campus Center for Conservation Biology, Walsh became interested in ways to make the conservation of the environment a public issue. Because of her interest in art, she decided to focus on public art as a way to change the way that people think about nature and environment issues.

The nation is ready to make the environment the key issue for 2000. Recent evidence of climate change is too drastic for anyone to ignore. . . . [W]ho can doubt that our climate is changing severely?
                                                                    —*Sierra Club Action Daily,* 26 Feb. 1999

If articulated properly, the environment can be the central issue of the next decade.
                                                                    —Dick Morris, *The Hill,* 24 Feb. 1999

The face of our planet is changing rapidly as a result of ecotastrophes such as global warming, pollution, and deforestation, but the average person cannot see it happening, even though scientists generate data everyday to support the reality of the changes. The problem is not how many facts and figures we receive about global warming, habitat destruction, and diversity loss—but how we perceive these facts. Frightening information about the degradation of

our environment is ignored as it flows over TV waves into nightly news programs and hides amongst editorial columns in newspapers. The current form
of communication has made people entirely apathetic to the destruction of the
world that we live in. To change the way that people and whole societies treat
the environment, the communication of environmental issues must change.
Communicating environmental issues through visual arts will force people to
actually *see* the change in their environment. Public murals, photography, and
billboards will make environmental issues immediate, changing apathy into urgency and catalyzing environmental action on local and global scales.

The current mode of communication to the public has led to the stagnation
of the environmental movement; emphatic, public visual arts will re-energize it.
Murals, photographs, and billboards actively engage people on a personal and
emotional level. Images activate the vivid memory bank of experiences that
each person has. The images of these experiences create the mental landscape
that we live our lives on; the contents of those images in turn can influence our
actions. As one looks at photographs of cracked, dry earth from the *Water in the
West Project,* a model for communication through visual arts, the images become part of the person's mental landscape. Later, when she sees a lush green
lawn in Arizona or her tap water left running, she will give it a second thought.

5   However, every person has a different collection of experiences and, consequently, a different level of visual literacy. "Visual literacy does not apply to our
society as a whole," regrets Margaret Moulton, professor of photography at Stanford University. Even though we are constantly bombarded with images, people
do not have a sophisticated level of literacy with visual images (Moulton). Public
images, though, are uniquely democratic. Every person who passes by a mural in
a park, regardless of her level of visual literacy, has the same opportunity to stop
for a moment and think about it. Art breaks cultural and literacy boundaries
that limit many people's abilities to communicate in other media.

The art must be displayed in public to be successful. It must be in city and
county parks, on the side of high rises and parking structures, and plastered on
the billboards that create a forest around expressways. Margaret Moulton
agrees that all people have the ability to respond to art but not all people have
the ability to see art because it is not in public. Art of this type cannot be in museums or galleries because it will become as esoteric as the conventional texts
that it is trying to improve upon. Many artists who are dealing with environmental issues display their art in places like The Ansel Adams Center for Photography. Sadly enough, the majority of the public does not go to The Ansel
Adams Center for Photography, but global warming still affects us all.

Social and political issues have already been communicated through visual
arts to the public outside of museums. Images have been intentionally and un-
intentionally changing the way that people live since pictographs first appeared
on rock faces. In modern times, despite the advent of the printing press, a few
specific images have dramatically changed people's perceptions of society
more than headlines. Visual images have made radical social and political
change and will make radical environmental change.

Environmental degradation is as much of a social and political issue as war, oppression, and eating disorders. Picasso changed people's perceptions of World War II more than most newspaper headlines with his painting *Guernica*. The twisted faces and contorted bodies scream out Picasso's message. *Guernica* embodies all that is corrupt, ugly, atrocious, and unbearable that now defines war for a person of the twentieth century. The Chicano movement forced people to recognize the more subtle forms of oppression occurring during peacetime using public murals. Murals and poster making became the emphasis of the movement's activism because they informed the literate and non-literate masses. A Chicano/a could "read" the message of the mural and be able to see "the social, economic, and political conditions forced onto the Chicano community" differently ("Brief History of Chicano Murals"). Through the Chicano Movement, visual arts became a tool for inciting people to take action. Robin Lasser and Catherine Sylva have proved that visual arts can also be a tool for educating people about themselves. They use billboards located in Sacramento to inform the commuters about the eating disorders that affect the majority of women today. The project, *Consuming Landscapes and Other Eating Disorders,* shows images of distorted bodies, flaming silver ware, and barbequed meat. The billboards are provocative because of their imagery and their ability to talk about a subject that most people are silent about. Public murals, photography, and billboards about any social, political, or environmental issue are provocative because they force the viewer to question the world in which they are viewing the art. When an environmental image forces the viewer to question the world around her, the answer she will find is that something has to change.

The success with social and political issues will be easily transferred to environmental issues because they are often more visual than social and political issues. Oppression of people can be silent and invisible; however, the destruction of old growth forests is loud and visible. Yet, environmental issues are still ignored because of our anthropomorphic sense of progress. Public displays of visual arts that use the affective characteristics of *Guernica,* the murals of the Chicano Movement, and the billboards of *Consuming Landscapes* will demand attention for environmental issues by questioning our progress.

10   Despite the inherent visual quality of environmental issues, visual arts have still not been addressed as seriously as a medium for communicating environmental issues as they have been for social and political issues. Fleeting television programs have been devoted to global warming or El Niño. However, television, a type of visual art, has a way of turning real problems into fantasies. The viewers of *Dateline* or *20/20* do not often leave the couch between these news shows and the next episode of *ER*. The real problems of global warming presented on *Dateline* special edition are then ignored because they seem as fantastic and distant as the people dying of multiple gun shot wounds on *ER*. These problems are also ignored because environmental issues are generally thought of as being strictly scientific. In between fantasy and science fiction, visual arts need to show reality. Murals, photography, and billboards have shown

the reality of social and political issues and now they will show the reality of the destruction of our environment because it is a social and political issue.

During the Industrial Revolution, J.M.W. Turner (1775–1851) and John Ruskin (1819–1900) recognized the environmental degradation of London as a social issue in their watercolor paintings. Through default, they made the first steps toward communicating environmental issues through visual arts. Clouds, smoke, and steam fill their work. Although the Turner and Ruskin's images were similar, the messages that they were trying to communicate were quite different: "where Turner celebrates the destructive energy of industrialization, Ruskin fears its affects on Nature" (Danahay 62). In Ruskin's work pollution is "a sign of social and spiritual disorder, a symptom of the blurring of the boundaries between the natural and the abominable, the sacred and the profane" (63). The connection of social ills to pollution made him a forerunner of the contemporary ecological movement. He was one of a group of experts who were just realizing the negative affects of what we call "pollution" (68). Connecting a change in environment to a social issue caused him difficulty when trying to reach his audience in lectures. Consequently, "Rather than exhort his audience to action, Ruskin frequently . . . [left] questions hanging and his points unarticulated" (70). If Ruskin had been successful in articulating his concerns about the trends in London's environment, it may not have taken until the 1970s to recognize the drastic changes in the environment that began in the 1870s.

If scientists and the general public could have learned from art at the turn of the century, can they learn from art now at the turn of the millennium? According to Cornelia Hesse-Honegger, the answer is yes. She began drawing *Dropsophilia* flies in the late 1960s at the Zoological Institute of the University of Zurich to supplement scientific research. In 1987, she upset the scientific community because her detailed paintings of insects and plants affected by radioactive emissions revealed mutations greater than those expected by scientists. When Hesse-Honegger published this in the Swiss periodical, *Das Magazine,* she received criticism from scientists who did not believe that such small doses of radiation could cause the mutations that Hesse-Honegger had recorded in her drawings. Dr. William Thompson, formerly a Professor of the humanities and social sciences at MIT, describes how "disorder broke out in Switzerland when Hesse-Honegger moved out of her place to use her art as a means of scientific analysis and political description of the modern technical world" (Hesse-Honegger and Thompson 18). In Hesse-Honegger's work, the role of art was to portray "an image: an image which reflects that which we actually have but do not want." She showed how we "destroy, poison and mutate" (18). Then, "we are faced with the awkward question, why does the gap between environmental destruction and taking action against it grow?" (17).

Hesse-Honegger's work shows how provocative communication of environmental issues through visual arts can be. She showed that "if we wish to think with art about science, we may find . . . a realism that is aesthetically unsettling precisely because it is neither horrific nor natural, but it is what we have made of a nature we once thought of as given" (19). Although it might be unsettling, the general public needs to be forced to *see* how we have changed nature as they walk through a park, down a side walk, or drive on the expressway. Artists are recognizing that their work can force this change where conventional forms of communication have failed to.

Successful work has come in a great variety of purpose and form. Artist's purposes range from simple environmental awareness to a call for specific action. Their forms range from public murals to photographic documentation. There is still not a perfect model. However, the current work is creating the guidelines for successful communication. Two examples with very different purposes and forms provide the foundation of these guidelines.

15   The popular ocean artist, Wyland, has been successful in promoting environmental awareness. He has confronted thousands of people with their relationship to oceanic animals through the life-size murals that he has painted in major cities all over the world. His sixty-seven, and counting, *Whaling Walls* represent an attempt to change attitudes on a large scale. Wyland says that "By painting them life-sized in public places, I hope to raise people's consciousness and get them involved in protecting the whales. . . . These murals will be seen by tens of millions of people each year. You can choose not to go into an art gallery or museum, but you can't ignore a giant mural" ("Wyland Brings Whaling Wall"). His majestic whales have become regular features in the lives of the people who live in those cities. Passersby recognize the beauty in the arc of a whale as it breeches up through aqua painted water on the side of their office building. The mural is an especially effective medium because it can be "'consumed' over and over again by the same person, it also can be "'consumed' simultaneously by many viewers" (Walker 74).

Wyland's *Whaling Walls* suggest change; the photographs of the *Water in the West* demand it. The *Water in the West* is a "photographic response to the growing water crisis that exists because our culture thinks of water as a commodity or an abstract legal right, rather than the most basic physical source of life" (Manchester i). Photographers Mark Wett, Terry Evans, Laurie Brown, Robert Dawson, Martin Stupich, Gregory Coniff, Wanda Hammerback, and Peter Goin wanted to answer the question: How can photography contribute to the urgent public debate over water use, allocation, and privilege? These photographers recognized that their medium is "uniquely qualified to offer information and visual insight" (i). Goin recalls that "A significant amount of our time was devoted to discussing the relationship of the photograph as a creative object to the photograph as a tool for political change. After a consensus, the project's goal was to create a collection of photos and related visual material that will contribute significantly to the dialogue about the future and quality of life on earth as sustained by increasingly limited natural resources such as water" (15).

At the same time as the *Water and the West Project* was formulating its plans, the Nevada Humanities Committee was sponsoring a conference entitled "Water in the Arid West." The two groups collaborated in their efforts to bring together historians, writers, ranchers, politicians, lawyers, students and

community members to discuss the water issue. The scholars were able to realize what the photographers had realized through their work: "The irony in
the American West today is that we have no water, yet seem to have plenty to
drink" (Manchester 1). *Water and the West* continues to be displayed, affecting
change and serving as a model for the communication of environmental issues through visual arts.

Wyland and the *Water in the West* show the range of the current work with visual arts to communicate environmental issues. In between these examples are
the violent images of the Headwaters campaign and the serene landscapes of
Adams. They are all models for how visual images can create change. Wyland
and Ansel Adams have changed the way that tens of thousands of people *see* nature. The Headwaters campaign and *Water in the West* have made their issues
immediate and have been catalysts for change. To improve upon these individual efforts, their strengths have to be combined. Communication of environmental issues through visual arts must address the issues that are being ignored
despite sufficient scientific data, then portray the issue so that people can *see* it
differently, make sure the image is accessible to the public, and emphasize the
immediacy of the issue and the need for action. These four guidelines will
make the communication of environmental issues through visual arts a catalyst
for local and global action. The environmental movement desperately needs
visual arts as a catalyst to propel it into the 21st Century. A commitment of significant amounts of federal money should be made to sponsor independent,
local artists to create murals, photography, and billboards that would become
permanent fixtures in communities nation-wide. The conventional means of
communication have led to the stagnation of the popular environmental movement. This radical, grass-root form of communication through visual arts will
re-energize the movement for the new millennium.

WORKS CITED

"A Brief History of Chicano Murals." L.A. Murals Home Page. Sep 1996. 13 Jan 1999
    <http://latino.sscnet.ucla.edu/murals/Sparc/muralhis.html>.

Danahay, Martin A. "Matter Out of Place: The Politics of Pollution in Ruskin and Turner." *CLIO*
    21.1 (Fall, 1991): 61.

Hesse-Honegger, Cornelia and William Thompson. "Painting Mutations." *Geographical Magazine*
    64.11 (Nov. 1992): 15.

Manchester, Ellen. *Arid Waters: Photographs From the Water and The West Project*. Ed. Peter Goin. Reno:
    University of Nevada Press, 1992.

Moulton, Margaret. Telephone interview. 14 Jan. 1999.

Walker, John A. and Sarah Chaplin. *Visual Culture: An Introduction*. Manchester, NY: Manchester
    U. P., 1997.

"Wyland Brings Whaling Wall to San Diego." *San Diego Earth Times* Aug. 1994. 3 March 1999.
    <http://www.sdearthtimes.com/et0894/et0894s6.html>.

QUESTIONS FOR DISCUSSION

1. How do Walsh's comments on environmental change and perceptions of
    change in the first paragraph help to establish a problem that needs to be

solved? At what point does Walsh state, in general terms, her proposed solution to the problem?

2. What examples of the way the media present environmental problems does Walsh provide, and what flaws and limits does she see in them? What are the limitations of some current venues for displaying environmental art, such as the Ansel Adams Center? How do the critical points Walsh makes about the media and the current places of exhibition help to strengthen her thesis and proposal?

3. How effectively does Walsh present past and current examples of effective environmental and protest art in order to strengthen her proposal? Could she have provided other examples?

4. Walsh originally used a number of visual illustrations to present her points more forcefully. Which of her points and references do you think could have been effectively reinforced by visuals? Does the essay make its points well without them?

5. Evaluate Walsh's specific proposal for change, which she develops in her final paragraphs. Is the proposal clear and convincing? Would her plan (assuming it were to get governmental funding) really engage people's understanding and concern about environmental degradation? Why or why not?

TOPICS FOR RESEARCH AND WRITING

1. Some of the essays in this chapter, such as those by Williams, Krakauer, and Webster, raise disturbing issues about the presence of humans in pristine natural spots. Do some research and write about the impact on the environment of ecotourism and other forms of recreational uses of the wilderness. Write about your findings with some conclusions about what kind of regulation could make such uses of nature less damaging and intrusive.

2. Develop an ideal program for educating today's children to live in harmony with nature. What emphasis would you put on science and technology? How would you introduce dreams, myths, and imaginative literature? How would you present history, social science, and politics? What books would you assign, and why? Discuss particular projects and field trip experiences that you might have your students complete.

3. Several of the texts in the chapter comment on the relationship between humans and natural creatures. Do some research into this subject and write an essay that examines several consequences of the severing of the relations between humans and other living beings.

4. We project human values, fears, and stereotypical beliefs onto animals, at times preventing us from seeing and appreciating them as they are. Do some research into this tendency on the part of humans to "anthropomorphize" living creatures, and write an essay in which you evaluate the problems it might cause.

5. The works in this chapter reveal a skilled ability to observe nature and its creatures. Using examples from the works in this chapter as well as other nature writing that you have read, write an essay in which you offer the beginning writer advice about improving his or her ability to observe closely and to make an accurate and interesting record of her or his observations of nature.

6. One of the most intriguing aspects of nature is the ceaseless process of change, which features a myriad of births, seeming deaths, transformations, and rebirths of living things over fairly short periods of time as well as larger historical changes to the environment. Taking the area where you live or another region with which you are familiar, do some research and then write an essay describing some of the changes in the "natural" and "artificial" landscapes, as well as in the populations of various living creatures, that have taken place over the past 50 to 100 years.

7. A number of films have been made that provide powerful images of nature as well as its relation to humanity and human values. Select and view a film that presents a vision of nature, then discuss the vision of the filmmaker. You might select a film from the following list: *Dreams* (by Akira Kurosawa), *Never Cry Wolf, Mindwalk, Erin Brockovich, Out of Africa, Gorillas in the Mist, The Horse Whisperer, The Medicine Man, Grizzly Man, Everest, Into the Void,* and *The Wild Parrots of Telegraph Hill.*

Journeys in Memory 3

Ralph Eugene Meatyard (1925–1972)
Untitled (1960)

After working for several years in Illinois as an optician, Ralph Meatyard began his dedication to photography in 1954 and continued to exhibit his work for the rest of his life. Meatyard's work is notable for its combination of realism with dream-like elements. Many of his photographs, like *Untitled*, are set in abandoned houses and use his family as characters in a mysterious interplay of memory and fantasy.

JOURNAL

Write about a memory that you find confusing, strange, and dreamlike.

In the New Age the Daughters of Memory shall become the Daughters of Inspiration.
                              WILLIAM BLAKE

If I approach writing from memory with the assumption that I know what I wish to say, I assume that intentionality is running the show. Things are not that simple.
                              PATRICIA HAMPL

Often I felt as though I was in a trance at my typewriter, that the shape of a particular memory was decided not by my conscious mind but by all that is dark and deep within me, unconscious but present.
                              BELL HOOKS
                              Writing Autobiography

NARRATION, MEMORY, AND SELF-AWARENESS

You will read a number of narrative accounts of childhood experiences in this chapter. Narratives serve two important functions for a writer: they can bring about a process of self-discovery, and they are fundamental sources and building blocks of both fiction and nonfiction writing. The brief stories or extended examples that develop, illustrate, and support points made in expository and argumentative essays are among the best resources writers have for presenting ideas in a clear, vivid, and convincing manner.

When you create a narrative, you draw on many inner resources and skills: memories of life experiences, dreams, your imagination, the ability to imitate the voices of others, and the skill required to develop a suspenseful plot that will hold your readers' attention. While not everyone can entertain friends with a natural storytelling ability, most of us can learn how to write a clear and engaging story.

Making Associations

As in other forms of writing, the first phase of narrative writing involves generating ideas and images to write about, experiences that come in part from your past and in part from your imagination that can later be shaped into a story with an overall theme. You can begin as Patricia Hampl does in her first draft of her essay, "Memory and Imagination," with what you think you remember: "When I was seven, my father . . . led me by the hand down a long, unlit corridor in St. Luke's basement, a sort of tunnel that ended in a room full of pianos." Later Hampl rereads her draft and realizes that her efforts to make emotional sense of a rather unpleasant childhood experience have led her to make numerous distortions of the actual facts of the first visit to her future piano teacher. She is willing to keep many of these alterations because they feel emotionally right if not factually so. This marks an important distinction between personal narrative and the kind of close description of nature that we saw in some of the essays in the previous chapter.

How do you find ideas and events for your writing, however, if the only memories you have of your early years are vague or sketchy? Notice the following initial account of a student's childhood in Sacramento: "As a child, I lived for five years on B Street in Sacramento. It was always hot in the summer there." Writing strategies such as drawing, freewriting, invisible writing, brainstorming, and clustering can help you to generate details, images, and ideas associated with a particular time and place in your life. For example, you could start with a significant part of an address and do a cluster or ten-minute freewrite around it, letting one detail lead to another: "B Street, hot, barren, dusty, fire hydrant out front turned on in the summer, the ice cream wagon's jingle." If you follow this process long enough, you will begin to imagine and re-create a number of details you thought you had forgotten, and you will have begun to gather the words, thoughts, and images that you can later shape into an essay.

Focusing and Concentration: The Inner Screen

In developing your narrative, it is also important to try to focus on the most significant aspect of your memory. For example, you might visualize a particular room or the backyard of your house on a summer day when something significant happened to you: a fateful accident, a moment of serious conflict, an unexpected gift, a moment of friendship or intimacy. Close your eyes and try to visualize all the objects, colors, forms, people, and expressions associated with that place and a particular time there. Then try to visualize the movements within the scene, as movements in time and space are essential elements of narration. When did certain people arrive and leave? How did they walk? What gestures did they make? What activities did they perform? What did they say to one another? After visualizing and naming specific colors, try to recall other sensations: textures, warmth or coolness, smells, tastes, and sounds. Take notes as you begin to remember and imagine sensations, forms, and movements.

Dialogue and Characters

While not all people have vivid auditory memories, including some conversation in your narrative will help bring it to life. Focus on the way each person in your scene speaks; jot down some of the typical brief exchanges that the group could have had, and then try to understand each character more fully through role-playing. Imagine that you have become each person in the scene, one at a time. As you role-play, speak out loud in the voice of each person, then write down a paragraph in which you try to capture their typical concerns and rhythms of speech. Finally, try to construct a conversation between the people in the scene.

Main Idea or Dominant Impression

Now you should be ready to write about the strong ideas or feelings that underlie or dominate your scene. Brainstorm or cluster around key details in your notes. Which emotions does the remembered moment call up for you? What ideas, what "lessons," does it suggest? Develop a statement that you can later clarify and qualify: "That evening was one of waiting and apprehension"; "The morning was a joyful one for my family, yet tinged by regret." Writing this type of dominant impression statement will guide you in adding more details and bits of dialogue and in selecting and ordering your material. A central idea for your narrative will help you to achieve a sense of focus and purpose that will help you to engage your readers' interest; most importantly, it will help you clarify what you have gained from the experience. The process of writing the narrative will contribute to your personal growth and self-awareness.

Drafting and Shaping the Narrative

Using your central idea or dominant impression as a guide in selecting and ordering details and events, write a rapid first draft, including what is relevant from the notes you generated in your preliminary brainstorming. Leave out any details or events that introduce a tone or feeling that conflicts with or detracts from the impression you want to emphasize. Relevant but not particularly interesting events and periods of time do not need to be narrated in detail and can be summed up in a sentence or two: "For hours I played with my dog, waiting eagerly for my father to return from work."

Try to order the events of your narrative to emphasize your main idea as well. Although most writers use a chronological sequence in shaping a narrative, your dominant idea may demand withholding a key event for purposes of suspense or creating a powerful conclusion, as Maya Angelou does with the powerful fantasy in "The Angel of the Candy Counter," included in this chapter. You might also consider the use of flashbacks, beginning perhaps with a brief scene that occurs at the end of the action and then revealing the sequence of events leading up to the initially described event. Any order is acceptable as long as you clarify shifts of time for the reader with transitions and make sure that your order serves the overall purpose of your story.

While writing different drafts of your narrative, don't hesitate to experiment with rearranging the parts of the story or essay until you find a clear, comfortable fit between the structure and the meaning of your work. This rearrangement process is made much easier if you are revising on a computer, as the cut-and-paste functions of your word processor make it easy to see how different sequences work. You might try saving different versions of your narrative with different file names, each using a different sequence of events, then printing each out and reading them over to see more clearly what may be the advantages of each version.

Revising the Narrative: Point of View, Transition, and Style

Point of View and Transition   As you move from the early stages into the final drafting of your narrative, pay special attention to your point of view and style. Your narrative will probably use the first person "I" pronoun, unless you are writing about someone else's experience. As is the case with the essays in this chapter, narrative essays are most frequently told from the perspective of an adult looking back on the past and are known as "memoir narratives." Be sure to maintain a consistent point of view. If you decide to move into your mind as a young person, indicate this shift with a clear transition ("Then I thought to myself . . . "), after which you could write in language that is typical of the younger "you."

Notice in Patricia Hampl's narrative of her piano lesson with Sister Olive how effectively she uses transition to indicate the shift of perspective and time that occurs with each next paragraph, beginning with a straightforward account of her trip through the corridor, moving in the second paragraph to a scene setting and extended description of the nun, then getting the father out of the picture in paragraph 3: "My father left me to discover the piano." She then gets down to the business of the lesson with paragraph 4—"But first Sister Olive must do her work"—moving through a series of stages until in paragraphs 11 and 12 we find Mary Katherine Reilly's final appraisal of young Hampl (and Hampl's appraisal of her): "Sized me up and found a person ready to be dominated."

Word Choice and Transition   Like descriptions, narratives are seldom written in highly formal, abstract, or generalized language, so try to make your narrative voice down to earth, using common and concrete language as you try to capture the mood and feeling of the events being revealed and the characters involved, as Hampl does in the passages quoted above. In refining the style of your narrative, ask yourself some questions about your word and sentence choices, questions similar to those you use in realistic descriptive writing, but with more emphasis on emotional tonality. For instance, have you used specific, concrete nouns, adjectives, verbs, and adverbs, and clear transitions indicating time lapses and movements, in order to capture the emotional feel of the experience you are describing? Always search for the word that best fits your meaning and mood. A thesaurus (paper or online) can be very helpful in finding specific replacements for tired, imprecise, general terms. When it seems as though no word exists to communicate your exact sensory impression or mood, try using literal or figurative comparisons as in descriptive writing, but with an imaginative twist. Always try for originality in your figurative comparisons, as clichés like "She looked like an angel" or "It was as dark as a dungeon" can tarnish the original impression that you are trying to create.

Sentence Patterns   Your writing style is also created through the way you put words together. Thus your sentence patterns are a vital part of your narrative, as they should be in everything you write. Vary your sentence length for emphasis, using short sentences to slow down the action and to emphasize climactic moments. Try, too, to capture the voice rhythms of your characters through your punctuation. Remember that you can use a number of different sentence patterns (simple, compound, complex) as well as different ordering possibilities for the parts of your sentences. Again, in writing on your computer, try saving different versions of key sentences with different strategies for combination and punctuation; print them out and decide which works best in context. Consult your grammar text repeatedly to review the range of sentence patterns and punctuation strategies; experiment to heighten the dramatic effects of your writing.

Writing an engaging narrative is a challenge. It can also be a fulfilling writing experience that will bring you in touch with your past experiences, feelings, values, and identity.

THEMATIC INTRODUCTION: JOURNEYS IN MEMORY

Self-concept, imagination, dreams, and memories—all are born in childhood. A person's identity as a writer begins there, too. Through writing about your memories, you will begin to rediscover yourself through places, people, events, and stories that are still alive in your mind. These formative memories may have kindled your dreams while creating the foundation of your self-concept. Because writing is a process of self-discovery that has its roots in childhood, some of the poems, essays, and stories that we have included address issues of childhood identity in relationship to dreams and fantasies, expectations, and goals. In many of the selections that follow, essayists and fiction writers create vividly narrated moments, some positive and some painful, from their earliest remembered experiences. Some of the selections present perspectives on the nature and the effects of memory itself.

The chapter begins with a poem by Mark Strand, "Where Are the Waters of Childhood?" which takes the reader on an imaginative journey backwards in time, from childhood back to birth, in search of the essence of childhood experience and the nature of life itself. Our next selection, Patricia Hampl's "Memory and Imagination," also journeys back into the past, but with the desire to re-create a childhood world in the form of a sustained memoir that acknowledges the immense role played by the imagination in our efforts to reenter and communicate worlds from the distant past. The second chapter essay, from Saira Shah's memoir "The Storyteller's Daughter," narrates the attempts of the author's father to re-create through literature and cuisine the feeling and sensations of a vanished homeland, prewar Afghanistan.

The next two selections present traumatic, turning-point memories of family life. In "The Angel of the Candy Counter," from Maya Angelou's autobiography, *I Know Why the Caged Bird Sings*, Angelou dramatizes a childhood encounter with virulent racism, while in "Silent Dancing," Judith Ortiz Cofer explores how her childhood memories of her native Puerto Rican culture and relatives continue to have a powerful influence on her understanding and fears about her life in the United States.

Do our memories represent the deepest truth, or do they sometimes cloud and distort our pasts? In our next essay, Rachel Naomi Remen's "Remembering," negative memories are perceived as repressed events that sometimes need to be relived in order to reclaim a lost happiness. In "Muller Bros. Moving & Storage," acclaimed scientist and writer Stephen Jay Gould reflects on his own relationship with his grandfather as he asks readers to think about why people continue to cherish memories of the past, despite the fact that these memories often do not represent the physical reality of events. The final professional essay in the chapter, Susan L. Engel's "The Past: Audiences and Perspectives," goes beyond memories that attempt to recall scenes from a personal, individual past to discuss efforts by writers and museum curators to re-create larger, collective visions of the past, the global events that touch us all indirectly.

The chapter closes with a student essay by Melissa Burns, "The Best Seat in the House," which explores poignant recollections of her grandfather, who helped to provide her with the motivation to succeed.

Although most people mature and learn to function in the rational world, the dreams and ghosts of their childhoods continue to shape, haunt, and inspire their waking lives. Writing about the past can be one of the best ways to face and come to terms with the ghosts of memory. This type of writing can help us to formulate and construct realistic and positive dreams for the future.

Mark Strand

Where Are the Waters of Childhood?

Former Poet Laureate of the United States Mark Strand was born in 1934 on Prince Edward Island in Canada but was raised and educated in the United States and South America. He received his B.A. at Antioch College and a B.F.A. from Yale, where he studied painting. In 1962 he completed his M.A. at the University of Iowa, and in 1965 he spent a year as Fulbright Lecturer at the University of Brazil, where he was deeply influenced by contemporary Latin American poets. Strand has taught at many American universities, including Columbia, Princeton, and Harvard. He currently teaches in the Committee on Social Thought at the University of Chicago. He is the author of ten books of poems, including The Story of Our Lives *(1973),* The Continuous Life *(1990),* Dark Harbor *(1993), and* Blizzard of One *(1998), which won the Pulitzer Prize. His honors include the Bollingen Prize, a National Institute of Arts and Letters Award, as well as fellowships from the Academy of American Poets and the MacArthur Foundation. Strand's poems often are dreamlike and mysterious; many of them, like "Where Are the Waters of Childhood?" (from* The Late Hour, *1978), deal with memory and the distant past.*

JOURNAL

Narrate a dream or memory involving a house or environment you lived in many years ago, trying to get in touch with emotions you feel now and felt then about this place as well as specific images and details that capture your feelings about it.

See where the windows are boarded up,
where the gray siding shines in the sun and salt air

and the asphalt shingles on the roof have peeled or fallen off,
where tiers of oxeye daisies float on a sea of grass?
5 That's the place to begin.

Enter the kingdom of rot,
smell the damp plaster, step over the shattered glass,
the pockets of dust, the rags, the soiled remains of a mattress,
look at the rusted stove and sink, at the rectangular stain
10 on the wall where Winslow Homer's *Gulf Stream* hung.

Go to the room where your father and mother
would let themselves go in the drift and pitch of love,
and hear, if you can, the creak of their bed,
then go to the place where you hid.

15 Go to your room, to all the rooms whose cold, damp air you breathed,
to all the unwanted places where summer, fall, winter, spring,
seem the same unwanted season, where the trees you knew have died
and other trees have risen. Visit that other place
you barely recall, that other house half hidden.

20 See the two dogs burst into sight. When you leave,
they will cease, snuffed out in the glare of an earlier light.
Visit the neighbors down the block; he waters his lawn,
she sits on her porch, but not for long.
When you look again they are gone.

25 Keep going back, back to the field, flat and sealed in mist.
On the other side, a man and a woman are waiting;
they have come back, your mother before she was gray,
your father before he was white.

Now look at the North West Arm, how it glows a deep cerulean blue.
30 See the light on the grass, the one leaf burning, the cloud
that flares. You're almost there, in a moment your parents
will disappear, leaving you under the light of a vanished star,
under the dark of a star newly born. Now is the time.

Now you invent the boat of your flesh and set it upon the waters
35 and drift in the gradual swell, in the laboring salt.
Now you look down. The waters of childhood are there.

QUESTIONS FOR DISCUSSION

1. What is the effect of having the first stanza of the poem function as a question rather than as a command? How is this stanza the beginning of an answer to the question in the title?

2. As the reader is asked to "Enter the kingdom of rot," what images and physical details are encountered? How does the voice of the speaker of the poem help to guide the reader through this "kingdom," which is designated by the pronouns "you" and "your" as the reader's own past?

3. What images of water/moisture appear in the poem, and what emotional impression do they create? Why is there a focus on a "stain" left on the wall from a reproduction of a painting by Winslow Homer, *The Gulf Stream* (1899)?

4. Why are the speakers' parents mentioned in their bed in "the drift and pitch of love," and why is the reader placed in hiding and commanded, "Go to your room"?

5. What is witnessed in the poem as the reader is invited further back into the past? Why do you think the North West Arm, a body of water in Nova Scotia near which Strand was born, is mentioned? How do Strand's parents change as the poem moves back into the distant past?

6. What is the significance of the final lines of the poem, which take place after the parents and homes have disappeared? What is meant by the final description of the waters of childhood, with their "gradual swell, in the laboring salt," and of the reader at last adrift in "the boat of your flesh"?

CONNECTION

Compare the journey back into childhood taken in Strand's journey with the psychotherapeutic journey taken by the patient in Remen's essay "Remembering" in this chapter. What kind of closure do both Anna and Strand's narrator reach at the end of their respective journeys? (See page 159.)

IDEAS FOR WRITING

1. Develop your journal entry into a narrative essay about a place where you lived in your childhood or youth. Focus on a particular event that happened there and how it changed you. Refer in your narrative to some of the lines in "Where Are the Waters of Childhood?"

2. Write an essay in which you try to answer the question posed by the title of Strand's poem: "Where are the waters of childhood?" How does the poem answer the question, and how would you answer it from your own perspective and experience?

RELATED WEB SITES

Interview with Mark Strand
`www.mipoesias.com/Volume19Issue2/strand.html`
In this interview Mark Strand discusses his life in poetry, as well as early experiences that may have contributed to some of the images and places named in "Where Are the Waters of Childhood?"

Patricia Hampl

Memory and Imagination

*Born in St. Paul, Minnesota, in 1946, Patricia Hampl is a poet and memoirist
who writes about the importance of history, place, and beauty as revealed through
memories. She earned her B.A. in English from the University of Minnesota in
1968 and her M.F.A. from the University of Iowa in 1970. Hampl has taught
English and creative writing at the University of Minnesota since 1984. In 1992
she was awarded the prestigious MacArthur Award for creative achievement.
Hampl is the author of* A Romantic Education *(1981);* Virgin Time *(1992),
her account of her quest for religious understanding; and* I Could Tell You Stories: Sojourns in the Land of Memory *(1999). The article that follows,
"Memory and Imagination," is included in* The Anatomy of Memory: An
Anthology, *edited by James Hofstadter (1996).*

> **JOURNAL**
>
> Write about a memory that has remained important to you although you have
> never recorded it in words.

When I was seven, my father, who played the violin on Sundays with a
nicely tortured flair which we considered artistic, led me by the hand
down a long, unlit corridor in St. Luke's School basement, a sort of tunnel that
ended in a room full of pianos. There many little girls and a single sad boy were
playing truly tortured scales and arpeggios in a mash of troubled sound. My father gave me over to Sister Olive Marie, who did look remarkably like an olive.

Her oily face gleamed as if it had just been rolled out of a can and laid on
the white plate of her broad, spotless wimple. She was a small, plump woman;
her body and the small window of her face seemed to interpret the entire alphabet of olive: her face was a sallow green olive placed upon the jumbo ripe
olive of her black habit. I trusted her instantly and smiled, glad to have my
hand placed in the hand of a woman who made sense, who provided the satisfaction of being what she was: an Olive who looked like an Olive.

My father left me to discover the piano with Sister Olive Marie so that one
day I would join him in mutually tortured piano-violin duets for the edification

of my mother and brother who sat at the table meditatively spooning in the last of their pineapple sherbet until their part was called for: they put down their spoons and clapped while we bowed, while the sweet ice in their bowls melted, while the music melted, and we all melted a little into each other for a moment.

But first Sister Olive must do her work. I was shown middle C, which Sister seemed to think terribly important. I stared at middle C and then glanced away for a second. When my eye returned, middle C was gone, its slim finger lost in the complicated grasp of the keyboard. Sister Olive struck it again, finding it with laughable ease. She emphasized the importance of middle C, its central position, a sort of North Star of sound. I remember thinking, "Middle C is the belly button of the piano," an insight whose originality and accuracy stunned me with pride. For the first time in my life I was astonished by metaphor. I hesitated to tell the kindly Olive for some reason; apparently I understood a true metaphor is a risky business, revealing of the self. In fact, I have never, until this moment of writing it down, told my first metaphor to anyone.

5   Sunlight flooded the room; the pianos, all black, gleamed. Sister Olive, dressed in the colors of the keyboard, gleamed; middle C shimmered with meaning and I resolved never—never—to forget its location: it was the center of the world.

Then Sister Olive, who had had to show me middle C twice but who seemed to have drawn no bad conclusions about me anyway, got up and went to the windows on the opposite wall. She pulled the shades down, one after the other. The sun was too bright, she said. She sneezed as she stood at the windows with the sun shedding its glare over her. She sneezed and sneezed, crazy little convulsive sneezes, one after another, as helpless as if she had the hiccups.

"The sun makes me sneeze," she said when the fit was over and she was back at the piano. This was odd, too odd to grasp in the mind. I associated sneezing with colds, and colds with rain, fog, snow and bad weather. The sun, however, had caused Sister Olive to sneeze in this wild way, Sister Olive who gleamed benignly and who was so certain of the location of the center of the world. The universe wobbled a bit and became unreliable. Things were not, after all, necessarily what they seemed. Appearance deceived: here was the sun acting totally out of character, hurling this woman into sneezes, a woman so mild that she was named, so it seemed, for a bland object on a relish tray.

I was given a red book, the first Thompson book, and told to play the first piece over and over at one of the black pianos where the other children were crashing away. This, I was told, was called practicing. It sounded alluringly adult, practicing. The piece itself consisted mainly of middle C, and I excelled, thrilled by my savvy at being able to locate that central note amidst the cunning camouflage of all the other white keys before me. Thrilled too by the shiny red book that gleamed, as the pianos did, as Sister Olive did, as my eager eyes probably did. I sat at the formidable machine of the piano and got to know middle C intimately, preparing to be as tortured as I could manage one day soon with my father's violin at my side.

But at the moment Mary Katherine Reilly was at my side, playing something at least two or three lessons more sophisticated than my piece. I believe she even struck a chord. I glanced at her from the peasantry of single notes, shy, ready to pay homage. She turned toward me, stopped playing, and sized me up.

10 Sized me up and found a person ready to be dominated. Without introduction she said, "My grandfather invented the collapsible opera hat."

I nodded, I acquiesced, I was hers. With that little stroke it was decided between us—that she should be the leader, and I the side-kick. My job was admiration. Even when she added, "But he didn't make a penny from it. He didn't have a patent"—even then, I knew and she knew that this was not an admission of powerlessness, but the easy candor of a master, of one who can afford a weakness or two.

With the clairvoyance of all fated relationships based on dominance and submission, it was decided in advance: that when the time came for us to play duets, I should always play second piano, that I should spend my allowance to buy her the Twinkies she craved but was not allowed to have, that finally, I should let her copy from my test paper, and when confronted by our teacher, confess with convincing hysteria that it was I, I who had cheated, who had reached above myself to steal what clearly belonged to the rightful heir of the inventor of the collapsible opera hat. . . .

There must be a reason I remember that little story about my first piano lesson. In fact, it isn't a story, just a moment, the beginning of what could perhaps become a story. For the memoirist, more than for the fiction writer, the story seems already *there,* already accomplished and fully achieved in history ("in reality," as we naively say). For the memoirist, the writing of the story is a matter of transcription.

That, anyway, is the myth. But no memoirist writes for long without experiencing an unsettling disbelief about the reliability of memory, a hunch that memory is not, after all, *just* memory. I don't know why I remembered this fragment about my first piano lesson. I don't, for instance, have a single recollection of my first arithmetic lesson, the first time I studied Latin, the first time my grandmother tried to teach me to knit. Yet these things occurred too, and must have their stories.

15 It is the piano lesson that has trudged forward, clearing the haze of forgetfulness, showing itself bright with detail more than thirty years after the event. I did not choose to remember the piano lesson. It was simply there, like a book that has always been on the shelf, whether I ever read it or not, the binding and title showing as I skim across the contents of my life. On the day I wrote this fragment I happened to take that memory, not some other, from the shelf and paged through it. I found more detail, more event, perhaps a little more entertainment than I had expected, but the memory itself was there from the start. Waiting for me.

Or was it? When I reread what I had written just after I finished it, I realized that I had told a number of lies. I *think* it was my father who took me the first time for my piano lesson—but maybe he only took me to meet my teacher and there was no actual lesson that day. And did I even know then that he played the violin—didn't he take up his violin again much later, as a result of my piano playing, and not the reverse? And is it even remotely accurate to describe as "tortured" the musicianship of a man who began every day by belting out "Oh What a Beautiful Morning" as he shaved?

More: Sister Olive Marie did sneeze in the sun, but was her name Olive? As for her skin tone—I would have sworn it was olive-like; I would have been willing to spend the better part of an afternoon trying to write the exact description of imported Italian or Greek olive her face suggested: I wanted to get it right. But now, were I to write that passage over, it is her intense black eyebrows I would see, for suddenly they seem the central fact of that face, some indicative mark of her serious and patient nature. But the truth is, I don't remember the woman at all. She's a sneeze in the sun and a finger touching middle C. That, at least, is steady and clear.

Worse: I didn't have the Thompson book as my piano text. I'm sure of that because I remember envying children who did have this wonderful book with its pictures of children and animals printed on the pages of music.

As for Mary Katherine Reilly. She didn't even go to grade school with me (and her name isn't Mary Katherine Reilly—but I made that change on purpose). I met her in Girl Scouts and only went to school with her later, in high school. Our relationship was not really one of leader and follower; I played first piano most of the time in duets. She certainly never copied anything from a test paper of mine: she was a better student, and cheating just wasn't a possibility with her. Though her grandfather (or someone in her family) did invent the collapsible opera hat and I remember that she was proud of that fact, she didn't tell me this news as a deft move in a childish power play.

20 So, what was I doing in this brief memoir? Is it simply an example of the curious relation a fiction writer has to the material of her own life? Maybe. That may have some value in itself. But to tell the truth (if anyone still believes me capable of telling the truth), I wasn't writing fiction. I was writing memoir—or was trying to. My desire was to be accurate. I wished to embody the myth of memoir: to write as an act of dutiful transcription.

Yet clearly the work of writing narrative caused me to do something very different from transcription. I am forced to admit that memoir is not a matter of transcription, that memory itself is not a warehouse of finished stories, not a static gallery of framed pictures. I must admit that I invented. But why?

Two whys: why did I invent, and then, if a memoirist must inevitably invent rather than transcribe, why do I—why should anybody—write memoir at all?

I must respond to these impertinent questions because they, like the bumper sticker I saw the other day commanding all who read it to QUESTION AUTHORITY, challenge my authority as a memoirist and as a witness.

It still comes as a shock to realize that I don't write about what I know: I write in order to find out what I know. Is it possible to convey to a reader the enormous degree of blankness, confusion, hunch and uncertainty lurking in the act of writing? When I am the reader, not the writer, I too fall into the lovely illusion that the words before me (in a story by Mavis Gallant, an essay by Carol Bly, a memoir by M. F. K. Fisher), which *read* so inevitably, must also have been *written* exactly as they appear, rhythm and cadence, language and syntax, the powerful waves of the sentences laying themselves on the smooth beach of the page one after another faultlessly.

25   But here I sit before a yellow legal pad, and the long page of the preceding two paragraphs is a jumble of crossed-out lines, false starts, confused order. A mess. The mess of my mind trying to find out what it wants to say. This is a writer's frantic, grabby mind, not the poised mind of a reader ready to be edified or entertained.

I sometimes think of the reader as a cat, endlessly fastidious, capable, by turns, of mordant indifference and riveted attention, luxurious, recumbent, and ever poised. Whereas the writer is absolutely a dog, panting and moping, too eager for an affectionate scratch behind the ears, lunging frantically after any old stick thrown in the distance.

The blankness of a new page never fails to intrigue and terrify me. Sometimes, in fact, I think my habit of writing on long yellow sheets comes from an atavistic fear of the writer's stereotypic "blank white page." At least when I begin writing, my page isn't utterly blank; at least it has a wash of color on it, even if the absence of words must finally be faced on a yellow sheet as truly as on a blank white one. Well, we all have our ways of whistling in the dark.

If I approach writing from memory with the assumption that I know what I wish to say, I assume that intentionality is running the show. Things are not that simple. Or perhaps writing is even more profoundly simple, more telegraphic and immediate in its choices than the grating wheels and chugging engine of logic and rational intention. The heart, the guardian of intuition with its secret, often fearful intentions, is the boss. Its commands are what a writer obeys—often without knowing it. Or, I do.

That's why I'm a strong adherent of the first draft. And why it's worth pausing for a moment to consider what first draft really is. By my lights, the piano lesson memoir is a first draft. That doesn't mean it exists here exactly as I first wrote it. I like to think I've cleaned it up from the first time I put it down on paper. I've cut some adjectives here, toned down the hyperbole there, smoothed a transition, cut a repetition—that sort of housekeeperly tidying-up. But the piece remains a first draft because I haven't yet gotten to know it, haven't given it a chance to tell me anything. For me, writing a first draft is a little like meeting someone for the first time. I come away with a wary acquaintanceship, but the real friendship (if any) and genuine intimacy—that's all down the road. Intimacy with a piece of writing, as with a person, comes from paying attention to the revelations it is capable of giving, not by imposing my own preconceived notions, no matter how well-intentioned they might be.

30   I try to let pretty much anything happen in a first draft. A careful first draft is a failed first draft. That may be why there are so many inaccuracies in the piano lesson memoir: I didn't censor, I didn't judge. I kept moving. But I would not

publish this piece as a memoir on its own in its present state. It isn't the "lies" in
the piece that give me pause, though a reader has a right to expect a memoir to
be as accurate as the writer's memory can make it. No, it isn't the lies themselves
that makes the piano lesson memoir a first draft and therefore "unpublishable."

The real trouble: the piece hasn't yet found its subject; it isn't yet about what
it wants to be about. Note: what *it* wants, not what I want. The difference has to
do with the relation a memoirist—any writer, in fact—has to unconscious or
half-known intentions and impulses in composition.

Now that I have the fragment down on paper, I can read this little piece as a
mystery which drops clues to the riddle of my feelings, like a culprit who wishes
to be apprehended. My narrative self (the culprit who has invented) wishes to
be discovered by my reflective self, the self who wants to understand and make
sense of a half-remembered story about a nun sneezing in the sun. . . .

We only store in memory images of value. The value may be lost over the passage of time (I was baffled about why I remembered that sneezing nun, for example), but that's the implacable judgment of feeling: *this,* we say somewhere
deep within us, is something I'm hanging on to. And of course, often we cleave
to things because they possess heavy negative charges. Pain likes to be vivid.

Over time, the value (the feeling) and the stored memory (the image) may
become estranged. Memoir seeks a permanent home for feeling and image, a
habitation where they can live together in harmony. Naturally, I've had a lot of
experiences since I packed away that one from the basement of St. Luke's
School; that piano lesson has been effaced by waves of feeling for other moments and episodes. I persist in believing the event has value—after all, I remember it—but in writing the memoir I did not simply relive the experience.
Rather, I explored the mysterious relationship between all the images I could
round up and the even more impacted feelings that caused me to store the images safely away in memory. Stalking the relationship, seeking the congruence
between stored image and hidden emotion—that's the real job of memoir.

35   By writing about the first piano lesson, I've come to know things I could not
know otherwise. But I only know these things as a result of reading this first draft.
While I was writing, I was following the images, letting the details fill the room
of the page and use the furniture as they wished. I was their dutiful servant—
or thought I was. In fact, I was the faithful retainer of my hidden feelings which
were giving the commands.

I really did feel, for instance, that Mary Katherine Reilly was far superior to
me. She was smarter, funnier, more wonderful in every way—that's how I saw it.
Our friendship (or she herself) did not require that I become her vassal, yet perhaps in my heart that was something I wanted; I wanted a way to express my feeling of admiration. I suppose I waited until this memoir to begin to find the way.

Just as, in the memoir, I finally possess that red Thompson book with the
barking dogs and bleating lambs and winsome children. I couldn't (and still
can't) remember what my own music book was, so I grabbed the name and image of the one book I could remember. It was only in reviewing the piece after

writing it that I saw my inaccuracy. In pondering this "lie," I came to see what I was up to: I was getting what I wanted. At last.

The truth of many circumstances and episodes in the past emerges for the memoirist through details (the red music book, the fascination with a nun's name and gleaming face), but these details are not merely information, not flat facts. Such details are not allowed to lounge. They must work. Their work is the creation of symbol. But it's more accurate to call it the *recognition* of symbol. For meaning is not "attached" to the detail by the memoirist; meaning is revealed. That's why a first draft is important. Just as the first meeting (good or bad) with someone who later becomes the beloved is important and is often reviewed for signals, meanings, omens and indications.

Now I can look at that music book and see it not only as "a detail," but for what it is, how it *acts*. See it as the small red door leading straight into the dark room of my childhood longing and disappointment. That red book *becomes* the palpable evidence of that longing. In other words, it becomes symbol. There is no symbol, no life-of-the-spirit in the general or the abstract. Yet a writer wishes—indeed all of us wish—to speak about profound matters that are, like it or not, general and abstract. We wish to talk to each other about life and death, about love, despair, loss, and innocence. We sense that in order to live together we must learn to speak of peace, of history, of meaning and values. Those are a few.

40   We seek a means of exchange, a language which will renew these ancient concerns and make them wholly and pulsingly ours. Instinctively, we go to our store of private images and associations for our authority to speak of these weighty issues. We find, in our details and broken and obscured images, the language of symbol. Here memory impulsively reaches out its arms and embraces imagination. That is the resort to invention. It isn't a lie, but an act of necessity, as the innate urge to locate personal truth always is.

All right. Invention is inevitable. But why write memoir? Why not call it fiction and be done with all the hashing about, wondering where memory stops and imagination begins? And if memoir seeks to talk about "the big issues," about history and peace, death and love—why not leave these reflections to those with expert and scholarly knowledge? Why let the common or garden variety memoirist into the club? I'm thinking again of the bumper sticker: why Question Authority?

My answer, of course, is a memoirist's answer. Memoir must be written because each of us must have a created version of the past. Created: that is, real, tangible, made of the stuff of a life lived in place and in history. And the down side of any created thing as well: we must live with a version that attaches us to our limitations, to the inevitable subjectivity of our points of view. We must acquiesce to our experience and our gift to transform experience into meaning and value. You tell me your story, I'll tell you my story.

If we refuse to do the work of creating this personal version of the past, someone else will do it for us. That is a scary political fact. "The struggle of man against power," a character in Milan Kundera's novel *The Book of Laughter and*

Forgetting says, "is the struggle of memory against forgetting." He refers to willful political forgetting, the habit of nations and those in power (Question Authority!) to deny the truth of memory in order to disarm moral and ethical power. It's an efficient way of controlling masses of people. It doesn't even require much bloodshed, as long as people are entirely willing to give over their personal memories. Whole histories can be rewritten. As Czeslaw Milosz said in his 1980 Nobel Prize lecture, the number of books published that seek to deny the existence of the Nazi death camps now exceeds one hundred.

What is remembered is what *becomes* reality. If we "forget" Auschwitz, if we "forget" My Lai, what then do we remember? And what is the purpose of our remembering? If we think of memory naively, as a simple story, logged like a documentary in the archive of the mind, we miss its beauty but also its function. The beauty of memory rests in its talent for rendering detail, for paying homage to the senses, its capacity to love the particles of life, the richness and idiosyncrasy of our existence. The function of memory, on the other hand, is intensely personal and surprisingly political.

45 Our capacity to move forward as developing beings rests on a healthy relation with the past. Psychotherapy, that widespread method of mental health, relies heavily on memory and on the ability to retrieve and organize images and events from the personal past. We carry our wounds and perhaps even worse, our capacity to wound, forward with us. If we learn not only to tell our stories but to listen to what our stories tell us—to write the first draft and then return for the second draft—we are doing the work of memoir.

Memoir is the intersection of narration and reflection, of story-telling and essay-writing. It can present its story *and* reflect and consider the meaning of the story. It is a peculiarly open form, inviting broken and incomplete images, half-recollected fragments, all the mass (and mess) of detail. It offers to shape this confusion—and in shaping, of course it necessarily creates a work of art, not a legal document. But then, even legal documents are only valiant attempts to consign the truth, the whole truth and nothing but the truth to paper. Even they remain versions.

Locating touchstones—the red music book, the olive Olive, my father's violin playing—is deeply satisfying. Who knows why? Perhaps we all sense that we can't grasp the whole truth and nothing but the truth of our experience. Just can't be done. What can be achieved, however, is a version of its swirling, changing wholeness. A memoirist must acquiesce to selectivity, like any artist. The version we dare to write is the only truth, the only relationship we can have with the past. Refuse to write your life and you have no life. At least, that is the stern view of the memoirist.

Personal history, logged in memory, is a sort of slide projector flashing images on the wall of the mind. And there's precious little order to the slides in the rotating carousel. Beyond that confusion, who knows who is running the projector? A memoirist steps into this darkened room of flashing, unorganized images and stands blinking for a while. Maybe for a long while. But eventually, as with any attempt to tell a story, it is necessary to put something first, then something else. And so on, to the end. That's a first draft. Not necessarily the truth, not even *a* truth sometimes, but the first attempt to create a shape.

The first thing I usually notice at this stage of composition is the appalling inaccuracy of the piece. Witness my first piano lesson draft. Invention is screamingly evident in what I intended to be transcription. But here's the further truth: I feel no shame. In fact, it's only now that my interest in the piece truly quickens. For I can see what isn't there, what is shyly hugging the walls, hoping not to be seen. I see the filmy shape of the next draft. I see a more acute version of the episode or—this is more likely—an entirely new piece rising from the ashes of the first attempt.

50 The next draft of the piece would have to be a true re-vision, a new seeing of the materials of the first draft. Nothing merely cosmetic will do—no rouge buffing up the opening sentence, no glossy adjective to lift a sagging line, nothing to attempt covering a patch of gray writing. None of that. I can't say for sure, but my hunch is the revision would lead me to more writing about my father (why was I so impressed by that ancestral inventor of the collapsible opera hat? Did I feel I had nothing as remarkable in my own background? Did this make me feel inadequate?). I begin to think perhaps Sister Olive is less central to this business than she is in this draft. She is meant to be a moment, not a character.

And so I might proceed, if I were to undertake a new draft of the memoir. I begin to feel a relationship developing between a former self and me.

And, even more compelling, a relationship between an old world and me. Some people think of autobiographical writing as the precious occupation of a particularly self-absorbed person. Maybe, but I don't buy that. True memoir is written in an attempt to find not only a self but a world.

The self-absorption that seems to be the impetus and embarrassment of autobiography turns into (or perhaps always was) a hunger for the world. Actually, it begins as hunger for *a* world, one gone or lost, effaced by time or a more sudden brutality. But in the act of remembering, the personal environment expands, resonates beyond itself, beyond its "subject," into the endless and tragic recollection that is history.

We look at old family photographs in which we stand next to black, boxy Fords and are wearing period costumes, and we do not gaze fascinated because there we are young again, or there we are standing, as we never will again in life, next to our mother. We stare and drift because there we are . . . historical. It is the dress, the black car that dazzle us now and draw us beyond our mother's bright arms which once caught us. We reach into the attractive impersonality of something more significant than ourselves. We write memoir, in other words. We accept the humble position of writing a version rather than "the whole truth."

55 I suppose I write memoir because of the radiance of the past—it draws me back and back to it. Not that the past is beautiful. In our commercial memoir, in history, the death camps *are* back there. In intimate life too, the record is

usually pretty mixed. "I could tell you stories . . . " people say and drift off, meaning terrible things have happened to them.

But the past is radiant. It has the light of lived life. A memoirist wishes to touch it. No one owns the past, though typically the first act of new political regimes, whether of the left or the right, is to attempt to re-write history, to grab the past and make it over so the end comes out right. So their power looks inevitable.

No one owns the past, but it is a grave error (another age would have said a grave sin) not to inhabit memory. Sometimes I think it is all we really have. But that may be a trifle melodramatic. At any rate, memory possesses authority for the fearful self in a world where it is necessary to have authority in order to Question Authority.

There may be no more pressing intellectual need in our culture than for people to become sophisticated about the function of memory. The political implications of the loss of memory are obvious. The authority of memory is a personal confirmation of selfhood. To write one's life is to live it twice, and the second living is both spiritual and historical, for a memoir reaches deep within the personality as it seeks its narrative form and also grasps the life-of-the-times as no political treatise can.

Our most ancient metaphor says life is a journey. Memoir is travel writing, then, notes taken along the way, telling how things looked and what thoughts occurred. But I cannot think of the memoirist as a tourist. This is the traveller who goes on foot, living the journey, taking on mountains, enduring deserts, marveling at the lush green places. Moving through it all faithfully, not so much a survivor with a harrowing tale to tell as a pilgrim, seeking, wondering.

Questions for Discussion

1. According to Hampl, what are the role and importance of a first draft? Why shouldn't a first draft be a "careful" draft?
2. Hampl states that the heart is the "boss" of her writing process. What do you think she means in this statement? Is your heart the boss of your writing process? In what ways is Hampl's insight significant to you?
3. Why does Hampl tell the story of Sister Olive and Mary Katherine Reilly only to later show that her memory could not possibly reflect the actual relationship that she had with them? Why is her memory more important to her than what actually happened?
4. How has reading this essay changed your understanding of the relationships among truth, fact, memory, and the imagination of a writer?
5. What does Hampl mean when she says that if you "[r]efuse to write your life . . . you have no life"? What examples does she provide in her memoir to support her claim? Do you agree or disagree with Hampl?
6. Identify several of Hampl's comparisons or metaphors that you found especially effective and persuasive. Explain how these metaphors help to illustrate her meanings.

CONNECTION

Compare Hampl's use of examples of the unreliability of memory to those used by Stephen Jay Gould in his essay in this chapter. What different conclusions do the authors draw from their examples (see page 163)?

IDEAS FOR WRITING

1. Working through several drafts, develop your journal entry above into a memory narrative. Then discuss how writing about the memory has affected you. Has it changed your understanding of the memory's meaning and importance? What did you learn about yourself through writing your memory narrative?

2. Write an essay that explores the differences and similarities between memoir and fiction. You should refer to Hampl's essay, but also do some research into the topic and explore the views of other writers to support your claims and conclusions.

RELATED WEB SITES

Patricia Hampl
`http://english.cla.umn.edu/faculty/hampl/hampl.htm`
Visit this URL for information on Patricia Hampl, including her achievements, works, background, and central interests. A link to her teaching philosophy is also included.

Memoir Writing Links
`www.kporterfield.com/memoir/Memoir_Links.html`
Several links to sites about memoir writing on the Web will be found at this URL as well as links to creativity, journaling, the arts, and healing.

Saira Shah

The Storyteller's Daughter

Saira Shah was born in Britain into an Afghan family. Her father, Idries Shah, was a famous Sufi writer, translator, and storyteller. Saira Shah has said, "Stories were a part of my childhood—and never considered just for children. This was a family tradition and a very Afghan one." She first visited Afghanistan at age 21 and worked there for three years covering the guerilla war against the Soviet occupiers; later, she reported stories for Britain's Channel 4 News about the NATO action in Kosovo, massacres in Algeria, the fall of President Mobutu Sésé Seko in Zaire, the Palestinian-Israeli conflict, and bombings in Northern Ireland. Her reporting for Channel 4 News won her awards from Amnesty International, the New

York Film Festival, and the Royal Television Society. She has produced two award-winning documentaries about Afghanistan: Beneath the Veil *and* Unholy War. *Her memoir,* The Storyteller's Daughter: Return to a Lost Homeland *(2003), is an account of her search for a cultural identity. The selection included here is from the beginning of her memoir; in it, Shah explores her protected yet alienated childhood living in England as an Afghani in exile.*

JOURNAL

Write a family story about a place of family origin in another area or country.

I am three years old. I am sitting on my father's knee. He is telling me of a magical place: the fairytale landscape you enter in dreams. Fountains fling diamond droplets into mosaic pools. Coloured birds sing in the fruitladen orchards. The pomegranates burst and their insides are rubies. Fruit is so abundant that even the goats are fed on melons. The water has magical properties: you can fill to bursting with fragrant *pilau,* then step to the brook and drink—and you will be ready to eat another meal.

On three sides of the plateau majestic mountains tower, capped with snow. The fourth side overlooks a sunny valley where, gleaming far below, sprawls a city of villas and minarets. And here is the best part of the story: it is true.

The garden is in Paghman, where my family had its seat for nine hundred years. The jewel-like city it overlooks is the Afghan capital, Kabul. The people of Paghman call the capital Kabul *jan:* beloved Kabul. We call it that too, for this is where we belong.

"Whatever outside appearances may be, no matter who tells you otherwise, this garden, this country, these are your origin. This is where you are truly from. Keep it in your heart, Saira *jan.* Never forget."

5   Any western adult might have told me that this was an exile's tale of a lost Eden: the place you dream about, to which you can never return. But even then, I wasn't going to accept that. Even then, I had absorbed enough of the East to feel I belonged there. And too much of the West not to try to nail down dreams.

My father understood the value of stories: he was a writer. My parents had picked Kent as an idyllic place to bring up their children, but we were never allowed to forget our Afghan background.

Periodically during my childhood, my father would come upon the kitchen like a storm. Western systematic method quickly melted before the inspiration of the East. Spice jars tumbled down from their neat beechwood rack and disgorged heaps of coloured powder on to the melamine sideboard. Every pan was pressed into service and extra ones were borrowed from friends and neighbours. The staid old Aga wheezed exotic vapours—*saffran, zeera, gashneesh;* their scents to this day are as familiar to me as my own breath.

In the midst of this mayhem presided my father, the alchemist. Like so many expatriates, when it came to maintaining the traditions, customs and food of his own country he was *plus royaliste que le roi.* Rather than converting lead into gold, my father's alchemical art transported our English country kitchen to the furthest reaches of the Hindu Kush.

We children were the sorcerer's apprentices: we chopped onions and split cardamom pods, nibbling the fragrant black seeds as we worked. We crushed garlic and we peeled tomatoes. He showed us how to steep saffron, to strain yoghurt and to cook the rice until it was *dana-dar,* possessing grains—that is, to the point where it crumbles into three or four perfect round seeds if you rub it between your fingers.

10   In the kitchen, my father's essential *Afghaniyat,* Afghanness, was most apparent. The Afghan love of *pilau* is as fundamental to the national character as the Italian fondness for spaghetti. The Amir Habibullah, a former ruler of Afghanistan, would demolish a vast meal of *pilau,* meatballs and sauce for lunch, then turn to his courtiers and ask: "Now, noblemen and friends, what shall we cook tonight?"

We knew to produce at least three times more *pilau* than anyone could ever be expected to eat. Less would have been an insult to our name and contrary to the Afghan character. As my great-great-great-grandfather famously roared: "How dare you ask me for a *small* favour?"

If, at any point, my father found himself with an unexpected disaster—rice that went soggy or an overboiling pan that turned the Aga's hotplate into a sticky mess—he would exclaim: "Back in Afghanistan, we had cooks to do this work!"

He would tell us, with Afghan hyperbole: "We are making a *Shahi pilau,* a *pilau* fit for kings. This recipe has been handed down through our family since it was prepared for up to four thousand guests at the court of your ancestors. It is far better than the *pilau* you will find when you visit homes in Afghanistan today."

On one notable occasion, my father discovered the artificial food colouring, tartrazine. A *pilau*-making session was instantly convened. Like a conjurer pulling off a particularly effective trick, he showed us how just one tiny teaspoon could transform a gigantic cauldron of *pilau* to a virulent shade of yellow. We were suitably impressed. From that moment on, traditional saffron was discarded for this intoxicating substance.

15   Years later, I learned that all of the Afghan dishes my father had taught me diverged subtly from their originals. His method of finishing off the parboiled rice in the oven, for example, was an innovation of his own. Straining yoghurt through cheesecloth turned out to be merely the first stage in an elaborate process. In Kent, rancid sheep's fat was hard to come by, so he substituted butter. Cumin was an Indian contamination. And so it went on.

Yet although his methods and even his ingredients were different, my father's finished dishes tasted indistinguishable from the originals. He had conveyed their essential quality; the minutiae had been swept away.

During these cookery sessions, we played a wonderful game. We planned the family trip to Afghanistan that always seemed to be just round the corner. How we would go back to Paghman, stroll in the gardens, visit our old family home and greet the relatives we had never met. When we arrived in the Paghman mountains, the men would fire their guns in the air—we shouldn't worry, that was the Afghan way of welcome and celebration. They would carry us on their shoulders, whooping and cheering, and in the evening we would eat a *pilau* that eclipsed even the great feasts of the court of our ancestors.

My mother's family background, which is Parsee from India, rarely got a look in. As far as my father was concerned, his offspring were pure Afghan. For years, the mere mention of the Return was enough to stoke us children into fits of excitement. It was so much more alluring than our mundane Kentish lives, which revolved round the family's decrepit Land Rover and our pet Labrador, Honey.

"Can we take the Land Rover?" asked my brother Tahir.

20   "We shall take a fleet of Land Rovers," said my father grandly.

My sister Safia piped up: "Can we take Honey?"

There was an uncomfortable pause. Even my father's flight of fantasy balked at introducing to Afghans as a beloved member of our family that unclean animal, the dog.

When I was fifteen, the Soviet Union invaded and occupied Afghanistan. During a *pilau*-making session quite soon after that, I voiced an anxiety that had been growing for some time now. How could my father expect us to be truly Afghan when we had grown up outside an Afghan community? When we went back home, wouldn't we children be strangers, foreigners in our own land? I expected, and possibly hoped for, the soothing account of our triumphant and imminent return to Paghman. It didn't come. My father looked tired and sad. His answer startled me: "I've given you stories to replace a community. They are your community."

"But surely stories can't replace experience."

25   He picked up a packet of dehydrated onion. "Stories are like these onions— like dried experience. They aren't the original experience but they are more than nothing at all. You think about a story, you turn it over in your mind, and it becomes something else." He added hot water to the onion. "It's not fresh onion—fresh experience—but it is something that can help you to recognize experience when you come across it. Experiences follow patterns, which repeat themselves again and again. In our tradition, stories can help you recognize the shape of an experience, to make sense of and to deal with it. So, you see, what you may take for mere snippets of myth and legend encapsulate what you need to know to guide you on your way anywhere among Afghans."

"Well, as soon as I'm eighteen I'm going to go to see for myself," I said, adding craftily: "Then perhaps I'll have fresh experiences that will help me grow up."

My father had been swept along on the tide of his analogy. Now, he suddenly became a parent whose daughter was at an impressionable age and whose country was embroiled in a murderous war.

"If you would only grow up a little in the first place," he snapped, "then you would realize that you don't need to go at all." . . .

For many years, in the secret cubbyhole where precious things were stored, my father kept a dusty file containing two pieces of paper. The first was the crumbling title deed to our estate in Paghman. The other was our family tree, stretching back before the Prophet Muhammad, two thousand years back, to the time before my family had even heard of Afghanistan.

both traditions, then draw some conclusions about the values inherent in both of them.

6. How does the Iranian Qur'an teacher hired by Saira's father represent the kind of change sweeping the Muslim world at the time? What is the teacher's view of the Shah household, and why is he dismissed?

CONNECTION

Compare Shah's memories of her childhood as an exile or immigrant with those of Judith Ortiz Cofer in her memoir "Recollections of a Puerto Rican Childhood" (see page 151). How do both writers recall rituals designed to keep the homeland culture alive in a new cultural environment?

IDEAS FOR WRITING

1. Develop your journal entry into an essay about childhood stories told to you about another place or country. Indicate the impact such stories had on you as you were growing up. If you were able to visit such a place, how did your firsthand experiences differ from the experiences and expectations derived from the stories you had been told?
2. Do some research into the conflict between "orthodox," or fundamentalist, Muslim beliefs and the philosophy and beliefs emphasized by the Baghawi of Herat compilation or another, less absolutist branch of the faith.

RELATED WEB SITES

Interview with Saira Shah

`www.identitytheory.com/interviews/birnbaum133.html`

In this interview, Saira Shah discusses the formative experiences that led her to travel from her protected home environment to Afghanistan and to become a journalist and documentary filmmaker.

Asia Source Interview with Saira Shah

`www.asiasource.org/news/special_reports/shah.cfm`

The Asia Source interview focuses on the audience for Shah's memoir and the East/West dichotomy the book emphasizes.

Maya Angelou

The Angel of the Candy Counter

Maya Angelou (b. 1928) grew up in Stamps, Arkansas, where she spent her childhood with her grandmother, a storekeeper and a leader in the African American community. Angelou has worked as a dancer, actress, teacher, and screenwriter;

currently she is a professor of American Studies at Wake Forest University. An-
gelou's works include Complete Collected Poems *(1994),* The Challenge of
Creative Leadership *(1996),* A Song Flying Up to Heaven *(2002), and*
Halleluyah! The Welcome Table: A Life Time of Memories with Recipes
(2004). Her autobiographical writings reflect on the impact of poverty and racism
on the black community, as well as present moments of joy, insight, and creative ex-
pression that sometimes can ease the pain of oppression, as can be seen in the fol-
lowing selection excerpted from the first book of her memoir, I Know Why the
Caged Bird Sings *(1970).*

JOURNAL

Write about a time in your childhood when you retreated into fantasy to help
protect yourself from feelings of rejection or loss. How did the fantasy help you to
cope with your situation?

The Angel of the candy counter had found me out at last, and was exacting
excruciating penance for all the stolen Milky Ways, Mounds, Mr. Goodbars
and Hersheys with Almonds. I had two cavities that were rotten to the gums.
The pain was beyond the bailiwick of crushed aspirins or oil of cloves. Only one
thing could help me, so I prayed earnestly that I'd be allowed to sit under the
house and have the building collapse on my left jaw. Since there was no Negro
dentist in Stamps, nor doctor either, for that matter, Momma had dealt with
previous toothaches by pulling them out (a string tied to the tooth with the
other end looped over her fist), pain killers and prayer. In this particular instance the medicine had proved ineffective; there wasn't enough enamel left to
hook a string on, and the prayers were being ignored because the Balancing
Angel was blocking their passage.

I lived a few days and nights in blinding pain, not so much toying with as seriously considering the idea of jumping in the well, and Momma decided I had
to be taken to a dentist. The nearest Negro dentist was in Texarkana, twenty-
five miles away, and I was certain that I'd be dead long before we reached half
the distance. Momma said we'd go to Dr. Lincoln, right in Stamps, and he'd
take care of me. She said he owed her a favor.

I knew that there were a number of whitefolks in town that owed her favors.
Bailey and I had seen the books which showed how she had lent money to
Blacks and whites alike during the Depression, and most still owed her. But I
couldn't aptly remember seeing Dr. Lincoln's name, nor had I ever heard of a
Negro's going to him as a patient. However, Momma said we were going, and
put water on the stove for our baths. I had never been to a doctor, so she told
me that after the bath (which would make my mouth feel better) I had to put
on freshly starched and ironed underclothes from inside out. The ache failed
to respond to the bath, and I knew then that the pain was more serious than
that which anyone had ever suffered.

Before we left the Store, she ordered me to brush my teeth and then wash my mouth with Listerine. The idea of even opening my clamped jaws increased the pain, but upon her explanation that when you go to a doctor you have to clean yourself all over, but most especially the part that's to be examined, I screwed up my courage and unlocked my teeth. The cool air in my mouth and the jarring of my molars dislodged what little remained of my reason. I had frozen to the pain, my family nearly had to tie me down to take the toothbrush away. It was no small effort to get me started on the road to the dentist. Momma spoke to all the passers by, but didn't stop to chat. She explained over her shoulder that we were going to the doctor and she'd "pass the time of day" on our way home.

5   Until we reached the pond the pain was my world, an aura that haloed me for three feet around. Crossing the bridge into whitefolks' country, pieces of sanity pushed themselves forward. I had to stop moaning and start walking straight. The white towel, which was drawn under my chin and tied over my head, had to be arranged. If one was dying, it had to be done in style if the dying took place in whitefolks' part of town.

On the other side of the bridge the ache seemed to lessen as if a whitebreeze blew off the whitefolks and cushioned everything in their neighborhood— including my jaw. The gravel road was smoother, the stones smaller and the tree branches hung down around the path and nearly covered us. If the pain didn't diminish then, the familiar yet strange sights hypnotized me into believing that it had.

But my head continued to throb with the measured insistence of a bass drum, and how could a toothache pass the calaboose, hear the songs of the prisoners, their blues and laughter, and not be changed? How could one or two or even a mouthful of angry tooth roots meet a wagonload of powhitetrash children, endure their idiotic snobbery and not feel less important?

Behind the building which housed the dentist's office ran a small path used by servants and those tradespeople who catered to the butcher and Stamps' one restaurant. Momma and I followed that lane to the backstairs of Dentist Lincoln's office. The sun was bright and gave the day a hard reality as we climbed up the steps to the second floor.

Momma knocked on the back door and a young white girl opened it to show surprise at seeing us there. Momma said she wanted to see Dentist Lincoln and to tell him Annie was there. The girl closed the door firmly. Now the humiliation of hearing Momma describe herself as if she had no last name to the young white girl was equal to the physical pain. It seemed terribly unfair to have a toothache and a headache and have to bear at the same time the heavy burden of Blackness.

10   It was always possible that the teeth would quiet down and maybe drop out of their own accord. Momma said we would wait. We leaned in the harsh sunlight on the shaky railings of the dentist's back porch for over an hour.

He opened the door and looked at Momma. "Well, Annie, what can I do for you?"

He didn't see the towel around my jaw or notice my swollen face.

Momma said, "Dentist Lincoln. It's my grandbaby here. She got two rotten teeth that's giving her a fit."

She waited for him to acknowledge the truth of her statement. He made no comment, orally or facially.

15   "She had this toothache purt' near four days now, and today I said, 'Young lady, you going to the Dentist.'"

"Annie?"

"Yes, sir, Dentist Lincoln."

He was choosing words the way people hunt for shells. "Annie, you know I don't treat nigra, colored people."

"I know, Dentist Lincoln. But this here is just my little grandbaby, and she ain't gone be no trouble to you . . . "

20   "Annie, everybody has a policy. In this world you have to have a policy. Now, my policy is I don't treat colored people."

The sun had baked the oil out of Momma's skin and melted the Vaseline in her hair. She shone greasily as she leaned out of the dentist's shadow.

"Seem like to me, Dentist Lincoln, you might look after her, she ain't nothing but a little mite. And seems like maybe you owe me a favor or two."

He reddened slightly. "Favor or no favor. The money has all been repaid to you and that's the end of it. Sorry, Annie." He had his hand on the doorknob. "Sorry." His voice was a bit kinder on the second "Sorry," as if he really was.

Momma said, "I wouldn't press on you like this for myself but I can't take No. Not for my grandbaby. When you come to borrow my money you didn't have to beg. You asked me, and I lent it. Now, it wasn't my policy. I ain't no moneylender, but you stood to lose this building and I tried to help you out."

25   "It's been paid, and raising your voice won't make me change my mind. My policy . . . " He let go of the door and stepped nearer Momma. The three of us were crowded on the small landing. "Annie, my policy is I'd rather stick my hand in a dog's mouth than in a nigger's."

He had never once looked at me. He turned his back and went through the door into the cool beyond. Momma backed up inside herself for a few minutes. I forget everything except her face which was almost a new one to me. She leaned over and took the doorknob, and in her everyday soft voice she said, "Sister, go on downstairs. Wait for me. I'll be there directly."

Under the most common of circumstances I knew it did no good to argue with Momma. So I walked down the steep stairs, afraid to look back and afraid not to do so. I turned as the door slammed, and she was gone.

Momma walked in that room as if she owned it. She shoved that silly nurse aside with one hand and strode into the dentist's office. He was sitting in his chair, sharpening his mean instruments and putting extra sting into his medicines. Her eyes were blazing like live coals and her arms had doubled themselves in length. He looked up at her just before she caught him by the collar of his white jacket.

"Stand up when you see a lady, you contemptuous scoundrel." Her tongue had thinned and the words rolled off well enunciated. Enunciated and sharp like little claps of thunder.

30   *The dentist had no choice but to stand at R.O.T.C. attention. His head dropped after a minute and his voice was humble. "Yes, ma'am, Mrs. Henderson."*

"You knave, do you think you acted like a gentleman, speaking to me like that in front of my granddaughter?" She didn't shake him, although she had the power. She simply held him upright.

"No, ma'am, Mrs. Henderson."

"No, ma'am, Mrs. Henderson, what?" Then she did give him the tiniest of shakes, but because of her strength the action set his head and arms to shaking loose on the ends of his body. He stuttered much worse than Uncle Willie. "No, ma'am. Mrs. Henderson, I'm sorry."

With just an edge of her disgust showing, Momma slung him back in his dentist's chair. "Sorry is as sorry does, and you're about the sorriest dentist I ever laid my eyes on." (She could afford to slip into the vernacular because she had such eloquent command of English.)

35 *"I didn't ask you to apologize in front of Marguerite, because I don't want her to know my power, but I order you, now and herewith. Leave Stamps by sundown."*

"Mrs. Henderson, I can't get my equipment . . ." He was shaking terribly now.

"Now, that brings me to my second order. You will never again practice dentistry. Never! When you get settled in your next place, you will be a veterinarian caring for dogs with the mange, cats with the cholera and cows with the epizootic. Is that clear?"

The saliva ran down his chin and his eyes filled with tears. "Yes, ma'am. Thank you for not killing me. Thank you, Mrs. Henderson."

Momma pulled herself back from being ten feet tall with eight-foot arms and said, "You're welcome for nothing, you varlet, I wouldn't waste a killing on the likes of you."

40 *On her way out she waved her handkerchief at the nurse and turned her into a crocus sack of chicken feed.*

Momma looked tired when she came down the stairs, but who wouldn't be tired if they had gone through what she had. She came close to me and adjusted the towel under my jaw (I had forgotten the toothache; I only knew that she made her hands gentle in order not to awaken the pain). She took my hand. Her voice never changed. "Come on, Sister."

I reckoned we were going home where she would concoct a brew to eliminate the pain and maybe give me new teeth too. New teeth that would grow overnight out of my gums. She led me toward the drugstore, which was in the opposite direction from the Store. "I'm taking you to Dentist Baker in Texarkana."

I was glad after all that I had bathed and put on Mum and Cashmere Bouquet talcum powder. It was a wonderful surprise. My toothache had quieted to solemn pain, Momma had obliterated the evil white man, and we were going on a trip to Texarkana, just the two of us.

On the Greyhound she took an inside seat in the back, and I sat beside her. I was so proud of being her granddaughter and sure that some of her magic must have come down to me. She asked if I was scared. I only shook my head and leaned over on her cool brown upper arm. There was no chance that a dentist, especially a Negro dentist, would dare hurt me then. Not with Momma there. The trip was uneventful, except that she put her arm around me, which was very unusual for Momma to do.

45 The dentist showed me the medicine and the needle before he deadened my gums, but if he hadn't I wouldn't have worried. Momma stood right behind

him. Her arms were folded and she checked on everything he did. The teeth were extracted and she bought me an ice cream cone from the side window of a drug counter. The trip back to Stamps was quiet, except that I had to spit into a very small empty snuff can which she had gotten for me and it was difficult with the bus humping and jerking on our country roads.

At home, I was given a warm salt solution, and when I washed out my mouth I showed Bailey the empty holes, where the clotted blood sat like filling in a pie crust. He said I was quite brave, and that was my cue to reveal our confrontation with the peckerwood dentist and Momma's incredible powers.

I had to admit that I didn't hear the conversation, but what else could she have said than what I said she said? What else done? He agreed with my analysis in a lukewarm way, and I happily (after all, I'd been sick) flounced into the Store. Momma was preparing our evening meal and Uncle Willie leaned on the door sill. She gave her version.

"Dentist Lincoln got right uppity. Said he'd rather put his hand in a dog's mouth. And when I reminded him of the favor, he brushed it off like a piece of lint. Well, I sent Sister downstairs and went inside. I hadn't never been in his office before, but I found the door to where he takes out teeth, and him and the nurse was in there thick as thieves. I just stood there till he caught sight of me." Crash bang the pots on the stove. "He jumped just like he was sitting on a pin. He said, 'Annie, I done tole you, I ain't gonna mess around in no niggah's mouth.' I said, 'Somebody's got to do it then,' and he said, 'Take her to Texarkana to the colored dentist' and that's when I said, 'If you paid me my money I could afford to take her.' He said, 'It's all been paid.' I tole him everything but the interest had been paid. He said, 'Twasn't no interest.' I said, 'Tis now. I'll take ten dollars as payment in full.' You know, Willie, it wasn't no right thing to do, 'cause I lent that money without thinking about it.

"He tole that little snippity nurse of his'n to give me ten dollars and make me sign a 'paid in full' receipt. She gave it to me and I signed the papers. Even though by rights he was paid up before, I figger, he gonna be that kind of nasty, he gonna have to pay for it."

50   Momma and her son laughed and laughed over the white man's evilness and her retributive sin.

I preferred, much preferred, my version.

Questions for Discussion

1. Why does Momma think the white dentist, Dr. Lincoln, will pull Maya's tooth? What type of woman is Maya's grandmother?
2. Angelou contrasts the physical pain of her toothache with the painful realization of the doctor's prejudice. Which pain do you think was more hurtful for Maya? Why?
3. Contrast the types of discrimination against blacks in the South and elsewhere in this country today to the discrimination that Angelou describes in her story.
4. What does Maya learn about Momma on her trip to Dr. Lincoln's?

5. What does Maya's revenge fantasy reveal about her self-concept and self-esteem? Why does she prefer her version of what happened?
6. Point out instances of effective dialogue, dialect, setting, details, and imagery that help make this an especially moving memoir.

CONNECTION

Compare Angelou's presentation of her childhood experience of discrimination with Cofer's exploration of memories of dislocation. How does each writer use memory in a unique way? How do the memories presented have a different long-term impact on the writers (see below)?

IDEAS FOR WRITING

1. Develop your journal entry into an essay that discusses what you have learned from living through situations when you were discriminated against, humiliated, or rejected.
2. Write about a childhood fantasy that helped you to overcome feelings of inadequacy and rejection and develop courage and inner strength. What conclusions can you make? What conclusions can you make about the role that childhood fantasies of power and heroism play in helping children to make the transition into adulthood?

RELATED WEB SITES

The History of Jim Crow

`www.jimcrowhistory.org/home.htm`

This site, designed for educators, contains historical essays, images, bibliographies, and other information designed to create an understanding of Jim Crow, or racial segregation, both in the North and South.

Maya Angelou

`www.empirezine.com/spotlight/maya/maya1.htm`

This Web site displays pictures, relevant links, and biographical and bibliographical information on Maya Angelou. It also shares excerpts from books and poetry, and has a special discussion forum.

Judith Ortiz Cofer

Silent Dancing

Born in Puerto Rico in 1952, Judith Ortiz Cofer came to New Jersey with her family when she was a child. After receiving an M.A. from Florida Atlantic University, Cofer taught English and Spanish at the University of Miami and currently teaches at the University of Georgia. Cofer's works include Silent Dancing: A Partial Remembrance of a Puerto Rican Childhood *(1990);* Latin Deli: Prose

and Poetry *(1993);* Island Like You: Stories of the Barrio *(1995);* Women
In Front of the Sun *(2000); and* Call Me Maria *(2004). In the following selection from* Silent Dancing, *Cofer recalls memories of a childhood spent in two
strikingly different cultures.*

JOURNAL

Write about a photograph or a home movie that evokes memories of your
childhood.

*We have a home movie of this party. Several times my mother and I have watched it
together, and I have asked questions about the silent revellers coming in and out of
focus. It is grainy and of short duration but a great visual aid to my first memory of life
in Paterson at that time. And it is in color—the only complete scene in color I can recall
from those years.*

We lived in Puerto Rico until my brother was born in 1954. Soon after, be-
cause of economic pressures on our growing family, my father joined the
United States Navy. He was assigned to duty on a ship in Brooklyn Yard, New
York City—a place of cement and steel that was to be his home base in the
States until his retirement more than twenty years later. He left the Island first,
tracking down his uncle who lived with his family across the Hudson River, in
Paterson, New Jersey. There he found a tiny apartment in a huge apartment
building that had once housed Jewish families and was just being transformed
into a tenement by Puerto Ricans overflowing from New York City. In 1955 he
sent for us. My mother was only twenty years old, I was not quite three, and my
brother was a toddler when we arrived at *El Building,* as the place had been
christened by its new residents.

My memories of life in Paterson during those first few years are in shades of
gray. Maybe I was too young to absorb vivid colors and details, or to discriminate between the slate blue of the winter sky and the darker hues of the snow-
bearing clouds, but the single color washes over the whole period. The
building we lived in was gray, the streets were gray with slush the first few
months of my life there, the coat my father had bought for me was dark in
color and too big. It sat heavily on my thin frame.

I do remember the way the heater pipes banged and rattled, startling all of
us out of sleep until we got so used to the sound that we automatically either
shut it out or raised our voices above the racket. The hiss from the valve punc-
tuated my sleep, which has always been fitful, like a nonhuman presence in
the room—the dragon sleeping at the entrance of my childhood. But the
pipes were a connection to all the other lives being lived around us. Having
come from a house made for a single family back in Puerto Rico—my
mother's extended-family home—it was curious to know that strangers lived
under our floor and above our heads, and that the heater pipe went through
everyone's apartment. (My first spanking in Paterson came as a result of playing tunes on the pipes in my room to see if there would be an answer.) My

mother was as new to this concept of beehive life as I was, but had been given strict orders by my father to keep the doors locked, the noise down, ourselves to ourselves.

5   It seems that Father had learned some painful lessons about prejudice while searching for an apartment in Paterson. Not until years later did I hear how much resistance he had encountered with landlords who were panicking at the influx of Latinos into a neighborhood that had been Jewish for a couple of generations. But it was the American phenomenon of ethnic turnover that was changing the urban core of Paterson, and the human flood could not be held back with an accusing finger.

"You Cuban?" the man had asked my father, pointing a finger at his name tag on the Navy uniform—even though my father had the fair skin and light brown hair of his northern Spanish family background and our name is as common in Puerto Rico as Johnson is in the U.S.

"No," my father had answered looking past the finger into his adversary's angry eyes, "I'm Puerto Rican."

"Same shit." And the door closed. My father could have passed as European, but we couldn't. My brother and I both have our mother's black hair and olive skin, and so we lived in El Building and visited our great-uncle and his fair children on the next block. It was their private joke that they were the German branch of the family. Not many years later that area too would be mainly Puerto Rican. It was as if the heart of the city map were being gradually colored in brown—*café-con-leche* brown. Our color.

The movie opens with a sweep of the living room. It is "typical" immigrant Puerto Rican decor for the time: the sofa and chairs are square and hard-looking, upholstered in bright colors (blue and yellow in this instance, and covered in the transparent plastic) that furniture salesmen then were adept at making women buy. The linoleum on the floor is light blue, and if it was subjected to the spike heels as it was in most places, there were dime-sized indentations all over it that cannot be seen in this movie. The room is full of people dressed in mainly two colors: dark suits for the men, red dresses for the women. I have asked my mother why most of the women are in red that night, and she shrugs, "I don't remember. Just a coincidence." She doesn't have my obsession for assigning symbolism to everything.

10   *The three women in red sitting on the couch are my mother, my eighteen-year-old cousin, and her brother's girlfriend. The "novia" is just up from the Island, which is apparent in her body language. She sits up formally, and her dress is carefully pulled over her knees. She is a pretty girl but her posture makes her look insecure, lost in her full skirted red dress which she has carefully tucked around her to make room for my gorgeous cousin, her future sister-in-law. My cousin has grown up in Paterson and is in her last year of high school. She doesn't have a trace of what Puerto Ricans call "la mancha" (literally, the stain: the mark of the new immigrant—something about the posture, the voice, or the humble demeanor making it obvious to everyone that that person has just arrived on the mainland; has not yet acquired the polished look of the city dweller). My cousin is wearing a tight red-sequined cocktail dress. Her brown hair has been lightened with peroxide around the bangs, and she is holding a cigarette very expertly between her fingers, bringing it up to her mouth in a sensuous arc of her arm to her as she talks animatedly with my*

mother, who has come up to sit between the two women, both only a few years younger than herself. My mother is somewhere halfway between the poles they represent in our culture.

It became my father's obsession to get out of the barrio, and thus we were never permitted to form bonds with the place or with the people who lived there. Yet the building was a comfort to my mother, who never got over yearning for *la isla*. She felt surrounded by her language: the walls were thin, and voices speaking and arguing in Spanish could be heard all day. *Salsas* blasted out of radios turned on early in the morning and left on for company. Women seemed to cook rice and beans perpetually—the strong aroma of red kidney beans boiling permeated the hallways.

Though Father preferred that we do our grocery shopping at the supermarket when he came home on weekend leaves, my mother insisted that she could cook only with products whose labels she could read, and so, during the week, I accompanied her and my little brother to *La Bodega*—a hole-in-the-wall grocery store across the street from *El Building*. There we squeezed down three narrow aisles jammed with various products. Goya and Libby's—those were the trademarks trusted by her Mamá, and so my mother bought cans of Goya beans, soups and condiments. She bought little cans of Libby's fruit juices for us. And she bought Colgate toothpaste and Palmolive soap. (The final *e* is pronounced in both those products in Spanish, and for many years I believed that they were manufactured on the Island. I remember my surprise at first hearing a commercial on television for the toothpaste in which Colgate rhymed with "ate.") We would linger at La Bodega, for it was there that mother breathed best, taking in the familiar aromas of the foods she knew from Mamá's kitchen, and it was also there that she got to speak to the other women of El Building without violating outright Father's dictates against fraternizing with our neighbors.

But he did his best to make our "assimilation" painless. I can still see him carrying a Christmas tree up several flights of stairs to our apartment, leaving a trail of aromatic pine. He carried it formally, as if it were a flag in a parade. We were the only ones in El Building that I knew of who got presents on both Christmas Day and on *Día de Reyes*, the day when the Three Kings brought gifts to Christ and to Hispanic children.

Our greatest luxury in El Building was having our own television set. It must have been a result of Father's guilty feelings over the isolation he had imposed on us, but we were one of the first families in the barrio to have one. My brother quickly became an avid watcher of Captain Kangaroo and Jungle Jim. I loved all the family series, and by the time I started first grade in school, I could have drawn a map of Middle America as exemplified by the lives of characters in "Father Knows Best," "The Donna Reed Show," "Leave It to Beaver," "My Three Sons," and (my favorite) "Bachelor Father," where John Forsythe treated his adopted teenage daughter like a princess because he was rich and had a Chinese houseboy to do everything for him. Compared to our neighbors in El Building, we were rich. My father's Navy check provided us with financial security and a standard of life that the factory workers envied. The only thing his money could not buy us was a place to live away from the barrio—his greatest wish and Mother's greatest fear.

15   *In the home movie the men are shown next, sitting around a card table set up in one corner of the living room, playing dominoes. The clack of the ivory pieces is a sound familiar. I heard it in many houses on the Island and in many apartments in Paterson. In "Leave It to Beaver," the Cleavers played bridge in every other episode; in my childhood, the men started every social occasion with a hotly debated round of dominoes: the women would sit around and watch, but they never participated in the games.*

Here and there you can see a small child. Children were always brought to parties and, whenever they got sleepy, put to bed in the host's bedrooms. Babysitting was a concept unrecognized by the Puerto Rican women I knew: a responsible mother did not leave her children with any stranger. And in a culture where children are not considered intrusive, there is no need to leave children at home. We went where our mother went.

Of my preschool years I have only impressions: the sharp bite of the wind in December as we walked with our parents towards the brightly lit stores downtown, how I felt like a stuffed doll in my heavy coat, boots and mittens; how good it was to walk into the five-and-dime and sit at the counter drinking hot chocolate.

On Saturdays our whole family would walk downtown to shop at the big department stores on Broadway. Mother bought all our clothes at Penney's and Sears, and she liked to buy her dresses at the women's specialty shops like Lerner's and Diana's. At some point we would go into Woolworth's and sit at the soda fountain to eat.

We never ran into other Latinos at these stores or eating out, and it became clear to me only years later that the women from El Building shopped mainly at other places—stores owned either by other Puerto Ricans, or by Jewish merchants who had philosophically accepted our presence in the city and decided to make us their good customers, if not neighbors and friends. These establishments were located not downtown, but in the blocks around our street, and they were referred to generically as *La Tienda, El Bazar, La Bodega, La Botánica.* Everyone knew what was meant. These were the stores where your face did not turn a clerk to stone, where your money was as green as anyone else's.

20   On New Year's Eve we were dressed up like child models in the Sears catalogue—my brother in a miniature man's suit and bow tie, and I in black patent leather shoes and a frilly dress with several layers of crinolines underneath. My mother wore a bright red dress that night, I remember, and spike heels; her long black hair hung to her waist. Father, who usually wore his Navy uniform during his short visits home, had put on a dark civilian suit for the occasion: we had been invited to his uncle's house for a big celebration. Everyone was excited because my mother's brother, Hernán—a bachelor who could indulge himself in such luxuries—had bought a movie camera which he would be trying out that night.

Even the home movie cannot fill in the sensory details such a gathering left imprinted in a child's brain. The thick sweetness of women's perfume mixing with the ever-present smells of food cooking in the kitchen: meat and plantain *pasteles,* the ubiquitous rice dish made special with pigeon peas—*gandules*—and seasoned with the precious *sofrito* sent up from the Island by somebody's mother or smuggled in by a recent traveler. *Sofrito* was one of the items that women hoarded, since it was hardly ever in stock at La Bodega. It was the flavor of Puerto Rico.

The men drank Palo Viejo rum and some of the younger ones got weepy. The first time I saw a grown man cry was at a New Year's Eve party. He had been reminded of his mother by the smells in the kitchen. But what I remember most were the boiled *pasteles*—boiled plantain or yucca rectangles stuffed with corned beef or other meats, olives, and many other savory ingredients, all wrapped in banana leaves. Everyone had to fish one out with a fork. There was always a "trick" pastel—one without stuffing—and whoever got that one was the "New Year's Fool."

There was also the music. Long-playing albums were treated like precious china in these homes. Mexican recordings were popular, but the songs that brought tears to my mother's eyes were sung by the melancholic Daniel Santos, whose life as a drug addict was the stuff of legend. Felipe Rodríguez was a particular favorite of couples. He sang about faithless women and broken-hearted men. There is a snatch of a lyric that has stuck in my mind like a needle on a worn groove: "De piedra ha de ser mi cama, de piedra la cabecera . . . la mujer que a mí me quiera . . . ha de quererme de veras. Ay, Ay, corazón, ¿por qué no amas . . . ?" I must have heard it a thousand times since the idea of a bed made of stone, and its connection to love, first troubled me with its disturbing images.

The five-minute home movie ends with people dancing in a circle. The creative filmmaker must have asked them to do that so that they could file past him. It is both comical and sad to watch silent dancing. Since there is no justification for the absurd movements that music provides for some of us, people appear frantic, their faces embarrassingly intense. It's as if you were watching sex. Yet for years, I've had dreams in the form of this home movie. In a recurring scene, familiar faces push themselves forward into my mind's eye, plastering their features into distorted close-ups. And I'm asking them: "Who is she? Who is the woman I don't recognize? Is she an aunt? Somebody's wife? Tell me who she is. Tell me who these people are."

25   "No, see the beauty mark on her cheek as big as a hill on the lunar landscape of her face—well, that runs in the family. The women on your father's side of the family wrinkle early; it's the price they pay for that fair skin. The young girl with the green stain on her wedding dress is *La Novia*—just up from the island. See, she lowers her eyes as she approaches the camera like she's supposed to. Decent girls never look you directly in the face. *Humilde,* humble, a girl should express humility in all her actions. She will make a good wife for your cousin. He should consider himself lucky to have met her only weeks after she arrived here. If he married her quickly, she will make him a good Puerto Rican-style wife; but if he waits too long, she will be corrupted by the city, just like your cousin there."

"She means me. I do what I want. This is not some primitive island I live on. Do they expect me to wear a black *mantilla* on my head and go to mass every day? Not me. I'm an American woman and I will do as I please. I can type faster than anyone in my senior class at Central High, and I'm going to be a secretary to a lawyer when I graduate. I can pass for an American girl anywhere—I've tried it—at least for Italian, anyway. I never speak Spanish in public. I hate these parties, but I wanted the dress. I look better than any of these *humildes* here. My life is going to be different. I have an American boyfriend. He is older and has a car. My parents don't know it, but I sneak out of the house late at night sometimes to be with him. If I marry him, even my name will be American. I hate rice and beans. It's what makes these women fat."

"Your *prima* is pregnant by that man she's been sneaking around with. Would I lie to you? I'm your great-uncle's common-law wife—the one he abandoned on the Island to marry your cousin's mother. I was not invited to this party, but I came anyway. I came to tell you that story about your cousin that you've always wanted to hear. Remember that comment your mother made to a neighbor that has always haunted you? The only thing you heard was your cousin's name and then you saw your mother pick up your doll from the couch and say: 'It was as big as this doll when they flushed it down the toilet.' This image has bothered you for years, hasn't it? You had nightmares about babies being flushed down the toilet, and you wondered why anyone would do such a horrible thing. You didn't dare ask your mother about it. She would only tell you that you had not heard her right and yell at you for listening to adult conversations. But later, when you were old enough to know about abortions, you suspected. I am here to tell you that you were right. Your cousin was growing an *Americanito* in her belly when this movie was made. Soon after she put something long and pointy into her pretty self, thinking maybe she could get rid of the problem before breakfast and still make it to her first class at the high school. Well, Niña, her screams could be heard downtown. Your aunt, her Mamá, who had been a mid-wife on the Island, managed to pull the little thing out. Yes, they probably flushed it down the toilet, what else could they do with it—give it a Christian burial in a little white casket with blue bows and ribbons? Nobody wanted that baby—least of all the father, a teacher at her school with a house in West Paterson that he was filling with real children, and a wife who was a natural blond.

"Girl, the scandal sent your uncle back to the bottle. And guess where your cousin ended up? Irony of ironies. She was sent to a village in Puerto Rico to live with a relative on her mother's side: a place so far away from civilization that you have to ride a mule to reach it. A real change in scenery. She found a man there. Women like that cannot live without male company. But believe me, the men in Puerto Rico know how to put a saddle on a woman like her. *La Gringa,* they call her. ha, ha. ha. *La Gringa* is what she always wanted to be . . . "

The old woman's mouth becomes a cavernous black hole I fall into. And as I fall, I can feel the reverberations of her laughter. I hear the echoes of her last mocking words: *La Gringa, La Gringa!* And the conga line keeps moving silently past me. There is no music in my dream for the dancers.

30   When Odysseus visits Hades asking to see the spirit of his mother, he makes an offering of sacrificial blood, but since all of the souls crave an audience with the living, he has to listen to many of them before he can ask questions. I, too,

have to hear the dead and the forgotten speak in my dream. Those who are still part of my life remain silent, going around and around in their dance. The others keep pressing their faces forward to say things about the past.

My father's uncle is last in line. He is dying of alcoholism, shrunken and shriveled like a monkey, his face is a mass of wrinkles and broken arteries. As he comes closer I realize that in his features I can see my whole family. If you were to stretch that rubbery flesh, you could find my father's face, and deep within *that* face—mine. I don't want to look into those eyes ringed in purple. In a few years he will retreat into silence, and take a long, long time to die. *Move back, Tío,* I tell him. *I don't want to hear what you have to say. Give the dancers room to move, soon it will be midnight. Who is the New Year's Fool this time?*

QUESTIONS FOR DISCUSSION

1. Which cultural and lifestyle differences affect Cofer most strikingly when she first arrived in Paterson? What prejudice does her family encounter there?
2. What do the television programs that she watches teach Cofer about American family life and how to adapt to it?
3. How do Cofer's father and mother relate differently to their neighborhood environment? With whose values does Cofer identify?
4. How does Cofer respond to the La Gringa story? Why does she respond in this way? What dream continues to haunt Cofer?
5. What dreamlike images and symbols does Cofer use in her narrative? How do these images contribute to the story and its power?
6. Interpret the meaning of the title, "Silent Dancing." Why is the dancing "silent"?

CONNECTION

Compare and contrast Cofer's way of adjusting to life in a new and foreign country with that of the patient described in Remen's "Remembering." What difficulties does each of them face, and how do they deal with their memories of a past homeland?

IDEAS FOR WRITING

1. Write an essay in which you discuss a conflict that you or a close friend experienced because you or your friend was not a member of the dominant cultural group in your community. What did you learn from this conflict, and how did it help shape your perceptions and expectations of the world?
2. Develop your journal entry into an essay. You might discuss a series of photographs or two or three films or videos made over a period of years. What do these images reveal to you about you and your family's evolving values and concerns?

Rachel Naomi Remen

Remembering

Nationally known for her leadership in the mind-body health movement, Rachel Naomi Remen, M.D., is the cofounder and medical director of the Commonweal Cancer Help Program in Bolinas, California. She is currently a clinical professor of family and community medicine at the University of California, San Francisco, School of Medicine. Her books include Humanistic Medicine *(1975),* The Human Patient *(1980),* Kitchen Table Wisdom *(1996), and* My Grandfather's Blessings *(2000). In her private practice, she has worked as a psycho-oncologist for more than 20 years. Her particular blend of caring and wisdom has developed through her professional life as a physician and her experience of living with a chronic illness. In the following selection from* Kitchen Table Wisdom, *Remen reflects on the power of memory to shape identity and to heal.*

JOURNAL

Write about how and why writing or talking about resolving issues from your past helped you feel better.

What we do to survive is often different from what we may need to do in order to live. My work as a cancer therapist often means helping people to recognize this difference, to get off the treadmill of survival, and to refocus their lives. Of the many people who have confronted this issue, one of the most dramatic was an Asian woman of remarkable beauty and style. Through our work together I realized that some things which can never be fixed can still heal.

She was about to begin a year of chemotherapy for ovarian cancer, but this is not what she talked about in our first meeting. She began our work together by telling me she was a "bad" person, hard, uncaring, selfish, and unloving. She delivered this self-indictment with enormous poise and certainty. I watched the light play across her perfect skin and the polish of her long black hair and thought privately that I did not believe her. The people I had known who were truly selfish were rarely aware of it—they simply put themselves first without doubt or hesitation.

In a voice filled with shame, Ana began to tell me that she had no heart, and that her phenomenal success in business was a direct result of this ruthlessness. Most important, she felt that it was not possible for her to become well, as she had earned her cancer through her behavior. She questioned why she had come seeking help. There was a silence in which we took each other's measure. "Why not start from the beginning?" I said.

It took her more than eight months to tell her story. She had not been born here. She had come to this country at ten, as an orphan. She had been adopted by a good family, a family that knew little about her past. With their support she had built a life for herself.

5   In a voice I could barely hear, she began to speak of her experiences as a child in Vietnam during the war. She began with the death of her parents. She had been four years old the morning the Cong had come, small enough to hide in the wooden box that held the rice in the kitchen. The soldiers had not looked there after they had killed the others. When at last they had gone and she ventured from hiding she had seen that her family had been beheaded. That was the beginning. I was horrified.

She continued on. It had been a time of brutality, a world without mercy. She was alone. She had starved. She had been brutalized. Hesitantly at first, and then with growing openness, she told story after story. She had become one of a pack of homeless children. She had stolen, she had betrayed, she had hated, she had helped kill. She had seen things beyond human endurance, done things beyond imagination. Like a spore, she had become what was needed to survive.

As the weeks went by, there was little I could say. Over and over she would tell me that she was a bad person, "a person of darkness." I was filled with horror and pity, wishing to ease her anguish, to offer comfort. Yet she had done these things. I continued to listen.

Over and over a wall of silence and despair threatened to close us off from each other. Over and over I would beat it back, insisting that she tell me the worst. She would weep and say, "I do not know if I can," and hoping that I would be able to hear it, I would tell her that she must. And she would begin another story. I often found myself not knowing how to respond, unable to do anything but stand with her here, one foot in this peaceful calm office on the water, the other in a world beyond imagination. I had never been orphaned, never been hunted, never missed a meal except by choice, never violently attacked another person. But I could recognize the whisper of my darkness in hers and I stood in that place in myself to listen to her, to try to understand. I wanted to jump in, I wanted to soothe, I wanted to make sense, yet none of this was possible. Once, in despair myself, I remember thinking, "I am her first witness."

Over and over she would cry out, "I have such darkness in me." At such times it seemed to me that the cancer was actually helping her make sense of her life, offering the relief of a feared but long-awaited punishment.

10   At the close of one of her stories, I was overwhelmed by the fact that she had actually managed to live with such memories. I told her this and added, "I am in awe." We sat looking at each other. "It helps me that you say that. I feel less alone." I nodded and we sat in silence. I *was* in awe of this woman and her ability to survive. In all the years of working with people with cancer, I had never met anyone like her. I ached for her. Like an animal in a trap that gnaws off its own leg, she had survived—but only at a terrible cost.

Gradually she began to shorten the time frame of her stories, to talk of more recent events: her ruthless business practices, how she used others, always serving her own self-interest. She began to talk about her contempt, her anger, her unkindness, her distrust of people, and her competitiveness. It seemed to me that she was completely alone. "Nothing has really changed," I thought. Her whole life was still organized around her survival.

Once, at the close of a particularly painful session, I found myself reviewing my own day, noticing how much of the time I was focused on surviving and not on living. I wondered if I too had become caught in survival. How much had I put off living today in order to do or say what was expedient? To get what I thought I needed. Could survival become a habit? Was it possible to live so defensively that you never got to live at all?

"You have survived, Ana," I blurted out. "Surely you can stop now." She looked at me, puzzled. But I had nothing further to say.

One day, she walked in and said, "I have no more stories to tell."

15   "Is it a relief?" I asked her. To my surprise she answered, "No, it feels empty."

"Tell me." She looked away. "I am afraid I will not know how to survive now." Then she laughed. "But I could never forget," she said.

A few weeks after this she brought in a dream, one of the first she could remember. In the dream, she had been looking in a mirror, seeing herself reflected there to the waist. It seemed to her that she could see through her clothes, through her skin, through to the very depths of her being. She saw that she was filled with darkness and felt a familiar shame, as intense as that she had felt on the first day she had come to my office. Yet she could not look away. Then it seemed to her as if she were moving, as if she had passed through into the mirror, into her own image, and was moving deeper and deeper into her darkness. She went forward blindly for a long time. Then, just as she was certain that there was no end, no bottom, that surely this would go on and on, she seemed to see a tiny spot far ahead. As she moved closer to it, she was able to recognize what it was. It was a rose. A single, perfect rosebud on a long stem.

For the first time in eight months she began to cry softly, without pain. "It's very beautiful," she told me. "I can see it very clearly, the stem with its leaves and its thorns. It is just beginning to open. And its color is indescribable: the softest, most tender, most exquisite shade of pink."

I asked her what this dream meant to her and she began to sob. "It's mine," she said. "It is still there. All this time it is still there. It has waited for me to come back for it."

20   The rose is one of the oldest archetypical symbols for the heart. It appears in both the Christian and the Hindu traditions and in many fairy tales. It presented itself now to Ana even though she had never read these fairy tales or heard of these traditions. For most of her life, she had held her darkness close to her, had used it as her protection, had even defined herself through it. Now, finally, she had been able to remember. There was a part she had hidden even from herself. A part she had kept safe. A part that had not been touched.

Even more than our experiences, our beliefs became our prisons. But we carry our healing with us even into the darkest of our inner places. *A Course in Miracles* says, "When I have forgiven myself and remembered who I am, I will bless everyone and everything I see." The way to freedom often lies through the open heart.

Questions for Discussion

1. Why does Ana believe that she is a bad person and that her cancer is a punishment? Do you think Ana recovers from her cancer? Why doesn't Remen tell us if Ana does or does not recover from her cancer?
2. Why do you think that Remen values memory? What is unique about her perspective on memory?
3. How and why is Remen able to help Ana? What has Remen learned from listening to Ana's struggle? What have you learned?
4. What is the significance of Ana's dream and the symbolism of the rose?
5. Why does Remen believe that "some things which can never be fixed can still heal"? Explain why you agree or disagree with Remen.
6. How does Remen's discussion of Ana support her conclusion that freedom can begin only after one can forgive oneself and have an open heart? Do you agree with Remen?

Connection

Compare Remen's insights into the need to integrate traumatic memories through dreams rather than to deny the past with Barasch's insights in "The Healing Dream" in Chapter 5 (see page 311).

Ideas for Writing

1. Explain Remen's claim, "What we do to survive is often different from what we may need to do in order to live." Develop the idea into an essay, using examples drawn from personal experience and observation to support your main ideas.

2. Write an essay that supports or refutes Remen's implied premise that peo-ple's beliefs about themselves affect their ability to live a healthy life and recover from an illness. You can research this issue on the Internet and also include examples from your own experience and observations of oth-ers to support your main ideas.

RELATED WEB SITES

Rachel Naomi Remen, M.D.
www.rachelremen.com
This Web site is an excellent introduction to the work and life of Naomi Re-men, a pioneer in the mind-body holistic health movement.

Trauma and Disease: The Sidran Traumatic Stress Institute
www.sidran.org/index.html
This organization provides online links and articles devoted to "education, advocacy and research related to the early recognition and treatment of trauma-related stress in children and the understanding and treatment of adults suffering from trauma-generated disorders."

Stephen Jay Gould

Muller Bros. Moving & Storage

A longtime professor of biology, geology, and the history of science at Harvard Uni-versity, Stephen Jay Gould (1941–2002) is well known for his views on evolution, creationism, and race. He is widely read by thinkers in many different disciplines as his works often point out relationships between scientific and humanistic thought, making technical subjects understandable to nonscientific readers. Gould was the recipient of a number of distinguished awards, including grants from the National Science Foundation and the MacArthur Foundation. His essay collections include Rocks of Ages: Science and Religion in the Fullness of Life *(1999);* The Structure of Evolutionary Theory *(2002); and* I Have Landed: The End of a Beginning in Natural History *(2002). As you read the following es-say, which first appeared in* Natural History Magazine *(1990), Gould examines the limitations and emotional power of memory.*

JOURNAL

Write about a possession a relative gave you that you cherish for the memories it embodies.

I own many old and beautiful books, classics of natural history bound in leather and illustrated with hand-colored plates. But no item in my collection comes close in personal value to a modest volume, bound in gray cloth and published in 1892: "Studies of English Grammar," by J. M. Greenwood, superintendent of schools in Kansas City. The book belonged to my grandfather, a Hungarian immigrant. He wrote on the title page, in an elegant European hand: "Prop. of Joseph A. Rosenberg, New York." Just underneath, he added in pencil the most eloquent of all possible lines: "I have landed. Sept. 11, 1901."

Papa Joe died when I was 13, before I could properly distill his deepest experiences, but long enough into my own ontogeny for the precious gifts of extensive memory and lasting influence. He was a man of great artistic sensibility and limited opportunity for expression. I am told that he sang beautifully as a young man, although increasing deafness and a pledge to the memory of his mother (never to sing again after her death) stilled his voice long before my birth.

He never used his remarkable talent for drawing in any effort of fine arts, although he marshaled these skills to rise from cloth-cutting in the sweatshops to middle-class life as a brassiere and corset designer. (The content of his chosen expression titillated me as a child, but I now appreciate the primary theme of economic emancipation through the practical application of artistic talent.)

Yet, above all, he expressed his artistic sensibilities in his personal bearing—in elegance of dress (a bit on the foppish side, perhaps), grace of movement, beauty of handwriting, ease of mannerism.

5   I well remember one manifestation of this rise above the ordinary—both because we repeated the act every week and because the junction of locale and action seemed so incongruous, even to a small child of 5 or 6. Every Sunday morning, Papa Joe and I would take a stroll to the corner store on Queens Boulevard to buy the paper and a half dozen bagels. We then walked to the great world-class tennis stadium of Forest Hills, where McEnroe and his ilk still cavort. A decrepit and disused side entrance sported a rusty staircase of three or four steps.

With his unfailing deftness, Papa Joe would take a section of the paper that we never read and neatly spread several sheets over the lowermost step (for the thought of a rust flake or speck of dust in contact with his trousers filled him with horror). We would then sit down and have the most wonderful man-to-man talk about the latest baseball scores, the rules of poker, or the results of the Friday night fights.

I retain a beautiful vision of this scene: The camera pans back and we see a tiny staircase, increasingly dwarfed by the great stadium. Two little figures sit on the bottom step—a well-dressed, elderly man gesturing earnestly; a little boy listening with adoration.

Certainty is both a blessing and a danger. Certainty provides warmth, solace, security—an anchor in the unambiguously factual events of personal observation and experience. I know that I sat on those steps with my grandfather because I was there, and no external power of suggestion has ever played havoc with this most deeply personal and private experience. But certainty is also a great danger, given the notorious fallibility—and unrivaled power—of the human mind. How often have we killed on vast scales for the "certainties" of nationhood and religion; how often have we condemned the innocent because the most prestigious form of supposed certainty—eyewitness testimony—bears all the flaws of our ordinary fallibility.

Primates are visual animals *par excellence,* and we therefore grant special status to personal observation—to being there and seeing directly. But all sights must be registered in the brain and stored somehow in its intricate memory. And the human mind is both the greatest marvel of nature and the most perverse of all tricksters, Einstein and Loge inextricably combined.

10   This special (but unwarranted) prestige accorded to direct observation has led to a serious popular misunderstanding about science. Since science is often regarded as the most objective and truth-directed of human enterprises, and since direct observation is supposed to be the favored route to factuality, many people equate respectable science with visual scrutiny—just the facts, ma'am, and palpably before my eyes.

But science is a battery of observational and inferential methods, all directed to the testing of propositions that can, in principle, be definitely proved false. A restriction of compass to matters of direct observation would stymie the profession intolerably. Science must often transcend sight to win insight. At all scales, from smallest to largest, quickest to slowest, many well-documented conclusions of science lie beyond the limited domain of direct observation. No one has ever seen an electron or a black hole, the events of picosecond or a geological eon.

One of the phoniest arguments raised for rhetorical effect by "creation scientists" tried to deny scientific status to evolution because its results take so much time to unfold and therefore can't be seen directly. But if science required such immediate vision, we could draw no conclusion about any subject that studies the past—no geology, no cosmology, no human history (including the strength and influence of religion), for that matter.

We can, after all, be reasonably sure that Henry V prevailed at Agincourt even though no photos exist and no one has survived more than 500 years to tell the tale. And dinosaurs really did snuff it tens of millions of years before any conscious observer inhabited our planet. Evolution suffers no special infirmity as a science because its grandest-scale results took so long to unfold during an unobservable past. (The small-scale results of agriculture and domestication have been recorded, and adequate evidence survives to document the broader events of a distant past.) The sciences of history rely on our ability to infer the past from signs of ancestry preserved in modern structures—as in the "panda's thumb" principle of current imperfection preserved as a legacy of ancestral inheritances originally evolved for different purposes.

Moreover, eyewitness accounts do not deserve their conventional status as ultimate arbiters even when testimony of direct observation can be marshaled in abundance. In her sobering book, *Eyewitness Testimony* (Harvard University Press, 1979), Elizabeth Loftus debunks, largely in a legal context, the notion that visual observation confers some special claim for veracity. She identifies three levels of potential error in supposedly direct and objective vision: misperception of the event itself and the two great tricksters of passage through memory before later disgorgement—retention and retrieval.

15   In one experiment, for example, Loftus showed forty students a three-minute videotape of a classroom lecture disrupted by eight demonstrators (a relevant subject for a study from the early 1970s!). She gave the students a questionnaire and asked half of them: "Was the leader of the twelve demonstrators . . . a male?" and the other half, "Was the leader of the four demonstrators . . . a male?" One week later, in a follow-up questionnaire, she asked all the students: "How many demonstrators did you see entering the classroom?" Those who had previously received the question about twelve demonstrators reported seeing an average of 8.9 people; those told of four demonstrators claimed an average of 6.4. All had actually seen eight, but compromised later judgment between their actual observation and the largely subliminal power of suggestion in the first questionnaire.

People can even be induced to "see" totally illusory objects. In another experiment, Loftus showed a film of an accident, followed by a misleading question: "How fast was the white sports car going when it passed the barn while traveling along the country road?" (The film showed no barn, and a control group received a more accurate question: "How fast was the white sports car going while traveling along the country road?") A week later, 17 percent of the students in the first group stated that they had seen the nonexistent barn; only 3 percent of the control group reported a barn.

Thus, we are easily fooled on all fronts of both eye and mind: seeing, storing and recalling. The eye tricks us badly enough; the mind is infinitely more perverse. What remedy can we possibly have but constant humility, and eternal vigilance and scrutiny? Trust your memory as you would your poker buddy (one of my grandfather's mottoes from the steps).

With this principle in mind, I went searching for those steps last year after more than thirty years of absence from my natal turf. I exited the subway at 67th Avenue, walked to my first apartment at 98–50, and then set off on my grandfather's route for Queens Boulevard and the tennis stadium.

I was walking in the right direction, but soon realized that I had made a serious mistake. The tennis stadium stood at least a mile down the road, too far for those short strolls with a bag of bagels in one hand and a five-year-old boy attached to the other. In increasing puzzlement, I walked down the street and, at the very next corner, saw the steps and felt the jolt and flood of memory that drives our *recherches du temps perdus.*

20   My recall of the steps was entirely accurate—three modest flagstone rungs, bordered by rusty iron railings. But the steps are not attached to the tennis stadium; they form the side entrance to a modest brick building, now crumbling, padlocked, and abandoned, but still announcing its former use with a commercial sign, painted directly on the brick in the old industrial style: "Muller Bros.

Inc. Moving & Storage"—with a telephone number below from the age before all-digit dialing: Illinois 9–9200.

Obviously, I had conflated the most prominent symbol of my old neighborhood, the tennis stadium, with an important personal place—and had constructed a juxtaposed hybrid for my mental image. Yet even now, in the face of conclusive correction, my memory of the tennis stadium soaring above the steps remains strong.

I might ask indulgence on the grounds of inexperience and relative youth for my failure as an eyewitness at the Muller Bros. steps. After all, I was only an impressionable lad of five or so, when even a modest six-story warehouse might be perceived as big enough to conflate with something truly important.

But I have no excuses for a second story. Ten years later, at a trustable age of fifteen, I made a western trip by automobile with my family; I have specially vivid memories of an observation at Devils Tower, Wyoming (the volcanic plug made most famous as a landing site for aliens in "Close Encounters of the Third Kind"). We approach from the east. My father tells us to look out for the tower from tens of miles away, for he has read in a guidebook that it rises, with an awesome near-verticality, from the dead-flat Great Plains—and that pioneer families used the tower as a landmark and beacon on their westward trek.

We see the tower, first as a tiny projection, almost square in outline, at the horizon. It gets larger as we approach, assuming its distinctive form and finally revealing its structure as a conjoined mat of hexagonal basalt columns. I have never forgotten the two features that inspired my rapt attention: the maximal rise of verticality from flatness, forming a perpendicular junction; and the steady increase in size from a bump on the horizon to a looming, almost fearful giant of a rock pile.

25   Now I know, I absolutely *know,* that I saw this visual drama, as described. The picture in my mind of that distinctive profile, growing in size, is as strong as any memory I possess. I see the tower as a little dot in the distance, as a midsized monument, as a full field of view. I have told the story to scores of people, comparing this natural reality with a sight of Chartres as a tiny toy tower twenty miles from Paris, growing to the overarching symbol and skyline of its medieval city.

In 1987, I revisited Devils Tower with my family—the only return since my first close encounter thirty years before. I planned the trip to approach from the east, so that they would see the awesome effect—and I told them my story, of course.

In the context of this essay, my denouement will be anticlimactic in its predictability, however acute my personal embarrassment. The terrain around Devils Tower is mountainous; the monument cannot be seen from more than a few miles away in any direction. I bought a booklet on pioneer trails westward, and none passed anywhere near Devils Tower. We enjoyed our visit, but I felt like a perfect fool. Later, I checked my old logbook for that high-school trip. The monument that rises from the plain, the beacon of the pioneers, is Scotts Bluff, Nebraska—not nearly so impressive a pile of stone as Devils Tower.

And yet I still see Devils Tower in my mind when I think of that growing dot on the horizon. I see it as clearly and as surely as ever, although I now know that the memory is false.

This has been a long story for a simple moral. Papa Joe, the wise old peasant in a natty and elegant business suit, told me on those steps to be wary of all blandishments and to trust nothing that cannot be proved. We must extend his good counsel to our own interior certainties, particularly those we never question because we regard eyewitnessing as paramount in veracity.

30   Of course we must treat the human mind with respect—for nature has fashioned no more admirable instrument. But we must also struggle to stand back and to scrutinize our own mental certainties. This last line poses an obvious paradox, if not an outright contradiction—and I have no solution to offer. Yes, step back and scrutinize your own mind. But with what?

QUESTIONS FOR DISCUSSION

1. Why is *Studies in English Grammar* Gould's most valued possession? Why was this book also cherished by Gould's grandfather?
2. Why does Gould remember his Sunday morning breakfasts with Papa Joe? Why does Gould admire his grandfather?
3. Gould is skeptical of the accuracy of direct visual observation. What evidence and descriptions does he present to support his point of view?
4. Gould is also skeptical of the accuracy of memory. Why do the subjects in the experiments he discusses come to different conclusions about what they saw and what they remembered?
5. When Gould goes back after 30 years to the place where he and Papa Joe had breakfast, what does Gould realize about his memory? Why does he still value his memory, despite its distortions? How does Gould's inaccurate recall of Devils Tower support the premise developed in his earlier example?
6. How does Gould effectively relate his personal experiences to broader scientific issues involving history, memory, and observation?

CONNECTION

Compare and contrast how Gould and Cofer reflect on the way that memories of family members are embodied in objects whose meaning is changed over time (see page 151).

IDEAS FOR WRITING

1. Develop your journal assignment into an essay in which you discuss how the memory you have of a relative is connected to and influenced by a physical possession that you keep to remind yourself of the relative. What feelings and values do you associate with the possession?

2. Write an essay in which you discuss the implications of the paradox Gould presents at the end of the essay: "Step back and scrutinize your own mind. But with what?" How can people become better at reflecting on and clarifying the memories and perceptions that they bring with them from their pasts?

RELATED WEB SITES

Stephen Jay Gould
http://prelectur.stanford.edu/lecturers/gould/
This Stanford University Web site on Stephen Gould includes biographical and bibliographical information, excerpts of various writings, reviews of Gould's works, and relevant links.

Elizabeth Loftus Web Site
http://faculty.washington.edu/eloftus/
This Web site for Professor Loftus, psychologist and researcher into the unreliability of memory and "false memory syndrome," contains several online articles she has written about memory. Gould discusses her research into memory in his essay.

Susan L. Engel

The Past: Audiences and Perspectives

Susan L. Engel earned her B.A. at Sarah Lawrence College in 1980 and received her Ph.D. in developmental psychology from the City University of New York (CUNY) Graduate Center in 1985. The cofounder and educational advisor to the Hayground School in Bridgehampton, New York, Engel currently is a senior lecturer in psychology and the director of the Program in Teaching at Williams College. She has published scholarly essays on child development in language and storytelling abilities, and is the author of two books: The Stories Children Tell: Making Sense of the Narratives of Childhood *(1995) and* Context Is Everything: The Nature of Memory *(1999), from which the following excerpt is drawn. In this essay Engel examines sources for our shared memories and diverse perspectives on the historical and collective past.*

JOURNAL

Write about a historical event you feel you have memory of, even though you did not directly experience it. What indirect experiences and stories have led to your feeling of the memory?

Finding an Audience for the Past

In a kibbutz about 40 miles south of Tel Aviv, there is a small museum dedicated to the memory of the Holocaust. Tom Segev, in his book *The Seventh Million*, writes: "In this place try to see what can no longer be seen, to hear what can no longer be heard, to understand what can never be understood." Knowing what others remember has become an increasingly central part of what we view as historical understanding and the function of memorials. But for the person who lives with terrible memories the private and internal ramifications of remembering are one thing, and the social or political uses of those memories are another.

For those who lived through the Holocaust, and particularly those who survived concentration and death camps, overpowering feelings of secrecy and shame kept them from talking about what they had been through. Many survivors interviewed by Tom Segev talked poignantly about the feeling that they couldn't speak about what they had lived through. One kibbutz member said that he could not speak of the Holocaust to those who had not experienced it:

> After the war, while still a prisoner in a maapilim [illegals] camp in Cyprus, he spent much time thinking about how he would tell people what had happened to him "there," what words he would choose to relate that the Jews of his town were no longer. He felt as if he were the last Jew on earth. When he arrived in the country [Israel] no one asked him, and that was horrible, he said. People did not want to know. The whole period was traumatic, he said.

Segev describes whole communities of survivors who couldn't even talk to one another about what they had all experienced. Living on a kibbutz provided many with a setting in which they could talk about what had happened to them. As many books have documented, and as any visitor to Israel can attest, one might say that the national identity of Israel is built on the notion of memorial. Museums, statues, holidays, and national customs all serve as physical embodiments of Israel's commitment to keep memories of the Holocaust alive and vivid for all who live there. What was so hard for people to talk about in the immediate aftermath of World War II became over time the bedrock of a whole national consciousness.

What does it take for someone to articulate a memory that has seemed too terrible to put into words? The unspoken memory is a different organism from the shared one. For survivors of the Holocaust, their excruciatingly vivid memories were personal. The historical significance, the use of those memories to shape an identity, was something that happened only later:

> For many students and teachers, the Holocaust was a personal trauma. The memories were too harsh, too close, and some of the questions were too distressing to discuss. People who were then in school [right after the war] recall their first encounter with the Holocaust as a kind of voyeurism—it was a forbidden secret, as discomfiting and tantalizing as death and sex.

5   The psychoanalyst might ask why people repress when the alternative frees them of symptoms. Many who survived the Holocaust suppressed rather than

repressed their memories. The decision (conscious or unconscious) to reveal the past had as much to do with where they lived as it does with any internal psychic balance between the costs of repression and the risk of consciousness. Revealing one's knowledge of a terrible event may have a huge impact on the individual doing the remembering. But much of the time the shift from secrecy to revelation has a great deal to do with what one's neighbors want to or can tolerate hearing.

When it was discovered in 1997 that Madeleine Albright, newly appointed U.S. secretary of state, was of Jewish descent, and that much of her family had perished in Europe during World War II, people wanted to know how this could have been a secret from us, and possibly from her. In explaining why her parents hid their Jewish heritage, Albright's mother explained, "To be Jewish was to risk persecution." She could not have meant this in any concrete way. At the time they were living in the United States, where there was little threat that Jews would be persecuted in any systematic way. But, based on their experiences and those of their family in Europe, their identity as Jews was dangerous to life itself. Albright's mother was explaining in a concrete way what has always been true about those aspects of the past that converge on some larger historical problem or condition. Remembering may in these instances have meaning beyond the personal and psychological.

In his study of Holocaust survivors and their uses of memory, psychologist Henry Greenspan discovered that for many, finding a space or context in which to tell their memories was essential:

> Constrained by both inner and outer silence, their goals become more modest. Survivors like Paula and Leon find more private, limited contexts of recounting. They retell what stories they can, choose the most promising situations for their recounting being heard, and bide their time.

One subject Greenspan interviewed put it this way:

> We didn't talk about it because we didn't want to be different . . . we didn't want to be pointed to as the abnormal people. We tried to get along, you know, "I'm an American too."

To bring out a dark memory and reveal it in the light of day poses internal as well as external risks. Whereas a private memory of childhood may emerge under the gaze of a loving friend or the guidance of a therapist, memories that have historical meaning for the listener emerge in a different kind of context. For each person who has revealed what happened to them during the Holocaust there have been two layers of audience, two spheres of meaning: the personal and immediate, and the social and conceptual.

In his book *Maus*, Art Spiegelman documents his father's story to him of living through the Nazi takeover, imprisonment, and its aftermath. His story is told twice, once to his son and then again to us, his son's readers. And it falls on two kinds of ears, the ears of a son who is finding out what his father endured and why his father is the way he is, and on the ears of his son and the rest of us, hearing the grim details that augment and bleakly enliven what we know about a distant time and place.

10 Just as Greenspan's subjects say, who you are talking to and what they make of your memories has an important effect on what you will or won't say. Once spoken, those most intimate details of one's past become, in these instances, part of everyone's past. They are no longer memories in the strictly psychological sense because they were never experienced by most of us. And yet, because they are part of our past, because they form the historical context in which we each developed our own more immediate identity, they provide us with a kind of borrowed memory.

The U.S. Holocaust Memorial Museum in Washington, D.C., has embodied this notion. When you arrive at the museum as a visitor, as soon as you pay your entrance fee, you are given a number and name identifying you as an actual victim of the Holocaust. The notion is that your experience of artifacts, demonstrations, text, and photographs will be that much more real and vivid if you are induced to try to experience it through the eyes of someone who actually lived in it. Of course, many of those whose names and numbers are used did not survive the experience. They didn't live to remember it. You are given the momentary illusion that you are remembering it for them.

Elie Wiesel begins his memoir of the Holocaust by telling us about what someone else heard and saw of the concentration camp. His description of his childhood experience of the Holocaust begins with the story of Moshe the Beadle, an innocuous neighbor liked by all. Then one day during the early part of the war, Moshe was transported along with other Jews from Wiesel's hometown. Wiesel recalls quickly forgetting about the deportees, assuming that they were happily resettled in another region. However, Moshe returned with horrific stories of what he had seen—Nazi soldiers ordering the Jews to dig massive graves and then calmly and methodically killing the deportees and dumping their bodies into the graves. Moshe tells all this to young Wiesel. This is, we are led to understand, his first intimation of what is to come, and it is ours too.

Wiesel begins his memoirs by looking through the eyes of another, just as we begin to learn about a past we didn't experience by looking through Wiesel's eyes. In that sense, his opening passages capture what all memory is as it is transformed from personal autobiography to everyone's history.

When we read about other people's experiences, we borrow their memories. Doing so gives us a sense of immediacy, texture, and insight that we could never acquire through objective accounts and artifacts alone. In addition, each memory carries with it other kinds of information, an aura of the past that gives us a broader sense of that time and place. The literary critic Mikhail Bakhtin has talked about this in a somewhat different context. He argues that any speaking character in a book (his most vivid examples are from the fiction of Dostoyevsky) gives voice to the perspectives, cultural habits, and characteristics of many people—in other words, each character is polyphonic. Bakhtin demonstrates the ways in which a character's words and phrases carry with them nuances, meanings, associations, and connotations that may reflect whole sectors of a society.

15   When we hear about someone's past we hear not only about that person, but also about the time that he or she recalls. In this way all kinds of memories are historical. In a stunning piece on not being able to remember his mother's voice, a writer talks about what we do and don't recall of the personal past, and what is and is not carried along with that thread of memory:

> My mother's mother said "pie-anna" for "piano." Like her daughter, she sat at that instrument between intervals of housework and played hymns. Her voice had the reediness that comes after a hard life. I know a lot of things about my grand-mother, but they are things a child knows, not adult information. I don't know a single sentence her parents ever spoke to her. My mom learned in school not to say "pie-anna," and I would wager that she never once used a phrase that was uniquely hers. She spoke, as we all do, a temporal dialect—a speech made up in the main of plain, enduring words but also of short-lived phrases that belong to a place and a moment.

The writer tells us he cannot recall his mother's voice. But he can recall the way that his mother's mother said certain words. Over time, what is recalled of one's past shifts? For this writer it is the historical context rather than the real people that is most easily evoked. But it reminds us that when we remember the past or visit someone else's memories, it gives us a view of a whole era, a community, a way of living beyond the specific events recalled. This, clearly, is one important way that people's individual memories offer the rest of us history.

The memories and autobiographies about the Holocaust discussed here all tend to converge on a common view of what happened. They don't, any longer, change what we know of what it was like for a Jew to live or die in the war, nor do they change what we think about those events. What they do is to give us a feeling of detail and immediacy, and evoke a level of emotion that no mere historical account could. In these instances, borrowing other people's memories brings us into the experience in a unique way and, therefore, changes our access to a historical event. When people talk of shared memory in a situation such as this, they are talking about a version or view of an event that people hold in common. The idea is that each person in the community, group, or society has an overlapping or similar narrative or collection of details and facts about an event. But not all shared memory involves convergence or similarity of representations. The psychologist Daniel Wegner has written lucidly and convincingly about another way in which people can remember collectively.

Converging Perspectives

Wegner suggests that people have been trying to explain collective thinking for a long time. Turn-of-the-[twentieth-] century explanations of collective thinking resorted to the notions of inherited thoughts or the supernatural. But the advent of behaviorism pushed all of that out of the way with its focus on the individual learning through specific experiences. How, then, in an era of empirical psychology and a firm idea of the individual, do we explain shared memories? Wegner argues that we have to look at the phenomenon in a new way. Instead of assuming that shared memory must involve a group of people all thinking or re-membering the same event in the same way, he shows how groups of people ex-change information about the past. What they know together is more than what any one of them knows alone. Part of his argument rests on the simple but strik-ing insight that much of our remembering is embodied in forms outside of the mind: writing, memorials, pictures, and lists. It is the norm, rather than the ex-ception, for us to fill in our internal representations of past events with informa-tion gleaned from these outside forms, including what other people can tell us.

In one study Wegner and his colleagues asked intimate couples to remem-ber long lists of information. In each list some of the information drew on the expertise of the woman in the couple, and other information rested on the ex-pertise of the man. Wegner showed that the couple acted as a team, each spon-taneously taking responsibility for the terms they would most easily remember. Wegner calls this kind of collaboration transactional memory. One of the inter-esting implications of his work is that people can have dissimilar memories of an event, or remember the event from different perspectives. The picture of that event that develops across people will be richer and more complex than the view any one of those people might have. The Vietnam War offers an inter-esting though troubled example of this phenomenon.

20   The situation in Vietnam, as almost every American over the age of 30 knows, was viewed from wildly divergent, even harshly conflicting points of view. Most people either ardently supported or violently disagreed with our military involvement in Indochina during the 1950s, 1960s, and early 1970s. At the time, our sources of information were skewed, to say the least. We only knew what the United States government would tell us. Few men coming back from the war in the early years would say much about it. Then the antiwar movement picked up momentum and we began to get a different picture of both the rationale (or lack of one) for being there and facts about what was happening there. Now, in retrospect, there have been two divergent sorts of memories the rest of us could draw on in thinking about that piece of our past. Some of the most compelling and disturbing information comes from men who fought in the war but only began communicating their experiences long after. This material has been made into several movies, all very potent in their effect—*Platoon, Apocalypse Now, The Deer Hunter, Born on the Fourth of July,* to name a few. However, each of those movies is so entwined with the imagina-tions of the filmmakers that it is hard to separate recollections.

There are, however, some notable books that draw from the memories of in-dividuals, giving us entrée into a kind of memory of Vietnam that changes the way we think about the war. Preeminent among those books is the writing of Tim O'Brien. In his collection of connected stories, *The Things They Carried,* O'Brien gives a visceral and compelling account of what it was like to be in the war. It is also, inevitably, a rumination on the nature of memory and truth. Like Holocaust survivors, American soldiers who were in Vietnam felt (and some still feel) that their experiences were shameful in some way. During the war they were surrounded by the silence of terror. And, like survivors of the Holocaust, many Vietnam veterans felt that once they returned home they were wrapped in a second kind of silence: the silence of a group of people who didn't really want to know. And like Holocaust survivors, they needed to tell as a way of surviving. Although the circumstances of their ordeal and the proximate causes of their subsequent sense of shame differed dramatically, they felt pressure to keep silent about horrendous experiences and the concomitant internal drive to tell those experiences to others is comparable.

Memories, and the stories in which they are wrapped, that come from people like Tim O'Brien allow us to smell and feel the stench or terror, the horror and desolation felt by young men totally disoriented by their presence in Vietnam.

> Forty-three years old, and the war occurred half a lifetime ago, and yet the remembering makes it now. And sometimes remembering will lead to a story, which makes it forever. That's what stories are for. Stories are for joining the past to the future. Stories are for those late hours in the night when you can't remember how you got from where you were to where you are. Stories are for eternity, when memory is erased, when there is nothing to remember except the story.

In 1994, an extremely important player in the decisions and actions carried out during the Vietnam War, Robert McNamara, published an autobiography presented as a kind of *mea culpa*. This too is a memory, but of a very different sort. To read McNamara's account and read an account such as Tim O'Brien's is to engage in what Wegner calls transactive memory—only to do so at a literary remove. McNamara's book, *In Retrospect,* begins with a chapter that recounts his early life. This is presented as a kind of foreshortened path that leads you directly to his life in government. The rest of the book describes his involvement with the Kennedy, Johnson, and Nixon administrations as it pertained to his role in the country's military activity in Indochina.

Unlike a book such as O'Brien's, which brings you into an experience through all your senses and emotions, McNamara's is a revelation of discussions and information that no one from within had yet told. It is what we learn, not what we are made to experience, that is important about his memoir. The most important point in his book is his admission that he and his colleagues never really thought through whether they had a chance of achieving their military or political aims through military involvement in Vietnam. Equally stunning is his admission that he came to believe years before the actual U.S. withdrawal that such an action should be taken. At the end of the second edition of the book is an intriguing collection of letters and other responses notable people had to the publication of the book. These reactions allow us to see how people responded to this important addition to our transactive, or collective, body of memories regarding the war. Some who wrote were impressed that McNamara was courageous enough to admit a mistake that had such catastrophic consequences for millions of people here and in Southeast Asia. Others were infuriated that he dared complain of sleepless nights and guilt that couldn't compare, in the writers' view, to what young men and their families went through as a result of the "mistakes" McNamara made all those years ago.

25   Many, if not all of the people writing, seemed already to know most of what
McNamara was admitting in his memoir. And yet, having him recount it as a
personal story changed its place in the body of information we consider to be
our collective memory of Vietnam. This has in part to do with the power of hearing about the past from someone's specific point of view. Having McNamara say
it, and say it in the form of a memoir, gives it a force that it didn't have when presented as pieces of authorless, subjectless information. As the layperson pieces
together an account of the Vietnam War, she or he must integrate a retrospec-
tive view such as McNamara's with the kind embodied in Tim O'Brien's writing.

Life as we live it in the United States at the end of the millennium presents a
special, perhaps paradoxical, context for historical remembering. On the one
hand, we live at a time when there is unprecedented interest in the experience
of the individual. Memoirs and autobiographies abound. Readers are drawn in
by subjective accounts of events, and we place high value on the reports and accounts of eyewitnesses. On the other hand, we are surrounded by events that,
while having obvious historical significance, are not directly experienced by
anyone. This means that we are constantly looking for ways to grasp personal
and direct experiences of ourselves and others. At the same time, we try to do
this with events with which we have had only indirect encounters.

QUESTIONS FOR DISCUSSION

1. Why has it been difficult for many who experienced the Holocaust to talk
   about it and to share their experiences with others? How did talking
   about these experiences and their aftermath become possible on a kibbutz and eventually become the "bedrock of a whole national consciousness" for Israelis?
2. Why does Engel believe that Madeleine Albright's family and other American Jews have hidden their Jewish heritage? What did they fear, and why
   did they try so hard to forget the past?
3. What is meant by calling Art Spiegelman's graphic novel about his father's
   life in the Nazi period and his imprisonment a "story . . . told twice"? What
   is the significance of retelling the story to a wider audience? How do such
   "borrowed memories" help us to understand our identities and what
   shaped them historically?
4. How and why does the U.S Holocaust Museum in Washington D.C., attempt to lead visitors to experience details and events of the Holocaust from
   the perspective of "someone who actually lived in it"? Do you think this is a
   valid and ethical use of borrowed memory? Explain your point of view.
5. How does psychologist David Wegner explain the phenomenon of
   "shared memories"? What "outside forms" help us to create such shared or
   "collective" memories?
6. How does Engel use Tim O'Brien's *The Things They Carried* and Robert
   McNamara's memoir, *In Retrospect,* to demonstrate different ways that the
   American people have gained a deeper, more complex "memory" of the
   war in Vietnam from authors than is possible by using firsthand personal
   experience?

CONNECTION

Engel and Steven Jay Gould (in his essay on page 163) both examine ways that memories of experiences we have not personally experienced can become part of our personal outlook on the past. Compare the views on such "secondhand" memories provided by the two authors.

IDEAS FOR WRITING

1. Interview someone, perhaps a relative, who has lived through a difficult historical period such as a war, a strike, or a time of extreme political unrest, here or abroad. Write up your findings in a reflective essay. How did thinking about and working with this individual's memories help you to broaden your own perspective and sense of experience/memory of the historical circumstances in question?

2. Pick an important social event that you lived through and that was also heavily covered in the media. Write a reflective essay in which you consider some of the personal and "borrowed memories" that helped to create the impressions and overall evaluation of the significance of the event and its effects and causes.

RELATED WEB SITES

Social Memory
`www.phil.mq.edu.au/staff/jsutton/Socialmemory.htm`
In this page from the Interdisciplinary Study of Memory site maintained by philosophy professor John Sutton of Macquarie University, Sydney, Australia, you will find many links and bibliographical references to information on the impact of cinema and other media, family memory, World War II, the Holocaust, and memorials on our sense of historical memory.

The Necessary Lie: A Process of Mediated Memory
`www.egs.edu/mediaphi/main/jay-stern-the-necessary-lie.html`
In this thesis, Jay Stern comments on the way photographs and family narratives create memories for us that, while not factually true, help us deal with trauma and loss.

Melissa Burns

The Best Seat in the House

Melissa Burns wrote this essay for her freshman writing class, Community Matters. As the essay suggests, Melissa is an accomplished bassoonist. Always active in dorm life and engaged in campus activities, Melissa Burns finds community life rewarding and is always willing to accept roles of leadership.

On my bookshelf at college sits a beautiful oak box, about six inches long by three inches wide and high. Its four sides, each with two triangular end pieces, are masterfully flush; they fit together so as to unfold fully into a flattened green, felt-lined surface. Well-placed brass hinges and tight fittings guarantee a smooth alignment when the box is latched shut. The top panel is stamped with a hot-iron oval and reads "PATENTED 1889 FEBRUARY." I have been told that my grandfather, Poppy, constructed this treasure box from a kit. My mother, a young girl at the time, remembers her father carefully gluing the velvet upholstery fabric, now faded and fraying, to the box's interior. For decades, it sat undisturbed on Poppy's dresser, the keeper of his rarely worn cufflinks. When Poppy passed away, my grandmother handed the box to my mother, who subsequently placed it into my hands. It is a memory of the grandfather I never knew, a man who loved me with all his heart. Today, this cherished oak box is known as the "reed graveyard," the place where good bassoon reeds go to die.

Poppy was a master craftsman, a WWII statistical officer in Italy, a peacemaker, a member of a bombardier squadron in the European Theater, a fighter pilot, a looker, a gentleman, a joke-teller. He traveled the globe, swam Lake Erie from Buffalo to Toronto, and constructed ornate and precision grandfather clocks, among numerous other works of art. Poppy fixed all things broken—electrical appliances, furniture, hearts. He was a gentle German giant: six foot four and slender, with an olive complexion and dark but graying hair. He wore a wicked grin, as if to forewarn all whom he met of his mischievous pranks, funny sayings, and unique brand of sarcasm. My grandfather awoke one freezing morning, concerned that the razor-sharp icicles dangling from the awning of his Amherst, New York, home might injure his family and friends. Instead, it was Poppy himself who succumbed to nature's wrath. While diligently chipping away at the deadly spikes, he suffered a massive coronary heart attack, dying immediately and painlessly. There were no good-byes. Poppy left my physical world on January 10, 1986, just four days after his 72nd birthday. I was two and a half years old.

My mother has shown me so many photographs of her father and me that sometimes I believe I can conjure the contours of his long, hollowed face and cheeks or his warm embrace as we snuggled in a lawn chair in the tall green grass of summertime in upstate New York. On other occasions, I realize that I possess no actual recollection of Poppy; I've simply deceived myself into believing false, picture-induced memories, all the while praying to God that I should someday reunite with my grandfather. Poppy is gone from the earth, but not from my soul. I embrace him through stories, maxims, and possessions. Over the years, I have learned to take comfort in his status as my guardian angel, protecting and sheltering me from the atrocities of this world.

Matt, my older brother and only sibling, bears an eerily striking resemblance to Poppy—he shares the height, the charm, the gait, and most of all, that devilish, cock-eyed smile. Growing up, however, it was I who captured my grandfather's precious attention. Poppy was well known to occupy our living room rocking chair, listening anxiously for the soft cries signaling that I had awoken from an afternoon nap. He would race upstairs, sweep me from my crib, and hold me soothingly against his broad chest. That was our special time together, my only grandfather and me.

5   When I was in a playful, alert mood, Poppy would lay me down on the family room floor and conduct a series of "tests." Very much the mathematician, calculating the release of bombs and their ensuing catastrophic destruction, Poppy transformed his wartime accuracy into tender, delicate, and methodical child rearing. He concealed my toys behind his back—Would I perceive their continued existence? He raided the kitchen for pots and pans and walked circles around the room, clanging them loudly in different locations while watching my tiny head move frantically from side to side. I have a vivid mental image of a photograph in which Poppy has placed colorful plastic rings around my arms to gauge my strength. Poppy's premature testing was often dismissed as playtime nonsense by the rest of the family, yet he was seriously equipping his only granddaughter with the resources necessary to grow up strong, healthy, independent, resourceful, smart, and intuitive. Poppy was preparing my two-year-old self for a life of struggles and achievements, failures and triumphs. He took great pride in his beautiful baby granddaughter, but he never felt the satisfaction or the joy of witnessing her metamorphosis into a little girl, a teenager, and now, a woman—a woman with a talent of which Poppy was entirely unaware.

I began to play the bassoon, an extremely difficult and intricate double-reed instrument, at the unprecedented age of ten. My decision to play this instrument was prompted by words of encouragement from family friends who recognized my musical aptitude for the piano, as well as the great orchestral demand for young bassoonists. This musical decision was to become perhaps the most consequential, life-altering choice of my life. My bassoon journeys have carried me from Williams College to New York City to Germany to Prague, and most recently, to Stanford University. Because of my musical performances, I have experienced the world's most amazing sights and sounds while interacting with extraordinarily talented and kindhearted members of society.

My story begins with a stroke of luck. I established contact with a renowned bassoon performer and instructor named Stephen Walt, a Williams College teacher in high demand, who had never before considered working with a beginning pupil. Instantaneously, I could tell that our personalities were well-suited, and he became my bassoon coach for the seven years I studied the instrument until moving to California. Mr. Walt is an inspiration, a musical virtuoso, and the most warm, encouraging, demanding instructor I can possibly imagine. My success as a musician is due in great part to his dedication and guidance. Every other weekend, my father drove me from Niskayuna, New York, to Williamstown, Massachusetts. Mr. Walt's lessons were worth every second of the hour-and-twenty-minute car ride along oftentimes slippery, snow-covered mountain roads.

As my years of practice accumulated, I steadily increased my skill level, becoming a proficient high school bassoonist. The summer before my sophomore year, I auditioned for, and gained acceptance to, one of America's premier youth orchestras, the Empire State Youth Orchestra. Although I was at first intimidated by the phenomenally talented musicians surrounding me in the orchestra, lengthy bus rides together, nights spent in hotels in foreign countries, and a sense of mutual admiration soon created an atmosphere in which these musicians became several of my closest friends. I will never forget the day our revered and beloved conductor, Francisco Noya, stood imposingly before us at the podium and announced in a thick Venezuelan accent, "Are you prepared to work extremely hard? Jes or no? Dis year, we play Carnegie Hall." I momentarily lost my grip on reality. Life for an orchestral musician does not reach a zenith more meaningful, more overwhelming, or more spectacular, than the opportunity to perform at *Carnegie Hall.*

For months, the idea of my orchestra's concert at Carnegie Hall constantly intruded on my thoughts. When I wasn't practicing the musical selections, my hands rehearsing complicated fingering passages, I imagined the sights and the sounds of the hall, and I stared at my monthly planner, scratching off each slowly passing day. One such day a week or so before the performance, I sat in my practice chair in the den trying to relax my aching mouth muscles, and I turned to look at the reed graveyard. Every reed I had used over the years, meticulously handcrafted from raw cane by Mr. Walt, inevitably found its way to the graveyard when it was worn-down, broken, cracked, weak, or simply no longer reliable. I carefully unfolded Poppy's box to examine its contents: hundreds of reeds, varying slightly in size, shape, cane discoloration, and string color—red, green, blue, even multi-hued—stuffed the box's interior. As I carefully lifted the reeds and let them sift through my fingers, each one evoked memories of a particular concert, practice session, summer camp, quintet, lesson, rehearsal, or pit orchestra. To this day, every tiny wooden relic, unique, beautiful, and delicate, tells a different, unforgettable story. The reed graveyard, I realized, is a metaphor for Poppy's undying love; it is representative of his personal contribution to my achievements. My greatest accomplishments, I now understood, were housed in this creation, crafted by his strong but gentle hands. Feeling revived, I closed the precious box, placed it on the shelf beside me, and resumed my practice.

10   My dream, from the moment that I began my avocation as a musician, was now materializing. I was standing in the wings of Carnegie Hall, placing my black patent leather shoes where all "the greats" had placed theirs. I peered around the velvet curtain, trembling slightly and sweating profusely. Scanning the sea of faces for a few seconds, I finally located my large cohort of immediate family and close friends. I found them sitting in the upper left-hand balcony in a private box protruding far from the wall. Matt, appropriately, was directly in front and practically falling over the railing, grinning with a true pride that I'd never seen before, and have not seen since. Poppy, I'm quite certain, was witnessing the entire scene from above. He undoubtedly had the best seat in the house. As Poppy's presence filled the air above my head, he beamed his joy through Matt, who served as a surrogate physical representation for a grandfather who would have loved, more than anyone else, to hug and hold his granddaughter on that emotional afternoon.

From the time I found my seat on the stage until the concert was over, my memories are blurred. I have been told that the show ran its entirety without a single hitch; I, for one, was too nervous, excited, ecstatic, and satisfied, to have known what was going on. Thankfully, my musical bodily functions—lungs, heart, fingers, and muscles—took over for a severely wandering mind. I simply cannot describe the fantastic, all-encompassing feeling of earning and achieving one's greatest goal.

I regained mental composure after the last note of our program finished resonating in Carnegie Hall. My attention was called immediately to my support group, cheering and clapping above all others. Beneath it all was the underlying essence of my grandfather's love. I breathed a sigh of relief, took my bows, and, bassoon clutched close to my heart, walked off the stage of the world-renowned Carnegie Hall. What happens to the dreamer when her dream becomes a reality? Is a new dream born? I currently attend Stanford University in northern California, a place I consider to be an ideal launching pad for the discovery of fresh and thrilling ambitions. I am searching for my calling, yet again.

As for Poppy, he resides in the heavens, continuing to protect his baby granddaughter as she matures, becoming stronger and more independent. Late on the night of the concert, when I arrived at my home in Niskayuna, I walked into the den and cradled the reed graveyard in my hands. I opened Poppy's box and placed the most absolutely perfect reed I had ever known inside, where it would retire among the masses that had come before. I latched the box shut as I positioned it in its resting place on the shelf, thus signifying the end to one marvelous chapter of my life. With Poppy as my copilot, I flew off in search of uncharted horizons.

QUESTIONS FOR DISCUSSION

1. What did Melissa learn from Poppy? In what ways was he her first "teacher"? Why has he remained such an important role model and source of support for her?
2. What personal and family qualities do you think led Melissa to become a successful bassoonist? What did playing at Carnegie Hall mean for her?
3. Why is the essay entitled "The Best Seat in the House"? How does this phrase help to clarify her ongoing relationship with "Poppy"?
4. Discuss the writer's central symbol of the reed box. Why does Melissa value her "reed graveyard"?

TOPICS FOR RESEARCH AND WRITING

1. Write an essay in which you discuss how readings such as those by Hampl, Cofer, Angelou, and Shah in this chapter, as well as outside readings and research, have affected your understanding of the importance of memories as a rich source for writing material.

2. After reading the essays by Maya Angelou and Judith Ortiz Cofer in this chapter, do some further research and write an essay about the relation between memories of discrimination in minority and/or immigrant groups and the writing that comes out of their communities.

3. Susan Engel and Naomi Remen explore the way that historical memory often is a mixture of personal remembered events and larger events that we learn about from outside reading or exposure to the media. Do some research into an event such as the Vietnam War or some more recent historical conflict such as 9/11 of which you have secondhand knowledge. How has the secondhand knowledge of the event created a sense of "memory" and emotional impact of the event for you?

4. After examining essays in this book such as the ones by Engel, Gould, and Remen, do some reading about the quality and improvability of memory. Can we improve our memories of recent and past events, or is memory simply a "given" ability that we can do nothing about? Write an essay that presents your findings and conclusions on this topic.

5. Hampl and Gould explore the reliability of memories of the past, questioning the extent to which the past and "history" are said to truly exist outside of what we recall and re-create through memory and imagination. Do some further research into the reliability of early memories, and draw some conclusions. Is there an "objective" past, or does each person or group of people invent a version of history? If so, what are our "versions" most often based upon? Write your conclusions in an essay.

6. Write an essay that explores your family's legacy by giving an account of several memories that have been crucial to its sense of identity and values. If possible, interview different family members, including extended family such as grandparents, uncles, aunts, and cousins.

7. Write about a film that focuses on the importance of memories and/or the reliability of memory, referring to elements such as dreams of characters, flashback sequences, and other cinematic devices for showing remembered scenes. Films to consider include *Wild Strawberries, Stand by Me, Cinema Paradiso, The Joy Luck Club, Lone Star, Memento, The Sixth Sense, Titanic, The Piano Lesson, The English Patient, The Butterfly Effect, I Know Why the Caged Bird Sings, The Eternal Sunshine of the Spotless Mind, Schindler's List, Garden State,* and *Angela's Ashes.*

Dreams, Myths, and Fairy Tales

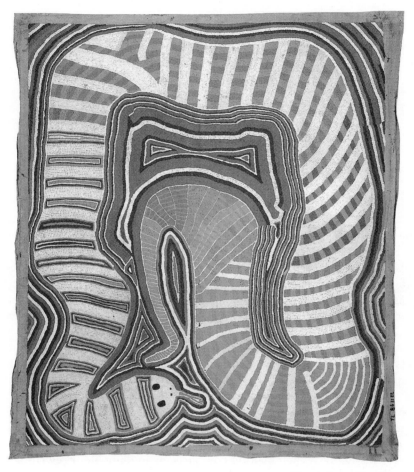

Tommy Lowry Tjapaltjarri
Warrmala the Serpent (1986)

This Aboriginal painting depicts Warrmala, a Rainbow Serpent, resting at Patjar-rnga, a deep desert waterhole in western Australia. Both waterholes and serpents are sacred in Aboriginal culture and religious art. The waterhole represents the place where life is nurtured in times of drought and in "dreamings," while the Rainbow Serpent is a creator god associated with the coming of the rainy season and with rebirth and spiritual renewal.

JOURNAL

Write and illustrate a creation story that explains how some natural phenomenon came into being—a certain star or constellation, the moon, the sun, the wind, fire, rain, or the like.

Myths are public dreams, dreams are private myths.
                                    JOSEPH CAMPBELL
                                    Hero with a Thousand Faces

Fantasy is the core of all writing for children, as I think it is for the writing of any book, for any creative act, perhaps for the act of living.
                                    MAURICE SENDAK

COMPARING AND CONTRASTING: STRATEGIES FOR THINKING AND WRITING

The readings selected for this chapter encourage you to think comparatively. You will find that dreams are compared to myths, myths to fairy tales, and traditional tales to modern forms of literature. Also included are different versions of the same basic myths from various cultures. We have designed the chapter in this way because comparing and contrasting are related and essential aspects of reading and writing and are crucial as well to the way the mind thinks and organizes experiences.

When you compare and contrast, you explore relationships between subjects that, despite apparent distinctions, have qualities in common. In this chapter, for example, Carl Jung uses comparison and contrast to emphasize the differences between his own ideas on dream analysis. Comparative writing demands sophisticated, analytical thinking and organization of ideas. Although everyone naturally makes comparisons while thinking, the structure of comparative writing is more balanced and complex than what one normally does when making comparisons in daily life. Prewriting is especially useful for gathering insights and details to use for comparison.

Prewriting for Comparison

You can do prewriting for a comparison paper using any of the techniques discussed in Chapter 1, such as freewriting or clustering. For example, to use brainstorming, begin by dividing a piece of paper down the middle, then create brainstorming lists of points or qualities you perceive in the subjects of your analysis. A student who wanted to develop a comparison between fairy tales and elementary school readers took the following notes:

Fairy Tales	*Elementary School Readers*
imaginative	seem written by "formula"
engage interest and feelings	don't involve students deeply

teach living skills and heroism	teach "basic reading skills"
encourage imagination	encourage conformity
raise some disturbing issues	avoid controversial issues

You can see some striking contrasts in the lists above. After eliminating some items and grouping the related points, the student could move from the list to a general, clearly worded thesis statement such as the following: "Fairy tales engage the feelings and mind of the child, while primary school texts often fail to attract the interests of children, and thus may actually turn children off to reading." In a very short time, this student writer has found several major points of contrast for possible development and a good central idea to unify a paragraph or essay.

Outlining and Transition

Use of an outline helps to structure extended comparison/contrast papers. An outline will help you to achieve a balanced treatment of each subject and major point in your paper. In preparing an outline, consider the kind of organization you want to use. Comparisons can be structured around points of similarity or difference. Use details to clarify and add interest to the comparison. In subject-by-subject comparing, points are made about two subjects in separate paragraphs or sections of a paper, and the two subjects are brought together in the conclusion for a final evaluation or summary of major points. In writing your comparison essay, make the basic points of your comparison clear to your readers through transitional statements. As you move from one comparative issue to another, use expressions such as "in comparison to," "similarly," and "likewise." If the differences between your subjects seem more striking than the similarities, use contrast as your major strategy for examining and noting distinctions, emphasizing your points with transitional expressions such as "in contrast to" and "another point of distinction." As student writer Josh Groban does in his comparison essay in this chapter between the Yao myth of creation and the story of Genesis in the Bible, order and develop your points with care, distinguishing between similarities and differences to retain a clear sense of the overall purpose of your comparison, to understand complex realities, and to evaluate.

Evaluation

Evaluating involves making a judgment based on a standard that you hold about a subject or issue. In the prewriting exercise above, the student who contrasted fairy tales with elementary school textbooks made an evaluation of each based on personal likes and dislikes: the student liked fairy tales and disliked textbooks. Although the student writer didn't discuss her standards for judging children's literature, we can assume that she likes reading that is entertaining and engaging and is bored by writing that exists simply as a tool for learning. The student might have even thought more critically about the standards that are appropriate for school readers. If she had, she might have considered the problems that schools have in selecting and judging materials for different types of learners. Regardless of your subject of comparison, you can come closer to seeing whether your values are realistic guides for belief and behavior by establishing guidelines for comparing your standards with those of other people.

Logical Fallacies of Comparison and Contrast

When you think and write comparatively, you may find yourself falling into misleading patterns of thought. A common problem involving comparison and contrast is drawing rigid distinctions that force a choice between artificially opposed positions. Often a contrastive statement will imply that one position is a bad choice: "America, love it or leave it"; "A person is either a God-fearing Christian or a sinful atheist"; or "You're either a real he-man or a spineless sissy." Such statements employ both an incorrect use of contrast and an inappropriate use of evaluation by setting up an either/or dilemma. There are occasions when any comparison oriented to evaluating may seem inappropriate. In comparing and contrasting the myths from different cultures included in this chapter, you may note that each myth of creation involves very different sets of images and values relative to the act and purpose of creation. When thinking about radically different cultures and values, it is more useful simply to make relevant distinctions than to attempt to evaluate one culture as superior or inferior to another.

In the faulty analogy, another common error in comparing, a person attempts to create a connection between two subjects when there are insufficient strong points of similarity. For example, a writer could argue that because life is dreamlike in certain ways, a person should go through life passively, accepting whatever happens just as one might in a dream. Analogies and imaginative, nonliteral comparisons, known as metaphors and similes, can be useful in writing, giving a sense of unexpected and imaginative connections, making descriptions clearer, and generating new insights. On the other hand, taking a metaphorical statement, such as "Life is a dream," and applying it too literally as a standard for conduct ignores real distinctions between the waking world and the sleeping world.

The section on dialogic argument in Chapter 7 discusses ways in which flexible stances in argument can allow you to move beyond rigid, unexamined standards of comparison and evaluation. For now, you should feel ready to use the strategy of comparison more systematically and productively to help you to perceive clear relationships between the public world and your inner world.

THEMATIC INTRODUCTION: DREAMS, MYTHS, AND FAIRY TALES

Once you understand how your memories of particular childhood events have shaped and continue to influence your identity and the direction of your life, you may enjoy comparing your personal history to myths and fairy tales. These universal stories have helped to connect humans to larger patterns of history, to their own cultures, and to one another, despite their historical and cultural differences. Myths are patterned stories that present the reader with ideal heroes and heroines acting through dreamlike plots and settings, representing the fundamental values of a culture and a society. Fairy tales satisfy the needs of younger people, and adults as well, for dangerous adventures where evil is ultimately banished and happiness and justice ultimately prevail. Both forms provide ethical lessons that help readers to discriminate between creative and destructive or good and evil behavior.

From Greek myths to nursery rhymes and fairy tales, images of heroism and of creation have marked our developing understanding of the cultural values and the workings of the human mind. The fundamental adventure and quest patterns of stories and legends are continually being transformed and adapted according to the values of each new age. Today's popular myths provide readers with revised values and reflections on changing cultural norms.

This chapter begins with a poem, an essay, and a story that reveal the power of myths in the lives of individuals and in communal existence. The first selection, "ego-tripping (there may be a reason why)," is a poem by the African American writer Nikki Giovanni. In this poem the speaker imagines herself living through the myths of her heritage as she realizes that identification with these myths protects her and gives her power. The next selection, Linda Seger's "Universal Stories," provides us with an illuminating analysis of the components of the hero myth as encountered in film and in literature. Next, we provide an example of a hero myth in the making through Gabriel García Márquez's tale, "The Handsomest Drowned Man in the World: A Tale for Children," which chronicles the creation of a peasant myth about the redemption brought by a drowned man to a remote seaside village.

Following these introductory readings on heroes, we present an essay about and several examples of creation myths. Physicist Marcelo Gleiser's "The Myths of Science—Creation" compares creation myths to scientific narratives of creation, while a portfolio of creation myths from around the world provides concrete examples of imaginatively charged mythical explanations of creation that embody the core values and beliefs of the cultures that produced the stories. We have included myths from the Book of Genesis as well as from ancient Australian, Greek, African, Native American, and Japanese traditions.

Just as dreams and myths give us clues to our unconscious selves and our connections to universal human concerns, fairy tales, a particular class of mythic stories, have been created for children to help them to understand the darker side of human nature. This section of the chapter begins with essays by psychologist Bruno Bettelheim and children's book author Jane Yolen on the importance of powerful, sometimes disturbing fairy tales for children. In "Fairy Tales and the Existential Predicament," Bruno Bettelheim asserts that children in our modern world need to read classic fairy tales that present the good and the bad sides of human nature and the conscious and unconscious needs and impulses of humans. Jane Yolen takes a historical and socially oriented perspective in her essay "American Cinderella," arguing that the modern story of Cinderella familiar to American youngsters displays a weak heroine who is a poor role model for girls.

To help you understand the different ways in which a fairy tale can be interpreted and transformed by particular cultures and historical periods, we have included four versions of the Cinderella myth: "Aschenputtel" by the Brothers Grimm; Charles Perrault's "Cendrillon"; a Native American version of the tale, "The Algonquin Cinderella"; and a Vietnamese Cinderella story, "Tam and Cam."

A student essay concludes the readings selected for this chapter. In his essay, "Two Myths," Joshua Groban compares the meanings of two creation myths to show the different values and beliefs held by the cultures that produced the myths.

Comparing myths and fairy tales from different cultures can help you gain new insights into your own culture as you see your world in a broader perspective of diverse values, emotional needs, and spiritual concerns. Drawing comparisons between versions of myths and fairy tales will help you to see how these universal forms can change and endure. Perhaps they will help you make sense of your contemporary world and see its connection to the past. Reflecting on and writing about the implications of your dreams and myths as well as the dreams and myths of others can comprise an essential path to your inward journey and a deeper appreciation of the world in which you live.

Nikki Giovanni

ego-tripping (there may be a reason why)

Nikki Giovanni (b. 1943) has written children's fiction, a memoir, and essays. Giovanni's poetry, which she frequently has read aloud on television and recordings, has been a significant influence on younger African American writers and poets, especially the new rap poets and musicians. She won a Ford Foundation grant and has received awards from the National Endowment for the Arts and the Harlem Cultural Council. Her first book, Black Feeling, Black Talk, *was written in 1968. Her recent publications include* Selected Poems *(1996);* Love Poems *(1997);* Blues: For All the Changes: New Poems *(1999);* Quilting the Black-Eyed Pea: Poems and Non Poems *(2002); and* The Collected Poetry of Nikki Giovanni *(2004). As you read her poem "ego-tripping" (there may be a reason why)" (1973), notice how she is able to use cultural myths and historical realities that are a source of pride for African Americans to create a new kind of female hero story.*

JOURNAL

Imagine yourself as related to the larger-than-life heroes and/or heroines you admire. Begin each sentence of your freewrite with "I"; exaggerate and have fun!

I was born in the congo
I walked to the fertile crescent and built
      the sphinx
I designed a pyramid so tough that a star
5   that only glows every one hundred years falls
      into the center giving divine perfect light
I am bad

I sat on the throne
      drinking nectar with allah
10 I got hot and sent an ice age to europe
      to cool my thirst
My oldest daughter is nefertiti
      the tears from my birth pains
      created the nile
15 I am a beautiful woman

I gazed on the forest and burned
      out the sahara desert
      with a packet of goat's meat
      and a change of clothes
20 I crossed it in two hours
I am a gazelle so swift
      so swift you can't catch me
For a birthday present when he was three
I gave my son hannibal an elephant
25   He gave me rome for mother's day
My strength flows ever on

My son noah built new\ark and
I stood proudly at the helm
      as we sailed on a soft summer day
30 I turned myself into myself and was
        jesus
        men intone my loving name

       All praises All praises
I am the one who would save
35 I sowed diamonds in my back yard
My bowels deliver uranium
        the filings from my fingernails are
        semi-precious jewels
        On a trip north
40 I caught a cold and blew
My nose giving oil to the arab world
I am so hip even my errors are correct
I sailed west to reach east and had to round off
        the earth as I went
45   The hair from my head thinned and gold was
        laid across three continents

I am so perfect so divine so ethereal so surreal
I cannot be comprehended
except by my permission

50 I mean . . . I . . . can fly
        like a bird in the sky . . .

QUESTIONS FOR DISCUSSION

1. To emphasize her pride in her African descent, Giovanni's narrator invokes a number of African cultures, mythologies, places, and historical figures. Identify several of the African references in the poem and explain how the narrator finds pride and power through these references and comparisons.

2. Giovanni's poem combines African references with African American expressions. Identify slang words and phrases in the poem, and explain how such expressions add to the power of the poem.

3. In addition to its references to the African Egyptian cultural tradition, the poem also alludes to biblical characters and mythologies. Point out references to the Old or New Testament of the Bible, and discuss how you think such references and implied comparisons help to develop the poem's tone and meaning.

4. Although the poem has a boisterous, buoyant feeling, at times it seems as if Giovanni may be questioning the narrator's boastfulness. Why do you think the poet built this self-critical perspective into the poem?

5. What does this poem suggest to you about the functions and power of myth in literature and in the inner life of the individual?

CONNECTION

Interpret the myths and fantasies in Giovanni's "heroic" poem using some of the ideas found in Seger's essay "Universal Stories" (see below).

IDEAS FOR WRITING

1. Try developing your ego-tripping freewriting into your own "rap" or "boast" poem. Refer to myths and cultural traditions that are familiar to you.
2. The speaker in Giovanni's poem seems to gain a sense of personal empowerment through making a series of mythical comparisons. Write an essay in which you argue for or against the importance of comparing yourself to and identifying with characters and situations in myths to gain a sense of pride and self-respect. Use examples of myths you or other people you know believe in that could help to develop a sense of self-esteem.

RELATED WEB SITES

The Poet and the Rapper
`www.findarticles.com/p/articles/mi_m1264/is_1_30/`
`ai_54492517`
This interesting article by Evelyn C. White, based on an interview with rap singer and actress Queen Latifah and "author/political activist" Nikki Giovanni, explores the connection between racism, rap, and politics.

The Hero-Myth Cycle
`www.geocities.com/Athens/Forum/8122/hero.html`
All cultures have myths, legends, and tales of heroes and their grand accomplishments. Follow the links here to get a basic introduction to the elements of the cycle of the hero myth.

Linda Seger

Universal Stories

Linda Seger earned a B.A. in English literature at Colorado College in 1967, an M.A. in dramatic arts at Northwestern University in 1968, an M.A. in religion and the arts at the Pacific School of Religion in 1973, a Th.D. in drama and theology from the Graduate Theological Union in 1976, and an M.A. in feminist theology from Immaculate Heart College Center. Seger has taught at many colleges, including Colorado College, the University of Southern California, and the Pacific School of Religion. Seger became a script consultant in 1981 and has worked on many scripts, feature films, and television projects. Her books include Making a Good Writer Great *(1999) and* Web-Thinking: Connecting, Not Competing for Success *(2002). The following selection on the myth of the hero in literature and films comes from Seger's* Making a Good Script Great *(1987).*

All of us have similar experiences. We share in the life journey of growth, development, and transformation. We live the same stories, whether they involve the search for a perfect mate, coming home, the search for fulfillment, going after an ideal, achieving the dream, or hunting for a precious treasure. Whatever our culture, there are universal stories that form the basis for all our particular stories. The trappings might be different, the twists and turns that create suspense might change from culture to culture, the particular characters may take different forms, but underneath it all, it's the same story, drawn from the same experiences.

Many of the most successful films are based on these universal stories. They deal with the basic journey we take in life. We identify with the heroes because we were once heroic (descriptive) or because we wish we could do what the hero does (prescriptive). When Joan Wilder finds the jewel and saves her sister, or James Bond saves the world, or Shane saves the family from the evil ranchers, we identify with the character, and subconsciously recognize the story as having some connection with our own lives. It's the same story as the fairy tales about getting the three golden hairs from the devil, or finding the treasure and winning the princess. And it's not all that different a story from the caveman killing the woolly beast or the Roman slave gaining his freedom through skill and courage. These are our stories—personally and collectively—and the most successful films contain these universal experiences.

Some of these stories are "search" stories. They address our desire to find some kind of rare and wonderful treasure. This might include the search for outer values such as job, relationship, or success; or for inner values such as respect, security, self-expression, love, or home. But it's all a similar search.

Some of these stories are "hero" stories. They come from our own experiences of overcoming adversity, as well as our desire to do great and special acts. We root for the hero and celebrate when he or she achieves the goal because we know that the hero's journey is in many ways similar to our own.

5   We call these stories *myths*. Myths are the common stories at the root of our universal existence. They're found in all cultures and in all literature, ranging from the Greek myths to fairy tales, legends, and stories drawn from all of the world's religions.

A myth is a story that is "more than true." Many stories are true because one person, somewhere, at some time, lived it. It is based on fact. But a myth is more than true because it is lived by all of us, at some level. It's a story that connects and speaks to us all.

Some myths are true stories that attain mythic significance because the people involved seem larger than life, and seem to live their lives more intensely than common folk. Martin Luther King, Jr., Gandhi, Sir Edmund Hillary, and Lord Mountbatten personify the types of journeys we identify with, because we've taken similar journeys—even if only in a very small way.

Other myths revolve around make-believe characters who might capsulize for us the sum total of many of our journeys. Some of these make-believe characters might seem similar to the characters we meet in our dreams. Or they might be a composite of types of characters we've met.

In both cases, the myth is the "story beneath the story." It's the universal pattern that shows us that Gandhi's journey toward independence and Sir Edmund Hillary's journey to the top of Mount Everest contain many of the same dramatic beats. And these beats are the same beats that Rambo takes to set free the MIAs, that Indiana Jones takes to find the Lost Ark, and that Luke Skywalker takes to defeat the Evil Empire.

10 In *Hero with a Thousand Faces,* Joseph Campbell traces the elements that form the hero myth. "In their own work with myth, writer Chris Vogler and seminar leader Thomas Schlesinger have applied this criteria to *Star Wars.* The myth within the story helps explain why millions went to see this film again and again."

The hero myth has specific story beats that occur in all hero stories. They show who the hero is, what the hero needs, and how the story and character interact in order to create a transformation. The journey toward heroism is a process. This universal process forms the spine of all the particular stories, such as the *Star Wars* trilogy.

The Hero Myth

1. In most hero stories, the hero is introduced in ordinary surroundings, in a mundane world, doing mundane things. Generally, the hero begins as a non-hero; innocent, young, simple, or humble. In *Star Wars,* the first time we see Luke Skywalker, he's unhappy about having to do his chores, which consists of picking out some new droids for work. He wants to go out and have fun. He wants to leave his planet and go to the Academy, but he's stuck. This is the setup of most myths. This is how we meet the hero before the call to adventure.

2. Then something new enters the hero's life. It's a catalyst that sets the story into motion. It might be a telephone call, as in *Romancing the Stone,* or the German attack in *The African Queen,* or the holograph of Princess Leia in *Star Wars.* Whatever form it takes, it's a new ingredient that pushes the hero into an extraordinary adventure. With this call, the stakes are established, and a problem is introduced that demands a solution.

3. Many times, however, the hero doesn't want to leave. He or she is a reluctant hero, afraid of the unknown, uncertain, perhaps, if he or she is up to the challenge. In *Star Wars*, Luke receives a double call to adventure. First, from Princess Leia in the holograph, and then through Obi-Wan Kenobi, who says he needs Luke's help. But Luke is not ready to go. He returns home, only to find that the Imperial Stormtroopers have burned his farmhouse and slaughtered his family. Now he is personally motivated, ready to enter into the adventure.

4. In any journey, the hero usually receives help, and the help often comes from unusual sources. In many fairy tales, an old woman, a dwarf, a witch, or a wizard helps the hero. The hero achieves the goal because of this help, and because the hero is receptive to what this person has to give.

   There are a number of fairy tales where the first and second son are sent to complete a task, but they ignore the helpers, often scorning them. Many times they are severely punished for their lack of humility and unwillingness to accept help. Then the third son, the hero, comes along. He receives the help, accomplishes the task, and often wins the princess.

   In *Star Wars*, Obi-Wan Kenobi is a perfect example of the "helper" character. He is a kind of mentor to Luke, one who teaches him the Way of the Force and whose teachings continue even after his death. This mentor character appears in most hero stories. He is the person who has special knowledge, special information, and special skills. This might be the prospector in *The Treasure of the Sierra Madre,* or the psychiatrist in *Ordinary People,* or Quint in *Jaws,* who knows all about sharks, or the Good Witch of the North who gives Dorothy the ruby slippers in *The Wizard of Oz.* In *Star Wars*, Obi-Wan gives Luke the light saber that was the special weapon of the Jedi Knight. With this, Luke is ready to move forward and do his training and meet adventure.

5. The hero is now ready to move into the special world where he or she will change from the ordinary into the extraordinary. This starts the hero's transformation, and sets up the obstacles that must be surmounted to reach the goal. Usually, this happens at the first Turning Point of the story, and leads into Act Two development. In *Star Wars*, Obi-Wan and Luke search for a pilot to take them to the planet of Alderaan, so that Obi-Wan can deliver the plans to Princess Leia's father. These plans are essential to the survival of the Rebel Forces. With this action, the adventure is ready to begin.

6. Now begin all the tests and obstacles necessary to overcome the enemy and accomplish the hero's goals. In fairy tales, this often means getting past witches, outwitting the devil, avoiding robbers, or confronting evil. In Homer's *Odyssey,* it means blinding the Cyclops, escaping from the island of the Lotus-Eaters, resisting the temptation of the singing Sirens, and surviving a shipwreck. In *Star Wars*, innumerable adventures confront Luke. He and his cohorts must run to the *Millennium Falcon,* narrowly escaping the Stormtroopers before jumping into hyperspace. They must make it through the meteor shower after Alderaan has been destroyed.

They must evade capture on the Death Star, rescue the Princess, and even survive a garbage crusher.

7. At some point in the story, the hero often hits rock bottom. He often has a "death experience," leading to a type of rebirth. In *Star Wars,* Luke seems to have died when the serpent in the garbage-masher pulls him under, but he's saved just in time to ask R2D2 to stop the masher before they're crushed. This is often the "black moment" at the second turning point, the point when the worst is confronted, and the action now moves toward the exciting conclusion.

8. Now, the hero seizes the sword and takes possession of the treasure. He is now in charge, but he still has not completed the journey. Here Luke has the Princess and the plans, but the final confrontation is yet to begin. This starts the third-act escape scene, leading to the final climax.

9. The road back is often the chase scene. In many fairy tales, this is the point where the devil chases the hero and the hero has the last obstacles to overcome before really being free and safe. His challenge is to take what he has learned and integrate it into his daily life. He *must* return to renew the mundane world. In *Star Wars,* Darth Vader is in hot pursuit, planning to blow up the Rebel Planet.

10. Since every hero story is essentially a transformation story, we need to see the hero changed at the end, resurrected into a new type of life. He must face the final ordeal before being "reborn" as the hero, proving his courage and becoming transformed. This is the point, in many fairy tales, where the Miller's Son becomes the Prince or the King and marries the Princess. In *Star Wars,* Luke has survived, becoming quite a different person from the innocent young man he was in Act One.

At this point, the hero returns and is reintegrated into his society. In *Star Wars,* Luke has destroyed the Death Star, and he receives his great reward.

This is the classic "Hero Story." We might call this example a *mission* or *task myth,* where the person has to complete a task, but the task itself is not the real treasure. The real reward for Luke is the love of the Princess and the safe, new world he had helped create.

A myth can have many variations. We see variations on this myth in James Bond films (although they lack much of the depth because the hero is not transformed), and in *The African Queen,* where Rose and Allnutt must blow up the *Louisa,* or in *Places in the Heart,* where Edna overcomes obstacles to achieve family stability.

15 The *treasure myth* is another variation on this theme, as seen in *Romancing the Stone.* In this story, Joan receives a map and a phone call which forces her into the adventure. She is helped by an American birdcatcher and a Mexican pickup truck driver. She overcomes the obstacles of snakes, the jungle, waterfalls, shootouts, and finally receives the treasure, along with the "prince."

Whether the hero's journey is for a treasure or to complete a task, the elements remain the same. The humble, reluctant hero is called to an adventure.

The hero is helped by a variety of unique characters. S/he must overcome a series of obstacles that transform him or her in the process, and then faces the final challenge that draws on inner and outer resources.

The Healing Myth

Although the hero myth is the most popular story, many myths involve healing. In these stories, some character is "broken" and must leave home to become whole again.

The universal experience behind these healing stories is our psychological need for rejuvenation, for balance. The journey of the hero into exile is not all that different from the weekend in Palm Springs, or the trip to Hawaii to get away from it all, or lying still in a hospital bed for some weeks to heal. In all cases, something is out of balance and the mythic journey moves toward wholeness.

Being broken can take several forms. It can be physical, emotional, or psychological. Usually, it's all three. In the process of being exiled or hiding out in the forest, the desert, or even the Amish farm in *Witness*, the person becomes whole, balanced, and receptive to love. Love in these stories is both a healing force and a reward.

20   Think of John Book in *Witness*. In Act One, we see a frenetic, insensitive man, afraid of commitment, critical and unreceptive to the feminine influences in his life. John is suffering from an "inner wound" which he doesn't know about. When he receives an "outer wound" from a gunshot, it forces him into exile, which begins his process of transformation.

At the beginning of Act Two, we see John delirious and close to death. This is a movement into the unconscious, a movement from the rational, active police life of Act One into a mysterious, feminine, more intuitive world. Since John's "inner problem" is the lack of balance with his feminine side, this delirium begins the process of transformation.

Later in Act Two, we see John beginning to change. He moves from his highly independent life-style toward the collective, communal life of his Amish hosts. John now gets up early to milk the cows and to assist with the chores. He uses his carpentry skills to help with the barn building and to complete the birdhouse. Gradually, he begins to develop relationships with Rachel and her son, Samuel. John's life slows down and he becomes more receptive, learning important lessons about love. In Act Three, John finally sees that the feminine is worth saving, and throws down his gun to save Rachel's life. A few beats later, when he has the opportunity to kill Paul, he chooses a nonviolent response instead. Although John doesn't "win" the Princess, he has nevertheless "won" love and wholeness. By the end of the film, we can see that the John Book of Act Three is a different kind of person from the John Book of Act One. He has a different kind of comradeship with his fellow police officers, he's more relaxed, and we can sense that somehow, this experience has formed a more integrated John Book.

QUESTIONS FOR DISCUSSION

1. Why does Seger believe that certain "universal stories" or myths serve as life patterns for people around the world, at all time periods? In what sense are these stories "more than true"? Do you agree that all cultures operate according to certain universal principles and narratives?

2. What examples does Seger provide for her belief that modern films represent a continuation of the universal myths of the past? Can you think of other, more recent films that could also serve as examples of this continuity, or as departures from it?

3. What does Seger mean by the expressions "story beneath the story" and "dramatic beats"? Are her explanations of the terms clear to you? Why or why not?

4. What are the specific "beats" of the hero myth, according to Seger and Joseph Campbell? How clearly does Seger define each stage?

5. How effectively does the author use examples from the film *Star Wars* in order to parallel modern hero myths to classical mythic narratives of the hero?

6. In the final paragraphs of her essay, Seger argues that the "task" or "mission" of the hero is not simply a material reward or treasure. What does she believe the reward or "transformation" of the hero to be in most myths and tales? How can the transformation involve a type of "healing"?

CONNECTION

Compare Seger's explanation of the hero myth to Bettelheim's ideas on the function of fairy tales (see page 215).

IDEAS FOR WRITING

1. Write an essay in which you compare and contrast two hero myths from widely different cultures and times. You might contrast a traditional myth with a modern myth from a film, television show, song, or comic book.

2. Develop your journal entry into a personal essay in which you examine a mythic story you have heard, seen, or read and demonstrate with examples its influence on your values and choices in life, positive and/or negative.

RELATED WEB SITES

Linda Seger
www.lindaseger.com
This site includes a biography, bibliography, seminar list, photos, and other information on Seger.

Heroes in Contemporary Works of Fantasy Literature
www.towson.edu/~flynn/swordsor.html
This site features three articles originally published in *The Encyclopedia Galactica* (1995), an encyclopedia devoted to science fiction and fantasy themes.

Gabriel García Márquez

The Handsomest Drowned Man in the World: A Tale for Children

Gabriel García Márquez (b. 1928) grew up in a small town in Colombia, the eldest of 12 children in a poor family. In 1947 he entered the National University in Bogotá, continuing his studies at the University of Cartagena, Colombia. His first book of stories, Leaf Storm and Other Stories *(1955), which includes "The Handsomest Drowned Man in the World," confirmed his commitment to politics and social change. From 1959 to 1961, he traveled extensively while working for a Cuban news agency. After the Cuban revolution, Márquez returned to Central America to encourage other revolutionary causes. His novels include* One Hundred Years of Solitude *(1967),* The Autumn of the Patriarch *(1975),* Love in the Time of Cholera *(1988), and* A Country for Children *(1998); his short stories can be found in* Collected Stories *(1984) and* Strange Pilgrims *(1993). He received the Nobel Prize for Literature in 1982. Márquez's work combines the realistic and the fantastic, and he often uses peasant fables as the basis of his stories, as in the tale that follows.*

JOURNAL

Write about a local hero in your community or neighborhood who achieved larger-than-life, "mythical" status after his or her death.

The first children who saw the dark and slinky bulge approaching through the sea let themselves think it was an empty ship. Then they saw it had no flags or masts and they thought it was a whale. But when it washed up on the beach, they removed the clumps of seaweed, the jellyfish tentacles, and the remains of fish and flotsam, and only then did they see that it was a drowned man.

They had been playing with him all afternoon, burying him in the sand and digging him up again, when someone chanced to see them and spread the alarm in the village. The men who carried him to the nearest house noticed that he weighed more than any dead man they had ever known, almost as much as a horse, and they said to each other that maybe he'd been floating too long and the water had got into his bones. When they laid him on the floor they said he'd been taller than all other men because there was barely enough room for him in the house, but they thought that maybe the ability to keep on growing after death was part of the nature of certain drowned men. He had the smell of the sea about him and only his shape gave one to suppose that it was the corpse of a human being, because the skin was covered with a crust of mud and scales.

They did not even have to clean off his face to know that the dead man was a stranger. The village was made up of only twenty-odd wooden houses that had stone courtyards with no flowers and which were spread about on the end of a desertlike cape. There was so little land that mothers always went about with the fear that the wind would carry off their children and the few dead that the years had caused among them had to be thrown off the cliffs. But the sea was calm and bountiful and all the men fit into seven boats. So when they found the drowned man they simply had to look at one another to see that they were all there.

That night they did not go out to work at sea. While the men went to find out if anyone was missing in neighboring villages, the women stayed behind to care for the drowned man. They took the mud off with grass swabs, they removed the underwater stones entangled in his hair, and they scraped the crust off with tools used for scaling fish. As they were doing that they noticed that the vegetation on him came from faraway oceans and deep water and that his clothes were in tatters, as if he had sailed through laybrinths of coral. They noticed too that he bore his death with pride, for he did not have the lonely look of other drowned men who came out of the sea or that haggard, needy look of men who drowned in rivers. But only when they finished cleaning him off did they become aware of the kind of man he was and it left them breathless. Not only was he the tallest, strongest, most virile, and best built man they had ever seen, but even though they were looking at him there was no room for him in their imagination.

5 They could not find a bed in the village large enough to lay him on nor was there a table solid enough to use for his wake. The tallest men's holiday pants would not fit him, nor the fattest ones' Sunday shirts, nor the shoes of the one with the biggest feet. Fascinated by his huge size and his beauty, the women then decided to make him some pants from a large piece of sail and a shirt from some bridal Brabant linen so that he could continue through his death with dignity. As they sewed, sitting in a circle and gazing at the corpse between stitches, it seemed to them that the wind had never been so steady nor the sea so restless as on that night and they supposed that the change had something to do with the dead man. They thought that if that magnificent man had lived in the village, his house would have had the widest doors, and highest ceiling, and the strongest floor; his bedstead would have been made from a midship frame held together by iron bolts, and his wife would have been the happiest woman. They thought that he would have had so much authority that he could have drawn fish out of the sea simply by calling their names and that he would have put so much work into his land that springs would have burst forth from among the rocks so that he would have been able to plant flowers on the cliffs. They secretly compared him to their own men, thinking that for all their lives theirs were incapable of doing what he could do in one night, and they ended up dismissing them deep in their hearts as the weakest, meanest, and most useless creatures on earth. They were wandering through that maze of fantasy when the oldest woman, who as the oldest had looked upon the drowned man with more compassion than passion, sighed:

"He has the face of someone called Esteban."

It was true. Most of them had only to take another look at him to see that he could not have any other name. The more stubborn among them, who were the youngest, still lived for a few hours with the illusion that when they put his clothes on and he lay among the flowers in patent leather shoes his name might be Lautaro. But it was a vain illusion. There had not been enough canvas, the poorly cut and worse sewn pants were too tight, and the hidden strength of his heart popped the buttons on his shirt. After midnight the whistling of the wind died down and the sea fell into its Wednesday drowsiness. The silence put an end to any last doubts: he was Esteban. The women who had dressed him, who had combed his hair, had cut his nails and shaved him were unable to hold back a shudder of pity when they had to resign themselves to his being dragged along the ground. It was then that they understood how unhappy he must have been with that huge body since it bothered him even after death. They could see him in life, condemned to going through doors sideways cracking his head on crossbeams, remaining on his feet during visits, not knowing what to do with his soft pink, sealion hands while the lady of the house looked for her most resistant chair and begged him, frightened to death, sit here, Esteban, please, and he, leaning against the wall, smiling, don't bother, ma'am, I'm fine where I am, his heels raw and his back roasted from having done the same thing so many times whenever he paid a visit, don't bother ma'am, I'm fine where I am to avoid the embarrassment of breaking up the chair, and never knowing perhaps that the one who said don't go, Esteban, at least wait till the coffee's ready, were the ones who later on would whisper the big boob finally left, how nice, the handsome fool has gone. That was what the women were thinking beside the body a little before dawn. Later, when they covered his face with a handkerchief so that the light would not bother him, he looked so forever dead, so defenseless, so much like their men that the first furrows of tears opened in their hearts. It was one of the younger ones who began the weeping. The others, coming to, went from sighs to wails, and the more they sobbed the more they felt like weeping, because the drowned man was becoming all the more Esteban for them, and so they wept so much, for he was the most destitute, most peaceful, and most obliging man on earth, poor Esteban. So when the men returned with the news that the drowned man was not from the neighboring villages either, the women felt an opening of jubilation in the midst of their tears.

"Praise the Lord," they sighed, "he's ours!"

The men thought the fuss was only womanish frivolity. Fatigued because of the difficult nighttime inquiries, all they wanted was to get rid of the bother of the newcomer once and for all before the sun grew strong on that arid, windless day. They improvised a litter with the remains of foremasts and gaffs, tying it together with rigging so that it would bear the weight of the body until they reached the cliffs. They wanted to tie the anchor from a cargo ship to him so that he would sink easily into the deepest waves, where the fish are blind and divers die of nostalgia, and bad currents would not bring him back to shore, as had happened with other bodies. But the more they hurried, the more the women thought of ways to waste time. They walked about like startled hens, pecking with the sea charms on their breasts, some interfering on one side to put a scapular of the good wind on the drowned man, some on the other side to put a wrist compass on him, and after a great deal of *get away from there woman, stay out of the way, look, you almost made me fall on top of the dead man*, the men began to feel mistrust in their livers and started grumbling about why so many main-altar decorations for a stranger, because no matter how many nails and holywater jars he had on him, the sharks would chew him all the same, but the women kept on piling on their junk relics, running back and forth, stumbling, while they released in sighs what they did not in tears, so that the men finally exploded with *since when has there ever been such a fuss over a drifting corpse, a drowned nobody, a piece of cold Wednesday meat*. One of the women, mortified by so much lack of care, then removed the handkerchief from the dead man's face and the men were left breathless too.

10   He was Esteban. It was not necessary to repeat it for them to recognize him. If they had been told Sir Walter Raleigh, even they might have been impressed with his gringo accent, the macaw on his shoulder, his cannibal-killing blunderbuss, but there could be only one Esteban in the world and there he was, stretched out like a sperm whale, shoeless, wearing the pants of an undersized child, and with those stony nails that had to be cut with a knife. They had only to take the handkerchief off his face to see that he was ashamed, that it was not his fault that he was so big or so heavy or so handsome, and if he had known that this was going to happen, he would have looked for a more discreet place to drown in; seriously, I even would have tied the anchor off a galleon around my neck and staggered off a cliff like someone who doesn't like things in order not to be upsetting people now with this Wednesday dead body, as you people say, in order not to be bothering anyone with this filthy piece of cold meat that doesn't have anything to do with me. There was so much truth in his manner that even the most mistrustful men, the ones who felt the bitterness of endless nights at sea fearing that their women would tire of dreaming about them and begin to dream of drowned men, even they and others who were harder still shuddered in the marrow of their bones at Esteban's sincerity.

That was how they came to hold the most splendid funeral they could conceive of for an abandoned drowned man. Some women who had gone to get flowers in the neighboring villages returned with other women who could not believe what they had been told, and those women went back for more flowers when they saw the dead man, and they brought more and more until there were so many flowers and so many people that it was hard to walk about. At the final moment it pained them to return him to the waters as an orphan and they chose a father and mother from among the best people, and aunts and uncles and cousins, so that through him all the inhabitants of the village became kinsmen. Some sailors who heard the weeping from a distance went off course, and people heard of one who had himself tied to the mainmast, remembering ancient fables about sirens. While they fought for the privilege of carrying him on

their shoulders along the steep escarpment by the cliffs, men and women became aware for the first time of the desolation of their streets, the dryness of
their courtyards, the narrowness of their dreams as they faced the splendor and
beauty of their drowned man. They let him go without an anchor so that he
could come back if he wished and whenever he wished, and they all held their
breath for the fraction of centuries the body took to fall into the abyss. They
did not need to look to one another to realize that they were no longer all present, that they would never be. But they also knew that everything would be different from then on, that their houses would have wider doors, higher ceilings,
and stronger floors so that Esteban's memory could go everywhere without
bumping into beams and so that no one in the future would dare whisper the
big boob finally died, too bad, the handsome fool has finally died, because they
were going to paint their house fronts gay colors to make Esteban's memory
eternal and they were going to break their backs digging for springs among the
stones and planting flowers on the cliffs so that in future years at dawn the passengers on great liners would awaken, suffocated by the smell of gardens on
the high seas, and the captain would have to come down from the bridge in his
dress uniform, with his astrolabe, his pole star, and his row of war medals and,
pointing to the promontory of roses on the horizon, he would say in fourteen
languages, look there, where the wind is so peaceful now that it's gone to sleep
beneath the beds, over there, where the sun's so bright that the sunflowers
don't know which way to turn, yes, over there, that's Esteban's village.

—Translated by Gregory Rabassa

QUESTIONS FOR DISCUSSION

1. What is revealed through the initial description of the drowned man? Why
   was "there . . . no room for him in their [the villagers'] imagination"?
2. Why and how does the drowned man make the women happy and the sea
   peaceful? Why does the community of women finally agree that this man
   must be Esteban?
3. How did the women feel about Esteban when he was alive? How do they
   feel about him now that he is dead?
4. Do the men of the village change their attitude toward the drowned man
   once they realize he is Esteban? Why or why not? Explain your point of
   view.
5. What is the significance of the villagers' making their island into a beautiful shrine dedicated to Esteban's size and beauty?
6. Why is the story subtitled "A Tale for Children"? What warnings and hope
   does the story offer?

CONNECTION

Compare this story about the origins of a myth with the qualities of the hero
myth as seen in Linda Seger's "Universal Stories" (see page 191). How is Mar-

quez's story of the birth of the hero more ironic than the hero stories portrayed in Seger's essay?

IDEAS FOR WRITING

1. Write an essay that examines the way the story weaves together realistic details and fantasy. How does this style help to emphasize and build the mythical quality of the story and its central character, Esteban?
2. Write an essay that interprets the myth and moral of "The Handsomest Drowned Man in the World." What truth and values are revealed in this portrait of a society in the process of creating a new myth?

RELATED WEB SITES

The Modern Word
`www.themodernword.com/gabo/`
Learn about the author, Gabriel García Márquez, at this Web site called "The Modern Word." Find many links, reviews, biographical, and bibliographical information here.

Magical Realism
`www.angelfire.com/wa2/margin/links.html`
Find a wide variety of information on the subject of magical realism—the genre of writing that Márquez is most famous for creating—here at this URL. Learn about other authors who write in this genre along with a special section devoted entirely to Márquez's work.

Marcelo Gleiser

The Myths of Science—Creation

Marcelo Gleiser was born in 1959 in Rio de Janeiro, Brazil, and received an M.Sc. in Rio de Janeiro in 1981. After completing his Ph.D. at the University of London in 1986, he immigrated to the United States, where he continued to study astronomy and physics. In 1995 he was hired as an associate professor of astrophysics at Dartmouth College, where he currently is the Appleton Professor of Physics. He has contributed articles to many professional journals and is widely known for his books The Dancing Universe: From Creation Myths to the Big Bang *(English translation, 1997), and* The Prophet and the Astronomer: A Scientific Journey to the End of Time *(2002). In the following article, Gleiser explores parallels between scientific and mythical accounts of the "creation" of the universe.*

JOURNAL
<hr>
Write about your idea of creation. Where did the world come from? How long did creation take? Was there any "agency" or being behind the creation of the world? How did you come to these conclusions?
<hr>

Myth, religion and science have more often than not proved inseparable in addressing the eternal imponderable: why something rather than nothing?

Since the dawn of civilization, humankind has marvelled at the skies and at Nature's myriad creations. This sense of wonder was deeply interwoven with a sense of fear: Nature's dual role as creator and destroyer has puzzled and polarized our perceptions of the cosmos. As a way of establishing a degree of control over the apparent unpredictability of natural phenomena, gods were held responsible for these conflicting manifestations. In short, Nature was deified.

The question of why there is something rather than nothing was a crucial part of this process. All cultures have attempted to provide an answer to the mystery of creation, and our modern scientific tradition is no exception. Perhaps more surprisingly, there is an intriguing correspondence between answers suggested by mythic narratives and those suggested by scientific research. The crucial difference, of course, is that the scientific process is capable of weeding out explanations which do not measure up to observations, while those based on myth are held true on the basis of faith alone.

Greece and Reason

Creation myths can be divided conveniently into two kinds: either the cosmos appeared at a specific moment in time marking the beginning of history, or it has always been "there." Myths with a creation event describe time in a linear fashion, with a beginning, middle and, as in the Christian narrative, an end. Myths without a creation event may consider time to be either unimportant or cyclic. Within these two sets, we encounter an enormous variety. Starting with the "no creation myths," the two possibilities are: an eternal, uncreated cosmos, as in the narrative of the Jains of India, or a cyclic cosmos, continuously created and destroyed, as beautifully represented in the Hindu tradition by the dance of Shiva.

5   The first and by far the most common "myth with creation" invokes a deity or deities who create the world, as in the Judaeo-Christian myth of Genesis. A second possibility is that the world was created out of nothing, without the interference of a god; this is what the Maori people of New Zealand have in mind when they sing, "from nothing the begetting, from nothing the increase. . . . " A final possibility is that the world appeared spontaneously from a primordial Chaos, where order coexists with disorder, Being with Non-Being.

The religious nature of the creation event has permeated scientific thought since its origins in Ancient Greece in the sixth century BC. As the Greek philosophers pondered the physical mechanisms that created the world and controlled its motions, many assumed an organizational principle based on rational design, attributed to a "Demiurge" by Plato or to the "Unmoved Mover" by Aristotle. Plato was a true heir of the Pythagorean tradition, which saw the world as a manifestation of Number, arranged and combined to create the harmonies perceived by the senses. The emphasis on a creation event was somewhat left aside, being substituted by the importance of reason in understanding the workings of Nature. The philosopher, in his search for rational meaning, was in effect elevating himself to a higher level of existence or that of the Demiurge's mind. To understand Nature was to understand God, or, in an oftquoted aphorism, to understand the mind of God.

This tradition reappeared in the West during the birth of modern science in the Renaissance. The great natural philosophers that spearheaded the so-called Copernican Revolution were all, to a greater or lesser degree, deeply religious men, who saw their scientific work as an integral part of their religious beliefs. Thus, Copernicus himself was a canon of the cathedral in Frauenberg, a reluctant revolutionary who sought to reconcile the arrangement of the celestial spheres with the Platonic ideal of circular motions with constant velocities. His model of the solar system was an elegant compromise between the old and the new, looking back at Plato and forward at the aesthetic principles of his time. His great opus, On the Revolutions of the Heavenly Orbs, was dedicated to Pope Paul III, in the hope that the Church would recognize the need for a reinterpretation of the Scriptures based on the new astronomical thought.

It was through the work of Giordano Bruno and, more importantly, Johannes Kepler and Galileo Galilei, that the Copernican Revolution was enacted. Kepler was deeply influenced by the Pythagorean tradition, a number mystic who believed geometry to be the key to the cosmic harmony. His three laws of planetary motion are a powerful illustration of how the scientific output of a great mind can be a byproduct of a belief system tempered by the analysis of data.

No Final Truths

Galileo's now famous tribulations with the Church were also a product of his beliefs. A pious (and overconfident) man, Galileo took as his personal mission to reset the course of Christian theology, preaching to the Church leaders the importance of accepting the new cosmic design. The clash was unavoidable, and in 1633 Galileo was forced to abjure his conviction in the Copernican system. Not for long, though, for soon after Isaac Newton put forward his three laws of motion and his universal theory of gravity in 1687, the sun-centered cosmos became widely accepted. To Newton, the cosmos was a manifestation of God's glory, infinite in extent and sublime in design.

During the twentieth century, the Newtonian universe was substituted by a curved Einsteinian universe; Einstein showed how matter and energy can bend space and alter the flow of time, endowing them with an unprecedented plasticity. Nowhere is this more spectacularly displayed than in the expansion of the universe itself, discovered by Edwin Hubble in 1929. Once again, the question of origins came back to haunt scientists: if the universe is expanding, there was a moment in time when all matter was squeezed into a very small volume. Astronomy was proclaiming that the universe did have an origin, after all. A cry of dissent emerged from Cambridge University via the proposal of the "steady-state model," where the universe never had a beginning in time. With the discovery that the whole cosmos is immersed in a bath of microwave radiation in the 1960s, the steady-state model was abandoned by most cosmologists; the "big-bang model" has since been accepted as the one which best fits the data.

Can science "explain" the age-old question of Creation? Certainly, physical models describing the origin of the cosmos can and have been proposed, at least since the 1970s. But these models face a serious technical obstacle: the lack of a proper theory to describe physical processes at the enormous energy scales prevalent during the first moments of cosmic history. They could be called scientific creation narratives, at least until they can be placed on more solid theoretical ground. We see old themes coming back, dressed in scientific jargon. In some models the universe was born out of "nothing," a quantum vacuum populated by all sorts of ephemeral energy fluctuations; others see the beginning as essentially chaotic, with an ordered cosmos emerging homogeneously in three dimensions.

Some of these models of creation make predictions about measurable properties of the universe, which can be used to test and refine them. Yet it may be hard to rule out all alternative models, which may also be compatible with these measurements. The best that we can hope for is a workable model of cosmic origins, compatible with observations but open to changes. Scientific inquiry is after all an ongoing process—there is no final truth, only approximations to the truth. Furthermore, science, at least as it is formulated at present, cannot answer questions concerning its own origin: we do not know why the universe operates according to the laws we have uncovered and not others. This essential incompleteness of science suggests a new form of complementarity between science and religion; religion does not exist to cover the holes of our scientific knowledge, but as a driving force behind scientific inspiration. Through our search for knowledge we uncover our true nature, fuelled by the same sense of mystery which filled our ancestors with awe.

QUESTIONS FOR DISCUSSION

1. Why does Gleiser believe that "Nature was deified" in the mythical age? What is the chief similarity and the chief difference between mythical narratives of creation and scientific explanations?
2. What does Gleiser believe are the two main types of creation myths and the different possibilities of each? Based on the readings in the "Portfolio of Creation Myths" later in this chapter, what other types and possibilities might there be?
3. According to Gleiser, how have religion-based notions of creation "permeated scientific thought" since long before the Christian era? How does

Plato's idea of the "Demiurge" serve as an example of "rational design" in the universe?

4. How was Copernicus a "reluctant revolutionary," in Gleiser's view? How did Copernicus attempt to reconcile his radical scientific views with traditional Christianity?

5. Although Newton managed to advance a sun-based center for the cosmos, how was his design still based on religious faith in "God's glory"? How did the twentieth century move beyond religious-based theories of the origin of life and matter?

6. What is missing in contemporary scientific theories of origins of the cosmos? Why does Gleiser call these theories "scientific creation narratives"? What is the "new form of complementarity between science and religion" that Gleiser refers to in his final paragraph?

CONNECTION

Compare Gleiser's idea of the purpose and possibilities of creation myths to one of the myths in the "Portfolio of Creation Myths" later in this chapter in order to determine how well the myth you have chosen fits into Gleiser's view of such myths.

IDEAS FOR WRITING

1. Do some research on the contemporary relation and/or conflict between science and religion in terms of theory, models, and narratives of creation. Write an essay that presents views of scientists who draw on religious models of creation and belief or religion-based creation narratives that make use of scientific theory and discovery. Do you think it is possible to see "complementarity" between these perspectives, or is conflict inevitable?

2. Write an essay in which you compare a particular scientific explanation of the origin and/or structure of the world such as those discussed in Gleiser's essay and a similar religious creation narrative/myth, such as one found in the "Portfolio of Creation Myths" or in a book or Internet site containing a variety of such myths.

RELATED WEB SITES

Marcelo Gleiser
www.unesco.org/courier/2001_05/uk/doss0.htm
This site includes information on research, lectures, and books by Marcelo Gleiser.

Science and Creation: The Riddle in the Skies
www.unesco.org/courier/2001_05/uk/doss0.htm
This issue of the *Unesco Courier* features several articles by Marcelo Gleiser and other scientists concerning the relationship between scientific and religious concepts of creation.

Portfolio of Creation Myths

We have selected the following myths from cultures around the world to encourage you to compare different fundamental beliefs and assumptions about reality. Preceding each myth is a note about the culture that produced it; following the portfolio is a set of questions for thought and writing.

JOURNAL

Discuss a creation myth or an experience of creating something very special to you. Develop imaginative comparisons and vivid details.

Genesis 2:4–23
(Old Testament of the Hebrew Bible)

This is the second account of creation in the Book of Genesis. Genesis 2 is thought to come from a different, less formal writing tradition (the "J," or Jehovah, tradition) from that of Genesis 1 and reveals an intimate relationship between God and his natural and human creations. The following passage portrays the God Jehovah, creating and watering the Garden of Eden, then creating animals, a man to till the fields, and finally a female helper for "the man." As you read the selection, consider the impact that the Book of Genesis has had on Western cultural assumptions and traditions.

Genesis 2:4: In the day that the Lord God made the earth and the heavens, (5) when no plant of the field was yet in the earth and no herb of the field had yet sprung up—for the Lord God had not caused it to rain upon the earth, and there was no man to till the ground; (6) but a mist went up from the earth and watered the whole face of the ground—(7) then the Lord God formed man of dust from the ground, and breathed into his nostrils the breath of life; and man became a living being. (8) And the Lord God planted a garden in Eden, in the east; and there he put the man whom he had formed. (9) And out of the ground the Lord God made to grow every tree that is pleasant to the sight and good for food, the tree of life also in the midst of the garden, and the tree of the knowledge of good and evil.

(10) A river flowed out of Eden to water the garden, and there it divided and became four rivers. (11) The name of the first is Pishon; it is the one which flows around the whole land of Hav'ilah, where there is gold; (12) and the gold of that land is good; bdellium and onyx stone are there. (13) The name of the second river is Gihon; it is the one which flows around the whole land of Cush.

(14) And the name of the third river is Tigris, which flows east of Assyria. And the fourth river is the Euphrates.

(15) The Lord God took the man and put him in the Garden of Eden to till it and keep it. (16) And the Lord God commanded the man, saying, "You may freely eat of every tree of the garden; (17) but of the tree of the knowledge of good and evil you shall not eat, for in the day that you eat of it you shall die."

(18) Then the Lord God said, "It is not good that the man should be alone; I will make him a helper fit for him." (19) So out of the ground the Lord God formed every beast of the field and every bird of the air, and brought them to the man to see what he would call them; and whatever the man called every living creature, that was its name. (20) The man gave names to all cattle, and to the birds of the air, and to every beast of the field; but for the man there was not found a helper fit for him. (21) So the Lord God caused a deep sleep to fall upon the man, and while he slept took one of his ribs and closed up its place with flesh; (22) and the rib which the Lord God had taken from the man he made into a woman and brought her to the man. (23) Then the man said, This at last is bone of my bones and flesh of my flesh; she shall be called Woman, because she was taken out of Man.

How the Sun Was Made: Dawn, Noontide and Night (Australian Aboriginal)

This aboriginal story of the sun's creation was adapted by W. J. Thomas, author of The Welsh Fairy-Tale Book *(1908), and appeared (using the flowery diction of his earlier anthology) in his collection* Some Myths and Legends of the Australian Aborigines *(1923).*

When the emu egg was hurled up to the sky it struck a great pile of wood which had been gathered by a cloud man named Ngoudenout. It hit the wood with such force that the pile instantly burst into flame, and flooded the earth with the soft, warm light of dawn. The flowers were so surprised that they lifted their sleepy heads to the sky and opened their petals so wide that the glistening dewdrops which night had given them fell to the ground and were lost. The little birds twittered excitedly on the trees, and the fairies, who kept the snow on the mountain tops, forgot their task, and allowed it to thaw and run into the rivers and creeks.

And what was the cause of this excitement? Away to the east, far over the mountains, the purple shadows of night were turning grey; the soft, pink-tinted clouds floated slowly across the sky like red-breasted birds winging their way to a far land. Along the dim sky-line a path of golden fire marked the parting of the grey shadows, and down in the valley the white mist was hiding the pale face of night.

Like a sleeper stirring softly at the warm touch of a kiss, all living things of the bush stirred at the caress of dawn. The sun rose with golden splendor in a clear blue sky, and, with its coming, the first day dawned. At first the wood pile burned slowly, but the heat increased, until at noonday it was thoroughly ablaze. But gradually it burnt lower and lower, until at twilight only a heap of glowing embers remained. These embers slowly turned cold and grey. The purple shadows and white mists came from their hiding-places, and once again the mantle of night was over the land.

When Ngoudenout saw what a splendid thing the sun was, he determined to give it to us for ever. At night, when the fire of the sun has burnt out, he goes to a dark forest in the sky and collects a great pile of wood. At dawn he lights it, and it burns feebly until noonday is reached, then it slowly burns away until twilight and night falls. Ngoudenout, the eternal wood gatherer, then makes his lonely way to the forest for the wood that lights the fire of the sun.

The Pelasgian Creation Myth (Ancient Greek)

This myth is the earliest known Greek creation myth. The Pelasgian stories were gathered in rural areas of Greece by a British scholar of mythology, Robert Graves, and published in his book The Pelasgian Myth *(1955). The following brief selection from the book describes the creation of all things out of the ritual dancing and coupling of the primal Eurynome, the "Goddess of All Things," with the snake Ophion.*

In the beginning, Eurynome, the Goddess of All Things, rose naked from Chaos, but found nothing substantial for her feet to rest upon, and therefore divided the sea from the sky, dancing lonely upon its waves. She danced towards the south, and the wind set in motion behind her seemed something new and apart with which to begin a work of creation.

Wheeling about, she caught hold of this north wind, rubbed it between her hands, and behold! the great serpent Ophion. Eurynome danced to warm herself, wildly and more wildly, until Ophion, grown lustful, coiled about those divine limbs and was moved to couple with her. Now, the North Wind, who is also called Boreas, fertilizes; which is why mares often turn their hind-quarters to the wind and breed foals without aid of a stallion. So Eurynome was likewise got with child.

Next, she assumed the form of a dove, brooding on the waves and, in due process of time, laid the Universal Egg. At her bidding, Ophion coiled seven times about this egg, until it hatched and split in two. Out tumbled all things that exist, her children: sun, moon, planets, stars, the earth with its mountains and rivers, its trees, herbs, and living creatures.

Eurynome and Ophion made their home upon Mount Olympus, where he vexed her by claiming to be the author of the Universe. Forthwith she bruised his head with her heel, kicked out his teeth, and banished him to the dark caves below the earth.

5   Next, the goddess created the seven planetary powers, setting a Titaness and a Titan over each. Theia and Hyperion for the Sun; Phoebe and Atlas for the Moon; Dione and Crius for the planet Mars; Metis and Coeus for the planet Mercury; Themis and Eurynmedon for the planet Jupiter; Tethys and Oceanus for Venus; Rhea and Cronus for the planet Saturn. But the first man was Pelasgus, ancestor of the Pelasgians; he sprang from the soil of Arcadia, followed by certain others, whom he taught to make huts and feed upon acorns and sew pig-skin tunics such as poor folk still wear in Euboea and Phocis.

The Chameleon Finds (Yao-Bantu, African)

"The Chameleon Finds" is a creation myth of the Yao, a Bantu tribe living by Lake Nyasa in Mozambique, Africa. Expressive of a close relationship with nature, this Yao myth, with a clever Chameleon and a helper Spider as the creator god's assistants, takes a critical view of human beings.

At first there were no people. Only Mulungu and the decent peaceful beasts were in the world. One day Chameleon sat weaving a fish-trap, and when he had finished he set it in the river. In the morning he pulled the trap and it was full of fish, which he took home and ate. He set the trap again. In the morning he pulled it out and it was empty: no fish.

"Bad luck," he said, and set the trap again.

The next morning when he pulled the trap he found a little man and woman in it. He had never seen any creatures like this.

"What can they be?" he said. "Today I behold the unknown." And he picked up the fish-trap and took the two creatures to Mulungu.

5   "Father," said Chameleon, "see what I have brought."

Mulungu looked. "Take them out of the trap," he said. "Put them down on the earth and they will grow."

Chameleon did this. And the man and woman grew. They grew until they became as tall as men and women are today.

All the animals watched to see what the people would do. They made fire. They rubbed two sticks together in a special way and thus made fire. The fire caught in the bush and roared through the forest and the animals had to run to escape the flames. The people caught a buffalo and killed it and roasted it in the fire and ate it. The next day they did the same thing. Every day they set fires and killed some animal and ate it.

"They are burning up everything!" said Mulungu. "They are killing my people!"

10   All the beasts ran into the forest as far away from mankind as they could get. Chameleon went into the high trees.

"I'm leaving!" said Mulungu. He called to Spider. "How do you climb on high?" he said.

"Very nicely," said Spider. And Spider spun a rope for Mulungu and Mulungu climbed the rope and went to live in the sky.

Thus the gods were driven off the face of the earth by the cruelty of man.

Spider Woman Creates the Humans (Hopi, Native American)

The following myth is only a brief selection from the much longer Hopi Emergence Story that uses birth imagery to explain a complex sequence of transformations in the act of creation. In the Hopi culture, the Emergence Story is told to the tribal initiates on the last evening of the year, after which the young men ascend a ladder to emerge from the kiva (Hopi dwelling) as full-fledged adult members of the Hopi community.

So Spider Woman gathered earth, this time of four colors, yellow, red, white, and black; mixed with tuchvala, the liquid of her mouth; molded them; and covered them with her white-substance cape which was the creative wisdom itself. As before, she sang over them the Creation Song, and when she uncovered them these forms were human beings in the image of Sotuknang. Then she created four other beings after her own form. They were wuti, female partners, for the first four male beings.

When Spider Woman uncovered them the forms came to life. This was at the time of the dark purple light, Qoyangnuptu, the first phase of the dawn of Creation, which first reveals the mystery of man's creation.

They soon awakened and began to move, but there was still a dampness on their foreheads and a soft spot on their heads. This was at the time of the yellow light, Sikangnuqua, the second phase of the dawn of Creation, when the breath of life entered man.

In a short time the sun appeared above the horizon, drying the dampness on their foreheads and hardening the soft spot on their heads. This was the time of the red light, Talawva, the third phase of the dawn of Creation, when man, fully formed and firmed, proudly faced his Creator.

5   "That is the Sun," said Spider Woman. "You are meeting your Father the Creator for the first time. You must always remember and observe these three phases of your Creation. The time of the three lights, the dark purple, the yellow, and the red reveal in turn the mystery, the breath of life, and warmth of love. These comprise the Creator's plan of life for you as sung over you in the Song of Creation."

The Beginning of the World (Japanese)

Like the other myths in this section, this Japanese story describes the process of cre-
ation (in this selection, of the islands of Japan) and focuses on issues such as the
proper social role of the sexes. The myth is from Genji Shibukawa's Tales from
the Kojiki *(712 C.E.), translated by Yaichiro Isobe. The* Kojiki *or* Records of
Ancient Matters *is the oldest work written in the Chinese kanji characters intro-*
duced to Japan through Korea in the sixth century. These were the original symbols
used to record the Japanese language.

Before the heavens and the earth came into existence, all was a chaos, unimaginably limitless and without definite shape or form. Eon followed eon: then, lo! out of this boundless, shapeless mass something light and transparent rose up and formed the heaven. This was the Plain of High Heaven, in which materialized . . . three divine beings are called the Three Creating Deities.

In the meantime what was heavy and opaque in the void gradually precipitated and became the earth, but it had taken an immeasurably long time before it condensed sufficiently to form solid ground. In its earliest stages, for millions and millions of years, the earth may be said to have resembled oil floating, medusa-like, upon the face of the waters. Suddenly like the sprouting up of a reed . . . many gods were thus born in succession, and so they increased in number, but as long as the world remained in a chaotic state, there was nothing for them to do.

Whereupon, all the Heavenly deities summoned the two divine beings, Izanagi and Izanami, and bade them descend to the nebulous place, and by helping each other, to consolidate it into terra firma. "We bestow on you," they said, "this precious treasure, with which to rule the land, the creation of which we command you to perform." So saying they handed them a spear . . . embellished with costly gems. The divine couple received the sacred weapon respectfully and ceremoniously and then withdrew from the presence of the Deities, ready to perform their august commission. Proceeding forthwith to the Floating Bridge of Heaven, which lay between the heaven and the earth, they stood awhile to gaze on that which lay below. What they beheld was a world not yet condensed, but looking like a sea of filmy fog floating to and fro in the air, exhaling the while an inexpressibly fragrant odor.

They were, at first, perplexed just how and where to start, but at length Izanagi suggested to his companion that they should try the effect of stirring up the brine with their spear. So saying he pushed down the jeweled shaft and found that it touched something. Then drawing it up, he examined it and observed that the great drops which fell from it almost immediately coagulated into an island, which is, to this day, the Island of Onokoro. Delighted at the result, the two deities descended forthwith from the Floating Bridge to reach the miraculously created island. In this island they thenceforth dwelt and made it the basis of their subsequent task of creating a country. Then wishing to become espoused, they erected in the center of the island a pillar, the Heavenly August Pillar, and built around it a great palace called the Hall of Eight Fathoms.

5   Thereupon the male Deity turning to the left and the female Deity to the right, each went round the pillar in opposite directions. When they again met each other on the further side of the pillar, Izanami, the female Deity, speaking first, exclaimed: "How delightful it is to meet so handsome a youth!" To which Izanagi, the male Deity, replied: "How delightful I am to have fallen in with such a lovely maiden!" After having spoken thus, the male Deity said that it was not in order that woman should anticipate man in a greeting. Nevertheless, they fell into connubial relationship, having been instructed by two wagtails which flew to the spot. Presently the Goddess bore her divine consort a son, but the baby was weak and boneless as a leech. Disgusted with it, they abandoned it on the waters, putting it in a boat made of reeds. Their second offspring was as disappointing as the first.

The two Deities, now sorely disappointed at their failure and full of misgivings, ascended to Heaven to inquire of the Heavenly Deities the causes of their misfortunes. The latter performed the ceremony of divining and said to them: "It is the woman's fault. In turning round the Pillar, it was not right and proper that the female Deity should in speaking have taken precedence of the male. That is the reason."

The two Deities saw the truth of this divine suggestion, and made up their minds to rectify the error. So, returning to the earth again, they went once more around the Heavenly Pillar. This time Izanagi spoke first saying: "How delightful to meet so beautiful a maiden!" "How happy I am," responded Izanami, "that I should meet such a handsome youth!" This process was more appropriate and in accordance with the law of nature. After this, all the children born to them left nothing to be desired. First, the island of Awaji was born, next, Shikoku, then, the island of Oki, followed by Kyushu; after that, the island Tsushima came into being, and lastly, Honshu, the main island of Japan. The name of . . . the Country of the Eight Great Islands was given to these eight islands. After this, the two Deities became the parents of numerous smaller islands destined to surround the larger ones.

QUESTIONS FOR DISCUSSION

1. What different images of the creator gods are presented in the various myths? Is the primary god in each clearly described? What powers and limits does the god have? Does the god operate alone or with other helping beings? What conclusions about the culture that produced each myth can you draw from these differences?

2. In the myths that present a clear picture of the physical world of the creation, how is the world described? How orderly and sequential is the act of creating the different elements and beings of the world? What conclusions can you draw from the varied presentation in these creation myths about the values of the culture that produced each myth?

3. Creation myths make significant comments on the roles and status of the sexes in various cultures. Compare and contrast the roles of sex and gender in the different creation myths included.
4. Another issue presented in some creation myths is the relationship of men and women to their creator. How do the humans in the various myths relate to the creator gods? How worshipful of God are the humans in the various myths?
5. Compare the ways that the different myths show the relationship between humans and nature. How harmonious a part of nature or how much at odds with nature do humans seem in the various myths? How are animals involved in the act of creation? Does part of the natural world need to be destroyed for creation to be completed?
6. Creation myths differ in tone. They can be imaginative and dreamlike, solemn and serious, philosophical, or even comical and mocking in tone. Compare the tone and attitude toward creation presented in each of the myths, then draw some conclusions about the values of each culture.

IDEAS FOR WRITING

7. Write your own creation myth, using characters, descriptions, and narration to illustrate the relationship between different aspects of creation: gods, animals, people, and the earth. At the end of your myth, comment on the values and ideas about the creative process and the world that your myth is designed to illustrate.
8. Develop an essay in the form of an extended comparison between two or three creation myths, each of which illustrates fundamental values and beliefs about gods, humans, and the natural world.

RELATED WEB SITES

Creation Myths—"Mything Links"
`www.mythinglinks.org/ct~creation.html`
Learn about creation myths from around the world at this Web site. Here you will find an annotated and illustrated collection of worldwide links to mythologies, fairy tales and folklore, sacred arts, and sacred traditions.

Bruno Bettelheim

Fairy Tales and the Existential Predicament

Born in Vienna and educated at the University of Vienna, Bruno Bettelheim (1903–1991) was imprisoned in a Nazi concentration camp for a time before immigrating to the United States. After settling in Chicago, he worked with autistic

*children, serving as director of the University of Chicago Orthogenic School from
1944 to 1973. Bettelheim's books, such as* On Learning to Read *(1981) and* A
Good Enough Parent *(1987), focus on the relationships between reading, parenting, and raising emotionally healthy children. The following selection from* The
Uses of Enchantment *(1976) presents a psychological perspective of the impact
that traditional fairy tales have on children. As you read the selection, think about
whether you agree with Bettelheim's theories about the role that fairy tales play in
creating healthy children.*

JOURNAL

Narrate the fairy tale that you remember most vividly from your childhood. Why
do you think you remember it? Would you share (or have you shared) this tale
with your own children? Why or why not?

In order to master the psychological problems of growing up—overcoming
narcissistic disappointments, oedipal dilemmas, sibling rivalries; becoming
able to relinquish childhood dependencies; gaining a feeling of selfhood and
of self-worth, and a sense of moral obligation—a child needs to understand
what is going on within his conscious self so that he can also cope with that
which goes on in his unconscious. He can achieve this understanding, and with
it the ability to cope, not through rational comprehension of the nature and
content of his unconscious, but by becoming familiar with it through spinning
out daydreams—ruminating, rearranging, and fantasizing about suitable story
elements in response to unconscious pressures. By doing this, the child fits unconscious content into conscious fantasies, which then enable him to deal with
that content. It is here that fairy tales have unequaled value, because they offer
new dimensions to the child's imagination which would be impossible for him
to discover as truly on his own. Even more important, the form and structure of
fairy tales suggest images to the child by which he can structure his daydreams
and with them give better direction to his life.

In child or adult, the unconscious is a powerful determinant of behavior.
When the unconscious is repressed and its content denied entrance into awareness, then eventually the person's conscious mind will be partially overwhelmed by derivatives of these unconscious elements, or else he is forced to
keep such rigid, compulsive control over them that his personality may become
severely crippled. But when unconscious material *is* to some degree permitted
to come to awareness and worked through in imagination, its potential for
causing harm—to ourselves or others—is much reduced; some of its forces can
then be made to serve positive purposes. However, the prevalent parental belief is that a child must be diverted from what troubles him most: his formless,
nameless anxieties, and his chaotic, angry, and even violent fantasies. Many
parents believe that only conscious reality or pleasant and wish-fulfilling images
should be presented to the child—that he should be exposed only to the sunny

side of things. But such one-sided fare nourishes the mind only in a one-sided way, and real life is not all sunny.

There is a widespread refusal to let children know that the source of much that goes wrong in life is due to our very own natures—the propensity of all men for acting aggressively, asocially, selfishly, out of anger and anxiety. Instead, we want our children to believe that, inherently, all men are good. But children know that *they* are not always good; and often, even when they are, they would prefer not to be. This contradicts what they are told by their parents, and therefore makes the child a monster in his own eyes.

The dominant culture wishes to pretend, particularly where children are concerned, that the dark side of man does not exist, and professes a belief in an optimistic meliorism. Psychoanalysis itself is viewed as having the purpose of making life easy—but this is not what its founder intended. Psychoanalysis was created to enable man to accept the problematic nature of life without being defeated by it, or giving in to escapism. Freud's prescription is that only by struggling courageously against what seem like overwhelming odds can man succeed in wringing meaning out of his existence.

5 This is exactly the message that fairy tales get across to the child in manifold form: that a struggle against severe difficulties in life is unavoidable, is an intrinsic part of human existence—but that if one does not shy away, but steadfastly meets unexpected and often unjust hardships, one masters all obstacles and at the end emerges victorious.

Modern stories written for young children mainly avoid these existential problems, although they are crucial issues for all of us. The child needs most particularly to be given suggestions in symbolic form about how he may deal with these issues and grow safely into maturity. "Safe" stories mention neither death or aging, the limits to our existence, nor the wish for eternal life. The fairy tale, by contrast, confronts the child squarely with the basic human predicaments.

For example, many fairy stories begin with the death of a mother or father; in these tales the death of the parent creates the most agonizing problems, as it (or the fear of it) does in real life. Other stories tell about an aging parent who decides that the time has come to let the new generation take over. But before this can happen, the successor has to prove himself capable and worthy. The Brothers Grimm's story "The Three Feathers" begins: "There was once upon a time a king who had three sons. . . . When the king had become old and weak, and was thinking of his end, he did not know which of his sons should inherit the kingdom after him." In order to decide, the king sets all his sons a difficult task; the son who meets it best "shall be king after my death."

It is characteristic of fairy tales to state an existential dilemma briefly and pointedly. This permits the child to come to grips with the problem in its most essential form, where a more complex plot would confuse matters for him. The fairy tale simplifies all situations. Its figures are clearly drawn; and details, unless very important, are eliminated. All characters are typical rather than unique.

Contrary to what takes place in many modern children's stories, in fairy tales evil is as omnipresent as virtue. In practically every fairy tale good and evil are given body in the form of some figures and their actions, as good and evil are omnipresent in life and the propensities for both are present in every man. It is this duality which poses the moral problem, and requires the struggle to solve it.

10   Evil is not without its attractions—symbolized by the mighty giant or dragon, the power of the witch, the cunning queen in "Snow White"—and often it is temporarily in the ascendancy. In many fairy tales a usurper succeeds for a time in seizing the place which rightfully belongs to the hero—as the wicked sisters do in "Cinderella." It is not that the evildoer is punished at the story's end which makes immersing oneself in fairy stories an experience in moral education, although this is part of it. In fairy tales, as in life, punishment or fear of it is only a limited deterrent to crime. The conviction that crime does not pay is a much more effective deterrent, and that is why in fairy tales the bad person always loses out. It is not the fact that virtue wins out at the end which promotes morality, but that the hero is most attractive to the child, who identifies with the hero in all his struggles. Because of this identification the child imagines that he suffers with the hero his trials and tribulations, and triumphs with him as virtue is victorious. The child makes such identifications all on his own, and the inner and outer struggles of the hero imprint morality on him.

The figures in fairy tales are not ambivalent—not good and bad at the same time, as we all are in reality. But since polarization dominates the child's mind, it also dominates fairy tales. A person is either good or bad, nothing in between. One brother is stupid, the other is clever. One sister is virtuous and industrious, the others are vile and lazy. One is beautiful, the others are ugly. One parent is all good, the other evil. The juxtaposition of opposite characters is not for the purpose of stressing right behavior, as would be true for cautionary tales. (There are some amoral fairy tales where goodness or badness, beauty or ugliness play no role at all.) Presenting the polarities of character permits the child to comprehend easily the difference between the two, which he could not do as readily were the figures drawn more true to life, with all the complexities that characterize real people. Ambiguities must wait until a relatively firm personality has been established on the basis of positive identifications. Then the child has a basis for understanding that there are great differences between people, and that therefore one has to make choices about who one wants to be. This basic decision, on which all later personality development will build, is facilitated by the polarizations of the fairy tale.

Furthermore, a child's choices are based, not so much on right versus wrong, as on who arouses his sympathy and who his antipathy. The more simple and straightforward a good character, the easier it is for a child to identify with it and to reject the bad other. The child identifies with the good hero not because of his goodness, but because the hero's condition makes a deep positive appeal to him. The question for the child is not "Do I want to be good?" but "Who do I want to be like?" The child decides this on the basis of projecting himself wholeheartedly into one character. If this fairy-tale figure is a very good person, then the child decides that he wants to be good, too.

Amoral fairy tales show no polarization or juxtaposition of good and bad persons; that is because these amoral stories serve an entirely different purpose. Such tales or type figures as "Puss in Boots," who arranges for the hero's success through trickery, and Jack, who steals the giant's treasure, build character not by promoting choices between good and bad, but by giving the child the hope that even the meekest can succeed in life. After all, what's the use of choosing to become a good person when one feels so insignificant that he fears he will never amount to anything? Morality is not the issue in these tales, but rather, assurance that one can succeed. Whether one meets life with a belief in the possibility of mastering its difficulties or with the expectation of defeat is also a very important existential problem.

The deep inner conflicts originating in our primitive drives and our violent emotions are all denied in much of modern children's literature, and so the child is not helped in coping with them. But the child is subject to desperate feelings of loneliness and isolation, and he often experiences mortal anxiety. More often than not, he is unable to express these feelings in words, or he can do so only by indirection: fear of the dark, of some animal, anxiety about his body. Since it creates discomfort in a parent to recognize these emotions in his child, the parent tends to overlook them, or he belittles these spoken fears out of his own anxiety, believing this will cover over the child's fears.

15   The fairy tale, by contrast, takes these existential anxieties and dilemmas very seriously and addresses itself directly to them: the need to be loved and the fear that one is thought worthless; the love of life, and the fear of death. Further, the fairy tale offers solutions in ways that the child can grasp on his level of understanding. For example, fairy tales pose the dilemma of wishing to live eternally by occasionally concluding: "If they have not died, they are still alive." The other ending—"And they lived happily ever after"—does not for a moment fool the child that eternal life is possible. But it does indicate that which alone can take the sting out of the narrow limits of our time on this earth: forming a truly satisfying bond to another. The tales teach that when one has done this, one has reached the ultimate in emotional security of existence and permanence of relation available to man; and this alone can dissipate the fear of death. If one has found true adult love, the fairy story also tells, one doesn't need to wish for eternal life. This is suggested by another ending found in fairy tales: "They lived for a long time afterward, happy and in pleasure."

An uninformed view of the fairy tale sees in this type of ending an unrealistic wish-fulfillment, missing completely the important message it conveys to the child. These tales tell him that by forming a true interpersonal relation, one escapes the separation anxiety which haunts him (and which sets the stage for many fairy tales, but it's always resolved at the story's ending). Furthermore, the story tells, this ending is not made possible, as the child wishes and believes, by holding on to his mother eternally. If we try to escape separation anxiety and death anxiety by desperately keeping our grasp on our parents, we will only be cruelly forced out, like Hansel and Gretel.

Only by going out into the world can the fairy-tale hero (child) find himself there; and as he does, he will also find the other with whom he will be able to live happily ever after; that is, without ever again having to experience separation anxiety. The fairy tale is future-oriented and guides the child—in terms he can understand in both his conscious and his unconscious mind—to relinquish his infantile dependency wishes and achieve a more satisfying independent existence.

Today children no longer grow up within the security of an extended family, or of a well-integrated community. Therefore, even more than at the times fairy tales were invented, it is important to provide the modern child with images of heroes who have to go out into the world all by themselves and who, although originally ignorant of the ultimate things, find secure places in the world by following their right way with deep inner confidence.

The fairy-tale hero proceeds for a time in isolation, as the modern child often feels isolated. The hero is helped by being in touch with primitive things—a tree, an animal, nature—as the child feels more in touch with those things than most adults do. The fate of these heroes convinces the child that, like them, he may feel outcast and abandoned in the world, groping in the dark, but, like them, in the course of his life he will be guided step by step, and given help when it is needed. Today, even more than in past times, the child needs the reassurance offered by the image of the isolated man who nevertheless is capable of achieving meaningful and rewarding relations with the world around him.

QUESTIONS FOR DISCUSSION

1. What does Bettelheim consider to be the primary positive psychological value of fairy tales? Do you agree?
2. According to Bettelheim, how do fairy tales help children to control destructive unconscious impulses? How does the polarization of good and evil in fairy tales help children?
3. Why does Bettelheim believe that children benefit more from reading traditional versions of fairy tales than modern stories for children?
4. How do fairy-tale endings help children to accept their isolation, their "existential predicament," while at the same time encourage them to believe in the possibility of creating meaningful relationships in their own world?
5. Why does Bettelheim believe that it is important for fairy tales to have happy endings? Do you agree with him? Why or why not?
6. What examples does Bettelheim give to support his ideas? What other examples might he have provided?

CONNECTION

After reading the Brothers Grimm's version of Cinderella (see page 229), included in this chapter, consider what place Bettelheim would see for this story within the theories he sets forth in "Fairy Tales and the Existential Predicament."

IDEAS FOR WRITING

1. Write a defense or refutation of Bettelheim's theory about the value of fairy tales for children. Refer specifically to both Bettelheim's ideas and your own ideas and experiences as a child reader or as an adult parenting or teaching young children.
2. Develop your journal entry into an essay. Expand on it by showing how your interpretation of the meaning of the fairy tale has changed as you have matured.

RELATED WEB SITES

Bruno Bettelheim
`http://peace.saumag.edu/faculty/kardas/courses/AHG/`
`Bettelheim.html`
Learn more about the controversial figure and work of Bruno Bettelheim at this simple but informative URL that shares many links to biographical and bibliographical information on Bettelheim.

Folklore, Myth and Legend for Children
`www.ucalgary.ca/~dkbrown/storfolk.html`
An annotated guide to major sites dealing with traditional literature geared toward children will be found at this URL from "the Children's Literature Web Guide" at the University of Calgary.

Jane Yolen

American Cinderella

Jane Yolen was born in New York in 1937 and earned her B.A. at Smith College in 1960 and her M.Ed. at the University of Massachusetts in 1976, where she also completed coursework for a doctorate in children's literature. Yolen has taught creative writing and children's literature at Smith College, worked as an editor for Harcourt Brace, and has written over 200 children's books. She has received many awards for her writing, including the Caldecott children's book award for The Emperor and the Kite *(1968) and for* Owl Moon *(1988), as well as the Parents' Choice Gold Medal for* Sword of the Rightful King *(2004). In her essay "American Cinderella," Yolen compares several older versions of the Cinderella story, which are strikingly different from the "Disney version" children are familiar with today.*

JOURNAL

Write about your first encounter with the Cinderella story as a child. What did you think of Cinderella: did she seem like a strong character to you, a good role model for young women? Why or why not? Explain.

It is part of the American creed, recited subvocally along with the pledge of allegiance in each classroom, that even a poor boy can grow up to become president. The unliberated corollary is that even a poor girl can grow up and become the president's wife. This rags-to-riches formula was immortalized in American children's fiction by the Horatio Alger stories of the 1860s and by the Pluck and Luck nickel novels of the 1920s.

It is little wonder, then, that Cinderella should be a perennial favorite in the American folktale pantheon.

Yet how ironic that this formula should be the terms on which "Cinderella" is acceptable to most Americans. "Cinderella" is *not* a story of rags to riches, but rather riches recovered; *not* poor girl into princess but rather rich girl (or princess) rescued from improper or wicked enslavement; *not* suffering Griselda enduring but shrewd and practical girl persevering and winning a share of the power. It is really a story that is about "the stripping away of the disguise that conceals the soul from the eyes of others. . . ."

We Americans have it wrong. "Rumpelstiltskin," in which a miller tells a whopping lie and his docile daughter acquiesces in it to become queen, would be more to the point.

5   But we have been initially seduced by the Perrault cinder-girl, who was, after all, the transfigured folk creature of a French literary courtier. Perrault's "Cendrillon" demonstrated the well-bred seventeenth-century female traits of gentility, grace, and selflessness, even to the point of graciously forgiving her wicked stepsisters and finding them noble husbands.

The American "Cinderella" is partially Perrault's. The rest is a spun-sugar caricature of her hardier European and Oriental forbears, who made their own way in the world, tricking the stepsisters with double-talk, artfully disguising themselves, or figuring out a way to win the king's son. The final bit of icing on the American Cinderella was concocted by that master candy-maker, Walt Disney, in the 1950s. Since then, America's Cinderella has been a coy, helpless dreamer, a "nice" girl who awaits her rescue with patience and a song. This Cinderella of the mass market books finds her way into a majority of American homes while the classic heroines sit unread in old volumes on library shelves.

Poor Cinderella. She has been unjustly distorted by storytellers, misunderstood by educators, and wrongly accused by feminists. Even as late as 1975, in the well-received volume *Womenfolk and Fairy Tales*, Rosemary Minard writes that Cinderella "would still be scrubbing floors if it were not for her fairy godmother." And Ms. Minard includes her in a sweeping condemnation of folk heroines as "insipid beauties waiting passively for Prince Charming."

Like many dialecticians, Ms. Minard reads the fairy tales incorrectly. Believing—rightly—that the fairy tales, as all stories for children, acculturate young readers and listeners, she has nevertheless gotten her target wrong. Cinderella is not to blame. Not the real, the true Cinderella. Ms. Minard should focus her sights on the mass-market Cinderella. She does not recognize the old Ash-girl for the tough, resilient heroine. The wrong Cinderella has gone to the American ball.

The story of Cinderella has endured for over a thousand years, surfacing in a literary source first in ninth-century China. It has been found from the Orient to the interior of South America and over five hundred variants have been located by folklorists in Europe alone. This best-beloved tale has been brought to life over and over and no one can say for sure where the oral tradition began. The European story was included by Charles Perrault in his 1697 collection *Histories ou Contes du temps passé* as "Cendrillon." But even before that, the Italian Straparola had a similar story in a collection. Since there had been twelve editions of the Straparola book printed in French before 1694, the chances are strong that Perrault had read the tale "*Peau d'Ane*" (Donkey Skin).

10   Joseph Jacobs, the indefatigable Victorian collector, once said of a Cinderella story he printed that it was "an English version of an Italian adaption of a Spanish translation of a Latin version of a Hebrew translation of an Arabic translation of an Indian original." Perhaps it was not a totally accurate statement of that particular variant, but Jacobs was making a point about the perils of folktale-telling: each teller brings to a tale something of his/her own cultural orientation. Thus in China, where the "lotus foot," or tiny foot was such a sign of a woman's worth that the custom of foot-binding developed, the Cinderella tale lays emphasis on an impossibly small slipper as a clue to the heroine's identity. In seventeenth-century France, Perrault's creation sighs along with her stepsisters over the magnificent "gold flowered mantua" and the "diamond stomacher." In the Walt Disney American version, both movie and book form, Cinderella shares with the little animals a quality of "lovableness," thus changing the intent of the tale and denying the heroine her birthright of shrewdness, inventiveness, and grace under pressure.

Notice, though, that many innovations—the Chinese slipper, the Perrault godmother with her midnight injunction and her ability to change pumpkin into coach—become incorporated in later versions. Even a slip of the English translator's tongue (*de vair*, fur, into *de verre*, glass) becomes immortalized. Such cross fertilization of folklore is phenomenal. And the staying power, across countries and centuries, of some of these inventions is notable. Yet glass slipper and godmother and pumpkin coach are not the common incidents by which a "Cinderella" tale is recognized even though they have become basic ingredients in the American story. Rather, the common incidents recognized by folklorists are these: an ill-treated though rich and worthy heroine in Cindersdisguise; the aid of a magical gift or advice by a beast/bird/mother substitute; the dance/festival/church scene where the heroine comes in radiant display; recognition through a token. So "Cinderella" and her true sister tales, "Cap o' Rushes" with its King Lear judgement and "Catskin" wherein the father unnaturally desires his daughter, are counted.

Andrew Lang's judgement that "a naked shoeless race could not have invented Cinderella," then, proves false. Variants have been found among the fur-wearing folk of Alaska and the native tribes in South Africa where shoes were not commonly worn.

"Cinderella" speaks to all of us in whatever skin we inhabit: the child mistreated, a princess or highborn lady in disguise bearing her trials with patience and fortitude. She makes intelligent decisions for she knows that wishing solves nothing without the concomitant action. We have each of us been that child. It is the longing of any youngster sent supperless to bed or given less than a full share at Christmas. It is the adolescent dream.

To make Cinderella less than she is, then, is a heresy of the worst kind. It cheapens our most cherished dreams, and it makes a mockery of the true magic inside us all—the ability to change our own lives, the ability to control our own destinies.

15   Cinderella first came to America in the nursery tales the settlers remembered from their own homes and told their children. Versions of these tales can still be found. Folklorist Richard Chase, for example, discovered "Rush Cape," an exact parallel of "Cap o' Rushes" with an Appalachian dialect in Tennessee, Kentucky, and South Carolina among others.

But when the story reached print, developed, was made literary, things began to happen to the hardy Cinderella. She suffered a sea change, a sea change aggravated by social conditions.

In the 1870s, for example, in the prestigious magazine for children *St. Nicholas,* there are a number of retellings or adaptations of "Cinderella." The retellings which merely translate European variants contain the hardy heroine. But when a new version is presented, a helpless Cinderella is born. G.B. Bartlett's "Giant Picture-Book," which was considered "a curious novelty [that] can be produced . . . by children for the amusement of their friends . . . " presents a weepy, prostrate young blonde (the instructions here are quite specific) who must be "aroused from her sad revery" by a godmother. Yet in the truer Cinderella stories, the heroine is not this catatonic. For example, in the Grimm "Cinder-Maid," though she weeps, she continues to perform the proper rites and rituals at her mother's grave, instructing the birds who roost there to:

Make me a lady fair to see,
Dress me as splendid as can be.

And in "The Dirty Shepherdess," a "Cap o' Rushes" variant from France, ". . . she dried her eyes, and made a bundle of her jewels and her best dresses and hurriedly left the castle where she was born." In the *St. Nicholas* "Giant Picture-Book" she has none of this strength of purpose. Rather, she is manipulated by the godmother until the moment she stands before the prince where she speaks "meekly" and "with downcast eyes and extended hand."

St. Nicholas was not meant for the mass market. It had, in Selma Lanes' words, "a patrician call to a highly literate readership." But nevertheless, Bartlett's play instructions indicate how even in the more literary reaches of children's books a change was taking place.

20   However, to truly mark this change in the American "Cinderella," one must turn specifically to the mass-market books, merchandised products that mas-

querade as literature but make as little lasting literary impression as a lollipop. They, after all, serve the majority the way the storytellers of the village used to serve. They find their way into millions of homes.

Mass market books are almost as old as colonial America. The chap-books of the eighteenth and nineteenth century, crudely printed tiny paperbacks, were the source of most children's reading in the early days of our country. Originally these were books imported from Europe. But slowly American publishing grew. In the latter part of the nineteenth century one firm stood out— McLoughlin Bros. They brought bright colors to the pages of children's books. In a series selling for twenty-five cents per book, *Aunt Kate's Series,* bowdlerized folk tales emerged. "Cinderella" was there, along with "Red Riding Hood," "Puss in Boots," and others. Endings were changed, innards cleaned up, and good triumphed with very loud huzzahs. Cinderella is the weepy, sentimentalized pretty girl incapable of helping herself. In contrast, one only has to look at the girl in "Cap o' Rushes" who comes to a great house and asks "Do you want a maid?" and when refused, goes on to say ". . . I ask no wages and do any sort of work." And she does. In the end, when the master's young son is dying of love for the mysterious lady, she uses her wits to work her way out of the kitchen. Even in Perrault's "Cinderilla," when the fairy godmother runs out of ideas for enchantment and "was at a loss for a coachman, I'll go and see, says Cinderilla, if there be never a rat in the rat-trap, we'll make a coachman of him. You are in the right, said her godmother, go and see."

Hardy, helpful, inventive, that was the Cinderella of the old tales but not of the mass market in the nineteenth century. Today's mass-market books are worse. These are the books sold in supermarket and candystore, even lining the shelves of many of the best bookstores. There are pop-up Cinderellas, coloring-book Cinderellas, scratch-and-sniff Cinderellas, all inexpensive and available. The point in these books is not the story but the *gimmick.* These are books which must "interest 300,000 children, selling their initial print order in one season and continuing strong for at least two years after that." Compare that with the usual trade publishing house print order of a juvenile book—10,000 copies which an editor hopes to sell out in a lifetime of that title.

All the folk tales have been gutted. But none so changed, I believe, as "Cinderella." For the sake of Happy Ever After, the mass-market books have brought forward a good, malleable, forgiving little girl and put her in Cinderella's slippers. However, in most of the Cinderella tales there is no forgiveness in the heroine's heart. No mercy. Just justice. In "Rushen Coatie" and "The Cinder-Maid," the elder sisters hack off their toes and heels in order to fit the shoe. Cinderella never stops them, never implies that she has the matching slipper. In fact, her tattletale birds warn the prince in "Rushen Coatie":

Hacked Heels and Pinched Toes
Behind the young prince rides,
But Pretty Feet and Little Feet
Behind the cauldron bides.

Even more graphically, they call out in "Cinder-Maid"

Turn and peep, turn and peep,
There's blood within the shoe;
A bit is cut from off the heel
And a bit from off the toe.

25   Cinderella never says a word of comfort. And in the least bowdlerized of the German and Nordic tales, the two sisters come to the wedding "the elder was at the right side and the younger at the left, and the pigeons pecked out one eye from each of them. Afterwards, as they came back, the elder was on the left, and the younger at the right, and then the pigeons pecked out the other eye from each. And thus, for their wickedness and falsehood, they were punished with blindness all their days." That's a far cry from Perrault's heroine who "gave her sisters lodgings in the palace, and married them the same day to two great lords of the court." And further still from Nola Langner's Scholastic paperback "Cinderella":

[The sisters] began to cry.
They begged Cinderella to forgive them for being so mean to her.
Cinderella told them they were forgiven.
"I am sure you will never be mean to me again," she said.
"Oh, never," said the older sister.
"Never, ever," said the younger sister.

Missing, too, from the mass-market books is the shrewd, even witty Cinderella. In a Wonder Book entitled "Bedtime Stories," a 1940s adaptation from Perrault, we find a Cinderella who talks to her stepsisters "in a shy little voice." Even Perrault's heroine bantered with her stepsisters, asking them leading questions about the ball while secretly and deliciously knowing the answers. In the Wonder Book, however, the true wonder is that Cinderella ever gets to be princess. Even face-to-face with the prince, she is unrecognized until she dons her magic ballgown. Only when her clothes are transformed does the Prince know his true love.

In 1949, Walt Disney's film *Cinderella* burst onto the American scene. The story in the mass market has not been the same since.

The film came out of the studio at a particularly trying time for Disney. He had been deserted by the intellectuals who had been champions of this art for some years. Because of World War II, the public was more interested in war films than cartoons. But when *Cinderella,* lighter than light, was released it brought back to Disney—and his studio—all of his lost fame and fortune. The film was one of the most profitable of all time for the studio, grossing $4.247 million dollars in the first release alone. The success of the movie opened the floodgates of "Disney Cinderella" books.

Golden Press's *Walt Disney's Cinderella* set the new pattern for America's Cinderella. This book's text is coy and condescending. (Sample: "And her best

friends of all were—guess who—the mice!") The illustrations are poor cartoons. And Cinderella herself is a disaster. She cowers as her sisters rip her
homemade ball gown to shreds. (Not even homemade by Cinderella, but by
the mice and birds.) She answers her stepmother with whines and pleadings.
She is a sorry excuse for a heroine, pitiable and useless. She cannot perform
even a simple action to save herself, though she is warned by her friends, the
mice. She does not hear them because she is "off in a world of dreams." Cinderella begs, she whimpers, and at last has to be rescued by—guess who—
the mice!

There is also an easy-reading version published by Random House, *Walt
Disney's Cinderella*. This Cinderella commits the further heresy of cursing her
luck. "How I did wish to go to the ball," she says. "But it is no use. Wishes never
come true."

30 But in the fairy tales wishes have a habit of happening—*wishes accompanied by
the proper action*, bad wishes as well as good. That is the beauty of the old stories
and their wisdom as well.

Take away the proper course of action, take away Cinderella's ability to
think for herself and act for herself, and you are left with a tale of wishes-come-
true-regardless. But that is not the way of the fairy tale. As P.L. Travers so wisely
puts it, "If that were so, wouldn't we all be married to princes?"

The mass-market American "Cinderellas" have presented the majority of
American children with the wrong dream. They offer the passive princess, the
"insipid beauty waiting . . . for Prince Charming" that Rosemary Minard objects
to, and thus acculturate millions of girls and boys. But it is the wrong Cinderella and the magic of the old tales has been falsified, the true meaning lost,
perhaps forever.

QUESTIONS FOR DISCUSSION

1. How is the American Cinderella related to the Horatio Alger "rags-to-
riches" stories? What other American and European influences have
molded this version, according to Yolen?

2. Of what unfair charges has Cinderella been unfairly accused, in Yolen's
view? In what sense is the core, ancient version of the story "about 'the
stripping away of the disguise that conceals the soul from the eyes of
others'"? What is the original story *not* about, according to Yolen?

3. What "recognizable" features and details of the American Cinderella story
are actually innovations, and what other incidents are common in the
older versions but missing in the American versions and in the "Cendrillon" of Charles Perrault? Look through the various versions included in
this book to see which ones have which features in common that depart
from the version popular in the United States.

4. How did the *St. Nicholas* children's magazine of the 1870s contribute to
the distortions or "innovations" in the original Cinderella persona? How
did older oral American versions of the story differ from the *St. Nicholas*
version and the "bowdlerized" *Aunt Kate's Series* versions?

5. How are issues of justice, punishment, and forgiveness for Cinderella's adversities handled differently in the American versions of the tale in contrast to older versions?
6. How did the Walt Disney version of Cinderella further weaken and degrade Cinderella's character? Why do you think his version of the tale became popular in the 1950s and continues to be popular today?

CONNECTION

Compare Yolen's view of fairy tales and the importance of the themes of struggle and violence with the views of Bruno Bettelheim on these themes in his essay in this chapter (see page 215).

IDEAS FOR WRITING

1. Write an essay in which you compare two versions of the Cinderella story not found in our textbook (one could be a film). How do the two versions reflect different cultural values? In what ways are they similar?
2. Write an essay in which you demonstrate how values and roles for women have been shaped by the American-style Cinderella myth. You can draw examples from personal experience as well as popular and commercial culture, such as films and television programs.

RELATED WEB SITES

Jane Yolen Web Site
www.janeyolen.com
The official Web site for Jane Yolen contains a bibliography of books by Yolen, a biography, a set of links for teachers on how to use children's books in the classroom, and an extensive links for writers.

The Children's Literature Web Guide: Cinderella Stories
www.acs.ucalgary.ca/~dkbrown/cinderella.html
This Web guide to Cinderella stories contains many full-text variants of the Cinderella story from around the world, a bibliography of books and articles on the stories, and an extensive list of picture books containing different versions.

Four Versions of Cinderella

Common tales are shared throughout the world in similar yet subtly distinct versions and are retold, generation after generation, over a period of many centuries. Following are four versions of the popular Cinderella fairy tale: the classic Brothers Grimm fairy tale, "Aschenputtel"; Charles Perrault's "Cendrillon"; the Native American "Algonquin Cinderella"; and "Tam and Cam," a Vietnamese folk version of Cinderella.

Write down a fairy tale that you remember from your childhood. Why was this story an important one to you when you were a child? What meaning does the story have for you today?

The Brothers Grimm

Aschenputtel

Jacob Grimm (1785–1863) and his brother Wilhelm Grimm (1786–1859) were scholars of the German language and of folk culture; they collected oral narratives that embodied the cultural values of the German peasant and reflected on universal human concerns. The Grimms' tales have been translated into more than seventy different languages. "Aschenputtel," a version of the Cinderella story, appears here in a version translated by Lucy Crane.

There was once a rich man whose wife lay sick, and when she felt her end drawing near she called to her only daughter to come near her bed, and said, "Dear child, be pious and good, and God will always take care of you, and I will look down upon you from heaven, and will be with you."

And then she closed her eyes and expired. The maiden went everyday to her mother's grave and wept, and was always pious and good. When the winter came the snow covered the grave with a white covering, and when the sun came in the early spring and melted it away, the man took to himself another wife.

The new wife brought two daughters home with her, and they were beautiful and fair in appearance, but at heart were black and ugly. And then began very evil times for the poor stepdaughter.

"Is the stupid creature to sit in the same room with us?" said they; "those who eat food must earn it. Out upon her for a kitchen-maid!"

5   They took away her pretty dresses, and put on her an old gray kirtle, and gave her wooden shoes to wear.

"Just look now at the proud princess, how she is decked out!" cried they laughing, and then they sent her into the kitchen. There she was obliged to do heavy work from morning to night, get up early in the morning, draw water, make the fires, cook, and wash. Besides that, the sisters did their utmost to torment her—mocking her, and strewing peas and lentils among the ashes, and setting her to pick them up. In the evenings, when she was quite tired out with her hard day's work, she had no bed to lie on, but was obliged to rest on the hearth among the cinders. And as she always looked dusty and dirty, they named her Aschenputtel.

It happened one day that the father went to the fair, and he asked his two stepdaughters what he should bring back for them.

"Fine clothes!" said one.

"Pearls and jewels!" said the other.

10 "But what will you have, Aschenputtel?" said he.

"The first twig, father, that strikes against your hat on the way home; that is what I should like you to bring me."

So he bought for the two stepdaughters fine clothes, pearls, and jewels, and on his way back, as he rode through a green lane, a hazel-twig struck against his hat; and he broke it off and carried it home with him. And when he reached home he gave to the stepdaughters what they had wished for, and to Aschenputtel he gave the hazel-twig. She thanked him, and went to her mother's grave, and planted this twig there, weeping so bitterly that the tears fell upon it and watered it, and it flourished and became a fine tree. Aschenputtel went to see it three times a day, and wept and prayed, and each time a white bird rose up from the tree, and if she uttered any wish the bird brought her whatever she had wished for.

Now it came to pass that the king ordained a festival that should last for three days, and to which all the beautiful young women of that country were bidden, so that the king's son might choose a bride from among them. When the two stepdaughters heard that they too were bidden to appear, they felt very pleased, and they called Aschenputtel, and said,

"Comb our hair, brush our shoes, and make our buckles fast, we are going to the wedding feast at the king's castle."

15 Aschenputtel, when she heard this, could not help crying, for she too would have liked to go to the dance, and she begged her stepmother to allow her.

"What, you Aschenputtel!" said she, "in all your dust and dirt, you want to go to the festival! you that have no dress and no shoes! you want to dance!"

But as she persisted in asking, at last the stepmother said,

"I have strewed a dish-full of lentils in the ashes, and if you can pick them all up again in two hours you may go with us."

Then the maiden went to the back-door that led into the garden, and called out,

"O gentle doves, O turtle-doves,
And all the birds that be,
The lentils that in ashes lie
Come and pick up for me!
The good must be put in the dish,
The bad you may eat if you wish."

20 Then there came to the kitchen-window two white doves, and after them some turtle-doves, and at last a crowd of all the birds under heaven, chirping and fluttering, and they alighted among the ashes; and the doves nodded with their heads, and began to pick, peck, pick, peck, and then all the others began to pick, peck, pick, peck, and put all the good grains into the dish. Before an hour was over all was done, and they flew away. Then the maiden brought the

dish to her stepmother, feeling joyful, and thinking that now she should go to the feast; but the stepmother said,

"No, Aschenputtel, you have no proper clothes, and you do not know how to dance, and you would be laughed at!"

And when Aschenputtel cried for disappointment, she added,

"If you can pick two dishes full of lentils out of the ashes, nice and clean, you shall go with us," thinking to herself, "for that is not possible." When she had strewed two dishes full of lentils among the ashes the maiden went through the backdoor into the garden, and cried,

"O gentle doves, O turtle-doves,
And all the birds that be,
The lentils that in ashes lie
Come and pick up for me!
The good must be put in the dish,
The bad you may eat if you wish."

So there came to the kitchen-window two white doves, and then some turtle-doves, and at last a crowd of all the other birds under heaven, chirping and fluttering, and they alighted among the ashes, and the doves nodded with their heads and began to pick, peck, pick, peck, and then all the others began to pick, peck, pick, peck, and put all the good grains into the dish. And before half-an-hour was over it was all done, and they flew away. Then the maiden took the dishes to the stepmother, feeling joyful, and thinking that now she should go with them to the feast; but she said "All this is of no good to you; you cannot come with us, for you have no proper clothes, and cannot dance; you would put us to shame."

25   Then she turned her back on poor Aschenputtel, and made haste to set out with her two proud daughters.

And as there was no one left in the house, Aschenputtel went to her mother's grave, under the hazel bush, and cried,

"Little tree, little tree, shake over me,
That silver and gold may come down and cover me."

Then the bird threw down a dress of gold and silver, and a pair of slippers embroidered with silk and silver. And in all haste she put on the dress and went to the festival. But her stepmother and sisters did not know her, and thought she must be a foreign princess, she looked so beautiful in her golden dress. Of Aschenputtel they never thought at all, and supposed that she was sitting at home, and picking the lentils out of the ashes. The King's son came to meet her, and took her by the hand and danced with her, and he refused to stand up with any one else, so that he might not be obliged to let go her hand; and when any one came to claim it he answered,

"She is my partner."

And when the evening came she wanted to go home, but the prince said he would go with her to take care of her, for he wanted to see where the beautiful maiden lived. But she escaped him, and jumped up into the pigeon-house. Then the prince waited until the father came, and told him the strange maiden had jumped into the pigeon-house. The father thought to himself,

30 "It cannot surely be Aschenputtel," and called for axes and hatchets, and had the pigeon-house cut down, but there was no one in it. And when they entered the house there sat Aschenputtel in her dirty clothes among the cinders, and a little oil-lamp burnt dimly in the chimney; for Aschenputtel had been very quick, and had jumped out of the pigeon-house again, and had run to the hazel bush; and there she had taken off her beautiful dress and laid it on the grave, and her bird had carried it away again, and then she had put on her little gray kirtle again, and had sat down in the kitchen among the cinders.

The next day, when the festival began anew, and the parents and stepsisters had gone to it, Aschenputtel went to the hazel bush and cried,

"Little tree, little tree, shake over me,
That silver and gold may come down and cover me."

Then the bird cast down a still more splendid dress than on the day before. And when she appeared in it among the guests every one was astonished at her beauty. The prince had been waiting until she came, and he took her hand and danced with her alone. And when any one else came to invite her he said,

"She is my partner."

And when the evening came she wanted to go home, and the prince followed her, for he wanted to see to what house she belonged; but she broke away from him, and ran into the garden at the back of the house. There stood a fine large tree, bearing splendid pears; she leapt as lightly as a squirrel among the branches, and the prince did not know what had become of her. So he waited until the father came, and then he told him that the strange maiden had rushed from him, and that he thought she had gone up into the pear-tree. The father thought to himself, "It cannot surely be Aschenputtel," and called for an axe, and felled the tree, but there was no one in it. And when they went into the kitchen there sat Aschenputtel among the cinders, as usual, for she had got down the other side of the tree, and had taken back her beautiful clothes to the bird on the hazel bush, and had put on her old gray kirtle again.

35 On the third day, when the parents and the stepchildren had set off, Aschenputtel went again to her mother's grave, and said to the tree,

"Little tree, little tree, shake over me,
That silver and gold may come down and cover me."

Then the bird cast down a dress, the like of which had never been seen for splendour and brilliancy, and slippers that were of gold.

And when she appeared in this dress at the feast nobody knew what to say for wonderment. The prince danced with her alone, and if any one else asked her he answered,

"She is my partner."

And when it was evening Aschenputtel wanted to go home, and the prince was about to go with her, when she ran past him so quickly that he could not follow her. But he had laid a plan, and had caused all the steps to be spread with pitch, so that as she rushed down them the left shoe of the maiden remained sticking in it. The prince picked it up, and saw that it was of gold, and very small and slender. The next morning he went to the father and told him that none should be his bride save the one whose foot the golden shoe should fit. Then the two sisters were very glad, because they had pretty feet. The eldest went to her room to try on the shoe, and her mother stood by. But she could not get her great toe into it, for the shoe was too small; then her mother handed her a knife, and said,

40   "Cut the toe off, for when you are queen you will never have to go on foot." So the girl cut her toe off, squeezed her foot into the shoe, concealed the pain, and went down to the prince. Then he took her with him on his horse as his bride, and rode off. They had to pass by the grave, and there sat the two pigeons on the hazel bush, and cried,

"There they go, there they go!
There is blood on her shoe;
The shoe is too small,
—Not the right bride at all!"

Then the prince looked at her shoe, and saw the blood flowing. And he turned his horse round and took the false bride home again, saying she was not the right one, and that the other sister must try on the shoe. So she went into her room to do so, and got her toes comfortably in, but her heel was too large. Then her mother handed her the knife, saying, "Cut a piece off your heel; when you are queen you will never have to go on foot."

So the girl cut a piece off her heel, and thrust her foot into the shoe, concealed the pain, and went down to the prince, who took his bride before him on his horse and rode off. When they passed by the hazel bush the two pigeons sat there and cried,

"There they go, there they go!
There is blood on her shoe;
The shoe is too small,
—Not the right bride at all!"

Then the prince looked at her foot, and saw how the blood was flowing from the shoe, and staining the white stocking. And he turned his horse round and brought the false bride home again.

"This is not the right one," said he, "have you no other daughter?"

45   "No," said the man, "only my dead wife left behind her a little stunted Aschenputtel; it is impossible that she can be the bride." But the King's son ordered her to be sent for, but the mother said,

"Oh no! she is much too dirty, I could not let her be seen."

But he would have her fetched, and so Aschenputtel had to appear.

First she washed her face and hands quite clean, and went in and curtseyed to the prince, who held out to her the golden shoe. Then she sat down on a stool, drew her foot out of the heavy wooden shoe, and slipped it into the golden one, which fitted it perfectly. And when she stood up, and the prince looked in her face, he knew again the beautiful maiden that had danced with him, and he cried,

"This is the right bride!"

50　　The stepmother and the two sisters were thunderstruck, and grew pale with anger; but he put Aschenputtel before him on his horse and rode off. And as they passed the hazel bush, the two white pigeons cried,

"There they go, there they go!
No blood on her shoe;
The shoe's not too small,
The right bride is she after all."

And when they had thus cried, they came flying after and perched on Aschenputtel's shoulders, one on the right, the other on the left, and so remained.

And when her wedding with the prince was appointed to be held the false sisters came, hoping to curry favour, and to take part in the festivities. So as the bridal procession went to the church, the eldest walked on the right side and the younger on the left, and the pigeons picked out an eye of each of them. And as they returned the elder was on the left side and the younger on the right, and the pigeons picked out the other eye of each of them. And so they were condemned to go blind for the rest of their days because of their wickedness and falsehood.

Related Web Sites

The Brothers Grimm
`www.pitt.edu/~dash/grimm.html`
Biographical information, studies of specific tales, electronic tales, and links to more resources on the Brothers Grimm can be found at this simple but informative URL.

Grimm Brothers @ NationalGeographic.com
`www.nationalgeographic.com/grimm/`
This attractive and entertaining Web site from *National Geographic* shares texts from many of Grimms' original fairy tales. It also includes audio samples of some of the stories, beautiful images, and interactive learning tools.

Charles Perrault

Cendrillon

This classic version of the Cinderella story, which is similar to the version Walt Disney used as the basis for his famous animated cartoon film, was written (based on earlier folk sources) by French author Charles Perrault (1628–1703) and collected in his Mother Goose Tales *(1697). "Cendrillon" was translated and adapted in an English version as "Cinderella, or the Little Glass Slipper" by English writer Andrew Lang for* The Blue Fairy Book *(1889).*

Once there was a gentleman who married, for his second wife, the proudest and most haughty woman that was ever seen. She had, by a former husband, two daughters of her own, who were, indeed, exactly like her in all things. He had likewise, by another wife, a young daughter, but of unparalleled goodness and sweetness of temper, which she took from her mother, who was the best creature in the world.

No sooner were the ceremonies of the wedding over but the stepmother began to show herself in her true colors. She could not bear the good qualities of this pretty girl, and the less because they made her own daughters appear the more odious. She employed her in the meanest work of the house. She scoured the dishes, tables, etc., and cleaned madam's chamber, and those of misses, her daughters. She slept in a sorry garret, on a wretched straw bed, while her sisters slept in fine rooms, with floors all inlaid, on beds of the very newest fashion, and where they had looking glasses so large that they could see themselves at their full length from head to foot.

The poor girl bore it all patiently, and dared not tell her father, who would have scolded her; for his wife governed him entirely. When she had done her work, she used to go to the chimney corner, and sit down there in the cinders and ashes, which caused her to be called Cinderwench. Only the younger sister, who was not so rude and uncivil as the older one, called her Cinderella. However, Cinderella, notwithstanding her coarse apparel, was a hundred times more beautiful than her sisters, although they were always dressed very richly.

It happened that the king's son gave a ball, and invited all persons of fashion to it. Our young misses were also invited, for they cut a very grand figure among those of quality. They were mightily delighted at this invitation, and wonderfully busy in selecting the gowns, petticoats, and hair dressing that would best become them. This was a new difficulty for Cinderella; for it was she who ironed her sister's linen and pleated their ruffles. They talked all day long of nothing but how they should be dressed.

5   "For my part," said the eldest, "I will wear my red velvet suit with French trimming."

"And I," said the youngest, "shall have my usual petticoat; but then, to make amends for that, I will put on my gold-flowered cloak, and my diamond stomacher, which is far from being the most ordinary one in the world."

They sent for the best hairdresser they could get to make up their head-pieces and adjust their hairdos, and they had their red brushes and patches from Mademoiselle de la Poche.

They also consulted Cinderella in all these matters, for she had excellent ideas, and her advice was always good. Indeed, she even offered her services to fix their hair, which they very willingly accepted. As she was doing this, they said to her, "Cinderella, would you not like to go to the ball?"

"Alas!" said she, "you only jeer me; it is not for such as I am to go to such a place."

10   "You are quite right," they replied. "It would make the people laugh to see a Cinderwench at a ball."

Anyone but Cinderella would have fixed their hair awry, but she was very good, and dressed them perfectly well. They were so excited that they hadn't eaten a thing for almost two days. Then they broke more than a dozen laces try-ing to have themselves laced up tightly enough to give them a fine slender shape. They were continually in front of their looking glass. At last the happy day came. They went to court, and Cinderella followed them with her eyes as long as she could. When she lost sight of them, she started to cry.

Her godmother, who saw her all in tears, asked her what was the matter.

"I wish I could. I wish I could." She was not able to speak the rest, being in-terrupted by her tears and sobbing.

This godmother of hers, who was a fairy, said to her, "You wish that you could go to the ball; is it not so?"

15   "Yes," cried Cinderella, with a great sigh.

"Well," said her godmother, "be but a good girl, and I will contrive that you shall go." Then she took her into her chamber, and said to her, "Run into the garden, and bring me a pumpkin."

Cinderella went immediately to gather the finest she could get, and brought it to her godmother, not being able to imagine how this pumpkin could help her go to the ball. Her godmother scooped out all the inside of it, leaving noth-ing but the rind. Having done this, she struck the pumpkin with her wand, and it was instantly turned into a fine coach, gilded all over with gold.

She then went to look into her mousetrap, where she found six mice, all alive, and ordered Cinderella to lift up a little the trapdoor. She gave each mouse, as it went out, a little tap with her wand, and the mouse was that mo-ment turned into a fine horse, which altogether made a very fine set of six horses of a beautiful mouse colored dapple gray.

Being at a loss for a coachman, Cinderella said, "I will go and see if there is not a rat in the rat trap that we can turn into a coachman."

20   "You are right," replied her godmother, "Go and look."

Cinderella brought the trap to her, and in it there were three huge rats. The fairy chose the one which had the largest beard, touched him with her wand, and turned him into a fat, jolly coachman, who had the smartest whiskers that eyes ever beheld.

After that, she said to her, "Go again into the garden, and you will find six lizards behind the watering pot. Bring them to me."

She had no sooner done so but her godmother turned them into six footmen, who skipped up immediately behind the coach, with their liveries all bedaubed with gold and silver, and clung as close behind each other as if they had done nothing else their whole lives. The fairy then said to Cinderella, "Well, you see here an equipage fit to go to the ball with; are you not pleased with it?"

"Oh, yes," she cried; "but must I go in these nasty rags?"

25 Her godmother then touched her with her wand, and, at the same instant, her clothes turned into cloth of gold and silver, all beset with jewels. This done, she gave her a pair of glass slippers, the prettiest in the whole world. Being thus decked out, she got up into her coach; but her godmother, above all things, commanded her not to stay past midnight, telling her, at the same time, that if she stayed one moment longer, the coach would be a pumpkin again, her horses mice, her coachman a rat, her footmen lizards, and that her clothes would become just as they were before.

She promised her godmother to leave the ball before midnight; and then drove away, scarcely able to contain herself for joy. The king's son, who was told that a great princess, whom nobody knew, had arrived, ran out to receive her. He gave her his hand as she alighted from the coach, and led her into the hall, among all the company. There was immediately a profound silence. Everyone stopped dancing, and the violins ceased to play, so entranced was everyone with the singular beauties of the unknown newcomer.

Nothing was then heard but a confused noise of, "How beautiful she is! How beautiful she is!"

The king himself, old as he was, could not help watching her, and telling the queen softly that it was a long time since he had seen so beautiful and lovely a creature.

All the ladies were busied in considering her clothes and headdress, hoping to have some made next day after the same pattern, provided they could find such fine materials and as able hands to make them.

30 The king's son led her to the most honorable seat, and afterwards took her out to dance with him. She danced so very gracefully that they all more and more admired her. A fine meal was served up, but the young prince ate not a morsel, so intently was he busied in gazing on her.

She went and sat down by her sisters, showing them a thousand civilities, giving them part of the oranges and citrons which the prince had presented her with, which very much surprised them, for they did not know her. While Cinderella was thus amusing her sisters, she heard the clock strike eleven and three-quarters, whereupon she immediately made a courtesy to the company and hurried away as fast as she could.

Arriving home, she ran to seek out her godmother, and, after having thanked her, she said she could not but heartily wish she might go to the ball the next day as well, because the king's son had invited her.

As she was eagerly telling her godmother everything that had happened at the ball, her two sisters knocked at the door, which Cinderella ran and opened.

"You stayed such a long time!" she cried, gaping, rubbing her eyes and stretching herself as if she had been sleeping; she had not, however, had any manner of inclination to sleep while they were away from home.

35   "If you had been at the ball," said one of her sisters, "you would not have been tired with it. The finest princess was there, the most beautiful that mortal eyes have ever seen. She showed us a thousand civilities, and gave us oranges and citrons."

Cinderella seemed very indifferent in the matter. Indeed, she asked them the name of that princess; but they told her they did not know it, and that the king's son was very uneasy on her account and would give all the world to know who she was. At this Cinderella, smiling, replied, "She must, then, be very beautiful indeed; how happy you have been! Could not I see her? Ah, dear Charlotte, do lend me your yellow dress which you wear every day."

"Yes, to be sure!" cried Charlotte; "lend my clothes to such a dirty Cinderwench as you are! I should be such a fool."

Cinderella, indeed, well expected such an answer, and was very glad of the refusal; for she would have been sadly put to it, if her sister had lent her what she asked for jestingly.

The next day the two sisters were at the ball, and so was Cinderella, but dressed even more magnificently than before. The king's son was always by her, and never ceased his compliments and kind speeches to her. All this was so far from being tiresome to her, and, indeed, she quite forgot what her godmother had told her. She thought that it was no later than eleven when she counted the clock striking twelve. She jumped up and fled, as nimble as a deer. The prince followed, but could not overtake her. She left behind one of her glass slippers, which the prince picked up most carefully. She reached home, but quite out of breath, and in her nasty old clothes, having nothing left of all her finery but one of the little slippers, the mate to the one that she had dropped.

40   The guards at the palace gate were asked if they had not seen a princess go out. They replied that they had seen nobody leave but a young girl, very shabbily dressed, and who had more the air of a poor country wench than a gentlewoman.

When the two sisters returned from the ball Cinderella asked them if they had been well entertained, and if the fine lady had been there.

They told her, yes, but that she hurried away immediately when it struck twelve, and with so much haste that she dropped one of her little glass slippers, the prettiest in the world, which the king's son had picked up; that he had done nothing but look at her all the time at the ball, and that most certainly he was very much in love with the beautiful person who owned the glass slipper.

What they said was very true; for a few days later, the king's son had it proclaimed, by sound of trumpet, that he would marry her whose foot this slipper would just fit. They began to try it on the princesses, then the duchesses and all the court, but in vain; it was brought to the two sisters, who did all they possibly could to force their foot into the slipper, but they did not succeed.

Cinderella, who saw all this, and knew that it was her slipper, said to them, laughing, "Let me see if it will not fit me."

45 Her sisters burst out laughing, and began to banter with her. The gentleman who was sent to try the slipper looked earnestly at Cinderella, and, finding her very handsome, said that it was only just that she should try as well, and that he had orders to let everyone try.

He had Cinderella sit down, and, putting the slipper to her foot, he found that it went on very easily, fitting her as if it had been made of wax. Her two sisters were greatly astonished, but then even more so, when Cinderella pulled out of her pocket the other slipper, and put it on her other foot. Then in came her godmother and touched her wand to Cinderella's clothes, making them richer and more magnificent than any of those she had worn before.

And now her two sisters found her to be that fine, beautiful lady whom they had seen at the ball. They threw themselves at her feet to beg pardon for all the ill treatment they had made her undergo. Cinderella took them up, and, as she embraced them, said that she forgave them with all her heart, and wanted them always to love her.

She was taken to the young prince, dressed as she was. He thought she was more charming than before, and, a few days after, married her. Cinderella, who was no less good than beautiful, gave her two sisters lodgings in the palace, and that very same day matched them with two great lords of the court.

Moral: Beauty in a woman is a rare treasure that will always be admired. Graciousness, however, is priceless and of even greater value. This is what Cinderella's godmother gave to her when she taught her to behave like a queen. Young women, in the winning of a heart, graciousness is more important than a beautiful hairdo. It is a true gift of the fairies. Without it nothing is possible; with it, one can do anything.

50 Another moral: Without doubt it is a great advantage to have intelligence, courage, good breeding, and common sense. These and similar talents come only from heaven, and it is good to have them. However, even these may fail to bring you success, without the blessing of a godfather or a godmother.

Related Web Site

Charles Perrault's Mother Goose Tales
`www.pitt.edu/~dash/perrault.html`
This site provides biographical information and useful links on Charles Perrault and his *Mother Goose Tales.*

The Algonquin Cinderella

This Native American version of the Cinderella story was anthologized by Idries Shah, father of Saira Shah and a student of world folklore and Sufism, in World Tales *(1979). As you read the tale, notice its emphasis on the spiritual power of beauty and vision.*

There was once a large village of the MicMac Indians of the Eastern Algonquins, built beside a lake. At the far end of the settlement stood a lodge, and in it lived a being who was always invisible. He had a sister who looked after him, and everyone knew that any girl who could see him might marry him. For that reason there were very few girls who did not try, but it was very long before anyone succeeded.

This is the way in which the test of sight was carried out: at evening-time, when the Invisible One was due to be returning home, his sister would walk with any girl who might come down to the lakeshore. She, of course, could see her brother, since he was always visible to her. As soon as she saw him, she would say to the girls:

"Do you see my brother?"

"Yes," they would generally reply—though some of them did say "No."

5   To those who said that they could indeed see him, the sister would say:

"Of what is his shoulder strap made?" Some people say that she would enquire: "What is his moose-runner's haul?" or "With what does he draw his sled?"

And they would answer:

"A strip of rawhide" or "a green flexible branch," or something of that kind.

10 Then she, knowing that they had not told the truth, would say:

"Very well, let us return to the wigwam!"

When they had gone in, she would tell them not to sit in a certain place, because it belonged to the Invisible One. Then, after they had helped to cook the supper, they would wait with great curiosity, to see him eat. They could be sure that he was a real person, for when he took off his moccasins they became visible, and his sister hung them up. But beyond this they saw nothing of him, not even when they stayed in the place all the night, as many of them did.

Now there lived in the village an old man who was a widower, and his three daughters. The youngest girl was very small, weak and often ill: and yet her sisters, especially the elder, treated her cruelly. The second daughter was kinder, and sometimes took her side: but the wicked sister would burn her hands and feet with hot cinders, and she was covered with scars from this treatment. She was so marked that people called her *Oochigeaskw*, the Rough-Faced-Girl.

When her father came home and asked why she had such burns, the bad sister would at once say that it was her own fault, for she had disobeyed orders and gone near the fire and fallen into it.

15 These two elder sisters decided one day to try their luck at seeing the Invisible One. So they dressed themselves in their finest clothes, and tried to look

their prettiest. They found the Invisible One's sister and took the usual walk by the water.

When he came, and when they were asked if they could see him, they answered: "Of course." And when asked about the shoulder strap or sled cord, they answered: "A piece of rawhide."

But of course they were lying like the others, and they got nothing for their pains.

The next afternoon, when the father returned home, he brought with him many of the pretty little shells from which wampum was made, and they set to work to string them.

That day, poor Little Oochigeaskw, who had always gone barefoot, got a pair of her father's moccasins, old ones, and put them into water to soften them so that she could wear them. Then she begged her sisters for a few wampum shells. The elder called her a "little pest," but the younger one gave her some. Now, with no other clothes than her usual rags, the poor little thing went into the woods and got herself some sheets of birch bark, from which she made a dress, and put marks on it for decoration, in the style of long ago. She made a petticoat and a loose gown, a cap, leggings and a handkerchief. She put on her father's large old moccasins, which were far too big for her, and went forth to try her luck. She would try, she thought, to discover whether she could see the Invisible One.

20 She did not begin very well. As she set off, her sisters shouted and hooted, hissed and yelled, and tried to make her stay. And the loafers around the village, seeing the strange little creature, called out "Shame!"

The poor little girl in her strange clothes, with her face all scarred, was an awful sight, but she was kindly received by the sister of the Invisible One. And this was, of course, because this noble lady understood far more about things than simply the mere outside which all the rest of the world knows. As the brown of the evening sky turned to black, the lady took her down to the lake.

"Do you see him?" the Invisible One's sister asked.

"I do, indeed—and he is wonderful!" said Oochigeaskw.

The sister asked:

25 "And what is his sled-string?"

The little girl said:

"It is the Rainbow."

"And, my sister, what is his bow-string?"

"It is The Spirit's Road—the Milky Way."

30 "So you *have* seen him," said his sister. She took the girl home with her and bathed her. As she did so, all the scars disappeared from her body. Her hair grew again, as it was combed, long, like a blackbird's wing. Her eyes were now like stars: in all the world there was no other such beauty. Then, from her treasures, the lady gave her a wedding garment, and adorned her.

Then she told Oochigeaskw to take the *wife's* seat in the wigwam: the one next to where the Invisible One sat, beside the entrance. And when he came in, terrible and beautiful, he smiled and said:

"So we are found out!"

"Yes," said his sister. And so Oochigeaskw became his wife.

Cinderella Stories

`www.ucalgary.ca/~dkbrown/cinderella.html`

Lists of variations on the Cinderella story can be found at this URL from the University of Calgary. Links to teaching ideas, articles, and essays will also be found here.

Tam and Cam (Vietnam)

"Tam and Cam" is a Vietnamese folk story that demonstrates how universal the Cinderella story is, as well as how unique each version is to the particular culture out of which it grew. The sensitive and resourceful Tam is similar in many ways to the Western Cinderella, yet she is very much a product of a strongly Buddhist, nature-oriented society. She is willing to use violence to attain her revenge, and she is re-born several times during the story as a different sort of being. "Tam and Cam" is retold by Vo Van Thang and Jim Larson in a bilingual version included in Vietnamese Folktales *(1993).*

There were once two stepsisters named Tam and Cam. Tam was the daughter of their father's first wife. She died when the child was young so her father took a second wife. Some years later the father died and left Tam to live with her stepmother and stepsister.

Her stepmother was most severe and treated the girl harshly. Tam had to labor all day and long into the night. When there was any daylight she had to care for the buffalo, carry water for the cooking, do the washing and pick vegetables and water-fern for the pigs to eat. At night she had to spend a lot of time husking the rice. While Tam worked hard her sister did nothing but play games. She was given pretty clothes to wear and always got the best food.

Early one morning the second-mother gave two creels to Tam and Cam and told them to go to the paddy fields to catch tiny shrimp and crab. "I will give a *yêm* of red cloth to the one who brings home a full creel," she promised.

Tam was very familiar with the task of finding shrimp and crab in the paddy fields, and by lunchtime she had filled her creel. Cam walked and waded from field to field but she could not catch anything. She looked at Tam's full creel and said to her, "Oh, my dear sister Tam, your hair is covered in mud. Get into the pond to wash it, or you will be scolded by mother when you return home."

5   Believing what her sister told her, Tam hurried to the pond to wash herself. As soon as her stepsister entered the water, Cam emptied the shrimp and crab into her own creel, and hurried home to claim the *yêm* of red cloth.

When she had finished washing and saw her empty creel Tam burst into tears.

A Buddha who was sitting on a lotus in the sky heard her sobs and came down beside her. "Why are you crying?" asked the Buddha.

Tam told him all that had happened and the Buddha comforted her. "Do not be tearful. Look into your creel and see if anything is left."

Tam looked into the creel and said to the Buddha, "There is only one tiny *bông* fish."

10 "Take the fish and put it in the pond near your home. At every meal you must save a bowl of rice with which to feed it. When you want the fish to rise to the surface to eat the rice you must call like this:

Dear *bông*, dear *bông*,
Rise only to eat my golden rice,
For that of others will not taste nice.

"Goodbye child, I wish you well." After saying this the Buddha disappeared.

15 Tam put the fish in the pond as she had been bidden, and every day, after lunch and the evening meal, she took some rice to feed it. Day by day the *bông* fish grew, and the girl became great friends with it.

Seeing Tam take rice to the pond after each meal the second-mother became suspicious, and bade Cam go to spy on her stepsister. Cam hid in a bush near the pond. When Tam called the *bông* fish the hidden girl listened to the words, and rushed to her mother to tell her of the secret.

That evening, the second-mother instructed Tam that on the following day she must take the buffalo to the far field.

"It is now the season for vegetables. Buffalo cannot graze in the village. Tomorrow you have to take the buffalo to the far field. If you graze in the village it will be taken by the notables."

Tam set off very early the next morning to ride the buffalo to the far field. When she was gone, Cam and her mother took rice to the pond and called the *bông* fish. It rose to the surface and the woman caught it. She then took it to the kitchen where she cooked and ate it.

20 Tam returned in the evening, and after eating her meal took rice to the pond to feed her friend. She called and called, again and again, but she saw only a drop of blood on the surface of the water. Tam knew that something terrible had happened to the *bông* fish and began to weep.

The Buddha appeared by her side again. "Why do you weep this time, my child?"

Tam sobbed out her story and the Buddha spoke. "Your fish has been caught and eaten. Now, stop crying. You must find the bones of the fish and put them in four jars. After doing this you must bury the jars. Put one under each of the legs of your bed."

Tam searched and searched for the bones of her beloved friend but could not find them anywhere. As she looked even further a rooster came and called to her.

Cock-a-doodle-do, cock-a-doodle-do,
25 A handful of rice,
And I'll find the bones for you.

Tam gave rice to the rooster, and when it had eaten it strutted into the kitchen. In no time at all the elegant fowl returned with the bones and laid them at Tam's feet. The girl placed the bones into four jars and buried one under each of the legs of her bed.

Some months later the king proclaimed that there would be a great festival. All the people of Tam's village were going to attend, and the road was thronged with well dressed people making their way to the capital. Cam and her mother put on their finest clothes in readiness to join them. When the woman saw that Tam also wanted to attend the gala day she winked at Cam. Then she mixed a basketful of unhusked rice with the basket of clean rice Tam had prepared the previous evening. "You may go to the festival when you have separated this grain. If there isn't any rice to cook when we return home you will be beaten."

With that, she and her daughter joined the happy people on their way to the festival, and left Tam to her lonely task. She started to separate the rice, but she could see that it was hopeless and she began to weep.

30 Once again the Buddha appeared by her side. "Why are there tears in your eyes?" he asked.

Tam explained about the rice grains that had to be separated, and how the festival would be over by the time she had finished.

"Bring your baskets to the yard," said the Buddha. "I will call the birds to help you."

The birds came and pecked and fluttered until, in no time at all, they had divided the rice into two baskets. Not one single grain did they eat, but when they flew away Tam began to weep again.

"Now why are you crying?" asked the Buddha.

35 "My clothes are too poor," sobbed Tam. "I thank you for your help, but I cannot go dressed like this."

"Go and dig up the four jars," ordered the Buddha. "Then you will have all you need."

Tam obeyed and opened the jars. In the first she found a beautiful silk dress, a silk *yêm* and a scarf of the same material. In the second jar she found a pair of embroidered shoes of a cunning design which fitted her perfectly. When she opened the third jar great was her surprise when she saw a miniature horse. It neighed once, and grew to become a noble steed. In the fourth jar there was a richly ornamented saddle and bridle which grew to fit the horse. She washed herself and brushed her hair until it shone. Then she put on her wonderful new clothes and rode off to the festival.

On the way she had to ride through a stream flowing over the road. As she did so, one of her embroidered shoes fell into the water and sank beneath the surface. She was in such a hurry that she could not stop to search for it, so she wrapped the other shoe in her scarf and rode on.

Shortly afterwards, the king and his entourage, led by two elephants, arrived at the same spot. The elephants refused to enter the water and lowered their tusks, bellowing and trumpeting. When no amount of goading would force them on, the king ordered his followers to search the water. One of them found the embroidered shoe and brought it to the king, who inspected it closely.

40   Finally he said, "The girl who wore a shoe as beautiful as this must herself be very beautiful. Let us go on to the festival and find her. Whoever it fits will be my wife."

There was great excitement when all the women learned of the king's decision, and they eagerly waited for their turn to try on the shoe.

Cam and her mother struggled to make it fit, but to no avail, and when they saw Tam waiting patiently nearby the woman sneered at her. "How can someone as common as you be the owner of such a shoe? And where did you steal those fine clothes? Wait till we get home. If there isn't any rice to cook I am going to beat you severely."

Tam said nothing, but when it came her turn to try on the shoe it fitted perfectly. Then she showed the other one that was wrapped in the scarf, and everyone knew that she was the future queen.

The king ordered his servants to take Tam to the palace in a palanquin, and she rode off happily under the furious and jealous gazes of her stepsister and stepmother.

45   Tam was very happy living in the citadel with the king, but she never forgot her father. As the anniversary of his death came nearer she asked the king if she could return to her village to prepare the offering.

When Cam and her mother saw that Tam had returned, their jealous minds formed a wicked plan. "You must make an offering of betel to your father," said the stepmother. "That areca tree over there has the best nuts. You are a good climber, so you must go to the top of the tree and get some."

Tam climbed the tree and when she was at the top her stepmother took an axe and began to chop at the trunk. The tree shivered and shook and Tam cried out in alarm. "What is happening? Why is the tree shaking so?"

"There are a lot of ants here," called her stepmother. "I am chasing them away."

She continued to chop until the tree fell. Its crown, with Tam in it, toppled into a deep pond and the beautiful young woman was drowned. The wicked murderer gathered Tam's clothes, gave them to Cam, and led her to the citadel. She explained about the terrible "accident" to the king and offered Cam as a replacement wife. The king was very unhappy, but he said nothing.

50   When Tam died she was transformed into a *vang anh* bird. The bird flew back to the palace gardens and there she saw Cam washing the king's clothes near the well. She called out to her. "Those are my husband's clothes. Dry the clothes on the pole, not on the fence, lest they be torn."

Then she flew to the window of the king's room, singing as she went. The bird followed the king everywhere and he, who was missing Tam greatly, spoke to it, "Dear bird, dear bird, if you are my wife, please come to my sleeve."

The bird sat on the king's hand and then hopped onto his sleeve. The king loved the bird so much that he often forgot to eat or sleep, and he had a golden cage made for it. He attended to it day and night and completely ignored Cam.

Cam went to her mother and told her about the bird. The woman advised that she must kill it and eat it, and make up a story to tell the king. Cam waited until the king was absent, then she did, as her mother had instructed. She threw the feathers into the garden afterwards.

When the king returned he asked about the bird and Cam answered, "I had a great craving for bird meat so I had it for a meal." The king said nothing.

55   The feathers grew into a tree. Whenever the king sat beneath it the branches bent down and made a parasol to shade him. He ordered a hammock to be placed under the tree and every day he rested there.

Cam was not happy about this, and once again she sought her mother's counsel.

"You must cut down the tree in secret. Use the wood to make a loom and tell the king you will weave some cloth for him."

On a stormy day Cam had the tree felled and made into a loom. When the king asked her about it she said that the wind had blown it over, and that now she would weave cloth for him on the loom made from its timber. When she sat down at the loom it spoke to her, "Klick klack, klick klack, you took my husband. I will take your eyes."

The terrified Cam went to her mother and told her of the loom's words. "Burn the loom and take the ashes far away from the palace," she told her daughter.

60   Cam did as she was bidden and threw the ashes at the side of the road a great distance from the king's home. The ashes grew into a green *thi* tree, and when the season came it bore one piece of fruit, with a wonderful fragrance that could be smelled from far away.

An old woman, who sold drinking water at a nearby stall, was attracted by the scent and she stood beneath the tree. She looked at the fruit, opened her pocket and called longingly, "Dear *thi,* drop into my pocket. I will only smell you, never eat you."

The fruit fell into her pocket, and she loved and treasured it, keeping it in her room to look at and to smell its fragrance.

Each day, when the old woman went to her stall, a small figure stepped from the *thi* fruit and grew into the form of Tam. She cleaned the house, put things in order, cooked the rice and made soup out of vegetables from the garden. Then she became tiny again and went back inside the *thi* fruit.

The old woman was curious and decided to find out who was helping her. One morning she pretended to go to her stall and hid behind a tree near the back door. She watched through a crack and saw Tam emerge from the *thi* fruit and grow into a beautiful girl. The old woman was very happy and rushed into the house and embraced her. She tore apart the skin of the fruit and threw it away. Tam lived happily with the old woman and helped her with the housework every day. She also made cakes and prepared betel to sell on the stall.

65 One day the king left his citadel and rode through the countryside. When he came to the old woman's stall he saw that it was neat and clean, so he stopped. The old woman offered him water and betel, and when he accepted it he saw that the betel had been prepared to look like the wings of an eagle. He remembered that his wife had prepared betel exactly in this fashion.

"Who prepared this betel?" he asked.

"It was done by my daughter," replied the old woman.

"Where is your daughter? Let me see her."

The old woman called Tam. When she came the king recognized his beloved wife, looking even younger and more beautiful. The king was very happy, and as the old woman told him the story he sent his servants to bring a rich palanquin to carry his wife back to the citadel.

70 When Cam saw that Tam had returned she was most fearful. She did her best to ingratiate herself and asked her stepsister the secret of her great beauty.

"Do you wish to be very beautiful?" asked Tam. "Come, I will show you how." Tam had her servants dig a hole and prepare a large jar of boiling water. "If you want to be beautiful you must get into this hole," Tam told her wicked stepsister.

When Cam was in the hole Tam ordered the servants to pour in the boiling water, and so her stepsister met her death. Tam had the body made into *mam,* a rich sauce, and sent it to her stepmother, saying that it was a present from her daughter.

Each day the woman ate some of the *mam* with her meals, always commenting how delicious it was. A crow came to her house, perched on the roof ridge and cawed, "Delicious! The mother is eating her own daughter's flesh. Is there any left? Give me some."

The stepmother was very angry and chased the bird away, but, on the day when the jar of *mam* was nearly empty, she saw her daughter's skull and fell down dead.

RELEVANT WEB SITE

Women In Vietnamese Folklore

`www.geocities.com/chtn_nhatrang/women.html`

This paper by Cong Huyen Trang was presented for the panel discussion *Southeast Asian Women Then and Now: A View from the Folklore of the Philippines, Thailand, and Vietnam,* at the University of Hawaii at Manoa in 1992.

QUESTIONS FOR DISCUSSION

1. What aspects of each tale help you to identify it as a Cinderella story? What would you consider to be the minimum set of motifs or key details to qualify as a Cinderella variant? (Note that the "glass slipper" in the Perrault story came from a mistranslation of a common French word that actually means "fur.")

2. How do you feel about rereading the "Cendrillon" ("Cinderella") tale, which is so much like the Disney version, as an adult? Does the Cinderella story hold a different meaning for you today than it did when it was first told to you? Why or why not?

3. Contrast the tone and theme of the four versions of the story. What different attitudes toward nature and the material world are expressed in each tale?

4. Were you surprised or shocked by the violent and punitive ending of the Grimms' version and "Tam and Cam"? Do you think these versions are suitable for children? Why do you think the popular fairy tales that most parents today read to their children are less violent than some of the older tales? Is this a positive development?

5. Comment on the themes of alienation and class exploitation in the various versions of Cinderella and the endings for each. What set of social values is implied in each story?

6. Comment on the use of supernatural or spiritual values implicit in each version of the tale. How are these values typical of the culture that produced each story?

Ideas for Writing

1. Write an essay that discusses how the Cinderella story helps to shape values for young women. Do you consider this story in its classic version to be sexist, or do you think it still has relevant meanings to convey? Explain your response.

2. Do a close comparison of any two of the Cinderella versions. You can consider such issues as nature, materialism, class dominance, and feminism.

Joshua Groban

Two Myths

Joshua Groban, who grew up in an artistic and literary family, has always been interested in mythology and issues related to creativity. In his freshman English class, Groban wrote a research paper comparing a number of different Native American accounts of the creation and was fascinated by the imagination and diversity of the visions he encountered in his reading. The following essay is Groban's comparative response to the two accounts of creation from the portfolio of myths presented in this chapter (see page 208).

An individual growing up in today's society is quickly indoctrinated into believing the predominant myth about creation. Our church, our parents, our teachers, and the media all reinforce such concepts as Adam and Eve and the Garden of Eden. However, every culture has its own unique myth to explain the birth of the planet and its inhabitants. By comparing the Bible's depiction of creation to that of the Yao myth, "The Chameleon Finds," one is reminded of the many different and imaginative ways people have presented such fundamental issues as gender relations, our connection with and responsibility to the environment, and the relationship of human beings to God.

First, we are struck by the different views of women in the two accounts of creation; the Bible's narration of creation depicts women as secondary to and subservient to men. In the Book of Genesis, "all cattle," "the birds of the air," and "every beast of the field" are created before women. This order of creation gives the impression that the beasts are more central to life on earth than women, and thus are created first. But, despite the abundance of these beasts, "there was not found a helper fit for him [man]." Genesis makes it clear that women are given life not as man's equal, but as his "helper" or assistant. When God finally creates females, they are divested from any sense of individuality; they are not created in the image of God, as man is, but from the rib of man. Thus, women are presented as owing their very existence to men. Genesis 2:4 concludes by emphasizing this idea, explaining that "she shall be called Woman, because she was taken out of Man." The Bible ties not only a woman's existence, but even her name to men. In this way, this creation myth clearly establishes women as subservient to men and lacking an equivalent sense of identity.

The Yao creation myth presents a different and more favorable portrayal of women. Women are not created as an afterthought in "The Chameleon Finds," to function as a helper to men, as they are in the Bible. Instead, men and women come into the world together, as companions. Males and females are given life when the Creator plucks them from the river in his trap. The myth says, "The next morning when he pulled the trap he found a little man and woman in it. He had never seen any creatures like this." In this way, the two sexes begin their existence in equality. Females do not come from males and are not granted life after men, cattle, birds, and beasts. The myth creates men and women together, and thus suggests that the two sexes should live their lives in this state of equality as well.

A juxtaposition of the Genesis and Yao stories in regard to their view of nature reveals a similar divergence. In the Bible, man dominates nature in much the same way as he dominates women. Both the environment and females are presented in Genesis as subservient "helpers" to man. Genesis 2:9 professes, "And out of the ground the Lord God made to grow every tree that is pleasant to the sight and good for food." Nature exists to serve and to help man; trees have life only to serve mankind by being "pleasant to the sight and good for food." Like women, the role of nature is to serve man rather than exist in equality with him. The Bible reads, "The Lord God took the man and put him in the Garden of Eden to till it and keep it." Man does not exist in the garden to coexist with the plants and animals of the garden. Instead, he is to "keep it," as if the earth were a possession.

5   The Yao story of creation sees humans as irresponsible and destructive in their relation to the earth. In the Yao tale, the first man and woman set fire to

the vegetation and kill animals that inhabit the earth. Their creator is appalled by this behavior: "'They are burning up everything'" he exclaims. "'They are killing my people!'" He is so disturbed by the way humans treat the earth that He decides to leave the planet. A spider makes him a ladder and He goes to live in the sky. The story ends, "Thus the gods were driven off the face of the earth by the cruelty of man." This myth, in contrast to the Bible, sets clear expectations about the consequences of man's mistreatment of the earth. In "The Chameleon Finds," nature, like women, has rights that should never be usurped. Genesis ignores these universal rights, affording them only to God and to man.

This contrast also exists in the way the two myths portray man's relationship to God. In Genesis, God is a distant, autocratic deity; he speaks and the act is performed. In this story, God "took" the man and "put him" in the Garden of Eden. Later, He "commands" man never to eat from the tree of good and evil. Humans are pawns controlled by this distant deity. They make no decisions in Genesis 2:4–23, but are instead "taken," "put," and "commanded." The Bible's God is one that controls humans and merely speaks in order to create.

The Yao Creator is an entirely different, more human sort of figure. This God is not presented as an all-powerful deity that merely speaks to create life. He unknowingly discovers humans in his trap, and no indication is given that He created them at all. This Creator does not command humans to do as He wants them to do. When humans destroy the earth, no punishment comes from a distant deity, as in the Bible. Instead, the Creator leaves the earth, leaving humans free to make their own decisions and choose their own destiny. This contrast impacts both man's relationship with God and his view of himself. In the Bible, The Creator is a force that has complete control over humans. He creates by merely speaking, commands humans, and punishes them. In contrast, the Yao Creator does not control every human action. He creates people not by speaking, but by discovering them. He does not command or punish, but leaves people to make their own choices about life on earth. This divergent approach functions to empower humans. The Yao myth enables people to feel in control of their life because no distant, supreme being controls them. Consequently, this fosters a heightened sense of morality and responsibility. "The Chameleon Finds" does not allow the individual to blame God or rely upon him. Instead, this creator deity, having set the world in motion and established His ideology, now leaves the decisions in the hands of humans, whose punishment for their crimes against nature is abandonment by the creator.

It would be misguided to contend that the discrepancy between the Bible and other myths on gender issues, the environment, and man's relationship with God proves that the Bible is responsible for the social ills of today. Religion does not create society; rather society creates religion. The Bible did not cause sexism or environmental disaster, and is not at the root of today's societal evils. However, comparing the account of the Creation in Genesis to similar myths from other cultures is of value in reminding the individual that there are no absolute truths. Every society has to define its origins and values as it sees fit. The dominance of Judeo-Christian thinking in our society does not make it more correct. There are alternative stories, such as "The Chameleon Finds," that present different visions of creation. This process of comparison can lead to an appreciation of a contrasting ideology; however, the appreciation of other religions and their view of creation comes only when someone begins to think about the validity of their own religion rather than blindly accepting it. The comparison of different creation myths is not antithetical to religion; it represents a reasoned approach to looking at God and creation and thus defines what true religious conviction really is.

QUESTIONS FOR DISCUSSION

1. What are the main points of comparison and contrast around which Groban structures his essay? Do they seem appropriate to the myths he studied, or would you have selected others?
2. How effectively does Groban use details and references to the two myths he contrasts to support his conclusions about their differences? Are there other details he might have used or different inferences he might have drawn based on the details he selects?
3. Although Groban states in some parts of his essay that all creation myths have validity, since "there are no absolute truths," he seems quite critical of the biblical version of Creation. Do you think that some views of creation are better than others, or is each version a product of the culture that produced it?
4. What are the criteria that Groban uses in his evaluation of the two myths he is comparing? Do his criteria seem appropriate, or would you substitute others? How would you set up criteria for evaluating myths of creation, if you believe that it is possible to do so?

TOPICS FOR RESEARCH AND WRITING

1. Write an essay that presents your own definition of a myth. Draw on your personal experiences and the readings in this chapter, as well as outside research into the nature of myths and mythology. How does a myth differ from a lie or falsehood?

2. Write your own myth, based on your view of yourself as a hero or heroine. Then write an analysis of your myth, comparing the "ideal" self that emerges in the story you have written to your "real" self. How does your myth reflect the concerns of your generation and your own values? In what ways is your myth traditional? Make connections between your myth and other hero myths that you read about in your research.

3. Over 500 different versions of the Cinderella tale are told in cultures around the world. Do some research to find two interesting versions from different cultures, then write a comparison paper of these two versions. What did you learn about the cultures that produced each story?

4. Compare and contrast a traditional myth or tale with a modern retelling of that myth, perhaps in a popular culture format such as a TV show or comic book. Reflect on how and why the original myth has been changed. Which of the two versions do you prefer, and why?

5. In what important ways do you think that myths function in people's lives and in society? Write an essay in which you do some research into this issue and discuss several ways that myths serve people. Support each main point you make with an example. (See particularly the essays by Seger, Gleiser, Bettelheim, and Yolen in this chapter.) Consider some of the problems that arise in a modern culture that has rejected many of its traditional myths and rituals.

6. Write your own modern version of a fairy tale such as Cinderella or one or the other popular Brothers Grimm tales such as Sleeping Beauty or Hansel and Gretel, or write your own creation or hero myth and explain your reasons for creating this tale. Refer to Bettelheim, Yolen, Gleiser, or Seger when explaining your reasons for creating the tale in the particular way that you did.

7. See one of the following films, or one that you choose, that explores the role of myth, either by yourself or with several of your classmates. Write an analysis of the film that discusses the ways in which the film explores the nature and meaning of myths or fairy tales and their relationship to dreams and the imagination. Choose from the following list: *Black Orpheus*, *Star Wars* (any episode), *The Princess Bride*, *Monty Python's Holy Grail*, *The Fisher King*, *Ever After*, *The Lion King*, *Harry Potter* (any episode), *Lord of the Rings* (any episode), *Spiderman*, *O Brother, Where Art Thou?*, *A Cinderella Story*, *Shrek*, and *Troy*.

Obsessions and Transformation 5

Vincent Van Gogh (1853–1890)
Starry Night (Saint-Remy, June 1889)

Dutch painter Vincent Van Gogh, one of the most famous modern artists, was a depressive who took his own life only one year after painting one of his greatest works, *Starry Night.* Van Gogh's expressionistic painting of a nighttime sky reminds us of how we transform the world as we view it through our own inner lenses of obsession, suffering, or joy.

JOURNAL

Describe a place or setting, urban or rural, interior or exterior, as you imagine a person who is emotionally distraught or disturbed might perceive it. Use figurative language and sensory appeal, but try to show how the mind distorts exterior reality according to inner pressures and concerns.

Yes indeed, I realized, looking into the mirror. There was a world in my eye. And I saw that it was possible to love it: that in fact, for all it had taught me of shame and anger and inner vision, I did love it.
ALICE WALKER

Even more than our experiences, our beliefs became our prisons. But we carry our healing with us even into the darkest of our inner places.
RACHEL NAOMI REMEN

These dreams refuse to go quietly, for they mean to change us utterly. If we look into their depths, we may behold a unique destiny struggling from its chrysalis, and watch, astonished and not a little afraid, as our unsuspected selfhood unfolds a new, wetly glistening wing.
MARK IAN BARASCH

DEFINITION: WORD BOUNDARIES OF THE SELF

Definition involves clarifying a term's meaning through precise use of language and through distinguishing among several words that may be difficult to use appropriately because they have similar or overlapping meanings. Definitions, both short and expanded, can be used not only as a way of clarifying the denotative or dictionary meanings of the crucial words and abstract terminology that you use in your writing, but also as a way of exploring personal definitions of terms based on feelings, values, and language.

Public Meanings and Formal Definition

In essay writing, definition is most often used as a method for clarifying meaning for your readers. If, for example, you are writing an essay on obsessions, you would first want to define what is meant by "obsession." Although you would first turn to a dictionary, an encyclopedia, or another reliable authority for a definition of this basic term, you would also need to use your own words to create your statement of meaning. Your own words will help you to develop control over the direction of your paper and capture your reader's interest. Begin by placing the term within a formal pattern. First, state the word you will be defining—in this case, "obsession"—then put the term in a larger class or group: "An obsession is a strong emotional response."

Next, you will need one or more details or qualifying phrases to distinguish your term from others in the larger group of strong emotions: "An obsession is an emotional response or preoccupation that is compulsive and highly repetitive, a response over which a person often has little or no control and that can have destructive consequences." If this definition still seems inadequate, you could add more details and develop the definition further with a typical example: "Overeating can be an obsessive form of behavior."

In writing an extended definition of a key term, carefully construct the initial definition. If you place the term in too large a class, do not distinguish it from others in the class, or merely repeat your original term or a form of the term, you will have difficulty developing your ideas clearly and will confuse your reader. You also need to decide how you plan to use your definition: what will its purpose be?

Once you have created the initial definition, you can proceed to develop your paragraph or essay using other analytical writing strategies such as process analysis, discussion of cause and effect, or comparative relationships. For example, you could discuss several of the qualities of a typical obsession, provide an ordered exploration of the stages of the obsession, or examine the kinds of human growth and interactions with which the obsession can interfere, as Sharon Slayton does in her essay on the obsession with being good. For clarity, reader interest, and development, examples and illustrations can be used effectively with any of the larger analytical structures that you might wish to take advantage of in your essay: examples from personal experience, friends, or your reading of fictional or factual sources.

Stipulative and Personal Definitions

Sometimes writers decide to develop a personal definition. This form of definition, referred to as a "stipulative definition," is based on the writer's personal ideals and values. In this case, you still need to be clear in making crucial distinctions. For example, if you are writing a paper on your own personal dream, you might begin with a dictionary definition of "dream" to contrast the qualities of your personal dream to the traditional connotations associated with the term as stated in the dictionary.

Freewriting and clustering will help you define what the term means to you and discover the term's deeper personal levels of meaning. Comparative thinking can also be useful. Write a series of sentences beginning with the words "My dream is . . ." or "My dream is like . . ." and make as many different associations with concrete objects or events as you can. Examine the associations you have made and construct a personal definition qualified with expressions such as "my," "to me," or "in my opinion," and include several personal distinguishing qualities.

A stipulative definition is often supported by personal experiences that help the reader understand the origins and basis of your views. Provide contrasts with qualities that others may associate with the term. For example, other people may believe that a dream as you have defined it is just "wishful thinking," an exercise in escapism. You could argue that, to the contrary, it is necessary to have a dream as a high ideal or aspiration; otherwise, one may too readily accept a version of reality that is less than what it could be and lose faith in the imagination that is necessary to solve problems and to move confidently into the future. Thus a stipulative definition can become a type of argument, an advocacy of one's perspective on life.

Contradiction

In developing your definition, be careful not to create contradictions. Contradiction or equivocation occurs when you define a term in one way and then shift the definition to another level of meaning. To base an argument intentionally on a contradiction is at best confusing and at worst dishonest and propagandistic. For example, if you begin your paper with a definition of "myth" as the cultural and social stories that bind a people together and then shift your paper to a discussion of private dreams and personal mythology, you will confuse your reader by violating the logic of your definition, and your essay will lose much of its credibility. A better strategy for dealing with the real complexity of certain words is to concede from the start (in your thesis) that this is an expression with seemingly contradictory or ironic shades of meaning—as in the case of the word "good" in Slayton's essay in this chapter—and then spell out the complexity clearly in your definition. Read your paper carefully before turning it in, checking to see that your definition and your arguments and examples are consistent. If not, your paper needs a revision, and you may want to modify your initial definition statement.

Writing objective and personal definitions will help you clarify your thoughts, feelings, and values. As you work to find the qualities, distinctions, and personal experiences that give a complex concept a meaning that reflects your inner self as well as the consensus of the public world, you will also be moving forward on your inward journey.

THEMATIC INTRODUCTION: OBSESSIONS AND TRANSFORMATIONS

Dreams and fantasies can be healthy; they can serve as a means for escape from trivial or tedious routines and demands. Popular entertainment, for example, often provides us with simple escapist fantasies that encourage us to identify with an idealized hero or heroine. We can become strong, beautiful, courageous, or very wise, and, for a moment, we may be able to forget the realities of our own lives. When our minds return from a fantasy, we may feel more refreshed, more capable of handling daily responsibilities. Often fantasies provide more than just possibilities of short-term escape; they can also offer insights that will lead to deeper self-understanding as well as psychological and/or spiritual transformation. Each individual has unique dreams and fantasies. When these messages from our unconscious minds and from our dream worlds are understood and interpreted, they can help us have more fulfilling and rewarding lives.

Some people suffer from personal obsessions and compulsions that can lead to behavior that can be limiting, repetitive, and sometimes even destructive to self or others. In such cases, the obsession controls the individual rather than the individual controlling the goal. Why do some people become possessed by their fantasies and obsessions, whereas others can maintain their psychological equilibrium and learn about themselves through their preoccupations, their unconscious dreams? How do people's unconscious obsessions influence their day-to-day life and decision-making processes? The essays, story, and poem included in this chapter provide you with a range of perspectives that will help you consider these and other issues related to how our inner lives, our unconscious, our dreams, nightmares, fantasies, and obsessions have a impact on political and social life.

In this chapter's first selection, "Fog-Horn" by W. S. Merwin, the poem's speaker reflects on the power of a forgotten, unconscious world of feelings that, if heeded, can serve as a valuable warning for people. Our second selection, Maressa Orzack's "Computer Addiction" reveals the way failure to stay in touch with our inner worlds can lead us into the repetitive, limiting behavior of addiction. Addictions are closely related to depression, which, as Andrew Solomon notes in his essay "Depression," if left untreated can lead to the decay of the inner self. Charlotte Perkins Gilman's classic short story "The Yellow Wallpaper" (1896) reveals how a character's depression leads her to obsessive hallucinations that distort and transform her character and relationships.

The next selections show how depressive frames of mind can be lived through and result in a profound transformation of personality. In her personal essay, "A Slender Thread," Diane Ackerman shows how a volunteer for a suicide hotline can help a depressed person to take a chance on starting a new life. In the next selection, "Hunger," Anne Lamott reveals how she transformed her addiction to alcohol and bulimia through learning to value herself and her own sensory world.

The last two professional selections examine holistic approaches to physical and psychological healing. Carrie Demer's "Chaos or Calm" reveals ways that meditation, yogic breathing, and other relaxation techniques can improve health and reduce stress. In our final professional selection, "What Is a Healing Dream?" Jungian analyst Mark Ian Barasch defines a healing dream while giving many examples of how individuals have used their dreams to enrich and improve their sense of physical and mental well-being.

The student essay that concludes this chapter also explores the power of obsession and transformation. In her essay "The Good Girl," Sharon Slayton analyzes her crippling obsession with being well-behaved and always living up to others' expectations.

The works in this chapter ask readers to look within, to listen to the questions and fears in their hearts and spirits. Through reading and reflecting on the selections in this chapter, we hope that you can recognize obsessive types of behavior and at the same time realize that they can be potential sources of creative inspiration, transformation, and love.

W. S. Merwin

Fog-Horn

W. S. Merwin (b. 1927) was raised in Pennsylvania. After graduating from Princeton University in 1947, he lived for several years in London, translating French and Spanish classics for the British Broadcasting Corporation. Merwin, who has published many collections of poems and translations, explores myths, cultural contrasts, and ecology. His style is often discontinuous, mysterious— wavering between waking and sleeping states, and creating a dialogue between the conscious and the unconscious mind. Merwin's writing often creates strong emotional responses. His books include Opening the Hand *(1983),* The Vixen *(1996),* The River Sound Poems *(2000), and* The Pupil *(2001). His recent essays appear in* Ends of the Earth: Essays *(2005). The poem "Fog-Horn" was included in Merwin's* The Drunk in the Furnace *(1958). As you read the poem, try to re-create the sound and image of the foghorn in your own imagination.*

JOURNAL

Write about a warning that came to you from your unconscious, a warning that might have taken the form of a dream, a fantasy, a minor accident, or a psychosomatic illness.

Surely that moan is not the thing
That men thought they were making, when they
Put it there, for their own necessities.
That throat does not call to anything human
5 But to something men had forgotten,
That stirs under fog. Who wounded that beast
Incurably, or from whose pasture
Was it lost, full grown, and time closed round it
With no way back? Who tethered its tongue
10 So that its voice could never come
To speak out in the light of clear day,
But only when the shifting blindness
Descends and is acknowledged among us,
As though from under a floor it is heard,
15 Or as though from behind a wall, always
Nearer than we had remembered? If it
Was we that gave tongue to this cry
What does it bespeak in us, repeating
And repeating, insisting on something
20 That we never meant? We only put it there
To give warning of something we dare not
Ignore, lest we should come upon it
Too suddenly, recognize it too late,
As our cries were swallowed up and all hands lost.

Questions for Discussion

1. How does Merwin personify the foghorn, making it more than just an object? Refer to specific details that you think are particularly effective.
2. What does the cry of the foghorn signify? What is its warning?
3. What words, images, and phrases make the poem seem like a dream or a nightmare?
4. Why can't the voice of the foghorn "speak out in the light of clear day"?
5. Why does the voice of the foghorn call to something "forgotten"? What parts of ourselves are we most likely to forget or ignore? What helps us to remember what we want to forget?
6. What is your interpretation of the poem? What state of mind is the poet attempting to define?

Connection

Compare the foghorn as a symbol of a human obsession in Merwin's poem with the yellow wallpaper in Gilman's story (see page 276). How does each symbol help to focus themes of psychic repression and denial as well as insights into the destructive consequences of obsessive behavior?

1. Write an essay in which you define and clarify with examples and comparisons the positive role that you think the unconscious mind can play in helping one to create a balanced and fulfilling life. Refer to the poem in shaping your response.
2. Write a narrative or a poem in which you use an object or an animal as a comparison to or as a way of defining and understanding the unconscious mind. Try to emphasize how the unconscious mind communicates with the conscious mind.

RELATED WEB SITES

The Academy of American Poets
www.poets.org
Learn more about American poetry at the Web site for "The Academy of American Poets." Find out about poets, poems, and events throughout the country.

Psych Central Web Site: The Unconscious Mind
www.psychcentral.com/psypsych/Unconscious_mind
This thorough site on psychological terms, issues, and problems gives a brief history of the idea of the unconscious mind and links to other sites and articles on the subject.

Maressa Hecht Orzack, Ph.D.

Computer Addiction: What Is It?

Maressa Hecht Orzack, a Massachusetts-licensed psychologist, is a faculty member with the Cognitive Behavior Therapy Program at Boston's McLean Hospital and a lecturer in the Department of Psychiatry at the Harvard Medical School. Dr. Orzack specializes in the treatment of addictive and impulsive behavioral problems such as gambling, substance and alcohol abuse, eating disorders, and sex addiction. In 1996 she founded and continues to serve as coordinator of the Computer Addiction Service at McLean Hospital. This program offers comprehensive evaluation and treatment services for individuals suffering from computer addiction and for people who are close to the computer addict. Orzack has described computer addiction as a "disorder suffered by people who find the virtual reality on computer screens more attractive than everyday reality." Notice how Orzack defines computer addiction by comparing it to other forms of "addictive" behavior.

JOURNAL

Write about your computer/Internet use or that of a friend. Do you think that the usage you have observed/experienced could be considered a form of addiction? Why or why not?

In 1995, I noticed that I was spending more and more time playing solitaire on my computer. I was trying to learn a new computer program and was very frustrated by it. My anger and inability to decipher the manuals led me to escape to solitaire. I became aware that I started my game program at an earlier time each evening, and at times I would avoid my primary reasons for using the computer. I was not alone.

Some of my patients told me about their computer use and how they were unable to stop spending time online or arranging electronic files.

I decided that these patterns might indicate a form of dysfunctional behavior associated with a new technology, and was worth investigating. I found support for my idea from colleagues, friends and reports in the media (Murray, 1996). As a trained cognitive behavior therapist, I often treat gamblers, alcoholics and people with obsessive-compulsive disorder, and have also studied mood changes resulting from the recreational use of psychotropic medication. I concluded that this inappropriate and excessive use of the computer might be a distinct disorder (Orzack et al., 1988).

This behavior has variously been called Internet addiction, pathological Internet use, problematic Internet use, and a mere symptom of other disorders. I am often asked why I call it computer addiction. I was not the first to use this term. Shotton (1989) coined the term in her book *Computer Addiction*. After searching the literature about alcoholism, gambling and other addictive behaviors, Shotton decided that she was witnessing computer addiction in a very specialized group of men who were developing hardware and software for computers. According to Shotton, these men were completely focused on their activities in the laboratory to the point of neglecting both family and friends.

5   The information superhighway did not exist when Shotton wrote her book. Few ordinary citizens outside of academia, the military and the computer industry had their own PCs, and fewer still had access to the Internet. Since then we have moved into the Information Age. The computer industry is now the fastest growing industry in the world. In 1997, the population of Internet users in the United States was estimated at 50 million to 80 million, and is projected to increase to 150 million to 200 million by the year 2000 (Pohly, 1995).

Any new technology requires a shakedown period in which the flaws and its effects on both society and individuals become evident. This is also true of the computer. As this rapidly evolving technology develops, so do the opportunities for negative consequences from its use. It is for these reasons that we must examine the phenomenon.

No epidemiological studies on computer addiction have been done. There have been online studies (Brenner, 1997; Young, 1998) and targeted group studies (Anderson, 1998; Scherer, 1997; Shotton, 1989), but to my knowledge no one has either interviewed a randomized sample of people about their computer use or recorded usage directly.

We have no idea what levels or kinds of computer usage are "normal." Therefore, we cannot state which behavior is always pathological. There have been heated and contentious arguments about these issues in an online forum devoted to research on the Internet (see *http://www.cmhc.com/mlists*). Discussions include topics such as the validity of scales to measure Internet addiction, with exact indicators defining a pathological or addictive behavior.

What is it about using computers that makes some people behave in ways in which they would not ordinarily? Is it the technology itself, or is it the way people interact with that technology? Is the behavior pathological or creative? Why are some people so connected to life on the screen that they have difficulty coming back to reality? Who are the people who act this way, and if they come to your office for help, how do you treat them?

Signs and Symptoms

10 Based on contact with my own patients, numerous requests for referrals from other therapists, and many online requests for help, I have designed a behavior list based on an impulse control model very similar to one used for gambling. These are the signs and symptoms of computer addiction, or, as I now prefer to call it, impulse-control disorder, not otherwise specified. I make no other claim for the validity of this diagnostic paradigm, since it is based on a highly selected population.

Tolerance, withdrawal and compulsive use are requisites for any diagnosis of dependency (American Psychiatric Association, 1994). Psychological tolerance is indicated by the need to spend increasing amounts of time on computer activities such as playing games, arranging files or participating in online discussion groups. Even though computer users are aware of problem behavior, they continue to use the computer compulsively. They often blame others for the problem. Withdrawal symptoms are indicated by an increase in irritability and anxiety when a person is unable to access a computer. Even though one investigator (Anderson, 1998) used a three-day abstinence as an indicator of problems, at least one patient has said that it is a matter of only hours before he starts to feel irritable, depressed or anxious.

The physical symptoms associated with computer addiction can have serious consequences. For instance, resulting carpal tunnel syndrome often requires months of care and may result in surgery. Eating habits change so that some people eat while at the computer and never exercise. Others may skip meals altogether. One patient has told me that she sometimes does not get to the bathroom in time. Failure to blink can cause migraines. Optometrists and ophthalmologists often prescribe special lenses for computer use because patients spend so much time looking at the screen.

The following cases illustrate the signs and symptoms described above:

Patient A, a recovering substance abuser, stated that she craved participating in an online chat and that she returned to it at earlier and earlier hours each day. She had such an intense relationship with a cyber friend that she lost her sobriety when that person suddenly disappeared from her screen.

15 Patient B also has a history of substance abuse, and compared his feelings when he was on a chat line to an amphetamine high.

Patient C said he feels an intense power and excitement when he plays interactive power games.

Patient D turned to a computer game for comfort after she wrecked her car.

A therapist who treats paraphilias tells me that a good proportion of his patients download pornography at their workplaces as well as at home (Kafka, personal communication, 1998). Other technologies have been considered addictive, including the telephone, television, pinball machines and video games. All these activities initially provide positive rewards for their use. Once someone is addicted to a behavior, however, the positive rewards are diminished. Gambling, for example, requires an early win to catch the player. Without a win, the gambler will leave in frustration. If the gambler wins and then loses, he or she will continue to play, taking more risks by raising the ante. The gambler chases losses by expecting to win on the next play.

For the Web surfer, satisfaction must come early, or the user will leave the site. Web pages are aptly named because of the many links attracting the computer user to new experiences, causing him or her to lose track of time. Patient D, who complained about the amount of time she spent online, said she could not leave the Web because the next connection might be just what she was looking for.

Socialization Online

20 The newest lure is Internet gambling. Shaffer (1996) points out that it is not the addictive quality of the games or program, but rather their capacity to influence the human experience that is the important element to be studied.

Buzzell (1997), who describes the effects in some children who have had seizures watching a TV screen, asks whether the same effect might occur in children who play computer games by the hour. Eastman (1998) goes even further, suggesting that the activity of watching a screen may be hypnotic, and may therefore contribute to the addictive process by maintaining the exposure for longer time periods.

What is it that makes participation in activities like MUD (multi-user domains), Internet relay chat groups, Internet support groups and surfing the Web so compelling? It is a combination of factors which are balanced in non-dependent individuals who can surf the Net, enter data, play games or engage in an online forum without it interfering with their other real life obligations. Those who cannot do this can be classified as dependent or addicted.

In the online world, people can become anyone they wish to be. Furthermore, they believe that they are part of a group. Being part of a MUD allows a participant to play a prescribed role that would be impossible in real life. As an example, a young patient fell asleep in class from staying up at night for hours directing a power game.

In addition to the actual activity there is a social connection with other players, which is highly reinforcing. Another patient, in recovery from several problems, described the sense of belonging he feels at a poker table. It is this same sense of belonging that I have heard expressed by people who belong to chat groups. A depressed patient continues to participate in chat groups even though she has had several traumatic experiences with men she arranged to meet offline.

25   One of the dormitory counselors at a major university reported that sports gambling on the Internet is a very popular group activity. Although gambling on the Internet is illegal in the United States; it thrives because it is hosted on offshore sites over which the U.S. has no regulatory authority. The other highly controversial topic is the number of sex and pornography sites that exist directly on the Internet and on CD-ROMs. How to regulate this is a subject of concern to many people.

Another view of computer addiction suggests that excessive and inappropriate computer use is a new symptom of other psychiatric problems. Shapira (1998) found that 14 self-selected Internet users who had problematic Internet use fit the *DSM-IV* criteria for a mean of five different psychiatric disorders. This data may suggest that this technology presents a new way to express affect.

One final consideration is treatment of this addiction. Whether or not this addiction is similar to substance dependency, impulse control disorder or a symptom of other disorders, its treatment cannot require abstinence. Computers are present in workplaces, schools, universities and households. Treatment must be similar to that given for an eating disorder where the aim is to help the patient normalize their behavior in order to survive. A combination of cognitive behavior therapy and motivational interviewing are the most helpful to the patient. Treating the depression and anxiety with antidepressants is also recommended. Shapira (1998) has had excellent results in prescribing serotonin reuptake inhibitors or other antidepressants for his patients.

Computer addiction is a combination of signs and symptoms that fit a dependency model, an impulse control disorder model, and are often comorbid with other psychiatric diagnoses. The treatment, therefore, must be for all three classifications. My hope is that an epidemiological study can be done which will define the limits of normal computer usage. Then we can decide what is pathological.

REFERENCES

American Psychiatric Association. 1994. *Diagnostic and statistical manual of mental disorders,* 4th ed. Washington, DC: American Psychiatric Association.

Anderson, K. 1998. Internet dependency among college students: Should we be concerned? Paper presented at the American College Personnel Association, March, St. Louis, Missouri.

Brenner, V. 1997. Psychology of computer use: XLVII. Parameters of Internet use, abuse, and addiction: The first 90 days of the Internet Usage Survey. *Psychological Reports* 80 (3, pt. 1): 879–82.

Buzzell, K. A. 1997. *The human brain and the influences of television viewing: An inquiry into meaning in the post-quantum world.* Denmark, ME: Cardinal Printing Company.

Eastman, G. 1998. The effect of electronic imaging on our experience of reality. Paper presented at the Eastern Psychology Association meeting, February, Boston.

Murray, J. B. 1996. Computer addictions entangle students. *APA Monitor* 27 (6): 38–39.

Orzack, M. H., L. Friedman, E. Dessain, et al. 1998. Comparative study of the abuse liability of alprazolam, lorazepam, diazepam, methaqualone, and placebo. *Int J Addict* 23 (5): 449–67.

Pohly, D. 1995. Selling in cyberspace. http://www.demographics.com/publications/mt/95_mt/9511_mt/mt368.htm (accessed July 7, 1998).

Scherer, K. 1997. College life online: Healthy and unhealthy Internet use. *J College Student Development* 38 (6): 655–64.

Shaffer, H. J. 1996. Understanding the means and objects of addiction, technology, the Internet and gambling. *J Gambling Studies* 12:461–69.

Shapira, N. A. 1998. Problematic Internet use. Paper presented at the annual meeting of the American Psychiatric Association, May, Toronto.

Shotton, M. A. 1989. *Computer addiction? A study of computer dependency.* New York: Taylor & Francis.

Young, K. S. 1989. *Caught in the net: How to recognize the signs of Internet addiction and a winning strategy for recovery.* New York: John Wiley & Sons.

QUESTIONS FOR DISCUSSION

1. What led Orzack to investigate the "dysfunctional behavior" associated with excessive computer use? How does she define this type of behavior?
2. What are the symptoms and withdrawal effects of computer addiction, in Orzack's view? Why does she define computer addiction as a compulsion?
3. What are the negative physical consequences of computer addiction? What cases and examples does Orzack use to support her discussion of consequences of computer addiction?
4. How do computer-addicted individuals misuse the computer world as a source of socialization? What negative consequences can come from the artificial socialization that occurs in computer chat groups and MUDs?
5. How is gambling, despite its illegality, a particularly difficult type of obsessive activity to control when it is played by computer? How is Internet addiction similar to gambling addiction?
6. Orzack concludes by speculating on possible therapies for computer addiction. What might work, and why is it necessary to determine what "normal" computer usage is before we can begin to define and properly treat "pathological" usage?

CONNECTION

Compare the description of symptoms and psychological interventions for addictions to compulsive drinking and overeating/bulimia in Anne Lamott's "Hunger" (see page 298) with the symptoms and interventions for computer addiction provided by Orzack.

IDEAS FOR WRITING

1. Do some research into Orzack's treatment methods and those of other therapists for individuals who have difficulties controlling their computer use, and draw some conclusions about how effective their strategies might be.
2. Do you agree with Orzack that "addiction" is an accurate description of what goes on when people spend large amounts of time working on computers or online? Write an essay in which you argue your position on this controversial subject.

Computer Addiction Services
`www.computeraddiction.com`
Maressa Orzack's site includes advice on recognizing computer addiction and its symptoms, questions and answers on the issue, as well as a bibliography of articles by and about Orzack, her ideas, and her work with computer addicts.

The Psychology of Cyberspace
`www.rider.edu/~suler/psycyber/psycyber.html`
This site, created and maintained by John Suler, a psychology professor at Rider College, covers all aspects of the psychological impact of computers and cyberspace, including computer addiction. The site contains an extensive collection to relevant online articles.

Andrew Solomon

Depression

Andrew Solomon was born in 1963. He grew up in New York and received a B.A. from Yale University as well as a B.A. and M.A. from Cambridge University. He has written for the New Yorker, Art Forum, *and the* New York Times Magazine. *His books include* The Irony Tower: Soviet Artists in a Time of Glasnost *(1991) and the novel* A Stone Boat *(1994). The following selection is drawn from his most recent work,* The Noonday Demon: An Atlas of Depression *(2001).*

JOURNAL

Write about a time when you felt "down" or somewhat depressed. Describe your feelings and how you coped with them.

Depression is the flaw in love. To be creatures who love, we must be creatures who can despair at what we lose, and depression is the mechanism of that despair. When it comes, it degrades one's self and ultimately eclipses the capacity to give or receive affection. It is the aloneness within us made manifest, and it destroys not only connection to others but also the ability to be peacefully alone with oneself. Love, though it is no prophylactic against depression, is what cushions the mind and protects it from itself. Medications and psychotherapy can renew that protection, making it easier to love and be loved, and that is why they work. In good spirits, some love themselves and some love others and some love work and some love God: any of these passions can furnish that vital sense of purpose that is the opposite of depression.

Love forsakes us from time to time, and we forsake love. In depression, the meaninglessness of every enterprise and every emotion, the meaninglessness of life itself, becomes self-evident. The only feeling left in this loveless state is insignificance.

Life is fraught with sorrows: no matter what we do, we will in the end die; we are, each of us, held in the solitude of an autonomous body; time passes, and what has been will never be again. Pain is the first experience of world-helplessness, and it never leaves us. We are angry about being ripped from the comfortable womb, and as soon as that anger fades, distress comes to take its place. Even those people whose faith promises them that this will all be different in the next world cannot help experiencing anguish in this one; Christ himself was the man of sorrows. We live, however, in a time of increasing palliatives; it is easier than ever to decide what to feel and what not to feel. There is less and less unpleasantness that is unavoidable in life, for those with the means to avoid. But despite the enthusiastic claims of pharmaceutical science, depression cannot be wiped out so long as we are creatures conscious of our own selves. It can at best be contained—and containing is all that current treatments for depression aim to do.

Highly politicized rhetoric has blurred the distinction between depression and its consequences—the distinction between how you feel and how you act in response. This is in part a social and medical phenomenon, but it is also the result of linguistic vagary attached to emotional vagary. Perhaps depression can best be described as emotional pain that forces itself on us against our will, and then breaks free of its externals. Depression is not just a lot of pain; but too much pain can compost itself into depression. Grief is depression in proportion to circumstance; depression is grief out of proportion to circumstance. It is tumbleweed distress that thrives on thin air, growing despite its detachment from the nourishing earth. It can be described only in metaphor and allegory. Saint Anthony in the desert, asked how he could differentiate between angels who came to him humble and devils who came in rich disguise, said you could tell by how you felt after they had departed. When an angel left you, you felt strengthened by his presence; when a devil left, you felt horror. Grief is a humble angel who leaves you with strong, clear thoughts and a sense of your own depth. Depression is a demon who leaves you appalled.

Depression has been roughly divided into small (mild or disthymic) and large (major) depression. Mild depression is a gradual and sometimes permanent thing that undermines people the way rust weakens iron. It is too much grief at too slight a cause, pain that takes over from the other emotions and crowds them out. Such depression takes up bodily occupancy in the eyelids and in the muscles that keep the spine erect. It hurts your heart and lungs, making the contraction of involuntary muscles harder than it needs to be. Like physical pain that becomes chronic, it is miserable not so much because it is intolerable in the moment as because it is intolerable to have known it in the moments gone and to look forward only to knowing it in the moments to come. The present tense of mild depression envisages no alleviation because it feels like knowledge.

5   Virginia Woolf has written about this state with an eerie clarity: "Jacob went to the window and stood with his hands in his pockets. There he saw three Greeks in kilts; the masts of ships; idle or busy people of the lower classes strolling or stepping out briskly, or falling into groups and gesticulating with their hands. Their lack of concern for him was not the cause of his gloom; but some more profound conviction—it was not that he himself happened to be lonely, but that all people are." In the same book, *Jacob's Room,* she describes how "There rose in her mind a curious sadness, as if time and eternity showed through skirts and waistcoats, and she saw people passing tragically to destruction. Yet, heaven knows, Julia was no fool." It is this acute awareness of transience and limitation that constitutes mild depression. Mild depression, for many years simply accommodated, is increasingly subject to treatment as doctors scrabble to address its diversity.

Large depression is the stuff of breakdowns. If one imagines a soul of iron that weathers with grief and rusts with mild depression, then major depression is the startling collapse of a whole structure. There are two models for depression: the dimensional and the categorical. The dimensional posits that depression sits on a continuum with sadness and represents an extreme version of something everyone has felt and known. The categorical describes depression as an illness totally separate from other emotions, much as a stomach virus is totally different from acid indigestion. Both are true. You go along the gradual path or the sudden trigger of emotion and then you get to a place that is genuinely different. It takes time for a rusting iron-framed building to collapse, but the rust is ceaselessly powdering the solid, thinning it, eviscerating it. The collapse, no matter how abrupt it may feel, is the cumulative consequence of decay. It is nonetheless a highly dramatic and visibly different event. It is a long time from the first rain to the point when rust has eaten through an iron girder. Sometimes the rusting is at such key points that the collapse seems total, but more often it is partial: this section collapses, knocks that section, shifts the balances in a dramatic way.

It is not pleasant to experience decay, to find yourself exposed to the ravages of an almost daily rain, and to know that you are turning into something feeble, that more and more of you will blow off with the first strong wind, making you less and less. Some people accumulate more emotional rust than others. Depression starts out insipid, fogs the days into a dull color, weakens ordinary actions until their clear shapes are obscured by the effort they require, leaves you tired and bored and self-obsessed—but you can get through all that. Not happily, perhaps, but you can get through. No one has ever been able to define the collapse point that marks major depression, but when you get there, there's not much mistaking it.

Major depression is a birth and a death: it is both the new presence of something and the total disappearance of something. Birth and death are gradual, though official documents may try to pinion natural law by creating categories such as "legally dead" and "time born." Despite nature's vagaries, there is definitely a point at which a baby who has not been in the world is in it, and a point at which a pensioner who has been in the world is no longer in it. It's true that at one stage the baby's head is here and his body not; that until the umbilical cord is severed the child is physically connected to the mother. It's true that the pensioner may close his eyes for the last time some hours before he dies, and that there is a gap between when he stops breathing and when he is declared "brain-dead." Depression exists in time. A patient may say that he has spent certain months suffering major depression, but this is a way of imposing a measurement on the immeasurable. All that one can really say for certain is that one has known major depression, and that one does or does not happen to be experiencing it at any given present moment.

The birth and death that constitute depression occur at once. I returned, not long ago, to a wood in which I had played as a child and saw an oak, a hundred years dignified, in whose shade I used to play with my brother. In twenty years, a huge vine had attached itself to this confident tree and had nearly smothered it. It was hard to say where the tree left off and the vine began. The vine had twisted itself so entirely around the scaffolding of tree branches that its leaves seemed from a distance to be the leaves of the tree; only up close could you see how few living oak branches were left, and how a few desperate little budding sticks of oak stuck like a row of thumbs up the massive trunk, their leaves continuing to photosynthesize in the ignorant way of mechanical biology.

10   Fresh from a major depression in which I had hardly been able to take on board the idea of other people's problems, I empathized with that tree. My depression had grown on me as that vine had conquered the oak; it had been a sucking thing that had wrapped itself around me, ugly and more alive than I. It had had a life of its own that bit by bit asphyxiated all of my life out of me. At the worst stage of major depression, I had moods that I knew were not my moods: they belonged to the depression, as surely as the leaves on that tree's high branches belonged to the vine. When I tried to think clearly about this, I felt that my mind was immured, that it couldn't expand in any direction. I knew that the sun was rising and setting, but little of its light reached me. I felt myself sagging under what was much stronger than I; first I could not use my ankles, and then I could not control my knees, and then my waist began to break under the strain, and then my shoulders turned in, and in the end I was compacted and fetal, depleted by this thing that was crushing me without holding me. Its tendrils threatened to pulverize my mind and my courage and my stomach, and crack my bones and desiccate my body. It went on glutting itself on me when there seemed nothing left to feed it.

I was not strong enough to stop breathing. I knew then that I could never kill this vine of depression, and so all I wanted was for it to let me die. But it had taken from me the energy I would have needed to kill myself, and it would not kill me. If my trunk was rotting, this thing that fed on it was now too strong to let it fall; it had become an alternative support to what it had destroyed. In the tightest corner of my bed, split and racked by this thing no one else seemed to be able to see, I prayed to a God I had never entirely believed in, and I asked for deliverance. I would have been happy to die the most painful death, though

I was too dumbly lethargic even to conceptualize suicide. Every second of being alive hurt me. Because this thing had drained all fluid from me, I could not even cry. My mouth was parched as well. I had thought that when you feel your worst your tears flood, but the very worst pain is the arid pain of total violation that comes after the tears are all used up, the pain that stops up every space through which you once metered the world, or the world, you. This is the presence of major depression.

I have said that depression is both a birth and a death. The vine is what is born. The death is one's own decay, the cracking of the branches that support this misery. The first thing that goes is happiness. You cannot gain pleasure from anything. That's famously the cardinal symptom of major depression. But soon other emotions follow happiness into oblivion: sadness as you had known it, the sadness that seemed to have led you here; your sense of humor; your belief in and capacity for love. Your mind is leached until you seem dim-witted even to yourself. If your hair has always been thin, it seems thinner; if you have always had bad skin, it gets worse. You smell sour even to yourself. You lose the ability to trust anyone, to be touched, to grieve. Eventually, you are simply absent from yourself.

Maybe what is present usurps what becomes absent, and maybe the absence of obfuscatory things reveals what is present. Either way, you are less than yourself and in the clutches of something alien. Too often, treatments address only half the problem: they focus only on the presence or only on the absence. It is necessary both to cut away that extra thousand pounds of the vines and to relearn a root system and the techniques of photosynthesis. Drug therapy hacks through the vines. You can feel it happening, how the medication seems to be poisoning the parasite so that bit by bit it withers away. You feel the weight going, feel the way that the branches can recover much of their natural bent. Until you have got rid of the vine, you cannot think about what has been lost. But even with the vine gone, you may still have few leaves and shallow roots, and the rebuilding of your self cannot be achieved with any drugs that now exist. With the weight of the vine gone, little leaves scattered along the tree skeleton become viable for essential nourishment. But this is not a good way to be. It is not a strong way to be. Rebuilding of the self in and after depression requires love, insight, work, and, most of all, time.

Diagnosis is as complex as the illness. Patients ask doctors all the time, "Am I depressed?" as though the result were in a definitive blood test. The only way to find out whether you're depressed is to listen to and watch yourself, to feel your feelings and then think about them. If you feel bad without reason most of the time, you're depressed. If you feel bad most of the time with reason, you're also depressed, though changing the reasons may be a better way forward than leaving circumstance alone and attacking the depression. If the depression is disabling to you, then it's major. If it's only mildly distracting, it's not major. Psychiatry's bible—the *Diagnostic and Statistical Manual,* fourth edition *(DSM-IV)*—ineptly defines depression as the presence of five or more on a list of nine symptoms. The problem with the definition is that it's entirely arbitrary. There's no particular reason to qualify five symptoms as constituting depression; four symptoms are more or less depression; and five symptoms are less severe than six. Even one symptom is unpleasant. Having slight versions of all the symptoms may be less of a problem than having severe versions of two symptoms. After enduring diagnosis, most people seek causation, despite the fact that knowing why you are sick has no immediate bearing on treating the sickness.

15   Illness of the mind is real illness. It can have severe effects on the body. People who show up at the offices of their doctors complaining about stomach cramps are frequently told, "Why, there's nothing wrong with you except that you're depressed!" Depression, if it is sufficiently severe to cause stomach cramps, is actually a really bad thing to have wrong with you, and it requires treatment. If you show up complaining that your breathing is troubled, no one says to you, "Why, there's nothing wrong with you except that you have emphysema!" To the person who is experiencing them, psychosomatic complaints are as real as the stomach cramps of someone with food poisoning. They exist in the unconscious brain, and often enough the brain is sending inappropriate messages to the stomach, so they exist there as well. The diagnosis—whether something is rotten in your stomach or your appendix or your brain—matters in determining treatment and is not trivial. As organs go, the brain is quite an important one, and its malfunctions should be addressed accordingly.

Chemistry is often called on to heal the rift between body and soul. The relief people express when a doctor says their depression is "chemical" is predicated on a belief that there is an integral self that exists across time, and on a fictional divide between the fully occasioned sorrow and the utterly random one. The word *chemical* seems to assuage the feelings of responsibility people have for the stressed-out discontent of not liking their jobs, worrying about getting old, failing at love, hating their families. There is a pleasant freedom from guilt that has been attached to *chemical.* If your brain is predisposed to depression, you need not blame yourself for it. Well, blame yourself or evolution, but remember that blame itself can be understood as a chemical process, and that happiness, too, is chemical. Chemistry and biology are not matters that impinge on the "real" self; depression cannot be separated from the person it affects. Treatment does not alleviate a disruption of identity, bringing you back to some kind of normality; it readjusts a multifarious identity, changing in some small degree who you are.

Anyone who has taken high school science classes knows that human beings are made of chemicals and that the study of those chemicals and the structures in which they are configured is called biology. Everything that happens in the brain has chemical manifestations and sources. If you close your eyes and think hard about polar bears, that has a chemical effect on your brain. If you stick to a policy of opposing tax breaks for capital gains, that has a chemical effect on your brain. When you remember some episode from your past, you do so through the complex chemistry of memory. Childhood trauma and subsequent difficulty can alter brain chemistry. Thousands of chemical reactions are involved in deciding to read this book, picking it up with your hands, looking at the shapes of the letters on the page, extracting meaning from those shapes, and having intellectual and emotional responses to what they convey. If time lets you cycle out of a depression and feel better, the chemical changes are no less particular and complex than the ones that are brought about by taking antidepressants. The external determines the internal as much as the internal invents the external. What is so unattractive is the idea that in addition to all other lines being blurred, the boundaries of what makes us ourselves are blurry. There is no essential self that lies pure as a vein of gold under the chaos of experience and chemistry. Anything can be changed, and we must understand the human organism as a sequence of selves that succumb to or choose one another. And yet the language of science, used in training doctors and, increasingly, in nonacademic writing and conversation, is strangely perverse.

The cumulative results of the brain's chemical effects are not well understood. In the 1989 edition of the standard *Comprehensive Textbook of Psychiatry,* for example, one finds this helpful formula: a depression score is equivalent to the level of 3-methoxy-4-hydroxyphenylglycol (a compound found in the urine of all people and not apparently affected by depression); minus the level of 3-methoxy-4-hydroxymandelic acid; plus the level of norepinephrine; minus the level of normetanephrine plus the level of metanepherine, the sum of those divided by the level of 3-methoxy-4-hydroxymandelic acid; plus an unspecified conversion variable; or, as *CTP* puts it: "D-type score = C_1 (MHPG) – C_2 (VMA) + C_3 (NE) – C_4 (NMN + MN)/VMA + C_0." The score should come out between one for unipolar and zero for bipolar patients, so if you come up with something else—you're doing it wrong. How much insight can such formulae offer? How can they *possibly* apply to something as nebulous as mood? To what extent specific experience has conduced to a particular depression is hard to determine; nor can we explain through what chemistry a person comes to respond to external circumstance with depression; nor can we work out what makes someone essentially depressive.

Although depression is described by the popular press and the pharmaceutical industry as though it were a single-effect illness such as diabetes, it is not. Indeed, it is strikingly dissimilar to diabetes. Diabetics produce insufficient insulin, and diabetes is treated by increasing and stabilizing insulin in the bloodstream. Depression is *not* the consequence of a reduced level of anything we can now measure. Raising levels of serotonin in the brain triggers a process that eventually helps many depressed people to feel better, but that is *not* because they have abnormally low levels of serotonin. Furthermore, serotonin does *not* have immediate salutary effects. You could pump a gallon of serotonin into the brain of a depressed person and it would not in the instant make him feel one iota better, though a long-term sustained raise in serotonin level has some effects that ameliorate depressive symptoms. "I'm depressed but it's just chemical" is a sentence equivalent to "I'm murderous but it's just chemical" or "I'm intelligent but it's just chemical." Everything about a person is just chemical if one wants to think in those terms. "You can say it's 'just chemistry,'" says Maggie Robbins, who suffers from manic-depressive illness. "I say there's nothing 'just' about chemistry." The sun shines brightly and that's just chemical too, and it's chemical that rocks are hard, and that the sea is salt, and that certain springtime afternoons carry in their gentle breezes a quality of nostalgia that stirs the heart to longings and imaginings kept dormant by the snows of a long winter. "This serotonin thing," says David McDowell of Columbia University, "is part of modern neuromythology." It's a potent set of stories.

20　　Internal and external reality exist on a continuum. What happens and how you understand it to have happened and how you respond to its happening are usually linked, but no one is predictive of the others. If reality itself is often a relative thing, and the self is in a state of permanent flux, the passage from slight mood to extreme mood is a glissando. Illness, then, is an extreme state of emotion, and one might reasonably describe emotion as a mild form of illness. If we all felt up and great (but not delusionally manic) all the time, we could get more done and might have a happier time on earth, but that idea is creepy and terrifying (though, of course, if we felt up and great all the time we might forget all about creepiness and terror).

Influenza is straightforward: one day you do not have the responsible virus in your system, and another day you do. HIV passes from one person to another in a definable isolated split second. Depression? It's like trying to come up with clinical parameters for hunger, which affects us all several times a day, but which in its extreme version is a tragedy that kills its victims. Some people need more food than others; some can function under circumstances of dire malnutrition; some grow weak rapidly and collapse in the streets. Similarly, depression hits different people in different ways: some are predisposed to resist or battle through it, while others are helpless in its grip. Willfulness and pride may allow one person to get through a depression that would fell another whose personality is more gentle and acquiescent.

Depression interacts with personality. Some people are brave in the face of depression (during it and afterward) and some are weak. Since personality too has a random edge and a bewildering chemistry, one can write everything off to genetics, but that is too easy. "There is no such thing as a mood gene," says Steven Hyman, director of the National Institute of Mental Health. "It's just shorthand for very complex gene-environment interactions." If everyone has the capacity for some measure of depression under some circumstances, everyone also has the capacity to fight depression to some degree under some circumstances. Often, the fight takes the form of seeking out the treatments that will be most effective in the battle. It involves finding help while you are still strong enough to do so. It involves making the most of the life you have between your most severe episodes. Some horrendously symptom-ridden people are able to achieve real success in life; and some people are utterly destroyed by the mildest forms of the illness.

Working through a mild depression without medications has certain advantages. It gives you the sense that you can correct your own chemical imbalances through the exercise of your own chemical will. Learning to walk across hot coals is also a triumph of the brain over what appears to be the inevitable physical chemistry of pain, and it is a thrilling way to discover the sheer power of mind. Getting through a depression "on your own" allows you to avoid the social discomfort associated with psychiatric medications. It suggests that we are accepting ourselves as we were made, reconstructing ourselves only with our own interior mechanics and without help from the outside. Returning from distress by gradual degrees gives sense to affliction itself.

Interior mechanics, however, are difficult to commission and are frequently inadequate. Depression frequently destroys the power of mind over mood. Sometimes the complex chemistry of sorrow kicks in because you've lost someone you love, and the chemistry of loss and love may lead to the chemistry of depression. The chemistry of falling in love can kick in for obvious external reasons, or along lines that the heart can never tell the mind. If we wanted to treat this madness of emotion, we could perhaps do so. It is mad for adolescents to rage at parents who have done their best, but it is a conventional madness, uniform enough so that we tolerate it relatively unquestioningly. Sometimes the same chemistry kicks in for external reasons that are not sufficient, by mainstream standards, to explain the despair: someone bumps into you in a crowded bus and you want to cry, or you read about world overpopulation and find your own life intolerable. Everyone has on occasion felt disproportionate emotion over a small matter or has felt emotions whose origin is obscure or that may have no origin at all. Sometimes the chemistry kicks in for no apparent external reason at all. Most people have had moments of inexplicable despair, often in the middle of the night or in the early morning before the alarm clock sounds. If such feelings last ten minutes, they're a strange, quick mood. If they last ten hours, they're a disturbing febrility, and if they last ten years, they're a crippling illness.

25   It is too often the quality of happiness that you feel at every moment its fragility, while depression seems when you are in it to be a state that will never pass. Even if you accept that moods change, that whatever you feel today will be different tomorrow, you cannot relax into happiness as you can into sadness. For me, sadness always has been and still is a more powerful feeling; and if that is not a universal experience, perhaps it is the base from which depression grows. I hated being depressed, but it was also in depression that I learned my own acreage, the full extent of my soul. When I am happy, I feel slightly distracted by happiness, as though it fails to use some part of my mind and brain that wants the exercise. Depression is something to do. My grasp tightens and becomes acute in moments of loss: I can see the beauty of glass objects fully at the moment when they slip from my hand toward the floor. "We find pleasure much less pleasurable, pain much more painful than we had anticipated," Schopenhauer wrote. "We require at all times a certain quantity of care or sorrow or want, as a ship requires ballast, to keep on a straight course."

There is a Russian expression: if you wake up feeling no pain, you know you're dead. While life is not only about pain, the experience of pain, which is particular in its intensity, is one of the surest signs of the life force. Schopenhauer said, "Imagine this race transported to a Utopia where everything grows of its own accord and turkeys fly around ready-roasted, where lovers find one another without any delay and keep one another without any difficulty: in such a place some men would die of boredom or hang themselves, some would fight and kill one another, and thus they would create for themselves more suffering than nature inflicts on them as it is . . . the polar opposite of suffering [is] boredom." I believe that pain needs to be transformed but not forgotten; gainsaid but not obliterated.

QUESTIONS FOR DISCUSSION

1. Solomon begins his definition of depression by claiming, "Depression is the flaw in love." What does he mean by this compelling statement, and how does he develop it further in his opening paragraphs?
2. In his third paragraph, Solomon contrasts grief with depression. What distinction does he draw, and how does this help to clarify his definition of depression?
3. How does Solomon contrast mild and major depression, and how does his example from Virginia Woolf's *Jacob's Room* help to clarify the point he is making about mild depression?
4. How does Solomon use rust as a metaphor to explain how major depression can overcome an individual? Is his metaphor effective? Explain your response.
5. How does Solomon use his personal observation of an oak tree choked by a vine to explain both depression's process and its cure through drug therapy?
6. Solomon has a complex opinion of the value of chemical therapy in treating depression. How does he explain its benefits, its limitations, and its misapplications?
7. According to Solomon, what valuable insights can grow out of depression? How do the quotations he uses from Schopenhauer help to reinforce his point at the end of the essay?

CONNECTION

Compare Solomon's and Remen's views of the therapy for the treatment of depression (see page 311).

IDEAS FOR WRITING

1. Using a series of metaphors and comparisons as Solomon does in the first part of his essay, write a definition of depression or some other type of mental or physical illness that reflects obsessive behavior.
2. Write an essay arguing for or against the concept that Solomon presents at the end of his essay: pain and suffering are positive because they relieve complacency, help us to understand ourselves more deeply, and develop in us a stronger appreciation of beauty. According to Solomon, how is the struggle to get through a depression a form of transformation?

Charlotte Perkins Gilman

The Yellow Wallpaper

A feminist and economist, Charlotte Perkins Gilman (1860–1935) was born in Hartford, Connecticut, and attended the Rhode Island School of Design. Her best-known work is Women and Economics *(1898); she also wrote* Herland *(1915), a feminist utopia. Gilman's "The Yellow Wallpaper" (1892), originally published as a ghost story, became popular with the rebirth of the feminist movement in the 1970s. The story is a fictionalized account of Gilman's severe depression after the birth of her daughter. While "The Yellow Wallpaper" gives us insights into the role of women at the turn of the twentieth century, many readers today can still identify with the struggles that the narrator in the story faces.*

JOURNAL

Describe a place about which you have dreamed or fantasized that embodies or symbolizes one of your fears or obsessions.

It is very seldom that mere ordinary people like John and myself secure ancestral halls for the summer.

A colonial mansion, a hereditary estate, I would say a haunted house and reach the height of romantic felicity—but that would be asking too much of fate!

Still I will proudly declare that there is something queer about it.

Else, why should it be let so cheaply? And why have stood so long untenanted?

5   John laughs at me, of course, but one expects that in marriage.

John is practical in the extreme. He has no patience with faith, an intense horror of superstition, and he scoffs openly at any talk of things not to be felt and seen and put down in figures.

John is a physician, and *perhaps*—(I would not say it to a living soul, of course, but this is dead paper and a great relief to my mind)—*perhaps* that is one reason I do not get well faster.

You see, he does not believe I am sick!

And what can one do?

10   If a physician of high standing, and one's own husband, assures friends and relatives that there is really nothing the matter with one but temporary nervous depression—a slight hysterical tendency—what is one to do?

My brother is also a physician, and also of high standing, and he says the same thing.

So I take phosphates or phosphites—whichever it is, and tonics, and air and exercise, and journeys, and am absolutely forbidden to "work" until I am well again.

Personally, I disagree with their ideas.

Personally, I believe that congenial work, with excitement and change, would do me good.

15   But what is one to do?

I did write for a while in spite of them; but it *does* exhaust me a good deal—having to be so sly about it, or else meet with heavy opposition.

I sometimes fancy that in my condition, if I had less opposition and more society and stimulus—but John says the very worst thing I can do is to think about my condition, and I confess it always makes me feel bad.

So I will let it alone and talk about the house.

The most beautiful place! It is quite alone, standing well back from the road, quite three miles from the village. It makes me think of English places that you read about, for there are hedges and walls and gates that lock, and lots of separate little houses for the gardeners and people.

20   There is a *delicious* garden! I never saw such a garden—large and shady, full of box-bordered paths, and lined with long grape-covered arbors with seats under them.

There were greenhouses, but they are all broken now.

There was some legal trouble, I believe, something about the heirs and co-heirs; anyhow, the place has been empty for years.

That spoils my ghostliness, I am afraid, but I don't care—there is something strange about the house—I can feel it.

I even said so to John one moonlight evening, but he said what I felt was a *draught*, and shut the window.

25   I get unreasonably angry with John sometimes. I'm sure I never used to be so sensitive. I think it is due to this nervous condition.

But John says if I feel so I shall neglect proper self-control; so I take pains to control myself—before him, at least, and that makes me very tired.

I don't like our room a bit. I wanted one downstairs that opened onto the piazza and had roses all over the window, and such pretty old-fashioned chintz hangings! But John would not hear of it.

He said there was only one window and not room for two beds, and no near room for him if he took another.

He is very careful and loving, and hardly lets me stir without special direction.

30   I have a schedule prescription of each hour in the day; he takes all care from me, and so I feel basely ungrateful not to value it more.

He said he came here solely on my account, that I was to have perfect rest and all the air I could get. "Your exercise depends on your strength, my dear," said he, "and your food somewhat on your appetite; but air you can absorb all the time." So we took the nursery at the top of the house.

It is a big, airy room, the whole floor nearly, with windows that look all ways, and air and sunshine galore. It was nursery first, and then playroom and gymnasium, I should judge, for the windows are barred for little children, and there are rings and things in the walls.

The paint and paper look as if a boys' school had used it. It is stripped off—the paper—in great patches all around the head of my bed, about as far as I can reach, and in a great place on the other side of the room low down. I never saw a worse paper in my life.

One of those sprawling, flamboyant patterns committing every artistic sin.

35   It is dull enough to confuse the eye in following, pronounced enough constantly to irritate and provoke study, and when you follow the lame uncertain curves for a little distance they suddenly commit suicide—plunge off at outrageous angles, destroy themselves in unheard-of contradictions.

The color is repellent, almost revolting: a smoldering unclean yellow, strangely faded by the slow-turning sunlight. It is a dull yet lurid orange in some places, a sickly sulphur tint in others.

No wonder the children hated it! I should hate it myself if I had to live in this room long.

There comes John, and I must put this away—he hates to have me write a word.

We have been here two weeks, and I haven't felt like writing before, since that first day.

40   I am sitting by the window now, up in this atrocious nursery, and there is nothing to hinder my writings as much as I please, save lack of strength.

John is away all day, and even some nights when his cases are serious.

I am glad my case is not serious!

But these nervous troubles are dreadfully depressing.

John does not know how much I really suffer. He knows there is no reason to suffer, and that satisfies him.

45   Of course it is only nervousness. It does weigh on me so not to do my duty in any way!

I meant to be such a help to John, such a real rest and comfort, and here I am a comparative burden already!

Nobody would believe what an effort it is to do what little I am able—to dress and entertain, and order things.

It is fortunate Mary is so good with the baby. Such a dear baby!

And yet I *cannot* be with him, it makes me so nervous.

50   I suppose John never was nervous in his life. He laughs at me so about this wallpaper!

At first he meant to repaper the room, but afterward he said that I was letting it get the better of me, and that nothing was worse for a nervous patient than to give way to such fancies.

He said that after the wallpaper was changed it would be the heavy bedstead, and then the barred windows, and then that gate at the head of the stairs, and so on.

"You know the place is doing you good," he said, "and really, dear, I don't care to renovate the house just for a three months' rental."

"Then do let us go downstairs," I said. "There are such pretty rooms there."

55   Then he took me in his arms and called me a blessed little goose, and said he would go down cellar, if I wished, and have it whitewashed into the bargain.

But he is right enough about the beds and windows and things.

It is as airy and comfortable a room as anyone need wish, and, of course, I would not be so silly as to make him uncomfortable just for a whim.

I'm really getting quite fond of the big room, all but that horrid paper.

Out of one window I can see the garden—those mysterious deep-shaded arbors, the riotous old-fashioned flowers, and bushes and gnarly trees.

60   Out of another I get a lovely view of the bay and a little private wharf belonging to the estate. There is a beautiful shaded lane that runs down there from the house. I always fancy I see people walking in these numerous paths and arbors, but John has cautioned me not to give way to fancy in the least. He says that with my imaginative power and habit of story-making, a nervous weakness like mine is sure to lead to all manner of excited fancies, and that I ought to use my will and good sense to check the tendency. So I try.

I think sometimes that if I were only well enough to write a little it would relieve the press of ideas and rest me.

But I find I get pretty tired when I try.

It is so discouraging not to have any advice and companionship about my work. When I get really well, John says we will ask Cousin Henry and Julia down for a long visit; but he says he would as soon put fireworks in my pillowcase as to let me have those stimulating people about now.

I wish I could get well faster.

65   But I must not think about that. This paper looks to me as if it *knew* what a vicious influence it had!

There is a recurrent spot where the pattern lolls like a broken neck and two bulbous eyes stare at you upside down.

I get positively angry with the impertinence of it and the everlastingness. Up and down and sideways they crawl, and those absurd unblinking eyes are everywhere. There is one place where two breadths didn't match, and the eyes go all up and down the line, one a little higher than the other.

I never saw so much expression in an inanimate thing before, and we all know how much expression they have! I used to lie awake as a child and get more entertainment and terror out of blank walls and plain furniture than most children could find in a toy store.

I remember what a kindly wink the knobs of our big old bureau used to have, and there was one chair that always seemed like a strong friend.

70   I used to feel that if any of the other things looked too fierce I could always hop into that chair and be safe.

The furniture in this room is no worse than inharmonious, however, for we had to bring it all from downstairs. I suppose when this was used as a playroom they had to take the nursery things out, and no wonder! I never saw such ravages as the children have made here.

The wallpaper, as I said before, is torn off in spots, and it sticketh closer than a brother—they must have had perseverance as well as hatred.

Then the floor is scratched and gouged and splintered, the plaster itself is dug out here and there, and this great heavy bed, which is all we found in the room, looks as if it had been through the wars.

But I don't mind it a bit—only the paper.

75   There comes John's sister. Such a dear girl as she is, and so careful of me! I must not let her find me writing.

She is a perfect and enthusiastic housekeeper, and hopes for no better profession. I verily believe she thinks it is the writing which made me sick!

But I can write when she is out, and see her a long way off from these windows.

There is one that commands the road, a lovely shaded winding road, and one that just looks off over the country. A lovely country, too, full of great elms and velvet meadows.

This wallpaper has a kind of subpattern in a different shade, a particularly irritating one, for you can only see it in certain lights, and not clearly then.

80   But in the places where it isn't faded and where the sun is just so—I can see a strange, provoking, formless sort of figure that seems to skulk about behind that silly and conspicuous front design.

There's sister on the stairs!

Well, the Fourth of July is over! The people are all gone, and I am tired out. John thought it might do me good to see a little company, so we just had Mother and Nellie and the children down for a week.

Of course I didn't do a thing. Jennie sees to everything now.

But it tired me all the same.

85   John says if I don't pick up faster he shall send me to Weir Mitchell in the fall.

But I don't want to go there at all. I had a friend who was in his hands once, and she says he is just like John and my brother, only more so!

Besides, it is such an undertaking to go so far.

I don't feel as if it was worthwhile to turn my hand over for anything, and I'm getting dreadfully fretful and querulous.

I cry at nothing, and cry most of the time.

90   Of course I don't when John is here, or anybody else, but when I am alone.

And I am alone a good deal just now. John is kept in town very often by serious cases, and Jennie is good and lets me alone when I want her to.

So I walk a little in the garden or down that lovely lane, sit on the porch under the roses, and lie down up here a good deal.

I'm getting really fond of the room in spite of the wallpaper. Perhaps *because* of the wallpaper.

It dwells in my mind so!

95 I lie here on this great immovable bed—it is nailed down, I believe—and follow that pattern about by the hour. It is as good as gymnastics, I assure you. I start, we'll say, at the bottom, down in the corner over there where it has not been touched, and I determine for the thousandth time that I *will* follow that pointless pattern to some sort of a conclusion.

I know a little of the principle of design, and I know this thing was not arranged on any laws of radiation, or alternation, or repetition, or symmetry, or anything else that I ever heard of.

It is repeated, of course, by the breadths, but not otherwise.

Looked at in one way, each breadth stands alone; the bloated curves and flourishes—a kind of "debased Romanesque" with delirium tremens go waddling up and down in isolated columns of fatuity.

But, on the other hand, they connect diagonally, and the sprawling outlines run off in great slanting waves of optic horror, like a lot of wallowing seaweeds in full chase.

100 The whole thing goes horizontally, too, at least it seems so, and I exhaust myself trying to distinguish the order of its going in that direction.

They have used a horizontal breadth for a frieze, and that adds wonderfully to the confusion.

There is one end of the room where it is almost intact, and there, when the crosslights fade and the low sun shines directly upon it, I can almost fancy radiation after all—the interminable grotesque seems to form around a common center and rush off in headlong plunges of equal distraction.

It makes me tired to follow it. I will take a nap, I guess.

I don't know why I should write this.

105 I don't want to.

I don't feel able.

And I know John would think it absurd. But I *must* say what I feel and think in some way—it is such a relief!

But the effort is getting to be greater than the relief.

Half the time now I am awfully lazy, and lie down ever so much. John says I mustn't lose my strength, and has me take cod liver oil and lots of tonics and things, to say nothing of ale and wines and rare meat.

110 Dear John! He loves me very dearly, and hates to have me sick. I tried to have a real earnest reasonable talk with him the other day, and tell him how I wish he would let me go and make a visit to Cousin Henry and Julia.

But he said I wasn't able to go, nor able to stand it after I got there; and I did not make out a very good case for myself, for I was crying before I had finished.

It is getting to be a great effort for me to think straight. Just this nervous weakness, I suppose.

And dear John gathered me up in his arms, and just carried me upstairs and laid me on the bed, and sat by me and read to me till it tired my head.

He said I was his darling and his comfort and all he had, and that I must take care of myself for his sake, and keep well.

115   He says no one but myself can help me out of it, that I must use my will and self-control and not let any silly fancies run away with me.

There's one comfort—the baby is well and happy, and does not have to occupy this nursery with the horrid wallpaper.

If we had not used it, that blessed child would have! What a fortunate escape! Why, I wouldn't have a child of mine, an impressionable little thing, live in such a room for worlds.

I never thought of it before, but it is lucky that John kept me here after all; I can stand it so much easier than a baby, you see.

Of course I never mention it to them any more—I am too wise—but I keep watch for it all the same.

120   There are things in the wallpaper that nobody knows about but me, or ever will.

Behind that outside pattern the dim shapes get clearer every day.

It is always the same shape, only very numerous.

And it is like a woman stooping down and creeping about behind that pattern. I don't like it a bit. I wonder—I begin to think—I wish John would take me away from here!

It is so hard to talk with John about my case, because he is so wise, and because he loves me so.

125   But I tried it last night.

It was moonlight. The moon shines in all around just as the sun does.

I hate to see it sometimes, it creeps so slowly, and always comes in by one window or another.

John was asleep and I hated to waken him, so I kept still and watched the moonlight on that undulating wallpaper till I felt creepy.

The faint figure behind seemed to shake the pattern, just as if she wanted to get out.

130   I got up softly and went to feel and see if the paper *did* move, and when I came back John was awake.

"What is it, little girl?" he said. "Don't go walking about like that—you'll get cold."

I thought it was a good time to talk, so I told him that I really was not gaining here, and that I wished he would take me away.

"Why, darling!" said he. "Our lease will be up in three weeks, and I can't see how to leave before."

"The repairs are not done at home, and I cannot possibly leave town just now. Of course, if you were in any danger, I could and would, but you really are better, dear, whether you can see it or not. I am a doctor, dear, and I know. You are gaining flesh and color, your appetite is better, I feel really much easier about you."

135　　"I don't weigh a bit more," said I, "nor as much; and my appetite may be better in the evening when you are here but it is worse in the morning when you are away!"

"Bless her little heart!" said he with a big hug. "She shall be as sick as she pleases! But now let's improve the shining hours by going to sleep, and talk about it in the morning!"

"And you won't go away?" I asked gloomily.

"Why, how can I, dear? It is only three weeks more and then we will take a nice little trip for a few days while Jennie is getting the house ready. Really, dear, you are better!"

"Better in body perhaps—" I began, and stopped short, for he sat up straight and looked at me with such a stern, reproachful look that I could not say another word.

140　　"My darling," said he, "I beg you, for my sake and for our child's sake, as well as for your own, that you will never for one instant let that idea enter your mind! There is nothing so dangerous, so fascinating, to a temperament like yours. It is a false and foolish fancy. Can you trust me as a physician when I tell you so?"

So of course, I said no more on that score, and we went to sleep before long. He thought I was asleep first, but I wasn't, and lay there for hours trying to decide whether that front pattern and the back pattern really did move together or separately.

On a pattern like this, by daylight, there is a lack of sequence, a defiance of law, that is a constant irritant to a normal mind.

The color is hideous enough, and unreliable enough, and infuriating enough, but the pattern is torturing.

You think you have mastered it, but just as you get well under way in following, it turns a back somersault and there you are. It slaps you in the face, knocks you down, and tramples upon you. It is like a bad dream.

145　　The outside pattern is a florid arabesque, reminding one of a fungus. If you can imagine a toadstool in joints, an interminable string of toadstools, budding and sprouting in endless convolutions—why, that is something like it.

That is, sometimes!

There is one marked peculiarity about this paper, a thing nobody seems to notice but myself, and that is that it changes as the light changes.

When the sun shoots in through the east window—I always watch for that first long, straight ray—it changes so quickly that I never can quite believe it.

That is why I watch it always.

150　　By moonlight—the moon shines in all night when there is a moon—I wouldn't know it was the same paper.

At night in any kind of light, in twilight, candlelight, lamplight, and worst of all by moonlight, it becomes bars! The outside pattern, I mean, and the woman behind it is as plain as can be.

I didn't realize for a long time what the thing was that showed behind, that dim subpattern, but now I am quite sure it is a woman.

By daylight she is subdued, quiet. I fancy it is the pattern that keeps her so still. It is so puzzling. It keeps me quiet by the hour.

I lie down ever so much now. John says it is good for me, and to sleep all I can.

155   Indeed he started the habit by making me lie down for an hour after each meal.

It is a very bad habit, I am convinced, for you see, I don't sleep.

And that cultivates deceit, for I don't tell them I'm awake—oh, no!

The fact is I am getting a little afraid of John.

He seems very queer sometimes, and even Jennie has an inexplicable look.

160   It strikes me occasionally, just as a scientific hypothesis—that perhaps it is the paper!

I have watched John when he did not know I was looking, and come into the room suddenly on the most innocent excuses, and I've caught him several times *looking at the paper!* And Jennie too. I caught Jennie with her hand on it once.

She didn't know I was in the room, and when I asked her in a quiet, a very quiet voice, and the most restrained manner possible, what she was doing with the paper, she turned around as if she had been caught stealing, and looked quite angry—asked me why I should frighten her so!

Then she said that the paper stained everything it touched, that she had found yellow smooches on all my clothes and John's, and she wished we would be more careful!

Did not that sound innocent? But I know she was studying that pattern, and I am determined that nobody shall find it out but myself!

165   Life is very much more exciting now than it used to be. You see, I have something more to expect, to look forward to, to watch. I really do eat better, and am more quiet than I was.

John is so pleased to see me improve! He laughed a little the other day, and said I seemed to be flourishing in spite of my wallpaper.

I turned it off with a laugh. I had no intention of telling him it was *because* of the wallpaper—he would make fun of me. He might even want to take me away.

I don't want to leave now until I have found it out. There is a week more, and I think that will be enough.

I'm feeling so much better!

170   I don't sleep much at night, for it is so interesting to watch developments; but I sleep a good deal during the daytime.

In the daytime it is tiresome and perplexing.

There are always new shoots on the fungus, and new shades of yellow all over it. I cannot keep count of them, though I have tried conscientiously.

It is the strangest yellow, that wallpaper! It makes me think of all the yellow things I ever saw—not beautiful ones like buttercups, but old, foul, bad yellow things.

But there is something else about that paper—the smell! I noticed it the moment we came into the room, but with so much air and sun it was not bad. Now we have had a week of fog and rain, and whether the windows are open or not, the smell is here.

175 It creeps all over the house.

I find it hovering in the dining room, skulking in the parlor, hiding in the hall, lying in wait for me on the stairs.

It gets into my hair.

Even when I go to ride, if I turn my head suddenly and surprise it—there is that smell!

Such a peculiar odor, too! I have spent hours in trying to analyze it, to find what it smelled like.

180 It is not bad—at first—and very gentle, but quite the subtlest, most enduring odor I ever met.

It used to disturb me at first. I thought seriously of burning the house—to reach the smell.

But now I am used to it. The only thing I can think of that it is like is the *color* of the paper! A yellow smell.

There is a very funny mark on this wall, low down, near the mopboard. A streak that runs round the room. It goes behind every piece of furniture, except the bed, a long straight, even *smooch,* as if it had been rubbed over and over.

I wonder how it was done and who did it, and what they did it for. Round and round and round—round and round and round—it makes me dizzy!

185 I really have discovered something at last.

Through watching so much at night, when it changes so, I have finally found out.

The front pattern *does* move—and no wonder! The woman behind shakes it!

Sometimes I think there are a great many women behind, and sometimes only one, and she crawls around fast, and her crawling shakes it all over.

Then in the very bright spots she keeps still, and in the very shady spots she just takes hold of the bars and shakes them hard.

190 And she is all the time trying to climb through. But nobody could climb through that pattern—it strangles so; I think that is why it has so many heads.

They get through and then the pattern strangles them off and turns them upside down, and makes their eyes white!

If those heads were covered or taken off it would not be half so bad.

I think that woman gets out in the daytime!

And I'll tell you why—privately—I've seen her!

195 I can see her out of every one of my windows!

It is the same woman, I know, for she is always creeping, and most women do not creep by daylight.

I see her in that long shaded lane, creeping up and down. I see her in those dark grape arbors, creeping all round the garden.

I see her on that long road under the trees, creeping along, and when a carriage comes she hides under the blackberry vines.

I don't blame her a bit. It must be very humiliating to be caught creeping by daylight!

200   I always lock the door when I creep by daylight. I can't do it at night, for I know John would suspect something at once.

And John is so queer now that I don't want to irritate him. I wish he would take another room! Besides, I don't want anybody to get that woman out at night but myself.

I often wonder if I could see her out of all the windows at once.

But, turn as fast as I can, I can only see out of one at one time.

And though I always see her, she *may* be able to creep faster than I can turn! I have watched her sometimes away off in the open country, creeping as fast as a cloud shadow in a wind.

205   If only that top pattern could be gotten off from the under one! I mean to try it, little by little.

I have found out another funny thing, but I shan't tell it this time! It does not do to trust people too much.

There are only two more days to get this paper off, and I believe John is beginning to notice. I don't like the look in his eyes.

And I heard him ask Jennie a lot of professional questions about me. She had a very good report to give.

She said I slept a good deal in the daytime.

210   John knows I don't sleep very well at night, for all I'm so quiet!

He asked me all sorts of questions too, and pretended to be very loving and kind.

As if I couldn't see through him!

Still, I don't wonder he acts so, sleeping under this paper for three months.

It only interests me, but I feel sure John and Jennie are secretly affected by it.

215   Hurrah! This is the last day, but it is enough. John is to stay in town overnight, and won't be out until this evening.

Jennie wanted to sleep with me—the sly thing; but I told her I should undoubtedly rest better for a night all alone.

That was clever, for really I wasn't alone a bit! As soon as it was moonlight and that poor thing began to crawl and shake the pattern, I got up and ran to help her.

I pulled and she shook. I shook and she pulled, and before morning we had peeled off yards of that paper.

A strip about as high as my head and half around the room.

220   And then when the sun came and that awful pattern began to laugh at me, I declared I would finish it today!

We go away tomorrow, and they are moving all my furniture down again to leave things as they were before.

Jennie looked at the wall in amazement, but I told her merrily that I did it out of pure spite at the vicious thing.

She laughed and said she wouldn't mind doing it herself, but I must not get tired.

How she betrayed herself that time!

225   But I am here, and no person touches this but me—not *alive!*

She tried to get me out of the room—it was too patent! But I said it was so quiet and empty and clean now that I believed I would lie down again and sleep all I could, and not to wake me even for dinner—I would call when I woke.

So now she is gone, and the servants are gone, and the things are gone, and there is nothing left but that great bedstead nailed down, with the canvas mattress we found on it.

We shall sleep downstairs tonight, and take the boat home tomorrow.

I quite enjoy the room, now it is bare again.

230   How those children did tear about here!

This bedstead is fairly gnawed!

But I must get to work.

I have locked the door and thrown the key down into the front path.

I don't want to go out, and I don't want to have anybody come in, till John comes.

235   I want to astonish him.

I've got a rope up here that even Jennie did not find. If that woman does get out, and tries to get away, I can tie her!

But I forgot I could not reach far without anything to stand on!

This bed will not move!

I tried to lift and push it until I was lame, and then I got so angry I bit off a little piece at one corner—but it hurt my teeth.

240   Then I peeled off all the paper I could reach standing on the floor. It sticks horribly and the pattern just enjoys it! All those strangled heads and bulbous eyes and waddling fungus growths just shriek with derision!

I am getting angry enough to do something desperate. To jump out of the window would be admirable exercise, but the bars are too strong even to try.

Besides I wouldn't do it. Of course not. I know well enough that a step like that is improper and might be misconstrued.

I don't like to *look* out of the windows even—there are so many of those creeping women, and they creep so fast.

I wonder if they all come out of that wallpaper as I did?

245   But I am securely fastened now by my well-hidden rope—you don't get *me* out in the road there!

I suppose I shall have to get back behind the pattern when it comes night, and that is hard!

It is so pleasant to be out in this great room and creep around as I please!

I don't want to go outside. I won't, even if Jennie asks me to.

For outside you have to creep on the ground, and everything is green instead of yellow.

250   But here I can creep smoothly on the floor, and my shoulder just fits in that long smooch around the wall, so I cannot lose my way.

Why, there's John at the door!

It is no use, young man, you can't open it!

How he does call and pound!

Now he's crying for an axe.

255   It would be a shame to break down that beautiful door!

"John, dear!" said I in the gentlest voice, "The key is down by the front steps, under a plantain leaf!"

That silenced him for a few moments.

Then he said, very quietly indeed, "Open the door, my darling!"

"I can't," said I. "The key is down by the front door under a plantain leaf!" And then I said it again, several times, very gently and slowly, and said it so often that he had to go and see, and he got it of course, and came in. He stopped short by the door.

260   "What is the matter?" he cried. "For God's sake, what are you doing!"

I kept on creeping just the same, but I looked at him over my shoulder.

"I've got out at last," said I, "in spite of you and Jane. And I've pulled off most of the paper, so you can't put me back!"

Now why should that man have fainted? But he did, and right across my path by the wall, so that I had to creep over him every time!

ACTIVITY

The drawings that follow were created by students using a computer drawing program. The students were asked to draw an image of the yellow wallpaper that for them was representative of the story's meaning. Try doing your own drawing of the wallpaper, and write a paragraph explaining your response.

QUESTIONS FOR DISCUSSION

1. Why are John and the narrator spending their summer at the colonial mansion? In what ways are the room's former function, the peculiarities of its location and decoration, and the objects left behind in it significant to the story's meaning? What is causing the narrator to be sick?
2. Characterize John and then contrast him to the narrator. Who is in control? Why? How does their relationship change as the story develops?
3. Why doesn't John think that the narrator should write? Why does she want to write?
4. Describe the yellow wallpaper. Why does it fascinate the narrator? What do the wallpaper and its changes signify about the narrator?

Vera Shimsky

My picture of "The Yellow Wallpaper" is a rather literal representation of the wallpaper as described in the story. The woman behind the bars is both the women imagined by the narrator and the narrator herself. She is shaking the bars, just as in the story, the narrator and the woman in the wallpaper try to free the woman from the image she has to put on for society, the bars on the wallpaper. Imagine a greenish tint to the wallpaper as the different view of it that comes with the change of the time of day. This tint is one of the things the narrator hates most about the paper. The upside-down faces with the eyes are portrayed here as circles with two glowing spots—the eyes.

Drawing this picture helped me understand even more intimately how much the narrator is the woman behind the wallpaper. In fact, the entire process of her growing more and more connected with the paper demonstrates the deterioration of her mental state. The eyes that stare at her from the wallpaper are the eyes of her husband and Jennie, as well as the rest of society who are watching her and observing whether or not she is improving. The confusing pattern of the wallpaper that the narrator cannot seem to figure out or follow all the way through represents the confusion and the struggle within her mine. The bars are what she is struggling against, both her mental condition and the pressures of the society put upon her that, instead of helping her, are making her worse. Having to visualize the wallpaper and put it into an image helped me transcend the story into a true understanding of the narrator's state of mind.

Shanney Yu

"The Yellow Wallpaper" is a story about one woman's struggle with postpartum depression. She is confined to a bedroom in order to regain her strength. The yellow wallpaper in this bedroom becomes the focal point of her attentions as its convoluted patter slowly drives her to the brink of insanity.

The narrator describes the design of the wallpaper:

> Looked at in one way, each breadth stands alone; the bloated curves and flourishes—a kind of "debased Romanesque" with delirium tremens go waddling up and down in isolated columns of fatuity . . . they connect diagonally . . . in great slanting waves of optic horror . . . The whole thing goes horizontally, too . . . and I exhaust myself trying to distinguish the order of its going in that direction.

The narrator is also convinced that the twisted design the wallpaper is the prison of one or more women. She feels as if the eyes of these women follow her every move. " . . . those absurd unblinking eyes are everywhere. . . I can see a strange, provoking, formless sort of figure that seems to skulk about behind that silly and conspicuous front design."

I tried to incorporate all of these elements into my drawing. I started by drawing vertical bars that run across the entire drawing, creating a sort of prison effect. In the tangled web of the pattern, I drew two "unblinking" eyes. The swirls around the eyes make up the face of a trapped woman and the swirls beneath this face are her arms. Her hands grasp the bars as she struggles to be freed. The circular swirls I drew next serve two purposes: to make the design all the more hypnotic as well as to represent the other "unblinking" eyes that taunt the narrator.

5. Why does John faint in the final scene? Is this scene comic or tragic? Do you assume that the narrator is insane or on the verge of an important discovery? What do you think will happen to the narrator?
6. Do you think the story makes a feminist statement about the causes for mental illness? Why or why not?

CONNECTION

Compare the narrator's obsession with the wallpaper and the trapped women behind it to Anne Lamott's obsession with thinness and eating in "Hunger" (see page 298). Which work takes a more feminist position in response to the obsession and its transformation into meaningful action?

IDEAS FOR WRITING

1. Write an essay in which you discuss the relevance of the story to the ways that men and women communicate with one another or try to control one another's behavior in modern society.
2. Write an essay in which you analyze and interpret the symbol of the wallpaper in the story, taking into consideration the student drawings and interpretations on pages 276–290.

RELATED WEB SITES

Charlotte Perkins Gilman

`www.womenwriters.net/domesticgoddess/gilman1.html`

Explaining the life and work of Charlotte Perkins Gilman, this Web site provides links, criticism, and a biography of Gilman. The site also features many other women writers, from the beginning of the nineteenth century, who wrote domestic fiction.

The Yellow Wallpaper

`http://itech.fgcu.edu/faculty/wohlpart/alra/gilman.htm`

This page, produced by students at Florida Gulf Coast University under the direction of Dr. Jim Wohlpart, contains essays, an annotated bibliography, and an annotated e-text of Gilman's story that emphasizes key characters, images, and symbols from the story.

Diane Ackerman

A Slender Thread

See the headnote in Chapter 2. The selection here comes from Ackerman's book A Slender Thread, *which examines the issue of suicide and her work at a suicide prevention hotline in upstate New York.*

Write about the experience of losing someone you know to illness or suicide. Try to define the experience of loss, how it changed you, and your understanding of the individual involved.

I'm afraid of losing Louise. *Losing her.* A shorthand for an avalanche of hurt, the phrase sounds too casual, the equivalent of misplacing a set of keys or an umbrella. I suppose it's my fundamental belief in the uniqueness of people that makes me cherish how irreplaceable they are. Louise has many talents, a lively mind, a quirky and unusual point of view, and a generous heart. I don't want life to lose her. I don't want society to lose her. I don't want to lose her from the pageant of humankind.

We use only a voice and a set of ears, somehow tied to the heart and brain, but it feels like mountaineering with someone who has fallen, a dangling person whose hands you are gripping in your own. But if she truly wishes to die? We don't hear from her when she's not depressed. In stabler times, I don't think she would choose death. But I respect her right to choose, and I tell her so.

"Look, you can always kill yourself. That's one option tonight. Why don't we put that up on the shelf for a moment and talk about what some other options might be."

Because she feels bereft of them, I want her to have choices. Choice is a signature of our species. We choose to live, sometimes we choose our own death, but most of the time we make choices just to prove choice is possible. Above all else, we value the right to choose one's destiny. The very young and some lucky few may find their days opening one onto another like a set of ornate doors, but most people make an unconscious vow each morning to get through the day's stresses and labors intact, without becoming overwhelmed or wishing to escape into death. Everybody has thought about suicide, or knows somebody who committed suicide, and then felt "pushed another inch, and it could have been me." As Emile Zola once said, some mornings you first have to swallow your toad of disgust before you can get on with the day. We choose to live. But suicidal people have tunnel vision—no other choice seems possible. A counselor's job is to put windows and doors in that tunnel.

5   "Options?" She says the word as if it were too large for her mouth. It probably seems tragically impersonal for what she is feeling. "You mean like eating dinner?" she asks acidly.

"Have you had anything to eat today?"

A dry little laugh. "I bought some lamb chops but couldn't face cooking them. I don't want to eat something more nervous than I am." I laugh. Her delivery was perfect. She laughs again. It is barely more than a chuckle.

"Cold . . ." She launches the word like a dark cloud, not attached to anything special, a nimbus of pure pain.

"How come so cold and lonely tonight?"

10   "I'm always lonely, lonelier than life," she says faintly; then rallying a little, she explains, "When I worked at Montessori, I used to meet people there, or when my kids were little, through their activities. Now I don't meet anyone. Not at work in that pathetic office. My job is horrible. Not hard, you know, just the same rain barrel full of soak everyday, boring and lonely, but it's the only one I could find. There's nothing out there for a middle-aged woman, and the minute they learn I've been hospitalized, they're afraid to hire me, like I'm going to napalm their filing cabinets or Crazy Glue their customers' thumbs to the counter or something."

A thought she has obviously entertained in some detail.

"I understand. You hate your job, you don't make friends there, and it's hard to find a new one. Every workday must feel like a wasteland." "Oppressive," she corrects. Not too little of a good thing, too much of a bad.

"Oppressive. Maybe we can figure out some other work . . ."

"It's hopeless. I've tried everywhere. There's nothing."

15   Before I can reply, she swerves to: ". . . and I haven't had a date in years, haven't been laid since I don't know when. And then there are my kids. I mean, they're teens, and suddenly Mom's a drag. We fight all the time. About ridiculous things, small things. I don't even know what we're fighting about half the time. They don't want me to hug and kiss them anymore. I can understand that, but it hurts."

Breathless, she sounds like a child trying to tell a story faster than her tumbling words. I was rushing her. She wasn't finished with her lamentation. She still needs to be heard, so I sit quietly and listen, a borrowed heart.

"There's no point to my life. I'm not doing anything of value with it. No one would miss me. No one would care if I were gone. Well, that's not true, it might change how a couple of people feel—give my ex a few sleepless nights, send a message to my Neanderthal boss, make my kids feel sorry about how cruel they can be . . ."

Magical thinking—the belief that suicide will change a relationship with someone. One of the warning signs. "I'm lonelier than life," she says again. She likes the phrase. "How do I get out of this?" she bleats. A primal cry, not a question. Then she says almost too low to hear, "I just want the pain to end. I only want to lose consciousness."

"What a heavy burden that must be. I can hear how low you're feeling, how meaningless life seems, how bleak things look. I'm so sorry you're suffering like this."

20   "Promise you won't send the police," she says, reading my mood.

"How about if I promise that I won't, and you promise not to give me reason to?" She doesn't answer.

"Too much?" I ask.

"Yeah," she says. Kindly, not critically. Her tone says: We are in this together. "I just don't want to be alone right now . . . in these last minutes." I think she said minutes.

"I'm worried about you," I say. "How about if I send someone over to be with you?" The tinkling of ice cubes against glass, and a small sip between sniffles. I didn't realize she was drinking. She doesn't sound drunk, but the alcohol won't help her mood and it might give her the wrong kind of courage.

25 "I'm not at home," she says. "Anyway, it's too late for that. I put my coat on, but I don't need to, do I, to be warm when I fly." She sounds wrung-out, exhausted, giving up. "At least it won't hurt much."

"Won't hurt much?"

"I took a bunch of Tylenol . . ."

My heart starts to pound, and with a huge effort at control I ask: "How much Tylenol did you take?"

"I don't know," she whines, "a bunch, enough."

30 That's it. I can't stand the risk any longer. Every call with Louise has seemed this dire, a last call for help, and she has survived. But suppose tonight is the exception, suppose this is the last of last times? What is different tonight? I'm not sure. Then it dawns on me. Something small. I'm frightened by how often she has been using the word "only," a word tight as a noose. Without letting her hear, I notify the police to trace the call and accompany her to the hospital, where a doctor will give her yet another type of medication.

"I'll stay with you." Which problem to focus on? Which section of the tunnel to drill windows in? Her job? Her family problems? Maybe her sense of isolation. The outer one, I mean, the one that can be eased by friends and acquaintances. The inner one is another matter. So often loneliness comes from being out of touch with parts of oneself. We go searching for those parts in other people, but there's a difference between feeling separate from others and separate from oneself.

"You said no one would care if you died. But I would care."

"I bet you say that to all the callers," she says, mustering a touch of coyness.

"Not so. You and I have had some good talks over the past few months."

35 Leaning on the desk, I focus my eyes on the wood grain's many streaks and knots. If it had color, it would look like a Navajo blanket. Hard as I try to concentrate solely on hearing, sights keep trickling in. So does the fragrance of coffee brewing in the kitchen. The long vowels of the wind. The chatter of the Venetian blinds against a drafty window frame.

"Yes," she says, "you've been swell. You've been my only friend, well, not friends exactly, not to you, I mean I'm just one of . . ."

"You'd be surprised how well you can get to know someone over the telephone. I bet you've gotten to know me a little, too, and the other counselors."

"Yes," she says, "I have actually. *You* always sound so calm and even. I envy how together you must be. My life is shooting out of my hands, and I wish I could have your . . . spirit level."

"I'm not always level. Believe me, my life has problems, too. It's easier to be calm when someone else is in trouble."

40 "Oh," she says, with a mixture of surprise and relief. "Anyway, you're a good person: patient, and kind, and strong . . ."

"So are you. All those things."

"Strong? That's a good one. If you could see how weak I am . . ." Her voice trails away.

"Amazingly strong." Be careful, I think, not to use the past tense. She might interpret that as an obituary. "Look how you've been fighting the torrents of depression—for years. That takes such courage. You've been working during that time, raising two kids, surviving the nightmare of an ugly divorce. Okay, you've lost jobs, but you've picked yourself up and found new jobs. You've even volunteered during the flood—filling sandbags and making sandwiches, I think you said once—and you've found the time and energy and heart to do volunteer work, and helped other people in trouble. You've been heroic. You're being strong tonight, calling us. Given how bad you're feeling, that takes real strength. I admire your courage."

"Admire?" she says, letting the word hover a long moment while she considers it. "You wouldn't want to live my life. It's only bad choices . . . except . . ." Sniffling.

45   "Death is always a possibility, but not the best."

Silence. I can feel her thinking it over.

"*Lonelier than life,* you said. Why don't we think of a few ways to help you solve that problem," I suggest. Broaden the perspective. The hardest job when someone is depressed.

"There aren't any."

"Sure there are." Off the top of my head, I list some ways for her to ease her loneliness—through classes, volunteer work, athletics, music, nature centers, city projects, and such. Not one appeals to her. I didn't think any would. Nonetheless, I ask her to consider the list and arrange it in order of preference, "even though we'll agree that you're too tired and fed up to do any of them and they all sound bad anyway." Despite her strong resistance to each item, she goes through the motions of ranking them, and that distracts her a little.

50   "Will you hold on?" she asks abruptly. "There's someone at the door."

Damn, the police. That was fast—she must be at home after all. Maybe I didn't need to send them. And she'll be angry, she'll feel lied to and betrayed. She does. I hear her screaming at me, at the telephone, at the world. She calls me a liar, and she's right. I lied to her. Not about what mattered, only about the trace, and only because her life is in danger, and only because I deduced that some part of her craves life or she wouldn't have called.

Maybe I could have calmed her and talked her round? Maybe someone else would have prevailed, someone who can do this slow tango of life and death with more grace and cunning. Suppose the hospital releases her right away and she heads straight for the gorge? Knowing and not knowing about callers, that's what gets to me. My chest feels rigid as a boat hull, my ribs tense. Taking a large breath and letting it out slowly, I press my open palms against my face, rub the eyebrows, then the cheekbones and jaw, and laugh. Not a ha-ha laugh, a small sardonic one, the kind we save for the ridiculous, as I catch myself slipping into a familiar trap. I did fine. I did the best I could. Maybe the best anyone could tonight.

My shoulders feel skewered, and a long grinding pain twitches down my right side. Rolling my head in slow circles, twisting my shoulders, stretching my arms, arching my spine, I realize that during the past two hours my back never touched the chair. The perfect recipe for backache. She'll hate me, hate me, I think, as I get up stiffly and go to the kitchen for tea. Yes, but she'll be *alive* to hate me. Until the next time, anyway, the next rock-bottom night when she longs to fly.

Helping Louise survive is always an ordeal. Tonight she sounded even more determined and death-bound than usual. It was the right choice. I think. Maybe. On the write-up sheet, under "Caller," I write "Louise," put the letter H for "high" in the box marked "suicide risk," attach a yellow Lethality Assessment sheet, and add a few details of the call. Pressing my fingertips to my face, I push again on the brow bones, as if I could rearrange them, but they ache from a place I can't reach with my hands.

55   A few weeks later, a new postcard on the Crisis Center bulletin board catches my eye. On one side is a reproduction of the Edward Hopper painting *Nighthawks,* in which three lonely souls sit drinking coffee in an overlit diner. Turning the card over, I find a neat, even handwriting, in blue ink, addressed to the agency. *I'm writing to thank whoever the counselor was I spoke with* . . . Notes to Suicide Prevention frequently begin that way. But when the large open loops and rounded *d's* mention the day and hour, my thoughts quicken. That was *my* shift. My eyes slide to the signature. It's from Louise, who has signed her real name.

Sitting down on the couch, I read the card carefully, and learn that she went from the emergency room to a psychiatric hospital in Pennsylvania, where she spent three weeks "in palatial bedlam." When she returned to town, she met an acquaintance who volunteers for Displaced Homemakers; Louise discovered a genial group of people there, and even took a paying job at the agency. A month later, she's "finally in a good place," by which I know she means several terrains, including her job and her mood. I cross the fingers of both hands and tap the interlocked fingertips together. May this small placard be true; may she find peace. She blesses the soul who "took my life in her hands that night," thanks us all for our good work, is just writing "to let you know what happened—I bet you don't hear very often." We don't.

—Adapted from *A Slender Thread: Rediscovering Hope at the Heart of Crisis*
(Vintage, 1998)

QUESTIONS FOR DISCUSSION

1. How does Ackerman try to define the experience of losing Louise in her first paragraph and in the essay that follows? Do you believe it is possible to experience authentic loss for someone whom you have only known indirectly, via a hotline, the media, or the Internet?

2. Do you agree with Ackerman that we should "respect [a person's] right to choose" suicide? How does Ackerman explain her position on choice? Why does she also believe that "suicidal people have tunnel vision" on the issue of choice?

3. As we get to know Louise through her telephone dialogue, what kind of personality and values emerge? Does her sense of humor surprise you? Do you think her wit helps her to fight her depression and stay alive?

4. Examine the role that Ackerman plays in the dialogue—in what ways does she act as a therapist would with a patient? In what ways does she intervene to help and advise Louise? How does Louise respond to her suggestions?

5. How does Ackerman feel after her conversation with Louise? What does her physical response suggest about her mental and emotional state at this time?

6. How does Ackerman interpret the card of thanks from Louise that she finds on the Crisis Center bulletin board? Does the card imply a real "happy ending"? What does this ending (and the selection as a whole) imply about the rewards and risks of working at crisis center hotlines?

CONNECTION

Compare the "therapeutic" interaction and evolving relationship between Ackerman and Louise with the evolving relationship between Naomi Remen and her depressed patient Ana in "Remembering" (see page 159).

IDEAS FOR WRITING

1. Interview people who have worked at suicide hotlines and do some further research on the subject of helping individuals vulnerable to suicide: How effective do the hotlines seem to be? What other approaches are effective in some cases? Write up your findings in a brief documented essay.

2. Although Diane Ackerman says initially that suicide is a choice that deserves respect, she concludes her conversation with Louise by sending the police to prevent her client from overdosing. Write an essay on suicide: do you agree that people should have the "right" to take their own lives, or should suicide be morally condemned and illegal?

RELATED WEB SITES

Review of Diane Ackerman's *A Slender Thread*
www.nytimes.com/books/97/03/02/reviews/970302.jennings. html? (registration required; no charge)
In this review, "Calling Out for Help," Kate Jennings discusses the setting and sense of community that underlie Ackerman's book about her work on a suicide hotline in upstate New York.

American Foundation for Suicide Prevention
www.afsp.org/index-1.htm

This Web site offers information on research, links, special programs, frequently asked questions, bibliographies, educational material, videos, and other material related to suicide prevention.

Anne Lamott

Hunger

Anne Lamott (b. 1954) grew up in Marin County, north of San Francisco, where she still lives. After attending two years of Goucher College from 1971 to 1973, Lamott began her career as a writer. To help support herself, she has also worked as an editor, a restaurant critic, a lecturer, and a writing teacher. Hard Laughter *(1980), about her father's struggle with brain cancer, was her first widely acclaimed book. Her prose works include* Operating Instructions: A Journal of My Son's First Year *(1993), and* Bird by Bird *(1994) in which Lamott explores the crucial human connections between writing and life. In 1997 Lamott's novel,* Crooked Little Heart, *became a best-seller immediately after its publication. The following selection, "Hunger," about her personal obsession with food and eating, is from her most recent collection of essays,* Traveling Mercies *(1998).*

JOURNAL

Explore your thoughts and feelings about eating disorders. You might want to write about the causes or the effects of the condition or your observations of people who have or have had an eating disorder.

This is the story of how, at the age of thirty-three, I learned to feed myself. To begin with, here's what I did until then: I ate, starved, binged, purged, grew fat, grew thin, grew fat, grew thin, binged, purged, dieted, was good, was bad, grew fat, grew thin, grew thinner.

I had been a lean and energetic girl, always hungry, always eating, always thin. But I weighed 100 pounds at thirteen, 130 at fourteen. For the next ten years, I dieted. It is a long, dull story. I had lots of secrets and worries about me and food and my body. It was very scary and obsessive, the way it must feel for someone who is secretly and entirely illiterate.

One week after my father was diagnosed with brain cancer, I discovered bulimia. I felt like I'd discovered the secret to life, because you could eat yourself into a state of emotional numbness but not gain weight. Then I learned how to do it more effectively by reading articles in women's magazines on how to stop doing it. I barfed, but preferred laxatives. It was heaven: I lost weight.

All right, OK: there were some problems. I was scared all the time, full of self-loathing, and my heart got funky. When you've lost too much water and electrolytes, your muscular heart cramps up; it races like a sewing machine. Sometimes it would skip beats, and other times there would be a terrible feeling of vacuum, as if there were an Alhambra water tank in my heart and a big bubble had just burbled to the surface.

5   I would try to be good, in the puritanical sense, which meant denying my appetites. Resisting temptation meant I was good—strong, counter-animal—and I'd manage to resist fattening foods for a while. But then the jungle drums would start beating again.

I looked fine on the outside: thin, cheerful, even successful. But on the inside, I was utterly obsessed. I went into a long and deep depression after seeing some photos of people on a commune, working with their hands and primitive tools and workhorses, raising healthy food. I could see that they were really tuned to nature, to the seasons, to a direct sense of bounty, where you plant something and it grows and you cut it down or pick it and eat it, savoring it and filling up on it. But I was a spy in the world of happy eating, always hungry, or stuffed, but never full.

Luckily I was still drinking at the time.

But then all of a sudden I wasn't. When I quit in 1986, I started getting healthier in almost every way and I had all these women helping me, and I told them almost every crime and secret I had, because I believed them when they said that we are as sick as our secrets. My life got much sweeter right away, and less dramatic; the pond inside me began to settle, and I could see through the water, which was the strangest sensation because for all those years I'd been taking various sticks—desperate men, financial drama, impossible deadlines—and stirring that pond water up. So now I was noticing beautiful little fish and dreamy underwater plants, and shells lying in the sand. I started getting along with myself pretty well for the first time in my life. But I couldn't or wouldn't tell anyone that for the last ten years I had been bingeing and purging, being on a diet, being good, getting thin, being bad, getting fat.

I remember hanging out with these people, letting their stories wash over me, when all of a sudden the thing inside would tap me on the shoulder and whisper, "OK, honey, let's go." And I'd cry out inwardly, No! No! "Sorry," it would say, "time to go shopping." And silently I'd cry out, Please don't make me go shopping! I'm not even hungry! "Shh, shh," it would whisper, "Let's go."

10   I felt that when I got sober, God had saved me from drowning, but now I was going to get kicked to death on the beach. It's so much hipper to be a drunk than a bulimic. Drunks are like bikers or wrestlers; bulimics are baton twirlers, gymnasts. The voice would say how sorry it was, but then glance down at its watch, tap its foot and sigh, and I'd sigh loudly too, and get up, and trudge behind it to the store.

It was actually more painful than that. It reminded me of the scene in Kazantzakis's *The Last Temptation of Christ,* when Jesus is walking along in the desert, really wanting to spend his life in a monastery praying, secluded and alone with God. Only of course God has different plans for him and, to get his attention, sends eagles down to wrap their talons around Jesus' heart, gripping him so that he falls to the sand in pain.

I did not feel eagle talons, but I felt gripped in the heart by a presence directing me to do exactly what it said. It said it was hungry and we had to go to the store.

So that voice and I would go buy the bad things—the chocolates, the Cheetos, the Mexican food—and big boxes of Epsom salts and laxatives. I grew weaker and more desperate until finally, one day in 1987, I called a woman named Rita Groszmann, who was listed in the Yellow Pages as a specialist in eating disorders. I told her what was going on and that I had no money, and she said to come in anyway, because she was afraid I was going to die. So I went in the next day.

I sat in her office and explained how I'd gotten started and that I wasn't ready to stop but that I was getting ready to be ready to stop. She said that was fine. I said that in fact I was going to go home that very night and eat chocolates and Mexican food and then purge. She said fine. I said, "Don't try to stop me." She said, "OK." I said, "There's nothing you can do to stop me, it's just the way it is," and we did this for half an hour or so, until she finally said very gently that she was not going to try to take my bulimia away from me. That she in fact was never going to take anything away from me, because I would try to get it back. But she said that I had some choices.

15   They were ridiculous choices. She proposed some, and I thought, This is the angriest person I've ever met. I'll give you a couple of examples. If I was feeling lonely and overwhelmed and about to binge, she said I could call someone up and ask them if they wanted to meet me for a movie. "Yeah," I said, "right." Or here's another good one: If I was feeling very *other,* sad and scared and overwhelmed, I could invite someone over for a meal, and then see if he or she felt like going for a walk. It is only because I was raised to be Politeness Person that I did not laugh at her. It was like someone detoxing off heroin, who's itching to shoot up, being told to take up macramé.

She asked if I was willing to make one phone call after I ate and buy time. I could always purge if I needed to, but she wanted me to try calling one person and see what happened. Now I'm not stupid. I knew she was up to something.

But I was really scared by the power the bad voice had over me, and I felt beaten up and out of control, scared of how sick I had somehow become, how often my pulse raced and my heart skipped beats, scared that one time when the eagle talons descended, they would grip too hard and pop me open. So I agreed. I got home, ate a more or less regular meal, called a friend, made contact, and didn't purge. The next day, I ate a light breakfast and lunch, and then a huge dinner, rooting around the fridge and cupboards like a truffle pig. But then I called my younger brother. He came over. We went for a walk.

Several weeks later, during one of our sessions, Rita asked me what I'd had for breakfast. "Cereal," I said.

"And were you hungry when you ate?"

20 "What do you mean?" I asked.

"I mean, did you experience hunger, and then make breakfast?"

"I don't really understand what you're asking," I said.

"Let me put it this way," she said. "Why did you have breakfast?"

"Oh! I see," I said. "I had breakfast because it was breakfast time."

25 "But were you hungry?"

I stared at her a moment. "Is this a trick question?" I asked.

"No," she said. "I just want to know how you know it's time to eat."

"I know it's time to eat because it's mealtime," I said. "It's morning, so I eat breakfast, or it's midday, so I eat lunch. And so on."

To make a long story ever so slightly shorter, she finally asked me what it felt like when I was hungry, and I could not answer. I asked her to explain what it felt like when she was hungry, and she described a sensation in her stomach of emptiness, an awareness of appetite.

30 So for the next week, my assignment was to notice what it felt like when I was hungry. It was so strange. I was once again the world's oldest toddler. I walked around peering down as if to look inside my stomach, as if it was one of those old-fashioned front-loading washing machines with a window through which you could see the soapy water swirling over your clothes. And I paid attention until I was able to isolate this feeling in my stomach, a gritchy kind of emptiness, like a rat was scratching at the door, wanting to be let in.

"Wonderful," Rita said, and then gave me my next assignment: first, to notice when I was hungry, and then—this blew my mind—to feed myself.

I practiced, and all of a sudden I was Helen Keller after she breaks the code for "water," walking around touching things, learning their names. Only in my case, I was discovering which foods I was hungry for, and what it was like to eat them. I felt a strange loneliness at first, but then came upon a great line in one of Geneen Roth's books on eating, which said that awareness was about learning to keep yourself company. So I'd feel the scratchy emptiness in my belly, and I'd mention to myself that I seemed hungry. And then I'd ask myself, in a deeply maternal way, what I felt like eating.

"Well, actually, I feel like some Cheetos," I might say. So I'd go and buy a bag of Cheetos, put some in a bowl, and eat them. God! It was amazing. Then I'd check in with myself: "Do you want some more?" I'd ask.

"No," I'd say. "But don't throw them out."

35 I had been throwing food out or wetting it in the sink since I was fourteen, ever since my first diet. Every time I broke down and ate forbidden foods, I would throw out or wet what I'd left uneaten, because each time I was about to start over and be good again.

"I'm hungry," I'd say to myself. "I'd like some frosting."

"OK."

"And some Cheetos."

So I'd have some frosting and some Cheetos for breakfast. I'd eat for a while. Then I'd check in with myself, kindly: "More?"

40   "Not now," I'd say. "But don't wet them. I might want some more later."

I ate frosting and Cheetos for weeks. Also, cookies that a local bakery made with M&M's instead of chocolate chips. I'd buy half a dozen and keep them on the kitchen counter. It was terrifying; it was like knowing there were snakes in my kitchen. I'd eat a little, stop when I was no longer hungry. "Want one more cookie?" I'd ask.

"No, thanks," I'd say. "But maybe later. Don't wet them."

I never wet another bag of cookies. One day I woke up and discovered that I also felt like having some oranges, then rice, then sautéed bell peppers. Maybe also some days the random pound of M&M's. But from then on I was always able at least to keep whatever I ate down—or rather, in my case, up. I went from feeling like a Diane Arbus character, viewed through the lens of her self-contempt, to someone filmed by a friendly cousin, someone who gently noted the concentration on my face as I washed a colander of tiny new potatoes.

Over the years, my body has not gotten firmer. Just the opposite in fact. But when I feel fattest and flabbiest and most repulsive, I try to remember that gravity speaks; also, that no one needs that plastic-body perfection from women of age and substance. Also, that I do not live in my thighs or in my droopy butt. I live in joy and motion and cover-ups. I live in the nourishment of food and the sun and the warmth of the people who love me.

45   It is, finally, so wonderful to have learned to eat, to taste and love what slips down my throat, padding me, filling me up, that I'm not uncomfortable calling it a small miracle. A friend who does not believe in God says, "Maybe not a miracle, but a little improvement," but to that I say, Listen! You must not have heard me right: I couldn't *feed* myself! So thanks for your input, but I know where I was, and I know where I am now, and you just can't get here from there. Something happened that I had despaired would ever happen. It was like being a woman who has despaired of ever getting to be a mother but now who cradles a baby. So it was either a miracle—Picasso said, "Everything is a miracle; it's a miracle that one does not dissolve in one's bath like a lump of sugar"—or maybe it was more of a gift, one that required some assembly. But whatever it was, learning to eat was about learning to live—and deciding to live; and it is one of the most radical things I've ever done.

QUESTIONS FOR DISCUSSION

1. Lamott writes in the first person about her own eating disorder. How does this influence the meaning of the essay for you? Do you think a more clinical or statistical approach to the subject would have been more or less effective? Explain your response.

2. After Lamott stops drinking, she says that "the pond inside me began to settle, and I could see through the water." What can she see? Why is she still unable to reveal her secret eating disorder?

3. What do the eagle talons symbolize? Why does Lamott finally call Rita Grossman to ask for help with her eating disorder? How do Rita and the choices she offers help Lamott?

4. What might Lamott's food-wetting ritual represent?
5. Why does she need to relearn what it feels like to be hungry and feed her-self? What allows her to take this responsibility for herself? How does she accomplish this simple but challenging task?
6. Why does Lamott conclude that deciding to feed herself and live was "one of the most radical things I've ever done"?

CONNECTION

Compare Lamott's obsession with her eating disorder with the depressed state of mind described by Andrew Solomon. Does an eating disorder seem to you to be a symptom of depression (see page 266)?

IDEAS FOR WRITING

1. Write an essay in which you discuss the positive aspects of Lamott's strug-gle to overcome her eating disorder. Consider how her obsession and struggle transform her life.
2. Write a paper on the causes and/or effects of eating disorders.

RELATED WEB SITES

Anne Lamott
www.barclayagency.com/lamott.html
Anne Lamott's life and work are presented at this URL through a brief text, links of interest, a schedule of her appearances, and an "Anne Lamott FAQ" section.

Eating Disorders Awareness and Prevention
www.edap.org
The National Eating Disorders Association hosts this Web site to provide in-formation, referrals, support, prevention, and conferences for individuals with eating disorders or people interested in learning about the issue.

Carrie Demers, M.D.

Chaos or Calm: Rewiring the Stress Response

Carrie Demers (b. 1961) is a holistically oriented physician who blends modern medicine with traditional approaches to health, such as yoga and meditation. Board certified in internal medicine, she received her medical degree from the Uni-versity of Cincinnati and completed a residency at Michael Reese Hospital in Chicago. Currently she is director of the Himalayan Institute's Center for Health and Living and on the faculty at the Institute's main campus in Honesdale, Penn-sylvania. Dr. Demers has been interviewed by numerous newspapers and maga-zines about her holistic approaches to health and is a frequent lecturer and guest on radio shows nationwide. She has written articles for Yoga International *and other magazines. The following article describes some of the health benefits of yoga and meditation in response to stress-related disorders.*

JOURNAL

Write about a time when you felt "stressed out." What caused this feeling, and what (if anything) did you do to relieve it?

R emember the tale "The Lady or the Tiger"? As it ends, the hero is standing before two identical doors: one conceals a beautiful maiden; the other, a ferocious tiger. The hero must open one of these doors—the choice is his—but he has no way of knowing which will bring forth the lady and which will re-lease the tiger.

I'm sometimes reminded of this story when a patient is describing one of the symptoms of chronic stress: headaches, indigestion, ulcers, tight muscles, high blood pressure or some combination of these. When I point out that the symp-tom is stress-related, the patient seems resigned—stress is such a constant in most people's lives that all the doors seem to have tigers lurking behind them. Most of the people who find their way to my office know the fight-or-flight re-sponse is hardwired into our nervous system and many have come to accept a constant feeling of tension as normal, even inevitable.

It isn't. Like the hero in the story, we have a choice. There is another door, another response to the challenges of everyday living that is also hardwired into our nervous system. And unlike the hero, whose destiny rests with chance, we can discover which door is which. A general understanding of the nervous system and how it responds to stress, coupled with training in three fundamen-tal yoga techniques, make it possible for us to distinguish one door from the other. Practicing these techniques gives us the power to choose the lady while leaving the door that unleashes the tiger firmly closed.

Releasing the Tiger

The autonomic nervous system controls all the body's involuntary processes: respiratory rate, heart rate, blood pressure, gastric juice secretion, peristalsis, body temperature, and so on. It has two main components or branches—the sympathetic and the parasympathetic. When we feel stressed, our brain acti-vates the sympathetic nervous system, which has come to be known as the fight-or-flight response. This causes the adrenal medulla to secrete adrenaline (also called epinephrine), a hormone that circulates through the bloodstream, af-fecting almost every organ. Adrenaline revs up the body to survive a threat to life and limb: The heart pumps faster and harder, causing a spike in blood pressure; respiration increases in rate and moves primarily into the chest; airways dilate to bring more oxygen into the body; blood sugar rises to provide a ready supply of fuel; some blood vessels constrict to shunt blood away from the skin and the core of the body, while others dilate to bring more blood to the brain and limbs. The result? A body pumped up to fight or run, and a mind that is hyper alert.

5   This response is a crucial reaction to a life-threatening event: when we find ourselves face-to-face with a mountain lion, the stress response dramatically increases our chances of surviving. And we've all heard stories of fantastic feats: the mom lifting a car off her trapped child, the firefighter carrying a man twice his size from a burning building. These are the benefits of the sympathetic nervous system. Any time we respond quickly and decisively when a life is at stake, this is the system to thank.

The fight-or-flight response is meant to be triggered sporadically, in those rare moments when we are actually in peril. Ideally, it remains dormant until the next close call (weeks, months, or even years later!). But in many of us this response is triggered daily, even hourly. Some people—soldiers, tightrope walkers, members of a SWAT team, for example—do find themselves in life-or-death situations frequently. But for most of us, such situations are rare: a mugging, a traffic accident, a close-up with a bear in the backcountry. Once the threatening event is over, hormonal signals switch off the stress response, and homeostasis is reestablished.

The problem is that for many of us the fight-or-flight response rarely switches off, and stress hormones wash through the body almost continuously. The source of our stress is psychological rather than physical—a perception that something crucial to us is threatened. Fear of the unknown, major changes in our circumstances, uncertainty about the future, our negative attitudes—all these are sources of stress. Today we worry more about our jobs, our relationships or getting stuck in traffic than we do about fighting off a wild animal, but even though the perceived threat is psychological, it still triggers the archaic survival response.

The upshot is that our bodies are in a constant state of tension, ready to fight or flee, and this causes a host of physical problems. You can see what some of these are if you look again at what happens when adrenaline courses through the body: elevated blood pressure, rapid shallow breathing, high blood sugar and indigestion. What is more, adrenaline makes our platelets stickier, so our blood will clot quickly if we are wounded. This increases our chances of surviving a physical injury—but chronically sticky platelets are more apt to clot and create blockages in our arteries. And this sets the stage for a heart attack or a stroke.

The damage doesn't end there. When we are constantly in fight-or-flight mode, the adrenal cortex begins to secrete cortisol, a steroid whose job it is to help us adapt to a prolonged emergency by ensuring that we have enough fuel. Cortisol acts on the liver and muscle tissues, causing them to synthesize sugars (glucose) and fats and release them into the bloodstream. From the body's viewpoint, this is a reasonable response—dumping fat and sugar into the blood will help us survive a shipwreck, for example. But when this fuel is not metabolized in response to prolonged physical duress, disease results. Excess sugar in the bloodstream leads to diabetes, and excess fat to high cholesterol/high triglycerides. Both conditions boost our chances of developing heart disease.

10   The steroids cortisol and cortisone quell inflammation in autoimmune diseases and asthma, and so are useful when used infrequently and for brief periods, but their constant presence in the bloodstream suppresses immune function. This causes the white blood cells—those hardy defenders against bacteria, viruses, cancer cells, fungi, and other harmful microorganisms—to become sluggish. And this makes us more prone to disease, especially cancer and chronic infections like Lyme disease, hepatitis, and the Epstein-Barr virus.

Sounds grim, doesn't it? It is. It's a tiger. A chronically activated sympathetic nervous system keeps the body under constant pressure. If we ignore early warning symptoms—tight shoulders, digestive upset, recurring headaches, an increasing tendency to lose our temper or become easily upset—sooner or later the tiger will tear us up. But we can make another choice. The autonomic nervous system has another component, the parasympathetic nervous system. Rather than living under the tyranny of a ramped-up sympathetic nervous system, we can learn to trigger the parasympathetic system, the rest-and-digest response, instead.

Just as the fight-or-flight response automatically kicks in at the threat of danger, the rest-and-digest response automatically responds to our sense of equilibrium. When it is activated, the heart rate drops, blood pressure falls, and respiration slows and deepens. Blood flow to the core of the body is reestablished—this promotes good digestion, supports the immune system and infuses us with a sense of well-being.

We unconsciously achieve this state on vacation, in the throes of a hearty laugh, or in deep sleep. It feels good, and it offers a much needed respite from the hectic pace we set for ourselves. But we have come to accept stress as the norm and to expect the feeling of relaxed well-being to come about only sporadically—and so it does. We release the tiger a dozen times a day, even though the other door is also there in every moment. Once we learn to open it at will, we can override the harmful habit of triggering our stress response by activating the rest-and-digest component of our nervous system instead.

Greeting the Lady

I use a variety of natural therapies in my medical practice, but the basic treatments are drawn from yoga—stretching, breathing, relaxation and meditation—and these techniques are especially effective when it comes to managing stress. You already know from personal experience that aerobic exercise is excellent for dissipating stress-created tension, and that sugar, caffeine and spicy food contribute to jangling your nervous system and shortening your temper. You are probably also familiar with the relaxing effects of practicing yoga postures—they teach us to move and stretch our tense, strained bodies and to focus on the breath. But do you know that breathing slowly and deeply is the easiest way to activate the rest-and-digest system? That is one reason yoga classes are so popular—they soothe frazzled nerves and quiet anxious minds. But yoga also works at an even deeper level: it reestablishes healthy breathing patterns, teaches us to relax consciously and systematically, and gives us the opportunity to explore the inner workings of our minds through meditation. These techniques, both separately and in combination, nourish and strengthen the parasympathetic nervous system so that the relax-and-digest response becomes our normal mode. The fight-or-flight response is then reserved for emergencies, as nature intended. So let's take a look at some ways we can open Door Number Two.

15 ***Diaphragmatic Breathing***   Babies and young children breathe deeply and fully, using the dome shaped diaphragm that separates the chest and abdominal cavities to move air in and out of their lungs. Their bellies are relaxed and move in concert with their breath. This is the natural, healthy way to breathe. But as we grow up we are taught to constrict the abdomen (Pull your stomach in and stand up straight!), and that training, coupled with an unconscious tendency to tighten the belly when we experience stress, disrupts the natural flow of our breath. With the abdomen pulled in, the breath is confined to the upper portion of the lungs (from about the nipple line up). And because this breathing pattern is perceived by the body to be a stress response, it reinforces the fight-or-flight reaction.

Diaphragmatic breathing, on the other hand, activates the relax-and-digest response by stimulating the primary mediator of the parasympathetic nervous system, the vagus nerve. This nerve travels from the brain to nearly all the thoracic and abdominal organs ("vagus" comes from the same root as "vagabond"), and triggers a cascade of calming effects. Most of the time we wait for it to be activated by something pleasant and hope for a trickle-down effect, not realizing that the nerve (and hence the entire parasympathetic nervous system) can be turned on from the bottom up by diaphragmatic breathing.

The fight-or-flight response is meant to be triggered sporadically, in those rare moments when we are actually in peril.

Of all the processes regulated by the autonomic nervous system (heart rate, blood pressure, secretion of gastric juices, peristalsis, body temperature, etc.), only breathing can be controlled consciously. And in doing so, we stimulate the branch of the vagus nerve that innervates the diaphragm (which carries a message to the other vagus branches and the brain) to activate the entire rest-and-digest response. This is why the first step in reversing our chronic stress response is to learn to breathe again the way we were born to breathe.

If you haven't been trained in diaphragmatic breathing, find an experienced teacher and practice every day until it once again becomes a habit. Then, as you develop the skill of breathing from the diaphragm in the course of your daily activities, you will begin to experience your breath as a barometer for the nervous system. As long as you are breathing deeply and from the diaphragm, you will find that you can access a feeling of calm and balance even when you are confronted with an unpleasant situation. And you will also notice that if you allow your breath to become shallow by breathing from your chest, anxiety creeps in, your muscles tighten, and your mind begins to race and spin. When this agitated breathing is prolonged, it creates an unsettled and defensive outlook on life. Once you know this from your own experience, you can make a different choice.

20   **Systematic Relaxation**   To activate the parasympathetic nervous system, diaphragmatic breathing makes an excellent beginning. But we need to do more, particularly when we have spent years unconsciously flinging open the door to the tiger's cage. Daily periods of relaxation are a must. When I tell my patients this, many of them say they relax while they watch TV or read or knit or socialize. The problem is that while these activities distract the mind from its usual worries (and so provide some relief), they do little to relieve the stress we hold in the form of muscular contraction and tension.

To reverse well-established habits of holding tension in our bodies, we need to work with what the yogis call the energy body (pranamaya kosha). Systematic relaxation practices offer a precise, orderly technique for releasing tension from head to toe. There are a number of these techniques, and like all yoga practices, they are best learned from an experienced teacher, and then honed through patient practice. They range in complexity from simple tension/relaxation exercises and point-to-point breathing practices to techniques that require making fine distinctions among various points in the energy body. But all involve moving our attention through the body in a methodical fashion, usually while resting in shavasana (corpse pose). And all require that we withdraw our attention—from the drama of our lives. For the duration of the practice, we let go of our memories, plans, worries, and fantasies, and focus on what we are doing here and now as we move our awareness calmly and quietly from one part of the body to another.

Breathing from the diaphragm, while systematically bringing our full attention to one point in the body after another, not only releases tension and fatigue in the places where we rest our attention, it also augments the energy flow among those points. This promotes both healing and cleansing. Further, because full engagement with a systematic relaxation practice requires that we clear our minds and attend fully to the present moment, we are also refining a skill that opens the door to meditation.

Meditation   Since stress begins with the perception that our lives (or at least our sense of wellbeing) are in danger, working with the mind to alter our perceptions is the most powerful technique for quieting our stress response. Most of what activates our fight-or-flight response is not a matter of life or death. We may feel pressured to accomplish a certain task or worried about what will happen at tomorrow's meeting—but our lives don't depend upon the outcome.

With rare exceptions, the habitual thought patterns that create the experience of stress for us are overreactions to events in our lives. Instead of responding in a way that floods the body with adrenaline, however, we can reframe the experience to make it not only less stressful, but also more accurate in reflecting what is really happening ("I'm only in a traffic jam, I'm not at death's door." "I want to please this person, but if I don't, I'm not going to be fired"). This goes a long way toward quieting the fight-or-flight response, and it is a skill that comes with experience in meditation.

Meditation helps us understand our mental habits by giving us the opportunity to observe them from a neutral vantage point. This is why I often prescribe meditation to my patients as a way to manage stress.

25 If we ignore early warning symptoms, sooner or later the tiger will tear us up.

I don't mean to minimize meditation as a means of spiritual transformation, but in its early stages, one of the most delicious benefits of meditation practice is seeing that it is possible to avoid getting sucked into the banter and hysteria of our mental chatter. Meditation allows us to witness that banter—to observe it impartially—without being smack in the middle of it. It's like watching a rainstorm from a warm, dry room. The peace we feel when we are watching our minds rather than identifying with our thoughts is the peace at our core.

When you are fast learning to meditate, the mind will wander away from the object of meditation to dwell on some other thought. This will happen again and again. Your job is to gently and repeatedly bring your attention back to your object of meditation, and to do it patiently, without judgment. Sometimes it may seem as if the distracting thoughts are like movie images projected onto a personal viewing screen in your mind. And some may be strange and wild. But you are in the rest-and-digest mode, and as strange as they are, your projections don't trigger the fight-or-flight response. The ability to simply observe them is evidence that they aren't you. And the ability to distinguish between the inner observer in you and the chaotic jumble in your mind means that you can respond with equanimity, rather than react and flood your body with stress hormones.

The more we practice meditation, the more we will be able to discriminate between what is real and what is not—between what is truly life-threatening and what is just a habitual overreaction. And once we begin to see that almost everything that triggers our sympathetic nervous system is merely a habitual overreaction, we can begin to make different choices. Instead of reacting to an unpleasant event, we can cushion the jarring effect on our nervous system by observing it in the same way that we observe our mental chatter in meditation and by consciously breathing from the diaphragm.

This is likely to prove challenging in the beginning. When your spouse or a coworker snaps at you, you may find yourself halfway into an angry retort before you notice that you have switched to chest breathing. Then you need to remind yourself to breathe from the diaphragm and to find a neutral vantage point. But this skill comes with time, particularly when you are sitting for meditation regularly, practicing diaphragmatic breathing, and punctuating your day with a systematic relaxation practice. And as you choose to activate your rest-and-digest response consciously and continuously, you will find yourself in fight-or-flight mode only when your car skids on a patch of ice or the cat knocks over a candle and sets the curtains on fire. Your health will improve, to say nothing of your outlook on life. You have learned to choose the right door.

QUESTIONS FOR DISCUSSION

1. How does Carrie Demers use the story "The Lady or the Tiger" to structure her essay? Point out examples where this strategy is used effectively. What do the "tiger" and the "lady" represent in the essay? What is the "other door" that Demers provides for us?
2. What is the autonomic nervous system? How does Demers define it and describe its functions? How does she make her definition clear?
3. What is problematic about the "fight-or-flight response" in the modern world? What physical problems does it create for us? What are the advantages of the naturally accruing steroids cortisol and cortisone? What can happen if they are always in the bloodstream?
4. What is the "rest-and-digest" response, and what happens when we learn to control it?
5. Describe the techniques Demers uses in her practice to help her clients open the "door" of the parasympathic nervous system. How do meditation and controlled breathing assist in this process?
6. How does yogic practice help people to become less anxious and more re-laxed? Why is relaxing while doing activities such as watching television or socializing not often successful in achieving these ends?

CONNECTION

Compare the program for holistic healing presented in Demers's essay with the ideas on healing explored in Mark Barasch's "Healing Dream" in this chapter (see page 311).

IDEAS FOR WRITING

1. Do some research into different programs that assist in stress reduction. Do any of these programs seem to be particularly effective in improving pa-tient health and well-being? Have any scientific studies been performed to demonstrate the positive effects? Write up your findings in the form of a documented essay.
2. Try using some form of systematic relaxation, meditation, and breath con-trol or a beginning yoga tape daily for a week or more, and keep track of your responses to this program in a journal. Write up your findings in the form of an essay that is supported by references to your journal. Alterna-tively, interview a person who has used a similar program over a signifi-cant period of time. Write up your findings in the form of an essay that is supported by references to your interview.

RELATED WEB SITES

Stress Management and Emotional Wellness Links
www.imt.net/~randolfi/StressLinks.html
This site from Optimal Health Concepts contains links and information on many stress reduction strategies including meditation, biofeedback, emotive therapy, humor, breathing, and hypnosis.

Yoga Online Mind and Body
http://yoga.org.nz/index.htm
Yoga Online's site contains extensive information on yoga as a means for stress reduction including definitions and types of yoga, as well as the exercise and spiritual dimensions of yoga.

Marc Ian Barasch

What Is a Healing Dream?

Marc Ian Barasch attended Yale University, where he studied literature, psychology, anthropology, and film. A longtime practitioner of Tibetan Buddhism, he was a founding member of the psychology department at Naropa University, Colorado. Barasch has worked as an editor-in-chief of New Age Journal, *as a contributing editor to* Psychology Today *and* Natural Health Magazine, *and as a producer/ writer for film and television. He has received the National Magazine Award and the Washington Monthly Award for Investigative Writing. His most widely read books include* The Healing Path: A Soul Approach to Illness *(1994);* Remarkable Recovery *(1995); and, most recently,* Healing Dreams: Exploring the Dreams That Can Transform Your Life *(2000), from which the following selection is excerpted.*

JOURNAL

Write about an unusual, especially memorable, or repeated dream, one that "stopped you in your tracks" and made you think about your life from a new perspective.

I have had a most rare vision. I have had a dream, past the wit of man to say what dream it was: man is but an ass, if he go about to expound this dream. . . . The eye of man hath not heard, the ear of man hath not seen, man's hand is not able to taste, his tongue to conceive, nor his heart to report, what my dream was.
　　　　　　　　　　　　　　—Bottom, in Shakespeare's *A Midsummer Night's Dream*

Most of us have had (or, inevitably, will have) at least one dream in our lives that stops us in our tracks. Such dreams tell us that we're not who we think we are. They reveal dimensions of experience beyond the everyday. They may shock us, console us, arouse us, or repulse us. But they take their place alongside our most memorable life events because they're so vivid and emblematic. Some are like parables, setting off sharp detonations of insight; others are like gripping mystery tales; still others are like mythic dramas, or horror stories, or even uproarious jokes. In our journey from childhood to age, we may count them on one hand. Yet once they have flared in the soul, they constellate there, emitting a steady, pulsarlike radiance.

The number of people I have discovered grappling with these powerful inner experiences has astounded me. In a time when the individual psyche is increasingly colonized by mass culture, when media images seem ever more intent on replacing dreams wholesale, here is an unvoiced parallel existence dreamers sometimes do not share with even their loved ones.

People often describe such striking dreams in a self-devised lexicon: "deep" dreams; "vibrational" dreams; "strong" dreams; "flash" dreams; "TV" dreams (a South African priestess); "lucky-feeling dreams" (a dog breeder in Quebec); "true" dreams (a Salish Indian healer in Oregon). A folk artist named Sultan Rogers, famous for his fancifully erotic woodcarvings, refers to his most powerful dreams as "futures," so filled are they with the urgency to be manifest in the world. (He makes a point of carving them immediately upon waking, while the sensuous images are still fresh.) Yet many I spoke with displayed a genuine reticence about discussing their dreams, as if exposing them to daylight might stunt some final germination still to come. Famed Jungian analyst Marion Woodman declined to share a dream she believed helped heal her of a serious physical illness, because, she told me, "I cannot let others into my holy of holies." Some said they feared the professional consequences of being seen as overly attentive to dreams. "I'm in the midst of putting together a multimillion-dollar deal based on a dream I had ten years ago," one man confided. His vision had become the polestar of his life. "But it wouldn't do," he said, "for my partners to think I'm relying on invisible consultants."

In the fifteen years since I began my exploration, a nascent field of research has arisen, along with a host of terms—*impactful, transformative, titanic, transcendent*—to differentiate big dreams from ordinary ones. I have coined the term *Healing Dreams*, because they seem to have a singular intensity of purpose: to lead us to embrace the contradictions between flesh and spirit, self and other, shadow and light in the name of wholeness. The very word for "dream" in Hebrew—*chalom*—derives from the verb meaning "to be made healthy or strong." With remarkable consistency, such dreams tell us that we live on the merest outer shell of our potential, and that the light we seek can be found in the darkness of a yet-unknown portion of our being.

5   Jung labeled them numinous (from the Latin *numen,* meaning "divine command"), but often just used the succinct shorthand, big. While most dreams, he wrote, were "nightly fragments of fantasy," thinly veiled commentaries on

"the affairs of the everyday," these significant dreams were associated with major life passages, deep relationship issues, and spiritual turning points.

Many cultures have had a terminology for such dreams of surpassing power. The Greek New Testament seems to contain more words for inner experience than Eskimos have for snow: *onar* (a vision seen in sleep as opposed to waking); *enypnion* (a vision seen in sleep that comes by surprise); *horama* (which could refer to visions of the night, sleeping visions, or waking visions); *horasis* (a supernatural vision); *optasia* (a supernatural vision that implies the Deity revealing Himself); and so on. By and large the English language has been impoverished of a working vocabulary; we have little at hand beyond *dream* and *nightmare.* Given our cultural paucity, it can be a struggle to define these signal occurrences.

"How do you know when you've had a special dream?" I once asked a Choctaw Indian acquaintance named Preston. A humorous man with rubbery features—his role in his tribe, he told me, was as a "backwards person," a trickster and comedian—he grew uncharacteristically serious at my question.

"These vision dreams are things that you follow," he said. "Things that you do. They show you a situation that needs to be taken care of, and a way to turn it around."

"But *how* do you know?" I pressed him.

10   "It's the way you feel. That kind of dream wakes you up very sudden-like. Maybe you wake up really, really happy." He looked at me, eyebrow cocked. "Or maybe you wake up with your bed so soaking wet you'da thought you'd peed on yourself!"

His ribald comment points to a universally reported attribute of Healing Dreams—what we might call ontological weight, the heft and immediacy of lived experience. Remarks from various dreamers return often to a common theme of "realer than real." They often comment on the acuity of the senses—taste, touch, sight, smell, and hearing. I, too, can recall awakening with my ears still ringing from a dream gunshot, or waking up momentarily blinded by a dream's burst of light.

There is often a depth of emotion that beggars normal waking life. The sixteenth-century rabbi and physician Solomon Almoli wrote: "If one dreams of powerful fantasy images that cause him to be excited or to feel anger or fear during the dream itself, this is a true dream; but if the images are insipid and arouse no strong feelings, the dream is not true." Such dreams are filled not with simple anxiety, but terror; not mere pleasantness, but heart-bursting joy. People report waking up on tear-soaked pillows, or laughing in delight. (The Bantu people of Africa have a specific term for the latter—*bilita mpatshi,* or blissful dreaming.)

Healing Dreams are analogous to ancient Greek theater, where actors in colorful, oversized costumes presented stories contrived to put an audience through the emotional wringer; to make it feel, viscerally, the heroes' agonies and ecstasies. Indeed, some Healing Dreams feature larger-than-life settings and personages—palatial buildings, sweeping landscapes, beings of supernatural goodness or terrible malignancy. Healing Dreams seem designed to produce a catharsis, to lead their "audience" to a metanoia, a change of heart.

Like drama, such dreams often have an unusually coherent narrative structure. Islamic dream texts refer to the ordinary dream as *azghas*—literally, "handful of dried grass and weeds," signifying a lack of arrangement—in contrast to the more coherent messages of *akham* ("genuine inspiration from the Deity, warning from a protecting power, or revelation of coming events"). The Healing Dream's storytelling tends to be more artful, often containing a rich array of literary or cinematic devices—subplots, secondary characters, sudden reversals and surprise endings, flashbacks and flashforwards, adumbration, even voice-over narration and background music.

15   Healing Dreams often involve a sense of the uncanny or paranormal. Within the dream, one may find one has special powers to telekinetically move objects; receive information as if via telepathy; levitate; transform oneself into other creatures; visit heavens or hells. Dreamers report of out-of-body experiences; actual events foreseen; talking with the departed; having a near-identical dream to that of a friend or loved one; and other strange synchronicities. Healing Dreams hum with so much energy that, like a spark from a Van de Graaf generator, they seem to leap the gap between the visible and invisible worlds.

In such dreams, symbols tend to be extraordinarily multilayered— exaggerated cases of what Freud referred to as "over-determination," where an image seems to be "chosen" by the unconscious for its multiplicity of associations. Language itself reveals a dense richness. A key dream-word may yield half a dozen definitions, each with a different or even opposing nuance. There is often a powerful aesthetic component—such dreams may depict dances and rituals, music and song, poetry, photos, paintings, and other art forms. There is frequently a collective dimension—the dream seems to transcend the dreamer's personal concerns, reaching into the affairs of family, clan, community, or the world at large.

Such dreams also have a peculiar persistence. People report waking up with the images still before their eyes. The dream lingers in memory long after common ones fade. New meanings emerge over time. One lives, as it were, into the dream. "The *findout*," the Native American sage Lame Deer told one researcher, "has taken me all my life."

Most important, Healing Dreams, if heeded, can be transformational— creating new attitudes toward ourselves and others, magnifying our spiritual understanding, deepening the feeling side of life, producing changes in careers and relationships, even affecting society itself. After a Healing Dream, one may never be the same again.

The Dream Uses You

Many people wonder why they should bother with their dreams at all. A common answer is that they will help us with our lives, and this is certainly true. Even the most extraordinary dream, properly investigated, will have much to say about bread-and-butter issues like work, love, and health. But the Healing Dream is less a defender of our waking goals—material achievement, perfect romance, a modest niche in history—than an advocate-general for the soul, whose aims may lay athwart those of the ego. Dreams are often uninterested in the self-enhancement stratagems we mistake for progress. "It's vulgarizing to say that we can use dreams as tools—like shovels!—to get ahead, or be more assertive, like a kid who prays his little sister will drop dead so he can have her candy," a dreamworker once told me with some passion. "It's more like"—and here he seemed to fluoresce with certainty—"the dream uses *you.*"

20   Such dreams "use" us only if we are willing to dwell for a time within their ambiguities without resolving them. The Jungian psychologist Robert Johnson tells of the time he had a dreamlike vision of a "spirit man" with burning orange fire coursing through his veins. The man plunged to the bottom of an indigo lake, but the fire was miraculously unquenched. Then the spirit man took Johnson by the hand and flew him to a great nebula coruscating like a diamond at the center of the universe. Standing on the very threshold of divine majesty, before vast, dazzling whorls of light eternal, Johnson tugged at the man's sleeve and asked impatiently, "This is fine, but *what is it good for?*"

"The spirit man looked at me," wrote Johnson, "in disgust: 'It isn't good for *anything.*'" Still, Johnson wondered for a long while afterward how his experience might tangibly change his life. Then he had a key insight: *He would never know.* "This magnificent power," he wrote "is transmuted into small things, day-to-day behavior, attitudes, the choices that we make in the ordinariness of daily human life."

Johnson's experience emphasizes that, contrary to a slew of popular works (starting with the dream manuals of the early Egyptians), there may be no surefire, direct method to utilize the power of dreams. We may be astonished by a bolt of lightning, but that doesn't mean we can harness it to flash down upon the grill to cook our steak. Healing Dreams offer few outright prescriptions. They often require us to live our questions rather than furnish instant answers.

How, then, should we see a Healing Dream? We might think of it as a window that enlarges our perspective, freeing us of a certain tunnel vision. It frames our daily concerns in a context beyond the confines of our room. The view from this dream window opens onto what we may think the exclusive province of mystics and philosophers—conundrums like the meaning of the sacred, the problem of evil, the nature of time, the quest for a true calling, the mysteries of death and love—making these issues intimately our own.

Or we might see the dream as a worthy opponent. It is often said that spiritual work is an *opus contra naturam,* going against the grain of what seems natural, normal, or even good. The unconscious is not just the repository of beauty and light, or the issuer of benign, firm-handed guidance, but the home of the trickster. The dream figure that bears the denied powers of the self often appears sinister and antithetical. Yet he may also be our secret ally: in spiritual life, what is merely pleasant can become the ego's friction-free way of sliding by without learning much of anything. By rubbing us the wrong way, the Healing

Dream kindles an inner heat, forcing us to include our obstacles and adversaries in our process of growth.

25   We might regard a Healing Dream as a work of art, something that evokes a feeling of meaningfulness that cannot be put into words. Like the glowing Vermeer painting of a simple woman with a pitcher, it is the extraordinary thing that sheds light on the ordinary. Like art, dreams create a shift in perspective in the very act of beholding them. Seeing things in a way we have not seen before—taking the stance of the appreciator rather than the analyst—changes us, as suggested by the remark by the phenomenologist Merleau-Ponty: "Rather than seeing the painting, I see according to or with it."

Healing Dreams might be conceived as visits to an otherworld with its own geography and inhabitants. From this perspective, we are explorers visiting a foreign land whose citizens have customs, beliefs, and language that are not entirely familiar. Dream images thus are experienced in their own right, not just as self-fabricated symbols. Through this sort of living encounter, dreams become the proverbial travel that broadens the mind.

Or we might regard the Healing Dream as a wise teacher, one who instructs us in the most personal way—embarrassingly so, for she knows our forbidden desires and deepest fears, our secret hopes and unexpressed gifts. This teacher tells us stories about ourselves, about our relationships to others, about our place in the larger schema. This approach may require a humility the ego finds discomforting. Jung told one dreamer: "Look here, the best way to deal with a dream is to think of yourself as a sort of ignorant child, ignorant youth, and to come to the two-million-year-old man or to the old mother of days and ask, 'Now, what do you think of me?'"

What *does* the dream think? Or is a Healing Dream itself more a question posed to *us*? If so, the most reasonable-seeming answer is often the wrong one. Such dreams play by rules that confound the waking mind. But at the heart of Healing Dreams are certain consistent, if challenging, attitudes. Before we set out to understand the big dream, it would be helpful to consider some of the principles and perspectives that will recur on the journey:

- ▪ *Nonself:* Dreams show us we are not who we think we are: "We walk through ourselves," wrote James Joyce, "meeting robbers, ghosts, giants, old men, young men, wives, widows, brothers-in-love." Dreams de-center us from our everyday identity, pushing us toward a richer multiplicity of being. Thus in dreams we may be startled to find, as one dream researcher puts it, that we are "a woman and not a man, a dog not a person, a child not an adult . . . [even] two people at once." As Alice in Wonderland says: "I know who I *was* this morning, but since then I have changed several times." What Healing Dreams attempt to cure is nothing less than the ego's point of view—that habitual "I" that clings to rigid certainties of what "I want," "I fear," "I hate," "I love." What is sometimes called the ego-self or the "I" figure in our dreams may be a mere side character, reacting or observing but not in control of events. We may experience the diminution of what in waking life we most prize in ourselves, and the elevation of what we find belittling. One sign of a healthy personality is the ability to acknowledge other selfhoods and inhabit other skins.

- *Nonsense:* From the ego's standpoint, dream logic is an oxymoron. It is a sure bet that whatever we deem most ridiculous upon waking is the fulcrum point of what the dream wants to tell us. Indeed, when we find ourselves disparaging an image as meaningless, it is a signal to retrieve it from the scrap heap and place it on the table. Like a magician, the dream may confuse us through misdirection, but only because we are paying too much attention to the right hand and not enough to the left. Like a fool in the court of a king, dreams use absurdity to tell the truth when none else dare; but the king must realize the joke is on him in order to get the punch line.

- *Balance:* A Healing Dream often comes to redress imbalance—something in the personality is askew, awry, not right (or perhaps, *too* right). If we have become inflated, it cuts us back down to human scale; if we wander in a dark vale, lost, it suddenly illumines the mountaintop. The psyche, Jung suggests, "is a self-regulating system that maintains its equilibrium just as the body does. Every process that goes too far immediately and inevitably calls forth compensations." The quickest way to the heart of a dream is to ask what one-sided conscious attitude it is trying to offset.

- *Reversal of value:* In dreams, our fixed reference points—our opinions, values, and judgments—may be revealed as mere tricks of perspective. What the conscious mind believes to be a precious gem may be a beach pebble to the spirit, while what it tosses aside may be the pearl of great price. Alice, on her journey through Wonderland's dreamscape, first drinks a potion that makes her large, and she weeps in misery. Then when another elixir makes her shrink, she finds herself literally drowning in her own tears. A few small tears, usually a matter of little import, suddenly become a matter of life or death—as indeed they may be to the dreaming soul.

- *Wholeness:* Healing Dreams point to the relatedness of all things, reveling in the union of opposites. They show us a vision of the divine that encompasses both growth and decay, horror and delight. We may crave a world of either/or, but the Dream says, *Both/and.* We build a wall between our social persona and our inner selves; the Dream bids us, *Demolish it.* We wish to believe we're separate from one another, but the Dream insists, *We are in this together.* We believe time to be a one-way river, flowing from past to present to future, yet the Dream reveals, *All three times at once.* We wish to be virtuous and free of taint, but the Dream insists, *The dark and the light are braided and bound.*

The Way of the Healing Dream

We live in a practical era, one that stresses the productive usage of things. Yet Healing Dreams are not easily reduced to the utilitarian. Although they may offer practical revelation, they have more in common with the realm of art, poetry, and music, where what you do with an experience is not the overriding issue. Such dreams open up a gap in the ordinary, allowing something new, and often indefinable, to enter our lives. We can work with our dreams, "unpack" them, analyze them, learn from them. But it is their residue of mystery that gives them enduring power, making them touchstones we return to again and again.

30   When we take our dreams seriously, their images and feelings subtly begin to alter our waking lives. Meaning seeps in through a kind of osmosis. We begin to glimpse the principle that connects each to all. Any sincere attention (and commitment) to our dreams renders us spiritually combustible. What was once inert now strikes sparks.

Healing Dreams seem to *want* something of us, and often will not let go until they receive it. But few of us pay them serious mind. Their images dissipate into air, dissolve like snowflakes on water. We dive back into the slipstream of our dailiness with something akin to relief. We sense that if we were to draw too near, the gravitational field of dreams might perturb, forever, the fixed orbit of our lives.

For this reason, I've chosen to focus as much as possible on these dreams that won't allow themselves to be tossed aside; the ones that yank off the bedclothes, spook us, amaze us, drag us below, lift us above, damn us, save us—in terms so strong, in presence so palpable, we simply can't ignore them. *These* dreams refuse to go quietly, for they mean to change us utterly. If we look into their depths, we may behold a unique destiny struggling from its chrysalis, and watch, astonished and not a little afraid, as our unsuspected selfhood unfolds a new, wetly glistening wing.

QUESTIONS FOR DISCUSSION

1. How does Barasch use similes in the first paragraph to reinforce some of the qualities of the "Healing Dream"? Why would it be (as Bottom says in the quotation from *A Midsummer Night's Dream*) so difficult to "conceive" and "report" what such a dream is about?

2. Why did some of the people Barasch interviewed express "reticence" to share and discuss their healing dreams? What does this reticence, combined with the lack of words in our language to name such dreams, suggest about the value placed on dreams in our culture?

3. Why does the author compare healing dreams to Greek theater and other dramatic forms of art?

4. In what sense are healing dreams "transformational"? How do they "use" us, changing our lives in subtle ways?

5. How do healing dreams "enlarge our perspective," serving as an opponent, a teacher, or an artwork?

6. Explain the five bulleted "attitudes . . . principles and perspectives" of the healing dream. How might these five attitudes help in the healing process?

CONNECTION

Compare and contrast Stephen King's views on the significance of dreams (see page 17) with Barasch's views.

IDEAS FOR WRITING

1. Analyze the dream you narrated in your journal entry above from the perspective of the five attitudes presented at the end of the essay. How did examining the dream using the attitudes delineated by Barasch help you to understand it better?
2. Write a definition of another type of dream than the healing dream, using some of the same techniques as Barasch does: listing qualities, principles, attitudes, similes, and analogies. You can also use examples of such dreams that you have had or read about.

RELATED WEB SITES

Marc Ian Barasch
`www.healingdreams.com/author.htm`
At this Web site you will find information about author, Marc Ian Barasch; his book, *Healing Dreams;* and his work surrounding the subject of harnessing the power of dreams to heal.

The International Center for the Study of Dreams
`www.asdreams.org`
This organization maintains a Web site with a large archive of professional articles on all aspects of dreams and dream research from their journal and magazine; there are also many useful educational materials available online through the site.

Sharon Slayton

The Good Girl

After growing up in Florida and spending several years in Denver working in the computer field, Sharon Slayton moved to California to complete her education. When she wrote this essay, she was a part-time student in psychology with plans to transfer to a four-year university and to become a lawyer. Slayton enjoys writing and has contributed several articles to small business newsletters. The following essay was written in response to a question posed in her critical thinking class that asked her to define a form of obsessive or addictive behavior about which she had personal knowledge.

Most people who meet me today see a very strong and confident individual. They see a young woman who has accomplished a great deal in a short time. They see a very responsible and reliable person who can be counted on to get a job done with skill and competency. Typically, I am spokesperson for any group of which I become part. I am looked to for leadership and guidance among my friends and colleagues. I am quite proud of my reputation; however, I wish that I had come by it through some other means. You see, all of these admirable characteristics were developed over the past twenty-five years through an obsession with being good.

Maybe I should rephrase that, because merely being "good" has never quite been "good" enough for me—not since I was six years old and my parents failed to believe me about the most important issue in my life. I went to them for protection against a child molester, and they refused to believe that such a thing could be happening in their world. Those things do not happen to "nice" people, to "good" people. Those things could not happen to *their* child. My parents defended themselves the only way they knew how, by denying the reality of my perceptions and telling me that I was "bad" for telling such stories. Their choice of the word "bad" affected everything I was ever to do afterwards. From that time on I understood only one thing, that I must be "good."

"Good" soon came to encompass everything in my world: school, friends, home, work, society. I had to be good; and, if at all possible, I had to be great. Every deed at which I excelled, every recognition I received, every honor bestowed meant that I was one step closer to no longer being "bad." As the years passed, I forgot why I was trying so hard and lost touch with the reasoning that had started this quest—yet I pursued my goal with a diligence and devotion that can only be termed as obsessive.

I knew just about everyone at school, but I never made many friends. I didn't have time to be bothered with people, except superficially, because I was totally preoccupied with my grades; I had to get all "A's." Nothing less would do. When I wasn't studying, I was deeply involved in clubs and organizations. I decided, while still in elementary school, when I saw my first high school yearbook, that I would have the longest senior listing in my high school class when I graduated. Out of a class of almost eight hundred students, I got what I wanted. I had hoped my parents would be proud, but they hardly seemed to notice.

5   By the time I was fifteen I was looking for more ways to show "them" that I could do anything, and do it well. I was a junior in high school and started working full time while attending classes all day. My day began at 7:20 a.m. when the first bell rang and ended around 1:00 a.m. when I arrived home from work. Neither I nor my family needed extra money, but for me, there was no other way: I always had to do more. I kept this schedule up until I graduated. Of course, I was an honor student; I was also a student council representative, vice president of two clubs, treasurer of one. I attended and received top awards in state foreign language competitions in two languages and was a member of two choral groups which gave concerts statewide and which participated in state-level competitions. No one ever seemed to notice or to care.

What I didn't notice was that my parents were immensely proud of me. They often bragged about me to their friends and relatives, but I wasn't paying attention. I was after something that they could never give. My "badness" no longer existed for them, and probably had not since about an hour after that episode when I was six—but it was very much a part of me. I picked everything apart, thinking that everything could always use improvement, that nothing was "good" enough as it was. My grades were good, but some of the subjects weren't as "easy" for me as I wished. I was popular, but there were always some people I didn't know. I was working, but I had to be the best at my job, the fastest, the most knowledgeable. I actually learned stock numbers and prices to over two hundred items of inventory by heart so I could impress my manager with how good I was.

Was I getting tired? Maybe. But I was also getting plenty of recognition for my accomplishments. I fed off of it; I lived for it; I required it. I needed every reward or approval I got to reinforce me in my feeling that I was on the right track, that I was getting better and better. I was no longer consciously aware of what I was seeking. The obsession had taken over my behavior, almost completely; being constantly challenged was now a way of life. Never resting, never relaxing, always striving, always achieving—these things were second nature to me by the time I was twenty.

My relationships were disastrous. My constant need for approval and recognition was very difficult for anyone to supply. Likewise, no matter how much praise I was given, I never felt like it was enough. I felt that people patronized me, so I had to prove to them that I could always do more than anyone else. I criticized anyone who was willing to settle for less than I. If someone told me that they loved me, I would pick it apart, frequently arguing with the people I was involved with: "How can you say you love me? If you loved me, then you would stop making me feel like nothing I ever do is good enough."

When I was twenty-three I started my own business, which was quite successful for a time. I had moved two thousand miles away from my family, determined that I would be a great success. I was really going to make them proud this time, but my plans went awry as moving away from my family helped dim the constant need to impress them. Because of distance, they were no longer privy to my life and to daily events. Lacking the "audience" for my constant efforts to prove myself, I began to lose the motivation to excel, to be the "good one." Slowly, I began to lose interest in my business, lacking the drive to devote myself utterly to something that was unrecognized by my family. I began to realize what I might never have discovered if I had stayed close to home. Without parental recognition and approval, my business success meant little.

10   In fact, I began to realize that I had been so damned "good" all my life that I had missed out on a great deal of fun. Suddenly my life began to change. I was involved in many things, but I derived little pleasure now from activities I had thoroughly enjoyed in the past. At twenty-seven years of age I knew nothing about myself. I had no idea what I really liked and had no concept of happiness. I only knew what I was capable of accomplishing. I set about enjoying

myself with the same devotion that I had given to everything else, and for the next few years my life became a set of extremes. Struggling constantly with a desire to be good and a need to be "bad," I would go out drinking with friends and get very drunk, but I was always the one who forced myself to try to act sober. I was always the one responsible for making sure that everyone else got home. I thought I was enjoying the first freedom that I had ever experienced in my life, but I had really only broadened my obsession to include being bad as well. Whatever mood I was in, whatever my particular focus was for the hour, whether being good or being bad, I accomplished either with an abandon and passion hard to match. And I was very, very unhappy.

What was the point? Did I really enjoy anything I was doing? No. I had no idea what I wanted, yet I demanded attention and recognition. If I couldn't get enough recognition from my family, then I would get it from everyone else. But that had proved unsatisfying as well. What could I do now? What was I after and what did I want? The only thing I really knew was that I didn't want to go on living like I was anymore. With the help of one of the few friends I had managed to make along the way, I started psychiatric counseling. The results of that counseling you see in what you have just read.

So, here I am today, thirty-two years old and just beginning to discover myself as a person who exists outside of the obsession to be good. Actually, I think I have an advantage over a lot of people my age in that I covered a lot of ground when I was young. Driven by an obsession for goodness, I tested my limits and discovered what many people never learn: that I really could accomplish anything to which I put my mind. In going from one subject to another to prove I could do it all, I was exposed to a wide variety of experiences and activities, some of which I have rejected, some of which I have made a part of my current lifestyle. Either way, the experiences I have picked up along the way have made my life rich and varied. My obsessive past has given me a strength with which to confront the future; I just wish I had arrived here by some other way.

QUESTIONS FOR DISCUSSION

1. Despite feeling proud of her achievements, why does Slayton now wish she "had arrived here by some other way"? Do you agree with her?
2. How did Slayton's parents respond to her story about a molestation? Does their response seem understandable? Would parents today be as likely to respond as Slayton's parents did in the early 1960s?
3. This essay is an example of what is known as an extended definition. What qualities make up Slayton's definition of the "good girl" obsession? Is her definition of the essay's key terms a clear one?
4. To develop her definition essay, Slayton uses her own case history and a number of examples from her life at different stages. What are the key incidents that Slayton emphasizes? Are there any that seem to need more development or detail? Do all of the incidents she mentions seem relevant to her definition?

TOPICS FOR RESEARCH AND WRITING

1. Write an extended definition of one of the following terms: "nightmare," "obsession," "addiction," "depression." Provide examples from your research and contrast to indicate how your sense of the term differs from the dictionary meaning, how readings in this text have influenced your current definition, and how your personal experiences have helped you to understand the term's meaning.

After reading the essay by Meressa Ozack in this chapter, do some research into different types of obsessive and potentially destructive behavior associated with computers and cyberspace—gambling, video game playing, overuse of online pornography and sex-based chatrooms, and so on. Write an essay about your findings and indicate what might be done to control some of these "computer abuses."

3. After reading Diane Ackerman's "The Slender Thread," Solomon's "Depression," and Gilman's "The Yellow Wallpaper," all of which deal with the possibility of suicide as the result of depressive disorders, do some research and write about what can be done to predict the possibility of suicide in depressed individuals, and how it might be possible to intervene to reduce the increasingly high rate of suicide.

4. Gilman's "The Yellow Wallpaper" concerns a nineteenth-century woman's obsession and nervous breakdown after childbirth. How were young women who suffered from "nervous disorders" such as postpartum depression treated in nineteenth-century medicine? Research this aspect of medical history and draw some conclusions. How do modern treatments differ?

5. Using Lamott's essay "Hunger" as a point of departure, do some research and write an essay defining the nature and origins of eating disorders such as anorexia and bulimia. What social, psychological, or chemical factors can lead to an eating disorder?

6. Marc Barasch writes about escape from depression and obsession through a form of spiritual transformation that comes from a "healing dream." Do some research into ways that strongly charged dreams can lead to mental healing and draw some conclusions about the efficacy of such approaches in contrast to more traditional forms of therapy or medications.

7. See one of the following films that explores the relationship between nightmares and obsessions, either by yourself or with several of your classmates. Write an individual or collaborative analysis of the film, focusing on the definition the film provides for the type of obsession it examines and whether it regards the obsession as a primarily negative or potentially positive state of mind. Here are some choices: *Field of Dreams, The Piano, House of Games, Jacob's Ladder, A Beautiful Mind, Tom and Viv, Moulin Rouge, Beloved, Traffic, What Dreams May Come, Insomnia, The Cell, Girl Interrupted, Virgin Suicides, Shine, Amadeus, Leaving Las Vegas, The Hours, Adaptation,* and *Sylvia.*

6 Journeys in Sexuality and Gender

Marc Chagall (1887–1985)
Birthday (1915)

Painted less than a year after Russian-born painter Marc Chagall's arrival in Paris, *Birthday* shows the romantic, bohemian influence of the artist's life in the city. This painting is typical of Chagall's work in its rejection of realism, physical laws, and visual logic for a visionary art that creates its own rules in order to reveal the reality of dreams, the passions, and the spirit.

JOURNAL

Write about a romantic relationship that made you feel the world was upside down, with all the normal rules of logic suspended.

No one who accepts the view that censorship is the chief reason for dream distortion will be surprised to learn from the results of dream interpretation that most of the dreams of adults are traced back by analysis to erotic wishes.
SIGMUND FREUD
Erotic Wishes and Dreams

She obeyed him; she always did as she was told.
MAXINE HONG KINGSTON
No Name Woman

No, it wasn't easy for any of us, girls and boys, as we forced our beautiful, free-flowing child-selves into those narrow, constricting cubicles labeled female and male.
JULIUS LESTER
Being a Boy

CAUSALITY AND THE INWARD JOURNEY

What causes people to have certain kinds of dreams or to remember a particular dream? Do people's gender concerns influence their dreams? How do dreams and sexual fantasies influence an individual's waking life and personal relationships? Why can certain people use their dreams to make their lives richer while others are overwhelmed by their unconscious fears? All of these questions, central to the issues raised in *Dreams and Inward Journeys*, are also issues of causality.

As you reflect on your dreams and emotions, working to understand what you read and to create clear, focused arguments, causal analysis will be a fundamental part of your thinking process. Causal analysis can help you to understand your inner life, to interpret your relationship to the public world, and to explain how and why things happen the way they do. Finding connections that exist between two events, understanding how one event led to or produced another event, and speculating about the consequences of earlier events—all involve causal reasoning.

Observing and Collecting Information

People naturally search for solutions to mental dilemmas and physical problems, wanting to explain why something occurred and how they can improve the situation. In most cases, the more confident we are about our explanations of any event, the better we feel. Observing and collecting information about both your inner and outer worlds will increase your chances of making accurate causal connections and inferences about the sources and meanings of your dreams and the public events that are influencing you. For example, if you are keeping a dream journal, you may find that after writing down your dreams for a while, you notice repeated images or situations that may reflect your psychological concerns and may help you to draw more accurate inferences about your inner needs. Similarly, keeping a media journal of newspaper clippings or stories downloaded from the Internet will help you become more alert to issues of cause and effect in the external world: immediate and long-term causes for our country's attack on another nation, for instance, or the effects of a series of "strategic" bombing raids on the ecological system, the rate of global pollution and disease, and the flow of refugees out of and into various countries in a region of the world.

Whether you are studying dreams, literature, or current events, be sure that the causal connections you make are sound ones. Observe carefully and consider all possible causes, not simply the obvious, immediate ones. For example, student writer Julie Bordner Apodaca began her preparation to write "Gay Marriage: Why the Resistance?" (included in this chapter) with her own personal observations of biased comments about gay relationships, comments that had come up in conversations she had with other students and people in her community. These comments led her to consider some of the deeper, underlying causes of homophobia. She searched for information about the causes through further conversations and interviews with students and with her own mother, who is a psychotherapist. Apodaca also read a number of books and magazine articles on the subject, some of which are referred to in the bibliography that accompanies her essay. Ultimately, she found so many causes of bias that she chose to classify them into several different categories: religious, sociopolitical, and medical.

In writing a causal analysis, whether of a dream, a short story, or a social issue, it is also essential that you provide adequate evidence, both factual and logical, for the conclusions that you draw. You may believe that you understand the causes involved quite clearly, but perceiving these connections for yourself is not enough; you must re-create for your reader, in clear and specific language, the mental process you went through to arrive at your conclusions. Methodically and carefully questioning your own thought process will help you clarify your insights, generate new ideas and evidence that can be used to support your analysis, and avoid logical fallacies.

Causal Logical Fallacies

People create connections between events or personal issues about which they feel strongly, often rushing their thinking process to a hasty conclusion. One of the most common errors, the post hoc fallacy ("after this, therefore because of this"), mistakenly attempts to create a causal connection between unrelated events that follow each other closely in time. But a sequence in time is not necessarily a causal sequence. In fact, most magical or superstitious thinking relative to dreams and daily life is based on faulty causal analysis of sequences in time. For instance, people may carry a burden of guilt because of accidental sequential parallels between their inner thoughts and outer events, such as a dream of the death of a loved one and that person's subsequent death or injury.

Another common problem in thinking and writing about causality is causal oversimplification, in which a person argues that one thing caused something to happen, when in fact a number of different elements worked together to produce a major effect or outcome. For example, one's dream of flying may have been inspired in part by watching a television program about pilots the night before, yet other causes may also be present: one's love for performing or "showing off," or one's joy about a recent accomplishment. When trying to apply a broad theory to explain many individual cases, thinkers often become involved in causal oversimplification. We can ask, for example, if Freud's theories about the sexual content and sources of dreams really explain the entire range of dream stories and imagery. What other causes and sources might he have neglected to consider? Asking about other possible causal relations not covered by a causal thesis will help you to test the soundness of your analysis.

The "slippery slope" fallacy is also of particular relevance to the issues explored in this text. In the slippery slope fallacy, a reasoned analysis of causes and effects is replaced by a reaction of fear, in which a person might argue that if one seemingly insignificant event is allowed to happen, there will be serious consequences. Of course, in some cases this may be true: if one isn't careful about sexually transmitted diseases, there is the possibility that a person may get AIDS and eventually die. In most cases, however, theorizing about dreadful future events can become a way of validating irrational fears and can become a way of providing an excuse for maintaining the status quo. Recognizing the slippery slope fallacies both in others' thinking and within one's own thinking can help you to free yourself from irrational anxiety and develop better critical thinking skills.

Good causal reasoning can lead you closer to understanding and developing theories and explanations for the multiple causes and effects of the issues and events you encounter in your reading and in your own life. With an awareness of the complexities of causal thinking, you should be able to think and write more critically, clearly, and persuasively.

THEMATIC INTRODUCTION: SEXUALITY AND GENDER

People in all cultures define themselves in relationship to gender roles and sexuality. Individuals develop a sense of their gender role through observation and participation in the values and rituals of their family, peer group, culture, and spiritual heritage. The shifting social definitions of acceptable gender role behavior have led many people today to feel confused about their gender identity and about what constitutes appropriate sexual behavior: How do we meet somebody we care about in a world without "arranged" relationships and marriage? Should sexual intercourse be a casual hookup, or only available within a stable, loving relationship? What if our gender orientation is other than mainstream heterosexual? What responsibility does each partner in a relationship have for birth control, for making decisions about child-bearing and child care responsibilities? While people often rebel consciously against their culture's gender roles, a person's sexuality is a much more intimate and unconscious aspect of her or his personality, one that is often manifested in sexually charged dreams and fantasies that may or may not need to be manifested in overt sexual behavior.

Each of the readings selected for this chapter relates to a particular issue of controversy related to sexuality and/or gender roles. We begin with a poem, Pablo Neruda's "The Dream," which seems to pose the question of what we gain in a loving relationship through conflict, struggle, and reaffirmation. The next reading, the essay "Erotic Wishes and Dreams" by Sigmund Freud, presents Freud's theories of dream symbols that reflect repressed sexual desire and erotic wish fulfillment. The results of sexual repression that Freud explores in his essay are examined in a social context in the story/memoir "No Name Woman" by Maxine Hong Kingston, which portrays a traditional Chinese village culture where women are subordinate to men, with rigid expectations of gender role and conduct that can result in terrible punishment for female sexual transgressors.

In contrast to the rigid gender roles seen in the regimented village society portrayed in Kingston's essay, modern American society is far less protective of young women, as Mary Pipher points out in our next selection, "Saplings in the Storm," an exploration of the troubled lives of today's preteen and teenage girls. Tajamika Paxton's autobiographical essay, "Loving a One-armed Man," also examines modern family life, but from the perspective of father-daughter relations in an urban African American family.

Our next two essays focus on gender conflicts that arise from issues concerning working wives and shared housekeeping. Rachel Lehmann-Haupt's "Multi-Tasking Man" discusses the need for both men and women to be "multitasking" in the modern dual-career family, and examines how men are failing in some cases to accept the need to adjust to new child care responsibilities and demands on their time. Kevin Canty's personal essay, "The Dog in Me," provides an example of the difficulties many working men have in meeting the needs of their working spouses when there are young children in the home.

The final professional selection in this chapter, David Sedaris's "I Like Guys," presents a tragicomic memoir of growing up gay in the late 1950s, pointing out how school integration did little to alleviate the sexual oppression experienced by gay youth of the period.

The two student essays that close the chapter also present points of view on current gender issues. In "On Not Being a Girl," Rosa Contreras discusses the difficulties she faced growing up in a Mexican American family that expected her to follow the gender roles of her traditional-culture immigrant family while also expecting her to attend college. In "Gay Marriage: Why the Resistance?" Julie Bordner Apodaca writes about the political and social struggles for gay relationships to be recognized as legitimate family units and considers some of the reasons why it is difficult for such relationships to gain acceptance.

As we enter the new millennium, the issues of gender identity and sexuality only promise to become more complex, particularly with the increasing social and political tension between orthodox, fundamentalist religion and sexually explicit youth culture and values. We think that the readings in this chapter will give you some insights into the customs of the past as well as provocative points of view about changing gender roles and nontraditional sexual orientation.

Pablo Neruda

The Dream

Pablo Neruda (1904–1973) was born and educated in Chile. When he was 25, he began a long career in politics as a Chilean consul in Ceylon and East Asia and went on to serve at the Chilean Embassy in Mexico City. He was a member of the World Peace Council from 1950 to 1973 and received many international peace prizes. Neruda is considered one of the greatest poets of the twentieth century, and his work has been translated into 20 different languages. In 1971 he received the Nobel Prize in Literature. Critics have noted that Neruda's poetry "structures itself on emotive association like the subconscious, and worlds in the flux of sensation and thought." These qualities are apparent in "The Dream" (from The Captain's Verses, *1972), a poem that can be read as an account of a turning point in a relationship.*

JOURNAL

Write about a time when you felt like ending a relationship that was becoming too all-involving or too stressful. Did you find a way to save or transform the relationship? If so, how?

Walking on the sands
I decided to leave you.

I was treading a dark clay
that trembled
5   and I, sinking and coming out,
decided that you should come out
of me, that you were weighing me down
like a cutting stone,
and I worked out your loss
10 step by step:
to cut off your roots,
to release you alone into the wind.

Ah in that minute,
my dear, a dream
15 with its terrible wings
was covering you.

You felt yourself swallowed by the clay,
and you called to me and I did not come,
you were going, motionless,
20 without defending yourself
until you were smothered in the quicksand.

Afterwards
my decision encountered your dream,
and from the rupture
25 that was breaking our hearts
we came forth clean again, naked,
loving each other
without dream, without sand,
complete and radiant,
30 sealed by fire.

QUESTIONS FOR DISCUSSION

1. What is the significance of the sands and the trembling "dark clay" that the speaker treads on in the first part of the poem? How do the speaker

and the "you" in the poem change and gain power over the clay and sand as the poem progresses? How does this change comment on the central relationship in the poem?

2. What leads the "I" in the poem to decide to leave the "you"? What kind of a crisis in a relationship might this decision suggest?

3. What is the meaning of the dream with "terrible wings" that covers the "you?"

4. What seems to cause the "I" to have a change of heart toward the "you"? What might be the "rupture" that cleanses and renews the couple's relationship?

5. What new definition of love emerges as the speaker comments on the lovers as "naked,/loving each other/without dream, without sand"? Does the kind of love suggested here seem erotic, spiritual, or something else entirely?

CONNECTION

Compare the portrayal of struggle, rejection, and acceptance in a close relationship in Neruda's poem with the father-daughter relationship in Paxton's "Loving a One-armed Man" in this chapter (see page 355).

IDEAS FOR WRITING

1. Write an essay in which you define an ideal love capable of overcoming obstacles in its path. Use personal examples as well as references to Neruda's poem.

2. Write an essay in which you analyze the poem from the perspective of gender roles. Argue which gender a reader would be most likely to assign to the "I" and to the "you" in the poem, and explain your choices, making specific references to the poem. What criticism and/or acceptance of traditional gender roles does the poem make or imply, and how does it make such points?

RELATED WEB SITES

Academy of American Poets: Pablo Neruda
`www.poets.org/poets/poets.cfm?45442B7C000C040D0C`
This page on Neruda contains a biography, translations of poems, and links to other sites and materials relevant to his work.

Interview with Martin Espada on Pablo Neruda
`www.democracynow.org/article.pl?sid=04/07/16/1442233`
This interview for *Democracy Now!* on NPR highlights Neruda's contributions to twentieth-century poetry and emphasizes his importance in Chilean history and culture.

Sigmund Freud

Erotic Wishes and Dreams

Known as the founder of the psychoanalytic method and of concepts such as the unconscious mind and the Oedipus complex, Sigmund Freud (1856–1939) was also a pioneer in the scientific study of dreams and human sexuality. Freud spent most of his life in Vienna, where he practiced psychoanalysis and published many important studies on psychology and dream interpretation as well as cultural studies that focus on psychological interpretations of art and history. His works include Interpretation of Dreams *(1900),* Totem and Taboo, *and* Leonardo da Vinci: A Study in Psychosexuality. *In "Erotic Wishes and Dreams," from his explanation of dream theory,* On Dreams *(1901), Freud presents his ideas on dream symbolism and expresses his conviction that dreams focus on erotic wishes and fantasies, although sometimes in a disguised form.*

JOURNAL

Write about a dream you have had that you consider explicitly or implicitly sexual in its content. Did you consider the dream to be a form of wish fulfillment, or could there have been some other explanation for the dream and its images?

No one who accepts the view that censorship is the chief reason for dream distortion will be surprised to learn from the results of dream interpretation that most of the dreams of adults are traced back by analysis to *erotic wishes.* This assertion is not aimed at dreams with an *undisguised* sexual content, which are no doubt familiar to all dreamers from their own experience and are as a rule the only ones to be described as "sexual dreams." Even dreams of this latter kind offer enough surprises in their choice of the people whom they make into sexual objects, in their disregard of all the limitations which the dreamer imposes in his waking life upon his sexual desires, and by their many strange details, hinting at what are commonly known as "perversions." A great many other dreams, however, which show no sign of being erotic in their manifest content, are revealed by the work of interpretation in analysis as sexual wish fulfillments; and, on the other hand, analysis proves that a great many of the thoughts left over from the activity of waking life as "residues of the previous day" only find their way to representation in dreams through the assistance of repressed erotic wishes.

There is no theoretical necessity why this should be so; but to explain the fact it may be pointed out that no other group of instincts has been submitted to such far-reaching suppression by the demands of cultural education, while at the same time the sexual instincts are also the ones which, in most people, find it easiest to escape from the control of the highest mental agencies. Since we have become acquainted with infantile sexuality, which is often so unobtrusive in its manifestations and is always overlooked and misunderstood, we are justified in saying that almost every civilized man retains the infantile forms of sexual life in some respect or other. We can thus understand how it is that repressed infantile sexual wishes provide the most frequent and strongest motive forces for the construction of dreams.[*]

There is only one method by which a dream which expresses erotic wishes can succeed in appearing innocently nonsexual in its manifest content. The material of the sexual ideas must not be represented as such, but must be replaced in the content of the dream by hints, allusions and similar forms of indirect representation. But, unlike other forms of indirect representation, that which is employed in dreams must not be immediately intelligible. The modes of representation which fulfill these conditions are usually described as "symbols" of the things which they represent. Particular interest has been directed to them since it has been noticed that dreamers speaking the same language make use of the same symbols, and that in some cases, indeed, the use of the same symbols extends beyond the use of the same language. Since dreamers themselves are unaware of the meaning of the symbols they use, it is difficult at first sight to discover the source of the connection between the symbols and what they replace and represent. The fact itself, however, is beyond doubt, and it is important for the technique of dream interpretation. For, with the help of a knowledge of dream symbolism, it is possible to understand the meaning of separate elements of the content of a dream or separate pieces of a dream or in some cases even whole dreams, without having to ask the dreamer for his associations. Here we are approaching the popular ideal of translating dreams and on the other hand are returning to the technique of interpretation used by the ancients, to whom dream interpretation was identical with interpretation by means of symbols.

Although the study of dream symbols is far from being complete, we are in a position to lay down with certainty a number of general statements and a quantity of special information on the subject. There are some symbols which bear a single meaning almost universally: thus the Emperor and Empress (or the King and Queen) stand for the parents, rooms represent women and their entrances and exits the openings of the body. The majority of dream symbols serve to represent persons, parts of the body and activities invested with erotic interest; in particular, the genitals are represented by a number of often very surprising symbols, and the greatest variety of objects are employed to denote them symbolically. Sharp weapons, long and stiff objects, such as tree trunks and sticks, stand for the male genital; while cupboards, boxes, carriages or ovens may represent the uterus. In such cases as these the *tertium comparationis,* the common element in these substitutions, is immediately intelligible; but there are other symbols in which it is not so easy to grasp the connection. Symbols such as a

---

[*]See my *Three Essays on the Theory of Sexuality* (1905) [author's note].

staircase or going upstairs, representing sexual intercourse, a tie or cravat for the male organ, or wood for the female one, provoke our unbelief until we can arrive at an understanding of the symbolic relation underlying them by some other means. Moreover a whole number of dream symbols are bisexual and can relate to the male or female genitals according to the context.

5   Some symbols are universally disseminated and can be met with in all dreamers belonging to a single linguistic or cultural group; there are others which occur only within the most restricted and individual limits, symbols constructed by an individual out of his own ideational material. Of the former class we can distinguish some whose claim to represent sexual ideas is immediately justified by linguistic usage (such, for instance, as those derived from agriculture, e.g., "fertilization" or "seed") and others whose relation to sexual ideas appears to reach back into the very earliest ages and to the most obscure depths of our conceptual functioning. The power of constructing symbols has not been exhausted in our own days in the case of either of the two sorts of symbols which I have distinguished at the beginning of this paragraph. Newly discovered objects (such as airships) are, as we may observe, at once adopted as universally available sexual symbols.

It would, incidentally, be a mistake to expect that if we had a still profounder knowledge of dream symbolism (of the "language of dreams") we could do without asking the dreamer for his associations to the dream and go back entirely to the technique of dream interpretation of antiquity. Quite apart from individual symbols and oscillations in the use of universal ones, one can never tell whether any particular element in the content of a dream is to be interpreted symbolically or in its proper sense, and one can be certain that the *whole* content of a dream is not to be interpreted symbolically. A knowledge of dream symbolism will never do more than enable us to translate certain constituents of the dream content, and will not relieve us of the necessity for applying the technical rules which I gave earlier. It will, however, afford the most valuable assistance to interpretation precisely at points at which the dreamer's associations are insufficient or fail altogether.

Dream symbolism is also indispensable to an understanding of what are known as "typical" dreams, which are common to everyone, and of "recurrent" dreams in individuals.

If the account I have given in this short discussion of the symbolic mode of expression in dreams appears incomplete, I can justify my neglect by drawing attention to one of the most important pieces of knowledge that we possess on this subject. Dream symbolism extends far beyond dreams: it is not peculiar to dreams, but exercises a similar dominating influence on representation in fairy tales, myths and legends, in jokes and in folklore. It enables us to trace the intimate connections between dreams and these latter productions. We must not suppose that dream symbolism is a creation of the dream work; it is in all probability a characteristic of the unconscious thinking which provides the dream work with the material for condensation, displacement and dramatization.

QUESTIONS FOR DISCUSSION

1. Why does Freud believe that "repressed infantile sexual wishes" are the strongest motivation behind dreams and their primary content? Does he provide convincing evidence for this belief?
2. How might a dream express erotic wishes and at the same time appear innocent of sexual content? What might cause this apparent contradiction?
3. How does Freud define "symbols" as they appear in dreams? What examples does he provide? Do these seem like sexual symbols to you?
4. How does Freud compare traditional, culturally universal dream symbols with more modern symbols based on technological inventions? Can you think of modern dream symbols that have sexual implications?
5. According to Freud, why is it always a mistake to create dream interpretations without investigating the dreamer's own associations with the symbols from his or her dreams? Do you agree with Freud that popular books that list the meanings of dream symbols are basically worthless? Explain your position.
6. What is the relationship between dream symbolism, the unconscious mind, and more literary works such as fairy tales, myths, and legends? Do you agree with Freud's comparison and analysis?

CONNECTION

Compare Freud's view of sexuality, gender, dreams, and fantasy to Maxine Hong Kingston's observations in "No Name Woman." How would Freud respond (see page 336)?

IDEAS FOR WRITING

1. Apply Freud's theory about the content and symbolism of dreams to a dream you have had. Write an interpretive essay about your dream. Did Freud's ideas help you to understand your dream and its causes more clearly? What else might have influenced the imagery and events in your dream?
2. Because Freud's theories about the repressed erotic content and symbolism in dreams can also be applied to fantasy literature such as myths and fairy tales, many critics have attempted "Freudian" analyses of imaginative literature. Using a "Freudian" or sexual-symbol approach, try to interpret the characters, symbolism, and events of one of the stories or myths in this text. Did you find this approach satisfactory? Why or why not?

RELATED WEB SITES

Sigmund Freud
www.freudfile.org
This Web site is dedicated to the life and work of Sigmund Freud. It offers information about his biography, self-analysis, and work, as well as about the personalities who interacted with his ideas and with the development of

psychoanalysis. Bibliographical notes, quotations, and references concerning Freud and his activity in the psychoanalysis field will also be found here.

The American Psychoanalytic Association
www.apsa.org
Learn about psychoanalysis at this large Web site devoted to the subject. It also includes many relevant links, essays, news, and information on upcoming conferences.

An Erotic Table D'hôte
www.haverford.edu/psych/ddavis/ftable.html#fn0
Psychology professor Doug Davis presents a brief analysis of one of Freud's own dreams. The site contains links to others of Freud's dreams and of modern analyses of his work, which provide a clear sense of how Freud approached gender issues and the erotic dream.

Maxine Hong Kingston

No Name Woman

Maxine Hong Kingston (b. 1940) is from Stockton, California, where she grew up listening to the stories her mother would tell about Chinese village life. Hong Kingston graduated from the University of California, Berkeley, and taught high school and college English in Hawaii for a number of years before returning to the San Francisco Bay area to write and teach at UC Berkeley. Books by Hong Kingston include a personal memoir, The Woman Warrior: Memories of a Childhood Among Ghosts *(1976); a historical account of Chinese American life,* China Men *(1980); and a novel,* Tripmaster Monkey: His Fake Book *(1989). Her most recent books are* To Be the Poet *(2002), and* The Fifth Book of Peace *(2003). The following selection from* The Woman Warrior *reflects on one of the stories Hong Kingston's mother told her about an aunt in China whose sexual indiscretion leads her to become a "no name woman" and to lose her place in the life of the community.*

JOURNAL

Retell a story that you heard from a family member when you were a child that warned you of the dangers of adult life and sexuality.

"You must not tell anyone," my mother said, "what I am about to tell you. In China your father had a sister who killed herself. She jumped into the family well. We say that your father has all brothers because it is as if she had never been born.

"In 1924 just a few days after our village celebrated seventeen hurry-up weddings—to make sure that every young man who went 'out on the road' would responsibly come home—your father and his brothers and your grandfather and his brothers and your aunt's new husband sailed for America, the Gold Mountain. It was your grandfather's last trip. Those lucky enough to get contracts waved good-bye from the decks. They fed and guarded the stowaways and helped them off in Cuba, New York, Bali, Hawaii. 'We'll meet in California next year,' they said. All of them sent money home.

"I remember looking at your aunt one day when she and I were dressing; I had not noticed before that she had such a protruding melon of a stomach. But I did not think, 'She's pregnant,' until she began to look like other pregnant women, her shirt pulling and the white tops of her black pants showing. She could not have been pregnant, you see, because her husband had been gone for years. No one said anything. We did not discuss it. In early summer she was ready to have the child, long after the time when it could have been possible.

"The village had also been counting. On the night the baby was to be born the villagers raided our house. Some were crying. Like a great saw, teeth strung with lights, files of people walked zigzag across our land, tearing the rice. Their lanterns doubled in the disturbed black water, which drained away through the broken bunds. As the villagers closed in, we could see that some of them, probably men and women we knew well, wore white masks. The people with long hair hung it over their faces. Women with short hair made it stand up on end. Some had tied white bands around their foreheads, arms, and legs.

5   "At first they threw mud and rocks at the house. Then they threw eggs and began slaughtering our stock. We could hear the animals scream their deaths—the roosters, the pigs, a last great roar from the ox. Familiar wild heads flared in our night windows; the villagers encircled us. Some of the faces stopped to peer at us, their eyes rushing like searchlights. The hands flattened against the panes, framed heads, and left red prints.

"The villagers broke in the front and the back doors at the same time, even though we had not locked the doors against them. Their knives dripped with the blood of our animals. They smeared blood on the doors and walls. One woman swung a chicken, whose throat she had slit, splattering blood in red arcs about her. We stood together in the middle of our house, in the family hall with the pictures and tables of the ancestors around us, and looked straight ahead.

"At that time the house had only two wings. When the men came back, we would build two more to enclose our courtyard and a third one to begin a second courtyard. The villagers rushed through both wings, even your grandparents' rooms, to find your aunt's, which was also mine until the men returned. From this room a new wing for one of the younger families would grow. They ripped up her clothes and shoes and broke her combs, grinding them underfoot. They tore her work from the loom. They scattered the cooking fire and rolled the new weaving in it. We could hear them in the kitchen breaking our bowls and banging the pots. They overturned the great waist-high earthenware jugs; duck eggs, pickled fruits, vegetables burst out and mixed in acrid torrents. The old woman from the next field swept a broom through the air and loosed the spirits-of-the-broom over our heads. 'Pig.' 'Ghost.' 'Pig,' they sobbed and scolded while they ruined our house.

"When they left, they took sugar and oranges to bless themselves. They cut pieces from the dead animals. Some of them took bowls that were not broken and clothes that were not torn. Afterward we swept up the rice and sewed it back up into sacks. But the smells from the spilled preserves lasted. Your aunt gave birth in the pigsty that night. The next morning when I went for the water, I found her and the baby plugging up the family well.

"Don't let your father know that I told you. He denies her. Now that you have started to menstruate, what happened to her could happen to you. Don't humiliate us. You wouldn't like to be forgotten as if you had never been born. The villagers are watchful."

10   Whenever she had to warn us about life, my mother told stories that ran like this one, a story to grow up on. She tested our strength to establish realities. Those in the emigrant generations who could not reassert brute survival died young and far from home. Those of us in the first American generations have had to figure out how the invisible world that the emigrants built around our childhoods fit in solid America.

The emigrants confused the gods by diverting their curses, misleading them with crooked streets and false names. They must try to confuse their offspring as well, who, I suppose, threaten them in similar ways—always trying to get things straight, always trying to name the unspeakable. The Chinese I know hide their names; sojourners take new names when their lives change and guard their real names with silence.

Chinese-Americans, when you try to understand what things in you are Chinese, how do you separate what is peculiar to childhood, to poverty, insanities, one family, your mother who marked your growing with stories from what is Chinese? What is Chinese tradition and what is the movies?

If I want to learn what clothes my aunt wore, whether flashy or ordinary, I would have to begin, "Remember Father's drowned-in-the-well sister?" I cannot ask that. My mother has told me once and for all the useful parts. She will add nothing unless powered by Necessity, a riverbank that guides her life. She plants vegetable gardens rather than lawns; she carries the odd-shaped tomatoes home from the fields and eats food left for the gods.

Whenever we did frivolous things, we used up energy; we flew high kites. We children came up off the ground over the melting cones our parents brought home from work and the American movie on New Year's Day—*Oh, You Beautiful Doll* with Betty Grable one year, and *She Wore a Yellow Ribbon* with John Wayne another year. After the one carnival ride each, we paid in guilt; our tired father counted his change on the dark walk home.

15   Adultery is extravagance. Could people who hatch their own chicks and eat the embryos and the heads for delicacies and boil the feet in vinegar for party

food, leaving only the gravel, eating even the gizzard lining—could such people engender a prodigal aunt? To be a woman, to have a daughter in starvation time was a waste enough. My aunt could not have been the lone romantic who gave up everything for sex. Women in the old China did not choose. Some man had commanded her to lie with him and be his secret evil. I wonder whether he masked himself when he joined the raid on her family.

Perhaps she encountered him in the fields or on the mountain where the daughters-in-law collected fuel. Or perhaps he first noticed her in the marketplace. He was not a stranger because the village housed no strangers. She had to have dealings with him other than sex. Perhaps he worked an adjoining field, or he sold her the cloth for the dress she sewed and wore. His demand must have surprised, then terrified her. She obeyed him; she always did as she was told.

When the family found a young man in the next village to be her husband, she stood tractably beside the best rooster, his proxy, and promised before they met that she would be his forever. She was lucky that he was her age and she would be the first wife, an advantage secure now. The night she first saw him, he had sex with her. Then he left for America. She had almost forgotten what he looked like. When she tried to envision him, she only saw the black and white face in the group photograph the men had had taken before leaving.

The other man was not, after all, much different from her husband. They both gave orders: she followed. "If you tell your family, I'll beat you. I'll kill you. Be here again next week." No one talked sex, ever. And she might have separated the rapes from the rest of living if only she did not have to buy her oil from him or gather wood in the same forest. I want her fear to have lasted just as long as rape lasted so that the fear could have been contained. No drawn-out fear. But women at sex hazarded birth and hence lifetimes. The fear did not stop but permeated everywhere. She told the man, "I think I'm pregnant." He organized the raid against her.

On nights when my mother and father talked about their life back home, sometimes they mentioned an "outcast table" whose business they still seemed to be settling, their voices tight. In a communal tradition, where food is precious, the powerful older people made wrongdoers eat alone. Instead of letting them start separate new lives like the Japanese, who could become samurais and geishas, the Chinese family, faces averted but eyes glowering sideways, hung on to the offenders and fed them leftovers. My aunt must have lived in the same house as my parents and eaten at an outcast table. My mother spoke about the raid as if she had seen it, when she and my aunt, a daughter-in-law to a different household, should not have been living together at all. Daughters-in-law lived with their husbands' parents, not their own; a synonym for marriage in Chinese is "taking a daughter-in-law." Her husband's parents could have sold her, mortgaged her, stoned her. But they had sent her back to her own mother and father, a mysterious act hinting at disgraces not told me. Perhaps they had thrown her out to deflect the avengers.

20   She was the only daughter; her four brothers went with her father, husband and uncles "out on the road" and for some years became western men. When

the goods were divided among the family, three of the brothers took land, and the youngest, my father, chose an education. After my grandparents gave their daughter away to her husband's family, they had dispensed all the adventure and all the property. They expected her alone to keep the traditional ways, which her brothers, now among the barbarians, could fumble without detection. The heavy, deep-rooted women were to maintain the past against the flood, safe for returning. But the rare urge west had fixed upon our family, and so my aunt crossed boundaries not delineated in space.

The work of preservation demands that the feelings playing about in one's guts not be turned into action. Just watch their passing like cherry blossoms. But perhaps my aunt, my forerunner, caught in a slow life, let dreams grow and fade and after some months or years went toward what persisted. Fear at the enormities of the forbidden kept her desires delicate, wire and bone. She looked at a man because she liked the way the hair was tucked behind his ears, or she liked the question-mark line of a long torso curving at the shoulder and straight at the hip. For warm eyes or a soft voice or a slow walk—that's all—a few hairs, a line, brightness, a sound, a pace, she gave up family. She offered us up for a charm that vanished with tiredness, a pigtail that didn't toss when the wind died. Why, the wrong lighting could erase the dearest thing about him.

It could very well have been, however, that my aunt did not take subtle enjoyment of her friend, but, a wild woman, kept rollicking company. Imagining her free with sex doesn't fit, though. I don't know any women like that, or men either. Unless I see her life branching into mine, she gives me no ancestral help.

To sustain her being in love, she often worked at herself in the mirror, guessing at the colors and shapes that would interest him, changing them frequently in order to hit on the right combination. She wanted him to look back.

On a farm near the sea, a woman who tended her appearance reaped a reputation for eccentricity. All the married women blunt-cut their hair in flaps about their ears or pulled it back in tight buns. No nonsense. Neither style blew easily into heart-catching tangles. And at their weddings they displayed themselves in their long hair for the last time. "It brushed the backs of my knees," my mother tells me. "It was braided, and even so, it brushed the backs of my knees."

25   At the mirror my aunt combed individuality into her bob. A bun could have been contrived to escape into black streamers blowing in the wind or in quiet wisps about her face, but only the older women in our picture album wear buns. She brushed her hair back from her forehead, tucking the flaps behind her ears. She looped a piece of thread, knotted into a circle between her index fingers and thumbs, and ran the double strand across her forehead. When she closed her fingers as if she were making a pair of shadow geese bite, the string twisted together catching the little hairs. Then she pulled the thread away from her skin, ripping the hairs out neatly, her eyes watering from the needles of pain. Opening her fingers, she cleaned the thread, then rolled it along her hairline and the tops of her eyebrows. My mother did the same to me and my sisters and herself. I used to believe that the expression "caught by the short

hairs" meant a captive held with a depilatory string. It especially hurt at the temples, but my mother said we were lucky we didn't have to have our feet bound when we were seven. Sisters used to sit on their beds and cry together, she said, as their mothers or their slave removed the bandages for a few minutes each night and let the blood gush back into their veins. I hope that the man my aunt loved appreciated a smooth brow, that he wasn't just a tits-and-ass man.

Once my aunt found a freckle on her chin, at a spot that the almanac said predestined her for unhappiness. She dug it out with a hot needle and washed the wound with peroxide.

More attention to her looks than these pullings of hairs and pickings at spots would have caused gossip among the villagers. They owned work clothes and good clothes, and they wore good clothes for feasting the new seasons. But since a woman combing her hair hexes beginnings, my aunt rarely found an occasion to look her best. Women looked like great sea snails—the corded wood, babies, and laundry they carried were the whorls on their backs. The Chinese did not admire a bent back; goddesses and warriors stood straight. Still there must have been a marvelous freeing of beauty when a worker laid down her burden and stretched and arched.

Such commonplace loveliness, however, was not enough for my aunt. She dreamed of a lover for the fifteen days of New Year's, the time for families to exchange visits, money, and food. She plied her secret comb. And sure enough she cursed the year, the family, the village, and herself.

Even as her hair lured her imminent lover, many other men looked at her. Uncles, cousins, nephews, brothers would have looked, too, had they been home between journeys. Perhaps they had already been restraining their curiosity, and they left, fearful that their glances, like a field of nesting birds, might be startled and caught. Poverty hurt, and that was their first reason for leaving. But another, final reason for leaving the crowded house was the never-said.

30 She may have been unusually beloved, the precious only daughter, spoiled and mirror gazing because of the affection the family lavished on her. When her husband left, they welcomed the chance to take her back from the in-laws; she could live like the little daughter for just a while longer. There are stories that my grandfather was different from other people, "crazy ever since the little Jap bayoneted him in the head." He used to put his naked penis on the dinner table, laughing. And one day he brought home a baby girl, wrapped up inside his brown western-style greatcoat. He had traded one of his sons, probably my father, the youngest, for her. My grandmother made him trade back. When he finally got a daughter of his own, he doted on her. They must have all loved her, except perhaps my father, the only brother who never went back to China, having once been traded for a girl.

Brothers and sisters, newly men and women, had to efface their sexual color and present plain miens. Disturbing hair and eyes, a smile like no other, threatened the ideal of five generations living under one roof. To focus blurs, people shouted face to face and yelled from room to room. The immigrants I know have loud voices, unmodulated to American tones even after years away from the village where they called their friendships out across the fields. I have not been able to stop mother's screams in public libraries or over telephones. Walking erect (knees straight, toes pointed forward, not pigeon-toed, which is Chinese-feminine) and speaking in an inaudible voice, I have tried to turn myself American-feminine. Chinese communication was loud, public. Only sick people had to whisper. But at the dinner table, where the family members came nearest one another, no one could talk, not the outcasts nor any eaters. Every word that falls from the mouth is a coin lost. Silently they gave and accepted food with both hands. A preoccupied child who took his bowl with one hand got a sideways glare. A complete moment of total attention is due everyone alike. Children and lovers have no singularity here, but my aunt used a secret voice, a separate attentiveness.

She kept the man's name to herself throughout her labor and dying; she did not accuse him that he be punished with her. To save her inseminator's name she gave silent birth.

He may have been somebody in her own household, but intercourse with a man outside the family would have been no less abhorrent. All the village were kinsmen, and the titles shouted in loud country voices never let kinship be forgotten. Any man within visiting distance would have been neutralized as a lover—"brother," "younger brother," "older brother"—one hundred and fifteen relationship titles. Parents researched birth charts probably not so much to assure good fortune as to circumvent incest in a population that has but one hundred surnames. Everybody has eight million relatives. How useless then sexual mannerisms, how dangerous.

As if it came from an atavism deeper than fear, I used to add "brother" silently to boys' names. It hexed the boys, who would or would not ask me to dance, and made them less scary and as familiar and deserving of benevolence as girls.

35   But, of course, I hexed myself also—no dates. I should have stood up, both arms waving, and shouted out across libraries, "Hey, you! Love me back." I had no idea, though, how to make attraction selective, how to control its direction and magnitude. If I made myself American-pretty so that the five or six Chinese boys in the class fell in love with me, everyone else—the Caucasian, Negro, and Japanese boys—would too. Sisterliness, dignified and honorable, made much more sense.

Attraction eludes control so stubbornly that whole societies designed to organize relationships among people cannot keep order, not even when they bind people to one another from childhood and raise them together. Among the very poor and the wealthy, brothers married their adopted sisters, like doves. Our family provided some romance, paying adult brides' prices and providing dowries so that their sons and daughters could marry strangers. Marriage promises to turn strangers into friendly relatives—a nation of siblings.

In the village structure, spirits shimmered among the live creatures, balanced and held in equilibrium by time and land. But one human being flaring up into violence could open up a black hole, a maelstrom that pulled in the sky. The frightened villagers, who depended on one another to maintain the real, went to my aunt to show her a personal, physical representation of the break she had made in the "roundness." Misallying couples snapped off the future, which was to be embodied in true offspring. The villagers punished her for acting as if she could have a private life, secret and apart from them.

If my aunt had betrayed the family at a time of large grain yields and peace, when many boys were born, the wings were being built on many houses, perhaps she might have escaped such severe punishment. But the men—hungry, greedy, tired of planting in dry soil, cuckolded—had had to leave the village in order to send food-money home. There were ghost plagues, bandit plagues, wars with the Japanese, floods. My Chinese brother and sister had died of an unknown sickness. Adultery, perhaps only a mistake during good times, became a crime when the village needed food.

The round moon cakes and round doorways, the round tables of graduated size that fit one roundness inside another, round windows and rice bowls— these talismans had lost their power to warn this family of the law: a family must be whole, faithfully keep the descent line by having sons to feed the old and the dead, who in turn look after the family. The villagers came to show my aunt and her lover-in-hiding a broken house. The villagers were speeding up the circling of events because she was too short-sighted to see that her infidelity had already harmed the village, that waves of consequences would return unpredictably, sometimes in disguise, as now, to hurt her. This roundness had to be made coin-sized so that she would see its circumference: punish her at the birth of her baby. Awaken her to the inexorable. People who refused fatalism because they could invent small resources insisted on culpability. Deny accidents and wrest fault from the stars.

40   After the villagers left, their lanterns now scattering in various directions toward home, the family broke their silence and cursed her. "Aiaa, we're going to die. Death is coming. Death is coming. Look what you've done. You've killed us. Ghost! Dead ghost! Ghost! You've never been born." She ran out into the fields, far enough from the house so that she could no longer hear their voices, and pressed herself against the earth, her own land no more. When she felt the birth coming, she thought that she had been hurt. Her body seized together. "They've hurt me too much," she thought. "This is gall, and it will kill me." With forehead and knees against the earth, her body convulsed and then relaxed. She turned on her back, lay on the ground. The black well of sky and stars went out and out and out forever; her body and her complexity seemed to disappear, without home, without a companion, in eternal cold and silence. An agoraphobia rose in her, speeding higher and higher, bigger and bigger; she would not be able to contain it; there would be no end to fear.

Flayed, unprotected against space, she felt pain return, focusing her body. This pain chilled her—a cold, steady kind of surface pain. Inside, spasmodically, the other pain, the pain of the child, heated her. For hours she lay on the ground, alternately body and space. Sometimes a vision of normal comfort obliterated reality: she saw the family in the evening gambling at the dinner table, the young people massaging their elder's backs. She saw them congratulating one another, high joy on the mornings the rice shoots came up. When these pictures burst, the stars drew yet further apart. Black space opened.

She got to her feet to fight better and remembered that old-fashioned women gave birth in their pigsties to fool the jealous, pain-dealing gods, who do not snatch piglets. Before the next spasms could stop her, she ran to the pigsty, each step a rushing out into emptiness. She climbed over the fence and knelt in the dirt. It was good to have a fence enclosing her, a tribal person alone.

Laboring, this woman who had carried her child as a foreign growth that sickened her every day, expelled it at last. She reached down to touch the hot, wet, moving mass, surely smaller than anything human, and could feel that it was human after all—fingers, toes, nails, nose. She pulled it up on to her belly, and it lay curled there, butt in the air, feet precisely tucked one under the other. She opened her loose shirt and buttoned the child inside. After resting, it squirmed and thrashed and she pushed it up to her breast. It turned its head this way and that until it found her nipple. There, it made little snuffling noises. She clenched her teeth at its preciousness, lovely as a young calf, a piglet, a little dog.

She may have gone to the pigsty as a last act of responsibility: she would protect this child as she had protected its father. It would look after her soul, leaving supplies on her grave. But how would this tiny child without family find her grave when there would be no marker for her anywhere, neither in the earth nor the family hall? No one would give her a family hall name. She had taken the child with her into the wastes. At its birth the two of them had felt the same raw pain of separation, a wound that only the family pressing tight could close. A child with no descent line would not soften her life but only trail after her, ghost-like, begging her to give it purpose. At dawn the villagers on their way to the fields would stand around the fence and look.

45   Full of milk, the little ghost slept. When it awoke, she hardened her breasts against the milk that crying loosens. Toward morning she picked up the baby and walked to the well.

Carrying the baby to the well shows loving. Otherwise abandon it. Turn its face into the mud. Mothers who love their children take them along. It was probably a girl; there is some hope of forgiveness for boys.

"Don't tell anyone you had an aunt. Your father does not want to hear her name. She has never been born." I have believed that sex was unspeakable and words so strong and fathers so frail that "aunt" would do my father mysterious harm. I have thought that my family, having settled among immigrants who had also been their neighbors in the ancestral land, needed to clean their name, and a wrong word would incite the kinspeople even here. But there is more to this silence: they want me to participate in her punishment. And I have.

In the twenty years since I heard this story I have not asked for details nor said my aunt's name; I do not know it. People who can comfort the dead can also chase after them to hurt them further—a reverse ancestor worship. The real punishment was not the raid swiftly inflicted by the villagers, but the family's deliberately forgetting her. Her betrayal so maddened them, they saw to it that she would suffer forever, even after death. Always hungry, always needing, she would have to beg food from other ghosts, snatch and steal it from those whose living descendants give them gifts. She would have to fight the ghosts massed at crossroads for the buns a few thoughtful citizens leave to decoy her away from village and home so that the ancestral spirits could feast unharassed. At peace, they could act like gods, not ghosts, their descent lines providing them with paper suits and dresses, spirit money, paper houses, paper automobiles, chicken, meat, and rice into eternity—essences delivered up in smoke and flames, steam and incense rising from each rice bowl. In an attempt to make the Chinese care for people outside the family, Chairman Mao encourages us now to give our paper replicas to the spirits of outstanding soldiers and workers, no matter whose ancestors they may be. My aunt remains forever hungry. Goods are not distributed evenly among the dead.

My aunt haunts me—her ghost drawn to me because now, after fifty years of neglect, I alone devote pages of paper to her, though not origamied into houses and clothes. I do not think she always means me well. I am telling on her, and she was a spite suicide, drowning herself in the drinking water. The Chinese are always very frightened of the drowned one, whose weeping ghost, wet hair hanging and skin bloated, waits silently by the water to pull down a substitute.

QUESTIONS FOR DISCUSSION

1. Why is this a "story to grow on"? What lesson is it designed to teach? Does the daughter, Maxine, accept her mother's purpose in telling the story, or does she interpret the story to create a new meaning from it?

2. What possible reasons for the aunt's pregnancy and suicide does the narrator propose? What do these different reasons suggest about the status of women in the Chinese family and about the double standard for male and female behavior in Chinese culture prior to World War II? Do you think that in today's Chinese families, men and women are treated equally?

3. Why was it so important for Chinese family members to "efface their sexual color" and to remain silent at meals? How is this ritual reflective of their culture's values?

4. What relationship exists between the individual and the community in the Chinese village of the "No Name Woman"? How is this relationship between the individual and the community different from the one in your neighborhood?

5. Why did the aunt's killing of her infant, combined with her suicide, reflect signs of loving? Why was the infant "probably a girl"?

6. Why does the aunt's ghost continue to haunt the narrator? What perspective on gender roles do they seem to share? In what ways are the two women different from one another?

CONNECTION

Compare the traditional status of women and the punishment of a pregnant woman in a Chinese village as seen in "No Name Woman" with the tragic story of Judith Cofer's pregnant Puerto Rican relative in "Silent Dancing" (see page 151).

IDEAS FOR WRITING

1. Write about a relative who continues to haunt your family or a relative about whom there is a family legend because of his or her sexual life. What does the legacy of this ghostlike figure reflect about your family's values? What impact has it had on your own values?
2. Write about a value or tradition related to gender role or sexuality that your grandparents or parents accepted and that you have rebelled against. What do you think influenced you to believe in values different from those that were accepted by your parents and grandparents? How does this generation gap influence the functioning of your family?

RELATED WEB SITES

Maxine Hong Kingston: Teacher Research Guide
`http://falcon.jmu.edu/~ramseyil/kingston.htm#D`
This site devoted to Maxine Hong Kingston contains lesson plans, bibliographies, links to critical articles, and several biographies.

The Asian-American Literature and the Importance of Social Context
`www.adfl.org/ade/bulletin/n080/080034.htm`
This online article by Elaine Kim is a good introduction to modern Asian American literature; it comments on Maxine Hong Kingston's *Woman Warrior* and places it in a social context along with other Asian American writings of the period.

Mary Pipher

Saplings in the Storm

Mary Pipher was born in 1947 and grew up in Springfield, Missouri. She earned a B.A. in cultural anthropology at the University of California, Berkeley, in 1969 and, at the University of Nebraska–Lincoln, completed her Ph.D. in clinical psychology in 1977. Pipher has a private practice and is a faculty member at the University of Nebraska. Her recent books include Another Country: Navigating the Emotional Terrain of Our Elders *(1999) and* Letters to a Young Therapist *(2003). She is best known for her writing on adolescent girls; her book* Reviving

Ophelia: Saving the Selves of Adolescent Girls *(1994) became an international best-seller and was awarded the American Psychological Association Presidential Citation for excellence. In the following selection from* Reviving Ophelia,
*Pipher describes some of the difficulties that girls today have in making a satisfac-
tory transition from childhood to adolescence.*

JOURNAL

Write about a time in your early adolescent years when you felt you were losing your identity and self-confidence. What factors led to your confusion and
sense of loss?

When my cousin Polly was a girl, she was energy in motion. She danced,
did cartwheels and splits, played football, basketball and baseball with
the neighborhood boys, wrestled with my brothers, biked, climbed trees and
rode horses. She was as lithe and as resilient as a willow branch and as unre-
strained as a lion cub. Polly talked as much as she moved. She yelled out orders and advice, shrieked for joy when she won a bet or heard a good joke,
laughed with her mouth wide open, argued with kids and grown-ups and in-
sulted her foes in the language of a construction worker.

We formed the Marauders, a secret club that met over her garage. Polly was
the Tom Sawyer of the club. She planned the initiations, led the spying expeditions and hikes to haunted houses. She showed us the rituals to become blood
"brothers" and taught us card tricks and how to smoke.

Then Polly had her first period and started junior high. She tried to keep up
her old ways, but she was called a tomboy and chided for not acting more lady-
like. She was excluded by her boy pals and by the girls, who were moving into
makeup and romances.

This left Polly confused and shaky. She had temper tantrums and withdrew
from both the boys' and girls' groups. Later she quieted down and reentered as
Becky Thatcher. She wore stylish clothes and watched from the sidelines as the
boys acted and spoke. Once again she was accepted and popular. She glided
smoothly through our small society. No one spoke of the changes or mourned
the loss of our town's most dynamic citizen. I was the only one who felt that a
tragedy had transpired.

5   Girls in what Freud called the latency period, roughly age six or seven
through puberty, are anything but latent. I think of my daughter Sara during
those years—performing chemistry experiments and magic tricks, playing her
violin, starring in her own plays, rescuing wild animals and biking all over town.
I think of her friend Tamara, who wrote a 300-page novel the summer of her
sixth-grade year. I remember myself, reading every children's book in the library
of my town. One week I planned to be a great doctor like Albert Schweitzer. The
next week I wanted to write like Louisa May Alcott or dance in Paris like Isadora
Duncan. I have never since had as much confidence or ambition.

Most preadolescent girls are marvelous company because they are interested in everything—sports, nature, people, music and books. Almost all the heroines of girls' literature come from this age group—Anne of Green Gables, Heidi, Pippi Longstocking and Caddie Woodlawn. Girls this age bake pies, solve mysteries and go on quests. They can take care of themselves and are not yet burdened with caring for others. They have a brief respite from the female role and can be tomboys, a word that conveys courage, competency and irreverence.

They can be androgynous, having the ability to act adaptively in any situation regardless of gender role constraints. An androgynous person can comfort a baby or change a tire, cook a meal or chair a meeting. Research has shown that, since they are free to act without worrying if their behavior is feminine or masculine, androgynous adults are the most well adjusted.

Girls between seven and eleven rarely come to therapy. They don't need it. I can count on my fingers the girls this age whom I have seen: Coreen, who was physically abused; Anna, whose parents were divorcing; and Brenda, whose father killed himself. These girls were courageous and resilient. Brenda said, "If my father didn't want to stick around, that's his loss." Coreen and Anna were angry, not at themselves, but rather at the grown-ups, who they felt were making mistakes. It's amazing how little help these girls needed from me to heal and move on.

A horticulturist told me a revealing story. She led a tour of junior-high girls who were attending a math and science fair on her campus. She showed them side oats grama, bluestem, Indian grass and trees—redbud, maple, walnut and willow. The younger girls interrupted each other with their questions and tumbled forward to see, touch and smell everything. The older girls, the ninth-graders, were different. They hung back. They didn't touch plants or shout out questions. They stood primly to the side, looking bored and even a little disgusted by the enthusiasm of their younger classmates. My friend asked herself, What's happened to these girls? What's gone wrong? She told me, "I wanted to shake them, to say, 'Wake up, come back. Is anybody home at your house?'"

10   Recently I sat sunning on a bench outside my favorite ice-cream store. A mother and her teenage daughter stopped in front of me and waited for the light to change. I heard the mother say, "You have got to stop blackmailing your father and me. Every time you don't get what you want, you tell us that you want to run away from home or kill yourself. What's happened to you? You used to be able to handle not getting your way."

The daughter stared straight ahead, barely acknowledging her mother's words. The light changed. I licked my ice-cream cone. Another mother approached the same light with her preadolescent daughter in tow. They were holding hands. The daughter said to her mother, "This is fun. Let's do this all afternoon."

Something dramatic happens to girls in early adolescence. Just as planes and ships disappear mysteriously into the Bermuda Triangle, so do the selves of girls go down in droves. They crash and burn in a social and developmental

Bermuda Triangle. In early adolescence, studies show that girls' IQ scores drop and their math and science scores plummet. They lose their resiliency and optimism and become less curious and inclined to take risks. They lose their assertive, energetic and "tomboyish" personalities and become more deferential, self-critical and depressed. They report great unhappiness with their own bodies.

Psychology documents but does not explain the crashes. Girls who rushed to drink in experiences in enormous gulps sit quietly in the corner. Writers such as Sylvia Plath, Margaret Atwood and Olive Schreiner have described the wreckage. Diderot, in writing to his young friend Sophie Volland, described his observations harshly: "You all die at 15."

Fairy tales capture the essence of this phenomenon. Young women eat poisoned apples or prick their fingers with poisoned needles and fall asleep for a hundred years. They wander away from home, encounter great dangers, are rescued by princes and are transformed into passive and docile creatures.

15 The story of Ophelia, from Shakespeare's *Hamlet,* shows the destructive forces that affect young women. As a girl, Ophelia is happy and free, but with adolescence she loses herself. When she falls in love with Hamlet, she lives only for his approval. She has no inner direction; rather she struggles to meet the demands of Hamlet and her father. Her value is determined utterly by their approval. Ophelia is torn apart by her efforts to please. When Hamlet spurns her because she is an obedient daughter, she goes mad with grief. Dressed in elegant clothes that weigh her down, she drowns in a stream filled with flowers.

Girls know they are losing themselves. One girl said, "Everything good in me died in junior high." Wholeness is shattered by the chaos of adolescence. Girls become fragmented, their selves split into mysterious contradictions. They are sensitive and tenderhearted, mean and competitive, superficial and idealistic. They are confident in the morning and overwhelmed with anxiety by nightfall. They rush through their days with wild energy and then collapse into lethargy. They try on new roles every week—this week the good student, next week the delinquent and the next, the artist. And they expect their families to keep up with these changes.

My clients in early adolescence are elusive and slow to trust adults. They are easily offended by a glance, a clearing of the throat, a silence, a lack of sufficient enthusiasm or a sentence that doesn't meet their immediate needs. Their voices have gone underground—their speech is more tentative and less articulate. Their moods swing widely. One week they love their world and their families, the next they are critical of everyone. Much of their behavior is unreadable. Their problems are complicated and metaphorical—eating disorders, school phobias and self-inflicted injuries. I need to ask again and again in a dozen different ways, "What are you trying to tell me?"

Michelle, for example, was a beautiful, intelligent seventeen-year-old. Her mother brought her in after she became pregnant for the third time in three years. I tried to talk about why this was happening. She smiled a Mona Lisa smile to all my questions. "No, I don't care all that much for sex." "No, I didn't plan this. It just happened." When Michelle left a session, I felt like I'd been talking in the wrong language to someone far away.

Holly was another mystery. She was shy, soft-spoken and slow-moving, pretty under all her makeup and teased red hair. She was a Prince fan and wore only purple. Her father brought her in after a suicide attempt. She wouldn't study, do chores, join any school activities or find a job. Holly answered questions in patient, polite monosyllables. She really talked only when the topic was Prince. For several weeks we talked about him. She played me his tapes. Prince somehow spoke for her and to her.

20   Gail burned and cut herself when she was unhappy. Dressed in black, thin as a straw, she sat silently before me, her hair a mess, her ears, lips and nose all pierced with rings. She spoke about Bosnia and the hole in the ozone layer and asked me if I liked rave music. When I asked about her life, she fingered her earrings and sat silently.

My clients are not different from girls who are not seen in therapy. I teach at a small liberal arts college and the young women in my classes have essentially the same experiences as my therapy clients. One student worried about her best friend who'd been sexually assaulted. Another student missed class after being beaten by her boyfriend. Another asked what she should do about crank calls from a man threatening to rape her. When stressed, another student stabbed her hand with paper clips until she drew blood. Many students have wanted advice on eating disorders.

After I speak at high schools, girls approach me to say that they have been raped, or they want to run away from home, or that they have a friend who is anorexic or alcoholic. At first all this trauma surprised me. Now I expect it.

Psychology has a long history of ignoring girls this age. Until recently adolescent girls haven't been studied by academics, and they have long baffled therapists. Because they are secretive with adults and full of contradictions, they are difficult to study. So much is happening internally that's not communicated on the surface.

Simone de Beauvoir believed adolescence is when girls realize that men have the power and that their only power comes from consenting to become submissive adored objects. They do not suffer from the penis envy Freud postulated, but from power envy.

25   She described the Bermuda Triangle this way: Girls who were the subjects of their own lives become the objects of others' lives. "Young girls slowly bury their childhood, put away their independent and imperious selves and submissively enter adult existence." Adolescent girls experience a conflict between their autonomous selves and their need to be feminine, between their status as human beings and their vocation as females. De Beauvoir says, "Girls stop being and start seeming."

Girls become "female impersonators" who fit their whole selves into small, crowded spaces. Vibrant, confident girls become shy, doubting young women. Girls stop thinking, "Who am I? What do I want?" and start thinking, "What must I do to please others?"

This gap between girls' true selves and cultural prescriptions for what is properly female creates enormous problems. To paraphrase a Stevie Smith poem about swimming in the sea, "they are not waving, they are drowning." And just when they most need help, they are unable to take their parents' hands.

Olive Schreiner wrote of her experiences as a young girl in *The Story of an African Farm.* "The world tells us what we are to be and shapes us by the ends it sets before us. To men it says, work. To us, it says, seem. The less a woman has in her head the lighter she is for carrying." She described the finishing school that she attended in this way: "It was a machine for condensing the soul into the smallest possible area. I have seen some souls so compressed that they would have filled a small thimble."

Margaret Mead believed that the ideal culture is one in which there is a place for every human gift. By her standards, our Western culture is far from ideal for women. So many gifts are unused and unappreciated. So many voices are stilled. Stendhal wrote: "All geniuses born women are lost to the public good."

30 Alice Miller wrote of the pressures on some young children to deny their true selves and assume false selves to please their parents. *Reviving Ophelia* suggests that adolescent girls experience a similar pressure to split into true and false selves, but this time the pressure comes not from parents but from the culture. Adolescence is when girls experience social pressure to put aside their authentic selves and to display only a small portion of their gifts.

This pressure disorients and depresses most girls. They sense the pressure to be someone they are not. They fight back, but they are fighting a "problem with no name." One girl put it this way: "I'm a perfectly good carrot that everyone is trying to turn into a rose. As a carrot, I have good color and a nice leafy top. When I'm carved into a rose, I turn brown and wither."

Adolescent girls are saplings in a hurricane. They are young and vulnerable trees that the winds blow with gale strength. Three factors make young women vulnerable to the hurricane. One is their developmental level. Everything is changing—body shape, hormones, skin and hair. Calmness is replaced by anxiety. Their way of thinking is changing. Far below the surface they are struggling with the most basic of human questions: What is my place in the universe, what is my meaning?

Second, American culture has always smacked girls on the head in early adolescence. This is when they move into a broader culture that is rife with girl-hurting "isms," such as sexism, capitalism and lookism, which is the evaluation of a person solely on the basis of appearance.

Third, American girls are expected to distance from parents just at the time when they most need their support. As they struggle with countless new pressures, they must relinquish the protection and closeness they've felt with their families in childhood. They turn to their none-too-constant peers for support.

35 Parents know only too well that something is happening to their daughters. Calm, considerate daughters grow moody, demanding and distant. Girls who loved to talk are sullen and secretive. Girls who liked to hug now bristle when touched. Mothers complain that they can do nothing right in the eyes of their

daughters. Involved fathers bemoan their sudden banishment from their daughters' lives. But few parents realize how universal their experiences are. Their daughters are entering a new land, a dangerous place that parents can scarcely comprehend. Just when they most need a home base, they cut themselves loose without radio communications.

Most parents of adolescent girls have the goal of keeping their daughters safe while they grow up and explore the world. The parents' job is to protect. The daughters' job is to explore. Always these different tasks have created tension in parent-daughter relationships, but now it's even harder. Generally parents are more protective of their daughters than is corporate America. Parents aren't trying to make money off their daughters by selling them designer jeans or cigarettes, they just want them to be well adjusted. They don't see their daughters as sex objects or consumers but as real people with talents and interests. But daughters turn away from their parents as they enter the new land. They befriend their peers, who are their fellow inhabitants of the strange country and who share a common language and set of customs. They often embrace the junk values of mass culture.

This turning away from parents is partly for developmental reasons. Early adolescence is a time of physical and psychological change, self-absorption, preoccupation with peer approval and identity formation. It's a time when girls focus inward on their own fascinating changes.

It's partly for cultural reasons. In America we define adulthood as a moving away from families into broader culture. Adolescence is the time for cutting bonds and breaking free. Adolescents may claim great independence from parents, but they are aware and ashamed of their parents' smallest deviation from the norm. They don't like to be seen with them and find their imperfections upsetting. A mother's haircut or a father's joke can ruin their day. Teenagers are furious at parents who say the wrong things or do not respond with perfect answers. Adolescents claim not to hear their parents, but with their friends they discuss endlessly all parental attitudes. With amazing acuity, they sense nuances, doubt, shades of ambiguity, discrepancy and hypocrisy.

Adolescents still have some of the magical thinking of childhood and believe that parents have the power to keep them safe and happy. They blame their parents for their misery, yet they make a point of not telling their parents how they think and feel; they have secrets, so things can get crazy. For example, girls who are raped may not tell their parents. Instead, they become hostile and rebellious. Parents bring girls in because of their anger and out-of-control behavior. When I hear about this unexplainable anger, I ask about rape. Ironically, girls are often angrier at their parents than at the rapists. They feel their parents should have known about the danger and been more protective; afterward, they should have sensed the pain and helped.

40   Most parents feel like failures during this time. They feel shut out, impotent and misunderstood. They often attribute the difficulties of this time to their daughters and their own failings. They don't understand that these problems go with the developmental stage, the culture and the times.

Parents experience an enormous sense of loss when their girls enter this new land. They miss the daughters who sang in the kitchen, who read them school papers, who accompanied them on fishing trips and to ball games. They miss the daughters who liked to bake cookies, play Pictionary and be kissed goodnight. In place of their lively, affectionate daughters they have changelings—new girls who are sadder, angrier and more complicated. Everyone is grieving.

Fortunately adolescence is time-limited. By late high school most girls are stronger and the winds are dying down. Some of the worst problems—cliques, a total focus on looks and struggles with parents—are on the wane. But the way girls handle the problems of adolescence can have implications for their adult lives. Without some help, the loss of wholeness, self-confidence and self-direction can last well into adulthood. Many adult clients struggle with the same issues that overwhelmed them as adolescent girls. Thirty-year-old accountants and realtors, forty-year-old homemakers and doctors, and thirty-five-year-old nurses and schoolteachers ask the same questions and struggle with the same problems as their teenage daughters.

Even sadder are the women who are not struggling, who have forgotten that they have selves worth defending. They have repressed the pain of their adolescence, the betrayals of self in order to be pleasing. These women come to therapy with the goal of becoming even more pleasing to others. They come to lose weight, to save their marriages or to rescue their children. When I ask them about their own needs, they are confused by the question.

Most women struggled alone with the trauma of adolescence and have led decades of adult life with their adolescent experiences unexamined. The lessons learned in adolescence are forgotten and their memories of pain are minimized. They come into therapy because their marriage is in trouble, or they hate their job, or their own daughter is giving them fits. Maybe their daughter's pain awakens their own pain. Some are depressed or chemically addicted or have stress-related illnesses—ulcers, colitis, migraines or psoriasis. Many have tried to be perfect women and failed. Even though they followed the rules and did as they were told, the world has not rewarded them. They feel angry and betrayed. They feel miserable and taken for granted, used rather than loved.

45   Women often know how everyone in their family thinks and feels except themselves. They are great at balancing the needs of their co-workers, husbands, children and friends, but they forget to put themselves into the equation. They struggle with adolescent questions still unresolved: How important are looks and popularity? How do I care for myself and not be selfish? How can I be honest and still be loved? How can I achieve and not threaten others? How can I be sexual and not a sex object? How can I be responsive but not responsible for everyone?

As we talk, the years fall away. We are back in junior high with the cliques, the shame, the embarrassment about bodies, the desire to be accepted and the doubts about ability. So many adult women think they are stupid and ugly.

Many feel guilty if they take time for themselves. They do not express anger or ask for help.

We talk about childhood—what the woman was like at ten and at fifteen. We piece together a picture of childhood lost. We review her own particular story, her own time in the hurricane. Memories flood in. Often there are tears, angry outbursts, sadness for what has been lost. So much time has been wasted pretending to be who others wanted. But also, there's a new energy that comes from making connections, from choosing awareness over denial and from the telling of secrets.

We work now, twenty years behind schedule. We reestablish each woman as the subject of her life, not as the object of others' lives. We answer Freud's patronizing question "What do women want?" Each woman wants something different and particular and yet each woman wants the same thing—to be who she truly is, to become who she can become.

Many women regain their preadolescent authenticity with menopause. Because they are no longer beautiful objects occupied primarily with caring for others, they are free once again to become the subjects of their own lives. They become more confident, self-directed and energetic. Margaret Mead noticed this phenomenon in cultures all over the world and called it "pmz," postmenopausal zest. She noted that some cultures revere these older women. Others burn them at the stake.

QUESTIONS FOR DISCUSSION

1. What point does Pipher make through the narrative about her cousin Polly? What specific details does Pipher use to make Polly's adolescent transformation vivid and disturbing?

2. Why and how does Pipher disagree with Freud about the "latency period"? What personal examples does she use to make her point about this important stage in a girl's life? Why do girls in this period of their lives seldom begin therapy?

3. How does the horticulturist's story about two different age groups of girls on a campus tour support Pipher's argument about the difference between preadolescent and adolescent girls? What other contrasting stories does Pipher use persuasively?

4. How does Pipher use the story of Ophelia and narratives from her own patients to support her argument about adolescent transformation?

5. What is Simone de Beauvoir's view of adolescent female power envy? How do adolescent girls become "female impersonators"? Why does culture pressure them to "assume false selves," in Pipher's view? Do you agree? Explain your point of view.

6. According to Pipher, what three factors make girls vulnerable to the "hurricane" of adolescence? How have the traditional pressures on girls increased in recent years? Why is the "reality of discrimination" even more confusing for modern girls than in the past?

CONNECTION

Compare Pipher's examples of the pressures and confusion of adolescent females today with Lamott's narrative of her own experiences as a young
woman from her essay "Hunger" in Chapter 5 (see page 298).

IDEAS FOR WRITING

1. Write an essay in which you argue whether girls entering adolescence
   today have greater pressures and difficulties than young women in previous generations. Do some research into this subject; try doing interviews
   with older women about problems they encountered in adolescence; contrast their views with those of young women you interview.
2. In an essay based on personal experience and research, present some
   possible solutions for the gender-based pressure adolescent girls experience today.

RELATED WEB SITES

Reading Group Guide to *Reviving Ophelia*
`www.readinggroupguides.com/guides/reviving_`
`ophelia-author.asp#bio`
This reading guide contains an interview with Mary Pipher, study questions, a
biography, and an excerpt from the text.

Girl Power!
`www.girlpower.gov/AdultsWhoCare/campinfo/hometown/`
`quickstats.htm`
Girl Power is a Web site for the national public education campaign sponsored by the U.S. Department of Health and Human Services to help encourage and motivate 9- to 13-year-old girls to make the most of their lives. The
site contains health messages and statistics related to typical problems encountered by this age group.

Tajamika Paxton

Loving a One-armed Man

*After graduating from Georgetown University, Tajamaka Paxton has held a cre-
ative executive position at MTV Films, where she worked on* The Wood *and the
Academy Award–nominated* Election. *She is currently the executive producer of
the feature film division of Forest Whitaker's Spirit Dance Entertainment, where
she produced* Green Dragon *(2001) and* Chasing Papi *(2003). Paxton is also*

a member of the Black Women's Network and the Board of Directors of Outfest, a nonprofit organization that exhibits high-quality gay, lesbian, bisexual, and transgender themed films and videos in an annual festival in southern California. She writes personal essays that analyze the gender and ethnic issues of her own experiences. The essay included here, "Loving a One-armed Man" (2004), is an examination of her evolving relationship and understanding of her father and his troubled vision of African American manhood.

| JOURNAL |

Write about a difficult time in your relationship with a parent or partner when you found it difficult to accept his or her personal vision or "myth" of masculinity or femininity.

There's a man coming toward me. Together we're in the middle of a city street: people move hurriedly around us, but he and I don't rush. He walks slowly, almost ambling. He's returning home from a war. He went into battle resilient and optimistic that the world would yield for him and if it didn't he would take it down or die trying, extricating from the struggle a sense of power and self-determination. Instead, he's left "head bloody but unbowed" with his jacket neatly folded over the space where his arm once was. He has stories to tell about how the arm was blown off and other battles fought, but no story can match the intensity of living through it, the lesions the living creates on your soul. This one-armed man is an image I get in a dream. He's the symbol of men being torn apart by the impossible demands of one-dimensional manhood. The real man, fully limbed, is my father, Cassius Paxton.

My father is a veteran not of war, but of life lived within the cage of conflicting expectations particular to Black men born in America. Men who are told to be powerful in spite of economic cycles and discrimination that leave them powerless, and ordered to be rugged when the centuries-old healing they so desperately require demands sensitivity. I remember him as easily threatened, his wrath easily ignited. Self-taught and thus well educated, but lacking the resolve to use that education for his own prosperity. Instead, he chose to become an opportunist, a hustler, someone willing to take from others in a world where Black men go to prison for the same crimes that put White men in office. He spent his youth arrogant. He believed being quite handsome and charming would sustain him, perhaps lead him to the good life he saw in men like Nat King Cole and Sam Cooke.

My daddy is 62 and that man he once was is long gone. Now, he wants to tell other men what he's learned so they can avoid roads paved with personal regrets, the lingering numbness of unrealized dreams or ex-wives and children they never see. He's living with the unanswered question of what to do with those years and the sinking thought that he could have done more. My daddy has prostate cancer and cirrhosis. My daddy is dying. Maybe not today or next year but soon, he thinks, and because no one else in my family speaks to him, I feel like I'm the only one watching. I'm witnessing the transformation of his manhood like a scripted Hollywood film where the debonair leading man comes to some conclusive arc that makes the time watching his character worthwhile.

We're growing closer now. An extension of where we were in the picture I keep on my shelf. Cheek to cheek, his strong amateur middleweight boxing hands wrapped around my tiny three-year-old ones. Closer because we're determined to keep our connection despite the past and because of the future. My mother, his ex-wife of 21 years, talks to him when she must. She makes no pretense of truly caring if he changes or not. My father and I acknowledge the pain of the absence of my brothers. One lives locally and is being ravaged by some of the same addictions that plagued my father. High or sober, it's emotionally difficult for him to face my father, to have a conversation like two adults. He resorts to sickening depictions of his masculinity, bragging about his inability to cook and how his wife prepares meals and how other women respond to him when he's in public. My father usually stares at him pitifully. He probably hears his own father's cryptic words, "One day, son, you'll understand," and wishes that my brother would stand still and engage in a realistic conversation about what it's going to take for him not to die dirty in some hallway.

5   The other brother lives far away with his six children. He thinks having so many children is manly but cries like a baby when he's arrested for not paying his child support. My father sends no money, only admonition. "Son, you made that bed, you lie in it. Don't run from it now. It's not going anywhere." Today his advice is simple, too simple for my psychoanalytic tastes. He says people make two choices: do or don't. It's this simple creed that gave him the resolve to give up narcotics years ago and in 1996, to stop drinking before his habit killed him. So my father is changing and I am alone, listening. Listening to the stories of what life was like for him at 35 and why he sometimes behaved horribly in the name of being a man.

I remember my father as two men, distinct but with the same form. A manchild, he would sit for hours and play Atari Pac-Man with me after school, but a trip to the store that same night could mean a four-day absence. I would walk home wondering if his car was safely back in the driveway, like a friend waiting for me in front of a rickety swing, faithful. When it wasn't there, I suppressed my loss, but it metastasized into a resounding mistrust of all men. I lived, and at times, continue to live, with a sense that I would inevitably be let down, left waiting and alone. When he returned home after those times he offered no explanations and grew sullen when asked. Instead of communicating through the vulnerable places, I learned from my father to get silent and the world will walk away. Not so different from my brothers, I too adapted my father's stoic veneer as protection when I felt emotionally vulnerable.

At a recent birthday lunch, he shared the pain and pressure of the responsibility of parenting when he felt like such a young man, incapable of taking care of himself. He explained and, in his way, apologized for being an inadequate provider; for not having the resilience to consistently raise his children or the patience and understanding to love his wife. When the pressures mounted, he took flight.

I appreciate his candor and experience it as a step toward me. I meet him there, trying to talk to him every day partially because I have so many unanswered questions. Questions like "Why did you get so sad during Christmas?" One Christmas morning we found him in the bathtub obviously high, pupils dilated and stinging from tears. Looking broken and attempting to be coy, he asked what I thought of the gold necklace he had bought and bragged about its cost. He wouldn't respond to our pleading eyes or to my mother's seething resentment. I remember thanking him and wondering what could make a grown man cry at Christmas. To this day I care little for gold.

We don't talk much about the violence. He has taken to believing that he hasn't harmed anyone. It's easier than believing that he's scarred someone beyond repair. I don't pretend to understand this approach but it works for him and after years of tantrums, I've given up the need for blame. Some things must stay in the past so they don't choke the life out of what you're trying to create. But I can't forget. On two occasions, he beat my brothers mercilessly, and I can see clearly the afternoon my mother was cleaning our room and he dragged her out of it by her hair, her leg tearing as the flesh caught ahold of the sharp metal of my brother's bike pedal. Along with horror I was flooded with guilt. Could we have pushed the bike closer to the wall? The sound of her screaming, her open mouth begging, but I can't see his face. I wanted it be someone else, a stranger, not my father. My father who propped me up on the armrest while we rode through the streets of Los Angeles telling me stories of city landmarks and the time he hung out all night with Dinah Washington. My father who played with my hair for hours determined that his baby have an Afro.

10   I found some aspect of this man everywhere I went to look for love. By the grace of God, he was never violent. He was edgy, intelligent, magnetic and usually unavailable. Armed. He was my roughneck, and I was faithful to his type, always wanting to get beneath the armor, to try to make him be gentle with me. They could all be summed up with one. We met at a club dancing to "O.P.P." He knew all the lyrics and recited them through gold teeth emblazoned with his initials as he guided me to the dance floor. Later, I rejoiced when underneath the sagging pants and the heavy New York accent, I uncovered a man who played lacrosse despite the rough inner city upbringing he feigned; a man who talked for hours about growing up mixed race in Long Island. We talked about many subjects but not each other's needs. We exchanged easy childhood stories, more song lyrics, warm laughs and sweaty, disconnected sex. But we quickly tired of playing games the wounded play, neither willing to truly disarm. And I returned to my pattern of reaching for cool, tough men like my father.

The father I know now would not strike out against those he loves. In fact he sits in agony as he hears his neighbors beating each other to signal they're alive. In this new man I see a strong desire to be forgiven and loved. His calls are frequent, usually establishing when we'll spend our next moments to-gether. The attention he wants from his family and the advice he needs to share is urgent to him, his sustenance.

Little of his old masculinity is of use to him now, not much of it can help him fight the diseases inside him. Not the white Cadillac, once a symbol of his street status and now delivering him to frequent doctors' appointments every week. Not the women he allowed to distract him from his marriage. Most of them are dead or just gone. There's a kind one by his side now. She makes it easier to bear but she can't save him. His gold jewelry can't buy him any more time. Not even his once perfect biceps and his right hook. Using our kitchen as a ring, he once showed my brothers and I how to throw and block punches and stay off the ropes. The irony is overwhelming. Even the dominator, the dark side of him, is rendered useless. Age doesn't respond to bullying and there's no one else to rule over. He is left cultivating life-affirming skills he never found relevant. He's relying on spiritual fortitude to keep him grounded and hopeful. He's learning more about the cancer-fighting benefits of an organic diet. He listens to his mother.

Twelve years ago when he was injured in a car accident he joked that he had earned a purple heart from the streets of Oakland: he'd been shot, stabbed with a knife and an ice pick and none of those things could take him out. But I know this illness is different. "It's going to be the fight of my life," he says. Indeed. The harrowing facts about the survival rate for Black men are hum-bling. The doctors tell him to keep a positive attitude and not to succumb to the fatigue. He says, "My attitude is positive. And I'm tired." In the next hour, he's buoyant again, doing the calisthenics recommended by the doctor to strengthen his body before the radiation begins.

I admire how he now accepts the range of his feelings, not forcing himself into some stoic display of strength. He plans his life in days, maybe weeks if he's feeling optimistic. He says he just simply doesn't want to go yet; there are more days of sunshine, more long drives, boxing on TV every Saturday night, and a longing for creative fulfillment. I talk to him about the summer road trips we'll take together, but it's hard to experience just coming to know someone who could leave so soon.

15   What we have is a return to tenderness. Much is said about returning to the maternal "womb." I consider what we're engaged in now a return to the pater-nal womb, that place upon my father's chest where as a little girl I would rest comfortably and listen to his heart beating and think it the most melodious sound, comforting and truly strong. I hug this "one-armed man" frequently, and love him for the way he hugs me back generously, and for the meals he pre-pares for me with care. I love him for the considerate way he sends me home before it gets too late, and for the way I can cry on the phone with him about a thwarted romance and he'll paint a picture of my tomorrows and all the loves I'll have. It reminds me that this part of him was always there, beneath the fury.

I greedily devour him all for me. My brothers don't want to hear him talk about responsibility; they're sharpening their weaponry. During the three years

I refused to speak to him, I did the same, but now I relate to him as a disarmed man, not just because that's what he, in the face of aging and death, has finally become, but because I need my own disarmament.

My life had been lacking true openness, an openness that says I am here, love me or not; and if you don't, I have what it takes to tend my own garden. I hadn't tended my garden. I was coping. In the wake of my internal chaos I had embarked on my own nightmare of working hard to achieve success and unconsciously hoping it would fill the neglected spaces in me, the voids created by unprocessed childhood pains and the slashes made by years of broken relationships. I was looking for a fulfillment that came from high-powered salaries and expense accounts. I adapted the masculinity myth for myself, suppressing yin gentility and overdeveloping yang aggression, convincing myself that aggressive people get farther faster and that the same aggression would repel those who might do me harm. I locked away my sense of play and simple pleasure convinced that only "girls" play and get hurt; tough women don't. I presented this armor proudly to the world until I began to suffocate inside the suit.

I loved the same way. Strong and tough but underneath, easily bruised and braced for inevitable disappointment. I was holding onto resentment for the apologies I hadn't received from my father and for all my failed attempts at disarmament. I relied on my relationships to feel that I was wanted, that what I had to offer was valuable. If a potential lover didn't respond to me, I sat dejected, a flood of insecurity overtaking me. From this desperate place I clung tightly to all lovers. When relationships ended, I was broken, trapped in romantic notions that someone could "steal my heart."

I had been avoiding the truth that I am emotionally responsible for delivering my happiness. In these last months I have come to see more clearly that I am responsible for my inner work, for spending quality time with me; for affirming my radiance, for saying yes to those deepest unspoken desires and living a life unbridled by comparisons or the judgments of others. With this awareness, I now see that no amount of protective covering can shield me. That what I needed and am finding is an inner fortification as essential as breath itself.

20   And so at 31, I shed my armor. As I do, I see that remarkable scene from *The Wiz*. After the witch has been killed, her former sweatshop slaves peel off their stifling furry costumes and begin to dance. They clap thunderously, gliding in a criss-cross formation stage left and stage right. They sing with rousing gospel harmonies, "Can you feel a brand-new day? Can you feel a brand-new day? Hello, world, it's like a different way of living now. Thank you, world, we always knew that we'd be free somehow."

It is a brand new day for relating—to my father, to my lovers, to myself. I'm learning to love the men in my life in a place beyond sex and romantic interest, with a genuine closeness that touches the strong and tender beating heart that I once knew. I've decided to love as an act of surrender, not a declaration of war, fighting for my protection and survival. I know now to look for those men disarmed of their own volition, willing to let me touch their soft places and I am willing to let them touch mine, with an understanding of how fragile we all really are. I move closer to a man who can raise his hand in protest to an unjust world and bring it to rest gently on my waist.

I'm one of a collective of people coming home from the same war trying to cross burned bridges with worn-out shoes; we're tired but we have not given up. We're marching forward to a new way of being with and for each other, offering gentleness and attention, exchanging bravado for emotional bravery. Taking responsibility for our individual pasts and sorting through which needs are our own to meet, and which we can expect to be met by others. Willing to offer each other our fidelity not because we're supposed to but because we respect the time it takes to make love in this inundated world. We're creating a space to collectively acknowledge that there has been a war going on and we are committed to the work of rebuilding.

My father and I are doing this work privately, learning how to love each other, to be tender with each other, to put down our guns together. With this newfound freedom, I can finally allow him to make me a promise and believe that he'll keep it, knowing that if he doesn't I can forgive him and he can forgive himself. So much of this has come because we're willing to strain the muscles of trust until they hurt but in the hurting, they expand our mutual compassion and love.

I no longer subscribe to the crippling belief that he, or other men, can't emotionally handle the delicate places in relationships. Perhaps the inner fortification I'm finding is what my father needed long ago to feel safe and truly powerful. He is finding his way to it now. I send grace for his journey and along with it blessings for all of the many men still gasping for air inside their suffocating suits of armor. These men hunger for a new code that will offer them liberation, a code found in books like this one and in nationwide barbershop and boardroom discussions.

25   I'm getting a glimpse of a new dream, different from the one-armed man trudging down the street. I'm imagining a world without battle-scarred soldiers of life who have to be maimed or die in order to become heroic, a world without men who have to wage war to prove their point. This world is full of men who are heroic because they have the courage to nurture their families with a gentle confident strength, to teach children, their own and others, how to be humane, how to live in harmony with those considered different, how to practice spirituality in a world that overvalues the material. Heroic because they know the task of transformation is difficult but they take action anyway because they know it must be done.

Heroic like my father. He is far from perfect and I am farther but together we're reaching. And I'm like a little West African girl going from village to village beating the drum, hailing the sound of the new arrival.

QUESTIONS FOR DISCUSSION

1. What is the significance of the author's dream of a one-armed veteran? Why does she begin the essay with this dream, and how does it relate to her own father, a veteran of a different type of war?

2. How would you describe Paxton's father's concept of masculinity? In what sense is it born out of "the cage of conflicting expectations" of black manhood in America? How did Paxton's father's idea of masculinity disconnect him from his family and destroy his health?
3. What advice would Paxton's father like to give his sons? What stories can he now share with his daughter? What influence on her values and choices in men has he had?
4. What does the author mean by "disarming"? Why was her father's disarmament important for her? In what sense had she "adapted the masculinity myth [for herself]"?
5. What does the author mean when she says that she now sees "love as an act of surrender"? Why does this signify a "brand new day for relating" for her?
6. Why does Paxton come to see herself as a veteran returning from war, "exchanging bravado for emotional bravery"? What is the difference between these two terms? How does her "new dream" contrast to the original dream narrated in the introduction?

CONNECTION

Compare the images and ideas of masculinity presented through Paxton's father to those of Kevin Canty in his autobiographical essay "The Dog in Me," (see page 369).

IDEAS FOR WRITING

1. Write an essay in which you describe the vision of masculinity presented in this essay. What social and cultural factors cause such a view of masculinity to emerge in an individual, and how is it destructive to family life and relationships? Present examples of such "one-dimensional manhood" from your own experience and reading.
2. Write an essay about a program that can help a man or woman to make the transition from a destructive attitude of "bravado" to a state of "emotional bravery" as described in the final paragraphs of Paxton's essay. Do some research into different types of support groups and/or a series of steps that an individual can take to make such a major life transition.

RELATED WEB SITES

Young Dads
`www.findarticles.com/p/articles/mi_m2248/is_148_37/`
`ai_97723206/pg_3`
This article from the magazine *Adolescence* (2002) examines a program that shows promise for encouraging responsibility for family on the part of urban African American adolescent fathers.

The American Prospect: The Politics of Family
`www.prospect.org/web/page.ww?name=View+Issue&section=root&`
`id=106`

This issue of *The American Prospect* focuses on politically sensitive and controversial issues of family life, featuring links and articles related to fatherhood and minority families, gay marriage, poverty and the family, and reproductive rights.

Rachel Lehmann-Haupt

Multi-Tasking Man

Rachel Lehmann-Haupt has a B.A. in English literature from Kenyon College and an M.A. from the Graduate School of Journalism at the University of California, Berkeley. While at UC Berkeley she was founding editor of F *magazine, a postfeminist zine. She currently writes fiction and essays about gender politics and media culture. Her articles have appeared in many publications including the* New York Times, Wired, Vogue, US News and World Report, *and* Business Week. *The essay that we have selected, "The Multi-Tasking Man," appeared in* What Makes a Man: 22 Writers Imagine the Future *(2004), and suggests alternatives to the current way that men handle the demands of work and family.*

JOURNAL

Do you consider yourself talented at "multitasking"? Give an example of one of your successes or failures at handling several activities at the same time.

Feminism's first supermodel was an ancient goddess. As the story goes, Mahisa, a rebellious and greedy god, seized the celestial kingdom when his creator, Brahman, denied him immortality. The gods became so incensed by this tyrant that in order to win back their kingdom they combined their powers to produce a divine force in the form of a beautiful woman. Durga was a shapely siren with eight wild arms wielding deadly weapons.

Whirling her mighty arms, Durga sought Mahisa and seduced him. When he fell in love with her, she smiled, batted her wide eyes, and whispered that she could only marry a man who could defeat her in battle. Mahisa was charmed by her challenge, and so sure that he could beat a woman that he took her on.

Their battle was fierce. Mahisa, slick and focused, maneuvered in between and around the swipes of Durga's weapons. The goddess struggled, but didn't give up. When Mahisa was convinced that he had won, she suddenly overwhelmed him with the whisk of her arms and won the battle with a deadly blow to his heart.

In 1972 this multiarmed goddess appeared on the premiere issue of *Ms.* magazine. This time she juggled new weapons: a telephone, a steering wheel, an iron, a clock, a feather duster, a frying pan, a mirror, and a typewriter. There she was in high gloss, with her head tilted in a luring glance, dainty smirk, and demure eyes. She was no longer delivering blows to the ancients, but a modern media message to thousands of housewives and husbands of post–World War II America. A woman's ancient power to juggle multiple tasks, she declared, was the key to the economic power that would free her from cloistered suburbia, house-bound ennui, and Freudian shackles that held that anatomy is destiny.

5   Helen Fisher, the feminist anthropologist, in her book *The First Sex,* says that a woman's skill to juggle multiple tasks evolved out of men and women's naturally separate worlds—and naturally different brain structures—that date back millions of years to the sunburnt plains of East Africa. The women of the tribal village were responsible for gathering more than half of the meal, taking care of the children, watching out for wild animals, and managing the social and marketing networks of the village. The village men were responsible for focusing on the hunt.

"As our male forebears tracked warthogs and wildebeests," Fisher writes, "they gradually evolved the brain architecture to screen out peripheral thought, focus their attention, and make step-by-step decisions." Women's brains, she argues, evolved to handle many tasks at the same time; what she calls "web thinking." There is even scientific evidence from studies that the corpus callosum, the bundle of millions of nerve fibers that connects the two hemispheres of the brain, is larger in women, and therefore allows for greater communication between each side.

By harnessing these ancient juggling powers, the second wave of feminism was supposed to wash away the wife's troubles and empower her from the bedroom to the boardroom. Rather than husbands and wives operating in separate fiefdoms, pulling their weight at the office and the home, respectively, women could liberate themselves by dominating both environments. Ms. Durga's many arms meant that the modern woman could have it all. She could be the working woman, the housemaid, and the sexy goddess, and her gallant god in shining gray flannel stability, unchanged, would still love her.

Thirty years later women have indeed come a long way. Women managers still make 76 cents for every dollar earned by their male counterparts, but women now account for almost half of the labor force. And that number is rising. The majority of men and women no longer live in separate and isolated worlds. Technology and the global economy have connected us together both at work and in our homes, and there are now ways for each sex to play more equal roles in each realm. Home offices and telecommuting options, on-line grocery shopping and home delivery services, high-speed breast milk pumps and web cams in day care centers allow us all to toggle more efficiently between the duties of work and home.

These profound cultural changes have created an opportunity for traditional gender roles to break down and evolve. Now that Ms. Durga has tipped the scales, for better or for worse, isn't it time for her to put down her weapons and take the focus off trying to hold it all? Isn't the next step a new and alto-gether different feminist supermodel? What about a multi-tasking man?

10   Despite feminist progess, the majority of modern men are still focused solely on the hunt. "My career, not my home life," as one young technology entre-preneur in his twenties, who works at home, put it. "The hunt is not the nest. It is the hunt."

Today American men are still only doing a fraction more of the work in the home than they were thirty years ago. A 2002 report by the Institute for Social Research at the University of Michigan found that American men are doing a mere four more hours of housework a week than they were in 1965. Women aren't doing as much housework, but they are still doing 27 hour more a week than men are. The nanny/housekeeper may act as a bejeweled arm for many upper-income goddesses, but then we must ask, how many of these appendages of privilege are men?

While the traditional corporate wife of the '50s has become all but obsolete, the corporate husband has yet to really define himself. There are now the few corporate superheroes such as Hewlett-Packard CEO Carlton Fiorino, who boasted in a 2002 *Fortune* magazine story that the stay-at-home husband is "The New Trophy Husband." The reality, however, is that most American women feel more overworked than men because the brunt of multi-tasking is not equally distributed.

It may simply be a communication problem. Women, in their quest to figure out how to have it all, may have lost track of the conversation with men. In the 1970s the ideal feminist woman became the tomboyish Charlie perfume girl. She didn't ask her man to change. She merely untied her apron strings and took long strides of bold suited confidence that told us that she bought her own seduction potion rather than waiting for that special gift from her man. In the 1980s she wore broad shoulder-padded suits, took the train to Wall Street, and competed with high-octane men, all without asking her man to make a similar conversion. He was still the head of the household, still the stoic Marlboro man at the center of every scene. He might have moved over a bit to share his office with the broad in the pants, but it was still his world. Despite a few sensitive moments, he was still focused mainly on the hunt. "We saw women as equals," said a lawyer in his forties. "But it was still about the boys' network and a female secretary who supported you."

As it turned out, women did not really resemble the cool and confident Charlie girl. They were exhausted, anxiety-ridden and overburdened. By the end of the 1980s women were suffering from what Arlie Hochschild, a sociol-ogy professor at the University of California–Berkeley, called "the stalled revo-lution." In her book *The Second Shift: Working Parents and the Revolution at Home,* she argued that men and the organizations that they worked for weren't help-ing take on the weight of domestic labor. "Workplaces have remained inflexi-ble in the face of family demands of their workers," she wrote. "At home most men have yet to really adapt to the changes in women."

15　　　In the 1990s the "stalled revolution" in some ways got worse. Men and women became even more alienated from each other. Women gained more economic power and more confidence about their innate feminine powers. Many even argued that a woman's natural abilities to multi-task gave her an advantage over men in a new technology age where everyone was bombarded from all directions with the web, instant messages, and cell phone conference calls from offices around the globe in an ever-growing—and feminized—service economy.

Ms. Durga transformed from the shoulder-padded career woman to the post-feminist power girl who could gracefully toggle between work and home; talk of politics and nail polish; Madeleine Albright's weapons strategy and Monica's thongs. Men were suddenly "stiffed," as Susan Faludi observed. They may have learned that it was cool to tap into their more gentle side, carry the Baby Björn, and push the stroller with both hands. They may have traded the bachelor party entertainment of silicon-enhanced strippers for silicon-enhanced facials, manicures and massages at day spas. They also lost track of what it meant to be men.

Many men reacted by running away to pound their chests in the woods. They became cigar aficionados. They joined Promise Keepers meetings in baseball stadiums. They did everything to grasp the last hold on traditional manliness. "That means Russell Crowe. Someone who has steely clear, focused confidence. Someone linear and ballsy. A brute. A guy who can fix things," said a writer in his thirties.

At the turn of the twenty-first century American women are still sent happy-ending messages through the media—and all the fairy tales that we read as kids—that we need a prince who will let us let down our hair and save us—both financially and emotionally. Many women still want this image, or at least are sexually attracted to it. They want "a man."

But rather than a half-liberated prince in a gray Armani suit, what women really need is Durga's twin brother. A multi-tasking mensch. A man who can take some of the weight off women's many arms by bringing home the bacon, frying it up in a pan, without ever letting us forget that he's "a man!" The problem with this vision is that anatomy may be destiny. Men might not have the neurological wherewithal to deliver. "I can see how it would make my relationship with a woman easier, but it's just not natural for me to multi-task," says a New York editor in his thirties. "I know women think I'm just being stubborn, but when I try I feel like the slow kid in the fast class."

20　　　In 2001, Alladi Vankatesh, a sociologist at the University of California at Irvine's Center for Research on Information Technology began studying this very issue by looking at how traditional gender roles are shifting in the information age. Vankatesh, a soft-spoken Indian man in his mid-forties, spent a year in the sprawling suburban homes of Los Angeles observing the different ways men and women respond to computer technology. After interviewing close to seventy families, he discovered that not much has changed in a million years. When men use computers, they tend to focus on a single task or an immediate goal. Play game! Win game! Find information!

Women on the other hand, he says, think about how the computer integrates into the rest of their lives. How it can help them toggle between working at home and maintaining a connection with their children's school and other parents in their community, for example. "The good news is that because computer technology does seem to be saving women time, they are feeling less pressure about the work of home," he says. The fact remains, however, that men are overwhelmingly still focusing on the hunt.

The human brain has not changed significantly in twenty thousand years. As Helen Fisher explains, even if women in the nations with the highest birth rates, such as Africa and India, begin to select partners who are inclined toward more feminine behavior—including multitasking—it's going to take a long time before an actual hard-wiring evolution occurs. A new breed of super multi-tasking man is not arriving any time soon.

Maybe the optimal partnership will have to be more like the Wonder Twins, the characters in the '80s television cartoon *The Super Friends*. Zan and Jayna were from the planet Exxor. Zan, the boy, had the power to change spontaneously into any water-based form. Jayna, the girl, could become any animal. In order to activate their shape-shifting powers, the twins needed to touch hands. "Wonder Twin Powers, activate!" they would shout. When fighting a villain, Jayna would shout "Shape of the Sphinx!" and Zan would yell "Form of an Ice Shovel!" The Sphinx would then hit the villain over the head with the ice shovel. Their super powers worked only when they combined their different strengths.

Clinging to evolutionary determinism, however, could also thwart social progress. As women's salaries become necessities for survival of the modern family, men, despite ill-wiring, can no longer afford to focus solely on the hunt. Many modern men, especially those of the generation who were nurtured in Ms. Durga's multiple arms and grew up in the multi-tasking world of computer technology, have therefore begun to adapt.

25   Even in the most neo-traditional households, where the husband still takes the train to the organization and the wife has set up her office at home in order to manage the house and child care, a new multi-tasking masculinity is beginning to emerge. "Fathering is all about multi-tasking," said a writer in his thirties. "Just last night, in fact, I was swinging my daughter in the car seat to try to coax her to sleep, while at the same time I was downloading music into our computer, checking e-mail, reading a Philip Roth novel, and tinkering with an upcoming article. I only have two hands but sometimes I feel like an octopus. I have literally begun to undertake certain tasks with my feet.

"I also do almost all the cooking," he continued. "Thas said, my father was fairly shocked when he came to visit, because he saw me doing a lot of things that he never had to worry about—and I think he found that somewhat inappropriate." For men of generations X and Y, the social effects of feminism are slowly taking hold, but the pressures for more change are mounting. As women become more economically independent, they are staying single longer, choosing to rely on their social networks of friends for support rather than settling for a male partner who may not necessarily meet their standards of companionship. A higher divorce rate is forcing more men to live alone, care for themselves and develop the skills of the home front that traditionally have fallen to women. As liberated gay couples become more prominent, gay men, who either through biological or social wiring fall into more traditionally feminine roles, are becoming new social role models.

Most major corporations still lack in-house day care. Most men are still not granted paternity leave. There are still strong cultural pressures on men that make them feel that if they scant their jobs in favor of the work of home and child care, they might appear wimpy or uncommitted. Despite these obstacles, men are progressing in the direction of Durga's twin. If the conversation continues, the balance of roles will improve even more.

There may even be the possibility for change in men's brain circuits. Eric Kandel, a neuroscientist at Columbia University, won the first Nobel Prize in medicine of the twenty-first century for his seminal work with the sea slug aplysia. By studying the way the slug's nerve cells respond to chemical signals that produce changes in its behavior, Kandel and his colleagues discovered that learning can produce physical changes in the brain by strengthening connections between nerve cells.

Men aren't sea slugs, but it could be that the more they multi-task between the work of the home and their work, the more their brains will learn and change. It could be that once upon a time in the future, Durga's multi-tasking twin in shining armor could come to her rescue, overthrow the tyranny of the pressure for her to do it all, and prove that anatomy isn't destiny, experience is.

QUESTIONS FOR DISCUSSION

1. What is the myth of the goddess Durga? Why did she appear on the cover of the first *Ms.* magazine?
2. To what ancient historical development does Helen Fisher attribute women's superior ability to "multitask"? What is meant by "web thinking"? How do studies of the corpus callosum help to support Fisher's theory?
3. How have the expectations of early feminists for the success of multitasking women failed to materialize? How have men played a role in the failure or imbalance in the lives of working women?
4. What is the significance of the "stalled revolution"? What are its causes? How and why did the stalled revolution worsen in the 1990s? How was "Ms. Durga" transformed in the late 1990s?
5. How did men react to the shifting burden of child care in recent years? Why does University of California, Irvine, sociologist Alladi Vankatesh believe that men haven't really changed "in a million years"?
6. How and why, according to Lehmann-Haupt, is a "new multi-tasking masculinity" becoming more common? How might this multitasking begin to rewire the male brain?

CONNECTION

Compare the ideal of masculine behavior set forth in Rachel Lehmann-Haupt's essay to Kevin Canty's approach to balancing work and family in "The Dog in Me" (see below).

IDEAS FOR WRITING

1. Interview several men who have been influenced by the changes in child care options in recent years. Write an essay about such men: How do they see themselves in relation to their partners? Do they appear ready to accept the "new multi-tasking masculinity"? Why or why not? Explain and include quotes from your interviewees in your essay.
2. Interview several working women. Write an essay about how they feel about the willingness or capability of the men in their lives to take on the burden of multitasking in relation to child care and managing the tasks of home maintenance.

RELATED WEB SITES

Rachel Lehmann-Haupt: Writer at Large
`www.lehmannhaupt.com`
This site includes links to much of Lehmann-Haupt's essays and reportage on cultural, family, and gender issues, along with a brief bio.

Battle of the Sexes
`www.abc.net.au/catalyst/stories/s680863.htm#transcript`
This transcript from the ABC program *Catalyst,* broadcast on September 26, 2002, examines the gender-based conflict and differences between men and women, many related to multitasking abilities.

Kevin Canty

The Dog in Me

Kevin Canty completed his B.A. in 1988 at the University of Montana, his M.A. in 1990 at the University of Florida, and his M.F.A. in 1993 at the University of Arizona. He is married with two children and is an associate professor of creative writing at the University of Montana, Missoula. His novels include Nine Below Zero *(1999) and* Winslow in Love *(2005); his short stories have appeared in the collections* Stranger in This World *(1994) and* Honeymoon and Other Stories *(2001). He also has written essays and articles for* Vogue, Details, *the* New York Times, *and many other publications. The essay that follows was first published in* Bastard on the Couch *(2003), a collection of essays by husbands about*

the conflicts that arise between spouses over issues related to child rearing and tak-
ing equal responsibility for children and work.

Write about something in a relationship that you resented. Did your resentment
have a negative effect on the relationship? What was it?

Guilty, guilty, guilty as charged. I'm the one, Officer; I've got a box of cigars
in the glove compartment of my truck and a condom rattling around in
the bottom of my toiletries kit. That was me who skipped my daughter's grade-
school Christmas show and then went out and got hog-drunk with the graduate
students later that night. I was the one who told my wife we didn't have the
money to buy a new couch and then bought a new fishing reel that same week.
In fact, don't get me started on fishing junk: I've got enough of that lying
around to convict two or three of us.

Deep into middle age I still have a band, and we play Muddy Waters into the
small hours of the morning in smoky bars full of disreputable people. If somebody hands me a joint at a party, I will smoke it. If someone hands me a bottle
of tequila, I will drink from it. And it's true, my idea of a fine evening at home
involves drinking beer and watching *Monday Night Football* while playing electric
guitar loudly enough to keep the children awake.

I am, in short, that well-known figure of fun, that feckless boy/man so many
married and ex-married women are so permanently pissed off at. They should
be pissed. It's all true: I do things sometimes for selfish reasons and not for the
good of the family. I can spend hours on solitary work (writing) that makes me
spaced-out and irritable and then spend further hours in solitary recreation
(fishing), which puts me in a fine mood, most of the time, but well away from
the house and its travails. I would rather eat broken glass and drink iodine than
do the dishes.

It's the dog in me. And you know what? I kind of like the dog in me. I kind
of trust him.

5   The dog in me has got a pretty good nose, for one thing—he notices things
that we're normally too polite to notice. Like, for instance, it's *a lot* easier to get
forgiveness than it is to get permission. It's way easier to just buy that electric
guitar and let the Loved One find out later, if she ever does. (The trick is to
leave the house with an empty case that will hold the new acquisition.) The
idea that the Loved One and I would be able to sit down and negotiate the purchase in a reasonable and rational fashion is a total fiction. If you want the guitar (fly rod/golf clubs/exhaust manifold), you had best go out and just buy it,
because you will never, ever get permission.

And even if you do, it won't matter. A few years ago I came into a decent pile
of unexpected money, not life-changingly large but a pile nevertheless. Out of
that pot of money I built a fence around the backyard, put up a deck, had the

old asbestos-covered furnace removed and a new one installed, and bought the biggest, flashiest electric guitar known to mankind, a Gibson ES-295 in Les Paul gold with an engraved floral pick guard and a Bigsby vibrato unit.

And how did that work out? You can guess. Three years later the virtue I hoped to accumulate with the deck, fence, and furnace has evaporated entirely (if ever it existed in the first place). And yet the solid-gold ES-295 is still around to cause offense. Every day I am guilty of continuing to own such an expensive and frivolous object.

Now, it may very well be that this kind of sin-first-and-ask-questions-later approach contributes to a certain amount of tension around the house, may even promote seething and sulking. It may be that a more straightforward approach would not.

But this purchase *was* negotiated in advance; it was contextualized with the good of the family in mind, it was talked about, given a seal of approval. Three years later, none of that makes any difference. Just wanting such a thing in the first place is wrong, and having such a thing is doubly wrong. No slack. No possibility of slack. The point here being—as the dog in me would like to suggest— that there is no way to win in this situation. There's no way for me to legitimately want what I want. And at that point, in choosing between what I want and what, according to the Loved One, I *ought to want*, it's really not that difficult.

10   Now, obviously the way to avoid all this friction is for men to act more like women: less impulsive, more cooperative, more rational and group-oriented and family-centered. The dog in me wonders, though, whether this is the way women *are*—or the way women *imagine themselves to be.* Just curious.

It's a fine line, though, isn't it? Something's come loose, something's come unglued in the last couple of decades. We no longer feel quite comfortable in our roles, no longer quite fit the people we imagine ourselves to be. It seems a lot clearer when I look back at my parents' lives: Dad made the money, Mom took care of the house and the kids. Sure there were limitations—Mom never really took her rightful place in the world until all of us were grown and gone, and we never saw a lot of Dad—but overall, they knew where they stood. They knew what they were supposed to do. They did what they were supposed to do, and everything worked out fine. The nice thing about these roles was that they were inherited; they didn't have to make anything up, didn't have to improvise. They were grounded in tradition and, at least in part, in economic reality.

In the aftermath of the feminist revolution, though, we all find ourselves scrambling to adapt to new ideas of equality and democracy, to find new roles that seem to make sense. Everything's suddenly up for grabs—and haunting the whole process is the knowledge that we are actually making all of this up, that none of these new roles are blessed by anything other than our own convictions. We are supposed to be open and equal and democratic and straightforward. All those old, unspoken compacts—all those chains that bound our parents to outdated roles—are to be brought out into the daylight of reason. In reason and equality we will proceed together into a new, bright future.

Well, maybe. But the dog in me can't help noticing that I'm still paying for everything. The dog in me wonders if this isn't just a way to make me take care of half of your business while I'm still taking care of all of mine.

Now before you come after me with the tar and feathers and the rail, let me point out that we started in the same place everybody else did. In the years before marriage and children, the Loved One and I practiced the new doctrine of independence and equality: our financial and professional lives (she a photographer; I a writer and teacher) were as separate as separate gets, the housework split unevenly but nearly equally. I did the cars and the cooking, the Loved One did the dusting and organized the bills. We lived in blissful independence for more than a decade, and in fact we still have separate friendships and separate checking accounts, and we like it that way.

15   Throw a couple of kids into the mix, though, and everything goes to hell. When I count around the circle of my acquaintance, I find exactly one couple with children who split fifty/fifty, a few (a *very* few) in which the woman is the primary breadwinner, and a slew of marriages in which the responsibility is centrally on the man. He's the one with the retirement plan and the health plan, he's the one making the mortgage payments, he's doing the car insurance.

Now, wait a minute, I hear you say. *Somebody's* got to take care of the children.

Well, yeah. And somebody's got to make a living. Somebody's got to put a floor under the family to make sure that when your fulfilling, interesting, entirely worthwhile job hits a dry spell, you won't have to auction off the children. Don't get me wrong—I like my job. I teach creative writing in a good master of fine arts program; it's engaging work and there's not too much of it, with summers off and all. There are times when I think I have the best job on earth.

But even the best job on earth is hell some days: the student from hell, the faculty meeting from hell, the class from hell, the crucial chapter broken off midsentence so I can attend a meeting of the faculty evaluation subcommittee. I know you don't feel sorry for me. I don't expect you to. My point is that even a good job can feel on some days like eating a peck of shit. And in a ten- or twenty- or thirty-year career, there are going to be plenty of days that feel like that; days when all you can do is soldier on and hope that things get better. And that most of the time, still, it's the man in the house that's doing the soldiering. We don't have the luxury of a return to school, a career crisis, a nervous breakdown.

Okay, I know: you work, I work, everybody works. Everybody struggles through.

20   And sometimes, it's true, it's the woman carrying the weight and the man— in my experience, writers and artists, mainly—who has the luxury of pursuing his ambitions regardless of his ability to make any money with those ambitions. But not often; not as often as you would think, given the revolutions of the last thirty years. And even more rare, in my experience, is the couple that shares the roles equally.

What happened? Where did this idea of equality go off the rails? It's those damn kids, is my opinion. Somebody's got to take care of the kids, it's true— and I don't think anybody who doesn't have kids can appreciate what vicious little time-suckers and energy-suckers and emotion-suckers they are. It's like being Miss America, or being blind: you can *imagine* the experience beforehand, but your imagination has nothing to do with the actual experience, which you will not understand until you have it.

When my first child was born, my son, Turner, he came into the world not breathing. A kind of purposeful hush fell over the room, then began a rush of activity that was quick and grim and terror-inspiring. And in that moment my life changed—I felt myself turned inside out, I saw that everything I had held as important up until that moment was trivial, and that what mattered, the only thing that mattered, was that child's life. I prayed, I bargained, I held my breath. And when he started to breathe again, no more than a minute later—though it felt like an hour—I was no longer the same person as a minute before. I am still not. Every day, every minute he breathes—he's fourteen now, taller than his mother, taking kick-boxing classes and preparing to kick my ass—feels like a gift, and I am grateful for it. Turner and Nora, my son and my daughter, go first. On the way out of the burning building, they go first. When we're trying to figure out where to live, how to spend the summer, when we're making the thousand large and small decisions about our lives together, their interests go first. If you have not had children, you will think I am dramatizing. If you have had children, though, you will understand that I am merely reporting.

Somebody's got to take care of the kids. It's nice and primal, isn't it? The dog in me has no trouble understanding this thing. There is no substitute for time and care.

I don't at all mean that the woman in the partnership has to do it; like you, I know households in which it is the man who is in the house, changing the diapers, holding hands, whispering nursery rhymes. And these days it's nearly unimaginable that this work is not shared in part. But still: somebody has got to sign up to be the primary homemaker and make sure that the child is taken care of. And somebody needs to be the breadwinner, to make sure there's food on the table and a roof over everybody's head. And there are not enough hours in the day or enough days in the week for this to be the same person.

25   Can't we share? Sure we can share. In fact I even know one couple that seem to be sharing everything equally: money, planning, child care. (Although, come to think of it, he's a couple of rungs up the career ladder already, and she's a little behind . . .) But nearly all the couples-with-children I know relapse into some version of the old roles, breadwinner and homemaker. Sometimes it's the man wearing the skirt—and the dog in me would like to talk to him about this—mostly it's the woman, but some version of this home-at-home versus home-in-the-world seems to resurface.

With one change: the primary parent, whether it's Mom or Dad, isn't staying home very much anymore.

Go to the day care. Watch the parents dropping their children off. Watch their faces. Mostly just busy, harried, preoccupied, late—always late—but sometimes you see the regret as well. Does anybody think this is entirely a good idea? Dropping little Alexandria into a nurturing place for a few hours while Mom goes to work or Dad hammers away on his novel, sure—no problem. Stashing the kids in day care for forty hours a week so both parents can have their careers? This is not just stressful, this is not just anxiety-producing; this is wrong.

So what are we supposed to do? you say. We need the money.

Well, exactly. The roles of homemaker and breadwinner—the roles we inherited from our parents, not to mention the Brady Bunch—evolved at a time when the average household could be supported on a single income. But those days are over.

30   We have been approaching this idea of who does what and where we all fit in terms of ideology and emotion, in terms of feminism and equality and injury and lovingness. I wonder, though, if it would not be better approached in terms of political economy. What I'm getting at is, how did we get priced out of the market for our own lives? My mother would say—has said, in fact—that she didn't have a fancy kitchen or a fancy second car; she didn't spend thirty dollars a week on coffee or two hundred dollars a month on telephones, Internet access, and cable TV. She's right, of course. On the other hand, even if we were making our own coffee, bringing our lunch to work, driving secondhand Volvos, and dialing (gasp) an actual telephone connected to the wall by an actual cord, we still couldn't afford little Susie's ballet classes and Timmy's tennis lessons—not to mention a decent house in a decent neighborhood.

Also: we grew up in affluent times. Many of us had cars and trips and nice clothes and spending money in high school and college. Not only do we want the same things for our children, but the prospect of living worse in midlife than we did in high school seems completely strange and unacceptable.

Maybe it's as simple as that: maybe it's not our lives we can't afford but our aspirations, the things we were brought up to believe we could get from life. The dog in me is balled up over in the corner, muttering something about yuppie perfectionism, about materialist greed and advertising culture, about how we think we can buy our way into happiness—and isn't this the desire behind all this "living simple" hoo-ha? The notion that we can somehow dematerialize our lives and return to that mythical homespun yesteryear, where love is truly all you need. Of course, what this turns into is a glossy *Living Simple* magazine and a range of simple, tasteful products for your easy, low-key lifestyle, all elegantly designed and yet, somehow, quite expensive . . .

Where did that money go, anyway? I'm not going to touch that one, except to say that the richest 5 percent of our population has seen their share of the wealth skyrocket while the middle class has seen their share fall. And our country, alone in the Western world, has decided to allocate almost no resources to support working families. Spend a minute and imagine how much easier all of this would be—work, children, marriage—if there was a real family-leave policy, or if there was a system of child care run by professionals, trained caregivers who were paid more than the help at McDonald's . . .

But here in the real world it's impossible to take the time off to care for small children without trashing your career. Here in the real world it's every family for itself to improvise child care.

35   Here in the real world the "breadwinner" role continues to make sense, though. I can work hard—get through whatever I have to get through—show some discipline and persistence and grit, and I can make the money to take care of my family. Maybe not entirely, but I can put money in the retirement account, pay for the health insurance, keep the cars in shape and relatively new. And you know what? I find this completely satisfying. When things go to hell at work, I can remember why I'm sticking it through; it gives me a sense of purpose, a place in the world. I know what I'm supposed to be doing. I do it. It makes me feel purposeful and whole, a feeling even the dog in me can understand.

I like having kids. I like taking care of them. It's not crazy complicated.

Where it gets crazy complicated is when you get to the "homemaker" role. Lately one person is supposed to assume primary responsibility for the day-to-day care of the children, plus maintain a fulfilling and profitable career, plus keep the household going? Even with whatever degree of help the breadwinner is willing to come up with (wildly variable, in my experience), it still seems impossible.

What it turns into in our house is a big Mexican standoff, with the Loved One saying, I'm making more money than my mother ever did! and the Jerk saying, I'm doing way more housework than my father ever did! and the Loved One saying, You don't even pick up your socks! and the Jerk saying, You wouldn't know an electric bill if it bit you in the ass! and the Loved One saying, It was supposed to be different.

Maybe.

40   This is the place where the dog in me checks out, takes himself for a nice little walk, sniffs around to see what's happening. Because, you know, I can't force it all to make sense. I can't take care of you that way. I can only do what I do: get up in the morning, punch the clock, keep the credit cards in line and change the oil and cook dinner a few times a week and go to a Christmas pageant when forced to. I can keep my own head above water, and I can make sure that, whatever else happens, you and the children are not going to go homeless or hungry or without modern-dance lessons.

Here's a confession: a couple of years ago the Loved One had a huge photographic project down on the Navaho Nation in Arizona and New Mexico. She spent the first half of the summer on and off shooting pictures in the Southwest and the second half in a frenzy of developing, sorting, and printing the resulting pictures, leaving me with the kids. And you know what? I really liked it. We went to the river. We went camping. We talked about why Turner's tennis instructor was cool and why Nora's dance teacher was a freak, and we sat around eating pizza and watching terrible movies, and for a few weeks, I felt like I understood what the world looked like to them. It turns out that they are actually interesting people, and good company. When the university cranked up again and the Loved One came home, I was even, for a moment, jealous of the life she led with the children.

But this was a summer more or less off—no deadlines, nothing looming. I nickel-and-dimed my way through a little magazine work and a couple of short stories, but really, I didn't get a lot done. I don't see how you could, to tell you the truth. I don't see how that script works, not with small children.

Here's another confession: that condom in my toiletries bag came from a campus safe-sex drive about five years ago, and it's still sitting there. Those cigars in my glove compartment have sat there untouched since I quit smoking on my daughter's birthday two years ago, on the grounds that if I wanted to see her married, I was going to have to live for another twenty years or so. The band, the parties, the occasional late nights with the grad students—all these are, it pains me to admit, entirely harmless ways of blowing off steam, of getting through the week. I do what I do, as best I can. I take care of the people I was put here to take care of. I take the dog in me out for a walk, every once in a while, just so he won't get too restless. But I don't let him off the leash, not anymore.

And the guitars? Womankind will rejoice to know that I finally sold the solid-gold ES-295 last week—just wasn't playing it enough. I did, though, keep the money in the guitar account, and right now I'm eyeing a National Reso-Phonic style 1 tricone resonator guitar in chrome-plated bell brass, with a little engraved band around the edge—the biggest, flashiest, loudest acoustic guitar in existence. The Loved One still thinks we need a new couch, but the dog in me wants this thing. We'll see.

QUESTIONS FOR DISCUSSION

1. How does Canty define "the dog in me" in the first paragraphs of his essay? Do you believe him when he admits to being "guilty" of several "boy/man" instances of immature masculine behavior? How does he justify his behavior, including the purchase of an expensive guitar rather than a couch, which his wife desires?

2. What is the "Loved One's" response to Canty's "boy/man" desires? Why does Canty feel he is in a "no-win" situation in respect to his personal wants?

3. Why does Canty believe that "something's come loose" in traditional male/female relations in the past 20 years? In what sense is "everything . . . suddenly up for grabs"? How does he contrast the duties and responsibilities he and his wife face with those his own parents faced?

4. Why, according to Canty, is it so much harder for a couple with children to raise to have an equal male-female relationship than it is for a childless couple? Is his support for his position convincing? Explain.

5. Do you agree with Canty that one member of a couple must be the primary homemaker in charge of the children while the other must be the "breadwinner"? Does he provide convincing support for his position from his analysis of the current economic system and the lack of support for modern families? Do you agree with his position on long-term child care? Why or why not?

6. What confessions does Canty make about his current lifestyle in his final paragraphs? How does he use the symbol of the guitar and the concept of walking the dog to help make his points clearer? Does he seem less of a "dog" because of these confessions, more or less sympathetic to you than he did at the beginning of the essay?

CONNECTION

Compare Canty's approach to and beliefs about the male role in parenting to the role and attitudes of Judith Ortiz Cofer's father in "Silent Dancing" in Chapter 3 (see page 151).

IDEAS FOR WRITING

1. Write a response to Canty's essay either from the perspective of a fellow "dog" or from that of the "Loved One." Indicate whether the speaker agrees with his position on family responsibilities, and try to point out, if possible, a solution for the dilemma he leaves the reader with at the end of his article.

2. Do some research into the problems that working couples have with sharing child care responsibilities. Write an essay in which you present the positions of men and women on the issue, and indicate which side of this gender debate you most agree with and why you believe the way you do.

RELATED WEB SITES

A Talk with Author Kevin Canty
www.leisuresuit.net/Webzine/articles/kevin_canty.shtml
This interview and commentary on Kevin Canty's life and writing from the male-oriented ezine *Leisuresuit* also contain photos of Canty and his book covers.

Am I Exploiting My Nanny?—Yes, Men Can Do Housework
http://slate.msn.com/id/2095545/entry/2095753/
In this lively exchange of letters between author Caitlin Flanagan and activist Barbara Ehrenreich (*Slate*, 2004), we can see signs of conflict among women today over men's role in housework and the appropriate use of nannies to reduce the pressure on working spouses over child care and other household chores.

David Sedaris

I Like Guys

David Sedaris was born in 1957 in Raleigh, North Carolina. He completed his degree from the Art Institute of Chicago in 1987. Sedaris has worked as a radio commentator and diarist for National Public Radio (NPR); has written short stories; and has worked as an apartment cleaner, moving company worker, and office worker. In 2000 Sedaris won the Lambda Literary Award in the humor category. Sedaris's books include Barrel Fever: Stories and Essays *(1994);* Naked *(1997);* Holidays on Ice *(short stories, 1997);* Me Talk Pretty One Day *(2000); and* Dress Your Family in Corduroy and Denim *(2004).*

How were gay students treated at the high school or middle school that you attended? Were they accepted by the other students and the teachers?

Shortly before I graduated from eighth grade, it was announced that, come
fall, our county school system would adopt a policy of racial integration by
way of forced busing. My Spanish teacher broke the news in a way she hoped
might lead us to a greater understanding of her beauty and generosity.

"I remember the time I was at the state fair, standing in line for a Sno-Kone,"
she said, fingering the kiss curls that framed her squat, compact face. "And a
little colored girl ran up and tugged at my skirt, asking if she could touch my
hair. 'Just once,' she said. 'Just one time for good luck.'"

"Now, I don't know about the rest of you, but my hair means a lot to me."
The members of my class nodded to signify that their hair meant a lot to them
as well. They inched forward in their seats, eager to know where this story
might be going. Perhaps the little Negro girl was holding a concealed razor
blade. Maybe she was one of the troublemakers out for a fresh white scalp.

I sat marveling at their naiveté. . . . Like all her previous anecdotes, this
woman's story was headed straight up her ass.

5   "I checked to make sure she didn't have any candy on her hands, and then I
bent down and let this little colored girl touch my hair." The teacher's eyes assumed the dewy, faraway look she reserved for such Hallmark moments. "Then
this little fudge-colored girl put her hand on my cheek and said, 'Oh,' she said,
'I wish I could be white and pretty like you.'" She paused, positioning herself
on the edge of the desk as though she were posing for a portrait the federal
government might use on a stamp commemorating gallantry. "The thing to remember," she said, "is that more than anything in this world, those colored
people wish they were white."

I wasn't buying it. This was the same teacher who when announcing her
pregnancy said, "I just pray that my firstborn is a boy. I'll have a boy and then
maybe later I'll have a girl, because when you do it the other way round, there's
a good chance the boy will turn out to be funny."

"'Funny,' as in having no arms and legs?" I asked.

"That," the teacher said, "is far from funny. That is tragic, and you, sir,
should have your lips sewn shut for saying such a cruel and ugly thing. When I
say 'funny,' I mean funny as in . . ." She relaxed her wrist, allowing her hand to
dangle and flop. "I mean 'funny' as in *that* kind of funny." She minced across
the room, but it failed to illustrate her point, as this was more or less her natural walk, a series of gamboling little steps, her back held straight, giving the
impression she was balancing something of value atop her empty head. My
seventh-period math teacher did a much better version. Snatching a purse off
the back of a student's chair, he would prance about the room, batting his
eyes and blowing kisses at the boys seated in the front row. "So fairy nice to
meet you," he'd say.

Fearful of drawing any attention to myself, I hooted and squawked along with the rest of the class, all the while thinking, *That's me he's talking about.* If I was going to make fun of people, I had to expect a little something in return, that seemed only fair. Still, though, it bothered me that they'd found such an easy way to get a laugh. As entertainers, these teachers were nothing, zero. They could barely impersonate themselves. "Look at you!" my second-period gym teacher would shout, his sneakers squealing against the basketball court. "You're a group of ladies, a pack of tap-dancing queers."

10   The other boys shrugged their shoulders or smiled down at their shoes. They reacted as if they had been called Buddhists or vampires; sure, it was an insult, but no one would ever mistake them for the real thing. Had they ever chanted in the privacy of their backyard temple or slept in a coffin, they would have felt the sting of recognition and shared my fear of discovery.

I had never done anything with another guy and literally prayed that I never would. As much as I fantasized about it, I understood that there could be nothing worse than making it official. You'd seen them on television from time to time, the homosexuals, maybe on one of the afternoon talk shows. No one ever came out and called them a queer, but you could just tell by their voices as they flattered the host and proclaimed great respect for their fellow guests. These were the celebrities never asked about their home life, the comedians running scarves beneath their toupees or framing their puffy faces with their open palms in an effort to eliminate the circles beneath their eyes. "The poor man's face lift," my mother called it. Regardless of their natty attire, these men appeared sweaty and desperate, willing to play the fool in exchange for the studio applause they seemed to mistake for love and acceptance. I saw something of myself in their mock weary delivery, in the way they crossed their legs and laughed at their own jokes. I pictured their homes: the finicky placement of their throw rugs and sectional sofas, the magazines carefully fanned just so upon the coffee tables with no wives or children to disturb their order. I imagined the pornography hidden in their closets and envisioned them powerless and sobbing as the police led them away in shackles, past the teenage boy who stood bathed in the light of the television news camera and shouted, "That's him! He's the one who touched my hair!"

It was my hope to win a contest, cash in the prizes, and use the money to visit a psychiatrist who might cure me of having homosexual thoughts. Electroshock, brain surgery, hypnotism—I was willing to try anything. Under a doctor's supervision, I would buckle down and really change, I swore I would.

My parents knew a couple whose son had killed a Presbyterian minister while driving drunk. They had friends whose eldest daughter had sprinkled a Bundt cake with Comet, and knew of a child who, high on spray paint, had set fire to the family's cocker spaniel. Yet, they spoke of no one whose son was a homosexual. The odds struck me as bizarre, but the message was the same: this was clearly the worst thing that could happen to a person. The day-to-day anxiety was bad enough without my instructors taking their feeble little potshots. If my math teacher were able to subtract the alcohol from his diet, he'd still be on the football field where he belonged; and my Spanish teacher's credentials were based on nothing more than a long weekend in Tijuana, as far as I could tell. I quit taking their tests and completing their homework assignments, accepting Fs rather than delivering the grades I thought might promote their reputations as good teachers. It was a strategy that hurt only me, but I thought it cunning. We each had our self-defeating schemes, all the boys I had come to identify as homosexuals. Except for a few transfer students, I had known most of them since the third grade. We'd spent years gathered together in cinder-block offices as one speech therapist after another tried to cure us of our lisps. Had there been a walking specialist, we probably would have met there, too. These were the same boys who carried poorly forged notes to gym class and were the first to raise their hands when the English teacher asked for a volunteer to read aloud from *The Yearling* or *Lord of the Flies*. We had long ago identified one another and understood that because of everything we had in common, we could never be friends. To socialize would have drawn too much attention to ourselves. We were members of a secret society founded on self-loathing. When a teacher or classmate made fun of a real homosexual, I made certain my laugh was louder than anyone else's. When a club member's clothing was thrown into the locker-room toilet, I was always the first to cheer. When it was my clothing, I watched as the faces of my fellows broke into recognizable expressions of relief. *Faggots,* I thought. *This should have been you.*

Several of my teachers, when discussing the upcoming school integration, would scratch at the damp stains beneath their arms, pulling back their lips to reveal every bit of tooth and gum. They made monkey noises, a manic succession of ohhs and ahhs meant to suggest that soon our school would be no different than a jungle. Had a genuine ape been seated in the room, I guessed he might have identified their calls as a cry of panic. Anything that caused them suffering brought me joy, but I doubted they would talk this way come fall. From everything I'd seen on television, the Negros would never stand for such foolishness. As a people, they seemed to stick together. They knew how to fight, and I hoped that once they arrived, the battle might come down to the gladiators, leaving the rest of us alone.

15   At the end of the school year, my sister Lisa and I were excused from our volunteer jobs and sent to Greece to attend a month-long summer camp advertised as "the Crown Jewel of the Ionian Sea." The camp was reserved exclusively for Greek Americans and featured instruction in such topics as folk singing and something called "religious prayer and flag." I despised the idea of summer camp but longed to boast that I had been to Europe. "It changes people!" our neighbor had said. Following a visit to Saint-Tropez, she had marked her garden with a series of tissue-sized international flags. A once discreet and modest woman, she now paraded about her yard wearing nothing but clogs and a flame-stitched bikini. "Europe is the best thing that can happen to a person, especially if you like wine!"

I saw Europe as an opportunity to re-invent myself. I might still look and speak the same way, but having walked those cobblestoned streets, I would be identified as Continental. "He has a passport," my classmates would whisper. "Quick, let's run before he judges us!"

I told myself that I would find a girlfriend in Greece. She would be a French tourist wandering the beach with a loaf of bread beneath her arm. Lisette would prove that I wasn't a homosexual, but a man with refined tastes. I saw us holding hands against the silhouette of the Acropolis, the girl begging me to take her accordion as a memento of our love. "Silly you," I would say, brushing the tears from her eyes, "just give me the beret, that will be enough to hold you in my heart until the end of time."

In case no one believed me, I would have my sister as a witness. Lisa and I weren't getting along very well, but I hoped that the warm Mediterranean waters might melt the icicle she seemed to have mistaken for a rectal thermometer. Faced with a country of strangers, she would have no choice but to appreciate my company.

Our father accompanied us to New York, where we met our fellow campers for the charter flight to Athens. There were hundreds of them, each one confident and celebratory. They tossed their complimentary Aegean Airlines tote bags across the room, shouting and jostling one another. This would be the way I'd act once we'd finally returned from camp, but not one moment before. Were it an all-girl's camp, I would have been able to work up some enthusiasm. Had they sent me alone to pry leeches off the backs of blood-thirsty Pygmies, I might have gone bravely—but spending a month in a dormitory full of boys, that was asking too much. I'd tried to put it out of my mind, but faced with their boisterous presence, I found myself growing progressively more hysterical. My nervous tics shifted into their highest gear, and a small crowd gathered to watch what they believed to be an exotic folk dance. If my sister was anxious about our trip, she certainly didn't show it. Prying my fingers off her wrist, she crossed the room and introduced herself to a girl who stood picking salvageable butts out of the standing ashtray. This was a tough-looking Queens native named Stefani Heartattackus or Testicockules. I recall only that her last name had granted her a lifelong supply of resentment. Stefani wore mirrored aviator sunglasses and carried an oversized comb in the back pocket of her hiphugger jeans. Of all the girls in the room, she seemed the least likely candidate for my sister's friendship. They sat beside each other on the plane, and by the time we disembarked in Athens, Lisa was speaking in a very bad Queens accent. During the long flight, while I sat cowering beside a boy named Seamen, my sister had undergone a complete physical and cultural transformation. Her shoulder-length hair was now parted on the side, covering the left half of her face as if to conceal a nasty scar. She cursed and spat, scowling out the window of the chartered bus as if she'd come to Greece with the sole intention of kicking its dusty ass. "What a shithole," she yelled. "Jeez, if I'd knowed it was gonna be dis hot, I woulda stayed home wit my headdin da oven, right, girls!"

20   It shamed me to hear my sister struggle so hard with an accent that did nothing but demean her, yet I silently congratulated her on the attempt. I

approached her once we reached the camp, a cluster of whitewashed buildings hugging the desolate coast, far from any neighboring village.

"Listen, asshole," she said, "as far as this place is concerned, I don't know you and you sure as shit don't know me, you got that?" She spoke as if she were auditioning for a touring company of *West Side Story*, one hand on her hip and the other fingering her pocket comb as if it were a switchblade.

"Hey, Carolina!" one of her new friends called.

"A righta ready," she brayed. "I'm comin', I'm comin'."

That was the last time we spoke before returning home. Lisa had adjusted with remarkable ease, but something deep in my stomach suggested I wouldn't thrive nearly as well. Camp lasted a month, during which time I never once had a bowel movement. I was used to having a semiprivate bathroom and could not bring myself to occupy one of the men's room stalls, fearful that someone might recognize my shoes or, even worse, not see my shoes at all and walk in on me. Sitting down three times a day for a heavy Greek meal became an exercise akin to packing a musket. I told myself I'd sneak off during one of our field trips, but those toilets were nothing more than a hole in the floor, a hole I could have filled with no problem whatsoever. I considered using the Ionian Sea, but for some unexplained reason, we were not allowed to swim in those waters. The camp had an Olympic-size pool that was fed from the sea and soon grew murky with stray bits of jellyfish that had been pulverized by the pump. The tiny tentacles raised welts on campers' skin, so shortly after arriving, it was announced that we could photograph both the pool *and* the ocean but could swim in neither. The Greeks had invented democracy, built the Acropolis, and then called it a day. Our swimming period was converted into "contemplation hour" for the girls and an extended soccer practice for the boys.

25   "I really think I'd be better off contemplating," I told the coach, massaging my distended stomach. "I've got a personal problem that's sort of weighing me down."

Because we were first and foremost Americans, the camp was basically an extension of junior high school except that here everyone had an excess of moles or a single eyebrow. The attractive sports minded boys ran the show, currying favor from the staff and ruining our weekly outdoor movie with their inane heckling. From time to time the rented tour buses would carry us to view one of the country's many splendors, and we would raid the gift shops, stealing anything that wasn't chained to the shelf or locked in a guarded case. These were cheap, plated puzzle rings and pint-size vases, little pompommed shoes, and coffee mugs reading SPARTA IS FOR A LOVER. My shoplifting experience was the only thing that gave me an edge over the popular boys. "Hold it like this," I'd whisper. "Then swivel around and slip the statue of Diana down the back of your shorts, covering it with your T-shirt. Remember to back out the door while leaving and never forget to wave good-bye."

There was one boy at camp I felt I might get along with, a Detroit native named Jason who slept on the bunk beneath mine. Jason tended to look away when talking to the other boys, shifting his eyes as though he were studying the weather conditions. Like me, he used his free time to curl into a fetal position, staring at the bedside calendar upon which he'd x-ed out all the days he had endured so far. We were finishing our 7:15 to 7:45 wash-and-rinse segment one morning when our dormitory counselor arrived for inspection shouting, "What are you, a bunch of goddamned faggots who can't make your beds?"

I giggled out loud at his stupidity. If anyone knew how to make a bed, it was a faggot. It was the others he needed to worry about. I saw Jason laughing, too, and soon we took to mocking this counselor, referring to each other first as "faggots" and then as "stinking faggots." We were "lazy faggots" and "sunburned faggots" before we eventually became "faggoty faggots." We couldn't protest the word, as that would have meant acknowledging the truth of it. The most we could do was embrace it as a joke. Embodying the term in all its clichéd glory, we minced and pranced about the room for each other's entertainment when the others weren't looking. I found myself easily outperforming my teachers, who had failed to capture the proper spirit of loopy bravado inherent in the role. *Faggot,* as a word, was always delivered in a harsh, unforgiving tone befitting those weak or stupid enough to act upon their impulses. We used it as a joke, an accusation, and finally as a dare. Late at night I'd feel my bunk buck and sway, knowing that Jason was either masturbating or beating eggs for an omelette. *Is it me he's thinking about?* I'd follow his lead and wake the next morning to find our entire iron-frame unit had wandered a good eighteen inches away from the wall. Our love had the power to move bunks.

Having no willpower, we depended on circumstances to keep us apart. *This cannot happen* was accompanied by the sound of bedsprings whining, *Oh, but maybe just this once.* There came an afternoon when, running late for flag worship, we found ourselves alone in the dormitory. What started off as namecalling escalated into a series of mock angry slaps. We wrestled each other onto one of the lower bunks, both of us longing to be pinned. "You kids think you invented sex," my mother was fond of saying. But hadn't we? With no instruction manual or federally enforced training period, didn't we all come away feeling we'd discovered something unspeakably modern? What produced in others a feeling of exhilaration left Jason and me with a mortifying sense of guilt. We fled the room as if, in our fumblings, we had uncapped some virus we still might escape if we ran fast enough. Had one of the counselors not caught me scaling the fence, I felt certain I could have made it back to Raleigh by morning, skittering across the surface of the ocean like one of those lizards often featured on television wildlife programs.

30 When discovered making out with one of the Greek bus drivers, a sixteen-year-old camper was forced to stand beside the flagpole dressed in long pants and thick sweaters. We watched her cook in the hot sun until, fully roasted, she crumpled to the pavement and passed out.

"That," the chief counselor said, "is what happens to people who play around."

If this was the punishment for a boy and a girl, I felt certain the penalty for two boys somehow involved barbed wire, a team of donkeys, and the nearest volcano. Nothing, however, could match the cruelty and humiliation Jason and I soon practiced upon each other. He started a rumor that I had stolen an athletic supporter from another camper and secretly wore it over my mouth like a surgical mask. I retaliated, claiming he had expressed a desire to become a dancer. "That's nothing," he said to the assembled crowd, "take a look at what I found on David's bed!" He reached into the pocket of his tennis shorts and withdrew a sheet of notebook paper upon which were written the words I LIKE GUYS. Presented as an indictment, the document was both pathetic and comic. Would I supposedly have written the note to remind myself of that fact, lest I forget? Had I intended to wear it taped to my back, advertising my preference the next time our rented buses carried us off to yet another swinging sexual playground?

I LIKE GUYS. He held the paper above his head, turning a slow circle so that everyone might get a chance to see. I supposed he had originally intended to plant the paper on my bunk for one of the counselors to find. Presenting it himself had foiled the note's intended effect. Rather than beating me with sticks and heavy shoes, the other boys simply groaned and looked away, wondering why he'd picked the thing up and carried it around in his pants pocket. He might as well have hoisted a glistening turd, shouting, "Look what he did!" Touching such a foul document made him suspect and guilty by association. In attempting to discredit each other, we wound up alienating ourselves even further.

Jason—even his name seemed affected. During meals I studied him from across the room. Here I was, sweating onto my plate, my stomach knotted and cramped, when *he* was the one full of shit. Clearly he had tricked me, cast a spell or slipped something into my food. I watched as he befriended a girl named Theodora and held her hand during a screening of *A Lovely Way to Die*, one of the cave paintings the head counselor offered as a weekly movie.

35   She wasn't a bad person, Theodora. Someday the doctors might find a way to transplant a calf's brain into a human skull, and then she'd be just as lively and intelligent as he was. I tried to find a girlfriend of my own, but my one possible candidate was sent back home when she tumbled down the steps of the Parthenon, causing serious damage to her leg brace.

Jason looked convincing enough in the company of his girlfriend. They scrambled about the various ruins, snapping each other's pictures while I hung back fuming, watching them nuzzle and coo. My jealousy stemmed from the belief that he had been cured. One fistful of my flesh and he had lost all symptoms of the disease.

Camp ended and I flew home with my legs crossed, dropping my bag of stolen souvenirs and racing to the bathroom, where I spent the next several days sitting on the toilet and studying my face in a hand mirror. *I like guys.* The words had settled themselves into my features. I was a professional now, and it showed.

I returned to my volunteer job at the mental hospital, carrying harsh Greek cigarettes as an incentive to some of the more difficult patients.

"Faggot!" a woman shouted, stooping to protect her collection of pinecones. "Get your faggoty hands away from my radio transmitters."

40   "Don't mind Mary Elizabeth," the orderly said. "She's crazy."

Maybe not, I thought, holding a pinecone up against my ear. She's gotten the faggot part right, so maybe she was onto something.

The moment we boarded our return flight from Kennedy to Raleigh, Lisa re-arranged her hair, dropped her accent, and turned to me saying, "Well, I thought that was very nice, how about you?" Over the course of five minutes, she had eliminated all traces of her reckless European self. Why couldn't I do the same?

In late August my class schedule arrived along with the news that I would not be bused. There had been violence in other towns and counties, trouble as far away as Boston; but in Raleigh the transition was peaceful. Not only students but many of the teachers had been shifted from one school to another. My new science teacher was a black man very adept at swishing his way across the room, mocking everyone from Albert Einstein to the dweebish host of a popular children's television program. Black and white, the teachers offered their ridicule as though it were an olive branch. "Here," they said, "this is something we each have in common, proof that we're all brothers under the skin."

QUESTIONS FOR DISCUSSION

1. Why does Sedaris introduce his selection with the fact that the school district will implement racial integration with forced busing? What does the Spanish teacher's anecdote about the "colored girl" at the state fair who wanted to touch the teacher's hair reflect about common attitudes of the time regarding racial integration in the schools?
2. Why is Sedaris critical of his teachers and especially their sense of humor? What does Sedaris fear? Why does Sedaris believe that he is a member of a secret society founded on self-loathing?
3. How and why does Sedaris identify with the African American students who will be coming to his school in the fall? Why does he welcome their arrival and feel that they have more power than he does?
4. Why is Sedaris anxious about his one-month trip to summer camp in Greece? Why is it easier for his sister Lisa to adjust to camp?
5. Why are Jason and Sedaris frightened by their sexual experience? Why does Sedaris become jealous of Jason?
6. Why does Sedaris end the essay with the observation of his new science teacher, "a black man very adept at swishing his way across the room, mocking everyone from Albert Einstein to the dweebish host of a popular children's television program"? What does he mean when he says, "Black and white, the teachers offered their ridicule as though it were an olive branch"?

CONNECTION

Compare Sedaris's recollections of antigay bias in school with the types of prejudice against gays described in Julie Apodaca's "Gay Marriage: Why the Resistance?" (see page 390).

IDEAS FOR WRITING

1. What purpose do you think that Sedaris had in mind when writing and publishing this selection? Write an essay in which you discuss his most important points. Do you think he is successful at what he set out to achieve?
2. Write an essay that compares the way students and teachers dealt with the issue of homosexuality at your own high school with Sedaris's experiences and insights. How were the comments and activities sanctioned at Sedaris's junior high both similar and different from what was happening at your high school? How do you feel about the way homosexuals were treated at your high school?

RELATED WEB SITES

David Sedaris
`http://home.pacifier.com/~paddockt/sedaris.html`
Learn about David Sedaris at this Web site dedicated to the author and comedian. Read articles about Sedaris, read or listen to his work and interviews, view his bibliography, talk to other fans, and find out where the author will speak next.

Gay Literature
`www.gayliterature.com/biblios.htm`
This Web site is devoted to sharing the works of the world's gay writers. One can also find several relevant links to other sites that discuss gay literature and its influence on society.

Rosa Contreras

On Not Being a Girl

Rosa Contreras was born in Jalisco, Mexico, and raised in Half Moon Bay, California. She majored in Latin American studies and anthropology. Writing the following essay—a response to Julius Lester's essay "On Being a Boy"—helped Contreras to think more analytically about the expectations that her family had for her when she was a young girl and about how both her expectations and those of her family changed as she prepared herself for college.

JOURNAL

Write about an experience during your teenage years in which you disagreed with your family over what your role or responsibilities should be as a girl or a boy.

As I grew into adolescence, I experienced constant conflict between being a girl and having what have been traditionally considered "masculine" qualities. At the same time that I wanted to be contemplative and artful, I also wanted to take the initiative and all the responsibility which is typically a male role. I envied the opposite sex and their advantages and often found myself frustrated by my culture's traditional views of gender roles; I tried actively to break away from the typical role of a girl as defined in the Mexican family. In fact, growing up in a Mexican household with strong cultural values while also experiencing American culture with its less clearly defined gender roles allowed me to criticize both cultures from different perspectives. This allowed me to take the ideals that I liked from both and reject those that I did not agree with. In this manner, I was able to build my own set of values, and naturally, I have tried to inculcate them into my family.

As the oldest child in my family, I was given by my parents responsibilities fit for an adult, while they insisted that I remain a little girl, innocent and oblivious to boys and sex. I, in turn, rebelled; I did not want to be seen as an obedient, subservient girl, with all the qualities that make for a good Mexican wife. Every day I pushed to assert myself as strong, able to take on anything and succeed. I wanted to show my father and every other male in my life that I could do everything a boy could, if not more.

By the time I was twelve, I was tired of being a girl, sick of girls' activities. By this time I had accumulated five baby dolls, fourteen Barbie dolls, three Ken dolls, and four younger siblings. The fact that I was a girl, and the oldest one at that, burdened me with the responsibility of watching over my sisters and brother. If they hurt themselves, or strayed away from home, no one was blamed except me. I still remember one day when my little brother ran into the house, crying because he had slipped on the gravel while running. Upon hearing my brother's shrill cries, my father became irritated and turned toward me: "Look what happened! You're supposed to watch them!" I became angry. Why was I being blamed? Why did I have to watch them all the time?

One day I finally yelled out to my parents what I had been feeling for a while: "Why do I always get yelled at for the things they do? It's not my fault!— I can't always be watching THEM. THEY'RE your kids; you chose to have them! I wasn't even asked! I never asked to be born, much less asked to be born first!"

5   Looking back, I realize that those were extremely cruel and ungrateful words. Nevertheless, with this outcry, I opened my parents' eyes, and they saw that they were, in fact, being unreasonable when they expected me to watch four children all the time. Maybe they had already realized the unfairness of the situation I was in, because they did not protest or reprimand me for telling them how I felt. Afterwards, I was no longer blamed for my siblings' actions, and was given more independence from caring for them.

Along with protesting against the rules of watchdog and disciplinarian, which, in Mexican culture, are commonly reserved for girls, I did not like it that my family members disapproved of my love of reading. Nobody in my immediate or extended family gives books the importance that I do. Maybe the fact that I am a girl meant that books should not be very important to me. In old Mexican tradition, there exists the idea that it is not good for women to know too much. Not good for whom? For their husbands. A man was not a "real" man if his wife knew more than he did. However, I suspect that the main problem my family had with my reading books was that I often neglected my household chores because I would, literally, spend all day submerged in learning about other people, other worlds.

By the time I was twelve, I had disappointed my parents in their quest to make me a productive and useful young lady, according to what Mexican custom decrees. While the rest of the house was clean, my room was a mess. I had other things to do, like homework, studying for tests, reading, and playing basketball. And horror of horrors! I couldn't even cook a pot of beans. My mother was often distressed at my inability (and lack of desire) to cook and do housework, which simply did not interest me. I felt housework was a waste of time, and I'd rather be doing something else. More importantly, though, I hated it because I associated it with the oppression and subservience of Latina women, including those in my family.

The different roles of men and women in Mexican society are clearly marked and instilled in children from a very young age. While in first and third grade, I went to elementary school in Mexico. While the boys were encouraged to excel in athletics and academics, the girls competed in crocheting and embroidering. At the end of the year, there was a contest to see whose work was the most beautiful. Approximately once every two weeks, each girl had to help in mopping, cleaning windows, or sweeping her classroom. Therefore, at a very young age, girls were taught to do housework and feminine things, like embroidery. My mother, all my aunts, and most Mexican women that I know were taught that the value of a woman consisted in keeping her family well-fed and a squeaky-clean house.

I realize that it was complicated for my mother to pass on these same values to me because we were no longer living in Mexico. But possibly because we were so far away from Mexico, it became very important for her to make this new home like her old one. Therefore, she tried to make sure that, although her daughters were being raised in a foreign country, we were still raised as she was taught. So when I refused to agree with the traditional Mexican ideals for raising a girl, she probably felt as though she had somehow failed. But I could not go along with what I truly felt was wrong. I could not please my older relatives in the way I was expected to because living in the United States, where the issue of women's rights is more openly debated, had opened my eyes to new and better possibilities for women.

10   From elementary school to high school, I went to school with a predominantly white population and came home to a Mexican household. At school I was taught what I liked. The teachers encouraged and praised me for my love of reading. Boys and girls were equally expected to do well in both sports and academics. Boys even took home economics! But often, when I brought home these ideas and chose to read rather than do housework or wait on my father and siblings, I was scolded. I was in a new environment that my parents had never experienced, so they did not understand why I felt so strongly about the way of life women had always led in Latin American cultures.

From reading, which allowed me to learn a lot about other people, other lifestyles, and achieving excellent grades in school, I often felt that I knew it all. I became very outspoken. At first, I scolded my mother privately when I saw her being subservient to my father. When she waited up for him, I would become angry and tell her: "Why are you doing this? I can't believe you're waiting up for him to feed him dinner! It's not like he can't get it himself!" Later, I became bolder. For example, when I'd hear my dad ask my mother for tortillas, I would say: "They're on the stove. You can get them." By the time I was twelve, I had my future laid out for me. I would always say that when I got older, I would have a career and my husband would share in the household responsibilities. I was not about to go out and work and then come home to do even more work. I understood that the status of my mother as a housewife required that she do this kind of work, but I felt it was unfair that she had to work all day, while my father could come home and not do anything for the rest of the evening.

I know that the many outbursts and arguments I have had (and still do, although less often now than before) concerning women's equality were the cause for much conflict in my household. However, I realize today that because of my efforts, my parents have changed their ideas about what women can accomplish. As a young girl, I refused to mold myself to be good and docile, with traditional moral values and knowledge. I understand that these ideas are very ingrained in Mexican society and they will be hard to change, but I cannot stand by and watch the oppression of these women and keep myself quiet. Now, as a young woman, I'm on my way to defying the role traditionally designated for women. During my high school days, my mother often encouraged me to study hard so that I could have a career. She would tell me, "Study, so that you can have a better life." She wanted me to have the option of being someone else rather than a full-time housewife, who always depends on her husband. I believe I have shown my father that I am capable of succeeding, just like all men and women can if given the opportunity. He has grown to accept me as I am and to understand my way of thinking. I have earned my parents' respect, and today they are extremely proud of all that I have achieved.

QUESTIONS FOR DISCUSSION

1. What aspects of Mexican American culture made it difficult for Contreras to feel comfortable in her family role?
2. What might have contributed to Contreras's mother's tendency to reinforce the old ways? How were her family's values influenced by living in the United States? How did her family respond to her rebellion?
3. How does Contreras use examples of her family's interactions and her responsibilities in the home to illustrate her thesis about not fitting into the mold of "proper" female behavior?
4. Why do you think that Contreras's parents finally supported her desire to become independent?

Julie Bordner Apodaca

Gay Marriage: Why the Resistance?

Julie Bordner Apodaca was a student at the College of Alameda in California when she wrote the following essay. She is a native of Alameda and an aspiring writer who returned to college part-time after ten years out of school, while also working and starting a family. Ever since her elementary school days, Apodaca has enjoyed argumentation and has tried to encourage her fellow students and cowork-ers to see beyond biases and misconceptions about people whom society has labeled as "different." Thus, when she was assigned to write a paper on a controversial issue for her critical thinking course, she chose to write on the subject of gay mar-riages and to examine the underlying causes for bias against such relationships.

JOURNAL

What are your feelings about gay marriage? Why is it such a controversial issue?

It has been over twenty years since the Stonewall riot triggered the civil rights movement in the gay and lesbian community. In the past two years, a good portion of the movement's focus has been on the issue of legalized marriage for homosexual couples, a move that many leaders in the gay community see as essentially conservative, as a sign that gays are opting for more traditional, sta-ble lifestyles and desire recognition as committed couples. Thus American soci-ety has been asked to expand the traditionally heterosexual institution of marriage to include gay and lesbian couples. The response from mainstream America has been largely negative, due in part to the homophobic attitudes that permeate our society.

To understand why society continues to have a negative reaction to the idea of legalizing gay marriage, we must first understand homophobia. Webster's defines "homophobia" as "hatred or fear of homosexuals or homosexuality." Homophobic attitudes, which are generally emotional and lacking in factual foundation, have many origins, some of which are religious, some political and sociological, some psychological, and some even medical in nature. In a gen-eral sense, it can be argued that the roots of homophobia in America can be found in the institutions and philosophy that are at the heart of our culture: our dominant religious tradition, our political and class systems, our moral per-spective, and our psychological makeup.

Some of the most passionate arguments against legalization of gay and les-bian marriages stem from the Judaic and Christian fundamentalist religions in our society. A common belief is that homosexuality is a sin; not only is it morally wrong, but it also mocks natural laws and the will of God. Marriage is a sanctified privilege of heterosexual union that constructs a foundation for the procreation and nurture of children. Despite the fact that many gays have dependent children from previous heterosexual unions, homosexuals are not seen by the religious fundamentalist as having the capacity for procreation within their relationships; thus sexual relations between homosexuals are viewed by many religious people as sinful and mocking, a way of undermining the essential meaning of marriage.

Some social thinkers hold views against homosexual marriage that coincide in some ways with those of the religious fundamentalists. Such individuals resist the legalization or wide acceptance of gay relationships, fearing the repercussions to the already threatened traditional family. With the stigma against homosexuality relaxed, perhaps the 20 percent of closeted homosexuals who marry heterosexual partners may instead choose gay partners. This could lead to a decline in the numbers of heterosexual marriages and even to the rise of other unusual social arrangements thought of as destabilizing to our society, such as polygamy or group marriage (Hartinger 682). The traditional two-partner heterosexual marriage, already on the decline, could become a rarity, and our basic social structure, which historically was designed around this form of relationship, may crumble. The weakness of this type of causal reasoning is that it is based upon an assumption that it is somehow unhealthy for a society to change and evolve, as well as upon a view of the "stable nuclear family unit" that denies historical realities such as abusive families, alcoholism in the nuclear family, and other causes for the decline of the nuclear family, such as the high cost of maintaining a home, the high divorce rate, and the trend toward dual-career families.

5　　Despite the weaknesses in the reasoning, arguments against gay marriages as contributors toward the undermining of traditional families often have been used by politicians in order to win the support of the populace who feel that family values are endangered. Vice President Dan Quayle's attacks on the "cultural elite" during the 1992 presidential campaign could be seen as a veiled attack on homosexuals and their relationships. According to Quayle, the cultural elite are those who "respect neither tradition or standards. They believe that moral truths are relative and all 'life styles' are equal" (qtd. in Salter A15). Quayle's comments stirred both praise and rage throughout America in the summer of 1992; his ideas touched a sympathetic chord for many who are painfully aware of the increased fragility of the traditional nuclear, heterosexual family unit.

However, it is not only religious, conservative sociologists and aspiring politicians who promote homophobia; our government and its official branches play a key role as well. For instance, the U.S. military continues to resist fully accepting homosexuals in the armed forces, despite any evidence that would suggest that these individuals generally are unfit for duty, are disruptive, or pose a security threat. The discrimination against homosexual relationships in the military is instrumental in fostering and maintaining the psychological fears and stereotypes associated with homosexuals: that they are unstable, immoral, and, in some vague sense, a threat to the security of our nation.

The AMA does not classify homosexuality as a disease or a disorder, due to scientific experiments done in the 1950s that discredited the notion of the homosexual as any more neurotic or maladjusted than any other group in society. However, many people continue to cling to the outmoded belief that homosexuality is a psychological disorder. Some, including a minority in the psychiatric profession, believe that homosexuality should be therapeutically treated, rather than sanctioned by recognition of homosexual unions as the equivalent to "normal" married relationships. However, psychologist Richard Isay does not believe that the fear of homosexuality is simply a reaction to the idea of a "deviant" sex act; Isay considers that the fear and hatred for homosexuality is related intimately to "the fear and hatred of what is perceived as being 'feminine' in other men and in oneself" (qtd. in Alter 27). Thus, for some people, insecurity and mistrust of one's own sexuality may cause irrational anxiety about or contempt toward the homosexual. If homosexual marriages were legal, gay couples might feel free publicly and physically to express their affections. This possibility of overt display of homosexuality in turn adds to the homophobic individual's fantasies that, rather than witnessing such encounters with "natural" revulsion, he or she could possibly experience an unwanted arousal.

Another common psychological concern about homosexual marriages, despite evidence that points to homosexuality as a quasi-biological sexual orientation rather than a learned or conditioned sexual response, is that legally sanctioned gay relationships will somehow influence children to become homosexual. The reasoning goes that adolescents and even younger children are often confused by the intense and unfamiliar sexual feelings stirring inside them; thus the adolescent confronted with the "normality" of homosexual relationships, in or out of their own family circle, might tend to gravitate toward this kind of sexual outlook. Furthermore, part of the stereotype of the homosexual as sexual deviant is that gays enjoy the company of young children and might, if not sufficiently isolated from mainstream society, take advantage of the vulnerability of naïve and confused adolescents, encouraging such children to engage in gay sex.

A more recent fear that fuels the hostility to gay marriages is medically based but, as so many of the fears discussed above, based upon causal oversimplification. Consider AIDS; this disease is really a nightmare for our entire society, not just confined to the gay community, and can be spread by both heterosexual sexual conduct and drug-related activity. Yet the fearful stereotype persists that AIDS is somehow a "gay" disease; in fact, some religious zealots have even spoken of AIDS as God's "divine retribution" against gays for their blasphemous behavior, despite the reality that gays didn't originate the disease and in spite of the fact that the gay community has made enormous progress in educating itself about AIDS and in discontinuing the unsafe sexual practices of the past. The legalization of homosexual marriage elicits the fear among those with a deep fear of both AIDS and homosexuality that, along with the resulting increase in the numbers of homosexuals, such legalization will somehow cause the AIDS epidemic to become even more severe. This is truly an ironic misconception, when we consider that monogamous marriage, gay or heterosexual, is one of the most conservative sexual practices, one of the least likely to lead to a spread of disease beyond the bounds of matrimony.

10   As we have seen, there are many causes for the fear that surrounds the legalization of homosexual marriages. The cumulative effect of these causes has prevented legislation supporting such relationships in almost all parts of the country. Although some of the arguments against homosexual marriages may seem on the surface to have some justification, most are based on ignorance, irrationality, and fear. Perhaps, as Ernest Van Den Haag puts it, "nothing will persuade heterosexuals to believe that homosexuality is psychologically or morally as legitimate as their own heterosexuality" (38); however, despite the resistance that is likely to occur, it seems to me that a national effort should be made to dispel the misconceptions regarding homosexuality. What benefit is there in hiding behind irrational fears? Homosexuality is not going to disappear; history has proven that. Society would benefit from a better understanding of homosexuality, for if people were able to think more critically about the myths and the issues surrounding homosexuality, perhaps there would be a decrease in the nation's homophobia and an increased understanding from which all people, gay and heterosexual alike, would benefit. We cannot expect a change overnight, but we can begin to educate the ignorant and break down some of the prejudice. As Martin Luther King, Jr., once said, "Take the first step in faith. You don't have to see the whole staircase, just take the first step."

WORKS CITED

Alter, Jonathan. "Degrees of Discomfort." *Newsweek* 12 Mar. 1992: 27.

Hartinger, Brent. "A Case for Gay Marriage." *Commonweal* 22 Nov. 1991: 681–83.

Salter, Stephanie. "The 'Cultural Elite' and the Rest of Us." San Francisco *Chronicle* 14 Jun. 1992: A15.

Van Den Haag, Ernest. "Sodom and Begorrah." *National Review* 29 Apr. 1991: 35–38.

QUESTIONS FOR DISCUSSION

1. What are the major causes of the resistance to gay marriage as explored in the essay? Could the student have discussed other causes? Which ones?

2. Apodaca refutes the reasoning that underlies most of the "fears" she discusses. Is her refutation effective and fair?

3. What factual evidence does Apodaca use to support her general statements and conclusions? What additional evidence might she have used?

4. This essay includes some quotations from authorities or spokespersons to support some of the writer's ideas and conclusions about social attitudes. Were such citations of authorities handled appropriately, or would you have liked to see either more or less reliance on citation of authority?

TOPICS FOR RESEARCH AND WRITING

1. Develop an extended definition of masculinity. When relevant, show how it relates to the ideas presented by Canty, Paxton, and Lehmann-Haupt. To what extent is masculinity primarily a cultural concept, and to what extent is it a biological reality or a product of evolution? Do some research to help find some answers to these questions.

2. After reading the selection by Maxine Hong Kingston, review what you have learned about the limits, challenges, or advantages of being born female in a traditional society, considering your own experiences as well as outside readings in this area. Write your findings in a documented essay.

3. Write an essay based on readings from the text, research, as well as your own thoughts and feelings about the role that sex plays in an individual's life, health, and sense of well-being. Consider if sex is primarily a procreative act, an expression of love, an erotic experience, or a combination of experiences. Does the importance of sex and the sexual act vary significantly from culture to culture?

4. Reread the selection by Freud in this chapter that reflects on the relationships among dreams, the unconscious, and sexuality, and do some further reading in this area. Write your conclusions in the form of a documented essay. To what extent are dreams the product of the unconscious repression of sexual desires, and to what extent are they related more to issues in waking life?

5. How are definitions of male and female identity continuing to change in the era of cyberspace? In addition to doing some outside reading, you might interview some people you know who spend a lot of time in chat rooms and/or visit some chat rooms where gender identity role-playing is common.

6. The works in this chapter by Sedaris and Apodaca explore societal fears and rejection of gays. Do some research into these fears and their origins, and write an essay about the causes and effects of homophobia.

7. Write about a film that portrays an issue of sexuality or gender. How does the film comment on certain issues raised in the readings in this chapter? You can select a film from the following list or one of your own choosing: *Oleanna, The Crying Game, The Wedding Banquet, Orlando, Wilde, Shakespeare in Love, Boys Don't Cry, Chasing Amy, Legally Blonde, Closer, Sideways, The Stepford Wives, American Beauty, Before Sunset, Talk to Her, Kinsey, What Women Want,* and *Million Dollar Baby.*

The Double/The Other

Pablo Picasso (1881–1973)
Girl Before a Mirror (1932)

Created at the height of Picasso's artistic power, *Girl Before a Mirror* incorporates
what he had learned through the great twentieth-century art movements to which
he contributed—Expressionism, Primitivism, Cubism, Classicism, and Surrealism.
The painting portrays a woman whose beautiful, masklike classical profile seems
to reflect in her mirror an image of her inner self.

JOURNAL

Write about what you see when you look at yourself in a mirror. Does the image you see
look like the self you know, or does it seem like someone else, not entirely familiar or acceptable to you?

Within each one of us there is another whom we do not know. He speaks to us in dreams and tells us how differently he sees us from how we see ourselves.
                                    CARL JUNG

Our challenge is to call forth the humanity within each adversary, while preparing for the full range of possible responses. Our challenge is to find a path between cynicism and naiveté.
                                    FRAN PEAVEY
                                    Us and Them

ARGUMENT AND DIALOGUE

Traditional Argument

Traditional argument begins by defining a problem or issue, then taking a position or stance. In this form of argument, the advocate develops a clear thesis and demonstrates its validity through a series of convincing logical arguments, factual supports, and references to authority. Often the major aim of argument is seen as an attack on the ideas and positions of an opponent with the goal of persuading the audience of the correctness of the proponent's position. Arguments that don't quite fit into the debater's viewpoint are sometimes ignored or are introduced as refutation of the principal argument. Such traditional debate is frequently linked to political rhetoric, where only one candidate can be elected. A fundamental part of public life, oppositional argument at its best can be a powerful method of presenting one's own position and beliefs. At its worst, traditional argument can be manipulative and one-sided, leading people to believe that debate is a matter of verbal warfare and that every decision implies an either/or choice rather than an attempt at genuine communication. For examples of oppositional argument that lead to verbal warfare, visit some politically oriented Web sites on the Internet—or read the editorial page of your daily newspaper.

Dialogic Argument

Dialogic argument is a form of argument based on thoroughly presenting facts and reasons for supporting a position. This type of argument acknowledges the importance of creating a bridge between opposing viewpoints that are often rigidly separated in a traditional argument. It may remind you of the literary dialogue between opposites that we see at work in some of this chapter's stories and poems; it is best exemplified in expository form here in Fran Peavey's essay, "Us and Them." The dialogic argument emphasizes the need for discussion and a genuine exchange of ideas, while making a conscious effort to bring together seemingly irreconcilable viewpoints in order to arrive at a synthesis of opposing perspectives and allow the writer and the audience to learn more about themselves. Through the dialogic approach, you can come to a new awareness of positions you may not have understood or considered. Working to understand these opposite positions does not necessarily imply that you totally accept them, or that you abandon your own ideas and viewpoints. What it does suggest is that you consider the possibilities of strong arguments, positions, and value systems that are different from your own, and that you make a real attempt to integrate these positions into your thinking.

Dialogue and Prewriting

An effective prewriting strategy for a balanced argument paper involves engaging your opponent in a dialogue. Begin by creating a dialogue that explores different positions relative to your subject, your thesis, and your supporting points. Following is an example of an excerpt from student dialogue on the subject of reading fairy tales to small children. We have labeled the two sides in the dialogue "I" and "Me." "I" stands for the position that the student really wants to present, while "Me" represents the side of the argument, perhaps a side of the self that the writer doesn't want to acknowledge and perceives as the opponent.

I: I think all children should read fairy tales. I always loved hearing them as a kid; I liked the scary parts and the adventures. Fairy tales are so much more engrossing than the trash on the boob tube.

ME: I can see that you really like fairy tales. But wouldn't a lot of kids who get upset easily be frightened by reading stories about mean stepmothers and wicked witches, like in "Hansel and Gretel"?

I: I understand what you're saying; fairy tales might frighten some children, especially if they were very young or if they had had some really horrible things happen in their own lives that the stories reminded them of. Still, I think I can handle your objections. Kids should be read fairy tales by an adult who makes time to explain the issues in the story and who can reassure them if they think the story is too scary; after all, a fairy tale is "only a story."

ME: Well, I can see the point in having adults read the stories and explain them, but you're wrong about TV. There are some great programs for kids, like *Sesame Street* and *Barney,* that teach children to have positive values. And what about the values in those fairy tales? *Sesame Street* teaches you to love everyone and to give girls equal opportunities to succeed! Fairy tales are so old-fashioned and sexist, with all those beautiful sleeping princesses waiting around for Prince Charming.

I: I know what you mean. The values in fairy tales aren't always very modern. That's why it's really important that the adult who reads the stories to the kids discusses the old-fashioned way of life that is being presented and compares the world of the tale with our own values and lifestyles. I can see letting kids watch

TV, too. Fairy tales are only a part of the imaginative experience of childhood, but they're still a very important part!

In this short dialogue, you see the "I" and "Me" positions being brought closer together. "I"'s initial position is now more clearly stated, with some important, commonsense qualifications brought in through the interaction with the "Me."

Prewriting and the Audience

Before you write your essay, try to establish a similar kind of dialogue with your imaginary audience as you did with yourself. As in traditional argument or in any type of writing, this involves trying to determine the interests and values of your audience. For example, the student writing about fairy tales would have to decide if the audience includes cautious parents of school-age children or liberal educators with a progressive philosophy of child rearing. Creating a clear mental image of the audience is essential before appropriate arguments can be selected. Once you have a clear image of the audience in mind, approach your readers directly and respectfully. Make the audience an integral part of your arguments. Do not try to manipulate or dazzle them with your facts and figures; instead, establish a common ground and state the positions you hold in common with them while designating areas of mutual agreement or possible compromise. This approach will remind you to keep your audience's point of view in mind and will facilitate meaningful communication.

Defining Key Terms

As in traditional argument, it is important for dialogic arguers to define their terms. Definitions support clear communication and help develop rapport in an argument. People feel more comfortable in a discussion when they understand what key terms mean. For example, if I am arguing for reading fairy tales to young children and am referring to fairy tales such as those of Hans Christian Andersen, while my audience thinks I am discussing modern fantasy children's stories such as those by Maurice Sendak, then we are really thinking about different definitions of a fairy tale and will be unlikely to come to a mutual understanding. When defining your terms, use simple, straightforward definitions; avoid connotative language designed to manipulate or trick your audience.

Evaluating Facts

If you have taken a statistics course or read articles in journals, you know that facts and statistics can be interpreted in a variety of ways. When reading the factual studies that will form an important part of the support in any argument paper, you need to consider a number of questions. Have the results of the social scientists or psychologists you are studying been confirmed by other researchers? Are the data current? Was it collected by qualified researchers using thorough and objective methods? Are the results expressed in clear and unambiguous language? These and other questions should be asked about your sources of information so that you can create a sound factual base for the arguments you use in your paper. In doing research for your argument, you might look at Web sites, even extremist ones, to get the feeling for some of the strong sentiments that different groups have about your issue—but don't rely on these partisan, advocacy sites to provide objective information. On the other hand, you do need to mention both widely believed facts and popular misconceptions that may *oppose* the argument you are making. You will need to respectfully show your audience how some of these beliefs are not factual, show how others are not relevant, and concede that some are relevant and either can be dealt with by your proposed argument or cannot within the practical limits of the situation at hand. Present your supporting facts clearly; avoid overstating your conclusions in absolute, unqualified terms or overgeneralizing from limited data.

Feelings in Argument

Emotions play such a significant role in our lives that any argument that tried to be totally rational, pretending that emotional concerns were unimportant and that only facts have significance, would be unrealistic and ineffective. Emotions, both your own and those of your audience, are a central concern in argument. Although you need to present your ideas in ways that won't offend your readers, when feelings are a central issue in the argument itself, emotional issues do need to be directly confronted. For example, it would be impossible to discuss a subject such as abortion without acknowledging your own feelings and those of the audience. In this case, sharing such feelings will help to create an open and trusting relationship with your audience.

However, an important distinction must be made between acknowledging your feelings and exploiting them to manipulate your readers. Often, strong arguments are based on emotions, which can be exaggerated in an attempt to strengthen your position and cause you to overlook important issues. Avoid language that could ignite emotional fireworks in a discussion. Bringing in irrelevant appeals for pity or fear can obscure the real issues involved in a discussion. Try to use language that is emotionally neutral in describing the positions and ideas taken by the opposition. By doing so, you are more likely to keep the confidence of readers who might otherwise be offended by an adversarial position and manipulative language.

Argument can be one of the most satisfying forms of writing, but it can be one of the most difficult. To satisfy the factual, logical, and emotional demands of shaping an effective argument, you can do the following:

- Use the inner dialogue as an aid to prewriting and exploring different positions.

- Empathize with and acknowledge the assumptions and needs of your audience.
- Define key terms.
- Evaluate and use relevant factual supports.
- Be honest and direct in your treatment of the emotional aspects of an issue.

All of these strategies will be of use to you in your efforts to find a stance in argument that allows you to build bridges between your inner world and the worlds of others. This type of argument, when thoughtfully developed with an audience in mind, can be one of the most effective means of communication that a writer can draw upon, both in academic discourse and in private and community life.

THEMATIC INTRODUCTION: THE DOUBLE/THE OTHER

Many of us are conscious of having an alternate self that, for whatever reasons, we do not make public. We sometimes see glimpses of an alternative or underground personality in a family member, friend, supervisor, colleague, or even media figure. From Greek myths to nursery rhymes and fairy tales, from Shakespearean doubles and disguises to Gothic tales of horror and revenge, from Victorian mysteries to the modern psychological short story, images of the double, of twins in spirit or twins in reality, have marked our developing understanding of the workings of the human mind.

The frequent recurrence and popularity of the double in mythology, literature, and popular culture are often attributed to the human need to explore, understand, and perhaps conquer divided feelings that individuals have about the parts of themselves that are in conflict. These conflicts are revealed in many forms: the good versus the evil self, the rational versus the irrational self, the civilized versus the antisocial or criminal self, the masculine self versus the feminine self, the physical self versus the spiritual self, the controlled conventional versus the wild self, and the practical versus the dreamy self.

Although literature and human experiences suggest that inward journeys into the mind's dual nature can lead to confusion, or even neurosis or psychosis, there is the possibility of integrating and balancing the opposing parts through developing an increased awareness of the inner self. In this way, through the main character of a poem or story, the writer or a reader can experience a form of rebirth, emerging with a more balanced and confident sense of self and purpose. Your journey through this chapter will provide you with new insights into the dualities within the human personality.

The chapter opens with two selections that explore the double nature of the self. First, in Judith Ortiz Cofer's poem, "The Other," the Hispanic American speaker acknowledges the power of her "other," who is sensual, uninhibited, even dangerous, and more in touch with her cultural roots than her well-behaved public self. The comic strip superheroes that Danny Fingeroth discusses in his essay "The Dual Identity" also have second selves that they keep secret from others, yet Fingeroth shows how the interplay of dual identities actually helps many of these mythical heroes to function more effectively and to appeal to some of our deeper needs.

The next three readings will help you to think about the importance of getting the oppositional sides of your mind and psyche to work together productively. Jungian therapist Robert Johnson, in his essay "Owning Your Own Shadow," explores the dangerous consequences, both to individuals and to their societies, of failing to recognize and heal inner divisions within the human mind. In a selection from his classic double novella, *The*

Strange Case of Dr. Jekyll and Mr. Hyde ("Henry Jekyll's Full Statement of the Case"), Robert Louis Stevenson illustrates through the voice of the doomed Dr. Jekyll the negative consequences of trying to separate the good or civilized side of the human character from its sensual and irrational side. In a lighter vein, another kind of "divided self" is seen in Kate Sullivan's essay/story "J. Lo vs. K. Sul," a fan's tale of the attempted rejection of a "superstar" persona, J. Lo, the object of envy and hatred on the part of K. Sul, a rock fan who currently lacks a career.

The next two selections discuss the crucial impact of citizens' inner conflict on political and social stances and decisions. In an effort to find some way out of the dilemma of the other in society in her essay "Us and Them," longtime peace activist Fran Peavey suggests a new approach to community organization and political action that avoids dehumanizing and dismissing the opposition. Bishop Desmond Mpilo Tutu would agree with Peavey, and presents in his essay, "No Future Without Forgiveness," a concrete example in the form of the South African Truth and Reconciliation Commission's accomplishments in healing the rift between Afrikaaners and black Africans in the wake of the dismantling of the apartheid system.

The student essays that conclude the chapter offer new ways of thinking about how the double-sided nature of social issues can be internalized and affect the development of an individual's self-concept. In the first student essay, "Mixed-Up," Susan Voyticky, the daughter of an African American mother and a white father, discusses some of the difficult decisions she had to make to create an identity that she could call her own. Jill Ho in "Affirmative Action: Perspectives from a Model Minority" reflects on how Asian Americans face a glass ceiling, a double-sided reward, after gaining access to mainstream jobs.

Exploring the duality of the human mind and spirit as reflected in the essays, stories, and poems included in this chapter should prove to be provocative and enlightening. Becoming aware of the voices that exist within you in addition to your dominant voice or persona can help you understand yourself more fully and can provide you with additional resources to draw upon in your writing.

Judith Ortiz Cofer

The Other

(See headnote on Judith Ortiz Cofer in Chapter 3.) As a poet, Cofer often explores issues of cultural identity and heritage. In the following poem, notice how Cofer presents the inner conflict of identity experienced by the speaker through a series of progressively disturbing images.

Write about a part of yourself that you have difficulty accepting because the "other" in you seems too unconventional, wild, or irresponsible.

A sloe-eyed dark woman shadows me.
In the morning she sings
Spanish love songs in a high
falsetto filling my shower stall
5   with echoes.
She is by my side
in front of the mirror as I slip
into my tailored skirt and she
into her red cotton dress.
10 She shakes out her black mane as I
run a comb through my close-cropped cap.
Her mouth is like a red bull's eye
daring me.
Everywhere I go I must
15 make room for her: she crowds me
in elevators where others wonder
at all the space I need.
At night her weight tips my bed, and
it is her wild dreams that run rampant
20 through my head exhausting me. Her heartbeats,
like dozens of spiders carrying the poison
of her restlessness over the small
distance that separates us,
drag their countless legs
25 over my bare flesh.

QUESTIONS FOR DISCUSSION

1. How would you characterize the "other" that Cofer creates in this poem? Is it anything like your own "other"?
2. Describe the speaker's main self. How does her main self differ from that of the "other"?
3. Which part of the speaker is dominant or will eventually win out in the struggle?
4. Why do you think the two sides of the speaker's personality are in conflict? What different cultural and gender roles does each side reflect?
5. What images help to vividly portray the "other" and to contrast her with the speaker's main self?
6. What dreams and nocturnal fantasies of the speaker help to convey the struggle between the two sides of her personality? What do you think is

meant by the fantasy image, "Her heartbeats,/like dozens of spiders carrying the poison/of her restlessness"? In what sense is the restlessness a poison?

CONNECTION

Analyze this poem as a statement of the shadow as defined in the selection by Robert Johnson (see page 415).

IDEAS FOR WRITING

1. Write an essay about an inner struggle you have experienced that reflects a cultural conflict between two of the following: the culture of your parents, your friends, your school, your workplace, or your church. Include examples of ways that your inner conflict is reflected in your dreams and fantasies.
2. Write an essay that could take the form of a dialogue in which you explore inner conflicts that you have about making an important decision in your life. You might want to discuss whether to change your position on political or social issues, or on ways of relating to a marriage partner, friend, parent, supervisor at work, or teacher. After exploring your options, which choice seems preferable?

RELATED WEB SITES

Illuminating the Shadow: An Interview with Connie Zweig
www.scottlondon.com/insight/scripts/zweig.html
This online interview with author and psychotherapist Connie Zweig, from a weekly radio series called *Insight & Outlook,* defines the Jungian concept of the shadow and discusses celebrity and public fascination with the idea of the shadow self. The interview also raises the question of how to best integrate the shadow and the self.

Contradictions in Identity
www.apa.org/divisions/div44/olivia.htm
"Contradictions in Identity in Therapeutic Intervention" is an essay presented by Oliva M. Espin of San Diego State University at the National Multicultural Conference and Summit, 2005. Espin's essay deals with the inner divisions that modern women in therapy experience around issues of identity related to gender, culture, and race.

Danny Fingeroth

The Dual Identity: Of Pimpernels and Immigrants from the Stars

With a B.A. in filmmaking and a minor in creative writing, Danny Fingeroth went to work at Marvel Comics as a young man and ran Marvel's Spider-Man editorial line for a number of years. He has written many comic scripts and consulted on film adaptations of them. He started the magazine Write Now! *which is considered the best publication about writing for comics, animation, and science fiction; he followed this publication with* Draw Magazine, *which features step-by-step demonstrations of how a new character is created with words and visuals. Fingeroth teaches comics and graphic novel writing at New York University. His newest book is* Superman on the Couch: What Superheroes Really Tell Us About Ourselves and Our Society *(2004), from which the essay "The Dual Identity" is excerpted. Fingeroth's essay explores the dual natures and secret identities of many comic book heroes.*

JOURNAL

Write about a character from literature or popular culture who uses a mask or dual identity. What was the purpose of the "mask," and what does it suggest about our cultural values?

Though a disguise, Kent is necessary for the [Superman] myth to work. This uniquely American hero has two identities, one based on where he comes from in life's journey, one on where he's going. One is real, one an illusion, and both are necessary for the myth of balance in the assimilation process to be complete. Superman's powers make the hero capable of saving humanity; Kent's total immersion in the American heartland makes him want to do it. The result is . . . an optimistic myth of assimilation. . . .

> —Gary Engle, "What Makes Superman So Darned American?" in *Superman at Fifty: The Persistence of a Legend,* edited by Dennis Dooley and Gary Engle

We are who we pretend to be, so we must be careful about who it is we pretend to be.
> —Kurt Vonnegut, *Mother Night*

W hy does a person disguise his or her identity? There can be myriad reasons, although the very act can seem counterintuitive. Most people want *credit* for acts they are proud of. That is the nature of pride: "I made this," as the child's voice—the real or imagined voice of creator Chris Carter—says at the end of every episode of *The X-Files.*

In real life, there are many reasons people have for habitually disguising their identities or their actions. The most obvious would be the criminal who wears a mask so he will not be identified for future pursuit and incarceration.

The same can be said for acts of political or social courage in societies where such activities would be punished severely. Think of the masked mob informant or the hooded dissident in the Middle East. Or think of the Ku Klux Klan and its hooded cross burners. Their friends certainly know who they are, but their hoods keep them from being identified by their victims and by law-enforcement organizations. Plus, a mask or hood injects an element of terror into an individual's presence and presentation. The sight of many such hooded individuals massed together is the stuff of nightmares.

There are anonymous philanthropists who modestly wish that their acts speak for themselves, not for their own personal glorification.

5   There are graffiti artists whose "tags" consistently identify that they were there, but not who they are when you pass them on the street.

There is the anonymity of the telephone and the Internet, and of radio call-in shows, where the cloak of mystery gives people the courage to do and say things—either socially accepted as "good" or "bad," "right" or "wrong"—without fear of repercussion. Again, depending on the context and the intent, the hidden identity can be used to positive or negative effect. What is the popular *Crank Yankers* TV series but the exploits of anonymous phone pranksters, individuals usually seen as at best annoying and at worst criminally harassing? Generally, no one is permanently harmed by a phone prankster. Still, you'd be hard pressed to admire one, even one you found amusing.

How then, does this idea of disguise fit into our popular culture, and why has it become a staple, indeed one of the very definitions of, the superhero mythos?

In his classic routine "Thank You, Masked Man" (also made into an animated short), Lenny Bruce commented on the cliché of the masked hero—in this case the Lone Ranger—not only keeping his identity secret, but not even waiting around to be thanked. The reason for both these cultural conventions, according to Bruce—himself the "secret identity" of Leonard Schneider—is that the masked man doesn't want to get used to being thanked. If he became too dependent on it, how would he feel if he ever wasn't thanked? He wants to keep his motive pure: to make sure he does what he does because it's right, not to get thanked. So that may be a piece of why masked heroes appeal to us. They want their deeds to stand alone. That's a valid human desire that we can sympathize with.

Where did dual identity stories begin? Was it when Jacob disguised himself as Esau to get his father's blessing? Or was it Odysseus disguising himself in the pages of *The Odyssey?* Was it in the story where Leah disguised herself so that Jacob would marry her and not her sister? Going to Shakespeare, where would he have been without the disguises and impersonations used in *Twelfth Night* and *A Midsummer Night's Dream?* Disguise and deception have a long and honorable tradition in fiction, if not in real life.

10   To take us into the realm of heroic and superheroic disguises, we would probably start with Baroness Orczy's *Scarlet Pimpernel* mythology. Published in 1905, the *Pimpernel* tells of the adventures of Sir Percy Blanckney, a fop and

layabout who, it turns out, is also a master of disguise. As portrayed in the 1935 movie, starring Leslie Howard, the Pimpernel's alter ego is that of the most shallow and vain, albeit charming and witty, type of English aristocrat. But his secret agenda is to rescue *French* aristocrats who are condemned en masse to death at the guillotine by Robespierre and the excesses of the French Revolution.

The Pimpernel is not so much a mask as an attitude and a series of disguises. When at last discovered by his French nemesis—and his own wife, from whom he conceals his secret life—the Pimpernel still looks the same physically, but his carriage is suddenly more serious and dangerous. You can see this device used to comic effect by Jerry Lewis in *The Nutty Professor,* or, indeed, by Superman himself when he puts on the glasses that allegedly fool the world into thinking he and Clark Kent are two different people. Even the genre of teen movies in which a "plain" girl becomes glamorous always involves her removing glasses (and undoing her hair) to show the "secret identity" of the sex-pot within.

What fantasy does the double identity appeal to? Perhaps, as in the case of the Pimpernel, it is to allow us to believe that, deep down, we are or could be so much more than we appear. "If they only knew how special I am," we think. Don't we all have secret identities, those sides of ourselves we feel we dare not risk revealing? The secret identity is where our fantasies and ambitions take hold and ferment. We eagerly seek the time when we can give free reign to the "superhero within." But there is risk in being one's true self. Indeed, what if people don't like the real you? Well then, you can always go back, at least temporarily, to the pretend-you that they did like. Of course, in our real lives, there's much overlap between the "real" and the façade. One is always seeping into and through the other. A mask, a dual identity, makes the demarcation so much easier for us as well as those to whom we want to project our identities.

When you think of a mask, your first thought is of a criminal. This writer still recalls with a shiver the bandanna-wearing "Western Bandits" who demanded "all your gold," at an amusement park when he was a child. A mask is scary. It reduces the person wearing it to a single, sinister element. They are a living threat. You cannot reason with them. Their expression betrays no meaning beyond what their words say. They cannot be up to any good—nor mean you anything but harm. If they did, why would they cover their faces—or at least their true identities—and eschew responsibility for their actions?

So how did the masked hero come to be? (And here, I use the term *masked* as the superheroes do, both literally and metaphorically. A physical mask is not necessary to conceal identity, at least not among the superheroes.)

15   Through time and across civilizations, the mask has had much power and magic associated with it. African and South American shamans and priests wore ceremonial garb to perform their rituals, often with a mask as part of their costume. Clearly, the mask in such cases is not intended to fool anyone as to the identity of the wearer. It is simultaneously intended to make the wearer special and nondescript, the Everyman raised to the level of interlocutor with the holy. The mask is recognized as bestower of power as well as disguiser of identity.

A mask is intimidating. So why *should* it be confined to use by criminals? Why not use that intimidation factor against those who would do individuals or society harm on whatever scale? In real life, this leads to the aforementioned Ku Klux Klan and other vigilante and terrorist organizations. In the world of heroic fiction, though, such an affectation can be used to turn the tables on those who would do harm.

In the modern era, Zorro may be thought of as the first masked adventurer. Created by Johnston McCulley in his novel *The Curse of Capistrano,* which began its serialization in the August 9, 1919, issue of *All-Story Weekly* (the same magazine that introduced Tarzan), Zorro was the archetypal indolent rich laggard whose laziness and ennui were a cover for a passionate fighter for freedom. In such a case, Zorro needed a secret identity so that he could continue his life as an insider in the halls of power and wealth, privy to the goings on of the rich and powerful whom he could protect from those who would plunder their wealth, and whose rotten apples he could ferret out untroubled. Zorro, especially his movie incarnation in *The Mark of Zorro* in 1920, was certainly one of the role models for later masked heroes.

The Phantom, by Lee Falk and Ray Moore, was the first masked hero in the comic strips, and the first hero to adopt the trunks and leotard outfit—a legacy from circus performers of the time—and combine it with a cowl and a black mask that revealed no visible eyeballs. The Phantom's reason for the mask was to create the illusion of immortality, as one Phantom after another passed the mantle to a son.

Then there is the classic reason heroes give for maintaining dual identities: it will protect my loved ones from my enemies. That has some credence, until you stop to think about it. Does the policeman on the neighborhood beat have a secret identity? Does the teacher who works with delinquent kids? Come to think of it—maybe they should. Except, for the fact that that sort of thinking is where phenomena such as death squads emerge. Masked justice is rarely blind justice. Masked justice has an agenda, and in real life, the agenda is rarely to just give the police an extra "edge."

20   Spies may be seen as a subset of the dual-identity character. Even the flamboyant James Bond is, technically, an undercover operative. Often, in real life, spies are who they say they are, though their agendas are not what they purport them to be. And spies, even ones on "our side," are generally thought of as sneaky and untrustworthy. We accept that they have to be to do a dirty job on our behalf. But when espionage is presented outside the worlds of the *Alias* TV series and James Bond, it does indeed seem . . . well, underhanded. The CIA agents of the recent series *The Agency* are not really very nice people. Part of the reason for this is, well, they're always lying about who they really are.

Only the superhero disguises his identity for a noble purpose and is able to maintain his integrity while so doing. Why?

The secret identity, as Gary Engle notes, is deeply rooted in the American immigrant experience. As the *Ur* superhero, Superman is also the easiest and most direct manifestation of the dual identity. As Engle points out in his essay "What Makes Superman So Darned American?":

> The brilliant stroke in the conception of Superman—the *sine qua non* that makes the whole myth work—is the fact that he has two identities. The myth simply wouldn't work without Clark Kent, mild-mannered newspaper reporter . . . Adopting the white-bread image of a wimp is first and foremost a moral act for the Man of Steel. He does it to protect his parents from nefarious sorts who might use them to gain an edge over the powerful alien. Moreover, Kent adds to Superman's powers the moral guidance of a Smallville upbringing. Clark Kent . . . is the epitome of visible invisibility, someone whose extraordinary ordinariness makes him disappear in a crowd. In a phrase, he is the consummate figure of total cultural assimilation, and significantly, he is not real. Implicit in this is the notion that mainstream cultural norms, however useful, are illusions.

So, according to Engle, the immigrant origin is at the heart of the Superman dual identity. It's just that Superman is from another planet instead of another country. Superman's story is not unlike that of the kid who at home speaks the language of his parents' immigrant roots, but outside adopts the identity of the mainstream, attempting to blend in and become one with the adopted homeland. But the "regular guy" is the sham persona—because the power underneath is just too dangerous for people to be allowed to observe it any time they desire. The immigrant wants to excel but stay anonymous. He wants to make his parents proud—but not make them ashamed of who they themselves are, though he may, himself, be ashamed of them in certain profound ways.

In Siegel and Shuster's case, the home was the Yiddish-speaking, or at least Yiddish-inflected, home of the Eastern European Jewish immigrant stock they came from. The duo struggled with many of the same issues Superman did. Immigration and assimilation were issues that even a space-born superbeing could not avoid. As Engle notes:

> Immigration, of course, is the overwhelming fact in American history. Except for the Indians, all Americans have an immediate sense of their origins elsewhere. No nation on Earth has so deeply embedded in its social consciousness the imagery of passage from one social identity to another. . . . —80

25 further,

> Superman's powers . . . are the comic book equivalents of ethnic characteristics, and they protect and preserve the vitality of the foster community in which he lives in the same way that immigrant ethnicity has sustained American culture linguistically, artistically, economically, politically and spiritually. **The myth of Superman asserts with total confidence and a childlike innocence the value of the immigrant in American culture.** [Emphasis mine.]—81

and,

> Clinging to an Old World identity meant isolation in ghettos, confrontation with a prejudiced mainstream culture, second-class social status and impoverishment.

> On the other hand, forsaking the past in favor of total absorption into the main-
> stream, while it could result in socio-economic progress, meant a loss of the reli-
> gious, linguistic, even culinary traditions that provided a foundation for
> psychological well-being.—83

For the readers of early superhero stories, many of whom were children and grandchildren of immigrants, the characters were a symbolic reenactment of their own ambivalent feelings about where their roots lay, and where their lives in America were taking them. Dual identity superheroes would enable these readers to inhabit both sides of their dilemma. "Am I who I am at home, or am I the person I am outside my home? Which is the real me? Which is true and which false? Who should I *want* to be?"

In many ways, don't we all feel like strangers in a strange land when we first venture outside our homes to school or to work? Love home or hate it, it is familiar. We know who we must be to survive and possibly thrive there. But who do we become when we have some choice in what faces we present to the world? These are hard and basic choices we all have to make from our earliest days, certainly at first without even being aware that we're making them.

The superheroes make these choices in grander, more melodramatic, more colorful levels. But they clearly echo our own choices as we venture from the familiar terrain of home out into the world.

30 But Superman isn't merely an immigrant. He is an immigrant *orphan!* He didn't come here with his parents but as a representative of his entire race, and yet one who left that race as an infant. He's an infant who knows he's from somewhere, but knows precious little about where he's from compared to where he's landed. The problem—and the challenge—and the opportunity— is that *he is free to invent his own history*. Moreover, as an orphan, he *has to* invent his own history, since the one thing he does know is: he is not from here. As Engle says: "Orphans aren't merely free to reinvent themselves. They are *obliged* to do so."

So the dual identity is perhaps Superman's greatest wish fulfillment aspect, more so than flying or bending steel in his bare hands. He is able to cherry pick from the best both societies have to offer. His powers, which he actually only attained because he came to Earth—on Krypton, he and his people had none—mark him as the exceptional immigrant. Whatever objectionable quali- ties Kryptonians may have, they are none of his problem. He left there as a baby. He's not a bug-eyed monster-type alien—he's an alien who looks like the rest of earth humans. (And a handsome one, at that, modeled as he was on John Barrymore.) He can fit in when he wishes and distance himself when he wishes. He can use what he's learned as Kent to enhance his life as Superman, and vice versa.

Again, would we not all like to integrate all the sides of our personalities to, as the psychologists would put it, become one "fully realized" person? Ironi- cally, Superman becomes integrated by splitting himself. That can be a com- forting thought: *our dilemma is its own solution! Unity equals duality!* It's a neat trick, and one we actually do live with daily.

As an immigrant, Kent/Superman evinces that ambivalence one would expect. After all, if Superman truly wanted to blend in would he enter a profession—journalism—where courage is necessary, yet continually act in a cowardly way—but always get the scoop? How much more conspicuous could a person become in a role allegedly chosen to enable him to walk among us inconspicuously? The simultaneous needs to blend in and to stand out, echoing the immigrant's insecurities and self-confidence, are there in the Man of Steel.

Needless to say, when the Superman mythology was created, no one was imagining a serious discussion of these issues some 65 years later, and perhaps it isn't fair to scrutinize such a creation so closely. By the same token, that very lack of self-consciousness may enable us to read cultural signposts that would be harder to discern in a cultural vein more knowingly developed. One thing we can say that separates Superman's dual identity from most others is this: Superman is the "real" person. Clark Kent is the fake. For most superheroes—with the exception of Wonder Woman and, in later years, the heroes derived from Asgardian and other pantheons—the *civilian* is the real, with the addition of powers, skills, magic or technology being what creates the heroic identity. Batman was the first in the endless procession of comics superheroes with extra identities grafted onto their identity bestowed at birth.

35   Is there a significant difference between the two types of secret identities? It would seem so. If you adapt an identity to disguise who you really are, so that you can have a "normal" life and a regular job, so you can have a respite from the unasked-for responsibility your power brings you, maybe that's understandable. Who would want to be incessantly bothered by people wanting their car towed or that unsightly tree stump pulled out of their front yard? Even Superman needs a break, if not a rest.

But what of the folks—the vast majority of heroes—whose civilian identities are the real ones? Are they more noble—and their villainous counterparts more ignoble—because they have a choice in what they do, and choose to do the right (or wrong, in the case of the villains) thing? After all, one can imagine that there must be plenty of people with amazing, superhuman abilities who keep it to themselves. They may be so unnerved by the power they've gained or the indestructible armor they've designed that that just want to put the whole thing out of their minds. Such was the conceit of the M. Night Shamayilan film *Unbreakable.*

Is it braver to be who you are, or to be who you *pretend* you are? This is the fundamental question of identity. The superhero asks the question in capital letters with triple question marks at the end of the sentence. Other questions, equally daunting, are suggested by the first: Who am I? Who would I like to be? Who would those I love like me to be? Who would those I hate like me to be? Who am I capable of being? Who must I be? And who says so?

The superhero's answers to these questions are generally: "I will be who I must be in order to fulfill my mission of doing good works. Whatever serves that purpose is who I will be both in and out of my costume." Whatever other annoying questions they may have—which echo our own quandaries—are quieted by this allegiance to duty. This may be the key to the societal identity crises the heroes reflect. For the superhero, the answer to the contradictory needs is: "Don't be selfish. Serve the community and the rest will fall into place. Who am I? I am the mechanism for perfecting and serving society. *And I know exactly what actions I must take to do that.*"

Wouldn't it be nice to know so clearly the right thing to do at the right time? To have to deceive and dissemble regarding something as intrinsic one's own identity in order to achieve the good seems a small price to pay. And in a fictional superhero's universe, with its clear parameters of moral correctness, it is no contradiction for lying to equal truth and honor. Again, we wish this were true in real life. We wish every one of our lies was done in the service of a greater purpose—not merely to get us out of unpleasant or inconvenient situations.

40 So the secret identity becomes, in the care of the superhero, a badge of honor instead of a concealment of shame. The real world vigilante becomes the fictional dispenser of justice. The secret identity accompanies the ability to know who needs punishing and just how much, and what type of, punishing they need.

The quantity of disguise is unimportant. One may be fooled by Spider-Man's full-face covering mask, but Superman? Even Batman and Captain America, with their half-face concealing masks, wouldn't fool anybody for long. And once they opened their mouths to speak, who could have any doubt who they were, never mind such telltale clues as body or cologne odor, aftershave, mouthwash, telltale scratches or moles, missing teeth, and so on. The conventions of the genre make it enough for most heroes—and villains—merely to *will* it that their identities be impenetrable, though those conventions also make it necessary that they make some kind of effort at deception. Once the effort is made, the rules of logic become malleable.

Over the decades, the role of the secret identity has become less significant in the comics themselves. One of the byproducts of the greater insistence on certain types of "realism" in superhero fiction has been that, the more "real" the characters become, the sillier the idea of the dual identity—at least the one concealed by a pair of glasses or a mask no more feature-distorting than a pair of glasses—has come to seem.

Marvel's Fantastic Four was the first to break down this tradition in Stan Lee and Jack Kirby's comparatively more realistic take on superheroes that ushered in the 1960s. But even they were to prove the exception, as Spider-Man, Iron Man, Thor, and most of the Marvel pantheon adopted dual identities and had many story lines that hinged on the existence of the dualities. Iron Man pretended to be the bodyguard of his civilian persona, Tony Stark, and spent a good while, when trapped in the armor for various reasons, being accused of murdering Stark. It seemed the audiences insisted that a superhuman adventurer be torn between two lives.

More and more in current comics the secret identity is at least severely compromised—the number of people who know Peter Parker is Spider-Man and Bruce Wayne is Batman must surely be in the triple digits by now—or ignored altogether. Do the X-Men in the comics have secret identities? One would be hard pressed to say for sure. It's an issue that often seems to be sidestepped in the printed adventures of the mutant sales sensations.

45 But in the current screen incarnations of the characters—the ones more familiar to the general public—the secret identity is alive and well. The Spider-Man of the movies is Peter Parker, and not even his girlfriend Mary Jane Watson knows that, despite her having kissed both Spider-Man and Peter. The X-Men are certainly unknown to the rest of the world. Daredevil's face is masked so even Elektra didn't catch on until late in the game. Batman and Superman, whether in movies, or on live or animated television, are definitely dual in their identities. TV versions of characters like Static and the Justice League (whose members, besides Superman, are Flash, Hawkgirl, Green Lantern, Wonder Woman, and Martian Manhunter) are secret-I.D. folks. It just seems that this is what the public wants—and needs—from its superheroes. The appeal of the secret identity is as primal as ever. Don't underestimate me. I may not be who you think I am. Or to put it another way:

IF ONLY THEY (*whoever your "they" may be*) KNEW THE TRUTH (*whatever that truth may be*) ABOUT ME (*whoever you believe yourself to be*), THEY'D BE SORRY FOR THE WAY THEY TREAT ME.

That's a powerful fantasy and a powerful human need. It's what makes people read and watch works of fiction. In some cases, it's what enables us to function on a daily basis. "This may seem like my life—but it is *not* my life. In my true life, I fly above buildings, I lift trucks in my bare hands, I defend the defenseless, and I am true to my truest self."

Maybe the "new realism" in the comics themselves is missing an important point that isn't lost on the creators of superhero fare for the screen. In the frenzy to get closer to some simulation of realism, perhaps an important part of the superhero fantasy is lost. The fantasy is a large part of what draws people to these heroes in the first place. After all, if a hero's identity is secret . . . then that cute guy or girl you've glanced across a crowded room may just think you are a Woman of Wonder or a Super Man. Maybe that possibility even gives you the momentary illusion/fantasy/thrill that you could indeed be superpowerful. Of course, the illusion and the fantasy are fleeting and momentary and then all parties remember that this is the real world and that there are no superhumans.

But maybe . . . just maybe. . . .

QUESTIONS FOR DISCUSSION

1. Describe some of the ways that disguises or masks are used to help hide or create an alternate identity/self. Why do people use these disguises, according to Fingeroth? How does the mask or alternate identity traditionally create power for the individual or hero figure?

2. How has the idea of wearing a mask/disguise changed in fiction and film throughout history and especially in recent years?

3. According to Fingeroth, how did the invention of the superhero change the way people think about using masks? Why do most superheroes create dual identities with the use of a disguise?

4. Why does Gary Engle believe that Superman represents the immigrant? How does Superman use his disguise of "cultural assimilation" (i.e., the Clark Kent persona) in order to benefit from (and contribute to) both the worlds of his dual identity?

5. In what sense does Superman paradoxically "become . . . integrated through splitting himself"? Does this seem like a strategy for psychological health? Why or why not?

6. Why is Superman an orphan? Why does Fingeroth believe that the "appeal of the secret identity is as primal as ever"? Do you agree? Why or why not?

CONNECTION

Compare the discussion of the shadow self in Robert Johnson's essay with the dual identity of Superman or other comic heroes (see page 415).

IDEAS FOR WRITING

1. Choose a superhero with a secret identity and do some research into his/her qualities and motivations. Examine cartoon strips, books, or films for examples of your superhero's personality and actions. Write an essay analyzing how he or she behaves and why in and out of disguise. In what ways is the disguise integrated into his or her character?

2. Write an essay about American immigrants and their dual identities. What is it about an immigrant that makes him or her particularly prone to having a dual identity, and why? In what ways can this dual identity be helpful and/or harmful?

RELATED WEB SITES

Danny Fingeroth Talks Superheroes and Society
www.ugo.com/channels/comics/features/dannyfingeroth/
interview.asp
In this interview with UnderGroundOnline, Danny Fingeroth discusses his comic strip work and his book, *Superman on the Couch.*

My Marvel Years
www.lrb.co.uk/v26/n08/leth01_.html
In this essay from the *London Review of Books,* novelist Jonathan Letham discusses his childhood identification with characters from Marvel Comics and how the comics helped shape his identity and the identity of two of his friends.

Robert Johnson

Owning Your Own Shadow

Distinguished Jungian therapist Robert Johnson has written extensively on person-
ality archetypes, healing and integration, and human relationships. His works in-
clude Inner Work: Using Dreams and Active Imagination for Personal
Growth *(1989);* Lying with the Heavenly Woman: Understanding and Integrating the Feminine Archetypes in Men's Lives *(1995);* Balancing
Heaven and Earth: A Memoir *(1998); and* Owning Your Own Shadow:
Understanding the Dark Side of the Psyche *(1993), from which the following*
selection is excerpted.

JOURNAL

Write about a dream in which you felt as if a character in the dream seemed to
represent an aspect of yourself. Describe the character in as much detail as you
can. Then explain when and why you think that you are like this dream character.

The shadow: What is this curious dark element that follows us like a saurian
tail and pursues us so relentlessly in our psychological world? What role
does it occupy in the modern psyche?

The persona is what we would like to be and how we wish to be seen by the
world. It is our psychological clothing and it mediates between our true selves
and our environment just as our physical clothing presents an image to those
we meet. The ego is what we are and know about consciously. The shadow is
that part of us we fail to see or know.*

How the Shadow Originates

We all are born whole and, let us hope, will die whole. But somewhere early on
our way, we eat one of the wonderful fruits of the tree of knowledge, things separate into good and evil, and we begin the shadow-making process; we divide
our lives. In the cultural process we sort out our God-given characteristics into
those that are acceptable to our society and those that have to be put away. This
is wonderful and necessary, and there would be no civilized behavior without
this sorting out of good and evil. But the refused and unacceptable characteristics do not go away; they only collect in the dark corners of our personality.
When they have been hidden long enough, they take on a life of their own—
the shadow life. The shadow is that which has not entered adequately into consciousness. It is the despised quarter of our being. It often has an energy

---

*Jung used the term "shadow" in this general sense early in his formulation. Later, the term indicated those
characteristics of our own sex that have been lost to us. We are using the term in its general meaning in
this book.

potential nearly as great as that of our ego. If it accumulates more energy than our ego, it erupts as an overpowering rage or some indiscretion that slips past us; or we have a depression or an accident that seems to have its own purpose. The shadow gone autonomous is a terrible monster in our psychic house.

The civilizing process, which is the brightest achievement of humankind, consists of culling out those characteristics that are dangerous to the smooth functioning of our ideals. Anyone who does not go through this process remains a "primitive" and can have no place in a cultivated society. We all are born whole but somehow the culture demands that we live out only part of our nature and refuse other parts of our inheritance. We divide the self into an ego and a shadow because our culture insists that we behave in a particular manner. This is our legacy from having eaten of the fruit of the tree of knowledge in the Garden of Eden. Culture takes away the simple human in us, but gives us more complex and sophisticated power. One can make a forceful argument that children should not be subjected to this division too soon or they will be robbed of childhood; they should be allowed to remain in the Garden of Eden until they are strong enough to stand the cultural process without being broken by it. This strength comes at different ages for different individuals and it requires a keen eye to know when children are ready to adapt to the collective life of a society.

5   It is interesting to travel about the world and see which characteristics various cultures affix to the ego and which to the shadow. It becomes clear that culture is an artificially imposed structure, but an absolutely necessary one. We find that in one country we drive on the right side of the road; in another, the left. In the West a man may hold hands with a woman on the street but not with another man; in India he may hold hands with a male friend but not with a woman. In the West one shows respect by wearing shoes in formal or religious places; in the East it a sign of disrespect to wear shoes when one is in a temple or house. If you go into a temple in India with your shoes on you will be put out and told not to come back until you learn some manners. In the Middle East one burps at the end of a meal to show pleasure; in the West this would be very bad manners.

The sorting process is quite arbitrary. Individuality, for instance, is a great virtue in some societies and the greatest sin in others. In the Middle East it is a virtue to be selfless. Students of a great master of painting or poetry will often sign their work with the name of their master rather than their own. In our culture, one brings to his or her own name the highest publicity possible. The clash of these opposing points of view is dangerous as the rapidly expanding communication network of the modern world brings us closer together. The shadow of one culture is a tinderbox of trouble for another.

It is also astonishing to find that some very good characteristics turn up in the shadow. Generally, the ordinary, mundane characteristics are the norm. Anything less than this goes into the shadow. But anything better also goes into the shadow! Some of the pure gold of our personality is relegated to the shadow because it can find no place in that great leveling process that is culture.

Curiously, people resist the noble aspects of their shadow more strenuously than they hide the dark sides. To draw the skeletons out of the closet is relatively easy, but to own the gold in the shadow is terrifying. It is more disrupting to find that you have a profound nobility of character than to find out you are a bum. Of course you are both; but one does not discover these two elements at the same time. The gold is related to our higher calling, and this can be hard to accept at certain stages of life. Ignoring the gold can be as damaging as ignoring the dark side of the psyche, and some people may suffer a severe shock or illness before they learn how to let the gold out. Indeed, this kind of intense experience may be necessary to show us that an important part of us is lying dormant or unused. In tribal cultures, shamans or healers often experience an illness that gives them the insight they need to heal themselves and then bring wisdom to their people. This is often the case for us today. We are still operating with the archetype of the wounded healer who has learned to cure himself and find the gold in his experience.

Wherever we start and whatever culture we spring from, we will arrive at adulthood with a clearly defined ego and shadow, a system of right and wrong, a teeter-totter with two sides.* The religious process consists of restoring the wholeness of the personality. The word religion means to re-relate, to put back together again, to heal the wounds of separation. It is absolutely necessary to engage in the cultural process to redeem ourselves from our animal state; it is equally necessary to accomplish the spiritual task of putting our fractured, alienated world back together again. One must break away from the Garden of Eden but one must also restore the heavenly Jerusalem.

10   Thus it is clear that we must make a shadow, or there would be no culture; then we must restore the wholeness of the personality that was lost in the cultural ideals, or we will live in a state of dividedness that grows more and more painful throughout our evolution. Generally, the first half of life is devoted to the cultural process—gaining one's skills, raising a family, disciplining one's self in a hundred different ways; the second half of life is devoted to restoring the wholeness (making holy) of life. One might complain that this is a senseless round trip except that the wholeness at the end is conscious while it was unconscious and childlike at the beginning. This evolution, though it seems gratuitous, is worth all the pain and suffering that it costs. The only disaster would be getting lost halfway through the process and not finding our completion. Unfortunately, many Westerners are caught in just this difficult place.

Balancing Culture and Shadow

It is useful to think of the personality as a teeter-totter or seesaw. Our acculturation consists of sorting out our God-given characteristics and putting the acceptable ones on the right side of the seesaw and the ones that do not conform

---

*"Ego" and "right" are thought to be synonymous in all cultures, while "shadow" and "wrong" are also to be paired. There is great cultural strength in knowing exactly what is right and what is wrong and to ally oneself appropriately. This is cultural "rightness," highly effective but very clumsy. When the Inquisition of the Middle Ages judged someone and often condemned him or her to be burned at the stake, there had to be an unquestioned basis for such a decision. The fact that individuality and the freedom of belief were evolving in the Western psyche added fuel to this one-sided attitude. Fanaticism always indicates unconscious uncertainty not yet registering in consciousness.

on the left. It is an inexorable law that no characteristic can be discarded; it can only be moved to a different point on the seesaw. A cultured person is one who has the desired characteristics visible on the right (the righteous side) and the forbidden ones hidden on the left. All our characteristics must appear somewhere in this inventory. Nothing may be left out.

A terrible law prevails that few people understand and that our culture chooses to ignore almost completely. That is, the seesaw must be balanced if one is to remain in equilibrium. If one indulges characteristics on the right side, they must be balanced by an equal weight on the left side. The reverse is equally true. If this law is broken, then the seesaw flips and we lose our balance. This is how people flip into the opposite of their usual behavior. The alcoholic who suddenly becomes fanatical in his temperance, or the conservative who suddenly throws all caution to the wind, has made such a flip. He has only substituted one side of his seesaw for the other and made no lasting gain.

The seesaw may also break at the fulcrum point if it is too heavily loaded. This is a psychosis or breakdown. Slang terms are exact in describing these experiences. One must keep the balance intact, though this often requires a very great expenditure of energy.

The psyche keeps its equilibrium as accurately as the body balances its temperature, its acid-alkaline ratio, and the many other fine polarities. We take these physical balances for granted but rarely do we recognize their psychological parallels.

15   To refuse the dark side of one's nature is to store up or accumulate the darkness; this is later expressed as a black mood, psychosomatic illness, or unconsciously inspired accidents. We are presently dealing with the accumulation of a whole society that has worshiped its light side and refused the dark, and this residue appears as war, economic chaos, strikes, racial intolerance. The front page of any newspaper hurls the collective shadow at us. We must be whole whether we like it or not; the only choice is whether we will incorporate the shadow consciously and with some dignity or do it through some neurotic behavior. George Bernard Shaw said that the only alternative to torture is art. This means we will engage in our creativity (in the ceremonial or symbolic world) or have to face its alternative, brutality.

Any repair of our fractured world must start with individuals who have the insight and courage to own their own shadow. Nothing "out there" will help if the interior projecting mechanism of humankind is operating strongly. The tendency to see one's shadow "out there" in one's neighbor or in another race or culture is the most dangerous aspect of the modern psyche. It has created two devastating wars in this century and threatens the destruction of all the fine achievements of our modern world. We all decry war but collectively we move toward it. It is not the monsters of the world who make such chaos but the collective shadow to which every one of us has contributed. World War II gave us endless examples of shadow projection. One of the most highly civilized nations on earth, Germany, fell into the idiocy of projecting its virulent shadow on the Jewish people. The world had never seen the equal of this kind of destruction and yet we naively think we have overcome it. At the beginning of the 1990s, with the collapse of the Berlin Wall and a new relationship with the Soviet Union, we entered a brief period of euphoria and were convinced that we had left the dark days behind. It seemed nothing less than a miracle that the shadow projection between the United States and the Soviet Union had subsided, after years of the Cold War. Yet here is an example of what human creativity can do: we unconsciously picked up the energy released from this relationship and put the shadow in another place!

Only months later, we were engaged in another struggle, with terrifying technological power behind it. When the United States went to war in the Persian Gulf, once again we saw the rise of primitive psychology—with both sides projecting devils and demons onto their opponents. This kind of behavior, backed up by nuclear arms, is more than the world can bear. Is there a way to prevent these catastrophic wars, which pit shadow against shadow?

Our Western tradition promises that if even a few people find wholeness, the whole world will be saved. God promised that if just one righteous man could be found in Sodom and Gomorrah, those cities would be spared. We can take this out of its historical context and apply it to our own inner city. Shadow work is probably the only way of aiding the outer city—and creating a more balanced world.

A horrible proverb states that every generation must have its war so that young men can taste the blood and chaos of the battlefield. Our armies and navies have a high place in our society and any parade or military band starts hot blood flowing in the veins of men, young and old. Though I consciously question warfare and its place in an intelligent society, I was not immune to that hot blood when I was in Strasbourg one cold evening. I saw a detachment of the French foreign legion marching down the street with their colorful uniforms, their comraderie, and their jaunty song, and I would have given anything to join them. My own shadow had surfaced and for a moment hot blood completely overruled intelligence and thought.

20   A whole generation can live a modern, civilized life without ever touching much of its shadow nature. Then predictably—twenty years is the alloted time—that unlived shadow will erupt and a war will burst forth that no one wanted but to which everyone—both men and women—has contributed. Apparently, the collective need for shadow expression supersedes the individual determination to contain the dark. And so it happens that an era of disciplined creativity is always followed by an astounding display of annihilation. There are better ways of coping with the shadow, but until they are common knowledge we will continue to have these outbursts in their most destructive form.

Dr. Jung has pointed out that it requires a sophisticated and disciplined society to fight a war as long and complicated as World Wars I and II. He said that primitive people would have tired of their war in a few weeks and gone home. They would not have had a great accumulation of shadow since they live more balanced lives and never venture as far from the center as we do. It was for us civilized people to bring warfare to its high development. And so the greater the civilization, the more intent it is upon its own destruction. God grant that evolution may proceed quickly enough for each of us to pick up our own dark side, combine it with our hard-earned light, and make something better of it all than the opposition of the two. This would be true holiness.

QUESTIONS FOR DISCUSSION

1. In his opening paragraphs, how does Johnson differentiate between the persona, the ego, and the shadow? If any of these terms are unclear to you, look them up in a dictionary of psychological terms or in an unabridged dictionary.
2. Why does Johnson believe that the shadow originated in the sorting of good/bad values within the cultural or civilizing process? What problems does he see developing from this arbitrary sorting process in terms of both modern multicultural society and within the individual?
3. Why does Johnson believe the religious process can help us heal ourselves and integrate ego with shadow? How does he contrast the religious process with the cultural process, and at what periods of life is each dominant?
4. Why does Johnson believe the two world wars were created by "the tendency to see one's shadow 'out there' in one's neighbor or in another race or culture"? Is his reasoning convincing here? Explain your point of view.
5. How does Johnson describe the way our country has tended to "put the shadow in another place" as soon as one enemy or crisis has subsided? What does this suggest to you about the power and persistence of shadow projections?
6. Why does Johnson believe that after 20 years of peace, "an era of disciplined creativity is always followed by an astounding display of annihilation"? Does he present a viable alternative to this tendency? Do you think that there is a positive alternative to this phenomenon? What is it?

CONNECTION

Compare and contrast the ways that Johnson and Stevenson explore the causes and effects of the rejected shadow self (see page 421).

IDEAS FOR WRITING

1. Write an essay about a current international conflict or pattern of prejudice that may come from an outward projection of our inner shadow of undesirable qualities onto our enemies. Discuss some of the ways that political propaganda heightens the attachment of shadow qualities to the enemy in the particular conflict that you are analyzing. How do you feel about the conflict, and what impact you can have on its outcome?
2. Narrate a dream or an experience in which you felt menaced by a person or symbolic representation that seemed to you to embody your shadow. Did you try to create some balance in yourself after this experience, to be-

come more accepting of the shadow within you? What did you do? Were you successful?

RELATED WEB SITES

Practice Shadow

www.spiritualityhealth.com/newsh/items/blank/item_205.html
"By *owning your shadow,* you embrace your full humanity," claims the Spirituality and Health Web site. This URL offers books, articles, and relevant links on how "to make peace with those parts of ourselves that we find to be despicable."

Beginning Within

www.context.org/ICLIB/IC16/Johnson.htm
The In Context Web site contains an interesting interview by Lila Forest with Robert Johnson entitled "Maintaining Personal Balance in a Shifting Culture."

Robert Louis Stevenson

Henry Jekyll's Full Statement of the Case from The Strange Case of Dr. Jekyll and Mr. Hyde

Scottish author Robert Louis Stevenson (1850–1894) wrote the short novel The Strange Case of Dr. Jekyll and Mr. Hyde *(1886) at a time when he was very ill with tuberculosis. In the following selection, the conclusion to Stevenson's classic tale of good and evil, the character Henry Jekyll, a highly respected London physician, has chemically altered his own inner nature, constructing a morally depraved "second self," Mr. Hyde. The following statement of Dr. Jekyll, written just before his death, sets forth his reasons for and the fatal consequences of tampering with his inner world. The letter was found by his friends who discovered only the body of Mr. Hyde with a crushed phial of cyanide poison in his hand.*

JOURNAL

Write about experiencing your "other" self, or antiself, through some change in your normal mental state, perhaps from an emotional crisis, chemical stimulation, an illness, or extreme fatigue.

I was born in the year 18_ to a large fortune, endowed besides with excellent parts, inclined by nature to industry, fond of the respect of the wise and good among my fellow-men, and thus, as might have been supposed, with

every guarantee of an honourable and distinguished future. And indeed the
worst of my faults was a certain impatient gaiety of disposition, such as has
made the happiness of many, but such as I found it hard to reconcile with my
imperious desire to carry my head high, and wear a more than commonly
grave countenance before the public. Hence it came about that I concealed
my pleasures; and that when I reached years of reflection, and began to look
round me and take stock of my progress and position in the world, I stood already committed to a profound duplicity of life. Many a man would have even
blazoned such irregularities as I was guilty of; but from the high views that I
had set before me, I regarded and hid them with an almost morbid sense of
shame. It was thus rather the exacting nature of my aspirations than any particular degradation in my faults, that made me what I was, and, with even a
deeper trench than in the majority of men, severed in me those provinces of
good and ill which divide and compound man's dual nature. In this case, I was
driven to reflect deeply and inveterately on that hard law of life, which lies at
the root of religion and is one of the most plentiful springs of distress.
Though so profound a double-dealer, I was in no sense a hypocrite; both sides
of me were in dead earnest; I was no more myself when I laid aside restraint
and plunged in shame, than when I laboured, in the eye of day, at the further-
ance of knowledge or the relief of sorrow and suffering. And it chanced that
the direction of my scientific studies, which led wholly towards the mystic and
the transcendental, reacted and shed a strong light on this consciousness
of the perennial war among my members. With every day, and from both sides
of my intelligence, the moral and the intellectual, I thus drew steadily nearer
to that truth, by whose partial discovery I have been doomed to such a dreadful shipwreck: that man is not truly one, but truly two. I say two, because the
state of my own knowledge does not pass beyond that point. Others will follow,
others will outstrip me on the same lines; and I hazard the guess that man will
be ultimately known for a mere polity of multifarious, incongruous and independent denizens. I, for my part, from the nature of my life, advanced infalli-
bly in one direction and in one direction only. It was on the moral side, and in
my own person, that I learned to recognise the thorough and primitive duality
of man; I saw that, of the two natures that contended in the field of my consciousness, even if I could rightly be said to be either, it was only because I was
radically both; and from an early date, even before the course of my scientific
discoveries had begun to suggest the most naked possibility of such a miracle,
I had learned to dwell with pleasure, as a beloved daydream, on the thought of
the separation of these elements. If each, I told myself, could be housed in
separate identities, life would be relieved of all that was unbearable; the unjust
might go his way, delivered from the aspirations and remorse of his more upright twin; and the just could walk steadfastly and securely on his upward path,
doing the good things in which he found his pleasure, and no longer exposed
to disgrace and penitence by the hands of his extraneous evil. It was the curse
of mankind that these incongruous faggots were thus bound together—that in
the agonized womb of consciousness, these polar twins should be continuously
struggling. How, then, were they dissociated?

I was so far in my reflections when, as I have said, a side light began to shine upon the subject from the laboratory table. I began to perceive more deeply than it has ever yet been stated, the trembling immateriality, the mist-like transience, of this seemingly so solid body in which we walk attired. Certain agents I found to have the power to shake and pluck back that fleshy vestment, even as a wind might toss the curtains of a pavilion. For two good reasons, I will not enter deeply into this scientific branch of my confession. First, because I have been made to learn that the doom and burden of our life is bound for ever on man's shoulders, and when the attempt is made to cast it off, it but returns upon us with more unfamiliar and more awful pressure. Second, because, as my narrative will make, alas! too evident, my discoveries were incomplete. Enough, then, that I not only recognised my natural body from the mere aura and effulgence of certain of the powers that make up my spirit, but managed to compound a drug by which these powers should be dethroned from their supremacy, and a second form and countenance substituted, none the less natural to me because they were the expression, and bore the stamp of lower elements in my soul.

I hesitated long before I put this theory to the test of practice. I knew well that I risked death; for any drug that so potently controlled and shook the very fortress of identity, might, by the least scruple of an overdose or at the least inopportunity in the moment of exhibition, utterly blot out that immaterial tabernacle which I looked to it to change. But the temptation of a discovery so singular and profound at last overcame the suggestions of alarm. I had long since prepared my tincture; I purchased at once, from a firm of wholesale chemists, a large quantity of a particular salt which I knew, from my experiments, to be the last ingredient required; and late one accursed night, I compounded the elements, watched them boil and smoke together in the glass, and when the ebullition had subsided, with a strong glow of courage, drank off the potion.

The most racking pangs succeeded: a grinding in the bones, deadly nausea, and a horror of the spirit that cannot be exceeded at the hour of birth or death. Then these agonies began swiftly to subside, and I came to myself as if out of a great sickness. There was something strange in my sensations, something indescribably new and, from its very novelty, incredibly sweet. I felt younger, lighter, happier in body; within I was conscious of a heady recklessness, a current of disordered sensual images running like a millrace in my fancy, a dissolution of the bonds of obligation, an unknown but not an innocent freedom of the soul. I knew myself, at the first breath of this new life, to be more wicked, tenfold more wicked, sold a slave to my original evil; and the thought, in that moment, braced and delighted me like wine. I stretched out my hands, exulting in the freshness of these sensations; and in the act, I was suddenly aware that I had lost in stature.

5   There was no mirror, at that date, in my room; that which stands beside me as I write, was brought there later on and for the very purpose of these transformations. That night, however, was far gone into the morning—the morning, black as it was, was nearly ripe for the conception of the day—the inmates of my house were locked in the most rigorous hours of slumber, and I determined,

flushed as I was with hope and triumph, to venture in my new shape as far as to my bedroom. I crossed the yard, wherein the constellations looked down upon me, I could have thought, with wonder, the first creature of that sort that their unsleeping vigilance had yet disclosed to them; I stole through the corridors, a stranger in my own house; and coming to my room, I saw for the first time the appearance of Edward Hyde.

I must here speak by theory alone, saying not that which I know, but that which I suppose to be most probable. The evil side of my nature, to which I had now transferred the stamping efficacy, was less robust and less developed than the good which I had just deposed. Again, in the course of my life, which had been, after all, nine tenths a life of effort, virtue and control, it had been much less exercised and much less exhausted. And hence, as I think, it came about that Edward Hyde was so much smaller, slighter and younger than Henry Jekyll. Even as good shone upon the countenance of the one, evil was written broadly and plainly on the face of the other. Evil besides (which I must still believe to be the lethal side of man) had left on that body an imprint of deformity and decay. And yet when I looked upon that ugly idol in the glass, I was conscious of no repugnance, rather of a leap of welcome. This, too, was myself. It seemed natural and human. In my eyes it bore a livelier image of the spirit, it seemed more express and single, than the imperfect and divided countenance I had been hitherto accustomed to call mine. And in so far I was doubtless right. I have observed that when I wore the semblance of Edward Hyde, none could come near to me at first without a visible misgiving of the flesh. This, as I take it, was because all human beings, as we meet them, are commingled out of good and evil: and Edward Hyde, alone in the ranks of mankind, was pure evil.

I lingered but a moment at the mirror: the second and conclusive experiment had yet to be attempted; it yet remained to be seen if I had lost my identity beyond redemption and must flee before daylight from a house that was no longer mine; and hurrying back to my cabinet, I once more prepared and drank the cup, once more suffered the pangs of dissolution, and came to myself once more with the character, the stature and the face of Henry Jekyll.

That night I had come to the fatal crossroads. Had I approached my discovery in a more noble spirit, had I risked the experiment while under the empire of generous or pious aspirations, all must have been otherwise, and from these agonies of death and birth, I had come forth an angel instead of a fiend. The drug had no discriminating action; it was neither diabolical nor divine; it but shook the doors of the prisonhouse of my disposition; and like the captives of Phillipi, that which stood within ran forth. At that time my virtue slumbered; my evil, kept awake by ambition, was alert and swift to seize the occasion; and the thing that was projected was Edward Hyde. Hence, although I had now two characters as well as two appearances, one was wholly evil, and the other was still the old Henry Jekyll, that incongruous compound of whose reformation and improvement I had already learned to despair. The movement was thus wholly toward the worse.

Even at that time, I had not conquered my aversion to the dryness of a life of study. I would still be merrily disposed at times; and as my pleasures were (to say the least) undignified, and I was not only well known and highly considered, but growing toward the elderly man, this incoherency of my life was daily growing more unwelcome. It was on this side that my new power tempted me until I fell in slavery. I had but to drink the cup, to doff at once the body of the noted professor, and to assume, like a thick cloak, that of Edward Hyde. I smiled at the notion; it seemed to me at the time to be humorous; and I made my preparations with the most studious care. I took and furnished that house in Soho, to which Hyde was tracked by the police; and engaged as a housekeeper a creature whom I knew well to be silent and unscrupulous. On the other side, I announced to my servants that a Mr. Hyde (whom I described) was to have full liberty and power about my house in the square; and to parry mishaps, I even called and made myself a familiar object, in my second character. I next drew up that will to which you so much objected; so that if anything befell me in the person of Dr. Jekyll, I could enter on that of Edward Hyde without pecuniary loss. And thus fortified, as I supposed, on every side, I began to profit by the strange immunities of my position.

10   Men have before hired bravoes to transact their crimes, while their own person and reputation sat under shelter. I was the first that ever did so for his pleasures. I was the first that could plod in the public eye with a load of genial respectability, and in a moment, like a schoolboy, strip off these lendings and spring headlong into the sea of liberty. But for me, in my impenetrable mantle, the safety was complete. Think of it—I did not even exist! Let me but escape into my laboratory door, give me but a second or two to mix and swallow the draught that I had always standing ready; and whatever he had done, Edward Hyde would pass away like the stain of breath upon a mirror; and there in his stead, quietly at home, trimming the midnight lamp in his study, a man who could afford to laugh at suspicion, would be Henry Jekyll.

The pleasures which I made haste to seek in my disguise were, as I have said, undignified; I would scarce use a harder term. But in the hands of Edward Hyde, they soon began to turn toward the monstrous. When I would come back from these excursions, I was often plunged into a kind of wonder at my vicarious depravity. This familiar that I called out of my own soul, and sent forth alone to do his good pleasure, was a being inherently malign and villainous; his every act and thought centered on self; drinking pleasure with bestial avidity from any degree of torture to another; relentless like a man of stone. Henry Jekyll stood at times aghast before the acts of Edward Hyde; but the situation was apart from ordinary laws, and insidiously relaxed the grasp of conscience. It was Hyde, after all, and Hyde alone, that was guilty. Jekyll was no worse; he woke again to his good qualities seemingly unimpaired; he would even make haste, where it was possible, to undo the evil done by Hyde. And thus his conscience slumbered.

Into the details of the infamy at which I thus connived (for even now I can scarce grant that I committed it) I have no design of entering; I mean but to point out the warnings and the successive steps with which my chastisement approached. I met with one accident which, as it brought on no consequence, I shall no more than mention. An act of cruelty to a child aroused against me the anger of a passerby, whom I recognised the other day in the person of your kinsman; the doctor and the child's family joined him; there were moments when I feared for my life; and at last, in order to pacify their too just resentment, Edward Hyde had to bring them to the door, and pay them in a cheque drawn in the name of Henry Jekyll. But this danger was easily eliminated from the future, by opening an account at another bank in the name of Edward Hyde himself; and when, by sloping my own hand backward, I had supplied my double with a signature, I thought I sat beyond the reach of fate.

Some two months before the murder of Sir Danvers, I had been out for one of my adventures, had returned at a late hour, and woke the next day in bed with somewhat odd sensations. It was in vain I looked about me; in vain I saw the decent furniture and tall proportions of my room in the square; in vain that I recognised the pattern of the bed curtains and the design of the mahogany frame; something still kept insisting that I was not where I was, that I had not wakened where I seemed to be, but in the little room in Soho where I was accustomed to sleep in the body of Edward Hyde. I smiled to myself, and, in my psychological way, began lazily to inquire into the elements of this illusion, occasionally, even as I did so, dropping back into a comfortable morning doze. I was still so engaged when, in one of my more wakeful moments, my eyes fell upon my hand. Now the hand of Henry Jekyll (as you have often remarked) was professional in shape and size: it was large, firm, white and comely. But the hand which I now saw, clearly enough, in the yellow light of a mid-London morning, lying half shut on the bedclothes, was lean, corded, knuckly, of a dusky pallor and thickly shaded with a swart growth of hair. It was the hand of Edward Hyde.

I must have stared upon it for near half a minute, sunk as I was in the mere stupidity of wonder, before terror woke up in my breast as sudden and startling as the crash of cymbals; and bounding from my bed, I rushed to the mirror. At the sight that met my eyes, my blood was changed into something exquisitely thin and icy. Yes, I had gone to bed Henry Jekyll, I had awakened Edward Hyde. How was this to be explained? I asked myself; and then, with another bound of terror—how was it to be remedied? It was well on in the morning; the servants were up; all my drugs were in the cabinet—a long journey down two pairs of stairs, through the back passage, across the open court and through the anatomical theatre, from where I was then standing horror-struck. It might indeed be possible to cover my face; but of what use was that, when I was unable to conceal the alteration in my stature? And then with an overpowering sweetness of relief, it came back upon my mind that the servants were already used to the coming and going of my second self. I had soon dressed, as well as I was able, in clothes of my own size; had soon passed through the house, where Bradshaw stared and drew back at seeing Mr. Hyde at such an hour and in such a strange array; and ten minutes later, Dr. Jekyll had returned to his own shape and was sitting down, with a darkened brow, to make a feint of breakfasting.

15   Small indeed was my appetite. This inexplicable incident, this reversal of my previous experience, seemed, like the Babylonian finger on the wall, to be spelling out the letters of my judgment; and I began to reflect more seriously than ever before on the issues and possibilities of my double existence. That part of me which I had the power of projecting, had lately been much exercised and nourished; it had seemed to me of late as though the body of Edward Hyde had grown in stature, as though (when I wore that form) I were conscious of a more generous tide of blood, and I began to spy a danger that, if this were much prolonged, the balance of my nature might be permanently overthrown, the power of voluntary change be forfeited, and the character of Edward Hyde become irrevocably mine. The power of the drug had not been always equally displayed. Once, very early in my career, it had totally failed me; since then I had been obliged on more than one occasion to double, and once, with infinite risk of death, to treble the amount; and these rare uncertainties had cast hitherto the sole shadow on my contentment. Now, however, and in the light of that morning's accident, I was led to remark that whereas, in the beginning, the difficulty had been to throw off the body of Jekyll, it had of late gradually but decidedly transferred itself to the other side. All things therefore seemed to point to this: that I was slowly losing hold of my original and better self, and becoming slowly incorporated with my second and worse.

Between these two, I now felt I had to choose. My two natures had memory in common, but all other faculties were most unequally shared between them. Jekyll (who was composite) now with the most sensitive apprehensions, now with a greedy gusto, projected and shared in the pleasures and adventures of Hyde; but Hyde was indifferent to Jekyll, or but remembered him as the mountain bandit remembers the cavern in which he conceals himself from pursuit. Jekyll had more than a father's interest; Hyde had more than a son's indifference. To cast in my lot with Jekyll, was to die to those appetites which I had long secretly indulged and had of late begun to pamper. To cast it in with Hyde, was to die to a thousand interests and aspirations, and to become, at a blow and forever, despised and friendless. The bargain might appear unequal; but there was still another consideration in the scales; for while Jekyll would suffer smartingly in the fires of abstinence, Hyde would be not even conscious of all that he had lost. Strange as my circumstances were, the terms of this debate are as old and commonplace as man; much the same inducements and alarms cast the die for any tempted and trembling sinner; and it fell out with me, as it falls with so vast a majority of my fellows, that I chose the better part and was found wanting in the strength to keep to it.

Yes, I preferred the elderly and discontented doctor, surrounded by friends and cherishing honest hopes; and bade a resolute farewell to the liberty, the comparative youth, the light step, leaping impulses and secret pleasures, that I had enjoyed in the disguise of Hyde. I made this choice perhaps with some unconscious reservation, for I neither gave up the house in Soho, nor destroyed the clothes of Edward Hyde, which still lay ready in my cabinet. For two months, however, I was true to my determination; for two months, I led a life of such severity as I had never before attained to, and enjoyed the compensations of an approving conscience. But time began at last to obliterate the freshness of my alarm; the praises of conscience began to grow into a thing of course; I began to be tortured with throes and longings, as of Hyde struggling after freedom; and at last, in an hour of moral weakness, I once again compounded and swallowed the transforming draught.

I do not suppose that, when a drunkard reasons with himself upon his vice, he is once out of five hundred times affected by the dangers that he runs through his brutish, physical insensibility; neither had I, long as I had considered my position, made enough allowance for the complete moral insensibility and insensate readiness to evil, which were the leading characters of Edward Hyde. Yet it was by these that I was punished. My devil had been long caged, he came out roaring. I was conscious, even when I took the draught, of a more unbridled, a more furious propensity to ill. It must have been this, I suppose, that stirred in my soul that tempest of impatience with which I listened to the civilities of my unhappy victim; I declare, at least, before God, no man morally sane could have been guilty of that crime upon so pitiful a provocation; and that I struck in no more reasonable spirit than that in which a sick child may break a plaything. But I had voluntarily stripped myself of all those balancing instincts by which even the worst of us continues to walk with some degree of steadiness among temptations and in my case, to be tempted, however slightly, was to fall.

Instantly the spirit of hell awoke in me and raged. With a transport of glee, I mauled the unresisting body, tasting delight from every blow; and it was not till weariness had begun to succeed, that I was suddenly, in the top fit of my delirium, struck through the heart by a cold thrill of terror. A mist dispersed; I saw my life to be forfeit; and fled from the scene of these excesses, at once glorying and trembling, my lust of evil gratified and stimulated, my love of life screwed to the topmost peg. I ran to the house in Soho, and (to make assurance doubly sure) destroyed my papers; thence I set out through the lamplit streets, in the same divided ecstasy of mind, gloating on my crime, light-headedly devising others in the future, and yet still hastening and still hearkening in my wake for the steps of the avenger. Hyde had a song upon his lips as he compounded the draught, and as he drank it, pledged the dead man. The pangs of transformation had not done tearing him, before Henry Jekyll, with streaming tears of gratitude and remorse, had fallen upon his knees and lifted his clasped hands to God. The veil of self-indulgence was rent from head to foot. I saw my life as a whole: I followed it up from the days of childhood, when I had walked with my father's hand, and through the self-denying toils of my professional life, to arrive again and again, with the same sense of unreality, at the damned horrors of the evening. I could have screamed aloud; I sought with tears and prayers to smother down the crowd of hideous images and sounds with which my memory swarmed against me; and still, between the petitions, the ugly face of my iniquity stared into my soul. As the acuteness of this remorse began to die away, it was succeeded by a sense of joy. The problem of my conduct was solved. Hyde was thenceforth impossible; whether I would or not, I was now confined to the better part of my existence; and O, how I rejoiced to think of it! With what willing humility I embraced anew the restrictions of natural life! With what sincere renunciation I locked the door by which I had so often gone and come, and ground the key under my heel!

20   The next day, came the news that the murder had been overlooked, that the guilt of Hyde was patent to the world, and that the victim was a man high in public estimation. It was not only a crime, it had been a tragic folly. I think I was glad to know it; I think I was glad to have my better impulses thus buttressed and guarded by the terrors of the scaffold. Jekyll was now my city of refuge; let but Hyde peep out an instant, and the hands of all men would be raised to take and slay him.

I resolved in my future conduct to redeem the past; and I can say with honesty that my resolve was fruitful of some good. You know yourself how earnestly, in the last months of the last year, I laboured to relieve suffering; you know that much was done for others, and that the days passed quietly, almost happily for myself. Nor can I truly say that I wearied of this beneficent and innocent life; I think instead that I daily enjoyed it more completely; but I was still cursed with my duality of purpose; and as the first edge of my penitence wore off, the lower side of me, so long indulged, so recently chained down, began to growl for licence. Not that I dreamed of resuscitating Hyde; the bare idea of that would startle me to frenzy; no, it was in my own person that I was once more tempted to trifle with my conscience; and it was as an ordinary secret sinner that I at last fell before the assaults of temptation.

There comes an end to all things; the most capacious measure is filled at last; and this brief condescension to my evil finally destroyed the balance of my soul. And yet I was not alarmed; the fall seemed natural, like a return to the old days before I had made my discovery. It was a fine, clear, January day, wet under foot where the frost had melted, but cloudless overhead; and the Regent's Park was full of winter chirrupings and sweet with spring odours. I sat in the sun on a bench; the animal within me licking the chops of memory; the spiritual side a little drowsed, promising subsequent penitence, but not yet moved to begin. After all, I reflected, I was like my neighbours; and then I smiled, comparing myself with other men, comparing my active goodwill with the lazy cruelty of their neglect. And at the very moment of that vainglorious thought, a qualm came over me, a horrid nausea and the most deadly shuddering. These passed away, and left me faint; and then, as in its turn faintness subsided, I began to be aware of a change in the temper of my thoughts, a greater boldness, a contempt of danger, a solution of the bonds of obligation. I looked down; my clothes hung formlessly on my shrunken limbs; the hand that lay on my knee was corded and hairy. I was once more Edward Hyde. A moment before I had been safe of all men's respect, wealthy, beloved—the cloth laying for me in the dining-room at home; and now I was the common quarry of mankind, hunted, house-less, a known murderer, thrall to the gallows.

My reason wavered, but it did not fail me utterly. I have more than once observed that, in my second character, my faculties seemed sharpened to a point and my spirits more tensely elastic; thus it came about that, where Jekyll perhaps might have succumbed, Hyde rose to the importance of the moment. My drugs were in one of the presses of my cabinet; how was I to reach them? That was the problem that (crushing my temples in my hands) I set to myself to solve. The laboratory door I had closed. If I sought to enter by the house, my own servants would consign me to the gallows. I saw I must employ another hand, and thought of Lanyon. How was he to be reached? how persuaded? Suppose that I escaped capture in the streets, how was I to make my way into his presence? and how should I, an unknown and displeasing visitor, prevail on the famous physician to rifle the study of his colleague, Dr. Jekyll? Then I remembered that of my original character, one part remained to me: I could write my own hand; and once I had conceived that kindling spark, the way that I must follow became lighted up from end to end.

Thereupon, I arranged my clothes as best I could, and summoning a passing hansom, drove to an hotel in Portland Street, the name of which I chanced to remember. At my appearance (which was indeed comical enough, however tragic a fate these garments covered) the driver could not conceal his mirth. I gnashed my teeth upon him with a gust of devilish fury; and the smile withered from his face—happily for him—yet more happily for myself, for in another instant I had certainly dragged him from his perch. At the inn, as I entered, I looked about me with so black a countenance as made the attendants tremble, not a look did they exchange in my presence; but obsequiously took my orders, led me to a private room, and brought me wherewithal to write. Hyde in danger of his life was a creature new to me; shaken with inordinate anger, strung to the pitch of murder, lusting to inflict pain. Yet the creature was astute; mastered his fury with a great effort of the will; composed his two important letters, one to Lanyon and one to Poole; and that he might receive actual evidence of their being posted, sent them out with directions that they should be registered. Thenceforward, he sat all day over the fire in the private room, gnawing his nails; there he dined, sitting alone with his fears, the waiter visibly quailing before his eye; and thence, when the night was fully come, he set forth in the corner of a closed cab, and was driven to and fro about the streets of the city. He, I say—I cannot say, I. That child of Hell had nothing human; nothing lived in him but fear and hatred. And when at last, thinking the driver had begun to grow suspicious, he discharged the cab and ventured on foot, attired in his misfitting clothes, an object marked out for observation, into the midst of the nocturnal passengers, these two base passions raged within him like a tempest. He walked fast, hunted by his fears, chattering to himself, skulking through the less frequented thoroughfares, counting the minutes that still divided him from midnight. Once a woman spoke to him, offering, I think, a box of lights. He smote her in the face, and she fled.

25   When I came to myself at Lanyon's, the horror of my old friend perhaps affected me somewhat: I do not know; it was at least but a drop in the sea to the abhorrence with which I looked back upon these hours. A change had come over me. It was no longer the fear of the gallows, it was the horror of being Hyde that racked me. I received Lanyon's condemnation partly in a dream; it was partly in a dream that I came home to my own house and got into bed. I slept after the prostration of the day, with a stringent and profound slumber which not even in the nightmares that wrung me could avail to break. I awoke

in the morning shaken, weakened, but refreshed. I still hated and feared the thought of the brute that slept within me, and I had not of course forgotten the appalling dangers of the day before; but I was once more at home, in my own house and close to my drugs; and gratitude for my escape shone so strong in my soul that it almost rivalled the brightness of hope.

I was stepping leisurely across the court after breakfast, drinking the chill of the air with pleasure, when I was seized again with those indescribable sensations that heralded the change; and I had but the time to gain the shelter of my cabinet, before I was once again raging and freezing with the passions of Hyde. It took on this occasion a double dose to recall me to myself; and alas! six hours after, as I sat looking sadly in the fire, the pangs returned, and the drug had to be re-administered. In short, from that day forth it seemed only by a great effort as of gymnastics, and only under the immediate stimulation of the drug, that I was able to wear the countenance of Jekyll. At all hours of the day and night, I would be taken with the premonitory shudder; above all, if I slept, or even dozed for a moment in my chair, it was always as Hyde that I awakened. Under the strain of this continually impending doom and by the sleeplessness to which I now condemned myself, ay, even beyond what I had thought possible to man, I became, in my own person, a creature eaten up and emptied by fever, languidly weak both in body and mind, and solely occupied by one thought: the horror of my other self. But when I slept, or when the virtue of the medicine wore off, I would leap almost without transition (for the pangs of transformation grew daily less marked) into the possession of a fancy brimming with images of terror, a soul boiling with causeless hatreds, and a body that seemed not strong enough to contain the raging energies of life. The powers of Hyde seemed to have grown with the sickliness of Jekyll. And certainly the hate that now divided them was equal on each side. With Jekyll, it was a thing of vital instinct. He had now seen the full deformity of that creature that shared with him some of the phenomena of consciousness, and was co-heir with him to death: and beyond these links of community, which in themselves made the most poignant part of his distress, he thought of Hyde, for all his energy of life, as of something not only hellish but inorganic. This was the shocking thing; that the slime of the pit seemed to utter cries and voices; that the amorphous dust gesticulated and sinned; that what was dead, and had no shape, should usurp the offices of life. And this again, that that insurgent horror was knit to him closer than a wife, closer than an eye; lay caged in his flesh, where he heard it mutter and felt it struggle to be born; and at every hour of weakness, and in the confidence of slumber, prevailed against him, and deposed him out of life. The hatred of Hyde for Jekyll was of a different order. His terror of the gallows drove him continually to commit temporary suicide, and return to his subordinate station of a part instead of a person; but he loathed the necessity, he loathed the despondency into which Jekyll was now fallen, and he resented the dislike with which he was himself regarded. Hence the apelike tricks that he would play me, scrawling in my own hand blasphemies on the pages of my books, burning the letters and destroying the portrait of my father; and indeed, had it not been for his fear of death, he would long ago have ruined himself in order to involve me in the ruin. But his love of life is wonderful; I go further: I, who sicken and freeze at the mere thought of him, when I recall the abjection and passion of this attachment, and when I know how he fears my power to cut him off by suicide, I find it in my heart to pity him.

It is useless, and the time awfully fails me, to prolong this description; no one has ever suffered such torments, let that suffice; and yet even to these, habit brought—no, not alleviation—but a certain callousness of soul, a certain acquiescence of despair; and my punishment might have gone on for years, but for the last calamity which has now fallen, and which has finally severed me from my own face and nature. My provision of the salt, which had never been renewed since the date of the first experiment, began to run low. I sent out for a fresh supply and mixed the draught; the ebullition followed, and the first change of colour, not the second; I drank it and it was without efficacy. You will learn from Poole how I have had London ransacked; it was in vain; and I am now persuaded that my first supply was impure, and that it was that unknown impurity which lent efficacy to the draught.

About a week has passed, and I am now finishing this statement under the influence of the last of the old powders. This, then, is the last time, short of a miracle, that Henry Jekyll can think his own thoughts or see his own face (now how sadly altered!) in the glass. Nor must I delay too long to bring my writing to an end; for if my narrative has hitherto escaped destruction, it has been by a combination of great prudence and great good luck. Should the throes of change take me in the act of writing it, Hyde will tear it in pieces; but if some time shall have elapsed after I have laid it by, his wonderful selfishness and circumscription to the moment will probably save it once again from the action of his ape-like spite. And indeed the doom that is closing on us both has already changed and crushed him. Half an hour from now, when I shall again and forever reindue that hated personality, I know how I shall sit shuddering and weeping in my chair, or continue, with the most strained and fearstruck ecstasy of listening, to pace up and down this room (my last earthly refuge) and give ear to every sound of menace. Will Hyde die upon the scaffold? or will he find courage to release himself at the last moment? God knows; I am careless; this is my true hour of death, and what is to follow concerns another than myself. Here then, as I lay down the pen and proceed to seal up my confession, I bring the life of that unhappy Henry Jekyll to an end.

QUESTIONS FOR DISCUSSION

1. What strengths, faults, and inner divisions of character does Jekyll describe in the first paragraph of the narrative? Why does he feel a need to conceal his pleasures?
2. Upon what fantasy or "beloved daydream" does Jekyll come to dwell? Why does he become so obsessed with this fantasy? What does he invent to make his fantasy a reality? Is his invention a success?
3. What are the differences in appearance, stature, power, and age between Dr. Jekyll and Mr. Hyde? How do these physical distinctions underscore

symbolically the differences in their characters as well as the flaws in Dr. Jekyll's original character and the folly of artificially separating the two parts of the self?

4. How does Jekyll first respond to the changes in his character? How do his response and the nature of the control over the double personality gradually change? What difficulty does he experience in deciding which of his sides to finally repress?

5. Why is Jekyll unable to stick with his decision to refrain from doubling his personality? How would you explain the mutual loathing that each side of the divided personality feels for the other?

6. From the evidence in the letter, which side of the personality do you think killed Mr. Hyde: Hyde himself, in an act of suicide, or Jekyll, in an act of combined murder/suicide of both sides of his personality? Explain your response using references to the text.

CONNECTION

Compare Stevenson's essay about double identity with Danny Fingeroth's essay about comic book superheroes, "The Dual Identity" (see page 405). What different causes for the split self are examined in each work?

IDEAS FOR WRITING

1. After reading the entire text of *The Strange Case of Dr. Jekyll and Mr. Hyde,* write an essay in which you interpret the story as a criticism of rigid social conventions and moral standards of acceptable or unacceptable, or good or bad, behavior. In what ways does the story suggest that such strict standards can heighten the division between an individual's good and bad side, the main self and the double or shadow self?

2. This story concerns the dual nature of the human psyche, the struggle between our good side and our bad side, between the conscious mind and the unthinking appetites of the body. What do you think can be done to ease such a struggle? Write a paper in which you argue for an approach to life that would help to heal the split between potential Jekyll and Hyde personalities within the human psyche.

RELATED WEB SITES

The Robert Louis Stevenson Web site
`http://dinamico.unibg.it/rls/rls.htm`
This site, maintained by Richard Drury of the University of Bergamo, Italy, contains a biography, criticism, links, images, and bibliographies related to Stevenson and his works.

Doctor Jekyll and Mr. Hyde
`www.novelguide.com/dr.jekyllandmr.hyde/`
This useful Web site provides a chapter-by-chapter book analysis, character profiles, theme analysis, and author biography.

Kate Sullivan

J. Lo vs. K. Sul

Kate Sullivan was born and raised in Los Angeles and has lived in Eastern Europe and Minnesota. Her parents encouraged her love for music and writing about music. Sullivan's first journalistic piece appeared in Prognosis, *an English-language newspaper in Czechoslovakia. Her writing has been published in a wide range of music publications including* Spin, Los Angeles Magazine, Nylon, *the* New York Times Magazine, *and* DaCapo Best Music Writing *(2002). She hosts the Minnesota radio talk show for music and pop culture,* Pop Vultures, *which won the Public Radio Exchange's "Most-Broadcast Series of 2004" award. Her essay included here provides an imaginary dialogue and contrast between the persona of the author and Jennifer Lopez as she is presented in celebrity-oriented periodicals and other media.*

JOURNAL

Write about your feelings about celebrities as alternative selves. Do you see elements of your "ideal" self in certain celebrities, you as you might dream of becoming? Do celebrities ever make you feel inferior by representing an "ideal" self of incredible beauty and success?

L ots of people are fine with celebrity magazines. They read them to *unwind*—which sounds to me like eating live mice to unwind. They just don't take magazines seriously. They toss them out after they read them. They distinguish between the real world and the magazine world.

Me, not so much. I try, but it's no good: Magazines are real to me. I believe in them the way I believe in storybooks, which is a whole bunch. It hurts me to throw one away. So I've got to be careful, especially nowadays. Every issue of *Rolling Stone* in its most recent model (sleeker, faster, sexier) ends up in a cardboard box in the closet, because it makes me sad and lonely to have Britney, Christina, Kate Hudson, or that booby-rexic Brazilian model blinking at me from the coffee table like drugged teen hookers. I half believe that magazines and books have individual *vibes,* if you will, and that a magazine created without love transmits a jangly signal of desperation to those within its range. (The superstring theorists will prove me right, you'll see.) Let *Mojo* pile up next to the bed, no problem. But *Rolling Stone*'s got to go in the box.

Some people skim magazines to calm themselves while waiting for the shrink. For me, they're a big reason I'm at the shrink. How do these people do it? Maybe they just don't think to compare themselves to people in magazines. (They probably don't feel guilty for every bad thing that happens in the world, either. How do they do it? I carry around personal shame for Neil Diamond's work in the early Eighties, just for starters, not to mention that version of "Da Do Do Do, Da Da Da Da" with Sting singing in Spanish.) On a bad day like yesterday, in the middle of my own, private Celebrate Melancholy! Week, I was no match for the snorting beast of American psychosexual pathology in my mailbox: Jennifer Lopez on the cover of *Rolling Stone,* in a metal Wonderbra.

I pull the thing out of the mailbox, and I know right away I'm going to read it, despite laundry and deadlines and my best Girl Power/Drew Barrymore/ *Crouching Tiger* training. I mean, how can I not? She's a one-woman freak show of metastasized success. She might as well be wearing a sandwich board that reads: "I AM RICHER, HOTTER, AND BETTER ORGANIZED THAN YOU COULD EVER HOPE TO BE, YOU ROTTING CORPSE OF A NOBODY." An internal debate ensues between two of my selves: the teen girl who loves to torture herself with unfavorable comparisons to others, and the concerned guru:

TEEN: Whee! A celebrity-magazine article about a woman my age who's way more successful than me!

GURU: Hmmm . . . what other mail is there? Look here, love, see the pretty pink stationery from—erm, the nice gas company people . . .

TEEN: She has a metal bikini!

GURU: How about this keen *Get Organized!* catalog? Porn for obsessive-compulsives! C'mon, let's go grab some coffee—

TEEN: She has golden skin!

GURU: Do I have to give you the business—*again?* Okay. See, *Rolling Stone* pushes celebrity T&A in order to sell advertising to the tobacco, liquor, and corporate-record industries, which consist of greedy bores and balding guys who wish they had been rock stars, who abuse and exploit *your people:* young people, and musicians! Furthermore, young lady, you're every bit as lovely as Jennifer Lopez and twice as smart. You're soulful and, and . . . and well, you're just a super person, and I don't want to hear another word about it.

TEEN: She has a metal bikini.

And so on.

5   My mom always said, Don't compare yourself. But my mom's a Jedi master. I'm a 30-year-old late bloomer who couldn't even afford Ecstasy on New Year's, forgets her groceries in the back of the car, believes in magazines, obsesses over music trivia (and trivial musicians), and is convinced an alternate realm of perfection and beauty exists just on the other side of the air we breathe. I'm like one of those sleeping fetus-people in *The Matrix,* trying to find the rabbit hole to Reality. I don't have anything figured out, unlike Jennifer Lopez. She's got it sussed—even if what she's sussed is the manufacture of cold illusion and exploitation of human insecurity.

So I read the hideous thing. I regret it immediately but, unlike a bulimic food binge, you can't un-read a bad article once you've read it. It sits there, curdling your juju. For the rest of the day, comparisons with this chick haunt me.

Jennifer Lopez says, "I don't smoke because I don't have the three minutes it takes to smoke a cigarette!" I have plenty of time. I just don't have the three bucks for a pack.

Lopez has a kicky nickname: "J. Lo" (also the title of her new album). I wonder if I should try it. Call me K. Sul. Yo, I'm K. Sul.

J. Lo is a glamorous movie star. I have some glamorous moments too. Just the other night, my roommate said my dinner (fish sticks and spinach) was very *Erin Brockovich.*

10   J. Lo's famous ex-boyfriend is hoping he doesn't go to jail for fleeing the scene of a nightclub shooting, with guns ("it was an unfortunate situation," Lopez sighs), because it would mess with his recording career. The guy who used to kind of be my boyfriend (it was an unfortunate situation) is hoping he doesn't get dropped from his record label, because it would mess with his recording career. People call him "puffy" too, because of what his face looks like when he drinks too much Bud Light, which is most of the time.

J. Lo likes to stay in and nest. Hey, K. Sul does too. I'm at home writing on a Friday night when young Hollywood is out snorting coke and sucking face. You think I care?

J. Lo is ambitious. "I'm looking forward to the ninth album, the thirtieth movie," she says. I feel you, J. It's nice to collect stuff. I own, like, five movies right now, but I notice where they're selling used tapes now at Video Hut. You might want to check it out, too, sister. Just a tip.

J. Lo knows how to keep it real. Says one of her many producers: "[J. Lo] still comes to the Bronx and sleeps on her mother's couch." Up in my crib, we keep it so real, I even sleep on my own couch sometimes.

"When we're in the studio," says the producer, "she orders Chinese from, like, the place next door." Me too, totally! "One day she left the studio and got in a cab because she didn't want to wait for a car," he says. "She's got a little bit of thug in her." In that case, I'm a regular gang-banger—I walk, drive, *and* take cabs. I put the "hug" in "thug," yo.

15   J. Lo also likes to have fun: "Wherever she's at, she's got her crew that rolls with her," says the producer, "and they *party.*" Apparently she spends more time with these dancers, managers, stylists, and publicists than with her family or boyfriend. Let's see. I must have a crew lying around here somewhere . . . I'm pretty sure I had a crew—

Good God! I forgot to let the crew out of the closet when I got home from Food 4 Less last week! They've had nothing to read but *Rolling Stone!*

Of course, J. Lo has a thoughtful side, too. She thinks about things, because she has lots of things to think about. Things like, you know, thoughts. For example: "Things I go through, things I see my friends go through. You get to a certain age and you start thinking about other things." Speak!

And still, I can't help but wonder what it would be like to be like J. Lo: "When she's not demanding everyone do as she does, everyone just seems to want to." That used to happen to me all the time—till I told everybody, *Look, Barbie—and Skipper, and you too, Cher: You're going to have to fend for yourselves some day.* It still happened after that, but at least I warned them.

Actually, I don't know J. Lo and I don't really mind if she pulls her Madonniest stunts to pop the superfame barrier. She's like an international diplomat for the shelf-asses of the world, and I'm personally grateful for that. She's an okay actress. She's not cloning babies or inventing sheep AIDS or giving money to the Scientologists (that we know of). So what the hell?

20   But still, she and her single, "Love Don't Cost a Thing"—in which her voice is reinvented by recording technology to resemble a set of robotic triplets, their programs set on "Destiny's Child-lite"—just leave me feeling cold and alone. When a person manages, after years of struggle, to capture the flaming baton of public attention, and they're really running with it, and they're actually starting to master it, I guess I kind of want them to do something with it. Say something. Give me something for my attention.

Not to be too predictable, but supposing you gave me a sign that you feel the things I feel: self-doubt, fear, loneliness, even wild obsession? (Sorry, but confessing you're "addicted to love!" doesn't cut the muffin.) Don't try to sell me that dorky lie that you're part of some immortal club of people who, having achieved humanity's lamest values—fame, wealth, and power—have shed all human qualities but greed and smugness. It only makes you look desperate.

If you can't do that, then sell me a dream, because I love dreams. But make it a goddamn beautiful one. Can you do that? Can you make a kick-ass dream that inspires ass kicking? Can you make it a multidimensional dream that contains hidden doors to larger dreams? Can you be a force for good in the world, and not just a force for you in the world?

You know what? I'd even be happy with a cool *bad* dream. Just don't give me this "I'm totally bland, have no imagination, and have been completely desalinated by the teams at corporate who have reprogrammed me for the pursuit of money and fame" bullshit.

When you get like that, J., you just remind me too much of reality.

QUESTIONS FOR DISCUSSION

1. What is the author's attitude toward magazines in general, and celebrity magazines in particular? Why does she dislike recent issues of *Rolling Stone?* Try examining a recent issue of that magazine and comparing it with one from ten or more years ago to see how the publication has changed over the years.

2. What particularly irks K. Sul about Jennifer Lopez? Why does K. Sul consider her a "one-woman freak show"?

3. Why does the author double or divide her personality? What two different "selves" does she use in her "internal debate"? What contrasting opinions do they have of J. Lo?

4. How does J. Lo's success make K. Sul more keenly aware of her own limitations? What ironic comparisons does K. Sul draw between herself and Lopez?

5. How does the author use humor to convey her message? How does the author's utilization of humor add to or diminish her ideas?

6. In what ways do you think the author believes celebrities should properly use their fame and influence? What does she think J. Lo's responsibility should be to her fans? Do you agree or disagree with K. Sul?

CONNECTION

Compare the divide between K. Sul and the rejected J. Lo identity as presented in this essay with ideas about the difficulty of integrating the shadow self as found in Robert Johnson's "Owning Your Own Shadow" (see page 415).

IDEAS FOR WRITING

1. Write an essay analyzing the content of a celebrity interview/profile from the opposed perspectives of two different "selves": yourself as a student, as aspiring artist, as teacher, and so on. Conclude by commenting on whether or not you think this celebrity has any meaningful message to either of your two selves.

2. Write an argument essay on the subject of celebrities and fans. Do celebrities help their fans by providing positive role models for success, or do they tend to make their fans feel inferior and/or help them escape into fantasy worlds through overidentification? You might use two or three modern celebrities as examples. Consult fan sites and celebrity interviews.

RELATED WEB SITES

Kate Sullivan's Rockblog
`http://katesullivan.blogspot.com`
Kate Sullivan's blog is a fan's site, a personal musings site, and at times a rock critic's site where she has begun posting essays she has written for the *LA Weekly* and other periodicals. Compare the tone and presentation of self in the blog with the persona of K. Sul; the blog also makes a good contrast with the J. Lo site (below).

Jennifer Lopez Official Site
`www.jenniferlopez.com`
This site features stills from films by Lopez, product- and career-related news, music, and a shop with official JLo items such as jewelry, fragrances, clothing, and swimwear.

Fran Peavey (with Myrna Levy and Charles Varon)

Us and Them

Fran Peavey is a longtime California peace activist, ecologist, and community organizer. Peavey's books include Heart Politics *(1984);* A Shallow Pool of Time: One Woman Grapples with the Aids Epidemic *(1989);* By Life's Grace: Musings on the Essence of Social Change *(1994), (with Radmila Manojlovic Zarkovic); the anthology* I Remember: Writings by Bosnian Women Refugees *(1996); and* Heart Politics Revisited *(2000). Peavey has also written articles for a number of alternative-press publications, and has served as a longtime observer of the Balkans struggle and the war in Kosovo. As you read her essay "Us and Them," from* Heart Politics, *consider how the people whom we feel are different from us politically or socially can be mistakenly perceived as alien beings with whom we have nothing in common, and how accepting the "other" outside of ourselves is something like accepting the rejected parts of our own identity.*

JOURNAL

Write about someone with whom you have trouble communicating because this individual is different from you in some way. What do you have in common with this person that could form the basis for better communication?

Time was when I knew that the racists were the lunch-counter owners who refused to serve blacks, the warmongers were the generals who planned wars and ordered the killing of innocent people, and the polluters were the industrialists whose factories fouled the air, water and land. I could be a good guy by boycotting, marching, and sitting in to protest the actions of the bad guys.

But no matter how much I protest, an honest look at myself and my relationship with the rest of the world reveals ways that I too am part of the problem. I notice that on initial contact I am more suspicious of Mexicans than of whites. I see that I'm addicted to a standard of living maintained at the expense of poorer people around the world—a situation that can only be perpetuated through military force. And the problem of pollution seems to include my consumption of resources and creation of waste. The line that separates me from the bad guys is blurred.

When I was working to stop the Vietnam War, I'd feel uneasy seeing people in military uniform. I remember thinking, "How could that guy be so dumb as to have gotten into that uniform? How could he be so acquiescent, so credulous as to have fallen for the government's story in Vietnam?" I'd get furious inside when I imagined the horrible things he'd probably done in the war.

Several years after the end of the war, a small group of Vietnam veterans wanted to hold a retreat at our farm in Watsonville. I consented, although I felt ambivalent about hosting them. That weekend, I listened to a dozen men and women who had served in Vietnam. Having returned home only to face ostracism for their involvement in the war, they were struggling to come to terms with their experiences.

5   They spoke of some of the awful things they'd done and seen, as well as some things they were proud of. They told why they had enlisted in the Army or cooperated with the draft: their love of the United States, their eagerness to serve, their wish to be brave and heroic. They felt their noble motives had been betrayed, leaving them with little confidence in their own judgment. Some questioned their own manhood or womanhood and even their basic humanity. They wondered whether they had been a positive force or a negative one overall, and what their buddies' sacrifices meant. Their anguish disarmed me, and I could no longer view them simply as perpetrators of evil.

How had I come to view military people as my enemies? Did vilifying soldiers serve to get me off the hook and allow me to divorce myself from responsibility for what my country was doing in Vietnam? Did my own anger and righteousness keep me from seeing the situation in its full complexity? How had this limited view affected my work against the war?

When my youngest sister and her husband, a young career military man, visited me several years ago, I was again challenged to see the human being within the soldier. I learned that as a farm boy in Utah, he'd been recruited to be a sniper.

One night toward the end of their visit, we got to talking about his work. Though he had also been trained as a medical corpsman, he could still be called on at any time to work as a sniper. He couldn't tell me much about this part of his career—he'd been sworn to secrecy. I'm not sure he would have wanted to tell me even if he could. But he did say that a sniper's work involved going abroad, "bumping off" a leader, and disappearing into a crowd.

When you're given an order, he said, you're not supposed to think about it. You feel alone and helpless. Rather than take on the Army and maybe the whole country himself, he chose not to consider the possibility that certain orders shouldn't be carried out.

10   I could see that feeling isolated can make it seem impossible to follow one's own moral standards and disobey an order. I leaned toward him and said, "If you're ever ordered to do something that you know you shouldn't do, call me immediately and I'll find a way to help. I know a lot of people would support your stand. You're not alone." He and my sister looked at each other and their eyes filled with tears.

How do we learn whom to hate and fear? During my short lifetime, the national enemies of the United States have changed several times. Our World War II foes, the Japanese and the Germans, have become our allies. The Russians have been in vogue as our enemy for some time, although during a few periods relations improved somewhat. The North Vietnamese, Cubans, and Chinese have done stints as our enemy. So many countries seem capable of incurring our national wrath—how do we choose among them?

As individuals, do we choose our enemies based on cues from national leaders? From our schoolteachers and religious leaders? From newspapers and TV? Do we hate and fear our parents' enemies as part of our family identity? Or those of our culture, subculture, or peer group?

Whose economic and political interests does our enemy mentality serve?

At a conference on holocaust and genocide I met someone who showed me that it is not necessary to hate our opponents, even under the most extreme circumstances. While sitting in the hotel lobby after a session on the German holocaust, I struck up a conversation with a woman named Helen Waterford. When I learned she was a Jewish survivor of Auschwitz, I told her how angry I was at the Nazis. (I guess I was trying to prove to her that I was one of the good guys.)

15 "You know," she said, "I don't hate the Nazis." This took me aback. How could anyone who had lived through a concentration camp not hate the Nazis?

Then I learned that Helen does public speaking engagements with a former leader of the Hitler Youth movement: they talk about how terrible fascism is as viewed from both sides. Fascinated, I arranged to spend more time with Helen and learn as much as I could from her.

In 1980, Helen read an intriguing newspaper article in which a man named Alfons Heck described his experiences growing up in Nazi Germany. When he was a young boy in Catholic school, the priest would come in every morning and say, "Heil Hitler," and then "Good Morning," and finally, "In the name of the Father and the Son and the Holy Spirit . . ." In Heck's mind, Hitler came before God. At ten, he volunteered for the Hitler Youth, and he loved it. It was in 1944, when he was sixteen, that Heck first learned that the Nazis were systematically killing the Jews. He thought, "This can't be true." But gradually he came to believe that he had served a mass murderer.

Heck's frankness impressed Helen, and she thought, "I want to meet that man." She found him soft-spoken, intelligent and pleasant. Helen had already been speaking publicly about her own experiences of the holocaust, and she asked Heck to share a podium with her at an upcoming engagement with a group of four-hundred schoolteachers. They spoke in chronological format, taking turns telling their own stories of the Nazi period. Helen told of leaving Frankfurt in 1934 at age twenty-five.

She and her husband, an accountant who had lost his job when the Nazis came to power, escaped to Holland. There they worked with the underground Resistance, and Helen gave birth to a daughter. In 1940 the Nazis invaded Holland. Helen and her husband went into hiding in 1942. Two years later, they were discovered and sent to Auschwitz. Their daughter was hidden by friends in the Resistance. Helen's husband died in the concentration camp.

20 Heck and Waterford's first joint presentation went well, and they decided to continue working as a team. Once, at an assembly of eight-hundred high school students, Heck was asked, "If you had been ordered to shoot some Jews, maybe Mrs. Waterford, would you have shot them?" The audience gasped. Heck swallowed and said, "Yes. I obeyed orders. I would have." Afterward he apologized to Helen, saying he hadn't wanted to upset her. She told him, "I'm

glad you answered the way you did. Otherwise, I would never again believe a word you said."

Heck is often faced with the "once a Nazi, always a Nazi" attitude. "You may give a good speech," people will say, "but I don't believe any of it. Once you have believed something, you don't throw it away." Again and again, he patiently explains that it took years before he could accept the fact that he'd been brought up believing falsehoods. Heck is also harassed by neo-Nazis, who call him in the middle of the night and threaten: "We haven't gotten you yet, but we'll kill you, you traitor."

How did Helen feel about the Nazis in Auschwitz? "I disliked them. I cannot say that I wished I could kick them to death—I never did. I guess that I am just not a vengeful person." She is often denounced by Jews for having no hate, for not wanting revenge. "It is impossible that you don't hate," people tell her.

At the conference on the holocaust and genocide and in subsequent conversations with Helen, I have tried to understand what has enabled her to remain so objective and to avoid blaming individual Germans for the holocaust, for her suffering and for her husband's death. I have found a clue in her passionate study of history.

For many people, the only explanation of the holocaust is that it was the creation of a madman. But Helen believes that such an analysis only serves to shield people from believing that a holocaust could happen to them. An appraisal of Hitler's mental health, she says, is less important than an examination of the historical forces at play and the ways Hitler was able to manipulate them.

25   "As soon as the war was over," Helen told me, "I began to read about what had happened since 1933, when my world closed. I read and read. How did the 'S.S. State' develop? What was the role of Britain, Hungary, Yugoslavia, the United States, France? How can it be possible that the holocaust really happened? What is the first step, the second step? What are people searching for when they join fanatical movements? I guess I will be asking these questions until my last days."

Those of us working for social change tend to view our adversaries as enemies, to consider them unreliable, suspect, and generally of lower moral character. Saul Alinsky, a brilliant community organizer, explained the rationale for polarization this way:

> One acts decisively only in the conviction that all the angels are on one side and all the devils are on the other. A leader may struggle toward a decision and weigh the merits and demerits of a situation which is 52 percent positive and 48 percent negative, but once the decision is reached he must assume that his cause is 100 percent positive and the opposition 100 percent negative. . . . Many liberals, during our attack on the then-school superintendent [in Chicago], were pointing out that after all he wasn't a 100-percent devil, he was a regular churchgoer, he was a good family man, and he was generous in his contributions to charity. Can you imagine in the arena of conflict charging that so-and-so is a racist bastard and then diluting the impact of the attack with qualifying remarks? This becomes political idiocy.

But demonizing one's adversaries has great costs. It is a strategy that tacitly accepts and helps perpetuate our dangerous enemy mentality.

Instead of focusing on the 52-percent "devil" in my adversary, I choose to look at the other 48 percent, to start from the premise that within each adversary I have an ally. That ally may be silent, faltering, or hidden from my view. It may be only the person's sense of ambivalence about morally questionable parts of his or her job. Such doubts rarely have a chance to flower because of the overwhelming power of the social context to which the person is accountable. *My* ability to be *their* ally also suffers from such pressures. In 1970, while the Vietnam War was still going on, a group of us spent the summer in Long Beach, California, organizing against a napalm factory there. It was a small factory that mixed the chemicals and put the napalm in canisters. An accidental explosion a few months before had spewed hunks of napalm gel onto nearby homes and lawns. The incident had, in a real sense, brought the war home. It spurred local residents who opposed the war to recognize their community's connection with one of its most despicable elements. At their request, we worked with and strengthened their local group. Together we presented a slide show and tour of the local military-industrial complex for community leaders, and we picketed the napalm factory. We also met with the president of the conglomerate that owned the factory.

We spent three weeks preparing for this meeting, studying the company's holdings and financial picture and investigating whether there were any lawsuits filed against the president or his corporation. And we found out as much as we could about his personal life: his family, his church, his country club, his hobbies. We studied his photograph, thinking of the people who loved him and the people he loved, trying to get a sense of his worldview and the context to which he was accountable.

30   We also talked a lot about how angry we were at him for the part he played in killing and maiming children in Vietnam. But though our anger fueled our determination, we decided that venting it at him would make him defensive and reduce our effectiveness.

When three of us met with him, he was not a stranger to us. Without blaming him personally or attacking his corporation, we asked him to close the plant, not to bid for the contract when it came up for renewal that year, and to think about the consequences of his company's operations. We told him we knew where his corporation was vulnerable (it owned a chain of motels that could be boycotted), and said we intended to continue working strategically to force his company out of the business of burning people. We also discussed the company's other war-related contracts, because changing just a small part of his corporation's function was not enough; we wanted to raise the issue of economic dependence on munitions and war.

Above all, we wanted him to see us as real people, not so different from himself. If we had seemed like flaming radicals, he would have been likely to dismiss our concerns. We assumed he was already carrying doubts inside himself, and we saw our role as giving voice to those doubts. Our goal was to introduce ourselves and our perspective into his context, so he would remember us and consider our position when making decisions.

When the contract came up for renewal two months later, his company did not bid for it.

Working for social change without relying on the concept of enemies raises some practical difficulties. For example, what do we do with all the anger that we're accustomed to unleashing against an enemy? Is it possible to hate actions and policies without hating the people who are implementing them? Does empathizing with those whose actions we oppose create a dissonance that undermines our determination?

35   I don't delude myself into believing that everything will work out for the best if we make friends with our adversaries. I recognize that certain military strategists are making decisions that raise the risks for us all. I know that some police officers will rough up demonstrators when arresting them. Treating our adversaries as potential allies need not entail unthinking acceptance of their actions. Our challenge is to call forth the humanity within each adversary, while preparing for the full range of possible responses. Our challenge is to find a path between cynicism and naiveté.

QUESTIONS FOR DISCUSSION

1. Why does Peavey no longer find it easy to feel clear about the distinctions between the good guys and the bad guys? What elements of the bad guys does she now perceive in herself?
2. What was Peavey's rationale for being angry at soldiers? What did Peavey learn from her experience hosting a group of Vietnam veterans on her farm?
3. What did Peavey learn from the visit with her sister and her sister's husband, a military sniper? Does Peavey feel that the husband should be forgiven? Do you agree?
4. How does Peavey's friendship with Helen Waterford break down preconceptions Peavey holds about Nazis and concentration camp survivors? Do you agree with Waterford and Peavey's new perspective on Nazis?
5. Through providing an example of her own successful organizing technique against a napalm factory, Peavey attempts to refute an argument by organizer Saul Alinsky against the folly of qualifying our attacks on our enemies. Is Peavey's argument a convincing one?
6. How effective is Peavey's conclusion in anticipating and resolving objections that readers might have to her position? What point does she concede? Does her concession weaken or strengthen her argument?

CONNECTION

Compare Peavey's view on effective activism that works toward accepting the socially defined "other" or antagonist with the views of Desmond Tutu on forgiveness and reconciliation (see page 445).

IDEAS FOR WRITING

1. After reading Peavey's essay and our discussion at the beginning of this chapter on the dialogic argument, write an essay where you argue either for or against Peavey's approach to resolving political differences. If you see her approach as working better in some situations than in others, provide examples of areas of conflict where the approach might or might not work.

2. Write an essay about an experience in which you separated yourself from another person or group of people because of a difference of opinion, but later were able to understand and identify with their behavior and accept their differences.

RELATED WEB SITES

Interview with Fran Peavey
`www.jobsletter.org.nz/hpx/fran98.htm`
Interview with Peavey by Australian journalist David Leser from *The Melbourne Age* (1998).

Crabgrass
`www.crabgrass.org`
Crabgrass is a small nongovernmental organization based in San Francisco that works globally and locally on environmental, social justice, and human rights issues. The site features articles by Fran Peavey.

Desmond Mpilo Tutu

No Future Without Forgiveness

Born in 1931 in a South African mining town, Desmond Tutu suffered from the insults and violence that were a part of every black person's life under apartheid. Ordained as a priest in 1961, in 1976 he was consecrated as a bishop for his continued activism against apartheid and received the Nobel Peace Prize in 1984. His books include Crying in the Wilderness: The Struggle for Justice in South Africa *(1982);* Hope & Suffering: Sermons & Speeches *(1984),* The Rainbow People of God: The Making of a Peaceful Revolution *(1994);* No Future Without Forgiveness *(1999); and* God Has a Dream *(2004). In 1996 Nelson Mandela made him chairman of the Truth and Reconciliation Commission, an organization designed to reduce through testimony and forgiveness the lingering pain and anger over the apartheid years. The essay that follows is a brief account of the important work of the commission and its significance for conflict resolution in a variety of cultural settings.*

JOURNAL

What is your view of the importance of forgiveness? Who benefits the most from
the act of forgiveness?

A year after the genocide in Rwanda, when at least half a million people
were massacred, I visited that blighted land. I went as the president of the
ecumenical body, the All Africa Conference of Churches. In my ten-year, two-
term presidency, I had tried to take the AACC to its member churches through
pastoral visits, especially to those countries that were experiencing crises of one
sort or another. Other officers and I also went to celebrate successes when, for
instance, democracy replaced repression and injustice in Ethiopia.

In Rwanda we visited Ntarama, a village near the capital, Kigali. In Ntarama,
Tutsi tribespeople had been mown down in a church. The new government
had not removed the corpses, so that the church was like a mortuary, with the
bodies lying as they had fallen the year before during the massacre. The stench
was overpowering. Outside the church building was a collection of skulls, some
still stuck with *pangas* (machetes) and daggers. I tried to pray. Instead I broke
down and wept.

The scene was a deeply disturbing and moving monument to the viciousness
that, as human beings, we are capable of unleashing against fellow human beings. Those who had turned against one another in this gory fashion had often
lived amicably in the same villages and spoken the same language. They had
frequently intermarried and most of them had espoused the same faith—most
were Christians. The colonial overlords had sought to maintain their European
hegemony by favoring the main ethnic group, the Tutsi, over the other, the
Hutu, thus planting the seeds of what would in the end be one of the bloodiest
episodes in modern African history.

A few kilometers from this church, some women had begun to build a settlement which they named the Nelson Mandela Village. It was to be a home for
some of the many widows and orphans created by the genocide. I spoke to the
indomitable leaders of this women's movement. They said, "We must mourn
and weep for the dead. But life must also go on, we can't go on weeping." Over
at Ntarama, we might say, there was Calvary, death and crucifixion. Here in the
Nelson Mandela Village was Resurrection, new life, new beginning, new hope.

5   I also attended a rally in the main stadium of Kigali. It was amazing that people who had so recently experienced such a devastating trauma could sing and
laugh and dance as they did at that rally. Most of the leading politicians were
present, from the president on down. I had been asked to preach. I began by
expressing the deepest condolences of all their sisters and brothers in other
parts of Africa, for people elsewhere had been profoundly shocked at the car-
nage and destruction.

I said that the history of Rwanda was typical of a history of "top dog" and
"underdog." The top dog wanted to cling to its privileged position and the underdog strove to topple the top dog. When that happened, the new top dog

engaged in an *orgy* of retribution to pay back the new underdog for all the pain and suffering it had inflicted when it was top dog. The new underdog fought to topple the new top dog, storing in its memory all the pain and suffering it was enduring, forgetting that the new top dog was in its view only retaliating for all that it remembered it had suffered when the underdog had been its master. It was a sad history of reprisal provoking counter reprisal.

I reminded the Tutsi that they had waited for thirty years to get their own back for what they perceived to be the injustices that had been heaped on them. I said that extremists among the Hutu were also quite capable of waiting thirty years or more for one day when they could topple the new government, in which the Tutsi played a prominent role, and in their turn unleash the devastation of revenge and resentment.

I said there was talk about tribunals because people did not want to tolerate allowing the criminals to escape punishment. But what I feared was that, if retributive justice was the last word in their situation, then most Hutu would feel that they had been found guilty not because they *were* guilty but because they were Hutu and they would wait for the day when they would be able to take revenge. Then they would pay back the Tutsi for the horrendous prison conditions in which they had been held.

I told them that the cycle of reprisal and counter reprisal that had characterized their national history had to be broken and that the only way to do this was to go beyond retributive justice to restorative justice, to move on to forgiveness, because without it there was no future.

10   The president of Rwanda responded to my sermon with considerable magnanimity. They were ready to forgive, he said, but even Jesus had declared that the devil could not be forgiven. I do not know where he found the basis for what he said, but he was expressing a view that found some resonance, that there were atrocities that were unforgivable. My own view was different, but I had been given a fair and indeed friendly hearing. Later I addressed the parliamentary and political leadership of that country and I was not shouted down as I repeated my appeal for them to consider choosing forgiveness and reconciliation rather than their opposites.

Why was I not rebuffed? Why did these traumatized people, who had undergone such a terrible experience, listen to an unpopular point of view? They listened to me particularly because something had happened in South Africa that gave them reason to pause and wonder. The world had expected that the most ghastly bloodbath would overwhelm South Africa. It had not happened. Then the world thought that, after a democratically elected government was in place, those who for so long had been denied their rights, whose dignity had been trodden underfoot, callously and without compunction, would go on the rampage, unleashing an orgy of revenge and retribution that would devastate their common motherland.

Instead there was this remarkable Truth and Reconciliation Commission to which people told their heart-rending stories, victims expressing their willingness to forgive and perpetrators telling their stories of sordid atrocities while also asking for forgiveness from those they had wronged so grievously. Was this not a viable way of dealing with conflict? Might those who had been at one another's throats try to live amicably together?

It was courageous leaders who gave the sides hope that negotiations could lead to a good outcome. At that time we were fortunate to have as President F. W. De Klerk, leader of the Nationalist Party. Whatever the reasons may have been that impelled him to do what he did, he deserves his niche in history for having announced those very courageous decisions in February of 1990: amongst them the unbanning of the African National Congress, the Pan African Congress, and the Communist Party and the release of political prisoners. That wasn't done lightly. Had De Klerk been maybe more apprehensive he might not have done it. Had he been his granite-like predecessor, we might still be struggling against a vicious system. It was even more fortunate for us that Mr. De Klerk had, as his opposite number, not someone consumed by bitterness, eager for revenge and retribution, saying we are going to give them the same dose of medicine that they gave us once we come to power.

It was our good fortune that on the other side De Klerk found Nelson Mandela, who despite twenty-seven years of incarceration, instead of being consumed by a lust for revenge, demonstrated an extraordinary magnanimity, a nobility of spirit wishing to be able to forgive. Very many in his constituency were saying "We're going to fight to the last drop of blood." There were many, especially young ones, who felt that they could no longer take what had happened to their people for so long and for their own integrity's sake they really had to clobber the other side. By agreeing to negotiations with the Nationalists, Nelson Mandela was putting his reputation and his life, in a sense, on the line. He knew how to inspire hope.

15   The world could not quite believe what it was seeing. South Africans managed an extraordinary, reasonably peaceful transition from the awfulness of repression to the relative stability of democracy. They confounded everyone by their novel manner of dealing with a horrendous past. They had perhaps surprised even themselves at first by how much equanimity they had shown as some of the gory details of that past were rehearsed. It was a phenomenon that the world could not dismiss as insignificant. It was what enabled me to address my sisters and brothers in Rwanda in a manner that under other circumstances could have been seen as insensitive and presumptuous.

Believers say that we might describe most of human history as a quest for that harmony, friendship, and peace for which we appear to have been created. The Bible depicts it all as a God-directed campaign to recover that primordial harmony when the lion will again lie with the lamb and they will learn war no more because swords will have been beaten into plowshares and spears into pruning hooks. Somewhere deep inside us we seem to know that we are destined for something better than strife. Now and again we catch a glimpse of the better thing for which we are meant—for example, when we work together to counter the effects of natural disasters and the world is galvanized by a spirit of compassion and an amazing outpouring of generosity;

when for a little while we are bound together by bonds of a caring humanity, a universal sense of *ubuntu;* when victorious powers set up a Marshall Plan to help in the reconstruction of their devastated former adversaries; when we establish a United Nations organization where the peoples of the Earth can parley as they endeavor to avoid war; when we sign charters on the rights of children and of women; when we seek to ban the use of antipersonnel land mines; when we agree as one to outlaw torture and racism. Then we experience fleetingly that we are made for community, for family, that we are in a network of interdependence.

There is a movement to reverse the awful centrifugal force of alienation, brokenness, division, hostility, and disharmony. God has set in motion a centripetal process, a moving toward harmony, goodness, peace, and justice, a process that removes barriers. Jesus says, "And when I am lifted up from the Earth I shall draw everyone to myself" as he hangs from His cross with outflung arms, thrown out to clasp all, everyone and everything, in a cosmic embrace, so that all, everyone, everything, belongs. None is an outsider—all are insiders, all belong. There are no aliens—all belong in the one family, God's family, the human family.

With all its imperfections, what we have tried to do in South Africa has attracted the attention of the world. This tired, disillusioned, cynical world, hurting so frequently and so grievously, has marveled at a process that holds out considerable hope in the midst of much that negates hope. People in the different places that I have visited and where I have spoken about the Truth and Reconciliation process see in this flawed attempt a beacon of hope, a possible paradigm for dealing with situations where violence, conflict, turmoil, and sectional strife have seemed endemic, conflicts that mostly take place not between warring nations but within the same nation. At the end of their conflicts, the warring groups in Northern Ireland, the Balkans, the Middle East, Sri Lanka, Burma, Afghanistan, Angola, the Sudan, the two Congos, and elsewhere are going to have to sit down together to determine just how they will be able to live together amicably, how they might have a shared future devoid of strife, given the bloody past that they have recently lived through.

God does have a sense of humor. Who in their right minds could ever have imagined South Africa to be an example of anything but the most ghastly awfulness, of how not to order a nation's race relations and its governance? We South Africans were the unlikeliest lot and that is precisely why God has chosen us. We cannot really claim much credit ourselves for what we have achieved. We were destined for perdition and were plucked out of total annihilation. We were a hopeless case if ever there was one. God intends that others might look at us and take courage. God wants to point to us as a possible beacon of hope, a possible paradigm, and to say, "Look at South Africa. They had a nightmare called apartheid. It has ended. Northern Ireland (or wherever), your nightmare will end too. They had a problem regarded as intractable. They are resolving it. No problem anywhere can ever again be considered to be intractable. There is hope for you too."

QUESTIONS FOR DISCUSSION

1. What lesson can be learned through Tutu's contrast between the church building at Ntarama and the new Nelson Mandela Village?
2. How does Tutu's top dog/underdog analogy help explain the slaughter in Rwanda? What vicious circle has been perpetuated in that country?
3. Why does Tutu criticize the idea of "tribunals" to punish the guilty parties in the slaughter? Do you agree with him? Why or why not?
4. What advantage does a truth and reconciliation commission such as the one held in South Africa have over retribution and punishment? How were the personalities of De Klerk and Mandela uniquely qualified to make such a commission work?
5. How does Tutu draw on Christian values in his search for a way to overcome division, hostility, and disharmony? What does he mean by the "centripetal process" set in motion by God? Do you think this kind of faith in Christian values is enough to overcome centuries of hostility and suspicion?
6. Why does Tutu believe that God has chosen South Africa as "a possible beacon of hope, a possible paradigm"? If this is so, why have few divided countries followed the South African example?

CONNECTION

Compare Tutu's ideas on the need for social reconciliation with those of Fran Peavey in this chapter (see page 439).

IDEAS FOR WRITING

1. Write an essay about a warring, divided society that you believe has need for a reconciliation committee. Why has this idea not been put into effect there, and what do you believe it would take to create in this particular society the kind of forgiveness that Tutu would like to see?
2. Write a research essay about the South African Truth and Reconciliation Commission. What did it accomplish for South Africans, in both the short and long term? Do divisions and hostility still linger in that country? Why or why not?

RELATED WEB SITES

The Desmond Tutu Peace Centre
`www.tutu.org/main.htm`
The Desmond Tutu Peace Centre is "primarily aimed at using the experience of the South African people and the example of Desmond Tutu to inspire a new generation of visionary peace builders."

Peacejam
`www.peacejam.org/index.html`
Peacejam is a Colorado-based charity active in many parts of the world. Their site features information on their efforts for peace, links to other peace-related sites, and an interview with Desmond Tutu.

Susan Voyticky

Mixed-Up

Susan Voyticky grew up in Brooklyn, New York. She enjoys traveling, studying genetics, and writing poetry. The following essay was written for her freshman English class in response to a question that asked students to reflect on an aspect of their ethnic heritage about which they have conflicting feelings.

Having parents from different ethnic groups and growing up mixed is not easy in this country; in fact, it can really mix a person up, culturally as well as socially. Often, mixed children are confused about the cultural group to which they belong, and sometimes these children are alienated from half or even all of their cultural background. Other times children exposed to two distinct cultures feel pressured by society to choose one culture and social group to fit into and to define themselves through. However, as a person of mixed background, I try, despite the pressures that society puts on me, to relate to both my European and to my African heritage. I realize that I have a unique and independent cultural identity.

My lack of wanting to identify with a particular culture defines who I am. For instance, I remember going shopping in a store when I was ten years old that had black and white floor tiles. I decided to play with two children, a boy and a girl who were my age. After a while the girl said, "We'll [she and the boy] step on the white tiles, and you [pointing to me] step on the black tiles 'cause you're black." I couldn't believe what she had said. Even at that age, I found the idea insulting to my existence—she was ignoring half of me. I replied indignantly, "You two can step on the white tiles, I'll step anywhere I want because I'm both." Then I quickly returned to my mother.

As a child, I quickly grew to realize that I was not ethnically "identifiable." During recess at my elementary school I often would try to play with the few African American girls at my school. Usually the game was double-dutch, but I didn't know how to play, and the African American kids said I turned the rope "like a white girl." To whites, I was black, and to blacks, I was less than black. I refused to be either; my ethnicity is an entirely different color—gray. If my mother is black and my father is white, then I most certainly must be gray. What else does one get by mixing black and white? Some would consider gray a "drab" color, but often one forgets gray comes in an infinite number of shades.

Because I have not chosen to identify with only one of my parents' cultures, I'll never know the comfort of belonging to a specific group of people with ancient customs and rituals. This society does not recognize my unique cross-cultural heritage of African American, Irish, Russian, Polish, and Czechoslovakian. Few people choose to be mixed, to accept everything about themselves, and sometimes they are not given the choice. I have lost something in not being "white"; I also have lost something in not being "black." However, I have gained something important: my cultural independence. My brother puts it best when he says, "God was making a bunch of cookies. The white people he took out of the oven too soon. The black people he took out too late. We are the perfect cookies. One day everyone will be perfect, like us."

5   I struggle to be accepted in this society for what I am and not for what others would make of me. The longer I live, the more I feel pressured by society to "label" myself. When standardized forms were handed out in school, I would ask the teachers, "What should I fill out?" Most replied that I could fill whichever I wished. Most of the time that's what I did. One year I was black, the next year I was white, the next year I'd fill out two ovals. In high school, I was told I was black, because the federal government has a rule that if one is one-fourth black, one is black. I ignored this and continued to fill out forms in my usual way.

Finally the true test of my "grayness" arrived—college applications. My mother said that I should fill out African American, for the ethnic question, considering that it would improve my chances of being accepted. I didn't listen to her, for it's not in my nature to lie. How could I not be honest about who I was? On half of my applications I wrote "Black-Caucasian"; on the other half I wrote, "White African-American." My mother was not amused by what seemed to her a completely inane act. She didn't understand that I can't be told what I am, because I know who I am. In my blood run the tears of slaves torn from their homeland and the sweat of poor farmers looking for a better life. Their struggle is part of my identity.

A large part of one's culture is internal and cannot be represented simply by the color of one's skin. In this society it is difficult to be accepted for anything more than face value, but each person must try to be who he or she is within, not simply in the eyes of society. I am proud of my choice of identity with both of my ethnic backgrounds. Although being mixed often means being "mixed-up" through being mistaken for something you are not by people too ignorant to care, identity is more than skin deep.

QUESTIONS FOR DISCUSSION

1. What aspects of her mixed ethnic background cause Voyticky the most difficulty? How has she tried to resolve her problem of identity?
2. Compare Voyticky's view of the consequences of a mixed cultural and ethnic background with that presented in the poem by Judith Ortiz Cofer, "The Other."
3. Do you agree with Voyticky's approach to choosing an ethnicity for her college applications, or do you think that she should have taken fuller advantage of the opportunities afforded her?
4. Voyticky illustrates her essay with several examples drawn from her experience of being of mixed heritage at different stages of her life. What does each example add to her essay's persuasiveness and its portrait of the dilemmas faced in our society by individuals from backgrounds similar to Voyticky's? What other kinds of evidence or examples would have helped to persuade you?

Jill Ho

Affirmative Action: Perspectives from a Model Minority

Born in Taipei, Taiwan, in 1979, Jill Ho immigrated to the United States with her family and was educated in this country. In high school she was involved in many student organizations and was the cofounder of the first Asian-American Student Organization in Wichita, Kansas. She completed a biology major and is pursuing a career in medicine. In her spare time, she enjoys rollerblading, doing crossword puzzles, keeping up with current events, and designing Web pages. Ho wrote the following essay as a response to a professional essay by Dinesh D'Souza that criticized affirmative action and hiring quotas.

*I*ntelligent. *Hardworking. Compliant.* These three words are used frequently to describe Asian Americans who succeed in educational and occupational spheres. When I hear these words, they make me cringe because they mask my individuality and define my identity according to stereotypical expectations. A widespread belief referred to by Asian American scholars as the Model Minority Myth holds that Asian Americans are more successful than other minority groups. This stereotype has led to the distorted perspective that Asian Americans do not really need affirmative action and racial preference programs for education and employment; thus, in practice, such programs for the most part do not benefit and often completely ignore Asians.

Being Asian was just a minor part of my identity until high school, when I realized that my "Asianness" affected how people perceived me, regardless of how I perceived myself. Since ninth grade, I have chosen to leave the racial background bubble blank on my standardized tests, because I strongly believe that my identity cannot be summarized in the three short words *Asian/Pacific Islander.* I am proud of my cultural background, which is similar to that of many other Asians who have grown up in the United States and who experience their culture not as all-Asian or all-American, nor as a combination of "partly Asian" and "partly American," but rather as something unique.

Despite my pride in my identity, being Asian American has forced me to deal with situations that have made me feel excluded from both Asian *and* American cultures through pervasive stereotyping. For example, I am currently enrolled in a first-year Chinese language class because my relatives tease me for not being able to speak my native tongue. On the first day of class, a student who apparently assumed I was already fluent in Chinese asked me why I was enrolled in the introductory class. It was strange that my relatives would think I wasn't "Asian enough" until I had learned how to speak Chinese, while my classmate thought I was "too Asian" to be in the beginners' class. My classmate's harmless question suggested that she thought most Asian Americans were bilingual. Other common misperceptions include the stereotypes of

Asians as hardworking, highly intelligent, socially awkward or even "nerdy," modest and passive, interested in math and science, and deficient in their command of spoken English (Cheng 278). While many traits associated with the Model Minority are positive, the myth supports a powerful stereotype that many Asians feel pressured to fit.

Not only does the Model Minority Myth tell Asians how they should behave, but it also silences the unique experiences of Asian Americans. Dinesh D'Souza points out how ludicrous it would be to "abolish racial preferences for all groups except African-Americans" (28). In a country as multiethnic as the United States, it would seem extremely unfair to propose affirmative action plans, which only focus on one minority group; yet Asians are already invisible minorities, excluded by most if not all racial preference programs, even though they are the fastest-growing minority group in the United States. In 1980, 3.5 million Asian Americans were living in the United States; by 1990 that figure had doubled to 7.3 million and numbers are still increasing (Cheng and Thatchenkery 270). Part of the reason Asians are frequently not considered as minorities for preferences is the widespread belief that Asians are successful without benefiting from racial preferences; therefore they aren't disadvantaged enough. While Asian Americans include the same spectrum of demographic diversity as any other minority group, the Model Minority Myth leads people to believe that most Asians are Ivy League overachievers, despite the fact that many live in poverty in the inner city.

5   Because people generally refuse to acknowledge their minority status, Asian Americans are often unfairly treated in the workplace. The Model Minority Myth frequently appears to give Asians an initial advantage in getting hired when compared to other groups; however, Asians are actually at a disadvantage if we consider their job-related qualifications. Even when more educated than white applicants, Asians are often underpaid and occupy positions lower than would be expected for their level of education and training. Because people generally believe Asians are intelligent and industrious, many Asians feel they have to prove they are extra qualified to be considered for a position; once hired, they have to be exceptional to be promoted. When education and experience are accounted for, Asian American high school graduates "earn 26 percent less than comparably educated white high school graduates, and Asian-American college graduates earn 11 percent less than white college graduates" (Narasaki 5). While other applicants need only prove they are well qualified, Asians are forced to prove they are qualified above and beyond the already high expectations the Model Minority Myth sets for them.

However, despite the problems Asian Americans have in the workplace, I agree with D'Souza that forcing companies to meet racial quotas may unfairly result in consideration of issues entirely unrelated to who is most qualified. Selecting the less competent over better qualified applicants who do not benefit from racial preference programs is not only unfair toward qualified candidates denied positions at that company, but also unfair for the companies forced to absorb the economic costs of rejecting the best applicants (D'Souza 30). Furthermore, as D'Souza explains, companies would be unlikely to reject a highly qualified minority applicant for racial reasons because it would make no economic sense to do so; in fact, it would only hurt companies trying to compete in the marketplace to ignore talented minority applicants (30).

At the same time, affirmative action programs are essential to help minorities combat promotion discrimination. While it is reasonable to assume that companies are unlikely to discriminate blatantly against minorities in the hiring process, D'Souza fails to recognize that minority employees are far less likely to receive promotions or pay increases. This glass ceiling effect is common for all members of minority groups, but especially so for Asian Americans, who are victims of the Model Minority Myth. Since the stereotype portrays Asians as diligent, hardworking, and compliant, many employers believe that Asians are ideal employees because they are nonconfrontational. After his 1992 interviews with human resource managers in the Silicon Valley, Edward Park concluded that "Asian-Americans are seen as expendable workers who may be hired and fired at will because they will take what is offered and are too passive to complain, let alone file wrongful termination lawsuits" (163).

The same notion that Asians are unlikely to complain makes it more difficult for Asians to receive promotions or pay raises. The glass ceiling that prevents minority members from advancing to upper-management positions especially affects Asian Americans. In top management fewer than 1 percent are minority members and even in companies where there are numerous overqualified Asian employees in lower positions, fewer than 0.3 percent of senior level positions are held by Asian Americans (Cheng 285). One possible explanation is that the same passive nature thought to prevent Asians from complaining if not promoted would also make them ineffective managers. Additionally, another aspect of the Model Minority Myth, poor English skills, may lead employers to believe that Asian supervisors would be unable to communicate clearly to employees. For many minorities, especially Asian Americans, discrimination within companies for promotions is a bigger problem than possible discrimination in initial hiring.

Eric Foner points out that we cannot pretend that "eliminating affirmative action will produce a society in which rewards are based on merit" because race is still an issue (925). Although few companies today would openly refuse to hire minority employees, the unusually low number of minorities with equal seniority and/or equal pay in companies still reflects the effects of promotion discrimination. To remedy this situation, racial preference programs should strive to create equal access to higher education for all minorities so anyone can have the training to be well qualified for the workplace. Furthermore, employers need to focus on breaking down barriers that limit opportunities for minority promotion to senior-level positions so anyone can break through the glass ceiling. All people, regardless of race, gender, religion, or sexual orientation, should be accepted in the workplace for who they are and rewarded for their competency and hard work on the job.

WORKS CITED

Cheng, Cliff. "Are Asian American Employees a Model Minority or Just a Minority?" *Journal of Applied Behavioral Sciences* Sep. 1997: 277–90.

Cheng, Cliff, and Tojo Joseph Thatchenkery. "Why Is There a Lack of Workplace Diversity Research on Asian Americans?" *Journal of Applied Behavioral Sciences* Sep. 1997: 270–76.

D'Souza, Dinesh. "Beyond Affirmative Action." *National Review* 9 Dec. 1996: 26–30.

Foner, Eric. "Hiring Quotas for White Males Only." *The Nation* 26 Jun. 1995: 924–95.

Narasaki, K.K. "Separate but Equal? Discrimination and the Need for Affirmative Action Legislation." *Perspectives on Affirmative Action*. Los Angeles: Asian Pacific American Public Policy Institute, 1995. 5–8.

Park, Edward. "Asians Matter: Asian American Entrepreneurs in the Silicon Valley High Technology Industry." *Reframing the Immigration Debate*. Ed. B. Hing and R. Lee. Los Angeles: UCLA Asian American Studies Center, 1996. 155–77.

QUESTIONS FOR DISCUSSION

1. What is the Model Minority Myth? How do the traits of the model influence the lives of Asian Americans?

2. What examples from her own experiences does Ho provide? Are they effective?

3. What position does this essay take on Dinesh D'Souza's "Beyond Affirmative Action"? How does Ho both agree and disagree with D'Souza?

4. What solutions does Ho offer for improving work opportunities for Asian Americans? Do you think her solutions are clearly stated and adequate?

TOPICS FOR RESEARCH AND WRITING

1. Do some research into the use of the double in Stevenson's *Dr. Jekyll and Mr. Hyde*. You should read the complete text, preferably an annotated version, and find some biographical information about Stevenson's life and the values of the time when he lived. How does the double of Jekyll/Hyde reveal typical preoccupations of Victorian England such as sexual repression and the hypocrisy of maintaining the façade of proper behavior in a society whose moral standards ignored the realities of violence, illegitimacy, drug use, and rampant prostitution? In what ways does the struggle that Stevenson portrays seem relevant to the struggles people go through today?

2. Danny Fingeroth and Kate Sullivan examine aspects of the doubled personality as it occurs in popular culture through heroes who lead a double life and celebrities who create a false persona that fans mistake for the "real" person. Write an essay in which you analyze the phenomenon of the "doubled self" in the celebrities and hero/ines of popular culture.

3. At its most extreme, an inability to incorporate the shadow self into one's dominant personality reveals itself in mental illness and breakdown. Do some research into a type of mental illness such as schizophrenia or multiple personality disorder in which the individual's personality tends to fragment into portions that cannot acknowledge one another or function together as a unified self. What are the causes of the particular disorder you have chosen to study? What treatments have been tried in the past, and which ones are currently available?

4. Although the double is often seen as having a primarily psychological origin, there are often social and practical reasons why someone may choose to lead a literal "double life." Do some research into those who have chosen to pass as the "other," such as women who choose to disguise themselves as men, blacks who choose to pass for white, gays who are "closeted" or pass for "straight," and so on. What are the social causes of this type of self-concealment? What are the psychological effects of having to conceal one's true self in society?

5. Desmond Tutu and Fran Peavey examine the need for understanding of the "other," forgiveness, and reconciliation as strategies for conflict resolution between individuals and groups. Do further research into programs advocating similar approaches to conflict resolution, and conclude with some evaluation of the effectiveness of such approaches.

6. People have long been fascinated by identical twins as literal doubles. Do some research on the inner world of identical twins, and consider some of the following issues: In what ways does each twin see himself or herself in the other? How are twins bonded with one another for life? What happens when identical twins are reared apart and later reunited? How does a surviving twin respond psychologically to the death of her or his sibling? Why and how does one twin often see his or her other as a shadow self?

7. Write an analysis of a film that dramatically portrays the double or divided personality. How does this film echo insights provided by one or more of the authors in this chapter? You might consider a film such as one of the following: *Three Faces of Eve, Dr. Jekyll and Mr. Hyde* (several versions of this film exist, each with a different view of the double), *Mary Reilly* (still another perspective on Jekyll and Hyde), *The Double Life of Veronique, True Lies, Sliding Doors, Multiplicity, Being John Malkovich, Cat Woman,* and *Spiderman.*

Pop Dreams

Roy Lichtenstein, one of the leading members of the American pop-art movement of the 1960s, devoted many of his paintings to enlargements of frames from comic books, as can be seen in *Hopeless*, based on a woman depicted in D.C. Comics' *Girls' Romances*. Lichtenstein's large, striking paintings question the relationship between commercial and fine art while looking beneath the surface of popular arts like the comic strip to reflect on the sexism, dehumanization, and mechanization revealed in the mass media.

JOURNAL

Find an interesting frame from a comic book, photograph, or magazine advertisement, and write an analysis of what the image reveals about popular culture's perspective on gender, romance, violence, or some other social issue.

The adspeak means nothing. It means worse than nothing. It is "anti-language"
that, whenever it runs into truth and meaning, annihilates it.
                                            KALLE LASN

It's easy to blame the media. . . . But the real celebrity spinmeister is our own mind,
which tricks us into believing the stars are our lovers and our social intimates.
                                            CARLIN FLORA

Parents,—if they are willing to listen to this music and examine it critically with
their children—might consider Eminem immersion as a form of inoculation.
                                            MARK COCHRANE

RESEARCH WRITING

More so than any other type of writing, the research paper is a journey out-ward, into the worlds of many other writers past and present who have ar-ticulated their thoughts and views on a subject of public interest. The challenge in developing a research paper is in the synthesizing and harmo-nizing of diverse voices that you encounter and respond to in the course of your research. At the same time, you need to intersperse your own perspec-tive, arguments, and conclusions. This writing process, if successful, can lead to a document that is clearly your own yet properly introduces and fairly credits the ideas and language of your sources.

The new skills needed to integrate and document facts and a variety of intellectual perspectives often overwhelm students as they begin a research paper. To minimize your anxiety, try to maintain a balance between your curious and creative self and your logical and rational self. The steps that follow will provide your rational side with a map to keep you on the main trail, but you should also allow your curious and creative mind to explore the many side paths and research possibilities that you will discover as you compose your paper. Above all, start early and pace yourself. A research paper needs to be completed in stages; it takes time to gather, to absorb, and to develop a response to the materials that will be incorporated into your paper.

For many students, being assigned a research paper raises a number of practical questions and issues: "How many sources will I be expected to use?" "What procedure should I follow in taking notes and doing a bibliog-raphy?" "How does the computer in the library catalog information?" "How can I access and evaluate information on the World Wide Web?" While these concerns are essential parts of the research paper–writing process, we do not discuss specific techniques of finding, quoting, and doc-

umenting source information in the library or on the World Wide Web because these issues are thoroughly covered in most standard writing hand-
books. Librarians are also available and willing to help you with your
research. We will discuss the process involved in producing a research paper and the importance of maintaining a sense of voice and control over the
information and point of view that you are presenting.

Research is more than a catalog of interesting facts and quotations; it also
helps writers understand and evaluate their own perspectives and see their
topic in relationship to their personal values and to broader issues. Professional writers naturally turn to outside sources to deepen their own personal perspective and to better inform and engage their readers. Because
their writing is thoughtfully constructed and thoroughly revised, their
source material becomes an integral part of their writer's voice and stance.
What was originally research doesn't sound strained, dry, or tacked on,
even though they may have used numerous brief quotations and paraphrases of their source material.

While it is natural to think about how your paper will be evaluated, it is
more important to remain curious and to have fun discovering your sources
and learning about your subject. It is helpful to keep a regular log of your
process, making journal entries as you move through each stage and gather
new insights and new understanding about how your mind works under the
pressure of research paper deadlines.

Finding a Topic

Spend some time exploring possible topics for your paper. Writing brief
summaries of several different topics may help you to decide on the topic
that interests you most. The best research papers are produced by students
who are thoroughly engaged in their topic and in communicating what they
have learned. Their enthusiasm and intellectual curiosity help them to work
through the inevitable frustrations associated with learning how to use a library and tracking down information that may not be easily available.

After you complete some preliminary research, reevaluate and narrow
your general topic further, if necessary, so that it can be covered within the
scope and limits of the assignment. Notice, for instance, how in her essay in
this chapter, Anne Ritchie has narrowed the focus of her essay from the
general topic of sex, drugs, and rock and roll. She focuses the scope by
choosing to examine only the impact of drugs on creativity. She made her
paper more manageable by focusing on a particular topic—one that she was
concerned with and knowledgeable about.

Timetable and Process

Make a timetable for your project and follow it. For example, you might allow yourself two to three weeks to do research and to establish a working
bibliography. Then schedule several work sessions to write the first draft,
and several more days to complete your research and revise the draft,

complete the final draft, check your documentation, and do the final proof-reading. At every stage in this process, you should seek out as much useful feedback and advice as you possibly can. Tell your family and friends about your topic; they may have ideas about where to find sources. Read your first draft to your friends, and give your teacher a copy. Make sure that your readers clearly understand your paper's purpose and that your writing holds their interest. Don't feel discouraged if you find that you need to do several revisions to clarify your ideas. This is a natural part of the research paper–writing process.

Your Voice and the Voices of Your Sources

Practice careful reading and accurate note taking as you prepare to write your paper. To avoid becoming bored or overwhelmed by the sources you are working with, treat them as outside voices, as people you want to have a dialogue with. Take every quotation you intend to use in your paper, and paraphrase it carefully into your own language to make sure that you really understand it. If you feel confused or intimidated by a source, freewriting may help you to get in touch with your feelings and responses to the authority. Are the assertions of this authority correct, or do your experiences suggest that some comments are questionable? In our study questions throughout this text, we've created models of questions you can ask as you analyze a text. Now it is time for you to begin posing and answering your own questions about your text sources. Undigested sources often produce a glorified book report, a rehash of ideas that you have not fully absorbed and integrated with your own point of view. For further information on evaluating sources and the facts they present, both from print media and from electronic media such as Web sites, newsgroups, and listservs, see the section on argument in Chapter 7 of *Dreams and Inward Journeys* and any of a number of recent texts and Web sites.

Purpose and Structure

Always keep focused on the purpose and structure in your essay. Your research paper should express an original central purpose and have a compelling thesis. Each major idea must be introduced by a clear topic sentence and supported by evidence and examples. While using an outline is very helpful, feel free to revise the outline as you do further research and make changes in your original perspective. A research paper brings together many different ideas into a unified, original vision of a subject that, as the writer, only you can provide.

Language and Style

As you write your first draft, and particularly as you work through later stages of the paper, continue to express your own writer's voice. Your point of view should be communicated in language with which you are comfortable. Your voice should always be your paper's guide. Read your paper aloud periodically. Is it tedious to listen to? Is it interesting? Do you sound like yourself in this essay? Check your vocabulary and compare it with the sense of language in your previous papers. Are you using more multi-syllabic words than usual or a specialized jargon that even you can hardly understand, one that is too derivative of your sources? Are your sentences more convoluted than usual? Have you lost touch with your own personal voice? Consider the answers to all of these questions. Make sure that your paper reflects your point of view. Remember that your sources are supporting what you think and believe.

The Computer as a Research Partner

Whether you work on a computer at home or use the computers in your library's resource center, please consider the advantage of using a computer at all stages of your research-writing process. The Internet can help you to identify and refine topics; you also should keep a record of your writing timetable and progress on your computer files. It is helpful to gather and store information from different sources on the computer to save the time of copying information. When it comes time to draft your research paper, you can just start writing and integrating the information you have already saved, moving major portions of the paper around. Fine editing is done more efficiently with the use of a computer. There are computer programs that allow you to search hundreds of libraries and databases and to automatically format your data into different bibliographic formats, including the MLA Works Cited format required for most English classes.

Writing a research paper is a challenge that provides you with the opportunity to develop, to utilize, and to integrate your research and writing skills as well as your creativity. A well-written research paper is a genuine accomplishment, a milestone on your inward journey.

THEMATIC INTRODUCTION: POP DREAMS

How does popular culture help to shape the content of our dreams and fantasies, our values, and our very identities? The readings in this chapter suggest different ways that media such as film, television, advertising, video games, and popular music help create our political ideology and influence our dreams and self-concepts. Although it would be naïve to imagine that we could have total control over our own dreams, creating them without being influenced by our culture, many of us aspire to be individualistic, first valuing our inner feelings and thoughts while forming impressions and evaluations of our social and political worlds. In modern society, however, individualism is often undermined and threatened by forces that seek to mold us into loyal citizens, passive consumers, avid fans, and/or productive and compliant workers. Eager to escape temporarily from our immediate problems or to conform to our social world, we may allow ourselves to deny the impact that overexposure to media and the steady barrage of consumerist and political propaganda can have on the development and integrity of our private selves.

Our first two selections explore different ways that we process what we learn from the media. In Louise Erdrich's poem "Dear John Wayne," we learn about the impact that Western film images of the settling of the West and the conquest of the "redskins" continue to have on Native Americans, not to mention the citizens of mainstream America. In "Pictures in Our Heads," social scientists Anthony Pratkanis and Elliot Aronson examine the exaggerated impressions held by heavy television viewers of the level of violence and risk in society.

Our next selections focus of the importance of the "image" in media. Young people in particular see themselves reflected in the models and stars seen in commercials, films, and television shows, and often try to model their choices in clothing and lifestyles after media images. Media critic Alissa Quart points out in her essay "Branded" how media-conscious preteens and teenagers have developed a heightened sense of the importance of name-brand clothing and products so intense that such products actually "infiltrate" their inner lives and values. Next, Carlin Flora, an editor for *Psychology Today*, in "Seeing by Starlight" examines recent research by social scientists that indicate how not only the images but also the personalities of celebrities are internalized by the media audience, who come to mistake celebrities as a part of their extended family or friendship group.

A controversial issue in media and popular culture studies is that of violence in the media. To what extent does the witnessing of countless violent acts on television or in films, or the fantasy participation in such acts in violent video games, have an effect on young people's tendency to accept or even participate in violence in real life? Philosopher Sissela Bok, in her essay "Aggression: The Impact of Media Violence," holds that there is a causal connection present, although hard proof may be lacking, and that violent media exposure should be limited for youngsters. In contrast, in "Evaluating the Research on Violent Video Games," psychologist Jonathan Freedman finds no convincing evidence for a direct effect of violent video games on violent behavior in young people.

Our final professional selection, Mark Cochrane's "Moral Abdication?" examines the possible impact on young children of rapper Eminem's often violent, sexist, and seemingly homophobic lyrics and fantasies, arguing that exposure to the "toxins" in the lyrics can serve to "inoculate" youngsters against real-world hatred and violence. Our student essay, Anne Ritchie's research argument, "Creativity, Drugs, and Rock 'n' Roll," takes a critical approach to the "myth" in the world of pop music that drugs enhance creativity and imagination.

We hope that by reading the selections in this chapter, you will come to think more deeply and more critically about the ways that your dreams and beliefs are being shaped by the mass media, social conventions, and political ideology. Becoming critically aware of how your own dreams and values are both influenced by and distinct from those provided by the media and popular culture can be both liberating and life affirming.

Louise Erdrich

Dear John Wayne

Louise Erdrich (b. 1954) was raised in Wahpeton, North Dakota, as a member of the Turtle Mountain Chippewa tribe. Erdrich attended Dartmouth College where she studied with writer Michael Dorris, whom she later married. She earned a B.A. from Dartmouth in 1976 and an M.F.A. in creative writing from Johns Hopkins University. Her first novel, Love Medicine *(1984, expanded edition 1993), won the National Book Critics Circle Award and introduces many of the characters and clan histories that are developed in her novels* The Beet Queen *(1986),* Tracks *(1988), and* The Bingo Palace *(1994). Her recent work includes* The Last Report on the Miracles at Little No Horse *(2001),* The Birchbark House *(2002), and* Four Souls *(2004). The poem that follows, "Dear John Wayne," is included in her first book of poetry,* Jacklight *(1984).*

JOURNAL

Write about a film that influenced your view of a particular cultural, ethnic, or national group.

August and the drive-in picture is packed.
We lounge on the hood of the Pontiac
surrounded by the slow-burning spirals they sell
at the window, to vanquish the hordes of mosquitoes.
5 Nothing works. They break through the smoke-screen
for blood.

Always the look-out spots the Indians first,
spread north to south, barring progress.
The Sioux, or Cheyenne, or some bunch
10 in spectacular columns, arranged like SAC missiles,
their feathers bristling in the meaningful sunset.

The drum breaks. There will be no parlance.
Only the arrows whining, a death-cloud of nerves
swarming down on the settlers
15 who die beautifully, tumbling like dust weeds
into the history that brought us all here
together: this wide screen beneath the sign of the bear.

The sky fills, acres of blue squint and eye
that the crowd cheers. His face moves over us,
20 a thick cloud of vengeance, pitted
like the land that was once flesh. Each rut,
each scar makes a promise: *It is*
not over, this fight, not as long as you resist.
Everything we see belongs to us.

25 A few laughing Indians fall over the hood
slipping in the hot spilled butter.
The eye sees a lot, John, but the heart is so blind.
How will you know what you own?
He smiles, a horizon of teeth
30 the credits reel over, and then the white fields
again blowing in the true-to-life dark.
The dark films over everything.
We get into the car
scratching our mosquito bites, speechless and small
35 as people are when the movie is done.
We are back in ourselves.

How can we help but keep hearing his voice,
the flip side of the sound-track, still playing:
Come on, boys, we've got them
40 *where we want them, drunk, running.*

They will give us what we want, what we need:
The heart is a strange wood inside of everything
we see, burning, doubling, splitting out of its skin.

QUESTIONS FOR DISCUSSION

1. What is the ironic significance of the setting of the poem: a drive-in movie in August, where "hordes of mosquitoes" attack Indian patrons?
2. How are the Native Americans characterized in the second stanza? How does Erdrich use ironic images and details to critique the stereotypical attitudes of Native Americans that the film reflects? Are Native Americans characterized differently in contemporary films?
3. What image of the "history that brought us all here/together" is presented in the poem? How do you think the Native Americans would have told the film's story?
4. What is the impact of the huge close-up face and eye of John Wayne described in the fourth stanza? What attitude toward Native Americans does Wayne's face portray? Why is the poem addressed to Wayne?
5. What criticisms of Wayne's values and the values of the Western film genre are made through the italicized lines in stanzas 5 and 6? Who is speaking in these lines?
6. Who is describing the heart in these lines: "the heart is so blind" and "The heart is a strange wood"? Interpret the meaning of these lines.

CONNECTION

Compare the views in Erdrich's poem about the impact of minority portrayals on the audiences of films and television shows with those discussed in Pratkanis and Aronson's "Pictures in Our Heads" (see page 468).

IDEAS FOR WRITING

1. Write a critique of a particular film that you believe exploits racist stereotypes and could possibly influence the public negatively against a particular group of people.
2. Write about a film that you believe challenges stereotypes and presents a positive or original, revealing view of a group of people who have been stereotyped negatively.

RELATED WEB SITES

Internet Resources on Native Americans
`http://falcon.jmu.edu/~ramseyil/native.htm`
This is the Internet School Library Media Center [ISLMC] Native American page. Find bibliographies, directories to pages of individual tribes, history and historical documents, periodicals, and general links.

United Native America Media Links
`www.unitednativeamerica.com/media.html#Media`
This site provides an extensive collection of links to community-based, national, and international media sites and political organizations dedicated to
spreading information about and improving the social and economic status of
Native Americans.

Anthony Pratkanis and Elliot Aronson

Pictures in Our Heads

*Anthony Pratkanis and Elliot Aronson are professors of psychology at the Univer-
sity of California, Santa Cruz. Pratkanis has taught courses in consumerism and
advertising at Carnegie Mellon. He has written many articles for both popular and
scholarly journals and is an editor of* Attitude Structure and Function *(1989)
and, with Aronson,* Social Psychology *(1993). Aronson is one of the world's
most highly regarded social psychologists. He is the author of many books, including* The Social Animal *(1972, 7th ed. 1995) and* The Jigsaw Classroom
(1978, 2nd ed. 1997). The following selection is from Pratkanis and Aronson's
The Age of Propaganda *(1992, 2nd ed. 2001), a book that focuses on the ways
in which people's views of society are molded by media propaganda as well as the
stories and images shown frequently on television news.*

JOURNAL

Write about an attitude you have toward a certain political or social issue, an attitude that you believe was influenced by the images from television news.

In *Public Opinion,* the distinguished political analyst Walter Lippmann tells
the story of a young girl, brought up in a small mining town, who one day
went from cheerfulness into a deep spasm of grief.[1] A gust of wind had suddenly cracked a kitchen windowpane. The young girl was inconsolable and
spoke incomprehensibly for hours. When she finally was able to speak intelligi-
bly, she explained that a broken pane of glass meant that a close relative had
died. She was therefore mourning her father, whom she felt certain had just
passed away. The young girl remained disconsolate until, days later, a telegram
arrived verifying that her father was still alive. It appears that the girl had constructed a complete fiction based on a simple external fact (a broken window),
a superstition (broken window means death), fear, and love for her father.

The point of Lippmann's story was not to explore the inner workings of ab-
normal personality, but to ask a question about ourselves: To what extent do
we, like the young girl, let our fictions guide our thoughts and actions?

Lippmann believed that we are much more similar to that young girl than we might readily admit. He contended that the mass media paint an imagined world and that the "pictures in our heads" derived from the media influence what men and women will do and say at any particular moment. Lippmann made these observations in 1922. Seven decades later, we can ask: What is the evidence for his claim? To what extent do the pictures we see on television and in other mass media influence how we see the world and set the agenda for what we view as most important in our lives?

Let's look at the world we see on television. George Gerbner and his associates have conducted the most extensive analysis of television to date.[2] Since the late 1960s, these researchers have been videotaping and carefully analyzing thousands of prime-time television programs and characters. Their findings, taken as a whole, indicate that the world portrayed on television is grossly misleading as a representation of reality. Their research further suggests that, to a surprising extent, we take what we see on television as a reflection of reality.

In prime-time programming, males outnumber females by 3 to 1, and the women portrayed are younger than the men they encounter. Nonwhites (especially Hispanics), young children, and the elderly are underrepresented; and members of minority groups are disproportionately cast in minor roles. Moreover, most prime-time characters are portrayed as professional and managerial workers: Although 67 percent of the work force in the United States are employed in blue-collar or service jobs, only 25 percent of TV characters hold such jobs. Finally, crime on television is ten times more prevalent than it is in real life. The average 15-year-old has viewed more than 13,000 TV killings. Over half of TV's characters are involved in a violent confrontation each week; in reality, fewer than 1 percent of people in the nation are victims of criminal violence in any given year, according to FBI statistics. David Rintels, a television writer and former president of the Writers' Guild of America, summed it up best when he said, "From 8 to 11 o'clock each night, television is one long lie."[3]

5   To gain an understanding of the relationship between watching television and the pictures in our heads, Gerbner and his colleagues compared the attitudes and beliefs of heavy viewers (those who watch more than four hours a day) and light viewers (those who watch less than two hours a day). They found that heavy viewers (1) express more racially prejudiced attitudes; (2) overestimate the number of people employed as physicians, lawyers, and athletes; (3) perceive women as having more limited abilities and interests than men; (4) hold exaggerated views of the prevalence of violence in society; and (5) believe old people are fewer in number and less healthy today than they were twenty years ago, even though the opposite is true. What is more, heavy viewers tend to see the world as a more sinister place than do light viewers; they are more likely to agree that most people are just looking out for themselves and would take advantage of you if they had a chance. Gerbner and his colleagues conclude that these attitudes and beliefs reflect the inaccurate portrayals of American life provided to us by television.

Let's look at the relationship between watching television and images of the world by looking more closely at how we picture criminal activity. In an analysis of "television criminology," Craig Haney and John Manzolati point out that crime shows dispense remarkably consistent images of both the police and criminals.[4] For example, they found that television policemen are amazingly effective, solving almost every crime, and are absolutely infallible in one regard: The wrong person is never in jail at the end of a show. Television fosters an illusion of certainty in crimefighting. Television criminals generally turn to crime because of psychopathology or insatiable (and unnecessary) greed. Television emphasizes criminals' personal responsibility for their actions and largely ignores situational pressures correlated with crime, such as poverty and unemployment.

Haney and Manzolati go on to suggest that this portrayal has important social consequences. People who watch a lot of television tend to share this belief system, which affects their expectations and can cause them to take a hard-line stance when serving on juries. Heavy viewers are likely to reverse the presumption of innocence, believing that defendants must be guilty of something, otherwise they wouldn't be brought to trial.

A similar tale can be told about other "pictures painted in our heads." For example, heavy readers of newspaper accounts of sensational and random crimes report higher levels of fear of crime. Repeated viewing of R-rated violent "slasher" films is associated with less sympathy and empathy for victims of rape. When television is introduced into an area, the incidence of theft increases, perhaps due partly to television's promotion of consumerism, which may frustrate and anger economically deprived viewers who compare their lifestyles with those portrayed on television.[5]

It should be noted, however, that the research just described—that done by Gerbner and colleagues and by others—is correlational; that is, it shows merely an association, not a causal relation, between television viewing and beliefs. It is therefore impossible to determine from this research whether heavy viewing actually causes prejudiced attitudes and inaccurate beliefs or whether people already holding such attitudes and beliefs simply tend to watch more television. In order to be certain that watching TV causes such attitudes and beliefs, it would be necessary to perform a controlled experiment in which people are randomly assigned to conditions. Fortunately, some recent experiments do allow us to be fairly certain that heavy viewing does indeed determine the pictures we form of the world.

10   In a set of ingenious experiments, the political psychologists Shanto Iyengar and Donald Kinder varied the contents of evening news shows watched by their research participants.[6] In their studies, Iyengar and Kinder edited the evening news so that participants received a steady dose of news about a specific problem facing the United States. For example, in one of their experiments, some participants heard about the weaknesses of U.S. defense capabilities; a second group watched shows emphasizing pollution concerns; a third group heard about inflation and economic matters.

The results were clear. After a week of viewing the specially edited programs, participants emerged from the study more convinced than they were before viewing the shows that the target problem—the one receiving extensive coverage in the shows they had watched—was a more important one for the country to solve. What is more, the participants acted on their newfound perceptions, evaluating the current president's performance on the basis of how he handled the target issue and evaluating more positively than their competitors those candidates who took strong positions on those problems.

Iyengar and Kinder's findings are not a fluke. Communications researchers repeatedly find a link between what stories the mass media cover and what viewers consider to be the most important issues of the day.[7] The content of the mass media sets the public's political and social agenda. As just one example, in a pioneering study of an election in North Carolina, researchers found that the issues that voters came to consider to be most important in the campaign coincided with the amount of coverage those issues received in the local media.[8] Similarly, the problems of drug abuse, NASA incompetence, and nuclear energy were catapulted into the nation's consciousness by the coverage of dramatic events such as the drug-related death of basketball star Len Bias, the *Challenger* explosion, and the nuclear-reactor accidents at Three Mile Island and Chernobyl. Former Secretary of State Henry Kissinger clearly understood the power of the news media in setting agendas. He once noted that he never watched the content of the evening news but was only interested in "what they covered and for what length of time, to learn what the country was getting."[9]

Of course, each of us has had extensive personal contact with many people in a myriad of social contexts; the media are just one source of our knowledge about political affairs and different ethnic, gender, and occupational groups. The information and impressions we receive through the media are relatively less influential when we can also rely on firsthand experience. Thus those of us who have been in close contact with several women who work outside the home are probably less susceptible to the stereotypes of women portrayed on television. On the other hand, regarding issues with which most of us have had limited or no personal experience, such as crime and violence, television and the other mass media are virtually the only vivid source of information for constructing our image of the world.

The propaganda value of the mass media in painting a picture of the world has not been overlooked by would-be leaders. Such social policy as a "get tough on crime" program, for example, can be easily sold by relating it to the prime-time picture of crime as acts committed by the psychopathic and the greedy, rather than dealing with situational determinants such as poverty and unemployment. In a similar vein, it is easier to sell a "war on drugs" after the drug-related death of a prominent basketball star or to promote an end to nuclear power after a fatal tragedy at a nuclear reactor.

15   It is even more important for a would-be leader to propagate his or her own picture of the world. The political scientist Roderick Hart notes that since the early 1960s, U.S. presidents have averaged over twenty-five speeches per

month—a large amount of public speaking.[10] Indeed, during 1976, Gerald Ford spoke in public once every six hours, on average. By speaking frequently on certain issues (and gaining access to the nightly news), a president can create a political agenda—a picture of the world that is favorable to his or her social policies. Indeed, one of President Bush's key advisors is Robert Teeter, a pollster who informs the president on what Americans think and what issues should be the topic of his speeches. This can be of great importance in maintaining power. According to Jeffery Pfeffer, an expert on business organizations, one of the most important sources of power for a chief executive officer is the ability to set the organization's agenda by determining what issues will be discussed and when, what criteria will be used to resolve disputes, who will sit on what committees, and, perhaps most importantly, which information will be widely disseminated and which will be selectively ignored.[11]

Why are the pictures of the world painted by the mass media so persuasive? For one thing, we rarely question the picture that is shown. We seldom ask ourselves, for example, "Why are they showing me this story on the evening news rather than some other one? Do the police really operate in this manner? Is the world really this violent and crime-ridden?" The pictures that television beams into our homes are almost always simply taken for granted as representing reality.

Once accepted, the pictures we form in our heads serve as fictions to guide our thoughts and actions. The images serve as primitive social theories—providing us with the "facts" of the matter, determining which issues are most pressing, and decreeing the terms in which we think about our social world. As the political scientist Bernard Cohen observed,

> [The mass media] may not be successful much of the time in telling people *what to think*, but it is stunningly successful in telling its readers *what to think about* . . . The world will look different to different people, depending . . . on the map that is drawn for them by writers, editors, and publishers of the papers they read.[12]

END NOTES

1. W. Lippmann, *Public Opinion* (New York: Harcourt Brace, 1922).
2. G. Gerbner, L. Gross, M. Morgan, and N. Signorielli. "Living with Television: The Dynamics of the Cultivation Process," in *Perspectives on Media Effects*, ed. J. Bryant and D. Zillman (Hillsdale, N.J.: Erlbaum, 1986), 17–40.
3. Quoted in *Newsweek*, December 6, 1982, 40.
4. C. Haney, and J. Manzolati, "Television Criminology: Network Illusions on Criminal Justice Realities," in *Readings About the Social Animal*, 3rd ed., ed. E. Aronson (New York: W. H. Freeman, 1981), 125–136.
5. See L. Heath, "Impact of Newspaper Crime Reports on Fear of Crime: Multimethodological Investigation," *Journal of Personality and Social Psychology* 47: 263–76; D. G. Linz, E. Donnerstein, and S. Penrod, "Effects of Long-Term Exposure to Violent and Sexually Degrading Depictions of Women," *Journal of Personality and Social Psychology* 55: 758–68; and K. Henningan, L. Heath, J. D. Wharton, M. Del Rosario, T. D. Cook, and B. Calder, "Impact of the Introduction of Television on Crime in the United States: Empirical Findings and Theoretical Implications," *Journal of Personality and Social Psychology* 42: 461–77.

6. S. Iyengar and D. R. Kinder, *News That Matters* (Chicago: University of Chicago Press, 1987).
7. E. M. Rogers, and J. W. Dearing, "Agenda-Setting Research: Where Has It Been, Where Is It Going?" In *Communication Yearbook* 11, ed. J. A. Anderson 555–94. Beverly Hills, Calif.: Sage.
8. M. E. McCombs and D. L. Shaw, "The Agenda Setting Function of Mass Media," *Public Opinion Quarterly* 36: 176–87.
9. R. L. Dilenschneider, *Power and Influence* (New York: Prentice-Hall, 1990).
10. R. P. Hart, *The Sound of Leadership* (Chicago: University of Chicago Press, 1987).
11. J. Pfeffer, *Power in Organizations* (Cambridge, Mass.: Ballinger, 1981).
12. Cited in Rogers and Dearing, "Agenda-Setting Research."

QUESTIONS FOR DISCUSSION

1. What is the point of Walter Lippmann's story of the young girl who superstitiously mourned her father? Why is this an effective way to begin the essay?
2. What are the "pictures in our heads" that Lippmann and the authors of the essay comment on? How do these pictures both resemble and differ from dreams and fantasies?
3. What conclusions can be drawn from George Gerbner's television program analysis? What comparisons did Gerbner and his associates make between different kinds of viewers and their beliefs?
4. How are criminals usually portrayed on television? What impact does this portrayal have on our attitudes and beliefs? How have politicians used stereotypical portrayals of criminals and crime to sell their programs to the public?
5. What flaw can be found in Gerbner's research? How have the experiments of Iyengar and Kinder on evening news shows and their viewers helped to correct and support Gerbner's research?
6. Explain Bernard Cohen's distinction between the media telling us what to think as opposed to telling us "what to think about." What does Cohen consider the media's most stunning success? What examples does he provide?

CONNECTION

Compare and contrast Pratkanis's and Bok's evaluation of the impact of television news, media images, and information overload (see page 490).

IDEAS FOR WRITING

1. Do some research into recent intensive media coverage of a political event or a controversial issue. Discuss the media's impact on the public's perceptions of the reality of the situation. You might take a look at some public opinion polls that were taken during the period you are discussing and examine typical stories aired on television and in the newspapers.
2. Write about your attitudes toward a political issue covered extensively by the mass media. Explain to what degree your political views and social outlook were influenced by the media in contrast to your direct experience and/or conversations about the event.

Elliot Aronson and Social Psychology
`http://aronson.socialpsychology.org`
Social psychologist Elliot Aronson's biography and work are featured at this
Web site entitled the "Social Psychology Network." The site claims to have
the largest social psychology database on the Internet, with over 5,000 links
to psychology-related resources.

Propaganda Critic
`www.propagandacritic.com`
This site, founded by Aaron Delwiche, an assistant professor in the Department of Communication at Trinity University, contains examples of prowar,
revolutionary, and corporate propaganda; film clips; and definitions of some
of the logical fallacies favored by propagandists.

Alissa Quart

Branded

*Alissa Quart finished her undergraduate degree at Brown University and gradu-
ated from the Columbia School of Journalism. She has been a freelance writer for
many years and has published articles in a variety of newspapers and magazines,
including the* New York Times, Film Comment, *the* Nation, Salon, *and*
Wired. *The following excerpt is from Quart's recent book* Branded: The Buying
and Selling of Teenagers *(2003), an account of how advertisers manipulate the
lives of preteens or "tweens," teenagers, and their parents through persuading
youth that brand-name consumer products are essential aspects of identity.*

JOURNAL

Write about your experience as a consumer of "brand-name" goods. Do you
consider owning a product from a well-known, "classy" brand an important factor in buying food, clothes, or other merchandise, or do you purchase goods
mainly because of factors such as need, affordability, and comfort? Do you have
other reasons for purchasing products?

Coming of age in the 1980s, I was aware of status signs and corporate logos
and the distinction between them. I knew that Beatrice owned Tropicana
(thanks to the chipper synergic advertising jingle tagline of the period "By
Beatrice!"), that when I wore Converse high tops and listened to Joy Division I
was branding myself, putting myself on the art punk nostalgic "college rock"
side of adolescent style. I considered myself in a style war against the "normal"

girls, who wore ZaZu-colored hair and blue jelly shoes, their Polo by Ralph Lauren logos standing proud and emblematic on their cotton shirts. Of course, being a girl whose identity arose from her lack of brands, I had to make sure that everyone knew I was destroying all the logos in my wake. I carefully scissored the labels off my Levi's and Guess jeans. I believed the shadowy tell-tale rectangles and triangles that remained were an aesthetic of renunciation that would speak for me.

Adolescence has been transformed radically since then. No longer can teens' interest in brands be reduced to an ordinary concern with differentiation, or to distinguishing one's identity from that of the group and the converse, that of conforming, or fitting in with the group. The reliance on brands has shifted: brands have infiltrated preteens and adolescents' inner lives.

You can see the commercial remaking of teenagers in the ads for investment services and credit card companies directed at teens in the high-gloss teen magazines. The companies feign ignorance about the rising rates of credit card debt among the very young, that those under twenty-five are now the fastest-growing group filing for bankruptcy. In blatant disregard for youth consumer debt, financial-services companies now create teenage-oriented credit and cash cards. Among these cards are Visa's Visa Buxx card and the Coca-Cola-owned RocketCash debit card, where parents or other adults can put cash onto a teen's RocketCash account through an advance from the parents' own credit card.

Marketers have expanded their purview to nine-to-thirteen-year-olds as well, rather like urban realtors set on gentrifying neglected neighborhoods. Teen marketers and product managers have expanded into this "tween" niche by prepping the kids to be the sort of teen consumers that companies wish for. Companies ranging from Eastman Kodak to the WB channel now explicitly target these childish attentions, and car manufacturers angle for them in the hopes that kids will nag their parents for SUVs. It's an important strategy for Radio Disney, which has gathered an audience of 2.2 million kids aged from six to eleven, sitting ducklings for on-air advertisements. As Radio Disney's brand manager crowed, 55 percent of the station's listening occurs in cars when mom and kid are together: "You get the gatekeeper and the 'nagger' together."

5   Tweens and younger teens are now the audience for the teen magazines that have also emerged in the last six years, a new welter of high-rolling ventures such as *Teen People, Teen Vogue,* and *Elle Girl.* These, the training wheels of the glossies, prepare girls and boys for the day when they will move on to *People, Vogue,* and *Elle.* The child-age target market makes these magazines' contents all the more alarming. In the 1980s, teen magazines "indicate[d] no uncompromising commitment to the latest fashion. Instead, the emphasis [was] on 'budget buys.' Good value, economy and ideas," as youth theorist Angela McRobbie wrote of the now-defunct British girls' magazine *Jackie.* McRobbie continues, "Similarly, its beauty features tend[ed] to deal with down-market classic images rather than high-fashion beauty styles." The teen mags of my youth, such as

Seventeen, were full of clumsy fashion spreads featuring down-market items. The lessons of beauty—the teen girl's realm of self-improvement—were cheap and cheerful and had no high-end, expensive brands attached. Today's teen magazines must have celebrities on their covers, one month Jennifer Lopez, the next James King. The magazines now all push pricey clothes, such as the costumery of Stuart Weitzman, Christian Dior, and DKNY. *Teen Vogue* details the costly label-fixated clothing tastes of the stars: Liv Tyler in a Jane Mayle dress, Keith Richards's teen daughter in Frankie B. jeans, Scarlet Johansson squeezed into a "Technicolor Dolce" dress (in deference to the brand Dolce & Gabbana). These magazines construct an unaffordable but palpable world of yearning for girls. We are all too familiar with the negative effects of the model body on girls' self-images, but these new magazines do something new: They help to solidify feelings of economic and taste inadequacy in girls. By introducing very young teens to female celebrity and the dressmakers who help create it, these magazines underline that girls are not complete or competitive if they don't wear label dresses at their junior high school dances.

These new teen magazines emerged in the late 1990s, at the same period as the new magalog genre, which crosses magazines with catalogues (the catalog for the clothing company Delia*s is a classic magalog, full of wistful, poetic copy about love and freedom that loops around outfits, sizes, and prices.) The teen magazines themselves are informal catalogues, and, like adult magazines, they often cross the line between editorializing and out-and-out selling. The difference is that these magazines are aimed at twelve-year-olds, readers who don't understand that the "Technicolor dress" is unattainable.

These same magazines frequently include accounts of adolescents in other countries in an attempt to show their similarity to American teens: their cache-mongering and the tribal subdivisions between punk and preppy and hip hop kids in Cape Town or Sao Paolo. And while these cool hunting articles in American teen magazines convince American teens that all the world is a mall promoting a global youth materialism and homogeneity, these international fashion round-ups also reflect a world-wide teen consumerism and an erasure of national youth identity. In recession-era Japan, fashion photographers lurk in the trendy Harajuku neighborhood, ready to capture images of modish teens who, in turn, may well have received their cues from half a dozen teen girl fashion magazines with such names as *Style on the Street* and *Cutie.* (Scholars have theorized that global luxury brands such as Louis Vuitton and Hermes are particularly desirable to contemporary Japan's young "trend slaves" because they help build a generation's fragile self-confidence about the future.) In England, tweenies and teens become the targets of pitches offering to add extras on their already ubiquitous brand-name mobile phones, plusses such as celebrity voice mail and ring tones; and the kids buy in. In Australia, a newspaper columnist dubbed selling to kids in his country nothing less than "corporate pedophilia." In Canada, a recent study by Laval University in Quebec found that their sample group of rich and poor kids had an equal and unslakeable thirst for designer clothes.

In 2002, the government in South Korea decided to create regulations for issuing credit cards to minors. The rulings were necessitated by a wave of robberies by unemployed teenagers seeking to steal money to pay off credit card debt. The credit card companies created the situation in the first place by competing to *issue* cards to unemployed teenagers and college students, jobless kids who later turned to crime in desperation. A resulting bill prevents the issuance of credit cards to those under the age of twenty without their parents' consent.

Welcome to the Dollhouse

The American and international teenage buying public has been a long time in the making. Marketers discovered, or invented, the American teen market during World War II and the early postwar era. They argued that teens would be spending their parents' money on movies, cosmetics, and records. In 1945, *Seventeen* wrote memos to advertisers promising that teen girls were "copycats" who could be trusted to imitate one another by wearing the same clothes and eating the same food. *Seventeen* also set in motion a classic advertising paradigm. The magazine assured its advertisers that a few ads in *Seventeen* would pay rich rewards later by sowing the seeds of desire within the girls for certain linens or kinds of china when they got married. Marketers still believe in the basic truth of the axiom "get 'em while they're young."

10   Marketing to kids took off in the 1980s, in the wake of two important events. The first was the release and overwhelming successes of the films *Jaws* in 1975 and *Star Wars* in 1977. Youth-oriented blockbusters, it turned out, could sell not just enormous numbers of tickets but also a huge and varied assortment of ancillary branded products, everything from action figures to bed sheets. The second important event occurred in 1978, when the Federal Trade Commission attempted to impose regulations regarding restrictions on child-oriented ads. Congress blocked it, claiming that its emphasis on unfair advertising was too vague. In the decades following, an utter lack of regulation ineluctably led to the widespread flogging of kiddy blockbuster toys and games and the huge success of products related to the Teenage Mutant Ninja Turtles.

With the stakes rising, marketers began plumbing kids' minds, recognizing for the first time the full extent of the potential monetary gains children had to offer. These kids were called "skippies" (school kids with purchasing power). Veteran marketer Peter Zollo has written that the idea of kids as worthy targets was so new back then that he had to persuade advertisers that skippies were a viable enough bracket even to bother researching.

Branding slowed during the economic recession of the late 1980s and early 1990s. But when the economy began to stir to life, branding returned, and with a vengeance. Corporations eager to gain a foothold went on the attack through the aggressive marketing of designer labels. The economy was growing fast, but ad spending grew faster. In 1991, ad spending in the United States equaled $126.4 billion; in 1994, it equaled $150 billion.

Given all the goods jostling for consumer attention, branding became one of the necessities for making products stick in consumers' minds. The companies doing the best were those that had over the years built up a strong brand and recognizable identity. Competition also led marketers to deploy ever more sophisticated and innovative sales techniques.

Cruel Story of Youth

The language of teen marketing is now so refined that it resembles youth sociology and psychology. One difference is, of course, its intent. Academic writing on adolescence has, for at least a century, been interested in either teens' liberation or self-betterment by way of moral guidance from the family, the teacher, or the state. The marketers who borrow the terms and methods used by scholars just want to sell.

15   In her 2000 book, *The $100 Billion Allowance,* marketing guru Elissa Moses breaks "teen orientation" and teen spending down into "me-directed," "other-directed," "nonconformist," and "conformist." Each category is further broken down into types of teen spending. These include "thrills & chills," "resigned," "bootstrappers," "world savers," "upholders," and "quiet achievers." World savers, according to Moses, include teen Brazilians and Hungarians. But although these "café altruists" are socially concerned, a marketer should not lose hope in their spending power. World savers like "piggyback" promotions, Moses writes, in which a product is marketed for a worthwhile cause.

The fancy language Moses uses echoes that of sociologists and cultural critics who imagine themselves champions of youth. Moses's terminology, in particular the phrase "other-directed," harks to popular sociology from the postwar period, especially the 1950 book *The Lonely Crowd.* Categories such as "mainstream" and "conformer" and "channeler" echo the comparisons within cultural studies of youth scholarship of the 1970s and 1980s. One of the classics from that period is Dick Hebdige's *Subculture: The Meaning of Style,* published in 1979. Hebdige claimed that the nonconformist fashions of 1970's Britain, such as punk, were not just irreverent posturing. Alternative style was part of a youth armamentarium, a defense against consumer capitalism. In contrast, Moses and her ilk deploy the category "nonconformist" style as another mode of teen consumerism, not a creative resistant force but a sliver of a market to be pandered to. Youth cultural studies of the 1970s, '80s, and '90s, which aimed to empower and elevate teen subcultures, now has an uncanny afterlife as mere spice at marketing meetings.

And the amount of research hours that go into these mercantile quasi-academic categorizations of kids is unparalleled. The advertising firm Ogilvy & Mather researches youth by using the techniques of social anthropology performed by the Discover Group: They videotape kids with small cameras in their homes, filming their product choices and behaviors. Meanwhile, Teenage Research Unlimited (TRU) peddles the ominously named *Omnibuzz,* a monthly survey of six hundred teens and a bonus segment of 250 tweens, all culled from

847 focus groups. (They are not the only ones to use this technique; so does Ally & Gargano, a New York City ad firm, and various other agencies). TRU company also provides a "Coolest Brand Meter" (Sony, Nike, Abercrombie & Fitch, and Old Navy were tops recently). These youth marketers aim to sell their products. And they do so even if it means playing on kids' fears of being social outcasts or physically unappealing. TRU's interest in only the "cool" teens creates a burlesque of high school politics—one that shows up in teen-oriented advertising.

Girlitude

Pornography has also mainstreamed as never before in the decade of Generation Y, and advertisers now pander to the heightened body-consciousness they've helped create. The clothing company Abercrombie & Fitch's ad agency blithely told *Women's Wear Daily* that teens "love sexy bodies and they're more conscious of that than ever." A&F makes sure they are. In 2000 and 2001, the company produced a quarterly magalog of underdressed college jocks, porn stars, and couples and trios wearing omnipresent branded underwear. The catalog was so tawdry that it was encased in plastic and was, at least in theory, available only to those age eighteen and over. The outraged lieutenant governor of Illinois, Corinne Wood, called for a boycott of the company, which she renewed in the spring of 2002 when the teen retailer started selling thongs featuring cherries and sayings such as "wink, wink" and "eye candy" to preteen girls. Although the Web site that carried the images of these thongs, as well as the A&F magalog, was attacked by moralists from the right on sexual grounds, to me the aggressive twinning of logos and sexual desire when marketing to kids seemed far worse. The clear message was that when you and your partner drop trou it had better be expensive trou—your underwear must have the legible letters of a good brand or you'll never get a sexy boy or girl to date you. I haven't seen a more blatant example of a rich corporation's exploiting teen horniness, as if an adolescent need only buy underwear to instantly attract partners.

Blackboard Jingle

Preteens and teens are not just cajoled by sexy ads and viral marketing in their private and recreational spaces. They are invaded at their schools as well. A growing number of high schools are sponsored by corporations. Teenagers not only play ball in gyms rimmed with logos but also spend their English classes coming up with advertising slogans for sponsors, all under the auspices of their so-called public high schools. One hundred and fifty school districts in twenty-nine states have Pepsi and Coke contracts. Textbooks regularly mention Oreo cookies, and math problems contain Nike logos. Companies from Disney to McDonald's promote themselves within secondary school walls by holding focus groups about their new flavors, toys, and ad campaigns. (Teens who register their resistance to the presence of sponsors at school can be punished for voicing their displeasure. In one instance, a student who wore a Pepsi shirt to a Coca-Cola sponsorship day at high school was suspended for the insurrection.) School sponsorship starts when children are very young, so that by the time kids are thirteen they are more than used to having companies and lobbyists pumping private interests into the curriculum. Recently, General Mills gave out free samples of Fruit Gushers and instructed kids to put them in their mouths as a supposed science experiment (the children were then asked to compare the sensation to volcano eruptions). Sixth-grade math textbooks, published by McGraw Hill, feature references to Nike and Gatorade. Exxon and Shell sponsor science videos. The American Nuclear Society hands out a brochure to schools titled "Let's Color and Do Activities with the Atoms Family"; and educational programs sponsored by the timber industry, according to one environmental science teacher, teach children how to visualize the thinning of the forest.

Selling Adulthood

20   Some of the latest extremes of marketing to the young involve pushing adult products upon adolescents, things that are jazzed up to appear young and fun. America's distillers spent $350 million in 2002 to sell "alcopops," sweetened, fruity alcohol that is ostensibly aimed at twenty-one-year-olds; but in the drinks' semblance to soda and juice and in their boppy names, such as BoDean's Twisted Tea, the products really target adolescents. Such drinks encourage an early adoption, to use the marketing term, of booze, and perhaps also alcoholism, in teenagers' lives. Similarly, the U.S. government, empowered to protect consumers, is not blind to the power of branding over the young, and it has enlivened its advertising to kids. Once the U.S. Army told teenagers to "Be All That You Can Be." Now it has become newly branded to attract youthful recruits. After September 11, 2001, army enlistment surged, but not because of 9/11, according to army personnel. Rather, it was thanks to the armed services' clever $150 million ad campaign launched since January 2001, which carries the tag line "An Army of One." This ad is designed to pander to Generation Y's self-interest and taste, and, in the words of one potential recruit, has "real cool" imagery. But the attempt to win over Generation Y doesn't stop there. The U.S. Army has even developed a video game: a "highly realistic and innovative" first-person shooter game that puts a player inside an army unit. In a radio interview in 2002, an army spokesman described the game as one of the new methods the military was using to "reach young people" over thirteen and to "inspire people regarding their career choices."

Over the Edge

Of course, all of this intrusive marketing would be fine—just the way the shilling game is played at this late date—if it didn't deeply affect teens themselves. The personae, self-images, ambitions, and values of young people in the United States have been seriously distorted by the commercial frenzy surrounding them. What do the advertising images of teens, breasts augmented and abs bared, do to teenagers? These images take their toll on a teen's sense of self and his or her community. "You have to be thin to be popular," one girl told me, and the array of flat, bare stomachs at her summer camp certainly backs this up. Other girls told me about their eating disorders and their friends' body-image problems. Their self-understanding doesn't change their behavior, though. They are like birds that know every bar of their gilded cage by heart. "Can you believe this ad? No one's body looks like that!" one fourteen-year-old told me, pointing to an ad in *Vogue*. "A bunch of old men are telling me how to look!" Thirteen-year-old girls expressed pained astonishment at "eleven-year-olds who get their eyebrows waxed"—but the thirteen-year-olds shave their legs every day. On Manhattan's Upper East Side, one salon runs a back-to-school waxing special.

Brand consciousness sets in early. One twelve-year-old murmured to me when a girl clad in Reebok gear passed by, "Adidas is cooler." A small child saw a friend's Paramount T-shirt and shouted "Blue's Clues!" She knew the snow-capped mountain symbol of the studio from the split second the logo appeared on the children's television show. A class of third graders on a school trip can almost all distinguish which beer brands had brown bottles (Amstel Light, Budweiser) and which had green (Heineken).

The heavy-duty marketing from the cradle onward has warped the social lives of today's teenagers and exacerbated caste snobbery in the classrooms. The standard "pretty and popular" refrain has changed. Now teens judge one another more for the brands they wear and how much money they or their families have. Girls ranging from Brooklyn Jamaican Americans to suburban princesses to Christian Midwesterners told me that if they wear "scrubby" non-brand clothes to their urban private schools or suburban or inner-city public schools, they know they will be shunted into the out group.

"You know what you're supposed to be wearing. You see it on TV," says Lenita, who is from Brooklyn. "They advertise on the buses: Levi's, FuBu. You've got to wear that gear to be in the in crowd." "Yeah, it's twisted. Clothes are very important at my school," adds Renee, a thirteen-year-old from affluent Westchester County, outside New York City. "Brands designate social position."

25   "What brand is that?" teen girls sitting in a New York City Starbucks ask as a platinum blonde woman in Manolo Blahnik heels clatters by. "Where did you get them?" The girls spend the next hour giving strangers in their twenties fiercely competitive once-overs.

The new brand obsession has also changed adolescent leisure time. Social-class pressures have intensified to the degree that middle-class teens now work to catch up with their wealthier peers. Laurie, a seventeen-year-old from Denver, worked four hours a day during her senior year of high school so that she might spend $250 a month on clothes. "People know who has money at school," says Shelly, clad entirely in Abercrombie & Fitch. "When there's a party, people look through each other's stuff and check out how much it cost. At my school, you can only justify not having money by being good at something else."

Today, 55 percent of American high school seniors labor more than three hours a day, while only 27 percent of foreign students report that they work at all. And all this hard work does more than just make it less likely that kids will do their homework. A study published in 2000 found that working is beneficial to teen girls only if the job is of a limited duration. Girls who work only a few hours tend to smoke and drink less and maintain more internal control. But girls who work long enough for it to interfere with their schoolwork tend to become depressed and self-derogating, and to drink and smoke more than their less-employed peers.

Work can be particularly hard on poorer kids because they are by no means exempt from the pressure to be properly branded. As Katherine S. Newman writes in *No Shame in My Game: The Working Poor in the Inner City,* the consequences of starting a life identified with low wage work can be serious. Poor teens have to "swallow hardship" at jobs at Burger Barn, the only jobs they can get. "Fast food jobs in particular are notoriously stigmatized and denigrated," writes Newman. "McJob' has become a common epithet for work without much redeeming value." She goes on: A swathe of parents and politicians like to think that teen labor is an unmitigated good, instilling a work ethic and giving pubescents emotional ballast. In one Colorado community, tweens, but also their parents and even a local mayor wanted kids ranging in age from between nine to fourteen be allowed to work—although it's illegal. In fact, while teens are not supposed to work more than twelve hours a week during the school year if they are under sixteen years old, in 1998, almost 150,000 minors were found to be illegally employed each week.

The popular impression is that today's teens are capitalism's happy children, but as one educator puts it, American teens' heavy labor is the "logical extension of materialism." Some have described teens as a new proletariat, kids who work primarily to consume more goods.

30   Parents are also an influence on Generation Y's fashion precocity and predilection for high fashion brands. When I was a teen and preteen, my style sense was low rent; it extended as far as $20 canvas sneakers and $10 T-shirts on which a dark lithograph of The Cure was bleached so the band was *only* their hair. The branded generation's obsession with opulent brands, including Dolce & Gabbana, Chanel, and Prada is so strong that the kids I interviewed regularly spoke of the luxury brands Gucci and Chloé and Burberry as if they were talking about their family and friends. But the knowledge and fixation on high fashion is not just an interest in classiness and elegance evinced by lower-middle-class and middle-class kids. It derives from a related interest adolescents have in obtaining the trappings of adulthood while still underage. Millennial teens now wear junior-sized versions of the DKNY and Ralph Lauren garb that adults wear; in an inversion of the youth cult explosion of thirty years ago, when adults dressed in young styles, teens now aspire to dress as if they were women in their twenties. It is common for mothers and daughters in upper-middle-class areas to wear the same expensive brand-name clothes. While the mother strives to look twelve years younger, the daughter strives to look twelve years older. They meet in between.

QUESTIONS FOR DISCUSSION

1. How does Quart contrast her own attitude as an adolescent toward brands with that of today's tweens? Based on your own experience, do you think the conclusions she draws about the attitude shift of brand consciousness to modern youths' "inner lives" are justified?
2. What formerly adult-oriented products, services, and consumer practices are now being marketed to teens and preteens today? What new types of media now are teen/tween oriented?
3. How, according to Quart, have commercial youth culture and branding contributed to "an erasure of national youth identity"?
4. How does Quart contrast marketer Elissa Moses's pseudo-sociological teen consumer categories such as "nonconformist" or "world saver" with the "alternative style" examined by Dick Hebdige in *Subculture* (1979)? What kind of specialized research by marketers now goes into monitoring and directing teen style trends and interests?
5. What distorted "self-images, ambitions, and values" does Quart believe are promoted by the excessive commercialism of modern teen-oriented advertising and media? What examples does Quart provide to illustrate her points?
6. Why does Quart believe that such a high percentage of American high school students work? Why is their work "the 'logical extension of materialism'"? Do you agree, or could they have other reasons for working?

CONNECTION

Compare the points that Quart makes about the negative mental impact of fast-paced commercial culture on youth with Mary Pipher's comment on youth culture in "Sapling in the Storm" (see page 346).

IDEAS FOR WRITING

1. Do a study of a particular advertising campaign targeting teens and/or tweens. What values are being sold along with the brand and product(s) being marketed, and how does the campaign differ visually and verbally to take advantage of the different media it appears in? Write up your findings in the form of a documented essay.
2. Write an essay based on interviews with several teenagers or college students about their consciousness of brands. To what extent do particular brands and the advertising for these brands influence their choices as consumers? Draw conclusions from what you have learned, and in writing up the essay include quotes from some of the people you interviewed.

RELATED WEB SITES

Branded For Life?

www.csmonitor.com/2002/0401/p15s02-wmcn.html

In this article from *Christian Science Monitor*, staff writer Noel Paul argues that brand consciousness and loyalty are built into children from infancy on.

Center for Communication and Civic Engagement: Culture Jamming
`http://depts.washington.edu/ccce/polcommcampaigns/`
`CultureJamming.htm`
This page from the CCCE site contains an explanation of culture jamming and
numerous links to articles related to culture jamming, a movement to build
resistance to hypercommercialism and branding, including an article by
Alissa Quart, "Cultural Sabotage Waged in Cyberspace."

Carlin Flora

Seeing by Starlight

An editor and longtime writer for Psychology Today, *Carlin Flora has published
many articles over the years on subjects including alternative therapies, memory,
indoctrination and brainwashing, marriage and family life, women in the workplace, consumerism, religion, music, psychotropic drugs, obsession, schizophrenia,
bipolar disorder, and the narcissistic personality. The essay we have included here,
"Seeing by Starlight" (2004), is one of several articles Flora has written that examine the causes and effects of our obsession with celebrities and their lifestyles.
Notice how she includes research findings from a variety of social scientists to support her arguments.*

JOURNAL

Write about why people are so fascinated by celebrities. Do you find them intriguing? Why or why not?

A couple of years ago, Britney Spears and her entourage swept through my
boss's office. As she sashayed past, I blushed and stammered and leaned
over my desk to shake her hand. She looked right into my eyes and smiled her
pageant smile, and I confess, I felt dizzy. I immediately rang up friends to report my celebrity encounter, saying: "She had on a gorgeous, floor-length
white fur coat! Her skin was blotchy!" I've never been much of a Britney fan, so
why the contact high? Why should I care? For that matter, why should any of
us? Celebrities are fascinating because they live in a parallel universe—one that
looks and feels just like ours yet is light-years beyond our reach. Stars cry to
Diane Sawyer about their problems—failed marriages, hardscrabble upbring-
ings, bad career decisions—and we can relate. The paparazzi catch them in wet
hair and a stained T-shirt, and we're thrilled. They're ordinary folks, just like
us. And yet . . .

Stars live in another world entirely, one that makes our lives seem woefully
dull by comparison. The teary chat with Diane quickly turns to the subject of a

recent $10 million film fee and honorary United Nations ambassadorship. The magazines that specialize in gotcha snapshots of schleppy-looking celebs also feature Cameron Diaz wrapped in a $15,000 couture gown and glowing with youth, money and star power. We're left hanging—and we want more.

It's easy to blame the media for this cognitive whiplash. But the real celebrity spinmeister is our own mind, which tricks us into believing the stars are our lovers and our social intimates. Celebrity culture plays to all of our innate tendencies: We're built to view anyone we recognize as an acquaintance ripe for gossip or for romance, hence our powerful interest in Anna Kournikova's sex life. Since catching sight of a beautiful face bathes the brain in pleasing chemicals, George Clooney's killer smile is impossible to ignore. But when celebrities are both our intimate daily companions and as distant as the heavens above, it's hard to know just how to think of them. Reality TV further confuses the picture by transforming ordinary folk into bold-faced names without warning. Even celebrities themselves are not immune to celebrity watching: Magazines print pictures of Demi Moore and "Bachelorette" Trista Rehn reading the very same gossip magazines that stalk them. "Most pushers are users, don't you think?" says top Hollywood publicist Michael Levine. "And, by the way, it's not the worst thing in the world to do."

Celebrities tap into powerful motivational systems designed to foster romantic love and to urge us to find a mate. Stars summon our most human yearnings: to love, admire, copy and, of course, to gossip and to jeer. It's only natural that we get pulled into their gravitational field.

Exclusive: Fan's Brain Transformed by Celebrity Power!

5 John Lennon infuriated the faithful when he said the Beatles were more popular than Jesus, but he wasn't the first to suggest that celebrity culture was taking the place of religion. With its myths, its rituals (the red carpet walk, the Super Bowl ring, the handprints outside Grauman's Chinese Theater) and its ability to immortalize, it fills a similar cultural niche. In a secular society our need for ritualized idol worship can be displaced onto stars, speculates psychologist James Houran, formerly of the Southern Illinois University School of Medicine and now director of psychological studies for True Beginnings dating service. Nonreligious people tend to be more interested in celebrity culture, he's found, and Houran speculates that for them, celebrity fills some of the same roles the church fills for believers, like the desire to admire the powerful and the drive to fit into a community of people with shared values. Leo Braudy, author of *The Frenzy of Renown: Fame and Its History,* suggests that celebrities are more like Christian calendar saints than like spiritual authorities (Tiger Woods, patron saint of arriviste golfers; or Jimmy Carter, protector of down-home liberal farmers?). "Celebrities have their aura—a debased version of charisma" that stems from their all-powerful captivating presence, Braudy says.

Much like spiritual guidance, celebrity-watching can be inspiring, or at least help us muster the will to tackle our own problems. "Celebrities motivate us to make it," says Helen Fisher, an anthropologist at Rutgers University in New Jersey. Oprah Winfrey suffered through poverty, sexual abuse and racial discrimination to become the wealthiest woman in media. Lance Armstrong survived advanced testicular cancer and went on to win the Tour de France five times. Star-watching can also simply point the way to a grander, more dramatic way of living, publicist Levine says. "We live lives more dedicated to safety or quiet desperation, and we transcend this by connecting with bigger lives—those of the stars," he says. "We're afraid to eat that fatty muffin, but Ozzy Osborne isn't."

Don't I know you?! Celebrities are also common currency in our socially fractured world. Depressed college coeds and laid-off factory workers both spend hours watching Anna Nicole Smith on late night television; Mexican villagers trade theories with hometown friends about who killed rapper Tupac Shakur; and Liberian and German businessmen critique David Beckham's plays before hammering out deals. My friend Britney Spears was, in fact, last year's top international Internet search.

In our global village, the best targets for gossip are the faces we all know. We are born to dish dirt, evolutionary psychologists agree; it's the most efficient way to navigate society and to determine who is trustworthy. They also point out that when our brains evolved, anybody with a familiar face was an "in-group" member, a person whose alliances and enmities were important to keep track of.

Things have changed somewhat since life in the Pleistocene era, but our neural hardwiring hasn't, so on some deeper level, we may think NBC's *Friends* really are our friends. Many of us have had the celebrity-sighting mishap of mistaking a minor star—a local weatherman, say, or a bit-part soap opera actor—for an acquaintance or former schoolmate. Braudy's favorite example of this mistake: In one episode of the cartoon show *King of the Hill*, a character meets former Texas Governor Ann Richards. "You probably know me," he says. "I've seen you on TV." That's also why we don't get bored by star gossip, says Bonnie Fuller, editorial director of American Media, which publishes *Star* and *The Enquirer:* "That would be like getting bored with information about family and friends!"

10   The brain simply doesn't realize that it's being fooled by TV and movies, says sociologist Satoshi Kanazawa, lecturer at the London School of Economics. "Hundreds of thousands of years ago, it was impossible for someone not to know you if you knew them. And if they didn't kill you, they were probably your friend." Kanazawa's research has shown that this feeling of friendship has other repercussions: People who watch more TV are more satisfied with their friendships, just as if they had more friends and socialized more frequently. Another study found that teens who keep up to date on celebrity gossip are popular, with strong social networks—the interest in pop culture indicates a healthy drive for independence from parents.

The penchant for gossiping about the stars also plays into our species' obsession with status. Humans naturally copy techniques from high-status individuals, says Francisco Gil-White, professor of psychology at University of

Pennsylvania. It's an attempt to get the same rewards, whether that's "attention, favors, gifts, [or] laudatory exclamations." Stars get all kinds of perks and pampering: Sarah Jessica Parker was allowed to keep each of her *Sex in the City* character's extravagant getups; Halle Berry borrowed a $3 million diamond ring to wear to the Oscars. Understandably, we look to get in on the game.

The impulse to copy is behind the popularity of celebrity magazines, says Fuller. Regular women can see what the stars are wearing, often with tips on how to buy cheap knockoffs of their outfits. Taken to extremes—which television is only too happy to do—the urge to copy produces spectacles like the MTV reality show *I Want a Famous Face.* By dint of extensive plastic surgery, ordinary people are made to look more like their famous heroes. In one episode, two gangly 20-year-old twin brothers are molded into Brad Pitt look-alikes. The brothers want to be stars, and they've decided that looking more like Pitt is the fastest road to fame. No wonder makeover shows are so popular, points out Joshua Gamson, an associate professor of sociology at the University of San Francisco. These shows offer drab nobodies a double whammy: simultaneous beauty and celebrity. The most fascinating measure of status is, of course, sex. "We want to know who is mating with whom," says Douglas Kenrick, professor of psychology at Arizona State University. He speculates that we look to stars to evaluate our own sexual behavior and ethics, and mistake them unconsciously for members of our prospective mating pool. Given this me-too drive to imitate and adore, why are celebrity flame-outs and meltdowns so fascinating? Even though we love to hear about the lavish rewards of fame—remember *Lifestyles of the Rich and Famous?*—we're quick to judge when stars behave too outrageously or live too extravagantly. We suspect some stars are enjoying society's highest rewards without really deserving them, says University of Liverpool anthropologist Robin Dunbar, so we monitor their behavior. "We need to keep an eye on the great-and-the-good because they create a sense of community for us, but also because we need to make sure that they are holding to their side of the bargain."

Diva Alert: Beauty Isn't Everything (Being Nice Helps!)

The beauty bias is well-known. We all pay more attention to good-looking people. Kenrick's eye-tracking research has shown that both men and women spend more time looking at beautiful women than at less attractive women. Babies as young as 8-months-old will stare at an attractive female face of any race longer than they will at an average-looking or unattractive female face. Certain human traits are universally recognized as beautiful: symmetry, regularity in the shape and size of the features, smooth skin, big eyes and thick lips, and an hourglass figure that indicates fertility. Men interpret these features as evidence of health and reproductive fitness. Women's responses are more complex, says psychologist and Harvard Medical School instructor Nancy Etcoff, author of *Survival of the Prettiest.* Women stare at beautiful female faces out of aesthetic appreciation, to look for potential tips—and because a beautiful woman could be a rival worth monitoring.

It's not surprising that gorgeous people wind up famous. What's less obvious is that famous people often wind up gorgeous: The more we see a certain face, the more our brain likes it, whether or not it's actually beautiful. Thanks to what is known as "the exposure effect," says James Bailey, a psychologist at George Washington University, the pleasurable biological cascade that is set off when we see a certain celebrity "begins to wear a neurochemical groove," making her image easier for our brains to process. It begins to explain why Jennifer Aniston—not exactly a classic cover girl—was again named one of *People* magazine's 50 "most beautiful" in the world this year.

15   On the flip side, celebrity overload—let's call it the J.Lo effect—can leave us all thoroughly sick of even the most beautiful celeb. With the constant deluge of celebrity coverage, says Etcoff, "they at first become more appealing because they are familiar, but then the ubiquity becomes tedious. That is why the stars who reign the longest—Madonna is the best example—are always changing their appearance." Every time Madonna reconfigures her look, she resets our responses back to when her face was recognizable but still surprising.

Just as in pageants, personality plays a part in the beauty contest, too. State University of New York at Binghamton psychology professors Kevin Kniffin and David Sloan Wilson have found that people's perceptions of physical appeal are strongly influenced by familiarity and likeability. "Almost all of the beauty research is based on subjects looking at strangers in photos or computer-generated images—but we don't live in a world of strangers!" Kniffin points out.

In one of Kniffin's experiments, students worked on an archeological dig together toward a shared goal. Those who were deemed cooperative and likable were rated as more attractive after the project was finished than they were at the outset. Conversely, students who were not as hardworking were rated as less attractive after the chore was done.

Kniffin believes this same mechanism is at work in our feelings toward celebrities, who rank somewhere between strangers and intimates. Athletes are an obvious example: Team spirit gives even ugly guys a boost. NBA great Wilt Chamberlain might have been a bit goofy-looking, but his astonishing abilities to propel his team to victory meant that he was a hero, surrounded with adoring—and amorous—fans. Kniffin points to William Hung, the talent-free and homely also-ran on the contest show *American Idol,* as evidence of his theory at work. In part because of his enthusiasm and his good-natured willingness to put up with ridicule, Hung became a bigger star after he was kicked off the show: His album, *Inspiration,* sold more than 37,000 copies in its first week. "William doesn't display the traits of universal attractiveness, but people who have seen the show would probably rate him as more attractive because of nonphysical traits of likeability and courage. He's even received some marriage proposals." Kniffin's theory also explains why models are less compelling objects of fascination than actresses or pop stars. They're beautiful, but they're enigmatic: We rarely get any sense of their personalities.

Saved from Oblivion!

What's the result of our simultaneous yearning to be more like celebrities and our desire to be wowed by their unattainable perfection? We've been watching it for the past decade. Reality television is an express train to fame, unpredictably turning nobodies into somebodies. Reality TV now gives us the ability to get inside the star factory and watch the transition to fame in real time.

20   "The appeal of reality stars is that they were possibly once just like you, sitting on the couch watching a reality TV program, until they leaped to celebrity," says Andy Denhart, blogger and reality TV junkie. "With the number of reality shows out there, it's inexcusable to not be famous if you want to be!" In the past, ambitious young men who idolized a famous actor might take acting lessons or learn to dance. Now, they get plastic surgery and learn to tell their life stories for the camera. In fact, says editor Fuller, the newly minted stars of reality TV are better at the celebrity game than many of the movie and television stars: "They are more accessible, more cooperative. They enjoy publicity. They will open up and offer insight, often more than a 'traditional' celeb, because they want the attention, whereas an actress might have ambivalent feelings about fame and how it is tied in with her 'craft.'" At the same time, shows like *The Simple Life* and *The Newlyweds* (and amateur videotapes like Paris Hilton's) let us gawk at the silly things that stars do in the privacy of their own home. As a result, the distance between celebrity stratosphere and living room couch dwindles even further.

Yet there's still something about that magic dust. A celebrity sighting is not just about seeing a star, author Braudy points out, but is about being seen by a star: "There is a sense that celebrities are more real than we are; people feel more real in the presence of a celebrity." It wasn't just that I saw Britney, it was that Britney saw me.

QUESTIONS FOR DISCUSSION

1. In what sense do celebrities live in a "parallel universe," and why is this a source of their appeal? What examples does Flora give to clarify this concept? What is the "real celebrity spinmeister," according to Flora? Why do we believe that stars are our friends, even our lovers?

2. How does reality TV confuse us further about our relationship to celebrities? Why do these shows make it seem "inexcusable to not be famous if you want to be"? Do you agree?

3. How does celebrity culture fill a spiritual need for worship, community, and guidance? What examples and authorities does Flora present to clarify her ideas on this subject?

4. How is the brain "fooled by TV and movies"? Why do individuals who watch large amounts of television tend to feel "satisfied with their friendships"? Does this "satisfaction" seem healthy to you?

5. Why do celebrities inspire imitation? What is the "exposure effect," and how does it explain why celebrities appear more beautiful than they actually are?

6. What is the significance of the final sentence of the essay: "It wasn't just that I saw Britney, it was that Britney saw me"? How does this sentence refer back to the introduction of the essay and help to explain the "magic dust" of celebrity interaction?

CONNECTION

Compare and contrast the allure of celebrities presented in Flora's essay to the revulsion with celebrity seen in "K. Sul vs. J. Lo" in Chapter 7 (see page 434). Are these two entirely distinct responses, or do they seem related in some way? If so, how?

IDEAS FOR WRITING

1. Write an analysis of a reality TV show that tries to create "instant celebrities" from its ordinary contestants. What is the source of popularity for this show? Make reference to Flora's article as well as your own experiences and those of your friends who have viewed the show.
2. Select one of the psychological effects that celebrities have on the public, according to one or more of the social scientists that Flora cites in her essay, and write an essay in which you evaluate their views based on your own reading and experience.

RELATED WEB SITES

Celebrity Links
`www.celebrity-link.com`
This giant celebrity links and photo site is ideal for studying the complex relationship between fans and celebrities. Contains links to many fan sites for particular celebrities, television shows, and bands.

Poppolitics
`www.poppolitics.com/siteguide.shtml`
This thought-provoking site with a political outlook contains reviews, interviews, and in-depth criticism on celebrities, popular entertainment, and culture.

Sissela Bok

Aggression: The Impact of Media Violence

Sissela Bok has made a major contribution to the contemporary debate over values and ethical issues in society. Born in Sweden to liberal economists and peace activists Alva and Gunnar Myrdal, Bok was influenced by her parents' devotion to public causes. Bok left Sweden at an early age to study abroad; she received her Ph.D. in philosophy from Harvard University in 1970. She has been a professor of philosophy at Brandeis University and is currently a Distinguished Fellow at the Harvard Center for Population and Development Studies. Bok's writings on ethical issues and values include Lying: Moral Choice in Public and Private Life *(1978);* Secrets: On the Ethics of Concealment and Revelation *(1983);* A Strategy for Peace: Human Values and the Threat of War *(1989);* Common Values *(1995); and, most recently,* Mayhem: Violence as Public Entertainment *(1998), which contains the following essay on the relationship between media and aggression.*

JOURNAL

Do you believe that media violence can cause a significant amount of actual violence in children? How could you prove your belief to be a fact?

Even if media violence were linked to no other debilitating effects, it would remain at the center of public debate so long as the widespread belief persists that it glamorizes aggressive conduct, removes inhibitions toward such conduct, arouses viewers, and invites imitation. It is only natural that the links of media violence to aggression should be of special concern to families and communities. Whereas increased fear, desensitization, and appetite primarily affect the viewers themselves, aggression directly injures others and represents a more clear-cut violation of standards of behavior. From the point of view of public policy, therefore, curbing aggression has priority over alleviating subtler psychological and moral damage.

Public concern about a possible link between media violence and societal violence has further intensified in the past decade, as violent crime reached a peak in the early 1990s, yet has shown no sign of downturn, even after crime rates began dropping in 1992. Media coverage of violence, far from declining, has escalated since then, devoting ever more attention to celebrity homicides and copycat crimes. The latter, explicitly modeled on videos or films and sometimes carried out with meticulous fidelity to detail, are never more relentlessly covered in the media than when they are committed by children and adolescents. Undocumented claims that violent copycat crimes are mounting in number contribute further to the ominous sense of threat that these crimes generate. Their dramatic nature drains away the public's attention from other, more mundane forms of aggression that are much more commonplace, and from . . . other . . . harmful effects of media violence.

Media analyst Ken Auletta reports that, in 1992, a mother in France sued the head of a state TV channel that carried the American series *MacGyver*, claiming that her son was accidentally injured as a result of having copied MacGyver's recipe for making a bomb. At the time, Auletta predicted that similar lawsuits were bound to become a weapon against media violence in America's litigious culture. By 1996, novelist John Grisham had sparked a debate about director

Oliver Stone's film *Natural Born Killers,* which is reputedly linked to more copy-cat assaults and murders than any other movie to date. Grisham wrote in protest against the film after learning that a friend of his, Bill Savage, had been killed by nineteen-year-old Sarah Edmondson and her boyfriend Benjamin Darras, eighteen: after repeated viewings of Stone's film on video, the two had gone on a killing spree with the film's murderous, gleeful heroes expressly in mind. Characterizing the film as "a horrific movie that glamorized casual may-hem and bloodlust," Grisham proposed legal action:

> Think of a film as a product, something created and brought to market, not too dis-similar from breast implants. Though the law has yet to declare movies to be prod-ucts, it is only a small step away. If something goes wrong with the product, either by design or defect, and injury ensues, then its makers are held responsible. . . . It will take only one large verdict against the like of Oliver Stone, and his production company, and perhaps the screenwriter, and the studio itself, and then the party will be over. The verdict will come from the heartland, far away from Southern California, in some small courtroom with no cameras. A jury will finally say enough is enough; that the demons placed in Sarah Edmondson's mind were not solely of her own making.

As a producer of books made into lucrative movies—themselves hardly de-void of violence—and as a veteran of contract negotiations within the enter-tainment industry, Grisham may have become accustomed to thinking of films in industry terms as "products." As a seasoned courtroom lawyer, he may have found the analogy between such products and breast implants useful for invok-ing product liability to pin personal responsibility on movie producers and di-rectors for the lethal consequences that their work might help unleash.

5   Oliver Stone retorted that Grisham was drawing "upon the superstition about the magical power of pictures to conjure up the undead spectre of cen-sorship." In dismissing concerns about the "magical power of pictures" as merely superstitious, Stone sidestepped the larger question of responsibility fully as much as Grisham had sidestepped that of causation when he attributed liability to filmmakers for anything that "goes wrong" with their products so that "injury ensues."

Because aggression is the most prominent effect associated with media vio-lence in the public's mind, it is natural that it should also remain the primary focus of scholars in the field. The "aggressor effect" has been studied both to identify the short-term, immediate impact on viewers after exposure to TV vio-lence, and the long-term influences. . . . There is near-unanimity by now among investigators that exposure to media violence contributes to lowering barriers to aggression among some viewers. This lowering of barriers may be as-sisted by the failure of empathy that comes with growing desensitization, and intensified to the extent that viewers develop an appetite for violence—something that may lead to still greater desire for violent programs and, in turn, even greater desensitization.

When it comes to viewing violent pornography, levels of aggression toward women have been shown to go up among male subjects who view sexualized violence against women. "In explicit depictions of sexual violence," a report by the American Psychological Association's Commission on Youth and Violence concludes after surveying available research data, "it is the message about violence more than the sexual nature of the materials that appears to affect the attitudes of adolescents about rape and violence toward women." Psychologist Edward Donnerstein and colleagues have shown that if investigators tell subjects that aggression is legitimate, then show them violent pornography, their aggression toward women increases. In slasher films, the speed and ease with which "one's feelings can be transformed from sensuality into viciousness may surprise even those quite conversant with the links between sexual and violent urges."

Viewers who become accustomed to seeing violence as an acceptable, common, attractive way of dealing with problems find it easier to identify with aggressors and to suppress any sense of pity or respect for victims of violence. Media violence has been found to have stronger effects of this kind when carried out by heroic, impressive, or otherwise exciting figures, especially when they are shown as invulnerable and are rewarded or not punished for what they do. The same is true when the violence is shown as justifiable, when viewers identify with the aggressors rather than with their victims, when violence is routinely resorted to, and when the programs have links to how viewers perceive their own environment.

While the consensus that such influences exist grows among investigators as research accumulates, there is no consensus whatsoever about the size of the correlations involved. Most investigators agree that it will always be difficult to disentangle the precise effects of exposure to media violence from the many other factors contributing to societal violence. No reputable scholar accepts the view expressed by 21 percent of the American public in 1995, blaming television more than any other factor for teenage violence. Such tentative estimates as have been made suggest that the media account for between 5 and 15 percent of societal violence. Even these estimates are rarely specific enough to indicate whether what is at issue is all violent crime, or such crimes along with bullying and aggression more generally.

10   One frequently cited investigator proposes a dramatically higher and more specific estimate than others. Psychiatrist Brandon S. Centerwall has concluded from large-scale epidemiological studies of "white homicide" in the United States, Canada, and South Africa in the period from 1945 to 1974, that it escalated in these societies within ten to fifteen years of the introduction of television, and that one can therefore deduce that television has brought a doubling of violent societal crime:

> Of course, there are many factors other than television that influence the amount of violent crime. Every violent act is the result of a variety of forces coming together—poverty, crime, alcohol and drug abuse, stress—of which childhood TV exposure is just one. Nevertheless, the evidence indicates that if hypothetically, television technology had never been developed, there would today be 10,000 fewer homicides each year in the United States, 70,000 fewer rapes, and 700,000 fewer injurious assaults. Violent crime would be half of what it now is.

Centerwall's study, published in 1989, includes controls for such variables as firearm possession and economic growth. But his conclusions have been criticized for not taking into account other factors, such as population changes during the time period studied, that might also play a role in changing crime rates. Shifts in policy and length of prison terms clearly affect these levels as well. By now, the decline in levels of violent crime in the United States since Centerwall's study was conducted, even though television viewing did not decline ten to fifteen years before, does not square with his extrapolations. As for "white homicide" in South Africa under apartheid, each year brings more severe challenges to official statistics from that period.

Even the lower estimates, however, of around 5 to 10 percent of violence as correlated with television exposure, point to substantial numbers of violent crimes in a population as large as America's. But if such estimates are to be used in discussions of policy decisions, more research will be needed to distinguish between the effects of television in general and those of particular types of violent programming, and to indicate specifically what sorts of images increase the aggressor effect and by what means; and throughout to be clearer about the nature of the aggressive acts studied.

Media representatives naturally request proof of such effects before they are asked to undertake substantial changes in programming. In considering possible remedies for a problem, inquiring into the reasons for claims about risks is entirely appropriate. It is clearly valid to scrutinize the research designs, sampling methods, and possible biases of studies supporting such claims, and to ask about the reasoning leading from particular research findings to conclusions. But to ask for some demonstrable pinpointing of just when and how exposure to media violence affects levels of aggression sets a dangerously high threshold for establishing risk factors.

We may never be able to trace, retrospectively, the specific set of television programs that contributed to a particular person's aggressive conduct. The same is true when it comes to the links between tobacco smoking and cancer, between drunk driving and automobile accidents, and many other risk factors presenting public health hazards. Only recently have scientists identified the specific channels through which tobacco generates its carcinogenic effects. Both precise causative mechanisms and documented occurrences in individuals remain elusive. Too often, media representatives formulate their requests in what appear to be strictly polemical terms, raising dismissive questions familiar from debates over the effects of tobacco: "How can anyone definitively pinpoint the link between media violence and acts of real-life violence? If not, how can we know if exposure to media violence constitutes a risk factor in the first place?"

15   Yet the difficulty in carrying out such pinpointing has not stood in the way of discussing and promoting efforts to curtail cigarette smoking and drunk driving. It is not clear, therefore, why a similar difficulty should block such efforts when it comes to media violence. The perspective of "probabilistic causation" . . . is crucial to public debate about the risk factors in media violence. The television industry has already been persuaded to curtail the glamorization of smoking and drunk driving on its programs, despite the lack of conclu-

sive documentation of the correlation between TV viewing and higher incidence of such conduct. Why should the industry not take analogous precautions with respect to violent programming?

Americans have special reasons to inquire into the causes of societal violence. While we are in no sense uniquely violent, we need to ask about all possible reasons why our levels of violent crime are higher than in all other stable industrialized democracies. Our homicide rate would be higher still if we did not imprison more of our citizens than any society in the world, and if emergency medical care had not improved so greatly in recent decades that a larger proportion of shooting victims survive than in the past. Even so, we have seen an unprecedented rise not only in child and adolescent violence, but in levels of rape, child abuse, domestic violence, and every other form of assault.

Although America's homicide rate has declined in the 1990s, the rates for suicide, rape, and murder involving children and adolescents in many regions have too rarely followed suit. For Americans aged fifteen to thirty-five years, homicide is the second leading cause of death, and for young African Americans, fifteen to twenty-four years, it is *the* leading cause of death. In the decade following the mid-1980s, the rate of murder committed by teenagers fourteen to seventeen more than doubled. The rates of injury suffered by small children are skyrocketing, with the number of seriously injured children nearly quadrupling from 1986 to 1993; and a proportion of these injuries are inflicted by children upon one another. Even homicides by children, once next to unknown, have escalated in recent decades.

America may be the only society on earth to have experienced what has been called an "epidemic of children killing children," which is ravaging some of its communities today. As in any epidemic, it is urgent to ask what it is that makes so many capable of such violence, victimizes so many others, and causes countless more to live in fear. Whatever role the media are found to play in this respect, to be sure, is but part of the problem. Obviously, not even the total elimination of media violence would wipe out the problem of violence in the United States or any other society. The same can be said for the proliferation and easy access to guns, or for poverty, drug addiction, and other risk factors. As Dr. Deborah Prothrow-Stith puts it, "It's not an either or. It's not guns or media or parents or poverty."

We have all witnessed the four effects that I have discussed . . . —fearfulness, numbing, appetite, and aggressive impulses—in the context of many influences apart from the media. Maturing involves learning to resist the dominion that these effects can gain over us; and to strive, instead, for greater resilience, empathy, self-control, and respect for self and others. The process of maturation and growth in these respects is never completed for any of us; but it is most easily thwarted in childhood, before it has had chance to take root. Such learning calls for nurturing and education at first; then for increasing autonomy in making personal decisions about how best to confront the realities of violence.

20   Today, the sights and sounds of violence on the screen affect this learning process from infancy on, in many homes. The television screen is the lens through which most children learn about violence. Through the magnifying

power of this lens, their everyday life becomes suffused by images of shootings, family violence, gang warfare, kidnappings, and everything else that contributes to violence in our society. It shapes their experiences long before they have had the opportunity to consent to such shaping or developed the ability to cope adequately with this knowledge. The basic nurturing and protection to prevent the impairment of this ability ought to be the birthright of every child.

QUESTIONS FOR DISCUSSION

1. What question does Bok believe John Grisham and Oliver Stone avoid in their debate over the impact of films on "copycat" violent crimes? Do their arguments seem reasonable to you, as she presents them here?
2. According to the research that Bok discusses, what circumstances tend to have the greatest impact on viewers' tendency to find violence acceptable?
3. According to Bok, what further research remains to be done before we can draw more definitive conclusions about the impact of such violence on actual patterns of aggression?
4. Bok points out the difficulty in making a clear-cut connection between smoking and cancer, even though we presume there is a cause. How effective is her analogy with media violence as a presumed cause of actual violence among heavy viewers? Do her conclusions here seem clear and reasonable?
5. What does Dr. Deborah Prothrow-Stith mean when she states, "It's not an either or. It's not guns or media or parents or poverty"? What conclusions does Bok suggest can be drawn from this statement about causes and solutions for the "problem" of media violence?
6. How, according to Bok, might excessive exposure to media violence thwart a child's ability to learn to resist aggression and to acquire such traits as empathy, respect, and self-control? Do you agree?

CONNECTION

Compare the way Bok tries to demonstrate a connection between TV violence and violence in the life of children with the efforts of Anthony Pratkanis and Elliot Aronson to show a relationship between viewing violence in the media and beliefs about violence in society. Which seems to make the most convincing connection (see page 468)?

IDEAS FOR WRITING

1. Write an essay in which you consider some alternative causes for the current outbreak of youth violence. For instance, what about parental neglect and abuse, the decay of our educational system, or the violence of war?
2. If you accept Bok's argument that there is too much media violence and that this can lead to more youth aggression, how do we cut back on the media violence to which young people are currently being exposed? Write an essay in the form of a proposal for change, considering some ideas that have been suggested and that are currently being tried on a limited basis.

Jonathan L. Freedman

Evaluating the Research on Violent Video Games

*Jonathan Freedman, a professor of psychology at the University of Toronto, argues
that there is no proven relationship between violent entertainment and violent behavior. He has published many articles analyzing research studies in the field, including "Effect of Television Violence on Aggressiveness" (1984); "Television
Violence and Aggression: What Psychologists Should Tell the Public" (1992); and
"Violence in the Mass Media and Violence in Society: The Link Is Unproven"
(1996). His book* Media Violence and Its Effect on Aggression *(2002) surveys the empirical studies and experiments in this field, and concludes that there is
not enough evidence to prove that violent entertainment causes children or adults
to act aggressively and violently in social situations. The article that follows focuses
on video games and their potential for arousing violence in young users, comparing a number of flawed research studies on the subject.*

JOURNAL

Write about your experience or observations of video games and their players.
Have you noticed any negative or violent effects from playing such games?

As human beings, we have difficulty accepting random or senseless occurrences. We want to understand why something has happened, and the
strength of this desire seems to be proportional to the horror of the event.

When a horrible crime occurs, we want to know why. If it was related to drugs or gangs or an armed robbery, I think we find those sufficient reasons. We do not hate the crime less, but at least we think we know why it occurred.

But consider the case of the two boys who walked into Columbine High School in Littleton, Colorado, and deliberately killed 12 students, a teacher and then themselves; or the case of the 14-year-old Canadian boy who walked into the WR Myers High School in Taber, Alberta, killed one and seriously injured another. It is difficult to imagine events more terrible than our young people deliberately killing each other. What makes it even worse (if that's possible) is that these appear to have been entirely senseless acts. Oh yes, we have heard that they (and others who have committed similar acts) were outsiders, that they had not been accepted, that they were teased and so on. These reports have sometimes turned out to be false. But even if they were true, nothing that was done to these boys or that they experienced even remotely explains their horrendous crimes.

It seems likely that what happened in most of the school killings was that some random combination of events and personalities and opportunities came together to cause the crime. With tens of millions of children in school, it is perhaps not surprising that every once in a while one of them does something terrible. This is not an explanation. You have all probably gone to your doctor with some ache or pain that appeared for no apparent reason, or gone to your computer expert with a machine that suddenly ceases to function properly or that wiped out a crucial file, and been told by doctor or computer expert that "These things happen." We can accept this with minor ailments and problems, but for most of us it is not an acceptable explanation for violence. We cannot accept that, oh yes, every once in a while a young boy will take out a gun and kill a classmate. We find it hard to live with this. We want something better.

Therefore, whenever these horrible crime[s] occur, people search for a reason. It was the parents' fault; it was Satanism and witchcraft; it was the lack of religion in the schools and at home; it was a moral breakdown in the countries; it was the availability of guns; it was the culture.

5   One answer that is often proposed is that the crimes are due to exposure to media violence. Children who watch television and go to the movies see thousands of murders and countless other acts of violence. Many people believe that being exposed to all this violence causes children to be more aggressive and to commit crimes. That's an explanation people can accept and, sure enough, many people in Canada and the United States believe that media violence is a major cause of violent crime.

Recently, attention has turned toward the violence in video games. It seems reasonable to many people that if passively watching violence in movies and on television causes aggression, actively participating in violence in video games should have an even greater effect. Surely, so the argument goes, spending hours shooting images of various creatures and of human beings and watching them blow up, break apart, scream in pain, spew blood all over, and so on must have a harmful effect on those who play—it must teach them that violence is acceptable, that it is a way to deal with problems, perhaps make them insensitive to real violence, and thus cause them to be more aggressive and more violent themselves.

While this seems obvious or even self-evident to some, it is less obvious to others. In any case, we know that what seems obvious is not always correct. The role of systematic research is to help determine whether it is correct. Therefore, the work on the effect of video games on aggression is potentially very important. Accordingly, it is essential that it be done very carefully and that the results be evaluated fairly and objectively. Anderson and Bushman (2001) have recently published a meta-analysis of the research. Their analysis concludes that exposure to violent video games has a negative effect on a variety of measures. The analysis of greatest import is the one indicating that playing violent video games causes an increase in aggressive behavior. On the basis of their overall analysis and presumably especially the one regarding aggressive behavior, the authors assert that video games pose a threat to public health. This is a serious paper and a very serious assertion. What should we make of it?

To begin, it should be clear that there has not been a great deal of research relevant to this question. In their meta-analysis Anderson and Bushman identified 35 research reports that included 54 independent samples of participants. Of these, 22 were published. And of these, only 9 studies dealt with aggressive behavior. In other words, conclusions about whether playing violent video games causes aggressive behavior must be based on nine published experiments. I cannot think of another important issue for which scientists have been willing to reach conclusions on such a small body of research. Even if the research had been designed and conducted perfectly, there is far too little evidence to reach any firm conclusions. And, as I shall discuss below, the research is far from perfect.

Before discussing some of the problems with the research, let me acknowledge that this is a very difficult issue to study. Only experimental research can provide a definitive answer to the question whether violent video games cause aggression. Yet, as with many issues of public concern, it is impossible to conduct the perfect experiment. To determine whether exposure to violent video games causes aggression, the ideal experiment would randomly assign children to playing or not playing video games containing violence. Some would play violent video games for a great many hours, some would play such games for less time or would play games with less violence, others would play no video games, and so on. They would continue to do this for many years, and during and after that time one would obtain measures of their aggressive behavior. If those who played violent video games engaged in more aggressive or violent behavior, it would indicate that the video games caused aggression; and if this difference did not emerge, it would provide evidence that playing violent video games did not cause aggression.

10   Of course, such a study is not possible. For ethical, legal, moral, and logistic reasons, one cannot assign children to play certain kinds of games for years even if one were willing to do so. Accordingly, the ideal experiment cannot be conducted and we must rely on less perfect studies in attempting to answer our question. Although it is difficult to reach firm conclusions about causality

without the kind of study I just described, it is not impossible. With sufficient ingenuity, resources and time, one can collect enough evidence of an effect that most scientists will be convinced. This is the case with the research on cigarette smoking and cancer—no perfect experiment can be done, but after a vast amount of research, few people doubt that smoking causes cancer. We are nowhere near the point at which we could have the same confidence in the video game research, but we can at least try to make sense out of the work that has been done. To do so requires a careful analysis of the methodology and logic of the studies and their findings. Accordingly, let me turn to a consideration of the research.

Non-experimental Studies

Most of the non-experimental work consists of relatively small-scale surveys. People are asked about their exposure to video games, to violent video games, and to various other media. They are also asked about their aggressive behavior, or occasionally others provide information on the respondents' aggressive behavior. Then the researchers conduct correlational analyses (or other similar analyses) to see if those who are exposed more to violent video games are more aggressive than those who are exposed less. Sometimes more detailed analyses are conducted to see if other factors mediate or reduce any relation that is found.

The findings of this research are similar to that of the survey research on other violent media and aggression. Despite some inconsistencies and complexities, the results seem to indicate that people who spend more time playing video games tend to be more aggressive than those who spend less time playing them; and, with less certainty, that this is especially true of playing violent video games. Because there are so few studies and the lack of representative samples, we cannot put much confidence in the size of these correlations. Nevertheless, it seems likely that the basic relation is true—those who like violent video games tend to be more aggressive than those who do not like them.

This is an important finding, because it raises the possibility that playing video games causes aggression. That is, one reason why playing violent games is related to aggressiveness could be that playing the games makes people more aggressive. However, there are other plausible explanations, such as that people with a more aggressive personality like violent video games and also engage in more aggressive behavior. Playing the games does not cause the aggression, nor does the aggression cause the preference for violent games. They are both caused by another factor—the person's personality. Other such explanations are also possible. Thus, the existence of the correlation between playing violent games and aggressiveness does not prove that one causes the other. It provides no evidence for causality. While interesting, this research is not relevant to the central question whether violent video games cause aggression. Therefore, I shall restrict my comments to the experimental research since that is the only work that is relevant to this question. (I should add that as Anderson and Bushman point out, other kinds of non-experimental research could provide some evidence for causality, but it has not been done and thus does not enter the debate.)

Experimental Research

The experimental work seems to have been patterned on laboratory experiments on the effects of film and television violence. The basic design is that people are brought into a laboratory, some play a video game containing violence while others play a video game with less violence or no violence, and in some studies others do not play any video games. Then various measures are obtained that are meant to indicate the participants' level of aggression. If those who played the violent video game score higher on these measures, it is interpreted to show that the violent video game caused aggression. As noted above, there are very few such experiments but according to the review by Anderson and Bushman, overall the results indicate a significant effect of violent video games on aggression. One can question some of the decisions those authors made in the classifications in their meta-analysis, but this paper is not meant as a critique of the meta-analysis so let us assume that their statistical conclusion is justified. That is, combining all of the research, there is a small but significant effect of playing violent video games on the measures of aggression employed in the studies.

15   This should not end the debate. The original question whether playing violent video games causes people to be aggressive is certainly not answered yet. We must still ask what this finding means. Or, to put it in other terms, should the results of this research be interpreted as indicating that playing violent video games causes aggression. The answer to this question depends on the details of how the research was designed and conducted. If it has been done perfectly, the findings would mean that violent video games do affect aggression; but if the research is flawed or limited, the findings may be open to other interpretations. Although there are all sorts of points that can be made about the work, let me focus on three: the comparability of the violent and non-violent games, the possibility of demand factors being present, and the measures of aggression.

The Choice of Games

One of the most basic requirements of good experimentation is that the various conditions be as similar as possible except for the variable of interest. As long as the conditions differ only in terms of that variable, any differences in the dependent measure can be attributed to that variable; but if the conditions differ in other ways, any differences in the dependent measure could be due to any of the ways in which the conditions differ. That is why great effort is usually made to equate the various experiment groups on every factor except the one of concern.

For example, imagine some researchers wanted to test the effectiveness of a new drug designed to reduce flu symptoms. The researchers design a study in which some people who have the flu get the drug three times a day while others get a placebo three times a day. Because the drug does not taste very good, it is mixed with a vitamin-rich fruit drink to make it more palatable, while the placebo is taken with water. The study shows that those who are given the drug report that their symptoms were less severe that those who were given the placebo. The researchers conclude that the drug works.

This conclusion is clearly not justified because the two conditions differ in more ways than just the presence or absence of the drug. Those who got the drug also drank the fruit drink. The difference between the conditions on the dependent variable could be due to the drug or to the fruit drink. This is so obvious that no serious scientist would make such a silly mistake. In good drug research the conditions are identical except for the drug—everyone gets the same instructions, everyone takes an identical-looking pill, takes the pill under identical circumstances, and every effort is made to have the drug-pill and the placebo-pill taste the same. In fact, as I'll discuss later, both patient and physician do not even know what condition the patients are in until after the experiment is completed. Only when all of this is done is it legitimate to attribute differences to the drug. Similarly, in any kind of experiment, only if the experimental and control conditions are identical in every respect except the variable of interest can one conclude that differences on the dependent variable are due to that variable.

This ideal level of comparability between conditions has never been realized in the research on video games, even when the experimenters tried to equate conditions. For example, Anderson and Dill (2000) compared Wolfenstein, a violent video game, with Myst. They selected these two programs with considerable care. They conducted a pilot study on several video programs and found that these two did not differ in the ratings they received on various important dimensions. In particular, there were no differences on physiological measures or on ratings of action. In other words, the authors tried to find games that were equivalent.

20   However, it seems obvious that their attempt was not entirely successful. In the first place, players rated Wolfenstein more exciting than Myst. But perhaps equally important, anyone familiar with the two knows that they are entirely different programs. Myst was a very popular program that sold millions—but it differs in many ways from the violent game. To begin, it is not really a game but a puzzle. The players find themselves on a strange island and must figure out what is going on. This involves finding esoteric clues, interpreting them, and then using them correctly. It is extremely difficult and requires great ingenuity to solve. Those who like the game find this interesting and fascinating. But there is no action (it is hard to imagine why it was rated similar to Wolfenstein on this dimension) and nothing that makes it similar to a game. So it is not really an appropriate comparison, since presumably the question is whether games that involve violence differ from games that do not involve violence in their effects on aggression—not whether playing games differs from engaging in problem solving. Or, to put it another way, as in any experiment, you do not compare apples and oranges, but rather two kinds of apples.

Ballard and Lindeberger (1999) did a better job. They compared NBA Jam, an exciting sports game, with three versions of Mortal Kombat that differed in the amount of violence (or at least the graphic nature of the violence). It is possible that Mortal Kombat was more exciting and had more action than the basketball game, but at least all of the programs were exciting, all were games, and it was possible to compare three level of Mortal Kombat to look for differences due to varying amounts of violence. Graybill et al. (1987) probably did still better. They used six games that did not differ in ratings of excitement, difficulty or enjoyment but only in ratings of violence. All of them were lively, action-packed games in which players compete against the computer. Presumably it is better to have six games than to have only two since this reduces the chance that any effects are due to the specific games.

My point here is not to say that all of the studies failed to equate the games or that those that did equate them found no effect on aggression. Rather, the point is that in considering all of the research, it is important to understand that few of the experiments came close to solving and none solved perfectly the tricky problem of making the violent and non-violent games comparable on all variables other than the amount of violence. It may be that this cannot be done, but we must recognize that it is a limitation of the work and a serious limitation in some of the experiments.

The lack of comparability of the video games is not a subtle or picky criticism—it is absolutely basic to the design and interpretation of the research because it leaves open the interpretation of any difference that is found between conditions. And as in other media violence research, one obvious interpretation is that any effect is due to differences in arousal. Indeed, in their review of the research Anderson and Bushman found that exposure to violent video games increased physiological arousal. If the violent video game is more arousing than the non-violent comparison program, one would expect more aggression (or almost anything else) in the condition with higher arousal. If so, there is no reason to attribute the effect to the violence—it might be just the arousal. Since all of this research compared games with violence to games (or programs) without violence, and since the two types of games differed in many ways, it is possible any effects on aggression could be due to arousal or other factors rather than to the presence of violence. Because of this problem, one must be extremely cautious in interpreting the results of this research and especially cautious in deciding that the effects are due to the amount of violence in the games.

Demand Factor

Another basic element in almost all experiments is the problem of experimenter or situational demand producing effects. Those who design experimental research know that there is always the possibility, indeed probability, that elements of the procedure will give the subject the impression that a particular response is expected or desired or allowed, and that this will affect how the subjects behave. This problem is so well recognized that virtually all drug research is designed so that neither the participants or the experiments know the participants' experimental condition. This avoids the possibility that those getting the drug would expect to get better and would therefore feel better or report that they feel better, and also that the experimenters would expect them to get better and would judge that they had gotten better. This procedure works very well for drug research, but cannot be used in the research on video games (since obviously the participants will know what game they have played).

25   The problem of experimenters demand effects is especially pronounced when the behavior of interest is one that is usually not allowed or is inhibited in the experimental situation. For example, imagine that a group of psychologists want to study the effect of rap music on children's tendency to use obscene language. To do this, they design an experiment in which some children listen to rap music and others listen to equally lively, equally popular heavy metal music. Note that they have been careful to equate the music in terms of arousal, popularity and so on. The children are brought into the laboratory in small groups, the music is playing in the room, and the children are asked to wait for a while. The experiments then have a long talk with the children or let them talk among themselves and they observe how much obscene language is used.

Although this is not a bad study in some respects, it suffers from the possibility of serious demand effects. The children will notice that the experimenters have chosen to play rap music and will infer that the experimenters like that music or at least approve of it. This will send the message that the language in the music is acceptable to the experimenters, or at least acceptable in the laboratory. This will give the children permission to use the language themselves, whereas without that message most of them would probably be inhibited by the formality of the situation and the presence of unknown adults.

Knowing this, careful experimenters will distance themselves from the music. That is, they will make it obvious that they did not choose the music and thus give no indication whether they approve of it or even tolerate it. They could do this in various ways. For example, the children could come first to a room some distance from the laboratory, and the music (rap or otherwise) could apparently be coming from outside the building. The children would thus be exposed to the music for a while, but there would be no suggestion and no reason to infer that the experimenters had anything to do with the music. When the children then came to the laboratory, their behavior might be affected by the music, but not through the effect of experimenter demand.

Turning now to the work on video games, when some subjects are told to play a violent game and others a non-violent game, there is the clear possibility of experimenter demand (broadly defined). When the experimenters choose a violent game, they may be giving the message that they approve of such games and might therefore approve of or even expect the subjects to behave violently or aggressively. This could be avoided by separating the experimenters from the choice of game. This is admittedly not easy, but no one ever said that designing research is simple. Only if "sponsorship" of the game is removed as a factor can any differences among conditions be unambiguously attributed to the presence of violence rather than the "permission" given to act aggressively by the choice of the game.

One of the most obvious weaknesses in much of the research on media violence and especially on video game violence is that so little attention appears to have been paid to how the study was structured for the participants. Often they were told virtually nothing about why the study was being conducted or even what they could expect to be doing. When there were cover stories, they were pretty flimsy or incomplete. Anderson and Dill (2000) provided one of the better cover stories, which was that the study concerned the learning curve—how people learn and develop a motor skill and how it affects other tasks. This is not bad, but it offers no explanation of why the particular game was chosen. Since as far as each participant knows, the experimenters are using only one game, they could infer that the experimenters liked that particular game or were interested in the learning of that game and this could affect the participants' responses. Imagine that the cover story were expanded a little and included the statement that to make their findings as general as possible they were using a large number of video games (which could be shown) and that the game each person would play is randomly selected from the group. If lots of games were shown, the participant would have no reason to infer anything from the fact that he or she was asked to play a violent game (except perhaps that the experimenters did not disapprove of these games so strongly that they excluded them). This would greatly reduce or even eliminate the possibility that the choice of game affected the participants' behavior.

30   Let me be clear that the possibility of demand causing the results is not unlikely or farfetched. It is a well-known phenomenon in experimental research and a continual almost ubiquitous source of problems in interpretation. That is why so much attention is usually devoted to setting up the situation to minimize this effect. Unfortunately, those studying the impact of video games have not generally been concerned enough with this problem to deal with it effectively. This leaves almost all of the results open to the alternative and uninteresting interpretation that they are caused by demand factors rather than the variable of interest, namely the direct effect of the amount of violence in the video game.

Measures of Aggression

As noted before, very few of the studies even try to measure aggression, and many of the measures have almost nothing to do with aggression. The most distant are measures of thoughts or as they are sometimes called, aggressive cognitions. In some of the studies, if the people in the violent game condition have more thoughts of aggression than those playing the non-violent game, this is considered an indication that violent games cause aggression. This interpretation is not justified. After eating a huge meal, you probably are thinking about food—but you are less rather than more likely to want to eat. After watching a war movie, you probably have thoughts of war, but no one would suggest that you are more likely to wage war unless the movie promoted war. After *Schindler's List,* I imagine that most people thought about war and torture and violence, but I hope that most people were less likely to be aggressive rather than more likely. Whatever stimulus you are exposed to, you are more likely to have thoughts related to that stimulus, but that does not mean that your behavior has been affected. Indeed, Graybill et al. used aggressive thoughts as a manipulation check to see if the aggressive content of the game was salient, not as a measure of aggression.

Similarly, some studies measure physiological arousal and consider that an indication of aggression. Again, this makes no sense. After playing a tense game that involves shooting and being shot at, people may be physiologically aroused. But there is no reason to think that this alone makes them more likely to be aggressive. As noted above, it is an indication that the violent game differed from the non-violent one in terms of arousal, which is a problem, not a finding that supports the notion that violent video games cause aggression.

I am not arguing that this research is uninteresting. It is interesting that people have violent thoughts after playing violent games and it is interesting (though less so) that they are more aroused after a violent game. Both the thoughts and the arousal may play a role in their behavior. But there is no evidence that it makes them more likely to act violently—perhaps it does the opposite. So the studies with these measures should be given little or no weight. They tell us nothing about whether playing violent video games makes people aggressive.

Most of the behavioral measures are analogues of aggression rather than the real thing. Anderson and Dill (2000) used as their measure of aggression the intensity and duration of a loud noise that one subject gave to another. Pressing a button that delivers a short burst of loud noise is pretty remote from real aggression. Cooper and Mackie (1986) observed whether the children in their study chose to play with "aggressive" or "non-aggressive" toys. Playing with an aggressive toy is hardly the same as being aggressive. One could even argue that this measure confuses the outcome with the question which is whether playing an aggressive game (i.e. video game) causes aggression. Showing that playing one aggressive game increases the likelihood that children will play another aggressive game does not tell us anything about effects on actual aggression.

35   Some of the measures were somewhat better than these, but it should be clear that almost all of the research involved analogues of aggression rather than the real thing. One can and I believe should question whether these analogues have anything to do with aggression—they may sound like aggression and they have often been used by other researchers to measure aggression, but they are not aggression and there is no good evidence that they indicate anything about aggressive behavior.

Conclusions

This body of research is not only extremely limited in terms of the number of relevant studies, but also suffers from many methodological problems. Insufficient attention has been paid to choosing games that are as similar as possible except for the presence of violence; virtually no attention has been paid to eliminating or at least minimizing experimenter demand; and the measures of aggression are either remote from aggression or of questionable value.

Given these problems and limitations in this body of research, what can we reasonably conclude from the findings? 1. There is substantial, though far from overwhelming or definitive evidence that people who like and play violent video games tend to be more aggressive than those who like and play them less. This is, of course, a purely correlational finding and tells us nothing about whether playing violence video games causes aggression. 2. There is some slight evidence that immediately after playing violent video games there is an increase in aggressiveness. As discussed above, the evidence for this is minimal and is greatly weakened by limitations in the research, which provide alternative explanations of the effect. 3. There is not the slightest evidence that playing violent video games causes any long-term or lasting increase in aggressiveness or violence. There is very little relevant research, and no longitudinal studies that might show such effects. It may well be that further research will indicate that playing violent video games is harmful. For the moment, however, there is no such work and no scientific reason to believe that violent video games have bad effects on children or on adults, and certainly none to indicate that such games constitute a public health risk.

REFERENCES

Anderson, C. A., and B. J. Bushman. 2001. Effects of violent video games on aggressive behavior, aggressive cognition, aggressive affect, physiological arousal, and prosocial behavior: A meta-analytic review of the scientific literature. *Psychological Science* 12: 353–59.

Anderson, C. A., and Dill, K. E. 2000. Video games and aggressive thoughts, feelings, and behavior in the laboratory and life. *Journal of Personality and Social Psychology* 78: 772–90.

Cooper, J., and Mackie, D. 1986. Video games and aggression in children. *Journal of Applied Social Psychology* 16: 726–744.

Graybill, D., M. Strawniak, T. Hunter, and M. O'Leary, 1987. Effects of playing versus observing violent versus nonviolent video games on children's aggression. *Psychology: A Quarterly Journal of Human Behavior* 24: 1–8.

QUESTIONS FOR DISCUSSION

1. How does Freedman link our desire to create a clear cause for "random" events to the blaming of media for violence in our society? Is his explanation convincing? Why or why not?
2. How does Freedman attempt to counter the assumption that violent video games can cause greater social violence than movies or TV? Do you agree?

3. How does Freedman attempt to refute the conclusions and methodology in Anderson and Bushman's study of 35 research reports on video game–related aggression? Is Freedman's refutation convincing? Why or why not?

4. Why does Freedman argue that it is very difficult to study and design experiments to demonstrate video game–related aggression? What is his argument based on, other than his own beliefs? Do his arguments seem logical and factual?

5. How does Freedman attempt to refute "non-experimental" studies? What is wrong, in his view, with "correlational" studies? How do issues such as choice of games to study and "experimental demand" influence the outcome of video game violence experiments, in Freedman's view?

6. What distinction does Freedman draw between experiments that note behavior in the area of "analogues of aggression" as opposed to "the real thing"? Why is this distinction important in considering the actual impact of the games upon aggressive behavior?

CONNECTION

Compare Freedman's views on violence in the media and its effects to the opinions of Sissela Bok on this subject (see page 490).

IDEAS FOR WRITING

1. Considering Freedman's overall response to the research on the causal relations between video games and violence, do some further research into the issue of violent video games. Write an essay in which you argue for or against further restrictions and prohibitions on such games.

2. Write an essay in which you present a hypothetical design for a video game that would not contain values that are violent and/or war oriented but that would still be challenging and exciting enough so that young people would enjoy playing it repeatedly. Discuss what you learned through attempting to design such a game.

RELATED WEB SITES

Studies and Research on Media Effects

`http://libertus.net/whatsnew.html`

This site contains a positive review of Jonathan Friedman's book on the effects of media violence, as well as many articles both critiquing and endorsing the view of video games and other electronic media as incitements to violence. In most cases, these articles draw the line at censorship.

Violent Video Games Can Increase Aggression

`www.apa.org/releases/videogames.html`

This APA press release sums up a 2000 study showing a link between video games and aggression. A link at this site also will take you to the full text of the study by psychological researchers Anderson and Dill.

Mark Cochrane

Moral Abdication?

Mark Cochrane was born in 1965 in Saskatchewan, did graduate work in English at Concordia University (Montreal) and the University of British Columbia, and currently lives in Vancouver. He teaches writing and literature at Kwantlen University College in Richmond, British Columbia. He is a freelance writer and the author of two poetry collections, Boy Am I *(1995) and* Change Room *(2000). His poems have appeared in* New American Writing, PRISM *International, and* Capilano Review. *In the following essay, published originally in the* Vancouver Sun, *Cochrane examines the quality of Eminem's lyrics and their impact on young people.*

JOURNAL

Write about a conversation you have had with a younger person or an older individual about some aspect of popular culture that is generally considered inappropriate for youngsters—gangsta rap, adult-themed films, and violent video games. How did this conversation affect your understanding both of the cultural practice and of the older or younger person involved?

In the car my son and I listen to *The Eminem Show,* and we know every word, every snarled and spit syllable. As fans of potty-mouthed, horrorshow American rapper Marshall Mathers III—aka Eminem, aka Slim Shady—my son and I could, I believe, perform the entire CD from start to finish in a karaoke bar. Not since the days of *Jelly Belly* and *Alligator Pie,* in fact, have we *spontaneously* committed verses to memory with such devotion.

Sometimes while driving, however, I watch as the boy in the passenger seat mouths profanities of a kind that would have been unimaginable in mainstream, popular art when I was twelve years old. Even more imaginable—surreal to me, and deeply worrying—becomes the fact that I am tolerating, sharing, and ultimately nurturing my grade seven's enthusiasm for a talented hatemonger. If this is father-son bonding, it's got a creepy edge. Some might call it moral abdication.

At least I know I am not alone in this shady parenting. One evening last summer, when "Without Me" was the best thing—well, since wrestling—we pulled into the driveway with the windows down and the system up. When I shut off the engine, the bevy of boys and girls shooting hoops next door finished the song for us—verbatim, *a cappalla,* and in the unexpurgated form, not the Gore-friendly "airplay" version. Since when did "cum on your lips & some on your tits" become playground singalong in my westside 'hood?

The combination of childishly catchy melodies with woman-hating lyrics (or bloody imaginary dramas) is part of Mathers' dangerous allure. Yet this same track continues with a passage that I like to discuss with my college English students; among other things, it offers examples of how verbs and participles can create implied metaphors:

5   I'm interesting, the best thing since wrestling
    Infesting in your kids ears and nesting

Holy wack, Marshall, you got that right. You are the king of the mind-poisoning kid-perverting earwigs. Children love this stuff, and my students always lift their foreheads from the desks whenever I mention your eminence by name.

Much has changed since the early nineties, when everybody I knew was a kneejerk-PC graduate student and my son was a newborn. But still the driveway episode left me with, say, conflicted goosebumps. I was both thrilled and chilled. Because whatever its content, these kids were memorizing *poetry*—there is not better term to describe what Mathers produces—and not teacher or drama coach was force-feeding them. They were revelling in sound, metrical precision, wordplay and characterization: the pure wicked vivacity of Eminem's lyrical theatre. While playing horse with a basketball, they were paying homage to the living master of internal rhyme.

"Shut the hell up / I'm tryin to develop these pictures of the devil to sell 'em."

10   Whatever condemnation I might formerly have heaped upon Mathers for his views toward women and gays, no living poet confined to the page can touch what this bleach-blonde brat has accomplished. Not even Canadian-born Classics professor Anne Carson, my other farourite poet, recently identified by Harold Bloom (author of *Genius*) as one of a handful of "living geniuses," can approach the impact that Mathers continues to have on our literary culture, both highbrow and low. His virulent persona has taken the English-speaking world by the throat, even as he threatens to slash it.

And therein, of course, lies the dilemma. I am glad that my kids and my students gravitate to a wordsmith who takes his language-play so seriously. But the language that Mathers speaks is frequently hate speech. In fact, his work is fundamentally concerned with hate speech and its connection to the self-conscious art of satire.

While the rapper's status as a literary figure may remain subject to debate, his dominion over the entertainment world is now secure. Tomorrow night he may lose the Grammy for Album of the Year to the long-snubbed Springsteen (most of whose *The Rising* is a saccharine snoozefest), but everybody knows that *The Eminem Show* is not only the bestselling, but also the most culturally significant (in *zeitgeist* terms), album of 2002. And now Mathers also boasts an Oscar nomination, for the song "Lose Yourself" from his acclaimed, quasi-autobiographical film *8 Mile.*

If he wins any of these awards, there will be outrage, because there always has been. Courting controversy is both Mathers' method and his subject matter. Everything we can possibly say about Eminem, his songs have anticipated. "I am whatever you say I am." All along the rapper has scripted both the reception of his work and the media analysis of that reception.

Mathers folds everything that transpires around him back into his writing, and this complex refraction—even the word "Eminem" is self-mirroring—is one of the reasons that the name of "genius" has not been misapplied by the legion of admirers marching in back of him.

15   Consider, for instance, the parent-mocking paradox that he introduces in the song "My Dad's Gone Crazy." "I don't blame you, I wouldn't let Hailie listen to me neither," Mathers concedes—just as the rapper's daughter, darling Hailie Jade herself, takes up the mike to chirp the song's chorus.

Eminem's oeuvre is rife with such ironies and euphonious wit. The line "Feminist women love Eminem," from the hit "The Real Slim Shady," is not just an infuriating and provocative falsehood. The sentence is also a marvel of assonance and consonance, recycled vowel and consonant sounds.

Yet, while many observers have caught a whiff of literary genius off Eminem's body of work, could Harold Bloom ever be convinced? Only, perhaps, if Bloom means what he says when he identifies vitality, audacity, originality and self-reliance as the hallmarks of genius.

Once more Anne Carson, who passes Bloom's test, offers useful comparison here, because at her worst she's as bad as Mathers. In Bloom's universe, however, a poet's candidacy for "genius" depends heavily on the quality of her allusions—the references he or she makes to cultural "authorities," and the tradition the poet aspires to. That's why Carson gets away with all kinds of dour vulgarity and downright sloppiness in her writing. Even as she beats to death the story of her broken marriage, she peppers her work with references to the Greeks—and to a myriad other great thinkers besides. She puts her learning to great subversive service.

Eminem's frame of reference, on the other hand, is confined to his own trashy and violent life—to sex, drugs, media . . . and his broken marriage. Like Carson, he makes brilliant use of the materials he's mastered, but self-centred pop cultural allusions, no matter how sophisticated in their puns and cross-referencing, don't buy you cred, or a shot at immortality, from the likes of Bloom.

20   Still, many writers in North America and the UK have credited Mathers with a resurgence of interest in the spoken and written word. Two years ago an article appearing in the *Guardian* compared Mathers, whose "Stan" then topped the charts, with a number of canonical poets, most notably Browning and Eliot, great practitioners of the dramatic monologue.

A more recent article in the *New York Observer* suggests that "the Eminem flavour" can be discerned in novels by young Americans whose other influences include Eggers and Foster Wallace. Zadie Smith of *White Teeth* fame is an avowed fan. And it was Vancouver writer Lee Henderson, another Eminem-ophile, who pointed out to me that Mathers, on the track "Business," takes up the age-old challenge of finding a word to rhyme with "orange." (The result is these weirdly beautiful lines containing *two* such words: ". . . set to blow college dorm room doors off the hinges / oranges, peach, pears, plums, syringes.")

Another article, on CNN.com, compares Marshall Mathers to Mark Twain, and suggests that Eminem's obscene ideas and vocabulary are analogous with the politically incorrect vernacular of Huckleberry Finn.

Are Mathers' alter egos—Eminem and the more diabolical Slim Shady— best understood, then, as fictional characters, unreliable first-person narrators, satirical personae? (*Spin* magazine once called this argument a "morally weak dodge" but nevertheless "totally legitimate.") Is Eminem his own Huck Finn, forever coming of age in the toxic street slang of his own time, lashing out at the world with that nasally, nerdish, pubescent twang?

If one is inclined to defend Mathers' work in a culture, in a city, where gay-bashing is a problem that never goes away, some such justification or rationale— what Sir Philip Sidney might have called an "apologie"—would seem necessary.

25   At the same time, it is worth noting that *The Slim Shady LP*, the first install-ment in Eminem's major-label trilogy, begins with a disclaimer: "The views and events expressed here are totally fucked, and are not necessarily the views of anyone." Likewise, on *Show*, Mathers avers, "when I speak, it' tongue-in-cheek, I'd yank my fuckin' teeth before I'd ever bite my tongue."

Opponents will understandably counter that Eminem creates reprehensible characters in order to pass off his own reprehensible views. As Jonathan Swift proved, satirical voicing can still get a writer in trouble, and readers of all stripes recognize that "satire" can be a ruse for strafing your victims while avoiding litigation or moral accountability.

A further weakness in the "satirical personae" argument is that Mathers' "real-life" pronouncements of sexuality and gender tend to echo those of "Eminem" and "Shady." Mathers' personae are not backed up by an authorial self that appears to know better, and this is either the most subversive, post-modern feature of Mathers' shtick, or it clearly proves that he's a bigot.

The best defence for Mathers I can muster is that he is a complete psycho-logical mess, out loud, all the time. In the 1999 single "My Name Is," Mathers' persona worries that his mother won't be able to breastfeed him because she has no breasts. Like, really—Paging Dr. Freud. It is Mathers' woundedness and vulnerability, the naked hurt no fog of rage can conceal, that makes him com-pelling to me.

Unlike some other rappers, Eminem tempers his boasts with un-macho revela-tions. Women cheat on him. His parents—disappearing gay father, pill-popping paranoiac mother—embarrass him. He feels insecure and, at times, just wants to give up. In *8 Mile*, the film's hero Rabbit wins the rap "battle" by belting out a litany of personal humiliations and badges of shame. This climax, it seems to me, marks a triumph of the confessional mode: everything his opponent might say about him, Rabbit says first. Likewise, on the soundtrack album, Eminem's best cuts ("Lose Yourself" and "Rabbit Run"—with its apparent Updike reference) are the ones that explore fear, loss of confidence, and writer's block.

30 Even the marketing for *8 Mile* emphasized Em's literariness. Here was a Hollywood film that lionized, with enormous posters on the sides of busses, a guy who scrawls poetry on the palm of his hand. And Mathers shoves those bloody hands deep into his own messed-up psyche, probing the raw nerves of cultural taboo. Like the great confessional poets (think Plath), Mathers delivers a barrage of personality, an explosion of ego that transcends mere egotism to become a study in character and Oedipal psychosis. Like Plath, he achieves his effects through a discordant combination of singsong rhythms with harrowing imagery, enormous technical ability joined to searing indignation.

For Marshall—the bullied, reticent little dopehead forever on the brink of thirteen—life is endless Junior High, a red haze of sexual jealousy and identity-panic. Misogyny and homophobia are the weapons teen boys use to police one another as they learn the masquerade of masculinity, and nothing smacks more vividly of that teen spirit than Eminem's rap daymares. He captures the cacophonous inner life of boys with great lucidity. "I could be one of your kids," he threatens, and he is right. His own arrested development is what enables his insights. Eminem is Peter Pan gone very wrong.

Boy George has gone on record to suggest that Mathers' homophobia is a cover, and that the MC is really gay. Quel shocker. For what it's worth, Mathers offers the same confession several times on *Show* ("I'm out the closet, I've been lyin' my ass off, / All this time me and Dre been fuckin' with hats off"), but this claim is just as "true" as every other in the rapper's repertoire. It's simply another verbal performance, without honest "intent" and never truly "meant." Identity is a game, and like Madonna or Michael Stipe, Mather enjoys playing it in our faces.

Still, some wonder why Mathers cannot flex his poetic muscles without also spewing hate. Why doesn't he keep the phat beats, the hooks, the cleverness, but jettison the verbal violence? Is it really true that hate is sexy, that hate sells? Aren't re-mixed, clean-up versions of his songs just as infectious, and far less scary?

Purists will celebrate the power of the unabridged texts, however, and might even argue that rhymes and hard consonants are particularly suited to the expulsion of bile. Perhaps it's a simple fact of language, and performance, that rage rocks.

35 That's why, ultimately, I think the merit of Eminem's work should be measured not against Bloom's genius template, but rather according the standards of "transgressive literature." In crossing social boundaries and rupturing liberal niceties, in his relentless quest to piss people off (God's alleged mission for him), Mathers belongs to a tradition that Bloom holds less dear, to a line of "geniuses" whose work has always occupied the uneasy border between subversion and hatred, and whose imaginative freedom has always needed protection.

Eminem's work seems to function partly as an antidote to itself. As an outlet, a preventative measure—a sort of homeopathic remedy. Mathers demystifies hate speech through exaggeration, through the blatant silliness of his trouble-making. Indeed, what many kids seem to intuit, what my own son understands without being told, is that Eminem's attitudes are the ones right-thinking people are supposed to reject.

Even under the seductive force of Mathers' misdirected anger, kids can still get the joke. And they get it because of, not despite, the work's most disturbing elements.

Parents—if they are willing to listen to this music *with* their children—might consider Eminem immersion as a form of inoculation. As the kids in the driveway taught me, Mathers' ideas are virulent antigens that children will ingest whether they are shielded or not. Like us, they need to develop immunities in order to reject hatred in their world, even as they get a twisted kick from it in their art. It may not be quite the same twisted kick they got out of *Garbage Delight* or *Alligator Pie,* but ultimately, it might be more **instructive.**

QUESTIONS FOR DISCUSSION

1. In what sense are Marshall Mathers/Eminem's lyrics a form of bonding for Cochrane and his son as well as a possible "moral abdication" for Cochrane?
2. What is disturbing about the ability of the boys and girls to finish the Eminem song they hear on Cochrane's car radio "in its unexpurgated version"? What comment does this make on the effectiveness of music censorship?
3. From his perspective as a college literature/creative writing teacher, what does Cochrane see as valuable about Eminem's work? What examples does Cochrane provide of the poetic talents of the rapper? Are you persuaded by Cochrane's point of view?
4. Why and how does Mathers have greater impact on literary culture than more academically respectable, traditionally "literate" poets such as Anne Carson? How does his frame of reference or source of allusions disqualify him from being considered a "genius" by critics such as Harold Bloom? Why does Cochrane consider Mathers akin to "confessional" poets such as Sylvia Plath and consider him an author of "transgressive literature"?
5. In what ways is Cochrane's essay exploring "hate speech and its connection to the self-conscious art of satire"? How is it that Mathers "demystifies hate speech through exaggeration"? Do you consider his use of hate speech to be appropriate in popular culture?
6. How does Cochrane use the concept of "inoculation" to describe Eminem's influence on children and the way parents can cope with this influence? How are Eminem's lyrics and thoughts like "virulent antigens"? Against what do they inoculate children?

CONNECTION

Compare Cochrane's discussions with his son and students about rock and rap to Kevin Canty's involvement with rock 'n' roll (see page 369). What is suggested by these two men's ties to pop music, despite their positions as parents, authors, and college creative writing teachers?

IDEAS FOR WRITING

IDEAS FOR WRITING

1. Write an essay in which you compare some of Eminem's "confessional" lyrics to those of poets from more traditional poetic backgrounds, such as Sylvia Plath. Do Eminem's "confessions" seem more "moving," sincere, and authentic than those of the traditional poets, or less? You might also compare his songs to those of "confessional" pop singers.

2. Write an essay in which you respond to Cochrane's comments on Mathers's songs as "virulent antigens." Do you agree that such songs help children understand and deal with the hate in our language and in society, or do they teach youngsters to hold hateful attitudes?

RELEVANT WEB SITES

Eminem World
www.eminemworld.com
This online site, part of the Rap Basement Hip Hop Network, features a biography, news, lyrics, reviews, and articles about Eminem.

Eminem versus Robert Frost
www.salon.com/books/feature/2004/03/18/poetry/
This article from the on line journal *Salon* discusses new directions in spoken word poetry and song including slam poetry, rap and hip hop, and Eminem.

Anne Ritchie

Creativity, Drugs, and Rock 'n' Roll

Anne Ritchie, a native Californian, wrote this research paper for her first-semester Writing and Rhetoric course at Stanford University in a section that focused on social and rhetorical issues in rock 'n' roll music. She is contemplating a career in journalism. Because of her love for the rock music of the 1960s and 1970s, she was interested in investigating the mythical correlation between drugs and rock 'n' roll.

We all know the scene: the show is over, the audience has left, the band has packed up the instruments, and back at the hotel, the musicians are celebrating another successful performance. On goes the music, in come the girls, and out come the drugs: cocaine, heroin, methamphetamines, LSD, marijuana, and, of course, alcohol. A common societal image of a rock star is that of a young performer addicted to drugs and sex, living the glorified lifestyle of a musician-celebrity. Through movies like Cameron Crowe's *Almost Famous,* the media illustrate the strong interdependence of sex, drugs, and rock 'n' roll. The recording industry bombards listeners with songs about smoking joints; "driving that train, high on cocaine" (Grateful Dead); and, for rap enthusiasts, "keepin' it real, packin' steel, gettin' high/Cause life's a bitch and then you die" (Nas). To the casual fan, drugs appear to be everywhere in pop music.

What, then, is the basis for this alleged necessary connection between drugs and rock 'n' roll? As social and political activist Abbie Hoffman put it, "[I]f you don't have sex and you don't do drugs, your rock 'n' roll better be awfully good" (qtd. in Driver xiii). Is this really the "truth" that drives the music industry? Do musicians need drugs to be successful? Many musicians and fans believe that drug use positively affects musical ability and creativity. As technological innovations allowed for the creation of more and more advanced drugs in the twentieth century, rock music evolved correspondingly, lending slight credence to this idea. However, despite the myths that link rock music and illegal drugs, musicians use drugs primarily for social reasons, and often find that drugs adversely affect their musical creativity. Thus, drugs are by no means necessary for a group's success, and can even have a detrimental effect on a single member of a band or the entire group.

A historical reason for the mythical connection between popular music and drugs lies with the advent of patent medicines in pre–World War I America. Patent medicines were tonics and elixirs containing opium, morphine, heroin, and cocaine, sold to cure any and all of the ills that plagued the general public (Shapiro 9). However, simple word-of-mouth popularity was not a good enough advertisement for the cure-alls, and so "medicine shows" were born (12). Designed to bring attention to the tonics, in the medicine shows, a salesman enthusiastically described the products' attributes while men who referred to themselves as doctors reassured the crowd that the "medicines" were safe and effective. A group of traveling entertainers, which included musicians, lured people to the shows and helped to build excitement for the products. As Harry Shapiro, author of *Waiting for the Man: The Story of Drugs and Popular Music*, observes, "[M]usic played an important part in the medicine show, which enabled those struggling to earn a living as musicians to find regular work and gave them a chance to travel" (14). In fact, most of the best blues musicians of the time worked in the medicine shows at one point or another, including "the King of Rock 'n' Roll, Little Richard" (16). These shows were the first significant events to connect music and drugs in the United States, to the extent that the traveling musicians were exposed to and often paid in drugs.

Traveling medicine shows ended with the Harrison Narcotics Act of 1914, which required the registration of all doctors, pharmacists, and vendors involved in drug transactions. Marijuana then became the drug of choice for musicians, as U.S. Treasury agents often used the new legislation to arrest anyone engaged in any way with the narcotic tonics. Thus, drug transactions through medicine shows came to an end, and musicians changed their focus to marijuana (Shapiro 17). With Prohibition in full swing, alcohol was only available illegally; three-quarters of all jazz clubs were Mob controlled during the 1920s (30). This connection with the underworld not only provided musicians with bootlegged alcohol, but also aligned them with a man named Milton "Mezz" Mezzerow, an instrumental figure in combining marijuana with jazz. Mezzerow was a central figure in a group of "marijuana musicians" who believed that marijuana smoking was crucial to producing good music. Although, as Shapiro explains, "it was widely felt among the jazz community that marijuana helped the creation of jazz by removing inhibitions and providing stimulation and confidence," not all musicians felt that way (32). Many musicians resented being associated with drugs; they shared clarinet player Artie Shaw's view that "during the twenties and thirties, a lot of good jazz went down in spite of marijuana rather than because of it" (qtd. in Shapiro 33). In the 1930s, the *Chicago Tribune* reported that marijuana addiction was "common among local musicians," marking the first time that concern was expressed regarding the intimate relationship between musicians and marijuana (qtd. in Shapiro 47). Furthermore, this connection to drugs gave birth to the idea of musicians as outlaw figures, rebelling against the norm. Since then, the media have played a large part in persuading the public about the link between musicians and drugs.

5   Music began to change dramatically in the 1950s, as did the drugs with which it was associated. Jazz musicians moved on from marijuana and became involved with heroin, which had become more accessible since its limited availability during World War II (Shapiro 64). Musicians took heroin and other drugs socially in order to become closer to other members of the band. One jazzman of the time noted that "it became such a habit with so many [musicians] that it was almost expected for any new man in the band to show his sense of brotherhood by sticking that needle into his arm, just like his buddies would" (qtd. in Shapiro 70). Many were taking heavier drugs because everyone else was, not because they made them any better at playing music. Once the heroin cycle began, musicians often would not be able to play gigs without the drug because their tolerance was so high that what they were once able to play sober now required the help of the illicit substance (67). Musical talent did not markedly improve with heroin usage, and the belief that jazz genius Charlie "Bird" Parker's heroin addiction somehow made heroin essential to jazz genius is illogical, because the correlation between one man's genius and his drug habit does not imply causation (78). Even though heroin did not contribute to the creation of music, the musician lifestyle, with its insecurities, temporary fame, high expectations, and constant, fatigue-inducing travel, led to the need for the drug and continues to support the illegal use of drugs today (Collins 19).

The social and political atmosphere of the 1950s deepened the role of rock music as a form of rebellion against the establishment. Elvis Presley's pelvis thrusting was controversial enough for the new genre, which developed out of a white appreciation for black rhythm and blues music. According to John Orman, professor of politics at Fairfield University in Connecticut and author of *The Politics of Rock Music*, the controversy of rock was compounded by the introduction of many new types of drugs to the United States' pop culture (3). The Central Intelligence Agency developed LSD in this time period, and the U.S. Army's mass distribution of performance-enhancing amphetamines to its troops spread their influence to the populace throughout the 1950s and 1960s (102). Elvis himself was exposed to amphetamines for the first time while on guard duty in the Army as a means to stay awake (104). Once the drugs had reached the general population through their introduction in the military, musicians promoted the substances through their lyrics, interviews, and onstage behavior. In the 1960s the drug lifestyle was popularized by a new set of rock songs and stars, from Eric Clapton's "Cocaine" to Rolling Stones guitarist Keith Richard's open discussions of his heroin addiction (57). Additionally, the psychedelic music genre acted as an advertisement for psychedelic drugs, and still does to this day (58). Pink Floyd's album *Dark Side of the Moon* can be found on Amazon.com under the subheading "Music Best Heard Under the Influence of Psychedelic Drugs" (Malone). The proliferation of songs about drugs and rock stars' lifestyles firmly cemented the connection between rock 'n' roll music and drugs.

The question of whether or not these drugs, from marijuana to cocaine to heroin to LSD to amphetamines, were necessary for the creation of good music and the success of bands can be answered in part by a case study of the Rolling Stones. The Rolling Stones established themselves as rock stars in 1965 with the release of "(I Can't Get No) Satisfaction," which, according to John Orman, is "perhaps the best rock song ever recorded" (91). They are also considered to have one of the worst reputations for on-the-road antics and drug abuse (Shapiro 216). The Rolling Stones not only are extremely successful, but also have a long history of drug use and abuse. The drug abuse, however, did not create the success.

Richards's addiction to heroin is so well known that he has become an iconic figure in association with the drug. In an interview with Jann Wenner for *Rolling Stone* magazine in 1995, Stones front man Mick Jagger discussed his bandmate's addiction: "Anyone taking heroin is thinking about taking heroin more than they're thinking about anything else. That's the general rule about most drugs. If you're really on some heavily addictive drug, you think about the drug and everything else is secondary" (qtd. in Wenner). Richards's focus was on his drug use, not on his music. Additionally, when asked about how Richards's heroin use affected the band, Jagger responded, "I think that people taking drugs occasionally are great. I think there's nothing wrong with it. But if you do it the whole time, you don't produce as good things as you could. It sounds like a puritanical statement, but it's based on experience . . . when Keith was taking heroin, it was very difficult to work. He was still creative, but it took a long time" (qtd. in Wenner). Clearly, Jagger thinks that drug use has a hindering effect on a band's ability to produce music. Although they may not completely destroy creativity, drugs slow the creation process. Jagger's authority on the subject of drugs is undeniable; as he himself puts it, "[I]t's based on experience" (qtd. in Wenner).

Many would disagree with Jagger's critical comments regarding drug use and creativity. In 1969, the Valentines were the first band to get arrested for possession of marijuana in Australia. In their defense, their lawyer, William Lennon, claimed that "under the influence of marijuana they became more perceptive to musical sounds . . . they could distinguish more clearly various instruments and how they were being played" (qtd. in Walker 154). When analyzing this idea, though, the context of the situation becomes extremely important. Who wouldn't say that drug use augmented their creativity when faced with jail time? Lennon's reasoning is obviously suspect. Often, drugs are thought to help capture the essence of the music, and, as Australian rock critic

Clinton Walker believes, "the music sounds like its drug of choice. Psychedelia— acid rock—sounds like, well, acid. Australian pub music sounds like beer. . . . Reggae sounds like da 'erb. Disco was the sound of amyl nitrate, or 'poppers.' Punk sounds like speed, as did the first wave of fifties rock 'n' roll and early 'beat' music" (154). This, however, is not necessarily a positive attribute for popularity and success. Many of the Grateful Dead's psychedelic rock songs are considered impossible to listen to unless one is in an altered state of consciousness (Shapiro 142). Thus, much of the population who does not approve of or does not partake of drugs, but still enjoys rock music, may feel alienated from the group's music. As a result, an extreme focus on drugs can be detrimental to a band's success. Fewer fans are attracted, and those who are interested may be involved with drugs themselves.

10   In the 1960s, some groups were able to enjoy mainstream musical success despite extensive drug use and drug references in their songs. In terms of success, the Beatles are incomparable. Often thought of as "opinion leaders" in the late 1960s, the Beatles were responsible for establishing much of what is known as "rock culture" (Orman 106). As the leaders of their generation of musicians, the Beatles' interactions with drugs reflect the general drug trend of the 1960s. Many of their songs contain drug references, including "Lucy in the Sky with Diamonds," which refers in the initials of its title to LSD, and "Day Tripper," which, according to Beatle member Paul McCartney, also is about acid. The image created by these songs, in conjunction with the Beatles' trip to India and their appreciation of marijuana and hashish, paints a drug-heavy picture. However, despite the prominence of drugs in the group's music, McCartney recently told the London *Daily Mirror* that although drugs did influence some of their songs, "[I]t's easy to overestimate the influence of drugs on the Beatles' music. Just about everyone was doing drugs in one form or another and we were no different, but the writing was too important for us to mess it up by getting off our heads all the time" ("McCartney"). In this interview, McCartney admits that using drugs is detrimental to creativity ("the writing"); thus, he is in agreement with Jagger of the Stones that too much drug use is detrimental to a group's production of original music. Rather than enhancing creativity, as drugs are thought to do, they most often impede it.

A discussion of individual bands' and groups' opinions regarding the effects of drug use on creativity, originality, and overall success (as more creative bands generally are more popular and successful) can help to demonstrate that drugs are not necessary for musical success. Even more effective, and quite graphic in illustrating the detrimental effects of drug use, is this list of names: Jimi Hendrix, Brian Jones, Janis Joplin, Jim Morrison, Elvis Presley, Sid Vicious, Hank Williams, Kurt Cobain, Brad Nowell (Driver ix). These musicians, and countless others, died from drug overdoses or drug-related incidents. Many of the deaths are still surrounded by mystery, like Morrison's sudden death in the bath of his Paris hotel and, of course, that of Presley, who, according to certain conspiracy theorists, still lives (Driver 592). More recently, in November 2004, rapper Ol' Dirty Bastard (O.D.B.) died from an overdose of cocaine mixed with the painkiller Tramadol. As a member of the Wu-Tang Clan rap group,

O.D.B. had been working on a solo album at the time of his death and was creating a reality TV show, *Stuck on Dirty*, which is yet to be released on television (Devenish). These youthful performers would have had great potential had they lived. Each overdose contributed to a great loss in musical innovation.

A 1995 poll conducted for the Massachusetts Mutual Life Insurance Company found "the sixties drug mentality to be the most negative societal development of the past forty years" (Bozell 28). Even worse than the hindering of creativity that drug use causes is overdosing. The risk of overdose is there with every hit, every injection, and every swallowed pill. Even doing drugs once can kill. Assuming that narcotics do not kill the musicians, the negative effects of the chemicals can be detrimental to their creative ability and overall health.

The threats to musicians' well-being caused by substance abuse are evidenced by the recent change of heart in music industry executives, who now are looking to get their performers off of drugs. The leaders of Capitol, MCA, Virgin, and Revolution record labels have agreed to supervise an industry antidrug program. The president of the National Academy of Recording Arts and Sciences, Michael Greene, has said that "anyone who profits off an artist has the obligation to stop whatever was going on—touring, recording—and put that individual into treatment" (qtd. in Bozell 28). Additionally, Sony Music Entertainment and Dreamworks Records have given their support to Road Recovery, a nonprofit organization comprised of music industry professionals who seek to share a substance-free message with the youth of the United States. Gene Bowen, Road Recovery's founder, is a former tour manager who once was responsible for supplying his bands with drugs. After realizing the dangers of substance abuse, Bowen switched his focus to Road Recovery in order to educate musicians as well as other young adults about addiction, and to publicize treatment options for addicts in the industry ("Who We Are"). MusiCares Foundation, established in 1989, is a group devoted to providing musicians with all kinds of support, from drug treatment to psychological therapy ("MusiCares"). When the industry executives, whose jobs require that they focus on the monetary success of their bands, begin to focus on treatment programs for their musicians, the evidence is clear: using drugs not only does not enhance musical creativity and overall band success; in contrast, it can be extremely detrimental to a band, and in extreme cases can effectively end a group or a musician's career.

Despite the obvious health risks of drug use, many people still believe that music is better with drugs as part of the package. Nick Cave, an Australian singer, produced several albums while in the throes of drug addiction. According to Australian rock critic Clinton Walker, "These albums have a special magic, an all-consuming ambience, that is sadly, it seems, in part a result of the drugs in which they were pickled" (154). Drugs affected the music created under their influence. While this can be good, as it is in some of Cave's work, it does not mean that it is the best. Cave finally reached his potential once he checked into rehab in 1988 and cleaned himself up. As Walker describes it, "[A]t the same time, Cave has confounded the stereotypes, since his early 'clean' albums such as *The Good Son* of 1990 and *Let Love In* of 1994 are perhaps his pinnacle" (154). Cave could only reach his peak once he had removed drugs from the creative process.

15   In conclusion, musical creativity is not dependent on drug use. Although the history of drugs is intertwined with the history of rock music, the connection is mainly a social one. The music industry is one of the only realms of American society in which drug use is condoned, expected, and even encouraged. While the legal system has sentenced musicians to jail time for drug violations, socially, it still is acceptable for musicians to use, abuse, and become addicted to drugs, and the legal repercussions are outweighed by the reputation gained by brushes with the law. According to Shapiro, "[D]rugs . . . have always been part of the social grease of the industry" (203). Although they may be socially acceptable, the myth that drugs enhance musical ability, creativity, and overall group success is simply untrue. True genius lies in the musician, and cannot be found in any drug.

WORKS CITED

Bozell, L. Brent III. "When Rock 'n' Roll Finally Says 'No.'" *Insight on the News* 29 Jul. 1996. 7 Mar. 2005 <http://www.findarticles.com/p/articles/mi_m1571/is_n28_v12/ai_18524894>.

Collins, Tim. "Everybody Must Not Get Stoned." *New York Times* 20 Jul. 1996, late ed.: 19.

Devenish, Colin. "ODB Died of Drug Overdose." *Rolling Stone* 14 Dec. 2004. 18 Apr. 2005 <http://www.rollingstone.com/news/story/_/id/6769257>.

Driver, Jim. *The Mammoth Book of Sex, Drugs & Rock 'n' Roll.* New York: Carroll & Graf, 2001.

Grateful Dead. "Casey Jones." *Steal Your Face* 1976. *LyricsXP.* 28 Feb. 2005 <http://www.lyricsxp.com/lyrics/c/casey_jones_grateful_dead.html>.

Malone, Jo Jo. "Music Best Heard Under the Influence of Psychedelic Drugs." *Amazon.com* Apr. 2005. 15 Apr. 2005 <http://www.amazon.com>.

"McCartney: Of Course Those Songs Were About Drugs." *Washington Post* 3 Jun. 2004. 22 Feb. 2005 <http://www.washingtonpost.com/wp-dyn/articles/A11258-2004Jun2.html>.

"MusiCares Foundation: Programs and Services." *Grammy* 2005. 18 Apr. 2005 <http://www.grammy.com/musicares/programs_services.aspx>.

Nas (Nasir Jones). "Life's a Bitch." *Illmatic* 1994. *LyricsXP* 4 May 2005 <http://www.lyricsxp.com/lyrics/l/life_s_a_bitch_nas.html>.

Orman, John. *The Politics of Rock Music.* Chicago: Nelson-Hall, 1984.

Shapiro, Harry. *Waiting for the Man: The Story of Drugs and Popular Music.* New York: William Morrow, 1988.

Walker, Clinton. "Codependent: A Potted History of Drugs and Australian Music." *Meanjin* 61.2 (2002). 7 Mar. 2005 <http://www.findarticles.com/p/articles/mi_hb200/is_200206/ai_n5785729>.

Wenner, Jann. "Jagger Remembers." *Rolling Stone* 14 April 1995. 7 Mar. 2005 <http://www.rollingstone.com/news/story/_/id/5938037>.

"Who We Are." *Road Recovery Foundation* 2005. 18 Apr. 2005 <http://www.roadrecovery.com>.

QUESTIONS FOR DISCUSSION

1. What is the main point or thesis of Anne Ritchie's essay on rock musicians and drug use? Do you think she is successful at making her main point and refuting possible counterarguments on the subject? Why or why not?

2. To what audience does this essay seem to be directed? If the article were being sent around to periodicals for publication, what kind of publication would be most likely to accept it? Give examples to support your position.

3. How effectively does Ritchie make use of source materials to support her argument? Do the sources she relies upon seem to you relevant and credible? Why or why not?
4. Ritchie uses a broad definition of "drugs" in her introduction. Do you agree that substances like marijuana, LSD, alcohol, heroin, and cocaine should all be placed in the same general category of substances? How might drawing distinctions between these substances and their effects have changed the focus or direction of her paper?
5. Although Ritchie's paper deals with the impact of drugs on musicians, very little emphasis is placed on the influence of the music on fans' patterns of drug use. Do you think raising such issues would have helped the paper to communicate its antidrug message more forcefully? Why or why not?

TOPICS FOR RESEARCH AND WRITING

1. Many critics have commented that mass communications media often portray a biased or stereotyped image of minority groups, sometimes excluding certain groups altogether. After reading the poem by Louise Erdrich and the essay by Pratkanis and Aronson, and doing further research into the media coverage of one or more minority groups, write your conclusions in the form of a documented research essay.

2. After reading the essay by Pratkanis and Aronson and doing further research into media bias and selective reporting, write a research paper that discusses the media's coverage and influence on the outcome of a significant event in your community, city, or state.

3. After doing some outside reading and Internet research, write an essay that focuses on the ways that the Internet and the electronic environment have influenced modern life and perceptions of reality. Consider whether communication through the World Wide Web is more positive than negative or more negative than positive.

4. Examine the current television schedule (cable as well as network TV) for programs that you think encourage imagination, creativity, and a concern for the inner life; then read some media reviews of these programs in print media or the Internet. After considering the media critiques made by Bok and by Pratkanis and Aronson, write an evaluative review of several such programs, trying to draw some conclusions about the potential the television medium has for improving the quality of modern life, as well as the ways it often fails to achieve its potential.

5. Considering the ideas of writers such as Freedman, Bok, and others in this chapter, write a research paper that addresses the negative, positive, or ambiguous impact of a particular aspect of pop culture on the self-concept and mental health of citizens in our society. You might consider video games, popular music, children's TV programs, MTV, commercials, branding, or sex and violence in films or on television.

6. Write a research essay that discusses the way that images of roles and behavior for people in other societies are created and/or reinforced by American mass media broadcasts and by other various forms available abroad.

7. Write about a film that examines issues of advertising, propaganda, or mass media on society, politics, and the inner life of the individual. Watch the film and take notes on the dialogue and any other details that can be used to support the conclusions you draw; also read some critical responses to the film, both in popular journals and in specialized magazines that critique films. You might select a film from the following list: *Network, Broadcast News, The Kiss of the Spider Woman, Pulp Fiction, The Matrix, The Truman Show, Wag the Dog, Pleasantville, Mean Girls, Freaky Friday, 8 Mile, Lost in Translation,* and *Be Cool.*

9 Voyages in Spirituality

Margaret Bourke-White (1904–1971)
Mahatma Gandhi

Born in the Bronx, New York, Margaret Bourke-White was a photojournalist who worked for the *New York Times* and *Life* magazine chronicling the Depression era, World War II, and the struggle for independence in India. Her classic photograph of Gandhi poses him next to the *chakra* (spinning wheel), a symbol for Gandhi of both spirituality and self-sufficiency from British colonialism.

JOURNAL

Write about an individual who represents to you some important spiritual quality or power. What is the source of his or her power?

Holiness is a force, and like the others can be resisted. It was given, but I didn't want to see it, God or no God.

                                   ANNIE DILLARD

With this faith we will be able to hew out of the mountain of despair a stone of hope. With this faith we will be able to transform the jangling discords of our nation into a beautiful symphony of brotherhood.

                                   MARTIN LUTHER KING JR.

We were children of the universe. In the gas of dust and life, we are voyagers.

                                   LINDA HOGAN

CREATIVITY, PROBLEM SOLVING, AND SYNTHESIS

Creativity and spirituality have many similar qualities. Both involve a new way of seeing—going beyond the surface appearance of things to find deeper and more complex meanings. These new insights may include a combination of information and experience into a new synthesis that solves problems and/or produces something that a person can value and respect. In the case of writing, that new thing may be a poem, story, or nonfiction work that is humanely and aesthetically satisfying, both to you and to others. While many people are inspired by the examples of creative visionaries in different fields and can learn from studying their techniques, creativity is in large part a generative rather than an imitative and technical process, a process of discovery that often originates in the unconscious mind, sometimes without a clear goal or defined product in mind—at least at the beginning. An open, receptive mental attitude encourages the initiation of the creative process.

Everyone is potentially creative; in fact, all people are creative when they dream, whether or not they are consciously aware of the process. As author John Steinbeck noted, a problem is often "resolved in the morning after the committee of sleep has worked it out." In waking life people are creative in a more conscious, directed manner, seeking solutions to problems in order to survive and to make their lives more comfortable and rewarding. For example, when you redecorate your room, look for a better job, or select a new course of study in school, you are working on creative solutions for the problems that you have recognized in your life, just as you are when you write a proposal for your job or for one of your classes at school. You may see what you are doing at work or school as competing for a raise or completing a course requirement—but there is also an element of creativity in every new solution, and it is usually the creative ideas that get the most attention.

Although it is true that everyone exercises some degree of creativity, it is equally true that most people have the potential to be far more creative in many aspects of their lives than they are. Writers, psychologists, and social scientists have identified patterns of behavior that are likely to block an individual's creativity. Understanding how these mental traps work may help you find a way to release yourself from nonproductive behavior and to become more creative.

Habit Versus Risk

Habit and self-image can be major blocks to creativity. If your inner self-image is that of a person stuck in a round of repetitive daily tasks and rituals, it is unlikely that you will feel that you have the capacity to be creative. You may have come to believe that you really need to follow a ritualized pattern in performing your job, relating to people, or writing. This type of thinking also protects you from taking risks: the risk of an original expression of a feeling or situation, the risk of a controversial solution to a problem, the risk of not being understood by others.

Furthermore, creative risk-taking approaches to problem solving can be quite time-consuming. Many people convince themselves that they don't have the time to explore a new and creative approach, and that it is more efficient to follow a method that has worked (or sort of worked) in the past. This inclination to play it safe and to be overly concerned with time management is typical of workers, managers, students, teachers, and writers who fear change and are wary of embarking on a new direction in their lives. Even if you see yourself as a non-risk-taking person, it is never too late to change. Fantasizing about new approaches and thinking about alternatives are positive first steps toward finding creative solutions. Try to develop your alternative fantasies, as do many of the writers in this chapter.

Reason Versus Intuition

You may be building another obstacle to uncovering your creativity if you value a linear, rational approach to handling problems to the extent that you ignore the imaginative, emotional, and intuitive side of the mind and the solutions that your imagination might suggest. Did you know that many landmark solutions to creative problems, both in the arts and in the sciences, were born in the unconscious mind and some specifically in dreams? Some examples are Descartes' philosophical system, the invention of the sewing machine needle, and the pattern of the benzene ring, as well as the basic concepts for classic works of literature such as Mary Shelley's *Frankenstein*, Samuel Taylor Coleridge's "Kubla Khan," and Robert Louis Stevenson's *The Strange Case of Dr. Jekyll and Mr. Hyde*.

We do not want you to think that all you have to do is to take a nap and allow your problems to solve themselves, or that if you sleep long enough, you will discover the seeds of great art and great ideas. We do encourage you to look to your dream mind for ideas and feelings and to allow your unconscious mind to have time to process and integrate ideas that are being developed by your rational mind. For example, after you have finished the first draft of a paper, go for a walk or a swim, listen to some music, or take a nap. Let your unconscious mind have a chance to think about what you have written. When you return to your first draft, you may find that your unconscious mind has sent you new ideas to work with or that you have a solution to a problem in your paper that was frustrating you.

Developing Self-Confidence: Learning to Trust Your Own Processes

Another barrier to the creative process can come from trying too hard to please an authority such as a teacher or employer. If you focus your energy on trying to please your teacher at the expense of what you think or believe, an inner conflict may keep you from writing your paper altogether. If you become too reliant on your instructor's assignment and approval, you will not be developing your own working style and sense of independence, which every writer must possess. Finally, if you rush to produce a finished paper in one draft, you will miss the excitement of discovery, the potential for personal involvement that is an essential part of the writing process; it is always preferable to relax and work within a writing project rather than to become too concerned with what it is supposed to be.

Evaluation and Application

The creative problem-solving process does include evaluation and application—but only after you give free expression to a range of imaginative solutions and ideas. Once you have finished the creative or generative part of your writing project, you will want to think about whether or not you have accomplished your goals. To evaluate your work, you need to establish clear standards so that you can compare your work with that of others. Always try to formulate standards that are challenging and yet realistic.

Peer sharing can be a useful comparative and evaluative process that will help you to create realistic standards for assessing your own writing in relationship to that of your classmates. Through sharing your work as well as reading and editing the work of your classmates, you will begin to develop realistic standards for the style, structure, and content of your writing. Learn to ask questions of yourself and of your peers. Develop criteria for evaluating papers as you go along. Soon you will find that you have established a vocabulary that allows you to talk about one another's papers and that you have defined some standards for effective writing.

Synthesis

Synthesis, the final step in the creative process, involves bringing a number of different ideas or solutions, which you may have considered separately, together to form an integrated solution. For example, if you are trying to decide on a method for presenting an essay on "How to Make Your Dreams Work for You," you will need to evaluate and then synthesize or integrate the different points of view of experts—as well as your own—on the subject of dream power. Synthesis is an excellent metaphor for the gathering and unifying of information from diverse sources that can produce a lively research proposal. In a sense, synthesis also defines the writing process itself, as writing involves bringing together a number of different skills to solve a variety of problems: engaging your reader's interest, persuading your reader, developing an overall structure and pattern, supporting your main ideas, and using language that is both appropriate and creative. The student essay in this chapter by Karen Methot-Chun ("Living Spirituality") contains examples of synthesis writing in her development of a complex philosophical definition that mediates between ideas and quotations from different writers while also employing strategies of illustration and contrast to build and support her argument.

Writing is a rewarding activity that can help you discover your thoughts and feelings and combine them in new ways. In any type of writing, you work through the stages and difficulties inherent in the creative process as a whole.

THEMATIC INTRODUCTION: VOYAGES IN SPIRITUALITY

From ancient times to the present, people have discovered solutions to personal, aesthetic, social, and scientific problems through spiritual messages brought to them from their dreams, their intuitions, and the religious communities of which they are a part. The selections in this chapter reflect the spiritual experiences of people from different cultures, denominations, generations, and social classes. They present a range of issues and experiences, all of which speak about a unique quality of spirituality. While many people connect their spirituality to a particular religion, in this chapter we are presenting spirituality more broadly, as being capable of embracing all religions and including all people, even those who have spiritual experiences and vocations that exist outside of any ordinary religious context.

We open our chapter with Emily Dickinson's poem "# 501, This World Is Not Conclusion." Her questioning of traditional religious piety and her continued feeling of being drawn to the world of the spirit will help you to think about the reasons why people continue to struggle with spiritual questions in an age of reason and science. The two essays that follow are narratives of spiritual doubt and discovery. In Annie Dillard's "A Field of Silence," the author experiences a moment of intense spiritual illumination while living a life of solitude on an isolated farm, even though she admits to having difficulty with accepting or making sense of her experience. "In the Forests of Gombe" tells of Jane Goodall's mystical experience of the interconnectedness of scientific and spiritual knowledge after returning to the place in Africa that has been her home with the chimpanzees that she came to study and to love.

Our next three selections discuss ways that spiritual beliefs and social activism can be joined. In his powerful speech, "I Have a Dream," the minister and civil rights leader Martin Luther King Jr. develops a politically charged spiritual vision that uses both modern and biblical language to create a plea for a future free of racial injustice and exploitation. King's essay is followed by Jim Wallis's "Taking Back the Faith," in which Wallis, whose activist ministry is dedicated to helping the poor, discusses ways in which many modern denominations have strayed from their mission by focusing on political issues and moralism rather than on doing good works. In Noah Levine's "Death Is Not the End My Friend," a former addict and punk rocker describes his spiritual movement out of grief over the death of a close friend to a renewed dedication to service for incarcerated youth.

Our final professional essay, Linda Hogan's "The Voyagers," develops a metaphor of earth-centered spiritual voyaging in the Native American tradition in counterpoint to the Voyager spacecraft's journey into an unknown, far-flung universe.

Each of the two student essays that conclude this chapter captures a sense of the meaning and importance of spirituality. Norman Yeung Bik

Chung in "A Faithful Taoist" tells the story of how his father's Taoist faith helped his father to make important decisions about his health that allowed his family to better cope with his death. Our final student essay, Karen Methot-Chun's "Living Spirituality," defines active spirituality in daily life and discusses issues of morality and service.

We hope that the readings in this chapter will encourage you to think and reflect more deeply on the enduring qualities of spiritual life. While spirituality has an individual meaning for each person, we can strive to nourish our spiritual lives, both in the public world and in our inner worlds of dreams. Our visions will create the future.

Emily Dickinson

 # 501, This World Is Not Conclusion

Emily Dickinson (1830–1886) lived nearly her entire life in her parents' home in Amherst, Massachusetts. She wrote more than seventeen hundred poems, although only ten appeared in print during her lifetime. All of her other work was published after her death, and her complete poems appear in The Poems of Emily Dickinson, *edited by Thomas H. Johnson (1955). Dickinson's approach to poetry was radical in both form and content. Her work was more concentrated and emotionally powerful than most nineteenth-century poetry, and it has had a strong influence on modern writers with its highly compressed quality, ambiguousness of language, irregular verse forms, and expressive punctuation. Her critical stance on accepted nineteenth-century views of society, spirituality, nature, and love also anticipates modern poetry. In many of her poems, Dickinson comments on spiritual issues with questioning, irony, and mixed emotions.*

JOURNAL

Write about a time when you were confused about a matter of religious faith or belief. Was your confusion ever resolved?

This World is not Conclusion.
A Species stands beyond—
Invisible, as Music—
But positive, as Sound—
5 It beckons, and it baffles—
Philosophy—don't know—
And through a Riddle, at the last—

Sagacity, must go—
To guess it, puzzles scholars—
10 To gain it Men have borne
Contempt of Generations
And Crucifixion, shown—
Faith slips—and laughs, and rallies—
Blushes, if any see—
15 Plucks at a twig of Evidence—
And asks a Vane, the way—
Much Gesture, from the Pulpit—
Strong Hallelujahs roll—
Narcotics cannot still the Tooth
20 That nibbles at the soul—

QUESTIONS FOR WRITING

1. By making the first line of the poem a clear declarative statement, what initial sense of the narrator's religious faith is given?
2. According to the narrator, what qualities of the "Species" that "stands beyond" make it difficult to define or to hold a common belief about? How do these same qualities make it desirable or alluring?
3. Give one or more examples of the type of questions, riddle, or paradoxes offered by the concept of the world "beyond" and its "Species." Why do you think these questions are intriguing to so many, and why would people risk contempt and even martyrdom for them?
4. Starting on line 12, six verbs are used to describe religious faith. What overall commentary on faith do these verbs make?
5. Lines 15–16 seem to make a comment on organized religion. What is the connotation here of the words "Much Gesture" combined with the "Strong Hallelujahs" that "roll"? Does the narrator seem to take the revivalist church service seriously, to join in the praising, or to take a more critical stance?
6. Examine the metaphor of a toothache in the final lines. What is the source of the toothache, what are the "narcotics" the narrator refers to?

CONNECTION

Compare and contrast the value and conflict that Emily Dickinson and Annie Dillard find in religion and/or spirituality (see page 532).

IDEAS FOR WRITING

1. Develop your journal entry into a reflective essay about your religious confusion and its resolution or aftermath.
2. After looking at the interpretive questions above, state what you believe to be the poet's view of religious speculation, faith, and organized religion. Then write an essay in which you state whether you agree or disagree

with the poet's ideas on religion. Include reasons and examples to support your ideas.

RELATED WEB SITES

Emily Dickinson
`www.poets.org/academy/news/edick`
Visit this Web site on poets to learn about the life and work of author Emily Dickinson. Here you will also find relevant links on Dickinson, as well as links to the writers that she admired.

The Agnostic Church
`www.agnostic.org/httoc.htm`
This URL, entitled the "Agnostic Bible Table of Contents," shares information on agnosticism and agnostic viewpoints on many topics such as the bible, God's existence, Western civilization, and even family values.

Annie Dillard

A Field of Silence

Poet, essayist, and naturalist Annie Dillard (b. 1945) was raised in Pittsburgh, Pennsylvania. She received an M.A. in 1968 from Hollins College in Virginia. Dillard has worked as an editor and college teacher and has written many essays and books, including Pilgrim at Tinker Creek *(1974), for which she received a Pulitzer Prize;* An American Childhood *(1987);* The Writing Life *(1989);* The Living: A Novel *(1992);* Mornings like These: Found Poems *(1995); and* For the Time Being *(1999). In her essay "A Field of Silence" (1978), Dillard explores a powerful vision she once had on a remote farm and reflects on the difficulty she has in accepting and sharing this kind of experience in a world that values rationality and scientific progress.*

JOURNAL

Write about a time when you were alone in nature and felt you made an abrupt break from your familiar perception of reality and began to experience the world from a new perspective.

There is a place called "the farm" where I lived once, in a time that was very lonely. Fortunately I was unconscious of my loneliness then, and felt it only deeply, bewildered, in the half-bright way that a puppy feels pain.

I loved the place, and still do. It was an ordinary farm, a calf-raising, haymaking farm, and very beautiful. Its flat, messy pastures ran along one side of the central portion of a quarter-mile road in the central part of an island, an island in Puget Sound, so that from the high end of the road you could look west toward the Pacific, to the Sound and its hundred islands, and from the other end—and from the farm—you could see east to the water between you and the mainland, and beyond it the mainland's mountains slicked smooth with snow.

I liked the clutter about the place, the way everything blossomed or seeded or rusted; I liked the hundred half-finished projects, the smells, and the way the animals always broke loose. It is calming to herd animals. Often a regular rodeo breaks out—two people and a clever cow can kill a morning—but still, it is calming. You laugh for a while, exhausted, and silence is restored; the beasts are back in their pastures, the fences not fixed but disguised as if they were fixed, ensuring the animals' temporary resignation; and a great calm descends, a lack of urgency, a sense of having to invent something to do until the next time you must run and chase cattle.

The farm seemed eternal in the crude way the earth does—extending, that is, a very long time. The farm was as old as earth, always there, as old as the island, the Platonic form of "farm," of human society itself and at large, a piece of land eaten and replenished a billion summers, a piece of land worked on, lived on, grown over, plowed under, and stitched again and again, with fingers or with leaves, in and out and into human life's thin weave. I lived there once.

5   I lived there once and I have seen, from behind the barn, the long roadside pastures heaped with silence. Behind the rooster, suddenly, I saw the silence heaped on the fields like trays. That day the green hayfields supported silence evenly sown; the fields bent just so under the even pressure of silence, bearing it, even, palming it aloft: cleared fields, part of a land, a planet, they did not buckle beneath the heel of silence, nor split up scattered to bits, but instead lay secret, disguised as time and matter as though that were nothing, ordinary— disguised as fields like those which bear the silence only because they are spread, and the silence spreads over them, great in size.

I do not want, I think, ever to see such a sight again. That there is loneliness here I had granted, in the abstract—but not, I thought, inside the light of God's presence, inside his sanction, and signed by his name.

I lived alone in the farmhouse and rented; the owners, Angus and Lynn, in their twenties, lived in another building just over the yard. I had been reading and restless for two or three days. It was morning. I had just read at breakfast an Updike story, "Packed Dirt, Churchgoing, A Dying Cat, A Traded Car," which moved me. I heard our own farmyard rooster and two or three roosters across the street screeching. I quit the house, hoping at heart to see Lynn or Angus, but immediately to watch our rooster as he crowed.

It was Saturday morning late in the summer, in early September, clear-aired and still. I climbed the barnyard fence between the poultry and the pastures; I watched the red rooster, and the rooster, reptilian, kept one alert and alien eye on me. He pulled his extravagant neck to its maximum length, hauled himself high on his legs, stretched his beak as if he were gagging, screamed, and blinked. It was a ruckus. The din came from everywhere, and only the most rigorous application of reason could persuade me that it proceeded in its entirety from this lone and maniac bird.

After a pause, the roosters across the street would start, answering the proclamation, or cranking out another round, arrhythmically, interrupting. In the same way there is no pattern nor sense to the massed stridulations of cicadas; their skipped beats, enjambments, and failed alterations jangle your spirits, as though each of those thousand insects, each with identical feelings, were stubbornly deaf to the others, and loudly alone.

10   I shifted along the fence to see if Lynn or Angus was coming or going. To the rooster I said nothing, but only stared. And he stared at me: we were both careful to keep the wooden fence slat from our line of sight, so that this profiled eye and my two eyes could meet. From time to time I looked beyond the pastures to learn if anyone might be seen on the road.

When I was turned away in this manner, the silence gathered and struck me. It bashed me broadside from nowhere, as if I'd been hit by a plank. It dropped from the heavens above me like yard goods; ten acres of fallen, invisible sky choked the fields. The pastures on either side of the road turned green in a surrealistic fashion, monstrous, impeccable, as if they were holding their breath. The roosters stopped. All the things of the world—the fields and the fencing, the road, a parked orange truck—were stricken and self-conscious. A world pressed down on their surfaces, a world battered just within their surfaces, and that real world, so near to emerging, had got struck.

There was only silence. It was the silence of matter caught in the act and embarrassed. There were no cells moving, and yet there were cells. I could see the shape of the land, how it lay holding silence. Its poise and its stillness were unendurable, like the ring of the silence you hear in your skull when you're little and notice you're living, the ring which resumes later in life when you're sick.

There were flies buzzing over the dirt by the henhouse, moving in circles and buzzing, black dreams in chips off the one long dream, the dream of the regular world. But the silent fields were the real world, eternity's outpost in time, whose look I remembered but never like this, this God-blasted, paralyzed day. I felt myself tall and vertical, in a blue shirt, self-conscious, and wishing to die. I heard the flies again; I looked at the rooster who was frozen looking at me.

Then at last I heard whistling, human whistling far on the air, and I was not able to bear it. I looked around, heartbroken; only at the big yellow Charolais farm far up the road was there motion—a woman, I think, dressed in pink, and pushing a wheelbarrow easily over the grass. It must have been she who was whistling and heaping on top of the silence those hollow notes of song. But the slow sound of the music—the beautiful sound of the music ringing the air like a stone bell—was isolated and detached. The notes spread into the general air and became the weightier part of silence, silence's last straw. The distant woman and her wheelbarrow were flat and detached, like mechanized and pink-painted properties for a stage. I stood in pieces, afraid I was unable to move. Something had unhinged the world. The houses and roadsides and pastures were buckling under the silence. Then a Labrador, black, loped up the distant driveway, fluid and cartoonlike, toward the pink woman. I had to try to turn away. Holiness is a force, and like the others can be resisted. It was given, but I didn't want to see it, God or no God. It was as if God had said, "I am here, but not as you have known me. This is the look of silence, and of loneliness unendurable: it too has always been mine, and now will be yours." I was not ready for a life of sorrow, sorrow deriving from knowledge I could just as well stop at the gate.

15   I turned away, willful, and the whole show vanished. The realness of things disassembled. The whistling became ordinary, familiar; the air above the fields released its pressure and the fields lay hooded as before. I myself could act. Looking to the rooster I whistled to him myself, softly, and some hens appeared at the chicken house window, greeted the day, and fluttered down.

Several months later, walking past the farm on the way to a volleyball game, I remarked to a friend, by way of information, "There are angels in those fields." Angels! That silence so grave and so stricken, that choked and unbearable green! I have rarely been so surprised at something I've said. Angels! What are angels? I had never thought of angels, in any way at all.

From that time I began to think of angels. I considered that sights such as I had seen of the silence must have been shared by the people who said they saw angels. I began to review the thing I had seen that morning. My impression now of those fields is of thousands of spirits—spirits trapped, perhaps, by my refusal to call them more fully, or by the paralysis of my own spirit at that time—thousands of spirits, angels in fact, almost discernible to the eye, and whirling. If pressed I would say they were three or four feet from the ground. Only their motion was clear (clockwise, if you insist); that, and their beauty unspeakable.

There are angels in those fields, and I presume, in all fields, and everywhere else. I would go to the lions for this conviction, to witness this fact. What all this means about perception, or language, or angels, or my own sanity, I have no idea.

QUESTIONS FOR DISCUSSION

1. How does the loneliness Dillard experiences on the farm help to set the stage for her vision?
2. What causes Dillard's vision? Why does her vision end?
3. How does Dillard make the abstract notion of absolute silence concrete, vibrant, and alive? How do you respond to her image?
4. Why is the stillness unendurable? What similes does Dillard use to express her concept? Why does she try to turn away from her vision? Why is her vision one of sorrow?
5. Why does Dillard reverse an accepted assumption by referring to the regular world as a dream? What does she mean by "regular" and "dream" in the context of her essay?
6. After having time to reflect, Dillard decides, "There are angels in those fields." How do you imagine the angels? Why is it significant that Dillard, who is usually so precise and perceptive, has no idea about the meaning of

her vision and has difficulty talking about it? How do you interpret her vision of spirituality?

CONNECTION

Compare and contrast Annie Dillard's spiritual vision with that of Jane Goodall. What different values and conclusions does each come to based upon their experiences (see below)?

IDEAS FOR WRITING

1. Write a reflective essay on a vision or an intense moment of natural insight you have had. Why was it difficult for you to share this experience? Were you able to do so? In what form?
2. Write an essay in which you attempt to interpret Dillard's vision, based on what you know about her from reading this essay. What does Dillard's vision reveal about her personality, values, and response to the natural world?

RELATED WEB SITES

The Ecotheology Of Annie Dillard: A Study In Ambivalence
`www.crosscurrents.org/dillard.htm`
Go to the "Cross Currents" Web site from the Association for Religion and Intellectual Life, and read Pamela A. Smith's article "The Ecotheology of Annie Dillard: A Study in Ambivalence."

Annie Dillard: Getting A Feel For The Place
`www.meadville.edu/carley_2_1.html`
This article by Burton Carley from the *Journal of Liberal Religion* (Fall 2000) focuses on the importance of physical and spiritual place in Annie Dillard's writing.

Jane Goodall

In the Forests of Gombe

Jane Goodall was born in London, England, in 1934. Dr. Louis Leakey, a pale-ontologist and anthropologist, chose Goodall to begin a study of wild chimpanzees on the shore of Lake Tanganyika. In 1960 she observed a chimpanzee using and making tools to fish for termites, a discovery that challenged the view of humans as being the only toolmakers in the animal kingdom. Although Jane Goodall had no formal education, she was awarded a Ph.D. at Cambridge University. She is a spokesperson for the conservation of chimpanzee habitats and for the humane treatment of captive primates. Her most recent books include Great Apes and Humans: The Ethics of Coexistence *(2001) and* The Ten Trusts: What We

Must Do to Care for the Animals We Love *(2002). In the following selection from her memoir,* A Reason for Hope *(1999), Goodall writes about a mystical experience in the forest of Gombe that helped her to recover from the death of her husband and gave her life a new spiritual perspective.*

JOURNAL

Discuss a time that you spent in a forest, at the seashore, or in any natural setting. Did the time you spent in this natural setting rejuvenate your mind and spirit? How?

I was taught, as a scientist, to think logically and empirically, rather than intuitively or spiritually. When I was at Cambridge University in the early 1960s most of the scientists and science students working in the Department of Zoology, so far as I could tell, were agnostic or even atheist. Those who believed in a god kept it hidden from their peers.

Fortunately, by the time I got to Cambridge I was twenty-seven years old and my beliefs had already been molded so that I was not influenced by these opinions. I believed in the spiritual power that, as a Christian, I called God. But as I grew older and learned about different faiths I came to believe that there was, after all, but One God with different names: Allah, Tao, the Creator, and so our God, for me, was the Great Spirit in Whom "we live and move and have our being." There have been times during my life when this belief wavered, when I questioned—even denied—the existence of God. At such times I felt there can be no underlying meaning to the emergence of life on earth.

Still, for me those periods have been relatively rare, triggered by a variety of circumstances. One was when my second husband died of cancer. I was grieving, suffering, and angry. Angry at God, at fate—the unjustness of it all. For a time I rejected God, and the world seemed a bleak place.

It was in the forests of Gombe that I sought healing after Derek's death. Gradually during my visits, my bruised and battered spirit found solace. In the forest, death is not hidden—or only accidentally, by the fallen leaves. It is all around you all the time, a part of the endless cycle of life. Chimpanzees are born, they grow older, they get sick, and they die. And always there are the young ones to carry on the life of the species. Time spent in the forest, following and watching and simply being with the chimpanzees, has always sustained the inner core of my being. And it did not fail me then.

5   One day, among all the days, I remember most of all. It was May 1981 and I had finally made it to Gombe after a six-week tour in America—six weeks of fund-raising dinners, conferences, meetings, and lobbying for various chimpanzee issues. I was exhausted and longed for the peace of the forest. I wanted nothing more than to be with the chimpanzees, renewing my acquaintance with my old friends, getting my climbing legs back again, relishing the sights, sounds, and smells of the forest. I was glad to be away from Dar es Salaam, with all its sad associations—the house that Derek and I had shared, the palm trees

we had bought and planted together, the rooms we had lived in together, the Indian Ocean in which Derek, handicapped on land, had found freedom swimming among his beloved coral reefs.

Back in Gombe. It was early in the morning and I sat on the steps of my house by the lakeshore. It was very still. Suspended over the horizon, where the mountains of the Congo fringed Lake Tanganyika, was the last quarter of the waning moon and her path danced and sparkled toward me across the gently moving water. After enjoying a banana and a cup of coffee, I was off, climbing up the steep slopes behind my house.

In the faint light from the moon reflected by the dew-laden grass, it was not difficult to find my way up the mountain. It was quiet, utterly peaceful. Five minutes later I heard the rustlings of leaves overhead. I looked up and saw the branches moving against the lightening sky. The chimps had awakened. It was Fifi and her offspring, Freud, Frodo, and little Fanni. I followed when they moved off up the slope, Fanni riding on her mother's back like a diminutive jockey. Presently they climbed into a tall fig tree and began to feed. I heard the occasional soft thuds as skins and seeds of figs fell to the ground.

For several hours we moved leisurely from one food tree to the next, gradually climbing higher and higher. On an open grassy ridge the chimps climbed into a massive mbula tree, where Fifi, replete from the morning's feasting, made a large comfortable nest high above me. She dozed through a midday siesta, little Fanni asleep in her arms, Frodo and Freud playing nearby. I felt very much in tune with the chimpanzees, for I was spending time with them not to observe, but simply because I needed their company, undemanding and free of pity. From where I sat I could look out over the Kasakela Valley. Just below me to the west was the peak. From that same vantage point I had learned so much in the early days, sitting and watching while, gradually, the chimpanzees had lost their fear of the strange white ape who had invaded their world. I recaptured some of my long-ago feelings—the excitement of discovering, of seeing things unknown to Western eyes, and the serenity that had come from living, day after day, as a part of the natural world. A world that dwarfs yet somehow enhances human emotions.

As I reflected on these things I had been only partly conscious of the approach of a storm. Suddenly, I realized that it was no longer growling in the distance but was right above. The sky was dark, almost black, and the rain clouds had obliterated the higher peaks. With the growing darkness came the stillness, the hush, that so often precedes a tropical downpour. Only the rumbling of the thunder, moving closer and closer, broke this stillness; the thunder and the rustling movements of the chimpanzees. All at once came a blinding flash of lightning, followed, a split second later, by an incredibly loud clap of thunder that seemed almost to shake the solid rock before it rumbled on, bouncing from peak to peak. Then the dark and heavy clouds let loose such torrential rain that sky and earth seemed joined by moving water. I sat under a palm whose fronds, for a while, provided some shelter. Fifi sat hunched over, protecting her infant; Frodo pressed close against them in the nest; Freud sat with rounded back on a nearby branch. As the rain poured endlessly down, my palm fronds no longer provided shelter and I got wetter and wetter. I began to feel first chilly, and then, as a cold wind sprang up, freezing; soon, turned in on myself, I lost all track of time. I and the chimpanzees formed a unit of silent, patient, and uncomplaining endurance.

10   It must have been an hour or more before the rain began to ease as the heart of the storm swept away to the south. At four-thirty the chimps climbed down, and we moved off through the dripping vegetation, back down the mountainside. Presently we arrived on a grassy ridge overlooking the lake. I heard sounds of greeting as Fifi and her family joined Melissa and hers. They all climbed into a low tree to feed on fresh young leaves. I moved to a place where I could stand and watch as they enjoyed their last meal of the day. Down below, the lake was still dark and angry with white flecks where the waves broke, and rain clouds remained black in the south. To the north the sky was clear with only wisps of gray clouds still lingering. In the soft sunlight, the chimpanzees' black coats were shot with coppery brown, the branches on which they sat were wet and dark as ebony, the young leaves a pale but brilliant green. And behind was the backcloth of the indigo sky where lightning flickered and distant thunder growled and rumbled.

Lost in awe at the beauty around me, I must have slipped into a state of heightened awareness. It is hard—impossible, really—to put into words the moment of truth that suddenly came upon me then. It seemed to me, as I struggled afterward to recall the experience, that *self* was utterly absent: I and the chimpanzees, the earth and trees and air, seemed to merge, to become one with the spirit power of life itself. The air was filled with a feathered symphony, the evensong of birds. I heard new frequencies in their music and also in the singing insects' voices—notes so high and sweet I was amazed. Never had I been so intensely aware of the shape, the color of the individual leaves, the varied patterns of the veins that made each one unique. Scents were clear as well, easily identifiable: fermenting overripe fruit; waterlogged earth; cold, wet bark; the damp odor of chimpanzee hair and, yes, my own too. I sensed a new presence, then saw a bushbuck, quietly browsing upwind, his spiraled horns gleaming and chestnut coat dark with rain.

Suddenly a distant chorus of pant-hoots elicited a reply from Fifi. As though waking from some vivid dream I was back in the everyday world, cold, yet intensely alive. When the chimpanzees left, I stayed in that place—it seemed a most sacred place—scribbling some notes, trying to describe what, so briefly, I had experienced.

Eventually I wandered back along the forest trail and scrambled down behind my house to the beach. Later, as I sat by my little fire, cooking my dinner of beans, tomatoes, and an egg, I was still lost in the wonder of my experience. Yes, I thought, there are many windows through which we humans, searching for meaning, can look out into the world around us. There are those carved out by Western science, their panes polished by a succession of brilliant minds. Through them we can see ever farther, ever more clearly, into areas which until recently were beyond human knowledge. Through such a scientific window I had been taught to observe the chimpanzees. For more than twenty-five years I had sought, through careful recording and critical analysis, to piece together their complex social behavior, to understand the workings of their minds. And this had not only helped us to better understand their place in nature but also helped us to understand a little better some aspects of our own human behavior, our own place in the natural world.

Yet there are other windows through which we humans can look out into the world around us, windows through which the mystics and the holy men of the East, and the founders of the great world religions, have gazed as they searched for the meaning and purpose of our life on earth, not only in the wondrous beauty of the world, but also in its darkness and ugliness. And those Masters contemplated the truths that they saw, not with their minds only but with their hearts and souls also. From those revelations came the spiritual essence of the great scriptures, the holy books, and the most beautiful mystic poems and writings. That afternoon it had been as though an unseen hand had drawn back a curtain and, for the briefest moment, I had seen through such a window.

15   How sad that so many people seem to think that science and religion are mutually exclusive. Science has used modern technology and modern techniques to uncover so much about the formation and the development of life forms on Planet Earth and about the solar system of which our little world is but a minute part. Alas, all of these amazing discoveries have led to a belief that every wonder of the natural world and of the universe—indeed, of infinity and time—can, in the end, be understood through the logic and the reasoning of a finite mind. And so, for many, science has taken the place of religion. It was not some intangible God who created the universe, they argue; it was the big bang. Physics, chemistry, and evolutionary biology can explain the start of the universe and the appearance and progress of life on earth, they say. To believe in God, in the human soul, and in life after death is simply a desperate and foolish attempt to give meaning to our lives.

But not all scientists believe thus. There are quantum physicists who have concluded that the concept of God is not, after all, merely wishful thinking. There are those exploring the human brain who feel that no matter how much they discover about this extraordinary structure it will never add up to a complete understanding of the human mind—that the whole is, after all, greater than the sum of its parts. The big bang theory is yet another example of the incredible, the awe-inspiring ability of the human mind to learn about seemingly unknowable phenomena in the beginning of time. Time as we know it, or think we know it. But what about before time? And what about beyond space? I remember so well how those questions had driven me to distraction when I was a child.

I lay flat on my back and looked up into the darkening sky. I thought about the young man I had met during the six-week tour I had finished before my return to Gombe. He had a holiday job working as a bellhop in the big hotel where I was staying in Dallas, Texas. It was prom night, and I wandered down to watch the young girls in their beautiful evening gowns, their escorts elegant in their tuxedos. As I stood there, thinking about the future—theirs, mine, the world's—I heard a diffident voice:

"Excuse me, Doctor—aren't you Jane Goodall?" The bellhop was very young, very fresh-faced. But he looked worried—partly because he felt that he should not be disturbing me, but partly, it transpired, because his mind was indeed troubled. He had a question to ask me. So we went and sat on some back stairs, away from the glittering groups and hand-holding couples.

He had watched all my documentaries, read my books. He was fascinated, and he thought that what I did was great. But I talked about evolution. Did I believe in God? If so, how did that square with evolution? Had we really descended from chimpanzees?

20   And so I tried to answer him as truthfully as I could, to explain my own beliefs. I told him that no one thought humans had descended from chimpanzees. I explained that I did believe in Darwinian evolution and told him of my time at Olduvai, when I had held the remains of extinct creatures in my hands. That I had traced, in the museum, the various stages of the evolution of, say, a horse: from a rabbit-sized creature that gradually, over thousands of years, changed, became better and better adapted to its environment, and eventually was transformed into the modern horse. I told him I believed that millions of years ago there had been a primitive, apelike, humanlike creature, one branch of which had gone on to become the chimpanzee, another branch of which had eventually led to us.

"But that doesn't mean I don't believe in God," I said. And I told him something of my beliefs, and those of my family. I told him that I had always thought that the biblical description of God creating the world in seven days might well have been an attempt to explain evolution in a parable. In that case, each of the days would have been several million years.

"And then, perhaps, God saw that a living being had evolved that was suitable for His purpose. *Homo sapiens* had the brain, the mind, the potential. Perhaps," I said, "that was when God breathed the Spirit into the first Man and the first Woman and filled them with the Holy Ghost."

The bellhop was looking considerably less worried. "Yes, I see," he said. "That could be right. That does seem to make sense."

I ended by telling him that it honestly didn't matter how we humans got to be the way we are, whether evolution or special creation was responsible. What mattered and mattered desperately was our future development. How should the mind that can contemplate God relate to our fellow beings, the other life forms of the world? What is our human responsibility? And what, ultimately, is our human destiny? Were we going to go on destroying God's creation, fighting each other, hurting the other creatures of His planet? Or were we going to find ways to live in greater harmony with each other and with the natural world? That, I told him, was what was important. Not only for the future of the human species, but also for him, personally. When we finally parted his eyes were clear and untroubled, and he was smiling.

25   Thinking about that brief encounter, I smiled too, there on the beach at Gombe. A wind sprang up and it grew chilly. I left the bright stars and went inside to bed. I knew that while I would always grieve Derek's passing, I could cope with my grieving. That afternoon, in a flash of "outsight" I had known timelessness and quiet ecstasy, sensed a truth of which mainstream science is merely a small fraction. And I knew that the revelation would be with me for the rest of my life, imperfectly remembered yet always within. A source of strength on which I could draw when life seemed harsh or cruel or desperate. The forest, and the spiritual power that was so real in it, had given me the "peace that passeth understanding."

QUESTIONS FOR DISCUSSION

1. Why did Goodall return to the forest?
2. Goodall says that living in the natural world "dwarfs yet somehow enhances human emotions." Explain her assertion within the context of her experience in the forest.
3. What precipitates Goodall's mystical experience? Why and how is her sense of reality altered? When does her mystical experience end? What insights does Goodall take away from this moment?
4. Describe Goodall's writing style. Does her style help to engage you in her experiences and beliefs? Give examples of effective use of time and unusual shifts of perspective in the essay.
5. How and why does Goodall contrast her Eastern mystical experience to her Western scientific and analytical study of the complex social behaviors of chimpanzees? What conclusions does she make?
6. How does Goodall help the bellhop and her readers to understand how both scientific and religious thinking can help us to find meaning in life? Do you agree or disagree with Goodall's perspective? Explain.

CONNECTION

Compare and contrast Jane Goodall's views on the connection between the spiritual and scientific experiences of the world with those of Marcelo Gleiser (see page 203).

IDEAS FOR WRITING

1. After the rainstorm Goodall looks over a ridge to see the lake in a new way. Write a descriptive narrative about an experience in the natural world that seemed to you spiritual or mystical in some way, and explain why you felt this way about the event.

2. Write an analysis of Goodall's conversation with the young hotel employee about the space for both spiritual and scientific explanations of the world to coexist. Do you agree with her reasoning here? Why or why not?

RELATED WEB SITES

The Jane Goodall Institute
`www.janegoodall.org`
The mission of the Jane Goodall Institute is to advance the power of individuals to take informed and compassionate action to improve the environment. Find out more about the institute, Jane Goodall's life and work, and how to get involved at this Web site.

Gombe National Park, Tanzania
`http://weber.ucsd.edu/~jmoore/apesites/Gombe/Gombe.html`
Learn about Gombe National Park, where Jane Goodall began her research on chimpanzees, at this Web site from the University of California, San Diego. The site also features a link to UCSD's "African Ape Study Site."

Martin Luther King Jr.

I Have a Dream

Martin Luther King Jr. (1928–1968), who came from a family of ministers, graduated from Morehouse University and received a Ph.D. in theology from Boston University. After graduation, King became a pastor and founded the Southern Christian Leadership Conference, developing the concept, derived from the teachings of Henry David Thoreau and Mahatma Gandhi, that nonviolent civil disobedience is the best way to obtain civil rights and to end segregation. King won the Nobel Peace Prize in 1964. Although his life ended in a tragic assassination, King wrote many speeches and essays on race and civil rights, which are collected in books such as I Have a Dream: Writings and Speeches That Changed the World *(1992) and* The Papers of Martin Luther King, Jr. *(1992). "I Have a Dream," King's most famous speech, was originally delivered in 1963 in front of the Lincoln Memorial in Washington, D.C., before a crowd estimated at 300,000. Notice how King uses powerful language, images, and comparisons to move his massive, diverse audience and to express his idealistic dream for America's future.*

JOURNAL

Write about a time when you found yourself moved by a minister or persuasive public speaker, in a speech you either heard live or saw on television. What skills of rhetoric and/or delivery do you remember as contributing to your strong feelings in response to this speech? If you saw it on television, what elements of video editing and soundtrack (music, applause, etc.) contributed to your response?

I am happy to join with you today in what will go down in history as the greatest demonstration for freedom in the history of our nation.

Five score years ago, a great American, in whose symbolic shadow we stand today, signed the Emancipation Proclamation. This momentous decree came as a great beacon light of hope to millions of Negro slaves who had been seared in the flames of withering injustice. It came as a joyous daybreak to end the long night of their captivity.

But one hundred years later, the Negro still is not free; one hundred years later, the life of the Negro is still sadly crippled by the manacles of segregation and the chains of discrimination; one hundred years later, the Negro lives on a lonely island of poverty in the midst of a vast ocean of material prosperity; one hundred years later, the Negro is still languished in the corners of American society and finds himself in exile in his own land.

So we've come here today to dramatize a shameful condition. In a sense we've come to our nation's capital to cash a check. When the architects of our republic wrote the magnificent words of the Constitution and the Declaration of Independence, they were signing a promissory note to which every American was to fall heir. This note was the promise that all men, yes, black men as well as white men, would be guaranteed the unalienable rights of life, liberty, and the pursuit of happiness.

5   It is obvious today that America has defaulted on this promissory note in so far as her citizens of color are concerned. Instead of honoring this sacred obligation, America has given the Negro people a bad check, a check which has come back marked "insufficient funds." But we refuse to believe that the bank of justice is bankrupt. We refuse to believe that there are insufficient funds in the great vaults of opportunity of this nation. And so we've come to cash this check, a check that will give us upon demand the riches of freedom and the security of justice.

We have also come to this hallowed spot to remind America of the fierce urgency of now. This is no time to engage in the luxury of cooling off or to take the tranquilizing drug of gradualism. Now is the time to make real the promises of democracy; now is the time to rise from the dark and desolate valley of segregation to the sunlit path of racial justice; now is the time to lift our nation from the quicksands of racial injustice to the solid rock of brotherhood; now is the time to make justice a reality for all of God's children. It would be fatal for the nation to overlook the urgency of the moment. This sweltering summer of the Negro's legitimate discontent will not pass until there is an invigorating autumn of freedom and equality.

Nineteen sixty-three is not an end, but a beginning. And those who hope that the Negro needed to blow off steam and will now be content, will have a rude awakening if the nation returns to business as usual. There will be neither rest nor tranquility in America until the Negro is granted his citizenship rights. The whirlwinds of revolt will continue to shake the foundations of our nation until the bright day of justice emerges.

But there is something that I must say to my people, who stand on the worn threshold which leads into the palace of justice. In the process of gaining our rightful place, we must not be guilty of wrongful deeds. Let us not seek to satisfy our thirst for freedom by drinking from the cup of bitterness and hatred. We must forever conduct our struggle on the high plain of dignity and discipline. We must not allow our creative protests to degenerate into physical violence. Again and again we must rise to the majestic heights of meeting physical force with soul force. The marvelous new militancy, which has engulfed the Negro community, must not lead us to a distrust of all white people. For many of our white brothers, as evidenced by their presence here today, have come to realize that their destiny is tied up with our destiny. And they have come to realize that their freedom is inextricably bound to our freedom. We cannot walk alone. And as we walk, we must make the pledge that we shall always march ahead. We cannot turn back.

There are those who are asking the devotees of Civil Rights, "When will you be satisfied?" We can never be satisfied as long as the Negro is the victim of the unspeakable horrors of police brutality; we can never be satisfied as long as our bodies, heavy with the fatigue of travel, cannot gain lodging in the motels of the highways and the hotels of the cities; we cannot be satisfied as long as the Negro's basic mobility is from a smaller ghetto to a larger one; we can never be satisfied as long as our children are stripped of their selfhood and robbed of their dignity by signs stating "For Whites Only"; we cannot be satisfied as long as the Negro in Mississippi cannot vote and a Negro in New York believes he has nothing for which to vote. No! No, we are not satisfied, and we will not be satisfied until "justice rolls down like waters and righteousness like a mighty stream."

10   I am not unmindful that some of you have come here out of great trials and tribulations. Some of you have come fresh from narrow jail cells. Some of you have come from areas where your quest for freedom left you battered by the storms of persecution and staggered by the winds of police brutality. You have been the veterans of creative suffering. Continue to work with the faith that unearned suffering is redemptive. Go back to Mississippi. Go back to Alabama. Go back to South Carolina. Go back to Georgia. Go back to Louisiana. Go back to the slums and ghettos of our Northern cities, knowing that somehow this situation can and will be changed. Let us not wallow in the valley of despair.

I say to you today, my friends, so even though we face the difficulties of today and tomorrow, I still have a dream. It is a dream deeply rooted in the American dream. I have a dream that one day this nation will rise up and live out the true meaning of its creed, "We hold these truths to be self-evident, that all men are created equal." I have a dream that one day on the red hills of Georgia, sons of former slaves and the sons of former slaves owners will be able to sit down together at the table of brotherhood. I have a dream that one day even the state of Mississippi, a state sweltering with the heat of injustice, sweltering with the heat of oppression, will be transformed into an oasis of freedom and justice. I have a dream that my four little children will one day live in a nation where they will not be judged by the color of their skin, but by the content of their character.

I HAVE A DREAM TODAY!

I have a dream that one day down in Alabama—with its vicious racists, with its Governor having his lips dripping with the words of interposition and nullification—one day right there in Alabama, little black boys and black girls will be able to join hands with little white boys and white girls as sisters and brothers.

I HAVE A DREAM TODAY!

15   I have a dream today that one day every valley shall be exalted, and every hill and mountain shall be made low. The rough places will be plain and the crooked places will be made straight, "and the glory of the Lord shall be revealed, and all flesh shall see it together."

This is our hope. This is the faith that I go back to the South with. With this faith we will be able to hew out of the mountain of despair a stone of hope. With this faith we will be able to transform the jangling discords of our nation into a beautiful symphony of brotherhood. With this faith we will be able to work together, to pray together, to struggle together, to go to jail together, to stand up for freedom together, knowing that we will be free one day. And this will be the day. This will be the day when all of God's children will be able to sing with new meaning, "My country 'tis of thee, sweet land of liberty, of thee I sing. Land where my fathers died, land of the pilgrims' pride, from every mountainside, let freedom ring." And if America is to be a great nation, this must become true.

So let freedom ring from the prodigious hilltops of New Hampshire; let freedom ring from the mighty mountains of New York; let freedom ring from the heightening Alleghenies of Pennsylvania; let freedom ring from the snow-capped Rockies of Colorado; let freedom ring from the curvaceous slopes of California. But not only that. Let freedom ring from Stone Mountain of Georgia; let freedom ring from Lookout Mountain of Tennessee; let freedom ring from every hill and mole hill of Mississippi. "From every mountainside, let freedom ring." And when this happens, and when we allow freedom to ring, when we let it ring from every village and every hamlet, from every state and every city, we will be able to speed up that day when all of God's children, black men and white men, Jews and Gentiles, Protestants and Catholics, will be able to join hands and sing in the words of the old Negro spiritual: "Free at last. Free at last. Thank God Almighty, we are free at last."

QUESTIONS FOR DISCUSSION

1. What is the dream to which the title of the essay refers? What techniques or strategies does King use to define his dream? Is his definition effective? Why or why not? Explain.

2. What does King mean by his analogy of a "promissory note"? Is this an effective metaphor? Why?

3. Who is the primary audience of King's speech: the "we" to whom he refers in paragraph 4, or the "you" in paragraph 10? How does King try to appeal to the needs and concerns of this audience?

4. Who is the secondary audience for the speech, other than those to whom he refers as having "come to our nation's capital to cash a check"? What rhetorical strategies in the speech are designed to stretch its message beyond the immediate needs and expectations of the present audience and to appeal to other audiences, including those who might see the speech on television or hear it on radio?

5. What does King mean by "creative suffering" in paragraph 10? How does this expression reflect different aspects of his spiritual vision of nonviolent resistance?

6. How does King use repetition of images, phrases, and entire sentences to help convey his dream to his audience? Refer to specific examples in his speech.

CONNECTION

Compare King's plan to achieve racial freedom through creative suffering with the ideas of Jim Wallis on the proper function of the activist church in modern society (see page 548).

IDEAS FOR WRITING

1. Write a speech in the form of an essay and/or multimedia presentation that discusses a dream that you have for our society. Express your dream in emotional and persuasive language and imagery, including slides, audio clips, or other multimedia features, in order to appeal to a specific audience. Indicate your intended audience.

2. Based on your understanding and reading about the current state of civil rights in America, write an essay in which you reflect on whether King, if he were alive today, would feel that his dream for African Americans had come true. What aspects of his dream might King feel still remain to be accomplished?

RELATED WEB SITES

The Martin Luther King Jr. Papers Project
www.stanford.edu/group/King/
Created by The King Papers Project at Stanford University, this Web site offers a major research effort to assemble and disseminate historical information concerning Martin Luther King Jr. and the social movements in which he participated.

The King Center
www.thekingcenter.org
In these Web pages, you will find valuable resources and information about Dr. King and the ongoing efforts to fulfill his great dream of "the Beloved Community for America and the World."

Jim Wallis

Taking Back the Faith

Jim Wallis (b. 1948) was raised in a Midwestern evangelical family and spent his student years involved in the civil rights and antiwar movements. Wallis founded and continues to edit Sojourners *a magazine for Christian activists working for justice and peace. In 1995, Wallis was instrumental in forming the Call to Renewal, a national federation of faith-based organizations from across the theological and political spectrum working to overcome poverty. He teaches a course on faith and politics at Harvard University and frequently speaks at conferences and meetings around the country. Wallis writes for major newspapers and has written several books, including* Who Speaks for God? A New Politics of Compassion, Community, and Civility *(1996), and* Faith Works *(2000). The selection that follows is taken from* God's Politics: Why the Right Gets It Wrong and the Left Doesn't Get It *(2005).*

JOURNAL

Write about your ideas of the place of religious faith in the area of politics. Do you believe that politics and religion should be intertwined? Why or why not?

Many of us feel that our faith has been stolen, and it's time to take it back. In particular, an enormous public misrepresentation of Christianity has taken place. And because of an almost uniform media misperception, many people around the world now think Christian faith stands for political commitments that are almost the opposite of its true meaning. How did the faith of Jesus come to be known as pro-rich, pro-war, and pro-American? What has happened here? And how do we get back to a historic, biblical, and *genuinely* evangelical faith rescued from its contemporary distortions? That rescue operation is even more crucial today, in the face of a deepening social crisis that literally cries out for more prophetic religion.

Of course, nobody can steal your personal faith; that's between you and God. The problem is in the political arena, where strident voices claim to represent Christians, when they clearly don't speak for *most* of us. It's time to take back our faith in the public square, especially in a time when a more authentic social witness is desperately needed.

The religious and political Right gets the public meaning of religion mostly wrong—preferring to focus only on sexual and cultural issues while ignoring the weightier matters of justice. And the secular Left doesn't seem to get the meaning and promise of faith for politics at all—mistakenly dismissing spirituality as irrelevant to social change. I actually happen to be conservative on issues of personal responsibility, the sacredness of human life, the reality of evil in our world, and the critical importance of individual character, parenting, and strong "family values." But the popular presentations of religion in our time (especially in the media) almost completely ignore the biblical vision of social justice and, even worse, dismiss such concerns as merely "left-wing."

It is indeed time to take back our faith.

5   Take back our faith from whom? To be honest, the confusion comes from many sources. From religious right-wingers who claim to know God's political views on every issue, then ignore the subjects that God seems to care the most about. From pedophile priests and cover-up bishops who destroy lives and shame the church. From television preachers whose extravagant lifestyles and crass fund-raising tactics *embarrass* more Christians than they know. From liberal secularists who want to banish faith from public life, and deny spiritual values to the soul of politics. And even from liberal theologians whose cultural conformity and creedal modernity serve to erode the foundations of historic biblical faith. From New Age philosophers who want to make Jesus into a non-threatening spiritual guru. And from politicians who love to say how religious they are but utterly fail to apply the values of faith to their public leadership and political policies.

It's time to reassert and reclaim the gospel faith—especially in our public life. When we do, we discover that faith challenges the powers that be to do justice for the poor, instead of preaching a "prosperity gospel" and supporting politicians that further enrich the wealthy. We remember that faith hates violence and tries to reduce it, and exerts a fundamental presumption against war, instead of justifying it in God's name. We see that faith creates community from racial, class, and gender divisions, [that it] prefers international community over nationalist religion, and that "God bless America" is found nowhere in the Bible. And we are reminded that faith regards matters such as the sacredness of life and family bonds as so important that they should never be used as ideological symbols or mere political pawns in partisan warfare.

The media likes to say, "Oh, then you must be the religious left." No, not at all, and the very question is the problem. Just because a religious right has fashioned itself for political power in one utterly predictable ideological guise does not mean that those who question this political seduction must be their opposite political counterpart. The best public contribution of religion is precisely *not* to be ideological predictable nor a loyal partisan. To always raise the moral issues of human rights, for example, will challenge both left and right-wing governments who put power above principles. Religious action is rooted in a much deeper place than "rights"—that being the image of God in every human being.

Similarly, when the poor are defended on moral or religious grounds it is certainly not "class warfare," as the rich often charge, but rather a direct response to the overwhelming focus on the poor in the Scriptures which claims they are regularly neglected, exploited, and oppressed by wealthy elites, political rulers and indifferent affluent populations. Those Scriptures don't simply endorse the social programs of the liberals or the conservatives, but make clear that poverty is indeed a religious issue, and the failure of political leaders to help uplift the poor will be judged a moral failing.

It is precisely because religion takes the problem of evil so seriously that it must always be suspicious of too much concentrated power—politically *and* economically—either in totalitarian regimes or in huge multi-national corporations which now have more wealth and power than many governments. It is indeed our theology of evil that makes us strong proponents of both political and economic democracy—not because people are so good, but because they often are not, and need clear safeguards and strong systems of checks and balances to avoid the dangerous accumulations of power and wealth.

10   It's why we doubt the goodness of *all* superpowers and the righteousness of empires in any era, *especially* when their claims of inspiration and success invoke theology and the name of God. Given the human tendencies of military and political power for self-delusion and deception, is it any wonder that hardly a religious body in the world regards the ethics of unilateral and pre-emptive war as "just"? Religious wisdom suggests that the more overwhelming the military might, the more dangerous its capacity for self and public deception. If evil in this world is deeply human and very real, and religious people believe it is, it just doesn't make spiritual sense to suggest that the evil all lies "out there" with our adversaries and enemies, and none of it "in here" with us—imbedded in our own attitudes, behaviors, and policies. Powerful nations dangerously claim to "rid the world of evil," but often do enormous harm in their self-appointed vocation to do so.

The loss of religion's prophetic vocation is terribly dangerous for any society. Who will uphold the dignity of economic and political outcasts? Who will question the self-righteousness of nations and their leaders? Who will question the recourse to violence and rush to wars, long before any last resort has been unequivocally proven? Who will not allow God's name to be used to simply justify ourselves, instead of calling us to accountability? And who will love the people enough to challenge their worst habits, coarser entertainments, and selfish neglects?

Prophetic religion always presses the question of the common good. Indeed, the question, "Whatever became of the common good?" must be a constant religious refrain directed to political partisans whose relentless quest for power and wealth makes them forget the "commonwealth" again and again. That common good should always be constructed from the deepest wells of our personal *and* social responsibility and the absolute insistence to never separate the two.

I am always amazed at the debate around poverty, with one side citing the need for changes in personal behaviors and the other for better social programs, as if the two were mutually exclusive. Obviously, both personal and social responsibility are necessary for overcoming poverty. When this absurd bifurcation is offered by ideological partisans on either side, I am quickly convinced that both sides must never have lived or worked anywhere near poverty or poor people. That there are behaviors that further entrench and even cause poverty is undisputable, as is the undeniable power of systems and structures to institutionalize injustice and oppression. Together, personal and social responsibility create the common good. Because we know these realities as *religious* facts, taught to us by our sacred Scriptures, religious communities can teach them to those still searching more for blame than solutions to pressing social problems.

But recovering the faith of the biblical prophets and Jesus is not just about politics; it also shapes the way we live our personal and communal lives. How do we live a faith whose social manifestation is compassion, and whose public expression is justice? And how do we raise our children by those values? That may be the most important battle of spiritual formation in our times, as I am personally discovering as a new father. Our religious congregations are not meant to be social organizations that merely reflect the wider culture's values, but dynamic counter-cultural communities whose purpose is to reshape both lives and societies. That realization perhaps has the most capacity to transform both religion and politics.

15   We contend today with both religious and secular fundamentalists, neither of whom must have their way. One group would impose the doctrines of a political theocracy on their fellow citizens, while the other would deprive the public square of needed moral and spiritual values often shaped by faith. In a political and media culture that squeezes everything into only two options of left and right, religious people must refuse the ideological categorization and actually build bridges between people of good will in both liberal and conservative camps. We must insist on the deep connections between spirituality and politics, while defending the proper boundaries between church and state which protect religious and non-religious minorities, and keep us all safe from state-controlled religion. We can demonstrate our commitment to pluralistic democracy *and* support the rightful separation of church and state without segregating moral and spiritual values from our political life.

QUESTIONS FOR DISCUSSION

1. Why do many people believe that religious faith needs to be taken back from those who have "stolen" it? Why does Wallis believe that people around the world now think that Christian faith is "pro-rich, pro-war, and pro-American"? Do you think that this is an accurate perception of world opinion?

2. How, according to Wallis, does the "political Right" misunderstand the "public meaning of religion"? How does the "secular Left" also misunderstand or underestimate the nature and power of faith? Do you agree with Wallis's assertions here?

3. What are some other mistaken attitudes toward religion that make it necessary to "take back" faith? Is it necessary for Wallis to list so many mistaken views? Is it perhaps inevitable that people will perceive and relate to religion differently in a secular society?

4. What positive suggestions for reclaiming true faith and authentic religious practice does Wallis begin to make in his sixth paragraph? How and why does he believe that "faith creates community"? How does faith heal divisions and go beyond "nationalist religion"? Why does an awareness of human evil make necessary a firm theological support for "political and economic democracy"?

5. What does Wallis believe to be the importance of helping the poor through religion, and why does he believe that no distinction or separation should be made between "personal and social responsibility" in order to advance "the common good"?
6. Despite his religious convictions, why does Wallis believe so strongly in the need for separation of church and state? Why does he believe that religious congregations should function as "dynamic counter-cultural communities"?

CONNECTION

Compare Jim Wallis's ideas and actions about religion, service, and politics with Martin Luther King's views and actions as found in his "I Have a Dream" speech (see page 543).

IDEAS FOR WRITING

1. Write an essay about a religious group or denomination in which you have participated. How well would this group measure up to Wallis's vision of the ideal spiritual community? How could it become more dynamic, more "counter-cultural"?
2. Write a response to Wallis's ideas about the importance of the separation between church and state. Do you agree or disagree with Wallis's position? Why or why not?

RELATED WEB SITES

Sojourners: Faith, Politics, Culture
`www.sojo.net/`
The *Sojourners* site (founded by Jim Wallis) features an electronic version of the group's magazine; a study guide to Jim Wallis's new book, *God's Politics*; news; and editorial articles.

God's Politics: An Interview With Jim Wallis
`www.motherjones.com/news/qa/2005/03/gods_politics_jim_`
`wallis.html`
In this interview with *Mother Jones* magazine, Jim Wallis clarifies his critique of the Republican Party, the religious right, the Democrats, and the "secular fundamentalists."

Noah Levine

Death Is Not the End My Friend

Noah Levine was born in 1971 and grew up in a New Age spiritual family in northern California. His father was Stephen Levine, a Buddhist convert and author of books on meditation and coping with loss. Angry at social injustice and troubled after the divorce of his parents, Noah Levine was arrested 17 times as a juvenile and was involved with punk rock culture, alcohol, and drugs. After achieving sobriety, Levine attended the California Institute of Integral Studies and trained at the Spirit Rock Meditation Center in Woodacre, California. He also has studied with the Dalai Lama, Thich Nhat Hanh, and many other spiritual teachers. He is the cofounder and director of the Mind Body Awareness Project, a nonprofit organization serving incarcerated young people. Levine now lives in San Francisco, where he teaches Buddhist meditation techniques and counsels young prisoners. He writes regularly for online Buddhist publications. The following selection, excerpted from Dharma Punx: A Memoir *(2003), reveals how meditation and service helped Levine to develop a spiritual self and to overcome deep anger, fear, and grief.*

JOURNAL

Write about the death of a friend or relative. In what sense did this loss change the direction of your life or give you new insights?

Driving fast with the music up loud, as usual, I didn't even hear my cell phone ring. Seeing that I had missed a call, I picked up the phone and checked my messages. I could tell by the sound of Alicia's voice that something terrible had happened; all she said was, "Noah, call me as soon as you get this, it's an emergency." Dialing her number, I could feel my belly get really tight, like I was bracing myself for a hard blow. When she answered the phone I heard the desperation in her voice. I said, "It's Noah, what happened?" and all she replied was, "Toby's dead." Everything became fuzzy and dark for a moment and I felt like my chest was being smashed, like a heavy weight was crushing my sternum. I didn't even reply. I couldn't speak; only a deep guttural sigh came out followed by a flood of tears. I started saying, "Fuck. What the fuck? Why? What happened? Fucking Toby." I had to pull my car to the side of the road and just cry and scream for a while. Alicia told me that she and Jerilyn, Toby's mom, had found him that morning, sitting up in bed, his skin cold and blue. They called the paramedics but it was too late—he had stopped breathing several hours earlier. She thought he probably overdosed but didn't really know; they hadn't found any dope or needles.

Alicia asked me to come down to Santa Cruz and be with her and Gage, Toby's son. I was crying so hard that I couldn't think. I was on my way to work at Spirit Rock, where I was supposed to meet with someone, but I couldn't remember whom. I was also supposed to be leading a weekend for a rites-of-passage boys' group at Tassajara Zen Center, but it didn't look like I was going to be able to make it to either commitment. I couldn't even think about trying to teach or work, my mind was foggy and confused, every cell in my body was in anguish.

I told Alicia that I would be there as soon as possible. After I got off the phone with her I immediately made several calls: to my dad and Ondrea in

New Mexico, to my mom in Santa Cruz, to Vinny, Joe, and Micah. Mostly I just left messages telling them what had happened and asking for some support. I talked to Vinny for a little while and he was very supportive—it was so nice to just hear a friendly voice. I felt so alone, so overwhelmed and distraught.

My heart felt like it had just been torn from my chest. I couldn't believe it. I wasn't ready for this, not now. Toby had been doing so well. He had been out of prison and going to recovery meetings and counseling, and as far as I knew he had been sober for almost a year. He was so in love with his son, and every time I talked to him he spoke about wanting to start helping kids like I was doing. He was trying to volunteer at some teen counseling programs in Santa Cruz and going to church every week with his family.

5   Not now! There was a time a few years ago when he was on the streets and I was just waiting for the call to come, but not now. He had just spent the weekend with me a few weeks ago in the city and had come to a teen retreat that I was leading at Spirit Rock. I had led a day of meditation and a sweat lodge in the afternoon. Toby had been great, sharing his life's experience with the teens and expressing his hope that they would never have to experience what he had. The kids had really loved him and it was so great to be sharing my role of Buddhist teacher with my oldest friend in the world.

Just the day before I had gotten an e-mail from him, something about being a spiritual porn star, another one of his punk rock fantasies. I wrote back telling him of my love for him and encouraging his continued commitment to the steps and spiritual practice. I said that I had been thinking about him a lot lately because of the meditation groups that I was doing in San Quentin. Thinking of the time he spent there, I was so glad he was back in my life and I never wanted him to have to go back to prison. I said that above everything else I hoped he was putting his recovery first, because without staying clean it seemed inevitable that he, that I, that we all would end up back in a cell, if not physically then at least spiritually.

He probably never even got it. Or maybe he did and since he was already relapsing it made him feel so bad that he had killed himself. I would never know.

My whole body was flushed with guilt and the tears flowed out of my empty eyes, soaking my face and sweatshirt. I made a quick stop at work to let them know that I would probably be out the rest of the week and drove directly to Santa Cruz to be with Alicia and Jerilyn and all the rest of our friends and family. I tried turning my stereo up so that it would be louder than my mind, but every song, every chord, and each beat reminded me of Toby.

It felt like nothing had prepared me for this; no amount of meditation, no amount of therapy, none of the spiritual practices or experiences I'd had, prepared me to lose my best friend. I felt like without him nobody in the world really knew me. It seemed like when I was ten years old I had left home and found my real family. The day I met Toby I finally felt understood. We had been through everything together. When we were kids on the streets getting high, chasing girls, when we couldn't relate to our parents and they couldn't understand us, we always had each other. The first time I had sex

Toby was there—the first punk rock show, first acid trip, first fucking everything. We fought together and stole together, we shared bottles, crack pipes, and needles. We did it all. Even when I got sober and turned into a fucking self-righteous Straight Edge asshole, Toby was still there. When he was strung out on the streets and needed somewhere to stay, my door was always open. Even when he ripped me and everyone else off and ended up in prison, our connection was still too strong and nothing could break our friendship; we were brothers. I sent him books in prison, he sent me letters. When he got out and met back up with Alicia and she got pregnant he asked me if I would be godfather.

10   We spent twenty years together, longer than with anyone else. My oldest friend in the world was dead. And with him died the only witness to see me both shoot dope and teach meditation. Now I was all alone, surrounded by people who I could tell about my past but who would never really know what it was like.

No amount of spiritual understanding or faith could make that feeling go away. I knew he was okay wherever he was, be it outside of his body or on to the next realm. But I wasn't okay. I was left behind to deal with his skeleton. I wished I believed that he was resting in peace, but I didn't. I knew that whatever his work was, it would be done, either this time or the next, in this realm or another.

When I finally spoke to my father he said that he felt that Toby might be feeling lost and confused and that what he really needed was my forgiveness. He suggested that I do as much forgiveness practice as possible to help set Toby free and guide him on his journey. I didn't even realize that I hadn't forgiven him, or that maybe I had but he just needed to hear it to help him navigate his strange journey, feeling confused and afraid. I hope my prayers and meditations touched him and helped him to let go and go back into the essence and into the next distressing disguise. I offered any merit that I might have accumulated to him, that he might take rebirth in a realm where he will come into contact with the Dharma.

In Santa Cruz I had to do everything for the funeral. Toby's mom was too overwhelmed with grief, his dad wasn't around, and Alicia had her hands full with taking care of Gage and getting them both out of the apartment where Toby had died. Lola was with Alicia when I arrived. Lola had been sober since just after that night in the hospital three years earlier. She was Alicia's sponsor. We had been in touch off and on and had been able to establish somewhat of a friendship. It was great to see her. I was in so much pain, her hug felt incredibly comforting. She just wanted to know what she could do to help.

We set up the funeral and got the word out as best we could, in the newspaper and by word of mouth. About two hundred people showed up, overflowing St. John's Church, the little chapel on the hill in Capitola where we grew up. People, some of whom I hadn't seen in fifteen years, lined the aisles and spilled out into the streets.

15   I stood at the pulpit in the front of the church. Pictures of Toby hung on the walls, and a large pile of flowers was being laid on the altar we had created. It

was the most important talk I would ever give, remembering Toby and honoring his life and his search for freedom. Looking out over the gathering of his family and friends, feeling inadequate and afraid, I spoke of his love for his family and friends, his son and his girlfriend, his humor, his style, and his struggle with addiction. I told the story of how our friendship had been one of the most important things in my life, how I might not have made it through some of the more difficult times without him. How he'd saved my life so many times by just being understanding and supportive, by just listening when we couldn't relate to our parents or anyone else.

I spoke of how we met at Little League, of our first punk shows and our first sexual experiences. I shared with the gathering of punks and parents, skaters and surfers, what I knew of Toby's life journey, of his search for love and happiness that led instead to addiction and confusion. Of his many loves and his son, of the honor I felt to be godfather to his child. Through my own tears and the tears of a church filled to the brim with love and grief, I did my best to memorialize Toby's life, his incredible sense of humor, and his uncanny ability to make anyone feel comfortable in any situation.

Before we ended the service I led the whole gathering in a short meditation of forgiveness and gratitude and we all offered our love and forgiveness, ending the period of reflection with a funny sound that Toby was famous for making. Everyone was laughing and crying at the same time.

I took some more time off from work and spent a lot of it just crying and reflecting on how lucky I had been to have such a good friend for so long, how rare and wonderful it was to ever connect with someone in such a deep way.

I kept coming back to the feeling of being lost, like a part of me had died, and it began to hit me that all of our other friends were dead also: Shooter, Mark, Darren, and even Toby's old girlfriend Jamie. My mind started swimming upstream, asking the useless question of "Why?" Why them and not me? Why was I surrounded by such wonderful spiritual teachers, all only a phone call away, all available to me? All of them helping me on the spiritual path.

20   After some time I realized that I was experiencing survivor's guilt. It was as if I had lived through a war and was one of the only ones left. And on some level it was true.

Talking to my parents and my teachers about my grief process, although helpful, also seemed to compound my feeling of guilt. There I was, being supported by some of the most wonderful teachers in the world, and all my friends were dying alone in ghetto apartments, shooting some more dope so that they wouldn't have to deal with the suffering for one more minute. That was me and where I came from, and I felt like I was somehow betraying them by surviving.

The guilt and doubt began to fade fairly quickly and were replaced by the realization that it was for Toby and all my other friends, all of the punks and kids who didn't make it, that I was continuing my spiritual quest, and for them that I had committed my life to sharing what I was finding with others—to teaching the simple meditation techniques that had so profoundly altered the course of my life.

Toby's death became the next teaching, opening my heart to the floods of grief and despair that we all hold at bay. No longer able to keep myself together, I fell apart and stumbled into a deeper understanding of what it means to be human. I began to see Toby's death and all of my life's experiences as teachings and tools to offer to others who will surely walk a similar path. I saw all of it as an opportunity for awakening, as grist for the mill.

Still processing all that had happened, I put one foot in front of the other and showed up for my life's work, using the grief and even the feelings of guilt and confusion over having escaped from a life of addiction and crime as the basis of my teachings. My heart was ripped open, raw and tender—I offered it to others so that they might benefit from my suffering.

25   A short time later Jack Kornfield invited me to join a small Buddhist teachers' training group that he was offering. I humbly accepted, knowing that it was the appropriate next step in actualizing my intention to share the Dharma with others. I decided that my time would be better spent working in juvenile halls and prisons, gave notice at Spirit Rock, and with a couple of friends started our own nonprofit organization to teach meditation to inmates, called the Mind Body Awareness project.

QUESTIONS FOR DISCUSSION

1. How would you interpret the title of this essay? Does Levine seem to believe in a literal afterlife, or is the statement true on another level? Explain your response.
2. Why is it significant that Levine receives his notification of his friend Toby's death via cell phone, while "[d]riving fast with the music up loud, as usual"? What is his immediate response to the news? What metaphors does he use to describe his response?
3. From whom does Levine ask for support? Why does he feel guilty about Toby's death, despite the fact that he sent warnings about the risks of returning to drugs and prison to his friend by e-mail?
4. What memories of his relationship with Toby does Levine share with his readers and with the many friends in attendance at the hastily organized funeral? Which details seem particularly vivid and poignant? Why does Levine consider this address "the most important talk I would ever give"?
5. In what sense was Toby's death "the next teaching"? What new insights about the meaning of Toby's death come to Levine in the days after the funeral?
6. To what active spirituality does Levine dedicate himself after his mourning for Toby and period of guilt and doubt? How does his new spiritual direction suggest both growth and leadership ability?

CONNECTION

Compare Levine's approach to spirituality and service with that of Jim Wallis in this chapter (see page 548).

IDEAS FOR WRITING

1. Write an essay about an abrupt change of direction in your life and/or about spiritual awareness that came to you through some form of trauma, crisis, or loss. As Levine does, try to capture both the physical and emotional impact of your loss as well as the type of reflection that it prompted in you. How did you change?
2. Do some research into meditation and recovery groups in prisons, and write an essay on your findings. How effective do such groups seem to be in helping inmates adjust to life in prison while maintaining hope and confidence that they can do something productive and rewarding with themselves, both in and out of incarceration?

RELATED WEB SITES

End Of Life And Dharma Talks
`www.aniccahouse.org/htm/buddhist_hindu_mp3_talks_hospice_dharma.htm`
The Anicca House site presents talks and guided meditations in MP3 format by Noah Levine, Stephen and Ondrea Levine, and Ajahn Amaro.

Buddha Was A Punk Rocker: Interview With Noah Levine
`www.satyamag.com/oct03/levine.htm`
In his interview with the emagazine *Satya,* Noah Levine discusses his Buddhist/ punk ethic and his classes in meditation and psychotherapy with inmates at San Quentin Prison.

Linda Hogan

The Voyagers

Linda Hogan (b. 1947), a member of the Chickasaw tribe, was raised in Denver, Colorado, and completed her M.A. at the University of Colorado at Boulder in 1978. Hogan began her career teaching creative writing and Native American literature at the University of Colorado at Boulder, and went on to teach poetry and literature in outreach programs in Colorado and Oklahoma. Since 1989 she has been an associate professor of English at the University of Colorado at Boulder. Her books include the novel Power *(1998),* Confronting the Truth *(2000), and* The Woman Who Watches Over the World: A Native Memoir *(2001). Hogan's work focuses on the survival of the family, community, and natural world as illuminated by Native American spirituality. The following selection from her essay collection,* Dwellings: A Spiritual History of the Living World *(1995), contrasts the "utopic" values implicit in the journey of the Voyager spacecraft with Hogan's Native American spiritual values as a voyager in the universe.*

Imagine that you are sending a message to another world, where the people know nothing about this planet and its inhabitants. What information would you want to share the most with the "aliens" about our earth and its people?

I remember one night, lying on the moist spring earth beside my mother. The fire of stars stretched away from us, and the mysterious darkness traveled without limit beyond where we lay on the turning earth. I could smell the damp new grass that night, but I could not touch or hold such black immensity that lived above our world, could not contain within myself even a small corner of the universe.

There seemed to be two kinds of people; earth people and those others, the sky people, who stumbled over pebbles while they walked around with their heads in clouds. Sky people loved different worlds than I loved; they looked at nests in treetops and followed the long white snake of vapor trails. But I was an earth person, and while I loved to gaze up at night and stars, I investigated the treasures at my feet, the veined wing of a dragonfly opening a delicate blue window to secrets of earth, a lusterless beetle that drank water thirstily from the tip of my finger and was transformed into sudden green and metallic brilliance. It was enough mystery for me to ponder the bones inside our human flesh, bones that through some incredible blueprint of life grow from a moment's sexual passion between a woman and a man, walk upright a short while, then walk themselves back to dust.

Years later, lost in the woods one New Year's eve, a friend found the way home by following the north star, and I began to think that learning the sky might be a practical thing. But it was the image of earth from out in space that gave me upward-gazing eyes. It was that same image that gave the sky people an anchor in the world, for it returned us to our planet in a new and loving way.

To dream of the universe is to know that we are small and brief as insects, born in a flash of rain and gone a moment later. We are delicate and our world is fragile. It was the transgression of Galileo to tell us that we were not the center of the universe, and now, even in our own time, the news of our small being here is treacherous enough that early in the space program, the photographs of Earth were classified as secret documents by the government. It was thought, and rightfully so, that the image of our small blue Earth would forever change how we see ourselves in context with the world we inhabit.

5   When we saw the deep blue and swirling white turbulence of our Earth reflected back to us, says photographer Steven Meyers, we also saw "the visual evidence of creative and destructive forces moving around its surface, we saw for the first time the deep blackness of that which surrounds it, we sensed directly, and probably for the first time, our incredibly profound isolation, and the special fact of our being here." It was a world whose intricately linked-together ecosystem could not survive the continuing blows of exploitation.

In 1977, when the Voyagers were launched, one of these spacecraft carried the Interstellar Record, a hoped-for link between earth and space that is filled with the sounds and images of the world around us. It carries parts of our lives all the way out to the great Forever. It is destined to travel out of our vast solar system, out to the far, unexplored regions of space in hopes that somewhere, millions of years from now, someone will find it like a note sealed in a bottle carrying our history across the black ocean of space. This message is intended for the year 8,000,000.

One greeting onboard from Western India says: "Greetings from a human being of the Earth. Please contact." Another, from Eastern China, but resembling one that could have been sent by my own Chickasaw people, says: "Friends of space, how are you all? Have you eaten yet? Come visit us if you have time."

There is so much hope in those greetings, such sweetness. If found, these messages will play our world to a world that's far away. They will sing out the strangely beautiful sounds of Earth, sounds that in all likelihood exist on no other planet in the universe. By the time the record is found, if ever, it is probable that the trumpeting bellows of elephants, the peaceful chirping of frogs and crickets, the wild dogs baying out from the golden needle and record, will be nothing more than a gone history of what once lived on this tiny planet in the curving tail of a spiral galaxy. The undeciphered language of whales will speak to a world not our own, to people who are not us. They will speak of what we value the most on our planet, things that in reality we are almost missing.

A small and perfect world is traveling there, with psalms journeying past Saturn's icy rings, all our treasured life flying through darkness, going its way alone back through the universe. There is the recorded snapping of fire, the song of a river traveling the continent, the living wind passing through dry grasses, all the world that burns and pulses around us, even the comforting sound of a heartbeat taking us back to the first red house of our mothers' bodies, all that, floating through the universe.

10   The Voyager carries music. A Peruvian wedding song is waiting to be heard in the far, distant regions of space. The Navajo Night Chant travels through darkness like medicine for healing another broken world. Blind Willie Johnson's slide guitar and deep down blues are on that record, in night's long territory.

The visual records aboard the Voyager depict a nearly perfect world, showing us our place within the whole; in the image of a snow-covered forest, trees are so large that human figures standing at their base are almost invisible. In the corner of this image is a close-up of a snow crystal's elegant architecture of ice and air. Long-necked geese fly across another picture, a soaring eagle. Three dolphins, sun bright on their silver sides, leap from a great ocean wave. Beneath them are underwater blue reefs with a shimmering school of fish. It is an abundant, peaceful world, one where a man eats from a vine heavy with grapes, an old man walks through a field of white daisies, and children lovingly touch a globe in a classroom. To think that the precious images of what lives on earth beside us, the lives we share with earth, some endangered, are now tumbling through time and space, more permanent than we are, and speaking the sacred language of life that we ourselves have only just begun to remember.

We have sent a message that states what we most value here on earth; respect for all life and ways. It is a sealed world, a seed of what we may become. What an amazing document is flying above the clouds, holding Utopia. It is more magical and heavy with meaning than the cave paintings of Lascaux, more wise than the language of any holy book. These are images that could sustain us through any cold season of ice or hatred or pain.

In *Murmurs of Earth,* written by members of the committee who selected the images and recordings, the records themselves are described in a way that attests to their luminous quality of being: "They glisten, golden, in the sunlight, . . . encased in aluminum cocoons." It sounds as though, through some magical metamorphosis, this chrysalis of life will emerge in another part of infinity, will grow to a wholeness of its own, and return to us alive, full-winged, red, and brilliant.

There is so much hope there that it takes us away from the dark times of horror we live in, a time when the most cruel aspects of our natures have been revealed to us in regions of earth named Auschwitz, Hiroshima, My Lai, and Rwanda, a time when televised death is the primary amusement of our children, when our children are killing one another on the streets.

15   At second glance, this vision for a new civilization, by its very presence, shows us what is wrong with our world. Defining Utopia, we see what we could be now, on earth, at this time, and next to the images of a better world, that which is absent begins to cry out. The underside of our lives grows in proportion to what is denied. The darkness is made darker by the record of light. A screaming silence falls between the stars of space. Held inside that silence are the sounds of gunfire, the wailings of grief and hunger, the last, extinct song of a bird. The dammed river goes dry, along with its valleys. Illnesses that plague our bodies live in this crack of absence. The broken link between us and the rest of our world grows too large, and the material of nightmares grows deeper while the promises for peace and equality are empty, are merely dreams without reality.

But how we want it, how we want that half-faced, one-sided God.

In earlier American days, when Catholic missions were being erected in Indian country, a European woman, who was one of the first white contacts for a northern tribe of people, showed sacred paintings to an Indian woman. The darker woman smiled when she saw a picture of Jesus and Mary encircled in their haloes of light. A picture of the three kings with their crowns and gifts held her interest. But when she saw a picture of the crucifixion, the Indian woman hurried away to warn others that these were dangerous people, people to fear, who did horrible things to one another. This picture is not carried by the Voyager, for fear we earth people would "look" cruel. There is no image of this man nailed to a cross, no saving violence. There are no political messages, no photographs of Hiroshima. This is to say that we know our own wrongdoings.

Nor is there a true biology of our species onboard because NASA officials vetoed the picture of a naked man and pregnant woman standing side by side, calling it "smut." They allowed only silhouettes to be sent, as if our own origins, the divine flux of creation that passes between a man and a woman, are unacceptable, something to hide. Even picture diagrams of the human organs, musculature, and skeletal system depict no sexual organs, and a photograph showing the birth of an infant portrays only the masked, gloved physician lifting the new life from a mass of sheets, the mother's body hidden. While we might ask if they could not have sent the carved stone gods and goddesses in acts of beautiful sexual intimacy on temple walls in India, this embarrassment about our own carriage of life and act of creative generation nevertheless reveals our feelings of physical vulnerability and discomfort with our own life force.

From an American Indian perspective, there are other problems here. Even the language used in the selection process bespeaks many of the failings of an entire system of thought and education. From this record, we learn about our relationships, not only with people, but with everything on earth. For example, a small gold-eyed frog seen in a human hand might have been a photograph that bridges species, a statement of our kinship with other lives on earth, but the hand is described, almost apologetically, as having "a dirty fingernail." Even the clay of creation has ceased to be the rich element from which life grows. I recall that the Chilean poet Pablo Neruda wrote "What can I say without touching the earth with my hands?" We must wonder what of value can ever be spoken from lives that are lived outside of life, without a love or respect for the land and other lives.

20   In *Murmurs of Earth,* one of the coauthors writes about hearing dolphins from his room, "breathing, playing with one another. Somehow," he says, "one had the feeling that they weren't just some sea creatures but some very witty and intelligent beings living in the next room." This revealing choice of words places us above and beyond the rest of the world, as though we have stepped out of our natural cycles in our very existence here on earth. And isn't our world full of those rooms? We inhabit only a small space in the house of life. In another is a field of corn. In one more is the jungle world of the macaw. Down the hall, a zebra is moving. Beneath the foundation is the world of snakes and the five beating hearts of the earthworm.

In so many ways, the underside of our lives is here. Even the metals used in the record tell a story about the spoils of inner earth, the laborers in the hot mines. Their sweat is in that record, hurtling away from our own galaxy.

What are the possibilities, we wonder, that our time capsule will be found? What is the possibility that there are lives other than our own in the universe? Our small galaxy, the way of the milk, the way of sustenance, is only one of billions of galaxies, but there is also the possibility that we are the only planet where life opens, blooms, is gone, and then turns over again. We hope this is not the case. We are so young we hardly know what it means to be a human being, to have natures that allow for war. We barely even know our human histories, so much having unraveled before our time, and while we know that our history creates us, we hope there is another place, another world we can fly to when ours is running out. We have come so far away from wisdom, a wisdom that is the heritage of all people, an old kind of knowing that respects a community of land, animals, plants, and other people as equal to ourselves. Where we know the meaning of relationship.

As individuals, we are not faring much better. We are young. We hardly know who we are. We face the search for ourselves alone. In spite of our search through the universe, we do not know our own personal journeys. We still wonder if the soul weighs half an ounce, if it goes into the sky at the time of our death, if it also reaches out, turning, through the universe.

But still, this innocent reaching out is a form of ceremony, as if the Voyager were a sacred space, a ritual enclosure that contains our dreaming the way a cathedral holds the bones of saints.

25   The people of earth are reaching out. We are having a collective vision. Like young women and men on a vision quest, we seek a way to live out the peace of the vision we have sent to the world of stars. We want to live as if there is no other place, as if we will always be here. We want to live with devotion to the world of waters and the universe of life that dwells above our thin roofs.

I remember that night with my mother, looking up at the black sky with its turning stars. It was a mystery, beautiful and distant. Her body I came from, but our common ancestor is the earth, and the ancestor of earth is space. That night we were small, my mother and I, and we were innocent. We were children of the universe. In the gas and dust of life, we are voyagers. Wait. Stop here a moment. Have you eaten? Come in. Eat.

QUESTIONS FOR DISCUSSION

1. Hogan makes a distinction between sky people, who wonder about the world beyond our planet, and earth people, who are content to observe the world around us. Which of these categories did she fit into as a child? What has made her see the world in a larger perspective? What does it mean for Hogan to "dream of the universe"?

2. What do the sounds and images chosen for inclusion in the Voyager's Interstellar Record reveal about our modern beliefs and values, what we take pride in, and what we consider a utopia?

3. What images and sounds are excluded from the Voyager's Record, and what do they reveal of our shame about "[t]he underside of our lives"? What aspects of religious history and practice, of violence to one another and to the earth, are excluded? Why?

4. What does Hogan feel is problematic about the Record from her own perspective as a Native American? Why does she quote the Chilean poet Pablo Neruda: "What can I say without touching the earth with my hands?" How do his words contrast with the view of "earth" provided by the images on the Record? Which view do you think has more credibility?

5. Why does Hogan consider the Voyager journey and Record "a ritual"? In what sense is the Voyager "a sacred place"? Why does she consider humans as "young" and "far away from wisdom"?

6. Why does Hogan shift away abruptly in her final paragraph from the Voyager and its "outer space"-oriented values to the scene at the beginning of the essay, where she lies with her mother on the "moist spring earth"? How does she bring her argument to a strong final point in this last scene?

CONNECTION

Compare Hogan's ideas on the relationship between mental health and connection with the earth with Theodore Roszak's beliefs as expressed in his essay in Chapter 2, "The Nature of Sanity." (See page 103.)

IDEAS FOR WRITING

1. Imagine you are making a new, more realistic media program for the Voyager. Write an essay that describes what images, sounds, and music you would include. What spiritual values and ideas about the earth and its people would you want to emphasize with your "sound track"?
2. After considering the facts about the Voyager included in Hogan's essay and after doing some outside research on the space program, write an essay in which you consider what spiritual needs underlie and motivate the continuance of this very complex and expensive attempt to journey to planets and solar systems far away from our own. Conclude by reflecting on whether you think the program is worth the effort and expense it is costing the United States and other societies around the world.

RELATED WEB SITES

Native American Authors Online: Linda Hogan
`www.hanksville.org/storytellers/linda/`
This page from the Storyellers site contains a biography, interviews, annotations, sample excerpts, and scholarly articles about Linda Hogan and her work.

Native American Religion
`www.nativeamericans.com/Religion.htm`
In the Native American Religion site, you will find links to many related Web pages featuring essays, images, and historical information.

Norman Yeung Bik Chung

A Faithful Taoist

Born in Hong Kong and raised in a traditional Chinese family, Norman Yeung left home to study abroad in England at 17. After immigrating to the United States, he worked in the high-tech industry as a software manager for many years before returning to school at De Anza College in Cupertino, California. He wrote the following essay for an English composition class to demonstrate the role that Taoist beliefs and rituals played in his father's capacity for hope in the face of life-threatening illness.

Faith is an important part of every religion. A strong belief in a higher order or power can help people in their daily life and gives many individuals a sense of purpose in this world. Because I grew up with both Eastern culture and Western religion, I have a difficult time accepting one main truth system; I have also come to believe that there are both good and evil aspects to every religion. Although I am not going to try to explain away the supernatural aspect of the spiritual experiences I have had, I can at least recollect them and reflect on how they happened and on how they helped my family and my father in particular.

Because my father was a strong believer of Taoism, an Eastern philosophy and religion that has many followers in Hong Kong, we had an altar in my home ever since I was very little. A beautifully painted portrait of Lao Tzu riding his ox hung on the wall by the altar along with some calligraphy. A small pot to hold the incense that filled the room with whatever fragrance my father chose was placed on a table in front of Lao Tzu. He devoted at least ten minutes twice a day, morning and evening, to meditation. He would light up three sticks of incense, bow three times, and chant, never missing a day until he had to go into the hospital. At that point he asked one of us to do the ritual for him, a practice that my oldest brother followed religiously until my father passed away.

In addition to the private ritual that he carried out at home, there was also a place of worship where he went to pray and to meditate. My father was among the many frequent visitors to a Taoist temple on the east side of Hong Kong. The first time I visited that temple with him, I was eighteen years old; and, having just come back from London for a summer vacation, I wanted to spend some time with him. Because my father was such a generous donor, I had always considered the temple as a place where con artists made money from the believers. The altar at this temple was very similar to the one I used to see at home, except it was bigger and has more space, enough room for forty to fifty people to stand in front of Lao Tzu's picture, chanting and mediating together.

On the first and fifteenth of each month, Taoist followers gathered at the temple to pray and ask for spiritual advice. On one side of the hall was a large table with a Chinese painting brush hanging from the ceiling. Like the ouija board that people use to seek spiritualistic or telepathic messages in the West, the "brush" composed and wrote poems and verses on large piece of papers in response to the believers' questions. Of course there was a person who helped to guide the brush, and my brothers, who visited the temple often with my father, told me that they often saw the priests there practicing the writing and composing of the poem beforehand—yet this knowledge had never altered my father's faith in Taoism.

5   My father was one of the few patients in Hong Kong in the early 1960s to have had heart surgery and to have had a pacemaker implanted. However, after twenty years, the battery inside his pacemaker stopped working. Considering his age and health condition, he was faced with a choice of having surgery to replace his battery, which would have necessitated a long and difficult period of recovery, or of letting nature take its course. No one in the family wanted to be responsible for that choice; after all, my father was a hardheaded person who usually had the last word in our domestic decisions.

On the evening of the first of July, 1982, my father and I went to the temple, where it was my first time to witness the "ghost painting" ritual. After the grand ceremony, the few people who wanted to ask for the gods' wisdom gathered around the table. In turn, each one lit three sticks of incense and said a prayer in private. Then the brush, assisted by a man who worked there, moved for each of them. Most of the worshippers got a symbol of luck, health or prosperity; only a few received a verse or a poem. Soon it was my father's turn. As he walked up to the altar, lit the sticks, and bowed down to pray, I knew he must be very worried; yet he never showed any emotions. As I eagerly watched close by, the pen began to move for him.

The verses that my father received gave him the answer he needed to hear: "Go and he will be healed." Taking this message as a sign of the need for surgery, he contacted the surgeon the next day and had the operation soon after. He lived for another fifteen years while he saw my mother gradually deteriorate with Alzheimer's disease. Just before he died, my mother lost consciousness, so she did not have to moan and suffer the loss of her dear husband. For two years, she had lain in bed with great physical pain, yet I think her devotion to my father for over sixty years brought them together in spirit from the day he died. We could feel my father's presence in the weeks that followed his death.

In Taoism, one believes that the spirit of the dead comes home every seventh day for seven weeks before it moves on permanently. Our family put fruit and food at the altar to honor my father every day during that period. On the first seventh day, a hummingbird came into our house and landed quietly on my sister-in-law's shoulder. "He" then went over to the altar and picked on the apple, which was my father's favorite fruit. A bat, which in Chinese rhymes with the word "blessing," came into our house on the second seventh day. It flew all over the room and stopped at the altar. Both creatures were taken as a sign of my father's presence. They symbolized my father who brought luck to our family. I would like to note that this happened in the city of Hong Kong in an apartment among many high-rise buildings; to have a bird or a bat come inside the house was unheard of in that area.

After a year abroad, I went back to Hong Kong for a visit. My family and I went to meet my brothers in their office, a place where my father had worked for over twenty years. As we entered the lift, we realized that no one remembered which floor the office was on; so we decided to go up to the top, the twentieth floor, and to walk back down, looking for the right level. Mystically, the lift opened on the eighth floor; I looked out and found that we were just outside my father's office. I can only relate this happening to the fact that his presence was still so strong within the building.

10   It is possible for me to dismiss all the events described above as coincidence or even as the work of my imagination. However, it is not important whether I think that the "ghost painting" was the result of the people who worked at the temple or not. What is important is that those few words in calligraphy strengthened my father's willpower to live and to seek the medical care he needed, and I will always be grateful to those who gave him the hope none of us in our family

could offer. For someone with a strong faith, the spirit will continue to live on; to me, the spirit of my father remains, continually looking over those whom he loved and worked for all his life, until one day we will meet again.

QUESTIONS FOR DISCUSSION

1. What is Chung's own position on religion and faith in supernatural events, and how does his position differ from that of his father?
2. In what way and for what reasons did the author change his initial view of the temple and those who worked there? Point out particular places in the essay where his spiritual perceptions and beliefs seem to shift and grow.
3. How do specific observed details and Chung's interpretations of them add to the mystery and emotional power of the essay? Give examples.
4. Comment on the title of the essay. How does the father's Taoism differ from what most Western people think Taoism means as a spiritual philosophy? Would it have been helpful for readers if Chung had discussed this distinction? Why or why not?

Karen Methot-Chun

Living Spirituality

Student writer Karen Methot-Chun works in human resources at a large computer company in Silicon Valley and attends classes at De Anza College in Cupertino, California, where she is working toward a degree in nursing. She comes from a nondenominational Christian household and has studied massage, meditation, Tai Chi, and yoga. In the following paper, Karen draws together ideas from several different texts and a television interview to help develop her definition of "living spirituality."

The term "spirituality" encompasses a very broad spectrum of definitions, emotions, and reactions. Although the *American Heritage Dictionary* defines "spiritual" as "not tangible or material; of, concerned with, or affecting the soul; of, from or relating to God; deific, sacred, supernatural," and "spirit" as "the vital principle or animating force within living beings," when we describe people who are engaged with a living spirituality, we generally assume that their lifestyle is moral, that they are conscious of a greater being or guiding force in life, and that they are in harmony with their surroundings and in communication with their inner being or soul. Most importantly, however, the word "living" implies that they are involved in putting their spirituality into action through living in a highly conscious and aware manner, in touch with the life inside them and around them, while maintaining a consistent desire to improve the way in which they live and interact with the people and the world around them.

Often the term "living spirituality" is used interchangeably with "morality," but morality can sometimes be confused with narrowly dogmatic and inflexible beliefs that might better be termed "dying spirituality." For instance, the emphasis on dogma in fundamentalist religions and in the Catholic Church often seeks to extinguish the lively debate over moral issues in today's society over subjects such as the role of women in the church, abortion, and gay marriage. In the selection of the new pope, Catholics seem to desire to move the church back to the strict conservative tradition of Roman Catholicism; however, a significant number of modern Catholics, particularly those in America and Western Europe, seek to push the Church forward to accept more modern concepts, such as allowing priests to marry, permitting women to lead the church, considering the needs of the impoverished, and welcoming gays and lesbians into the Church community without judgment. As people who practice a living spirituality, we need to be aware of each other's differences in order to accept and acknowledge them, and to recognize that common spiritual ground that binds us to one another and to our shared humanity.

Living spirituality can be tarnished and deadened by extreme political agendas. Jim Wallis writes in "Taking Back the Faith" that Christianity has been stolen from the Christians and redefined by the New Right's political, media, and social agenda. Wallis poses the question "How did the faith of Jesus come to be known as pro-rich, pro-war, and pro-American?" Here Wallis is arguing that political extremists often use God and religion to support their own agenda. Wallis goes on to argue that both the left- and right-wing politicians have a very limited view of religion: "[R]ight-wingers . . . ignore the subjects that God seems to care the most about . . . [f]rom pedophile priests and cover-up bishops who destroy lives and shame the church . . . [f]rom television preachers whose extravagant lifestyles and crass fund-raising tactics *embarrass* more Christians than they know." On the other end of the spectrum, Wallis states that the "liberal secularists . . . want to banish faith from public life, and deny spiritual values to the soul of politics."

Frustrated by the lack of understanding of our media and politicians in the area of religious and spiritual values, Wallis "support[s] the rightful separation of church and state [but] without segregating moral and spiritual values from our political life." Politics neglects to see religion and spirituality for what they truly are—a set of guiding principles with which we should model our lives and our interactions with one another in order to give us a moral and spiritual "safe haven" when we can no longer cope with the world around us, and to provide us with motivation, through living spirituality, to help the less fortunate.

5   Summing up the concept of religious manipulation and the need for a living spirituality, Wallis states, "It is precisely because religion takes the problem of evil so seriously that it must always be suspicious of too much concentrated power—politically *and* economically—either in totalitarian regimes or in huge multi-national corporations which now have more wealth and power than many governments." It is this kind of "suspicious" theology that Wallis believes "makes us strong proponents of both political and economic democracy—not

because people are so good, but because they often are not, and need clear safeguards and strong systems of checks and balances to avoid the dangerous accumulations of power and wealth."

Living spirituality is a structure that provides an emotional and sometimes a physical haven to the downtrodden. When people encounter difficulties or struggles in life, their spiritual faith and guidance become the rock in which they find their stability, coping, and endurance. Ironically many people in their time of suffering turn and blame their religion or spiritual leader for not protecting them, only later to discover the path to healing is through living, active spiritual faith. In his memoir *Dharma Punx,* Noah Levine writes about his experience as a recovering drug user who has devoted his life to teaching meditation and counseling youth prisoners and drug abusers. When Levine loses his best friend to an overdose he "felt like nothing had prepared [him] for this; no amount of meditation, no amount of therapy, none of the spiritual practices or experiences . . . prepared [him] to lose [his] best friend" (237). Levine felt a sense of guilt and remorse for having a plethora of spiritual guidance in his own life, while his friend did not. Although he suffered from "survivor guilt," he used these emotions to further engage with his "spiritual quest . . . [to] teach the simple meditation techniques that had so profoundly altered the course of [his] life" (240). Levine discovered a new strength within himself through spiritual awareness, and then used this gift to guide others to do the same.

Although spirituality relates to the belief in a higher power and the concept of a greater harmony or energy among us, so that each of us is a part of a bigger whole. For instance, when Natascha McElhone, an actress on the television series *Revelations,* was asked during an interview with the *Today Show* about the issues of religion and spirituality, she stated, "I think the whole issue of whether we're religious and spiritual or not is kind of confusing, because it's more in the practice of living that that stuff comes out than in what we say we believe." In her life and in the process of filming *Revelations,* she came to realize that people may believe a certain way, yet their lifestyle often is inconsistent with their claims. She now feels that society is "looking for something more spiritual that can't necessarily be bought . . . religious or otherwise." McElhone clearly sees the need to dig deep within ourselves in order to find another method of fulfilling our emotional needs, and for many, this spiritual void is filled by a living spirituality rather than through the mechanism of religion.

McElhone's suspicion of religious moralism is echoed in many of the works of Duane Michals, an accomplished photographer. Michals has a controversial work titled <u>Salvation</u>, in which a person is being held figuratively at gunpoint where the "gun" is a crucifix and the gunman is a collared priest. In an interview with *Photo/Design* magazine, Michals states that he is a "fallen-away Catholic [and that he] never confuse[s] religiosity with spirituality." He further claims, "I hate organized religions . . . there is no bigger bigot than a professionally religious person." Michals believes that self-discovery is the essence of spirituality: we must be able to discover our self in order to understand spirituality, and to do so, we must be able to "let go" of everything, for by doing this we can capture the essence of what it means to possess living spirituality by abandoning selfishness and materiality .

In conclusion, we can see that a person can be spiritual and not be religious, or highly "religious" and not truly spiritual at all. Living spirituality is something within us that sees the innocence in the laughter of a child, the familiarity and comfort in the eyes of a loved one, the allure of the clouds of an afternoon sunset, the natural beauty in the wilderness. The beauty in life itself is a spiritual reality, and an artist with living spirituality may seek to capture that beauty in his or her work, in order to share it with others and inspire them on their own spiritual quest, much as Noah Levine brought his abilities as a spiritual healer through meditation to the prisoners of San Quentin Prison, a place where the inmates are truly in need of spiritual hope and rebirth. When people find the ability to grasp that which is in front of them, they can see the beauty in everyone and everything and can see beyond face value, depression, and confusion to a solution for the problems of others. This is spiritual growth and enlightenment. This is living spirituality.

Works Cited

Levine, Noah. "Death Is Not the End My Friend." *Dharma Punx: A Memoir.* New York: Harper-Collins, 2003.

McElhone, Natascha. Interview with Katie Couric. *Today Show.* NBC. KNTV, San Francisco. 27 Apr. 2005.

Michals, Duane, and Joel-Peter Witkin. "Theater of the Forbidden." *Photo/Design* Jan./Feb. 1989. 25 Apr. 2005 <http://lestblood.imagodirt.net/uploads/pictures/DuaneMichals_Salvation.jpg>.

"Spirit," "Spiritual." *American Heritage Dictionary.* 4th ed. 2000.

Wallis, Jim. "Taking Back the Faith." *God's Politics* Jan. 2005. 6 May 2005 <http://www.beliefnet.com/story/159/story_15987_1.html>.

Questions for Discussion

1. How clear is Methot-Chun's initial definition of "living spirituality"? How does she contrast her definition of this complex term to the dictionary definitions for "spiritual" and "spirit"? Is this contrast effective? Why or why not?

2. How do Methot-Chun's comments on the Catholic Church's movement to reaffirm traditional positions on issues such as gay marriage, women in the clergy, and so on help or detract from her core definition of living spirituality? Would citations of opinion on these issues from different authorities within the Church have helped make her positions clearer or more powerful? Why or why not?

3. How do the position statements on religion versus spirituality from Jim Wallis and Noah Levine help to support Methot-Chun's definition and position on living spirituality? What makes these "authorities" credible?

4. Later in the essay, Methot-Chun brings in testimony from an actress and a photographer on the issue of living spirituality. How do these individuals' positions as artists provide a new and thought-provoking insight into the issue in question? Are their statements as convincing as those of the more spiritually committed authorities, Wallis and Levine? Why or why not?

TOPICS FOR RESEARCH AND WRITING

1. Emily Dickinson and Annie Dillard both indicate a conflicting desire for authentic religious experience combined with doubt and perhaps embarrassment with some of the more traditional forms of religious belief and practice. Do some further research into the place of religion in modern life. Do other writers whom you have encountered express similar views of doubt and confusion about religion?

2. Jane Goodall addresses the relationship between science and religious practices such as meditation. Do some further research into modern relations between science and religion, and write an essay in which you discuss ways that science and religion can reinforce and shed light on one another.

3. Do some further research into the use of prayer in religious and secular devotion. Why do people pray, and what do they derive from this practice?

4. Do some further research on the importance of ritual observances such as those described in Norman Chung's essay in both religious and secular life, and write an essay in which you consider what purpose such observances serve for people and for society.

5. Annie Dillard and Jane Goodall describe religious experiences that could be described as mystical. After doing some further research into this subject, write an essay in which you define and discuss what it means to have a mystical experience, and what the positive effects of such experiences might be.

6. King, Wallis, Methot-Chun, and Levine discuss the ways that spiritual love and service can be used to effect social change. Do some further research into spiritual social activism and service. What is particularly effective about social activist movements that use love and kindness as their source of energy?

7. The following films portray spiritual leaders (positive and negative), and elements of spirituality in action. Pick one of these films—*The Seventh Seal, Little Buddha, The Last Temptation of Christ, Gandhi, The Last Wave, Seven Years in Tibet, Kundun,* or *The Passion of Christ*—and write an essay in which you analyze the film and its spiritual message. What makes this film memorable, more than just a "preachy" experience?

Credits

Text Credits

Diane Ackerman, excerpt from *A Slender Thread*. Copyright © 1996 by Diane Ackerman. Reprinted by permission of Random House, Inc.

Diane Ackerman, "Preface" from *Deep Play*. Copyright © 1999 by Diane Ackerman. Reprinted by permission of Random House, Inc.

Maya Angelou, "The Angel of the Candy Counter" from *I Know Why the Caged Bird Sings*. Copyright © 1969 by Maya Angelou, Reprinted by permission of Random House, Inc.

Julie Bordner Apodaca, "Gay Marriage: Why the Resistance?" Reprinted by permission of the author.

Marc Ian Barasch, "What is a Healing Dream?" from *Healing Dreams*. Copyright © 2000 by Marc Ian Barasch. Used by permission of Riverhead Books, an imprint of Penguin Putnam Inc.

Bruno Bettelheim, "Fairy Tales and the Existential Predicament". Copyright © 1975, 1976 by Bruno Bettelheim. Reprinted by permission of Alfred A. Knopf, Inc., a division of Random House, Inc.

Sissela Bok, "Agression" from *Mayhem: Violence as Public Entertainment*. Copyright © 1998 by Sissela Bok. Reprinted by permission of Perseus Books PLC, a member of Perseus Books, L.L.C.

Melissa Burns, "The Best Seat in the House." Reprinted by permission of the author.

Kevin Canty, "The Dog in Me" from Bastard on the Couch: *27 Men Try Really Hard to Explain Their Feelings About Love, Loss, Fatherhood and Freedom*, Ed. Daniel Jones © 2004. Reprinted by permission of the author.

Joyce Chang, "Drive Becarefully." Reprinted by permission of the author.

Norman Chung, "A Faithful Taoist." Reprinted by permission of the author.

Mark Cochrane, "Moral Abdication or Just Father-Son Bonding With a Creepy Edge" from the *Vancouver Sun*, February 22, 2003. Copyright © 2003 by Mark Cochrane. Reprinted by permission of the author.

Judith Ortiz Cofer, "The Other" from *Reaching Mainland & Selected New Poems*. Copyright © 1995 by Judith Ortiz Cofer. Reprinted by permission of The Bilingual Press.

Judith Ortiz Cofer, "Silent Dancing" from *Silent Dancing: A Partial Remembrance of a Puerto Rican Childhood*. (Houston: Arte Publico Press-University of Houston, 1990). Copyright © 1990 by Judith Ortiz Cofer. Reprinted by permission of Arte Publico Press.

Rosa Contreras, "On Not Being a Girl." Reprinted by permission of the author.

Carrie Demers, M.D., "Chaos or Calm" from *Yoga International*, March 2004. Carrie Demers, M.D. is the medical director of the Center for Health and Healing at the Himalayan Institute in Honesdale, PA. Reprinted by permission of the Himalayan Institute.

Emily Dickinson, "This world is not conclusion" from *The Poems of Emily Dickinson*, edited by Thomas H. Johnson. Copyright © 1951, 1955, 1979, 1983 by the President and Fellows of Harvard College. Reprinted by permission of the publishers and the Trustees of Amherst College.

Annie Dillard, "A Field of Silence" from *Teaching a Stone to Talk: Expeditions and Other Encounters*. Copyright © 1982 by Annie Dillard. Reprinted by permission of HarperCollins Publishers inc.

Susan Engel, "Finding an audience for the past" from *Context Is Everything: The Nature of Memory*. Copyright © 1999 by Susan Engel. Reprinted by permisison of Henry Holt and Company, LLC.

Louise Erdrich, "Dear John Wayne" from *Jacklight*. Copyright © 1984 by Louise Erdrich. Reprinted by permission of the Wylie Agency Inc.

Danny Fingeroth, "The Dual Identity: Of Pimpernels and Immigrants" from *The Stars* from *Superman on the Couch*. Copyright © 2004 by Danny Fingeroth. Reprinted by permission of the publisher, The Continuum International Publishing Group.

Carlin Flora, "Seeing by Starlight" from *Psychology Today*, July/August 2004. Copyright © 2004 Psychology Today. Reprinted by permission of Psychology Today.

Jonathan L. Freedman, "Evaluating the Research on Violent Video Games" from a University of Chicago Cultural Policy Program Conference held on October 26–27, 2001 from a Panel on Videogame Violence. Copyright © 2001 by Jonathan L. Freedman. Reprinted by permission of the author.

Sigmund Freud, "Erotic Wishes and Dreams" from *The Standard Edition of the Complete Psychological Works of Sigmund Freud*, translated by and edited by James Strachey. Copyright © The Institute of Psycho-Analysis and The Hogarth Press. Reprinted by permission of The Random House Group Ltd.

Nikki Giovanni, "Ego Tripping" from *The Selected Poems of Nikki Giovanni*. Copyright © 1996 by Nikki Giovanni. Reprinted by permission of HarperCollins Publishers Inc.

Marcelo Gleiser, "The Myths of Science" from *UNESCO Courier*, May 2001. Copyright © 2001 UNESCO. Reproduced by permission of UNESCO.

Jane Goodall, excerpt from *Reason to Hope*. Copyright © 1999 by Soko Publications Ltd. and Phillip Berman. Reprinted by permission of Warner Books, Inc.

Stephen Jay Gould, "Muller Bros. Moving and Storage" from *Natural History: The Magazine of Nature and Culture*. Copyright © 2002 by Stephen Jay Gould. Reprinted by the Estate of Stephen Jay Gould c/o Art Science Research Laboratory, New York, NY.

"The Pelasgian Creation Myth" 1955 excerpt from *Ancient Greek*: retold by Robert Graves. Reprinted by permission of George Braziller Inc.

Joshua Groban, "Two Myths." Reprinted by permission of the author.

Patricia Hampl, "Memory and Imagination" from *I Could Tell You Stories: Sojourns in the Land of Memory*. Reprinted by permission of Marly Rusoff & Associates.

Jill Ho, "Affirmative Action: Perspectives from a Model Minority." Reprinted by permission of the author.

Steven Holtzman, "Don't Look Back" from *Digital Mosaics: The Aesthetics of Cyberspace*. Copyright © 1997 by Steven Holtzman. Reprinted by permission of Simon & Schuster Adult Publishing Group.

Robert Johnson, "The Shadow" from *Owning Your Own Shadow*. Copyright © 1991 by Robert A. Johnson. Reprinted by permission of HarperCollins Publishers.

David Kerr, "Strawberry Creek: A Search for Origins" from *Responding Voices*. Copyright © 1997 by Macmillan/McGraw Hill. Reprinted by permission of Macmillan/McGraw Hill.

Martin Luther King, Jr, "I Have a Dream." Copyright © 1963 Martin Luther King, Jr., renewed 1991 by Coretta Scott King. Reprinted by permission of the Estate of Martin Luther King, Jr., c/o Writers House as agent for the proprietor New York, NY.

Stephen King, "The Symbolic Language of Dreams" from *Writer's Dreaming* by Naomi Epel. Copyright © 1993 by Naomi Epel. Reprinted by permission of Carol Southern Books, a division of Crown Publishers, Inc.

Maxine Hong Kingston, "No Name Woman" from *The Woman Warrior*. Copyright © 1975, 1976 by Maxine Hong Kingston. Reprinted by permission of Alfred A. Knopf, Inc.

Jon Krakauer, excerpt from *Into Thin Air*. Copyright © 1997 by Jon Krakauer. Used by permission of Villard Books, a division of Random House, Inc.

Anne Lamott, "Hunger" from *Travelling Mercies*. Copyright © 1999 by Anne Lamott. Reprinted by permission of Pantheon Books, a division of Random House, Inc.

Kalle Lasn, "The Ecology of Mind" from *Culture Jam: The Uncooling of America* by Kalle Lasn. Copyright © 1997 by Kalle Lasn. Originally published by William Morrow. Reprinted by permission of HarperCollins Publishers Inc.

Ursula K. Le Guin, "A Matter of Trust" from *The Waves of the Mind: Talks and Essays on the Writer, Reader and the Imagination*. Copyright © 2004 by Ursula K. Le Guin. Reprinted by permission of The Virginia Kidd Agency, Inc.

Rachel Lehmann-Haupt, "Multi-Tasking Man" from *What Makes a Man* by Rebecca Walker, ed. Copyright © 2004 by Rachel Lehmann-Haupt. Reprinted by permission of the author.

Denise Levertov, "The Secret" from *Poems 1960–1967*. Copyright © 1964 by Denise Levertov. Reprinted by permission of New Directions Publishing Corp.

Noah Levine, "Death is Not the End My Friend" from *Dharma Punx: A Memoir*. Copyright © 2003 by Noah Levine. Reprinted by permission of HarperCollins Publishers.

Mary Mackey, "The Distant Cataract About Which We Do Not Speak" from *My California*, edited by Donna Wares. Copyright © 2004 by Mary Mackey. Reprinted by permission of the author.

Gabriel Garcia Marquez, "The Handsomest Drowned Man in the World" from *Leaf Storm and Other Stories*. Copyright © 1971 by Gabriel Garcia Marquez. Reprinted by permission of HarperCollins Publishers.

W.S. Merwin, "Fog-Horn" from *The Drunk in the Furnace*. Copyright © 1960 by W. S. Merwin. Reprinted by permission of the Wylie Agency, Inc.

Karen Methot-Chun, "Living Spirituality." Reprinted by permission of the author.

Pablo Neruda, "The Dream" from *The Captain's Verses*. Copyright © 1972 by Pablo Neruda and Donald D. Walsh. Reprinted by permission of New Directions Publishing Corp.

Naomi Shihab Nye, "Fireflies" from *Red Suitcase*. Copyright © 1994 by Naomi Shihab Nye. Reprinted by permission of BOA Editions, Ltd.

Maressa Hecht Orzack, Ph.D., "Computer Addiction" from *Psychiatric Times*, August 1998, Vol. XV, Issue 8. Copyright © 1998 by Maressa Hecht Orzack, Ph.D. Reprinted by permission of the author.

Mary Pipher, Ph.D, "Saplings in the Storm." From *Reviving Ophelia*. Copyright © 1994 by Mary Pipher, Ph.D. Reprinted by permission of G.P. Putnam's Sons, a division of Penguin Group (USA) Inc.

Tajamika Paxton, "Loving a One-Armed Man" from *What Makes a Man*. Copyright © 2004 by Tajamika Paxton. Reprinted by permission of the author.

Fran Peavey, "Us and Them" from *Heart Politics*. Copyright © 1984 by Fran Peavey. Reprinted by permission of New Society Publishers, Philadelphia, PA.

Anthony R. Pratkanis and Elliot Aronson, "Pictures in Our Heads" from *Age of Propoganda: The Everyday Use and Abuse of Persuasion*, by Anthony R. Pratkanis and Elliot Aronson. Copyright © 2001, 1992 by W. H. Freeman and Company. Reprinted by permission of Henry Holdt and Company, LLC.

Alissa Quart, "Branded" from *Branded: The Buying and Selling of Teenagers*. Copyright © 2003 by Alissa Quart. Reprinted by permission of Perseus Books PLC, a member of Perseus Books, L.L.C.

Photo Credits

Index